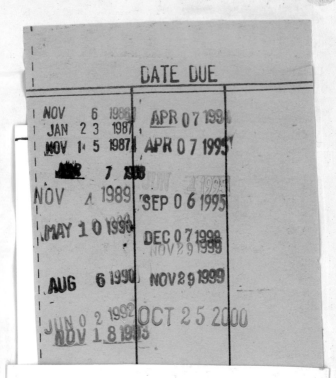

Y0-BUD-226

DATE DUE

| | |
|---|---|
| NOV 6 1986 | APR 07 1994 |
| JAN 2 3 1987 | APR 07 1995 |
| NOV 1 5 1987 | |
| APR 7 1988 | |
| NOV 4 1989 | SEP 0 6 1995 |
| MAY 1 0 1990 | DEC 0 7 1998 |
| | NOV 2 9 1999 |
| AUG 6 1990 | NOV 2 9 1999 |
| JUN 0 2 1992 | OCT 2 5 2000 |
| NOV 1 8 1993 | |

DISCARDED
Richmond Public Library

THE KOJIKI

# THE KOJIKI

## Records of Ancient Matters

translated by
## Basil Hall Chamberlain

RICHMOND
PUBLIC
LIBRARY
CALIFORNIA

## Charles E. Tuttle Company

Rutland, Vermont &
Tokyo, Japan

MAIN
952.01 Kojiki. English.
    The Kojiki : 1st
    Tuttle ed.

31143003886059          c.1

*Representatives*

*Continental Europe:* BOXERBOOKS, INC., *Zurich*

*British Isles:* PRENTICE-HALL INTERNATIONAL, INC., *London*

*Australasia:* BOOK WISE (AUSTRALIA) PTY. LTD.
*104-108 Sussex Street, Sydney 2000*

*Published by the Charles E. Tuttle Company, Inc.*
*of Rutland, Vermont & Tokyo, Japan*
*with editorial offices at*
*Suido 1-chome, 2-6, Bunkyo-ku, Tokyo, Japan*

© *1981 by Charles E. Tuttle Co., Inc.*

*All rights reserved*

*Library of Congress Catalog Card No. 81-52934*
*International Standard Book No. 0-8048-1439-2*

*First Tuttle edition, 1982*
*Second printing, 1986*

PRINTED IN JAPAN

# PUBLISHER'S FOREWORD

The *Kojiki* (Records of Ancient Matters) provides a panorama of Japan in the throws of its formation. As a compendium of history and mythology, and a record of early Japanese life and beliefs, it offers invaluable insight into the historical roots of the Japanese people.

The *Kojiki* was taken down by one Yasumaro from the lips of Hiyeda no Are, a man of extraordinary memory, and presented to the imperial court in A.D. 712, making it the oldest surviving Japanese book. A more factual history called the *Nihongi* or *Nihon Shoki* (Chronicles of Japan) was completed in A.D. 720, but the *Kojiki* remains the better known, perhaps because of its special concern with the legends of the gods, with the divine descent of the imperial family, and with native Shinto. Both works have immense value as records of the development of Japan into a unified state with a well-defined character. Indeed, even the mythological aspects were accepted as fact throughout most of subsequent Japanese history—until the defeat and disillusionment of the nation in 1945.

Basil Hall Chamberlain was one of the pioneering Western scholars on Japan. In 1882 he read this, the first translation of the *Kojiki*, before the Asiatic Society of Japan. It was published as a Supplement to Vol. X of the *Transactions* of the Asiatic Society, and later reprinted in 1919 and 1920. It is upon these latter that the present edition is based.

At the turn of the century, Professor Chamberlain remarked that "to have lived through the transition stage of modern Japan makes a man feel preternaturally old; for here he is in modern times, with

*Publisher's Foreword*

the air full of talk about bicycles and bacilli and 'spheres of influence,' and yet he can himself distinctly remember the Middle Ages." How much more has Japan changed in the decades since that was written. And yet the *Kojiki*, relating as it does the origins of the race, remains a key to this country of jammed commuter trains and ultramodern industrial technology.

# A Translation of the "Ko-ji-ki,"

OR

## "RECORDS OF ANCIENT MATTERS."
## (古 事 記)

By Basil Hall Chamberlain.

[*Read before the Asiatic Society of Japan April 12th, May 10th, and June 21st,* 1882.]
[*Reprinted, May,* 1919.]

## INTRODUCTION.

Of all the mass of Japanese literature, which lies before us as the result of nearly twelve centuries of book-making, the most important monument is the work entitled "*Ko-ji-ki*"[1] or "Records of Ancient Matters," which was completed in A. D. 712. It is the most important because it has preserved for us more faithfully than any other book the mythology, the manners, the language,

---

1. Should the claim of Accadian to be considered an Altaic language be substantiated, then Archaic Japanese will have to be content with the second place in the Altaic family. Taking the word Altaic in its usual acceptation, viz., as the generic name of all the languages belonging to the Mantchu, Mongolia, Turkish and Finnish groups, not only the Archaic, but the Classical, literature of Japan carries us back several centuries beyond the earliest extant documents of any other Altaic tongue.—For a discussion of the age of the most ancient Tamil documents see the Introduction to Bishop Caldwell's "Comparative Grammar of the Dravidian Languages," p. 91 *et seq.*

2 and the traditional history of Ancient Japan. Indeed it
is the earliest authentic connected literary product of that
large division of the human race which has been variously denominated Turanian, Scythian and Altaic, and it even
precedes by at least a century the most ancient extant
literary compositions of non-Aryan India. Soon after the
date of its compilation, most of the salient features of
distinctive Japanese nationality were buried under a
superincumbent mass of Chinese cultnre, and it is to these
"Records" and to a very small number of other ancient
works, such as the poems of the "Collection of a Myriad
Leaves" and the Shintō Rituals, that the investigator
must look, if he would not at every step be misled in
attributing originality to modern customs and ideas, which
have simply been borrowed wholesale from the neighbouring
continent.

It is of course not pretended that even these "Records"
are untouched by Chinese influence : that influence is
patent in the very characters with which the text is
written. But the influence is less, and of another kind.
If in the traditions preserved and in the customs alluded
to we detect the Early Japanese in the act of borrowing
from China and perhaps even from India, there is at least
on our author's part no ostentatious decking out in
Chinese trappings of what he believed to be original
matter, after the fashion of the writers who immediately
succeeded him. It is true that this abstinence on his
part makes his compilation less pleasant to the ordinary
native taste than that of subsequent historians, who put
fine Chinese phrases into the mouths of emperors and
heroes supposed to have lived before the time when
intercourse with China began. But the European student,

who reads all such books, not as a pastime but in order
to search for facts, will prefer the more genuine composition. It is also accorded the first place by the most learned
of the native *literati.*

Of late years this paramount importance of the " Records
of Ancient Matters " to investigators of Japanese subjects
generally has become well-known to European scholars ;
and even versions of a few passages are to be found
scattered through the pages of their writings. Thus Mr.
Aston has given us, in the Chrestomathy appended to
his "Grammar of the Japanese Written Language," a
couple of interesting extracts ; Mr. Satow has illustrated
by occasional extracts his elaborate papers on the Shintō
Rituals printed in these " Transactions," and a remarkable essay by Mr. Kempermann published in the Fourth 3
Number of the " Mittheilungen der Deutschen Gesellschaft
für Natur und Völkerkunde Ostasiens," though containing
no actual translations, bases on the account given in the
" Records " some conjectures regarding the *origines* of
Japanese civilization which are fully substantiated by more
minute research. All that has yet appeared in any European language does not, however, amount to one-
twentieth part of the whole, and the most erroneous views
of the style and scope of the book and its contents have
found their way into popular works on Japan. It is
hoped that the true nature of the book, and also the true
nature of the traditions, customs, and ideas of the Early
Japanese, will be made clearer by the present translation
the object of which is to give the entire work in a continuous English version, and thus to furnish the European
student with a text to quote from, or at least to use as
a guide in consulting the original. The only object aimed

at has been a rigid and literal conformity with the Japanese text. Fortunately for this endeavour (though less fortunately for the student), one of the difficulties which often beset the translator of an Oriental classic is absent in the present case. There is no beauty of style, to preserve some trace of which he may be tempted to sacrifice a certain amount of accuracy. The "Records" sound queer and bald in Japanese, as will be noticed further on; and it is therefore right, even from a stylistic point of view, that they should sound bald and queer in English. The only portions of the text which, from obvious reasons, refuse to lend themselves to translation into English after this fashion are the indecent portions. But it has been thought that there could be no objection to rendering them into Latin,—Latin as rigidly literal as is the English of the greater part.

After these preliminary remarks, it will be most convenient to take the several points which a study of the "Records" and the turning of them into English suggest, and to consider the same one by one. These points are :

    I.—Authenticity and Nature of the Text, together with Bibliographical Notes.

    II.—Details concerning the Method of Translation.

    III.—The "*Nihon-Gi*" or "Chronicles of Japan."

    IV.—Manners and Customs of the Early Japanese.

    V.—Religious and Political Ideas of the Early Japanese. Beginnings of the Japanese Nation, and Credibility of the National Traditions.

I.

The latter portion of the Preface to the " Records of
Ancient Matters " is the only documentary authority for
the origin of the work. It likewise explains its scope.
But though in so doing the author descends to a more
matter of fact style than the high-sounding Chinese phrases
and elaborate allusions with which he had set forth, still
his meaning may be found to lack somewhat of clearness,
and it will be as well to have the facts put into language
more intelligible to the European student. This having
already been done by Mr. Satow in his paper on the
" Revival of Pure Shintō,"[2] it will be best simply to quote
his words. They are as follows : " The Emperor Temmu,
at what portion of his reign is not mentioned, lamenting
that the records possessed by the chief families contained
many errors, resolved to take steps to preserve the true
traditions from oblivion. He therefore had the records
carefully examined, compared, and weeded of their faults.
There happened to be in his household a person of marvellous memory named Hiyeda no Are, who could repeat
without mistake the contents of any document he had
ever seen, and never forgot anything that he had heard.
Temmu Tennō[3] took the pains to instruct this person in
the genuine traditions and ' old language of former ages,'
and to make him repeat them until he had the whole by
heart. ' Before the undertaking was completed,' which
probably means before it could be committed to writing,

2. Published in Vol. iii, Pt. I, of these " Transactions."
3. *I.e.*, the Emperor Tem-mu.

the Emperor died, and for twenty-five years Are's memory was the sole depository of what afterwards received the title of *Kojiki*[4] or *Furu-koto-bumi* as it is read by Motoori. At the end of this interval the Empress Gemmiō ordered 5 Yasumaro to write it down from the mouth of Are, which accounts for the completion of the manuscript in so short a time as four months and a half.    Are's age at this date is not stated, but as he was twenty-eight years of age some time in the reign of Temmu Tennō, it could not possibly have been more than sixty-eight, while taking into account the previous order of Temmu Tennō in 681 for the compilation of a history, and the statement that he was engaged on the composition of the Kojiki at the time of his death in 686, it would not be unreasonable to conclude that it belongs to about the last year of his reign, in which case Are was only fifty-three in 711."

The previous order of the Emperor Temmu mentioned in the above extract is usually supposed to have resulted in the compilation of a history which was early lost. But Hirata gives reasons for supposing that this and the project of the "Records of Ancient Matters" were identical. If this opinion be accepted, the "Records," while the oldest *existing* Japanese book, are, not the third, but the second historical work of which mention has been preserved, one such having been compiled in the year 620, but lost in a fire in the year 645.    It will thus be seen that it is rather hard to say whom we should designate as the author of the work.

4.  *I.e.*, "Records of Ancient Matters."  The alternative reading, which is probably but an invention of Motowori's, gives the same meaning in pure Japanese (instead of Sinico-Japanese) sounds.

The Emperor Tem-mu, Hiyeda no Are, Yasumaro may all three lay claim to the title. The question, however, is of no importance to us, and the share taken by Are may well have been exaggerated in the telling. What seems to remain as the residue of fact is that the plan of a purely national history originated with the Emperor Temmu and was finally carried out under his successor by Yasumaro, one of the Court Nobles.

Fuller evidence and confirmatory evidence from other sources as to the origin of our "Records" would doubtless be very acceptable. But the very small number of readers and writers at that early date, and the almost simultaneous compilation of a history (the "Chronicles of Japan") which was better calculated to hit the taste of the age, make the absence of such evidence almost unavoidable. In any case, and only noticing in passing the fact that Japan was never till quite recent years noted for such wholesale literary forgeries (for Motowori's condemnation of the "Chronicles of Old Matters of Former Ages" has been considered rash by later scholars),—it cannot be too much emphasized that in this instance authenticity is sufficiently proved by internal evidence. It is hard to believe that any forger living later than the eighth century of our era should have been so well able to discard the Chinese "padding" to the old traditions, which after the acceptance by the Court of the "Chronicles of Japan," had come to be generally regarded as an integral portion of those very traditions ; and it is more unlikely still that he should have invented a style so little calculated to bring his handiwork into repute. He would either have written in fair Chinese, like the mass of early Japanese prose writers (and his Preface

shows that he could do so if he were so minded); or, if
the tradition of there having been a history written in
the native tongue had reached him, he would have made
his composition unmistakably Japanese in form by arranging consistent use of characters employed phonetically to denote particles and terminations, after the fashion
followed in the Rituals, and developed (apparently before
the close of the ninth century) into what is technically
known as the "Mixed Phonetic Style" (*Kana-mazhiri*),
which has remained ever since as the most convenient
vehicle for writing the language.  As it is, his quasi-
Chinese construction, which breaks down every now and
then to be helped up again by a few Japanese words
written phonetically, is surely the first clumsy attempt at
combining two divergent elements.  What however is
simply incredible is that, if the supposed forger lived even
only a hundred years later than A.D. 712, he should so
well have imitated or divined the archaisms of that early
period.  For the eighth century of our era was a great
turning point in the Japanese language, the Archaic
Dialect being then replaced by the Classical ; and as the
Chinese language and literature were alone thenceforward
considered worthy the student's attention, there was no
means of keeping up an acquaintance with the diction of
earlier reigns, neither do we find the poets of the time
ever attempting to adorn their verse with obsolete phraseology.  That was an affectation reserved for a later epoch,
when the diffusion of books rendered it possible.  The
poets of the seventh, eighth, and ninth centuries apparently wrote as they spoke ; and the test of language alone
would almost allow of our arranging their compositions
half century by half century, even without the dates

which are given in many instances in the "Collection of a Myriad Leaves" and in the "Collection of Songs 7 Ancient and Modern,"—the first two collections of poems published by imperial decree in the middle of the eighth, and at the commencement of the tenth, century respectively.

The above remarks are meant to apply more especially to the occasional Japanese words,—all of them Archaic, —which, as mentioned above, are used from time to time in the prose text of the "Records," to help out the author's meaning and to preserve names whose exact pronunciation he wished handed down. That he should have invented the Songs would be too monstrous a supposition for any one to entertain, even if we had not many of the same and other similar ones preserved in the pages of the "Chronicles of Japan," a work which was undoubtedly completed in A.D. 720. The history of the Japanese language is too well known to us, we can trace its development and decay in too many documents reaching from the eighth century to the present time, for it to be possible to entertain the notion that the latest of these Songs, which have been handed down with minute care in a syllabic transcription, is posterior to the first half of the eighth century, while the majority must be ascribed to an earlier, though uncertain, date. If we refer the greater number of them in their present form to the sixth century, and allow a further antiquity of one or two centuries to others more ancient in sentiment and in grammatical usage, we shall probably be making a moderate estimate. It is an estimate, moreover, which obtains confirmation from the fact that the first notice we have of the use of writing in Japan dates from early in the fifth century; for it is natural to suppose that the Songs believed to · have been composed by the gods and heroes of antiquity should have been among the first things to be written down, while the reverence in which they were held would in some cases cause them to be transcribed exactly as tradition had bequeathed them, even if unintelligible or nearly so, while in others the same feeling would lead to the correction of what were supposed to be errors or inelegancies.   Finally it may be well to observe that the authenticity of the " Records " has never been doubted, though, as has already been stated, some of the native commentators have not hesitated to charge with spuriousness another of their esteemed ancient histories.   Now it is unlikely 8 that, in the war which has been waged between the partisans of the " Records " and those of the " Chronicles," some flaw in the former's title to genuineness and to priority should not have been discovered and pointed out if it existed.

During the Middle Ages, when no native Japanese works were printed, and not many others excepting the Chinese Classics and Buddhist Scriptures, the " Records of Ancient Matters " remained in manuscript in the hands of the Shintō priesthood.   They were first printed in the year 1644, at the time when, peace having been finally restored to the country and the taste for reading become diffused, the great mass of the native literature first began to emerge from the manuscript state.   This very rare edition (which was reprinted in fac-simile in 1798) is indispensable to any one who would make of the " Records " a special study.   The next edition was by a Shintō priest, Deguchi Nobuyoshi, and appeared in 1687.   It has mar-

ginal notes of no great value, and several emendations of
the text. The first-mentioned of these two editions is
commonly called the "Old Printed Edition" (舊印本), but
has no title beyond that of the original work,—"Records
of Ancient Matters with Marginal Readings" (鼇頭古事記).
Each is in three volumes. They were succeeded in
1789–1822 by Motowori's great edition, entitled "Exposition of the Records of Ancient Matters" (古事記傳).
This, which is perhaps the most admirable work of which
Japanese erudition can boast, consists of forty-four large
volumes, fifteen of which are devoted to the elucidation
of the first volume of the original, seventeen to the second,
ten to the third, and the rest to prolegomena, indexes,
etc. To the ordinary student this Commentary will furnish
all that he requires, and the charm of Motowori's style
will be found to shed a glamour over the driest parts of
the original work. The author's judgment only seems to
fail him occasionally when confronted with the most
difficult or corrupt passages, or with such as might be
construed in a sense unfavourable to his predilections as
an ardent Shintoist. He frequently quotes the opinions
of his master Mabuchi, whose own treatise on this subject
is so rare that the present writer has never seen a copy
of it, nor does the public library of Tōkyō possess one.
Later and less important editions are the "Records of
Ancient Matters with the Ancient Reading" (古訓古事記),
a reprint by one of Motowori's pupils of the Chinese
text and of his Master's *Kana* reading of it without his
Commentary, and useful for reference, though the title is [9]
a misnomer, 1803; the "Records of Ancient Matters with
Marginal Notes" (古事記標註), by Murakami Tadanori,
1874; the "Records of Ancient Matters in the Syllabic

Character" (假名古事記), by Sakata no Kaneyasu, 1874, a
misleading book, as it gives the modern *Kana* reading
with its arbitrarily inserted Honorifics and other depar-
tures from the actual text, as the *ipissima verba* of the
original work; the "Records of Ancient Matters Revised"
(校正古事記), by Uematsu Shigewoka, 1875. All these
editions are in three volumes, and the "Records of
Ancient Matters with the Ancient Reading" has also been
reprinted in one volume on beautiful thin paper. Another
in four volumes by Fujihara no Masaoki, 1871, entitled
the "Records of Ancient Matters in the Divine Character"
(神法古事記), is a real curiosity of literature, though otherwise of no value. In it the editor has been at the pains
of reproducing the whole work, according to its modern
*Kana* reading, in that adaptation of the Korean alphabetic
writing which some modern Japanese authors have supposed to be characters of peculiar age and sanctity, used
by the ancient gods of their country and naméd "Divine
Characters" accordingly.

Besides these actual editions of the "Records of Ancient
Matters, there is a considerable mass of literature bearing less directly on the same work, and all of which
cannot be here enumerated. It may be sufficient to mention the "Correct Account of the Divine Age" (神代正語)
by Motowori, 3 Vols. 1789, and a commentary thereon
entitled "*Tokiha-Gusa*" (神代正語常盤草) by Wosada Tominobu, from which the present translator has borrowed a
few ideas; the "Sources of the Ancient Histories" (古史徵)
and its sequel entitled "Exposition of the Ancient Histories" (古史傳), by Hirata Atsutane, begun printing in
1819,—works which are specially admirable from a philological point of view, and in which the student will find

the solution of not a few difficulties which even to Motowori had been insuperable;[5] the "*Idzu no Chi-Waki*"
(稜威道別), by Tachibana no Moribe, begun printing in 1851,
a useful commentary on the "Chronicles of Japan"; the 19
"*Idzu no Koto-Waki*" (稜威語別), by the same author,
begun printing in 1847, an invaluable help to a comprehension of the Songs contained in both the "Records"
and the "Chronicles"; the Examination of Difficult
Words" (難語考, also entitled 山彦冊子), in 3 Vols., 1831,
a sort of dictionary of specially perplexing terms and
phrases, in which light is thrown on many a verbal crux
and much originality of thought displayed; and the
"Perpetual Commentary on the Chronicles of Japan"
(日本書記通證), by Tanigaha Shisei, 1762, a painstaking
work written in the Chinese language, 23 Vols. Neither
must the "*Kō Gan Shō*," (厚題抄), a commentary on the
Songs contained in the "Chronicles" and "Records"
composed by the Buddhist priest Keichiū, who may be
termed the father of the native school of criticism, be
forgotten. It is true that most of Keichiū's judgments
on doubtful points have been superseded by the more
perfect erudition of later days; but some few of his interpretations may still be followed with advantage. The
"*Kō Gan Shō*" which was finished in the year 1691,
has never been printed. It is from these and a few others
and from the standard dictionaries and general books of
reference, such as the "Japanese Words Classified and

5. Unfortunately the portion already printed does not carry the history
down even to the close of the "Divine Age." The work is as colossal
in extent as it is minute in research, forty-one volumes (including the
eleven forming the "Sources") having already appeared. The "*Idzu no
Chi-Waki*" and "*Idzu no Koto-Waki*" are similarly incomplete.

Explained" (和名類聚鈔), the "Catalogue of Family
Names" (姓氏錄), and (coming down to more modern
times) Arawi Hakuseki's "*Tōga*" (東雅), that the translator has derived most assistance. The majority of the
useful quotations from the dictionaries, etc., having been
incorporated by Motowori in his "Commentary," it has
not often been necessary to mention them by name in the
notes to the translation. At the same time the translator
must express his conviction that, as the native authorities
cannot possibly be dispensed with, so also must their
assertions be carefully weighed and only accepted with
discrimination by the critical European investigator. He
must also thank Mr. Tachibana no Chimori, grandson of
the eminent scholar Tachibana no Moribe, for kindly
allowing him to make use of the unpublished portions of
the "*Idzn no Chi-Waki*" and the "*Idzu no Katō-Waki*,"
works indispensable to the comprehension of the more
difficult portion of the text of the "Records." To Mr.
Satow he is indebted for the English and Latin equivalents of the Japanese botanical names, to Capt. Blakiston
and Mr. Namiye Motokichi for similar assistance with
regard to the zoological names.

11      Comparing what has been said above with what the
author tells us in his Preface, the nature of the text, so
far as language is concerned, will be easily understood.
The Songs are written phonetically, syllable by syllable,
in what is technically known as *Manyō-Gana, i. e.* entire
Chinese characters used to represent sound and not sense.
The rest of the text, which is in prose, is very poor
Chinese, capable (owing to the ideographic nature of the
Chinese written character[6]), of being read off into
Japanese. It is also not only full of "Japonisms," but

irregularly interspersed with characters which turn the
text into nonsense for a Chinaman, as they are used
phonetically to represent certain Japanese words, for which
the author could not find suitable Chinese equivalents.
These phonetically written words prove, even apart from
the notice in the Preface, that the text was never meant
to be read as pure Chinese. The probability is that
(sense being considered more important than sound) it
was read partly in Chinese and partly in Japanese, according to a mode which has since been systematized and
has become almost universal in this country even in the
reading of genuine Chinese texts. The modern school of
Japanese *literati*, who push their hatred of everything
foreign to the bounds of fanaticism, contend however
that this, their most ancient and revered book, was from
the first intended to be read exclusively into Japanese.
Drawing from the other sources of our knowledge of the
Archaic Dialect, Motowori has even hazarded a restoration of the Japanese reading of the entire prose text, in
the whole of which not a single Chinese word is used,
excepting for the titles of the two Chinese books (the
" Confucian Analects " and the " Thousand Character
Essay ") which are said to have been brought over to
Japan in the reign of the Emperor O-jin, and for the
names of a Korean King and of three or four other

6. The translator adopts the term "ideographic," because it is that
commonly used and understood, and because this is not the place to demonstrate its inappropriateness. Strictly speaking, "logographic" would
be preferable to "ideographic," the difference between Chinese characters
and alphabetic writing being that the former represent in their entirety
the Chinese words for things and ideas, whereas the latter dissects into
their component sounds the words of the languages which it is employed
to write.

Koreans and Chinese. Whatever may be their opinion
on the question at issue, most European scholars, to
11 whom the superior sanctity of the Japanese language is
not an article of faith, will probably agree with Mr.
Aston[7] in denying to this conjectural restoration the credit
of representing the genuine words into which Japanese
eighth century students of history read off the text of
the " Records."

## II.

### METHODS OF TRANSLATION.

To the translator the question above mooted is not
one of great importance. The text itself must form the
basis of his version, and not any one's,—not even Motowori's—private and particular reading of it. For this
reason none of the Honorifics which Motowori inserts as
prefixes to nouns and terminations to verbs have been
taken any notice of, but the original has been followed,
character by character, with as great fidelity as was attainable. The author too has his Honorifics; but he does
not use them so plentifully or so regularly as it pleases
Motowori to represent him as having intended to do.
On the other hand, Motowori's occasional emendations of
the text may generally be accepted. They rarely extend
to more than single words; and the errors in the earlier
editions may frequently bc shown to have arisen from
careless copying of characters originally written, not in
the square, but in the cursive form. The translator has
separately considered each case where various readings

7. "Grammar of the Japanese Written Language," Second Edition,
Appendix II., p. VI.

occur, and has mentioned them in the Notes when they seemed of sufficient importance. In some few cases he has preferred a reading not approved by Motowori, but he always mentions Motowori's reading in a Foot-note.

The main body of the text contains but little to perplex any one who has made a special study of the early Japanese writings, and it has already been noticed that there is an admirable exegetical literature at the student's command. With the Songs embedded in the prose text the case is different, as some of them are among the most difficult things in the language, and the commentators frequently arrive at most discordant interpretations of the obscurer passages. In the present version particulars concerning each Song have, except in a very few cases where comment appeared superfluous, been given in a Foot-note, the general sense being usually first indicated, the meaning of particular expressions then explained, and various opinions mentioned when they seemed worthy of notice. Besides one or two terms of Japanese grammar, the only technical knowledge with which the readers of the Notes are necessarily credited is that of the use by the Japanese poets of what have been styled Pillow-Words, Pivots, and Prefaces; and those Pillow-Words which are founded on a *jeu-de-mots* or are of doubtful signification form, with the one exception mentioned below, the only case where anything contained in the original is omitted from the English version.[8] After some consideration, it has been deemed

13

---

8. For a special account of the Pillow-Words, etc., see a paper by the present writer in Vol. V, Pt. I, pp. 79 *et seq.* of these "Transactions," and for a briefer notice, his "Classical Poetry of the Japanese," pp. 5 and 6.

advisable to print in an Appendix the Japanese text of all the Songs, transliterated into Roman. Students will thus find it easier to form their own opinion on the interpretation of doubtful passages. The importance likewise of these Songs, as the most ancient specimens of Altaïc speech, makes it right to give them as much publicity as possible.

The text of the " Records " is, like many other Japanese texts, completely devoid of breaks corresponding to the chapters and paragraphs into which European works are divided. With the occasional exception of a pause after a catalogue of gods or princes, and of notes inserted in smaller type and generally containing genealogies or indicating the pronunciation of certain words, the whole story, prose and verse, runs on from beginning to end with no interruptions other than those marked by the conclusion of Vol. I and by the death of each emperor in Vols. II and III. Faithfulness however scarcely seems to demand more than this statement ; for a similarly continuous printing of the English version would attain no end but that of making a very dry piece of reading more arduous still. Moreover there are certain traditional names by which the various episodes of the so-called " Divine Age " are known to the native scholars, and according to which the text of Vol. I may naturally be divided. The reigns of the emperors form a similar foundation for the analysis of Vols. II and III, which contain the account of the " Human Age." It has been thought that it would be well to mark such natural 14 divisions by the use of numbered Sections with marginal headings. The titles proposed by Motowori in the Prolegomena to his Commentary have been adopted with scarcely any alteration in the case of Vol. I. In Vols. II and III, where his sections mostly embrace the whole reign of an emperor, and the title given by him to each Section consists only of the name of the palace where each emperor is said to have resided, there is less advantage in following him; for those Sections are often inordinately long, and their titles occasionally misleading and always inconvenient for purposes of reference, as the Japanese emperors are commonly known, not by the names of their places of residence, but by their "canonical names." Motowori, as an ardent nationalist, of course rejected these "canonical names," because they were first applied to the Japanese emperors at a comparatively late date in imitation of Chinese usage. But to a foreigner this need be no sufficient reason for discarding them. The Sections in the translation of Vols. II and III have therefore been obtained by breaking up the longer reigns into appropriate portions; and in such Sections, as also in the Foot-notes, the emperors are always mentioned by their "canonical names."[9] The Vol. mentioned in brackets on every right-hand page is that of Motowori's Commentary which treats of the Section contained in that page.

The Notes translated from the original are indented, and are printed small when they are in small type in

---

9. The practice of bestowing a canonical name (*okurina* 諡) on an emperor after his decease dates from the latter part of the eighth century of our era when, at the command of the emperor Kuwam-mu, a scholar named Mifune-no-Mahito selected suitable "canonical names" for all the previous sovereigns, from Jim-mu down to Kuwan-mu's immediate predecessor. From that time forward every emperor has received his "canonical name" soon after death, and it is generally by it alone that he is known to history.

the Japanese text. Those only which give directions for pronouncing certain characters phonetically have been omitted, as they have no significance when the original tongue and method of writing are exchanged for foreign vehicles of thought and expression. The songs have likewise been indented for the sake of clearness, and each one printed as a separate paragraph. The occasionally unavoidable insertion in the translation of important words not occurring in the Japanese text has been indicated by printing such words within square brackets. The translator's Notes, which figure at the bottom of each page, do not aim at anything more than the exegesis of the actual text. To illustrate its subject-matter from other sources, as Motowori does, and to enlarge on all the subjects connected with Japanese antiquity which are sometimes merely alluded to in a single phrase, would require several more volumes the size of this one, many years of labour on the part of the investigator, and an unusually large stock of patience on the reader's part. The Notes terminate with the death of the Emperor Kenzō, after which the text ceases to offer any interest, except as a comment on the genealogies given in the "Chronicles of Japan."

Without forgetting the fact that so-called equivalent terms in two languages rarely quite cover each other, and that it may therefore be necessary in some cases to render one Japanese word by two or three different English words according to the context, the translator has striven to keep such diversity within the narrowest limits, as it tends to give a false impression of the original, implying that it possesses a versatility of thought which is indeed characteristic of Modern Europe, but not at all of Early Japan. With reference to this point a certain class of words must be mentioned, as the English translation is unavoidably defective in their case, owing to the fact of our language not possessing sufficiently close synonyms for them. They are chiefly the names of titles, and are the following :—

| | | | |
|---|---|---|---|
| *Agata-no-atahe* | roughly rendered by | | *Departmental Suzerain.* |
| *Agata-nushi* | " | " | " *Departmental Lord.* |
| *Asomi (Ason)* | " | " | " *Court Noble.* |
| *Atahe* | " | " | " *Suzerain.* |
| *Hiko* | " | " | " *Prince.* |
| *Hime* | " | " | " *Princess.* |
| *Inaki* | " | " | " *Territorial Lord.* |
| *Iratsuko* | " | " | " *Lord.* |
| *Iratsume* | " | " | " *Lady.* |
| *Kami* | " | " | " *Deity.* |
| *Kimi* | " | " | " *Duke.* |
| *Ma* | " | " | " *True.* |
| *Miko* (王) | " | " | " *King.* |
| *Mi Ko* (御子) | " | " | " *August Child.* |
| *Mikoto* | " | " | " *Augustness.* |
| *Miyatsuko* | " | " | " *Ruler.* |
| *Murazhi* | " | " | " *Chief.* |
| *Omi* | " | " | " *Grandee.* |
| *Sukune* | " | " | " *Noble.* |
| *Wake* (in the names of human beings) | | | *Lord.* |

It must be understood that no special significance is to be attached to the use of such words as "Duke," "Suzerain," etc. They are merely, so to speak, labels by which titles that are distinct in the original are sought to be kept distinct in the translation. Many of them also are used as that species of hereditary titular designation which the translator has ventured to call the "gentile name."[10] Where possible, indeed, the etymological

16

---

10. See Sect. IV. of this Introduction and Sect. XIV, Note 5 of the Translation.

meaning of the Japanese word has been preserved. Thus *omi* seems to be rightly derived by Motowori from *ohomi*, "great body"; and "grandee" is therefore the nearest English equivalent. Similarly *murazhi*, chief," is a corruption of two words signifying "master of a tribe." On the other hand, both the etymology and the precise import of the title of *wake* are extremely doubtful. *Hiko* and *hime* again, if they really come from *hi ko*, "sun-child" and *hi me*, "sun-female" (or "fire child" and "fire female"), have wandered so far from their origin as, even in Archaic times, to have been nothing more than Honorific appellations, corresponding in a loose fashion to the English words "prince and princess," or "lord and lady,"—in some cases perhaps meaning scarcely more than "youth and maiden."

The four words *kami*, *ma*, *miko* and *mikoto* alone call for special notice; and *ma* may be disposed of first. It is of uncertain origin, but identified by the native philologists with the perpetually recurring honorific *mi*, rendered "august." As, when written ideographically, it is always represented by the Chinese character 眞, the translator renders it in English by "true"; but it must be understood that this word has no force beyond that of an Honorific.

*Mikoto*, rendered "Augustness," is properly a compound, *mi koto*, "august thing." It is used as a title, somewhat after the fashion of our words "Majesty" and "Highness," being suffixed to the names of exalted human personages, and also of gods and goddesses. For the sake of clearness in the English translation this title is prefixed and used with the possessive pronoun, thus: *Yamato-Take-no-Mikoto*, His Augustness Yamato-Take.

With regard to the title read *miko* by the native commentators, it is represented in two ways in the Chinese text. When a *young* prince is denoted by it, we find the characters 御子, "august child," reminding us of the Spanish title of *infante*. But in other cases it is written with the single character 王, "King," and it may be questioned whether the reading of it as *miko* is not arbitrary. Many indications lead us to suppose that in Early Japan something similar to the feudal system, which again obtained during the Middle Ages, was in force; and if so, then some of these "kings" may have been kings indeed after a fashion; and to degrade their title, as do the modern commentators, to that of "prince" is an anachronism. In any case the safest plan, if we would not help to obscure this interesting political question, is to adhere to the proper signification of the character in the text, and that character is 王, "King."[11]

Of all the words for which it is hard to find a suitable English equivalent, *Kami* is the hardest. Indeed there is no English word which renders it with any near approach to exactness. If therefore it is here rendered by the word "deity" ("deity" being preferred to "god" because it includes superior beings of both sexes), it must be clearly understood that the word "deity" is taken in a sense not sanctioned by any English dictionary; for *kami*, and "deity" or "god," only correspond to each other in a very rough manner. The proper meaning of the word "*kami*" is "top," or "above"; and it is still constantly so used. For this reason it has the secondary sense of "hair of the head;" and only the hair on the *top*

11. *Conf.* Section LVI, Note 7.

of the head,—not the hair on the face,—is so designated. Similarly the Government, in popular phraseology, is *O Kami,* literally "the honorably above"; and down to a few years ago *Kami* was the name of a certain titular 11 provincial rank. Thus it may be understood how the word was naturally applied to superiors in general, and especially to those more than human superiors whom we call "gods." A Japanese, to whom the origin of the word is patent, and who uses it every day in contexts by no means divine, does not receive from the word *Kami* the same impression of awe which is produced on the more earnest European mind by the words "deity" and "god," with their very different associations. In using the word "deity," therefore; to translate the Japanese term *Kami* we must, so to speak, bring it down from the heights to which Western thought has raised it. In fact *Kami* does not mean much more than "superior." This subject will be noticed again in Section V of the present Introduction; but so far as the word *Kami* itself is concerned, these remarks may suffice.

To conclude this Section, the translator must advert to his treatment of Proper Names, and he feels that he must plead guilty to a certain amount of inconsistency on this head. Indeed the treatment of Proper Names is always an embarrassment, partly because it is often difficult to determine what *is* a Proper Name, and partly because in translating a text into a foreign tongue Proper Names, whose meanings are evident in the original and perhaps have a bearing on the story, lose their significance; and the translator has therefore first of all to decide whether the name is really a Proper Name at all or simply a description of the personage or place, and next whether he will sacrifice the meaning because the word is used as a name; or preserve the original name and thus fail to render the meaning,—a meaning which may be of importance as revealing the channels in which ancient thought flowed. For instance *Oho-kuni-nushi-no-kami*, " the Deity Master of the Great Land," is clearly nothing more than a description of the god in question, who had several other names, and the reason of whose adoption of this special one was that the sovereignty of the "Great Land," *i.e.* of Japan (or rather of Idzumo and the neighbouring provinces in north-western Japan), was ceded to him by another god, whom he deceived and whose daughter he ran away with.[12] Again *Toyo-ashi-hara-no-chi-aki-no-naga-i-ho-aki-no-midzu-ho-no-kuni*, which signifies "the Luxuriant Reed-Moor, the Land of Fresh Rice-ears,—of a Thousand Autumns,—of Long Five Hundred Autumns" cannot possibly be regarded as more than an honorific *description* of Japan. Such a catalogue of words could never have been used as a name. On the other hand it is plain that *Tema* was simply the proper name of a certain mountain, because there is no known word in Archaic Japanese to which it can with certainty be traced. The difficulty is with the intermediate cases,—the cases of those names which are but partly comprehensible or partly applicable to their bearers ; and the difficulty is one of which there would seem to be no satisfactory solution possible. The translator may therefore merely state that in Vol. I of these "Records," where an unusual number of the Proper Names have a bearing on the legends related in the text, he has, wherever feasible, translated all those which

12. See the legend in Sect. XXIII.

are borne by persons, whether human or divine. In the
succeeding Volumes he has not done so, nor has he,
except in a very small number of instances, translated
the Proper Names of places in any of the three volumes.
In order, however, to convey all the needful information
both as to sound and as to sense, the Japanese original
is always indicated in a Foot-note when the translation
has the name in English, and *vice versâ*, while all
doubtful etymologies are discussed.

## III.

### THE "CHRONICLES OF JAPAN."

It will have been gathered from what has been already
said, and it is indeed generally known, that the "Records
of Ancient Matters" do not stand alone. To say nothing
of the "Chronicles of Old Matters of Former Age" whose
genuineness is disputed, there is another undoubtedly
authentic work with which no student of Japanese antiquity can dispense. It is entitled *Nihon-Gi*, i.e., "Chronicles of Japan," and is second only in value to the
"Records," which it has always excelled in popular favour.
It was completed in A.D. 720, eight years after the
"Records of Ancient Matters" had been presented to
the Empress Gem-miyo.

The scope of the two histories is the same; but the
language of the later one and its manner of treating the
national traditions stand in notable contrast to the unpre-
20 tending simplicity of the elder work. Not only is the
style (excepting in the Songs, which had to be left as
they were or sacrificed altogether) completely Chinese,—in
fact to a great extent a cento of well-worn Chinese

phrases,—but the subject-matter is touched up, re-arranged, and polished, so as to make the work resemble a Chinese history so far as that was possible. Chinese philosophical speculations and moral precepts are intermingled with the cruder traditions that had descended from Japanese antiquity. Thus the naturalistic Japanese account of the creation is ushered in by a few sentences which trace the origin of all things to *Yin* and *Yang* (陰陽), the Passive and Active Essences of Chinese philosophy. The legendary Emperor Jim-mu is credited with speeches made up of quotations from the " *Yi Ching*,"[13] the " *Li Chi*,"[14] and other standard Chinese works. A few of the most childish of the national traditions are omitted, for instance the story of the "White Hare of Inaba," that of the gods obtaining counsel of a toad, and that of the hospitality which a speaking mouse extended to the deity Master-of-the Great-Land.[15] Sometimes the original tradition is simply softened down or explained away. A notable instance of this occurs in the account of the visit of the deity Izanagi[16] to Hades, whither he goes in quest of his dead wife, and among other things has to scale the "Even Pass (or Hill) of Hades."[17] In the tradition preserved in the "Records" and indeed even in the "Chronicles," this pass or hill is mentioned as a literal geographical fact. But the compiler of the latter work, whose object it was to appear and to make his forefathers appear, as reasonable as a learned Chinese, adds a gloss to the effect that "One account

13. 易經. 14. 禮記
15. See Sects. XXI., XXVII and XXIII.
16. Rendered in the English translation by "the Male-Who-Invites."
17. *Yomo tsu Hira-Saka.*

says that the Even Hill of Hades is no distinct place,
but simply the moment when breathing ceases at the
time of death ";—not a happy guess certainly, for this
pass is mentioned in connection with Izanagi's return to
the land of the living. In short we may say of this
work what was said of the Septuagint,—that it *rationalizes*.

21  Perhaps it will be asked, how can it have come to pass
that a book in which the national traditions are thus unmistakably tampered with, and which is moreover written
in Chinese instead of in the native tongue, has enjoyed
such a much greater share of popularity than the more
genuine work ?

The answer lies on the surface : the concessions made
to Chinese notions went far towards satisfying minds
trained on Chinese models, while at the same time the
reader had his respect for the old native emperors increased, and was enabled to preserve some sort of belief
in the native gods. People are rarely quite logical in
such matters, particularly in an early stage of society ;
and difficulties are glossed over rather than insisted upon.
The beginning of the world, for instance, or, to use
Japanese phraseology. the " separation of heaven and
earth " took place a long time ago ; and perhaps, although there could of course be no philosophical doubt
as to the course of this event having been the interaction
of the Passive and Active Essences, it might also some-
how be true that Izanagi and Izanami (the " Male Who-
Invites " and the " Female-Who-Invites ") were the pro-
genitor and progenitrix of Japan. Who knows but what in
them the formative principles may not have been embodied,
represented, or figured forth after a fashion not quite determined, but none the less real ? As a matter of fact, the

two deities in question have often been spoken of in Japanese books under such designations as the "*Yin* Deity" and the "*Yang* Deity," and in his Chinese Preface the very compiler of these "Records" lends his sanction to the use of such phraseology, though, if we look closely at the part taken by the gods in the legend narrated in Sect. IV, it would seem but imperfectly applicable. If again early sovereigns, such as the Empress Jin-gō, address their troops in sentences cribbed from the "*Shu Ching*,"[18] or, like the Emperor Kei-kō, describe the Ainos in terms that would only suit the pages of a Chinese topographer,—both these personages being supposed to have lived prior to the opening up of intercourse with the continent of Asia,—the anachronism was partly hidden by the fact of the work which thus recorded their doings being itself written in the Chinese language, where such phrases only sounded natural. In some instances, too, the Chinese usage had so completely superseded the native 22 one as to cause the latter to have been almost forgotten excepting by the members of the Shintō priesthood. This happened in the case of the Chinese method of divination by means of a tortoise-shell, whose introduction caused the elder native custom of divination through the shoulder-blade of a deer to fall into desuetude. Whether indeed this native custom itself may not perhaps be traced back to still earlier continental influence is another question. So far as any documentary information reaches, divination through the shoulder-blade of a deer was the most ancient Japanese method of ascertaining the will of the gods. The use of the Chinese sexagenary cycle for counting years, months, and days is another instance of the im-

---

18.  書經

ported usage having become so thoroughly incorporated
with native habits of mind as to make the anachronism
of employing it when speaking of a period confessedly
anterior to the introduction of continental civilization pass
unnoticed.  As for the (to a modern European) grotesque
notion of pretending to give the precise months and days
of events supposed to have occurred a thousand years
before the date assigned to the introduction of astronomi-
cal instruments, of observatories, and even of the art of
writing, that is another of those inconsistencies which,
while lying on the very surface, yet so easily escape the
uncritical Oriental mind.[19]  Semi-civilized people tire of
asking questions, and to question antiquity, which fills so
great a place in their thoughts, is the last thing that
would occur to any of their learned men, whose mental
attitude is characteristically represented by Confucius when
he calls himself "A transmitter and not a maker, believing in and loving the ancients."[20]  As regards the
question of language, standard Chinese soon became easier
to understand than Archaic Japanese, as the former
23 alone was taught in the schools and the native language
changed rapidly during the century or two that followed
the diffusion of the foreign tongue and civilization.  We

---

19.  Details as to the adoption by the Japanese of the Chinese system
of computing time will be found in the late Mr. Bramsen's "Japanese
Chronological Tables," where that lamented scholar brands "the whole
system of fictitious dates applied in the first histories of Japan," as one
of the greatest literary frauds over perpetrated, from which we may infer
how little trust can be placed in the early Japanese historical works.
See also Motowori's "Inquiry into the True Chronology," pp. 33-36, and
his second work on the same subject entitled "Discussion of the Objections
to the Inquiry into the True Chronology," pp. 46 *et seq*.

20.  "Confucian Analects," Book VII. Chap. I. Dr. Legge's translation.

have only to call to mind the relative facility to most of ourselves of a Latin book and of one written in Early English. Of course, as soon as the principles of the Japanese *Renaissance* had taken hold of men's minds in the eighteenth century, the more genuine, more national work assumed its proper place in the estimation of students. But the uncouthness of the style according to modern ideas, and the greater amount of explanation of all sorts that is required in order to make the "Records of Ancient Matters" intelligible, must always prevent them from attaining to the popularity of the sister history. Thus, though published almost simultaneously, the tendencies of the two works were very different, and their fate has differed accordingly.

To the European student the chief value of the "Chronicles of Japan" lies in the fact that their author, in treating of the so-called "Divine Age," often gives a number of various forms of the same legend under the heading of "One account says," suffixed in the form of a note to the main text. No phrase is more commonly met with in later treatises on Japanese history than this, —"One account in the 'Chronicles of Japan' says," and it will be met with occasionally in the Foot-notes to the present translation. There are likewise instances of the author of the "Chronicles" having preserved, either in the text or in "One account," traditions omitted by the compiler of the "Records." Such are, for instance, the quaint legend invented to explain the fact that the sun and moon do not shine simultaneously,[21] and the curious development of the legend of the expulsion of the deity [24]

---

21. It may perhaps be worth while to quote this legend in full. It is as follows:

*Susa-no-wo* ("Impetuous Male"), telling us of the hospitality which was refused to him by the other gods
when he appeared before them to beg for shelter. Many
of the Songs, too, in the "Chronicles" are different from
those in the "Records," and make a precious addition to
our vocabulary of Archaic Japanese. The prose text,
likewise, contains in the shape of notes, numbers of readings by which the pronunciation of words written ideographically, or the meaning of words written phonetically
in the "Records" may be ascertained. Finally the
"Chronicles" give us the annals of seventy-two years not
comprised in the plan of the "Records," by carrying
down to A.D. 700 the history which in the "Records"
stops at the year 628. Although therefore it is a mistake

"One account says that the Heaven-Shining Great Deity, being in
Heaven said: 'I hear that in the Central Land of Reed-Plains (*i.e.* Japan)
there is a Food-Possessing Deity. Do, thou, Thine Augustness Moon-Night
Possessor, go and see.' His Augustness the Moon-Night Possessor, having
received these orders, descended [to earth], and arrived at the place where
the Food-Possessing Deity was. The Food-Possessing Deity forthwith, on
turning her head towards the land, produced rice from her mouth; again, on
turning to the sea, she also produced from her mouth things broad of fin and
things narrow of fin; again, on turning to the mountains, she also produced from her mouth things rough of hair and things soft of hair.
Having collected together all these things, she offered them [to the
Moon-God] as a feast on a hundred tables. At this time His Augustness the Moon-Night-Possessor, being angry and colouring up, said:
'How filthy! how vulgar! What! shalt thou dare to feed me with
things spat out from thy mouth?' [and with these words], he drew his
sabre and slew her. Afterwards he made his report [to the Sun-God-
dess]. When he told her all the particulars, the Heaven-Shining Great
Deity was very angry, and said: 'Thou art a wicked Deity, whom it
is not right for me to see;'—and forthwith she and His Augustness the
Moon-Night-Possessor dwelt separately day and night." The partly
parallel legend given in these "Records" forms the subject of Sect. XVII
of the Translation.

to assert, as some have done, that the "Chronicles of Japan" must be placed at the head of all the Japanese historical works, their assistance can in no wise be dispensed with by the student of Japanese mythology and of the Japanese language.[22]

## IV.

### MANNERS AND CUSTOMS OF THE EARLY JAPANESE.

The Japanese of the mythical period, as pictured in the legends preserved by the compiler of the "Records of Ancient Matters," were a race who had long emerged from the savage state, and had attained to a high level of barbaric skill. The Stone Age was forgotten by them —or nearly so,—and the evidence points to ·their never having passed through a genuine Bronze Age, though the knowledge of bronze was at a later period introduced from the neighbouring continent. They used iron for manufacturing spears, swords, and knives of various shapes, and likewise for the more peaceful purpose of making hooks wherewith to angle, or to fasten the doors of their huts. Their other warlike and hunting implements (besides traps and gins, which appear to have been used equally for catching beasts and birds and for destroying human enemies) were bows and elbow-pads,—the latter seemingly of skin, while special allusion is made to the fact that the arrows were feathered. Perhaps clubs should be added to the list. Of the bows and arrows, swords and knives, there is perpetual mention ; but nowhere do we hear of the tools

---

22. Compare Mr. Satow's remarks on this subject in Vol. III, Pt. I, pp. 21-23 of these "Transactions."

with which they were manufactured, and there is the
same remarkable silence regarding such widely spread
domestic implements as the saw and the axe, We hear,
however, of the pestle and fire-drill, of the wedge, of
the sickle, and of the shuttle used in weaving.

Navigation seems to have been in a very elementary
stage.  Indeed the art *of sailing was, as we know from
the classical literature of the country, but little practised
in Japan even so late as the middle of the tenth century
of our era subsequent to the general diffusion of Chinese
civilization, though rowing and punting are often mentioned by the early poets.  In one passage of the
" Records " and in another of the " Chronicles," mention
is made of a " two-forked boat " used on inland pools
or lakes ; but, as a rule, in the earlier portions of those
works, we read only of people going to sea or being sent
down from heaven in water-proof baskets without oars,
and reaching their destination not through any efforts of
their own, but through supernatural inter-position.[23]

To what we should call towns or villages very little
reference is made anywhere in the " Records " or in
that portion of the " Chronicles " which contains the
account of the so-called " Divine Age."  But from what

---

23.  A curious scrap of the history of Japanese civilization is preserved in the word *kaji*, whose exclusive acceptation in the modern
tongue is "rudder."  In archaic Japanese it meant "oar," a signification
which is now expressed by the term *ro*, which has been borrowed from
the Chinese.  It is a matter of debate whether the ancient Japanese
boats possessed such an appliance as a *rudder*, and the word *tagishi* or
*iaishi* has been credited with that meaning.  The more likely opinion
seems to be that both the thing and the word were specialized in later
times, the early Japanese boatmen having made any oar do duty for a
rudder when circumstances necessitated the use of one.

we learn incidentally, it would seem that the scanty population was chiefly distributed in small hamlets and isolated dwellings along the coast and up the course of the larger streams. Of house-building there is frequent mention,—especially of the building of palaces or temples for sovereigns or gods,—the words " palace " and " temple " being (it should be mentioned) represented in Japanese by the same term. Sometimes, in describing the construction of such a sacred dwelling, the author of the " Records," abandoning his usual flat and monotonous style, soars away on poetic wings, as when, for instance, he tells how the monarch of Idzumo, on abdicating in favour of the Sun-Goddess's descendant, covenanted that the latter should " make stout his temple pillars on the nethermost rock-bottom, and make high the cross-beams to the plain of High Heaven."[24] It must not, however, be inferred from such language that these so-called palaces and temples were of very gorgeous and imposing aspect. The more exact notices to be culled from the ancient Shintō Rituals (which are but little posterior to the " Records " and in no wise contradict the inferences to be drawn from the latter) having been already summarized by Mr. Satow, it may be as well to quote that gentleman's words. He says:[25] " The palace of the Japanese sovereign was a wooden hut, with its pillars planted in the ground, instead of being erected upon broad flat stones as in modern buildings. The whole frame-work, consisting of posts, beams, rafters, door-posts and window-frames, was tied together with cords made by twisting the long fibrous stems of climbing plants, such as Pueraria

24. See the end of Sect. XXXII.
25. See Vol. IX, Pt. II, pp. 191-192, of these "Transactions."

Thunbergiana (*kuzu*) and Wistaria Sinensis (*fuji*). The
floor must have been low down, so that the occupants of
the building, as they squatted or lay on their mats, were
exposed to the stealthy attacks of venomous snakes, which
were probably far more numerous in the earliest ages when
the country was for the most part uncultivated, than at the
present day . . . There seems some reason to think that
the *yuka*, here translated floor, was originally nothing but
a couch which ran round the sides of the hut, the rest
27 of the space being simply a mud-floor, and that the
size of the couch was gradually increased until it occupied the whole interior. The rafters projected upward
beyond the ridge-pole, crossing each other as is seen
in the roofs of modern Shin-tau temples, whether their
architecture be in conformity with early traditions (in
which case all the rafters are so crossed) or modified
in accordance with more advanced principles of construction, and the crossed rafters retained only as ornaments at the two ends of the ridge. The roof was
thatched, and perhaps had a gable at each end, with a
hole to allow the smoke of the wood-fire to escape, so
that it was possible for birds flying in and perching on
the beams overhead, to defile the food, or the fire with
which it was cooked." To this description it need only
be added that fences were in use, and that the wooden
doors, sometimes fastened by means of hooks, resembled
those with which we are familiar in Europe rather than
the sliding, screen-like doors of modern Japan. The
windows seem to have been mere holes. Rugs of skins
and rush matting were occasionally brought in to sit
upon, and we even hear once or twice of "silk rugs"
being used for the same purpose by the noble and wealthy.

The habits of personal cleanliness which so pleasantly distinguish the modern Japanese from their neighbours in continental Asia, though less fully developed than at present, would seem to have existed in the germ in early times, as we read more than once of bathing in rivers, and are told of bathing-women being specially attached to the person of a certain imperial infant. Lustrations, too, formed part of the religious practices of the race. Latrines are mentioned several times. They would appear to have been situated away from the houses and to have generally been placed over a running stream, whence doubtless the name for latrine in the Archaic Dialect,— *kaha-ya* i.e. "river house." A well-known Japanese classic of the tenth century, the "Yamato Tales,"[26] tells us indeed that "in older days the people dwelt in houses raised on "plat-forms built out on the river Ikuta," and goes on to relate a story which presupposes such a method of architecture.[27] A passage in the account of the reign of the Emperor Jim-mu which occurs both in the "Records" and in the "Chronicles," and another in the reign of the Emperor Sui-nin occurring in the "Records" only, might be interpreted so as to support this statement.[28] But both are extremely obscure, and beyond the fact that people who habitually lived near the water *may* have built their houses after the aquatic fashion practised in different parts of the world by certain savage tribes both ancient and modern, the present writer is not aware of any authority for the assertion that they actually

---

26. *Yamato Monogatari.*

27. For a translation of this story see the present writer's "Classical Poetry of the Japanese," pp. 42.44.

28. See Sect. XLIV, Note 12 and Sect. LXXII, Note 29.

did so except the isolated passage in the "Yamato Tales"
just quoted.

A peculiar sort of dwelling-place which the two old
histories bring prominently under our notice, is the so-
called "parturition-house,"—a one-roomed hut without
windows which a woman was expected to build and retire into for the purpose of being delivered unseen.[29] It
would also appear to be not unlikely that newly-married
couples retired into a specially built hut for the purpose
29 of consummating the marriage, and it is certain that

---

29. Mr. Ernest Satow, who in 1898 visited the island of Hachijo,
gives the following detail concerning the observance down to modern
times in that remote corner of the Japanese Empire of the custom mentioned in the text: "In Hachijo women, when about to become mothers,
were formerly driven out to the huts on the mountain-side, and according
to the accounts of native writers, left to shift for themselves, the result
not unfrequently being the death of the newborn infant, or if it survived
the rude circumstances under which it first saw the light, the seeds of
disease were sown which clung to it throughout its after life.   The rule
of non-intercourse was so strictly enforced, that the woman was not allowed to leave the hut even to visit her own parents at the point of death,
and besides the injurious effects that this solitary confinement must have
had on the wives themselves, their prolonged absence was a serious loss
to households, where there were elder children and large establishments
to be superintended.   The rigour of the custom was so far relaxed in
modern times, that the huts were no longer built on the hills, but were
constructed inside the homestead.   It was a subject of wonder to people
from other parts of Japan that the senseless practice should still be kept
up, and its abolition was often recommended, but the administration of
the Shoguns was not animated by a reforming spirit, and it remained for
the Government of the Mikado to exhort the islanders to abandon this
and the previously mentioned custom.   They are therefore no longer
sanctioned by official authority and the force of social opinion against
them is increasing, so that before long these relics of ancient ceremonial
religion will in all probability have disappeared from the group of islands."
(Trans. of the Asiat. Soc. of Japan, Vol. VI, Part III, pp. 455-6.)

for each sovereign a new palace was erected on his accession.

Castles are not distinctly spoken of till a period which, though still mythical in the opinion of the present writer, coincides according to the received chronology with the first century B. C. We then first meet with the curious term " rice-castle," whose precise signification is a matter of dispute among the native commentators, but which, on comparison with Chinese descriptions of the Early Japanese, should probably be understood to mean a kind of palisade serving the purpose of a redoubt, behind which the warriors could ensconce themselves.[30] If this conjecture be correct, we have here a good instance of a word, so to speak, moving upward with the march of civilization, the term, which formerly denoted something not much better than a fence, having later come to convey the idea of a stone castle.

To conclude the subject of dwelling-places, it should be stated that cave-dwellers are sometimes alluded to. The legend of the retirement of the Sun-Goddess into a cavern may possibly suggest to some the idea of an early period when such habitations were the normal abodes of the ancestors of the Japanese race.[31] But at the time when the national traditions assumed their present shape, such a state of things had certainly quite passed away, if it ever existed, and only barbarous Ainos and rough bands of robbers are credited with the construction of such primitive retreats. Natural caves

---

30. See Sect. LXX, Note 6. The Japanese term is *ina-ki*, *ki* being an Archaic term for "castle."

31. See Sect. XVI. Mention of cave-dwellers will also be found in Sects. XLVIII, and LXXX.

(it may be well to state) are rare in Japan, and the caves that are alluded to were mostly artificial, as may be gathered from the context.

The food of the Early Japanese consisted of fish and of the flesh of the wild creatures which fell by the hunter's arrow or were taken in the trapper's snare,—an animal diet with which Buddhist prohibitions had not yet interfered, as they began to do in early historical times. Rice is the only cereal of which there is such mention made as to place it beyond a doubt that its 30 cultivation dates back to time immemorial. Beans, millet, and barley are indeed named once, together with silk-worms, in the account of the "Divine Age."[32] But the passage has every aspect of an interpolation in the legend, perhaps not dating back long before the time of the eighth century compiler. A few unimportant vegetables and fruits, of most of which there is but a single mention, will be found in the list of plants given below. The intoxicating liquor called *sake* was known in Japan during the mythical period [33] and so were chopsticks for eating the food with. Cooking-pots and cups and dishes—the latter both of earthenware and of leaves of trees,—are also mentioned; but of the use of fire for warming purposes we hear nothing. Tables are named several times, but never in connection with food. They would seem to have been exclusively used for the purpose of presenting offerings on, and were probably quite small and low,—in fact rather trays than tables according to European ideas.

In the use of clothing and the specialization of garments

32. See the latter part of Sect. XVII.
33. See Sect. XVIII, Note 16.

the Early Japanese had reached a high level. We read in the most ancient legends of upper garments, skirts, trowsers, girdles, veils, and hats, while both sexes adorned themselves with necklaces, bracelets, and head-ornaments of stones considered precious,—in this respect offering a striking contrast to their descendants in modern times, of whose attire jewelry forms no part. The material of their clothes was hempen cloth and paper-mulberry bark, coloured by being rubbed with madder, and probably with woad and other tinctorial plants. All the garments, so far as we may judge, were woven, sewing being nowhere mentioned, and it being expressly stated by the Chinese commentator on the " *Shan Hai Ching*,"[34] who wrote early in the fourth century, that the Japanese had no needles.[35] From the great place which the chase occupied in daily life we are led to suppose that skins also were used to make garments of. There is in the " Records " at least one passage which favours this supposi-tion,[36] and the " Chronicles " in one place mention the straw rain-coat and broad-brimmed hat, which still form the Japanese peasant's effectual protection against the incle-mencies of the weather. The tendrils of creeping plants served the purposes of string, and bound the warrior's sword round his waist. Combs are mentioned, and it is evident that much attention was devoted to the dressing of the hair. The men seem to have bound up their hair in two bunches, one on each side of the head, whilst the young boys tied theirs into a topknot, the unmarried girls let their locks hang down over their necks, and the

31

---

34. 山海經.
35. See, however, the legend in Sect. LXV.
36. See beginning of Sect. XXVII.

married women dressed theirs after a fashion which apparently combined the two last-named methods.   There is no mention in any of the old books of cutting the hair or beard except in token of disgrace; neither do we gather that the sexes, but for this matter of the headdress, were distinguished by a diversity of apparel and ornamentation.

With regard to the precious stones mentioned above as having been used as ornaments for the head, neck, and arms, the texts themselves give us little or no information as to the identity of the stones meant to be referred to.   Indeed it is plain (and the native commentators admit the fact) that a variety of Chinese characters properly denoting different sort of jewels were used indiscriminately by the early Japanese writers to represent the single native word *tama* which is the only one the language contains to denote any hard substance on which a special value is set, and which often refers chiefly to the rounded shape, so that it might in fact be translated by the word "bead" as fittingly as by the word "jewel." We know, however, from the specimens which have rewarded the labours of archæological research in Japan that agate, crystal, glass, jade, serpentine, and steatite are the most usual materials, and carved and pierced cylindrical shapes (*maga-tama* and *kuda-tama*), the commonest forms.[37]

The horse (which was ridden, but not driven), the

37.  For details on this subject and illustrations, see Mr. Henry von Siebold's "Notes on Japanese Archæology," p. 15 and Table XI, and a paper by Professor Milne on the "Stone Age in Japan," read before the Anthropological Society of Great Britain on the 25th May, 1880, pp. 10 and 11.

barn-door fowl, and the cormorant used for fishing, are the only domesticated creatures mentioned in the earlier traditions, with the doubtful exception of the silkworm, to which reference has already been made.[38] In the later portions of the " Records " and " Chronicles," dogs and cattle are alluded to ; but sheep, swine, and even cats were apparently not yet [introduced. Indeed sheep were scarcely to be seen in Japan until a few years ago, goats are still almost unknown, and swine and all poultry excepting the barn-door fowl extremely uncommon.

The following enumeration of the animals and plants mentioned in the earlier portion[39] of the " Records " may be of interest. The Japanese equivalents, some few of which are obsolete, are put in parenthesis, together with the Chinese characters used to write them :

MAMMALS.

Bear, (*kuma* 熊).

Boar, (*wi* 猪).

Deer, (*shika* 鹿).

Hare, (*usagi* 兎).

Horse, (uma 馬 and *koma* 駒).

Mouse or Rat (*nedzumi* 鼠).

"Sea-ass" [Seal or Sea-lion?] (*michi* 海鱸).

Whale, (*kujira* 鯨).

---

38. The tradition preserved in Sect. CXXIV, shows that in times almost, if not quite, historical (the 4th century of our era) the silkworm was a curious novelty, apparently imported from Korea. It is not only possible, but probable, that silken fabrics were occasionally imported into Japan from the mainland at an earlier period, which would account for the mention of "silk rugs" in Sects XL and LXXXIV.

39. The (necessarily somewhat arbitrary) line between earlier and later times has been drawn at the epoch of the traditional conquest of Korea by the Empress Jin-go at the commencement of the third century of our era, it being then, according to the received opinions, that the Japanese first came in contact with their continental neighbours, and began to borrow from them. (See however the concluding Section of this Introduction for a demonstration of the untrustworthiness of all the so-called history of JJapan down to the commencement of the fifth century of the Christian era).

### BIRDS.

Barndoor-fowl, (*kake* 鷄)

Cormorant, (*u* 鵜.)

Crow *or* Raven, (*karasu* 烏)

Dotterel *or* Plover *or* Sand-piper, (*chidori* 千鳥).

Heron *or* Egret (*sagi* 鷺)

Kingfisher (*soni-dori* 翠鳥).

*Nuye* (鵼).[40]

Pheasant (*kigishi* 雉).

Snipe, (*shigi* 鳴).

Swan, (*shiro-tori* 白鳥).

Wild-duck, (*kámo* 鴨).

Wild-goose, (*kari* 鴈).

### REPTILES.

Crocodile, (*wani* 鰐).[41]

Tortoise (*kame* 龜).

Toad *or* Frog, (*taniguku*, written phonetically).

Serpent, (*worochi* 蛇).

Snake [smaller than the preceding], (*hemi* 蛇).

### INSECTS.

Centipede, (*mukade* 蜈松).

Dragon-fly, (*akidzu* 蜻蛉).

Fly, (*hahi* 蠅).

Louse, (*shirami* 虱).

Silk-worm, (*kahiko* 蠶).

Wasp *or* Bee, (*hachi* 蜂).

### FISHES, ETC.

*Pagrus cardinalis* [probably], (*aka-dahi* 赤鯛) [or perhaps the *Pagrus cardinalis* (*tai* 鯛) is intended.]

Perch [*Percalabrax japonicus*] *su-dzuki* 鱸).

Beche-de-mer [genus *Pentacta*] (*ko* 海鼠).

Medusa, (*kurage*, written phonetically).

---

40. See Sect. XXIV, Note 4.

41. Mr. Satow, in his translation of a passage of the "Records of Ancient Matters" forming part of a note to his third paper on the "Rituals" in Vol. IX, Pt. II of these "Transactions," renders *wani* by "shark." There is perhaps some want of clearness in the old historical books in the details concerning the creature in question, and its *fin* is mentioned in the "Chronicles." But the accounts point rather to an amphibious creature, conceived of as being somewhat similar to the serpent, than to a fish, and the Chinese descriptions quoted by the Japanese commentators unmistakably refer to the crocodile. The translator therefore sees no sufficient reason for abandoning the usually accepted interpretation of *wani* (鰐) as "crocodile." It should be noticed that the *wani* is never introduced into any but patently fabulous stories, and that the example of other nations, and indeed of Japan itself, shows that myth-makers have no objection to embellish their tales by the mention of wonders supposed to exist in foreign lands.

### SHELLS.

*Arca Subcrenata* [ ? ] *hirabu-kahi,* written phonetically).

Cockle [*Arca Inflata*](*kisa-gahi* 蛼貝).

*Turbinidæ* [a shell of the family] (*shitadami* 細螺).

### PLANTS.

*Ampelopsis serianæfolia* [?] (*kagami* 羅摩).

*Aphananthe aspera,* (*muku,* written phonetically).

*Aucuba japonica* [probably] *aha-gi,* written phonetically).

Bamboo, (*take* 竹).

Bamboo-grass [*Bambusa chino*], *sasa* 小竹).

Barley [or wheat?], (*mugi* 麥).

Beans [two kinds, viz., *Soja glycine* and *Phaselus radiatus* (the general name is *mame* 豆, that of the latter species in particular *adzuki* 小豆).

Bulrush [*Typha japonica*] (*kama* 蒲黃).

Bush-clover [*Lespedeza* of various species], (*hagi* 萩).

*Camellia japonica* (*tsuba-ki* 椿).

Cassia [Chinese mythical; or perhaps the native *Cercidiphyllum japonica*], (*katsura,* variously written).

*Chamæcyparis obtusa,* (*hi-no-ki* 檜).

*Cleyera japonica* [and another allied but undetermined species], *saka-ki* 榊).

Clubmoss, (*hi-koge* 日景).

*Cocculus thunbergi* [probably] (*tsu-dzura* 黑葛).

*Cryptomeria japonica,* (*sugi* 椙).

*Eulalia japonica* (*kaya* 萱草).

*Evonymus japonica,* (*masa-ki* 眞賢木).

Ginger, [or perhaps the *Xanthoxylon* is intended] *hazhikami* 薑).

*Halocholoa macrantha* [but it is not certain that this is the sea-weed intended] *komo* 海藻).

Holly [or rather the *Olea aquifolium,* which closely resembles/ holly], *hihira-gi* 柊).

Knot-grass [*Polygonum tinctorium* (*awi* 藍).

Lily, (*sawi* written phonetically, *yamayuri-gusa* 山由理草, and *saki-kusa* 三枝草).

Madder, (*akane* 茜).

Millet [*Panicum italicum*], (*aha* 粟).

Moss, *koke* 蘿).

Oak (two species, one evergreen and one deciduous,—*Quercus myrsinæfolia, Q. dentata* (*kashi* 白檮, *kashi-wa* 柏)].

Peach, (*momo* 桃).

*Photinia glabra* [?], *soba,* written phonetically.

Pine-tree, (*matsu* 松).

*Pueraria thunbergiana,* (*kudzu* 葛).

Reed, (*ashi* 葦).

Rice, (*ine* 稻).

Sea-weed [or the original term may designate a particular species], (*me* 海布).

Sedge [*Scripus maritimus*], (*suge* 菅).

Spindle-tree [*Evonymus radicans*], (*masaki no kadzura* 眞栬蔓).

Vegetable Wax-tree [*Rhus succeda-nea*], (*hazhi* 櫨).

Vine, *yebi-kadzura* 蒲蒲).

Wild cherry [or birch?], *hahaka* 朱櫻).

Wild chive [or rather the *allium odorum*, which closely resembles t], (*ka-mira* 臭韮).

Winter-cherry [*Physalis alkekengi*] *aka-kagachi* written phonetically, and also *hohodzuki* 酸醬).

The later portions of the work furnish in addition the following :—

### ANIMALS.

Cow (*ushi* 牛).

Dog, (*inu* 犬).

Crane, [genus *Grus*] *tadzu* 鶴).

35 Dove *or* Pigeon, (*hato* 鳩).

Grebe, (*niho-dori* 鸊鷉).

Lark, (*hibari* 雲雀).

Peregrine falcon, (*hayabusa* 隼).

Red-throated quail (*udzura* 鶉).

Tree-sparrow (*suzume* 雀).

Wag-tail, [probably] |*mana-bashira*), written phonetically).

Wren, (*sazaki* 鷦鷯).

Dolphin, (*iruka* 入鹿魚).

Trout, [*Plecoglossus altivelis*] (*ayu* 年魚).

Tunny, [a kind of, viz. *Thynnus sibi*] (*shibi* 鮪).

Crab, (*kani* 蟹).

Horse-fly (*amu* 虻).

Oyster (*kaki* 蠣.

### PLANTS.

Alder [*Alnus maritima*] *hari-no-ki* 榛).

Aralia (*mi-tsuna gashiwa* 御綱柏).

*Brasenia peltata* (*nunaha*) 蓴.

Cabbage [*brassica*] (*aona* 菘菜).

*Catalpa Kaempfri* [but some say the cherry is meant (*adzusa* 梓).

Chestnut (*kuri* 栗).

*Dioscorea quinqueloba* (*tokoro-dzura* 解葛).

*Evonymus sieboldianus mayumi* 木檀).

Gourd (*hisago* 瓠).

*Hedysarum esculentum* (*wogi* 荻).

*Hydropyrum latifolium* (*komo* 菰).

*Kadzura japonica* (*sen kadzura* 蒅).

*Livistona sinensis* (*aji-masa* 檳榔).

Lotus [*nelumbium*] (*hachisu* 蓮).

Musk-melon (*hozoahi* 熟瓜).

Oak, [three species, *Quercus serrata* (*kunugi* 櫪木) and *Q. glandulifera* (*nara* 楢), both deciduous; *Q. gilvà* (*ichihi* 赤檮) [evergreen].

Orange (*tachibana* 橘).

*Podocarpus macrophylla* (*maki* 檜).

Radish, [*Raphanus sativus*] *oho-ne* 大根).

*Sashibu* (written phonetically) [not identified].

Water caltrop, [*Trapa bispinosa*] (*hishi* 菱).

Wild garlic [*Allium nipponicum*] (*nubiru* 野蒜).

*Zelkowa keaki* [probably] (*tsuki* 槻),

A few more are probably preserved in the names of places. Thus in Shinano, the name of a province, we seem to have the *shina* (*Tilia cordata*), and in Tadetsu the *tàde* (*Polygonum japonicum*). But the identification in these cases is mostly uncertain. It must also be remembered that, as in the case of all non-scientific nomenclatures, several species, and occasionally even more than one genus, are included in a single Japanese term. The *chi-dori* (here always rendered " dotterel ") is the name of any kind of sand-piper, plover or dotterel. *Kari* is a general name applied to geese, but not to all the species, and also to the great bustard. Again it should not be forgotten that there may have been, and probably were, in the application of some of these terms, differences of usage between the present day and eleven or twelve centuries ago. Absolute precision is therefore not attainable.[42]

Noticeable in the above lists is the abundant mention of plant-names in a work which is in no ways occupied with botany. Equally noticeable is the absence of some of those which are most common at the present day, such as the tea-plant and the plum-tree, while of the orange we are specially informed that it was introduced from abroad.[43] The difference between the various stones and metals seems, on the other hand, to have attracted 36 very little attention from the Early Japanese. In late

---

42. Sect. CXXVIII preserves a very early ornithological observation in the shape of the Songs composed by the Emperor Nin-toku and his Minister Take-Uchi on the subject of a wild-goose laying eggs in Central Japan. These birds are not known to breed even so far South as the island of Yezo.

43. See the legend in Sect. LXXIV.

times the chief metals were named mostly according to
their colour, as follows :

| | | | | |
|---|---|---|---|---|
| Yellow metal | .... | .... | .... .... | (gold). |
| White ,, | .... | .... | .... .... | (silver). |
| Red ,, | .... | .... | .... .... | (copper). |
| Black ,, | .... | .... | .... .... | (iron). |
| Chinese (or Korean) | | .... | .... | (bronze). |

But in the "Records" the only metal of which it is
implied that it was in use from time immemorial is iron,
while "various treasures dazzling to the eye, from gold
and silver downwards," are only referred to once as
existing in the far-western land of Korea. Red clay is
the sole kind of earth specially named.

> Black.
> Blue (including Green).
> Red.
> Piebald (of horses).
> White.

Yellow is not mentioned (except in the foreign Chinese
phrase "the Yellow Stream," signifying Hades, and not
to be counted in this context), neither are any of the
numerous terms which in Modern Japanese serve to
distinguish delicate shades of colour. We hear of the
"blue (or green) *i.e.* black[44]) clouds" and also of the
"blue (or green), sea"; but the "blue sky" is conspicuous by its absence here as in so many other early
literatures, though strangely enough it does occur in the
oldest written monuments of the Chinese.

With regard to the subject of names for the different
degrees of relationship,—a subject of sufficient interest

to the student of sociology to warrant its being discussed at some length,—it may be stated that in modern Japanese parlance the categories according to which relationship is conceived of do not materially differ from those that are current in Europe. Thus we find father, grandfather, great-grandfather, uncle, nephew. stepfather, stepson, 37 father-in-law, and the corresponding terms for females, —mother, grandmother etc.,—as well as such vaguer designations as parents, ancestors, cousins, and kinsmen, The only striking difference is that brothers and sisters, instead of being considered as all mutually related in the same manner, are divided into two categories, viz :

| | | | | | | | |
|---|---|---|---|---|---|---|---|
| *Ani* | 兄 | … | … | … | … | elder brother(s), |
| *Otouto* | 弟 | … | … | … | … | younger brother(s), |
| *Ane* | 姉 | … | … | … | … | elder sister(s), |
| *Imouto* | 妹 | … | … | … | … | younger sister(s). |

in exact accordance with Chinese usage.

Now in Archaic times there seems to have been a different and more complicated system, somewhat resembling that which still obtains among the natives of Korea, and which the introduction of Chinese ideas and especially the use of the Chinese written characters must have caused to be afterwards abandoned. There are indications of it in some of the phonetically written fragments of the "Records." But they are not of themselves sufficient to furnish a satisfactory explanation, and the subject has puzzled the native *literati* themselves. Moreover the English language fails us at this point, and elder and younger brother, elder and younger sister are the only terms at the translator's command. It may therefore be as well to quote *in extenso* Motowori's elucidation of the Archaic usage to be found in vol. XIII, p. 63–4 of his "Exposition of the Records of Ancient Matters."[45] He says: "Anciently, when brothers and sisters were spoken of, the elder brother was called *se* or *ani* in contradistinction to the younger brothers and younger sisters, and the younger brother also was called *se* in contradistinction to the elder sister. The elder sister was called *ane* in contradistinction to the younger sister, and the younger brother also would use the word *ane* in speaking of his elder sister himself. The younger brother was called *oto* in contradistinction to the elder brother, and the younger sister also was called *oto* in contradistinction to the elder sister. The younger sister was called *imo* in contradistinction to the elder brother, and the elder sister also was called *imo* in 38 contradistinction to the younger brother. It was also the custom among brothers and sisters to use the words *iro-se* for *se*, *iro-ne* for *ane*, and *iro-do* for *oto*, and analogy forces us to conclude that *iro-mo* was used for *imo*." (Motowori elsewhere explains *iro* as a term of endearment identical with the word *iro*, "love"; but we may hesitate to accept this view.) It will be observed that the foundation of this system of nomenclature was a subordination of the younger to the elder-born modified by a subordination of the females to the males. In the East, especially in primitive times, it is not "*place aux dames*," but "*place aux messieurs*."

Another important point to notice is that, though in a few passages of the "Records" we find a distinction drawn between the chief and the secondary wives,— perhaps nothing more than the favorite or better-born,

---

45. Only the foot-notes of the original are omitted, as not being essential.

and the less well-born, are meant to be thus designated,
—yet not only is this distinction not drawn throughout,
but the wife is constantly spoken of as *imo, i.e.* "younger
sister." It fact sister and wife were convertible terms
and ideas; and what in a later stage of Japanese, as of
Western, civilization is abhorred as incest was in Archaic
Japanese times the common practice. We also hear of
marriages with half-sisters, with stepmothers, and with
aunts; and to wed two or three sisters at the same time
was a recognized usage. Most such unions were naturally
so contrary to Chinese ethical ideas, that one of the first
traces of the influence of the latter in Japan was the stig-
matizing of them as incest; and the conflict between the
old native custom and the imported moral code is seen
to have resulted in political troubles.[46] Marriage with
sisters was naturally the first to disappear, and indeed it
is only mentioned in the legends of the gods; but unions
with half-sisters, aunts, etc., lasted on into the historic
epoch. Of exogamy, such as obtains in China, there is
no trace in any Japanese document, nor do any other
artificial impediments seem to have stood in the way of
the free choice of the Early Japanese man, who also (in
some cases at least) received a dowry with his bride or
brides.

\* \* \*

If, taking as our guides the incidental notices which
are scattered up and down the pages of the earlier 39
portion of the "Records" we endeavour to follow an
Archaic Japanese through the chief events of his life

---

46. See the story of Prince Karu, which is probably historical, in
Sects. CXLI *et seq.*

from the cradle to the tomb, it will be necessary to begin by recalling what has already been alluded to as the "parturition-house" built by the mother, and in which, as we are specially told that it was made windowless, it would perhaps be contradictory to say that the infant first saw the light. Soon after birth a name was given to it,—given to it by the mother,—such name generally containing some appropriate personal reference. In the most ancient times each person (so far as we can judge) bore but one name, or rather one string of words compounded together into a sort of personal designation. But already at the dawn of the historical epoch we are met by the mention of surnames and of what, in the absence of a more fitting word, the translator has ventured to call "gentile names," bestowed by the sovereign as a recompense for some noteworthy deed.[47]

It may be gathered from our text that the idea of calling in the services of wet-nurses in exceptional cases had already suggested itself to the minds of the ruling class, whose infants were likewise sometimes attended by special bathing-women. To what we should call education, whether mental or physical, there is absolutely no reference made in the histories. All that can be inferred is that, when old enough to do so, the boys began to follow one of the callings of hunter or fisherman,

---

47. The custom of using surnames was certainly borrowed from China, although the Japanese have not, like the Koreans, gone so far as to adopt the actual surnames in use in that country. The "gentile names" may have sprung up more naturally, though they too show traces of Chinese influence. Those most frequently met with are *Agata-nushi*, *Ason*, *Atahe*, *Kimi*, *Miyatsuko*, *Murazhi*, *Omi*, *Sukune*, and *Wake*. See above, pp. xv-xvi.

while the girls staid at home weaving the garments of
the family. There was also a great deal of fighting,
generally of a treacherous kind, in the intervals of which
the warriors occupied themselves in cultivating patches
of ground. The very little which is to be gathered
concerning the treatment of old people would seem to
indicate that they were well cared for.

We are nowhere told of any wedding ceremonies
except the giving of presents by the bride or her father,
the probable reason being that no such ceremonies 40
existed. Indeed late on into the Middle Age cohabitation alone constituted matrimony,—cohabitation often
secret at first, but afterwards acknowledged, when, instead
of going round under cover of night to visit his mistress,
the young man brought her back publicly to his parents'
house. Mistress, wife, and concubine were thus terms
which were not distinguished, and the woman could
naturally be discarded at any moment. She indeed was
expected to remain faithful to the man with whom she
had had more than a passing intimacy, but no reciprocal
obligation bound him to her. Thus the wife of one of
the gods is made to address her husband in a poem
which says :

" Thou . . . indeed, being a man, probably hast on
the various island-headlands that thou seest, and on
every beach-headland that thou lookest on, a wife like
the young herbs. But I, alas ! being a woman, have no
spouse except thee," etc., etc.[48]

In this sombre picture the only graceful touch is the
custom which lovers or spouses had of tieing each other's
girdles when about to part for a time,—a ceremony by

48. See Sect. XXV (the second Song in that Section).

which they implied that they would be constant to each
other during the period of absence.[49] What became of
the children in cases of conjugal separation does not
clearly appear. In the only instance which is related at
length, we find the child left with the father; but this
instance is not a normal one.[50] Adoption is not mentioned in the earliest traditions; so that when we meet
with it later on we shall probably be justified in tracing
its introduction to Chinese sources.

Of death-bed scenes and dying speeches we hear but
little, and that little need not detain us. The burial
rites are more important. The various ceremonies
observed on such an occasion are indeed not explicitly
detailed. But we gather thus much: that the hut
tenanted by the deceased was abandoned,—an ancient
custom to whose former existence the removal of
the capital at the commencement of each reign long
41 continued to bear witness,—and that the body was
first deposited for some days in a "mourning-house,"
during which interval the survivors (though their tears
and lamentations are also mentioned) held a carousal,
feasting perhaps on the food which was specially prepared
as an offering to the dead person. Afterwards, the
corpse was interred, presumably in a wooden bier, as the
introduction of stone tombs is specially noted by the
historian as having taken place at the end of the reign
of the Emperor Sui-nin, and was therefore believed by
those who handed down the legendary history to have
been a comparatively recent innovation, the date assigned
to this monarch by the author of the "Chronicles" coin-

49. See Sect. LXXI, Note 12.
50. See Sect. XLII.

ciding with the latter part of our first, and the first half of our second centuries. To a time not long anterior is attributed the abolition of a custom previously observed at the interments of royal personages. This custom was the burying alive of some of their retainers in the neighbourhood of the tomb. We know also, both from other early literary sources and from the finds which have recently rewarded the labours of archæologists, that articles of clothing, ornaments, etc., were buried with the corpse. It is all the more curious that the " Records " should nowhere make any reference to such a custom, and is a proof (if any be needed) of the necessity of not relying exclusively on any single authority, however respectable, if the full and true picture of Japanese antiquity is to be restored. A few details as to the abolition of the custom of burying retainers alive round their master's tomb, and of the substitution for this cruel holocaust of images in clay will be found in Sect. LXIII, Note 23, and in Sect. LXXV, Note 4, of the following translation.[51] If the custom be one which is properly included under the heading of human sacrifices, it is the only form of such sacrifices of which the earliest recorded Japanese social state retained any trace. The absence of slavery is another honourable feature. On the other hand, the most cruel punishments were dealt out to enemies and wrongdoers. Their nails were extracted, the sinews of their knees were cut, they were buried up to the neck so that their eyes burst, etc. Death, too, was inflicted for the 42

---

51. Representations of these clay images (*Tsuchi-nin-giyō*) will be found in Table XII of Mr. Henry von Siebold's "Notes on Japanese Archæology," and in Mr. Satow's paper on " Ancient Sepulchral Mounds in Kaudzuke " published in Vol. VII, Pt. III, pp. 313 *et seq.* of these " Transactions."

most trivial offences, Of branding, or rather tattooing,
the face as a punishment there are one or two incidental
mentions. But as no tattooing or other marking or painting of the body for any other purpose is ever alluded to,
with the solitary exception in one passage of the painting
of her eyebrows by a woman, it is possible that the penal
use of tattooing may have been borrowed from the
Chinese, to whom it was not unknown.

The shocking obscenity of word and act to which
the " Records " bear witness is another ugly feature
which must not quite be passed over in silence. It is
true that decency, as we understand it, is a very modern
product, and is not to be looked for in any society in
the barbarous stage. At the same time, the whole range
of literature might perhaps be ransacked in vain for a
parallel to the naïve filthiness of the passage forming
Sect. IV of the following translation, or to the extraordinary topic which the hero Yamato-Take and his
mistress Miyazu are made to select as the theme of
poetical repartee.[52] One passage likewise would lead us
to suppose that the most beastly crimes were commonly
committed.[53]

To conclude this portion of the subject, it may be
useful for the sake of comparison to call attention to a
few arts and products with which the early Japanese were
*not* acquainted, Thus they had no tea, no fans, no porce-
lain, no lacquer,—none of the things, in fact, by which
in later times they have been chiefly known. They did
not yet use vehicles of any kind. They had no accurate
method of computing time, no money, scarcely any

52.  See Sect. LXXXVII.
53.  See Sect. XCVII.

knowledge of medicine. Neither, though they possessed some sort of music, and poems a few of which at least are not without merit,[54] do we hear anything of the art of drawing. But the most important art of which they were ignorant is that of writing. As some misapprehension has existed on this head, and scholars in Europe have been misled by the inventions of zealous champions of the Shintō religion into a belief in the so-called "Divine Characters," by them alleged to have been invented by the Japanese gods and to have been used by the Japanese people prior to the introduction of the Chinese ideographic writing, it must be stated precisely that all the traditions of the "Divine Age," and of the reigns of the earlier Emperors down to the third century of our era according to the received chronology, maintain a complete silence on the subject of writing materials, and records of every kind. Books are nowhere mentioned till a period confessedly posterior to the opening up of intercourse with the Asiatic continent, and the first books whose names occur are the "Lun Yü" and the "Ch'ien Tzŭ Wên,"[55] which are said to have been brought over to Japan during the reign of the Emperor O-jin,—according to the same chronology in the year 284 after Christ. That even

43

---

54. A translation,—especially a literal prose translation,—is not calculated to show off to best advantage the poetry of an alien race. But even subject to this drawback, the present writer would be surprised if it were not granted that poetic fire and grace are displayed in some of the Love-Songs (for instance the third Song in Sect. XXIV and both Songs Yamato-Take's address to his "elder brother the pine-tree," and in his Death-Songs contained in Sect. LXXXIX).

55. 論語 and 千字文.

this statement is antedated, is shown by the fact that
the "Ch'ien Tzŭ Wên" was not written till more than
two centuries later,—a fact which is worthy the attention
of those who have been disposed simply to take on
trust the assertions of the Japanese historians. It should
likewise be mentioned that, as has already been pointed
out by Mr. Aston, the Japanese terms *fumi* "written
document," and *fude* "pen," are probably corruptions
of foreign words.[56] The present, indeed, is not the
44 place to discuss the whole question of the so-called
"Divine Characters," which Motowori, the most patriotic
as well as the most learned of the Japanese *literati*,
dismisses in a note to the Prolegomena of his "Exposition of the Records of Ancient Matters" with the remark
that they "are a late forgery over which no words need
be wasted." But as this mare's nest has been imported
into the discussion of the Early Japanese social state,
and as the point is one on which the absolute silence
of the early traditions bears such clear testimony, it was
impossible to pass it by without some brief allusion.

---

56. Viz. of the Chinese 文 and 筆 (in the modern Mandarin
pronunciation *wên* and *pi* ). Mr. Aston would seem to derive both the
Japanese term *fude* and the Korean *put* independently from the Chinese
筆. The present writer thinks it more likely that the Japanese *fude* was
borrowed mediately through the Korean *put*. In any case, as it regularly
corresponds with the latter according to the laws of letter-change subsisting
between the two languages, it will be observed that the Japanese term
would still have to be considered borrowed, even if the derivation of *put*
from 筆 had to be abandoned ; for we can hardly suppose Korean and
Japanese to have independently selected the same root to denote such a
thing as a "pen." As to the correctness of the derivation of *fumi* from
文 there can be little doubt, and it had long ago struck even the
Japanese themselves, who are not prompt to acknowledge such loans.
They usually derive *fude* from *fumi-te*, "document hand," and thus again
we are brought back to the Chinese 文 as the origin of the Japanese
word for "pen."

## V.

### RELIGIOUS AND POLITICAL IDEAS OF THE EARLY JAPANESE, BEGINNINGS OF THE JAPANESE NATION, AND CREDIBILITY OF THE NATIONAL RECORDS.

The religious beliefs of the modern upholders of Shintō[57] may be ascertained without much difficulty by a perusal of the works of the leaders of the movement which has endeavoured during the last century and a half to destroy the influence of Buddhism and of the Chinese philosophy, and which has latterly succeeded to some extent in supplanting those two foreign systems. But in Japan, as elsewhere, it has been impossible for men really to turn back a thousand years in religious thought and act; and when we try to discover the primitive opinions that were entertained by the Japanese people prior to the introduction of the Chinese culture, we are met by difficulties that at first seem insuperable. The documents are scanty, and the modern commentaries untrustworthy, for they are all written under the influence of a preconceived opinion. Moreover, the problem is apparently complicated by a mixture of races and my-thologies, and by a filtering in of Chinese ideas previous to the compilation of documents of any sort, though these are considerations which have hitherto scarcely been taken into account by foreigners, and are designedly neglected and obscured by such narrowly patriotic native writers as Motowori and Hirata.

---

57.　The Chinese characters used to write this word are 神道, which signify the "Way of the Gods." The term was adopted in order to distinguish the old native beliefs from Buddhism and Confucianism.

In the political field the difficulties are not less, but
45 rather greater; for when once the Imperial house and
the centralized Japanese polity, as we know it from the
sixth or seventh century of our era downwards, became
fully established, it was but too clearly in the interest of
the powers that be to efface as far as possible the trace
of different government arrangements which may have
preceded them, and to cause it to be believed that, as
things were then, so had they always been. The Emperor Tem-mu, with his anxiety to amend "the deviations
from truth and the empty falsehoods" of the historical
documents preserved by the various families, and the
author of the "Chronicles of Japan" with his elaborate
system of fictitious dates, recur to our minds, and we ask
ourselves to what extent similar garblings of history,—
sometimes unintentional,—may have gone on during earlier
ages, when there was even less to check them than there
was in the eighth century. If, therefore, the translator
here gives expression to a few opinions founded chiefly
on a careful study of the text of the "Records of Ancient
Matters" helped out by a study of the "Chronicles of
Japan," he would be understood to do so with great
diffidence, especially with regard to his few (so to speak)
constructive remarks. As to the destructive side of the
criticism, there need be less hesitation; for the old histories
bear evidence too conclusively against themselves for it
to be possible for the earlier portions of them, at least,
to stand the test of sober investigation. Before endeavouring to piece together the little that is found in the
"Records" to illustrate the beliefs of Archaic Japanese
times, it will be necessary, at the risk of dullness, to give
a summary of the old traditions as they lie before us in

their entirety, after which will be hazarded a few speculations on the subject of the earlier tribes which combined
to form the Japanese people; for the four questions of
religious beliefs, of political arrangements, of race, and of
the credibility of documents, all hang closely together
and, properly speaking, form but one highly complex
problem.

Greatly condensed, the Early Japanese traditions amount
to this: After an indefinitely long period, during which
were born a number of abstract deities, who are differently
enumerated in the "Records" and in the "Chronicles,"
two of these deities, a brother and sister named Izanagi
and Izanami (*i.e.*, the "Male who Invites" and the
"Female Who Invites"), are united in marriage, and
give birth to the various islands of the Japanese archi- 46
pelago. When they have finished producing islands,
they proceed to the production of a large number of
gods and goddesses, many of whom correspond to
what we should call personifications of the powers of
nature, though personification is a word which, in its
legitimate acceptations, is foreign to the Japanese mind.
The birth of the Fire-God causes Izanami's death, and
the most striking episode of the whole mythology then
ensues, when her husband, Orpheus-like, visits her in
the under-world to implore her to return to him. She
would willingly do so, and bids him wait while she
consults with the deities of the place. But he, impatient
at her long tarrying, breaks off one of the end-teeth
of the comb stuck in the left bunch of his hair, lights
it and goes in, only to find her a hideous mass of corruption, in whose midst are seated the eight Gods
of Thunder. This episode ends with the deification of

[58] three peaches[58] who had assisted him in his retreat before the armies of the under-world, and with bitter words exchanged between him and his wife, who herself pursues him as far as the "Even Pass of Hades."

Returning to Himuka in south-western Japan, Izanagi purifies himself by bathing in a stream, and, as he does so, fresh deities are born from each article of clothing that he throws down on the river-bank, and from each part of his person. One of these deities was the Sun-Goddess, who was born from his left eye, while the Moon-God sprang from his right eye, and the last born of all, Susa-no-Wo, whose name the translator renders by "the Impetuous Male," was born from his nose. Between these three children their father divides the inheritance of the universe.

At this point the story loses its unity. The Moon-God is no more heard of, and the traditions concerning the Sun-Goddess and those concerning the "Impetuous Male Deity" diverge in a manner which is productive of inconsistencies in the remainder of the mythology. The Sun-Goddess and the "Impetuous Male Deity" have a violent quarrel, and at last the latter breaks a hole in the roof of the hall in Heaven where his sister is sitting at work with the celestial weaving-maidens, and through it lets fall "a heavenly piebald horse which he had flayed with a backward flaying." The consequences of this act were so disastrous, that the Sun-Goddess withdrew for a season into a cave, from which the rest of the eight hundred myriad (according to the "Chronicles" eighty

---

58. *Conf.* p. xvii, last paragraph for the modified sense in which alone the word "deification" can be used in speaking of the Early Japanese worship.

myriad) deities with difficulty allured her. The "Impetuous Male Deity" was thereupon banished, and the Sun-
Goddess remained mistress of the field. Yet, strange to
say, she thenceforward retires into the background, and
the most bulky section of the mythology consists of
stories concerning the "Impetuous Male Deity" and his
descendants, who are represented as the monarchs of
Japan, or rather of the province of Idzumo. The "Impetuous Male Deity" himself, whom his father had charged
with the dominion of the sea, never assumes that rule,
but first has a curiously told amorous adventure: and an
encounter with an eight-forked serpent in Idzumo, and
afterwards reappears as the capricious and filthy deity of
Hades, who however seems to retain some power over
the land of the living, as he invests his descendant of
the sixth generation with the sovereignty of Japan. Of
this latter personage a whole cycle of stories is told, all
centering in Idzumo. We learn of his conversations with
a hare and with a mouse, of the prowess and 'cleverness
which he displayed on the occasion of a visit to his ancestor in Hades, which is in this cycle of traditions a
much less mysterious place than the Hades visited by
Izanagi, of his amours, of his triumph over his eighty
brethren, of his reconciliation with his jealous empress,
and of his numerous descendants, many of whom have
names that are particularly difficult of comprehension.
We hear too in a tradition, which ends in a pointless
manner, of a microscopic deity who comes across the sea
to ask this monarch of Idzumo to share the sovereignty
with him.

This last-mentioned legend repeats itself in the sequel.
The Sun-Goddess, who on her second appearance is con-

stantly represented as acting in concert with the "High
August Producing Wondrous Deity,"—one of the abstrac-
tions mentioned at the commencement of the "Records,"
—resolves to bestow the sovereignty of Japan on a child
of whom it is doubtful whether he were hers or that of
her brother the "Impetuous Male Deity." Three embassies are sent from Heaven to Idzumo to arrange
matters, but it is only a fourth that is successful, the
final ambassadors obtaining the submission of the monarch
48 or deity of Idzumo, who surrenders his sovereignty and
promises to serve the new dynasty (apparently in the
under-world), if a palace or temple be built for him and
he be appropriately worshipped. Thereupon the child of
the deity whom the Sun-Goddess had originally wished
to make sovereign of Japan, descends to earth,—not to
Idzumo in the north-west, be it mentioned, as the logical
sequence of the story would lead one to expect,—but to
the peak of a mountain in the south-western island of
Kiushiu.

Here follows a quaint tale accounting for the old appearance of the bèche-de-mer, and another to account for
the shortness of the lives of mortals, after which we are
told of the birth under peculiar circumstances of the
heaven-descended deity's three sons. Two of these,
Ho-deri and Howori, whose names may be Englished as
"Fire-Shine" and "Fire-Subside," are the heroes of a
very curious legend, which includes an elaborate account
of a visit paid by the latter to the palace of the God of
Ocean, and of a curse or spell which gained for him the
victory over his elder brother, and enabled him to dwell
peacefully in his palace at Takachiho for the space of
five hundred and eighty years,—the first statement re-

sembling a date which the "Records" contain. This personage's son married his own aunt, and was the father of four children, one of whom "treading on the crest of the waves, crossed over to the Eternal Land," while a second "went into the sea plain," and the two others moved eastward, fighting with the chiefs of Kibi and Yamato, having adventures with gods both with and without tails, being assisted by a miraculous sword and a gigantic crow, and naming the various places they passed through after incidents in their own career, as "the Impetuous Male" and other divine personages had done before them. One of these brothers was Kamu-Yamato-Ihare-Biko, who (the other having died before him) was first given the title of Jim-mu Ten-nō more than fourteen centuries after the date which in the "Chronicles" is assigned as that of his decease.

Henceforth Yamato, which had scarcely been mentioned before, and the provinces adjacent to it become the centre of the story, and Idzumo again emerges into importance. A very indecent love-tale forms a bridge which unites the two fragments of the mythology ; and the "Great Deity of Miwa," who is identified with the deposed monarch of Idzumo, appears on the scene. Indeed during the rest of the story this "Great Deity of Miwa," and 49 his colleague the "Small August Deity" (Sukuna-Mi-Kami[59]), the deity Izasa-Wake, the three Water-Gods of Sumi, and the "Great Deity of Kadzuraki," of whom there is so striking a mention in Sect. CLVIII, form, with the Sun-Goddess and with a certain divine sword

---

59. In Sect. XXVII, where this deity is first mentioned, he is called *Sukuna Biko-Na-no-Kami*, the "Little Prince the Renowned Deity."

preserved at the temple of Isonokami in Yamato, the only objects of worship specially named, the other gods and goddesses being no more heard of. This portion of the story is closed by an account of the troubles which inaugurated the reign of Jim-mu's successor, Sui-sei, and then occurs a blank of (according to the accepted chronology) five hundred years, during which absolutely nothing is told us excepting dreary genealogies, the place where each sovereign dwelt and where he was buried, and the age to which he lived,—this after the minute details which had previously been given concerning the successive gods or monarchs down to Sui-sei inclusive. It should likewise be noted that the average age of the first seventeen monarchs (counting Jim-mu Ten-nō as the first according to received ideas) is nearly 96 years if we follow the "Records," and over a hundred if we follow the accepted chronology which is based chiefly on the constantly divergent statements contained in the "Chronicles." The age of several of the monarchs exceeds 120 years.[60]

The above-mentioned lapse of an almost blank period of five centuries brings us to the reign of the Emperor known to history by the name of Sū-jin, whose life of one hundred and sixty-eight years (one hundred and twenty according to the "Chronicles") is supposed to have immediately preceded the Christian era. In this reign the former monarch of Idzumo or god of Miwa again appears and produces a pestilence, of the manner of staying which Sū-jin is warned in a dream, while a curious but highly indecent episode tells us how a person called Oho-Taka-Ne-Ko was known to be a son of the

60. See Appendix II.

deity in question, and was therefore appointed high priest of his temple. In the ensuing reign an elaborate legend, involving a variety of circumstances as miraculous as any in the earlier portion of the mythology, again centres in the necessity of pacifying the great god of 50 Idzumo; and this, with details of internecine strife in the Imperial family, of the sovereign's amours, and of the importation of the orange from the "Eternal Land," brings us to the cycle of traditions of which Yamato-Take, a son of the Emperor Kei-kō, is the hero. This prince, after slaying one of his brothers in the privy, accomplishes the task of subduing both western and eastern Japan; and, notwithstanding certain details which are unsavoury to the European taste, his story, taken as a whole, is one of the most striking in the book. He performs marvels of valour, disguises himself as a woman to slay the brigands, is the possessor of a magic sword and fire-striker, has a devoted wife who stills the fury of the waves by sitting down upon their surface, has encounters with a deer and with a boar who are really gods in disguise, and finally dies on his way westward before he can reach his home in Yamato. His death is followed by a highly mythological account of the laying to rest of the white bird into which he ended by being transformed.

The succeeding reign is a blank, and the next after that transports us without a word of warning to quite another scene. The sovereign's home is now in Tsuku-shi, the south-western island of the Japanese archipelago, and four of the gods, through the medium of the so-vereign's wife, who is known to history as the Empress Jin-gō, reveal the existence of the land of Korea, of

which, however, this is not the first mention. The
Emperor disbelieves the divine message, and is punished
by death for his incredulity. But the Empress, after a
special consultation between her prime minister and the
gods, and the performance of various religious ceremonies,
marshals her fleet, and, with the assistance of the fishes
both great and small and of a miraculous wave, reaches
Shirai[61] (one of the ancient divisions of Korea), and
subdues it. She then returns to Japan, the legend ending
with a curiously naïve tale of how she sat a-fishing
one day on a shoal in the river Wo-gawa in Tsukushi
with threads picked out of her skirt for lines.

The next section shows her going up by sea to
Yamato,—another joint in the story, by means of which
the Yamato cycle of legends and the Tsukushi cycle
are brought into apparent unity. The " Chronicles of
Japan " have even improved upon this by making Jin-
gō's husbands dwell in Yamato at the commencement of
his reign and only remove to Tsukushi later, so that if
the less elaborated " Records " had not been preserved,
the two threads of the tradition would have been still
more difficult to unravel. The Empress's army defeats
the troops raised by the native kings or princes, who
are represented as her step-sons ; and from that time
forward the story runs on in a single channel and always
centres in Yamato. China likewise is now first mentioned, books are said to have been brought over from the
mainland, and we hear of the gradual introduction of
various useful arts. Even the annals of the reign of
O-jin however, during which this civilizing impulse from
abroad is said to have commenced, are not free from

---

61.  新羅.

details as miraculous as any in the earlier portions of the book. Indeed Sects. CXIV-CXVI of the following translation, which form part of the narrative of his reign, are occupied with the recital of one of the most fanciful tales of the whole mythology. The monarch himself is said to have lived a hundred and thirty years, while his successor lived eighty-three (according to the "Chronicles," O-jin lived a hundred and ten and his successor Nin-toku reigned eighty-seven years). It is not till the next reign that the miraculous ceases, a fact which significantly coincides with the reign in which, according to a statement in the "Chronicles," historiographers were first appointed to all the provinces to record words and events, and forward archives from all directions." This brings us to the commencement of the fifth century of our era, just three centuries before the compilation of our histories, but only two centuries before the compilation of the first history of which mention has been preserved. From that time the story in the "Records," though not well told, gives us some very curious pictures, and reads as if it were reliable. It is tolerably full for a few reigns, after which it again dwindles into mere genealogies, carrying us down to the commencement of the seventh century. The "Chronicles," on the contrary, give us full details down to A.D. 701, that is to within nineteen years of the date of their compilation.

The reader who has followed this summary, or who will take the trouble to read through the whole text for himself will perceive that there is no break in the story, —at least no chronological break,—and no break between the fabulous and the real, unless indeed it be at the commencement of the fifth century of our era, *i.e.* more

than a thousand years later than the date usually accepted
as the commencement of genuine Japanese history. The
only breaks are,—not chronological,—but topographical.

This fact of the continuity of the Japanese mythology
and history has been fully recognized by the leading
native commentators, whose opinions are those considered
orthodox by modern Shintoists; and they draw from it
the conclusion that everything in the standard national
histories must be equally accepted as literal truth. All
persons however cannot force their minds into the limits
of such a belief; and early in the last century a celebrated
writer and thinker, Arawi Hakuseki, published a work
in which, while accepting the native mythology as an
authentic chronicle of events, he did so with the reservation of proving to his own satisfaction that all the
miraculous portions thereof were allegories, and the gods
only men under another name. In this particular, the
elasticity of the Japanese word for "deity," *kami*, which
has already been noticed, stood the eastern Euhemerus
in good stead. Some of his explanations are however
extremely comical, and it is evident that such a system
enables the person who uses it to prove whatever he has
a mind to.[62] In the present century a diluted form of
the same theory was adopted by Tachibana no Moribe,
who, although endeavouring to remain an orthodox Shintoist, yet decided that some of the (so to speak) useless-

---

62. As a specimen of the flexibility of his system, the reader to
whom the Japanese language and Japanese legend are familiar is recommended to peruse pp. 13-24 of Vol. I of Arawi Hakuseki's " *Ko Shi
Tsŭ* " (古史通), where an elaborate rationalistic interpretation is applied
to the story of the amours of Izanagi and Izanami. It is amusing in its
very gravity, and one finds it difficult to believe that the writer can have
been in earnest when he penned it.

ly miraculous incidents need not be believed in as revealed truth. Such, for instance, are the story of the speaking mouse, and that of Izanagi's head-dress turning into a bunch of grapes. He accounts for many of these details by the supposition that they are what he calls *wosana-goto*, i.e. "child-like words," and thinks that they were invented for the sake of fixing the story in the minds of children, and are not binding on modern adults as articles of faith. He is also willing to allow that some passages show traces of Chinese influence, and he blames 53 Motowori's uncompromising championship of every iota of the existing text of the "Records of Ancient Matters." As belonging to this same school of what may perhaps be termed "rationalistic believers" in Japanese mythology, a contemporary Christian writer, Mr. Takahashi Gorō, must also be mentioned. Treading in the foot-steps of Arawi Hakuseki, but bringing to bear on the legends of his own country some knowledge of the mythology of other lands, he for instance explains the traditions of the Sun-Goddess and of the Eight-Forked Serpent of Yamada by postulating the existence of an ancient queen called Sun, whose brother, after having been banished from her realm for his improper behaviour, killed an enemy whose name was Serpent, etc., while such statements as that the microscopic deity who came over the waves to share the sovereignty of Idzumo would not tell his name, are explained by the assertion that, being a foreigner, he was unintelligible for some time until he had learnt the language. It is certainly strange that such theorists should not see that they are undermining with one hand that which they endeavour to prop up with the other, and that their own individual fancy is made by them the sole standard of historic truth. Yet Mr. Takahashi confidently asserts that "his explanations have nothing forced or fanciful" in them, and that "they cannot fail to solve the doubts even of the greatest of doubters."[63]

The general habit of the more sceptical Japanese of the present day,—*i.e.* of ninety-nine out of every hundred of the educated,—seems to be to reject, or at least to ignore, the history of the gods, while implicitly accepting the history of the emperors from Jim-mu downwards; and in so doing they have been followed with but little reserve by most Europeans,—almanacs, histories and cyclopædias all continuing to repeat on the antiquated authority of such writers as Kaempfer and Titsingh, that Japan possesses an authentic history covering more that two thousand years, while Siebold and Hoffmann even go the length of discussing the *hour* of Jim-mu's accession in the year 660 B. C.! This is the attitude of mind now sanctioned by the governing class. Thus, in the historical compilations used at text-books in the schools, 54 the stories of the gods,—that is to say the Japanese traditions down to Jim-mu exclusive,—are either passed over in silence or dismissed in a few sentences, while the annals of the human sovereigns,—that is to say the Japanese traditions from Jim-mu inclusive,—are treated precisely as if the events therein related had happened yesterday, and were as incontrovertibly historical as later statements, for which there is contemporary evidence. The same plan is pursued elsewhere in official publications. Thus, to take out one example among many, the Imperial Commissioners to the Vienna Exhibition, in their

63. Mr. Takahashi Gorō's book here alluded to is his "Shintō Discussed Afresh."

"Notice sur l'Empire du Japan," tell us that "L'histoire de la dynastie impériale remonte très-haut. L'obscurité entoure ses débuts, vu l'absence de documents réguliers ou d'un calendrier parfait. Le premier Empereur de la dynastie présente, dont il reste des annales dignes de confiance, est Jin-mou-ten-nô[64] qui organisa un soulèvement dans la province de Hiuga, marcha à l'Est avec ses compagnons, fonda sa capitale dans la vallée de Kashihara dans le Yamato, et monta sur le trône comme Empereur. C'est de cet Empereur que descend, par une succession régulière, la présente famille régnante du Japon. C'est de l'année de l'avènement de Jin-mou-ten-nô que date l'ère japonaise (Année 1—660 avant Jésus-Christ)."

As for the *ère Japonaise* mentioned by the commissioners, it may be permitted to observe that it was only introduced by an edict dated 15th Dec., 1872[65] that is to say just a fortnight before the publication of their report. *And this era, this accession, is confidently placed thirteen or fourteen centuries before the first history which records it was written, nine centuries before (at the earliest computation) the art of writing was introduced into the country, and on the sole authority of books teeming with miraculous legends ! !* Does such a proceeding need any comment after once being formulated in precise terms, and can any unprejudiced person continue to accept the early Japanese chronology and the first thousand years of the so-called history of Japan.

\*        \*        \*

Leaving this discussion, let us now see whether

---

64.  *I. e.* the emperor Jim-mu,—*ten-nō* written 天皇, being simply the Sinico-Japanese word for "emperor."

65.  15th day of 11th moon of 5th year of Meiji.

55 any information relative to the early religious and political
state of the Japanese can be gleaned from the pages of
the "Records" and of the "Chronicles." There are
fragments of information,—fragments of two sorts,— some
namely of clear import, others which are rather a matter
for inference and for argument. Let us take the positive
fragments first—the notice as to cosmological ideas,
dreams, prayers, etc.

The first thing that strikes the student is that what,
for want of a more appropriate name, we must call the
religion of the Early Japanese, was not an organized
religion. We can discover in it nothing corresponding to
the body of dogma, the code of morals, and the sacred
book authoritatively enforcing both, with which we are
familiar in civilized religions, such as Buddhism, Christ-
ianity, and Islam. What we find is a bundle is miscellaneous superstitions rather than a co-ordinated system.
Dreams evidently were credited with great importance,
the future being supposed to be foretold in them, and
the will of the gods made known. Sometimes even an
actual object, such as a wonderful sword, was sent down
in a dream, thus to our ideas mixing the material with
the spiritual. The subject did not, however, present itself
in that light to the Early Japanese, to whom there was
evidently but one order of phenomena,—what we should
call the natural order. Heaven, or rather the Sky, was
an actual place,—not more ethereal than earth, nor thought
of as the abode of the blessed after death,—but simply
a "high plain" situated above Japan and communicating
with Japan by a bridge or ladder, and forming the residence of some of those powerful personages called *kami*,—
a word which we must make shift to translate by "god"

or "goddess," or "deity." An arrow shot from earth could reach Heaven, and make a hole in it. There was at least one mountain in Heaven, and one river with a broad stony bed like those with which the traveller in Japan becomes familiar, one or two caves, one or more wells, and animals, and trees. There is, however, some confusion as to the mountain,—the celebrated Mount Kagu,—for there is one of that name in the Province of Yamato.

Some of the gods dwelt here on earth, or descended hither from Heaven, and had children by human women. Such, for instance, was the emperor Jim-mu's great-grandfather. Some few gods had tails or were otherwise personally remarkable ; and "savage deities" are often mentioned as inhabiting certain portions of Japan, both in the so-called "Divine Age" and during the reigns of the human emperors down to a time corresponding, according to the generally received chronology, with the first or second century of the Christian era. The human emperors themselves, moreover, were sometimes spoken of as deities, and even made personal use of that designation. The gods occasionally transformed themselves into animals, and at other times simple tangible objects were called gods,—or at least they were called *kami ;* for the gulf separating the Japanese from the English term can never be too often recalled to mind. The word *kami*, as previously mentioned, properly signifies "superior," and it would be putting more into it than it really implies to say that the Early Japanese "deified,"—in our sense of the verb to "deify,"—the peaches which Izanagi used to pelt his assailants with, or any other natural objects whatsoever. It would, indeed, be to attribute to them a

flight of imagination of which they were not capable,
and a habit of personification not in accordance with the
genius of their language.   Some of the gods are mentioned collectively as "bad Deities like unto the flies in
the fifth moon"; but there is nothing approaching a
systematic division into good spirits and bad spirits.   In
fact the word "spirit" itself is not applicable at all to
the gods of Archaic Japan.   They were, like the gods of
Greece, conceived of only as more powerful human beings.
They were born, and some of them died, though here
again there is inconsistency, as the death of some of
them is mentioned in a manner leading one to suppose
that they were conceived of as being then at an end,
whereas in other cases such death seems simply to denote
transference to Hades, or to what is called "the One
Road," which is believed to be a synonym for Hades.
Sometimes, again, a journey to Hades is undertaken by
a god without any reference to his death.   Nothing,
indeed, could be less consistent than the various details.

Hades[66] itself is another instance of this inconsistency.
In the legend of Oho-Kuni-Nushi (the "Master of the
Great Land"),—one of the Idzumo cycle of legends,—
57 Hades is described exactly as if it were part of the land
of the living, or exactly as if it were Heaven, which
indeed comes to the same thing.   It has its trees, its
houses, its family quarrels, etc., etc.   In the legend of
Izanagi, on the other hand, Hades means simply the
abode of horrible putrefaction and of the vindictive dead,
and is fitly described by the god himself who had ventured thither as "a hideous and polluted land."   The

66.  For the use of this word to represent the Japanese *Yomo* or
*Yomi*, see Sect. IX., Note 1.

only point in which the legends agree is in placing between the upper earth and Hades a barrier called the "Even Pass (or Hill) of Hades." The state of the dead in general is nowhere alluded to, nor are the dying ever made to refer to a future world, whether good or evil.

The objects of worship were of course the gods, or some of them. It has already been stated that during the later portions of the story, whose scene is laid almost exclusively on earth, the Sun-Goddess, the deity Izasa-Wake, the Divine Sword of Isonokami, the Small August Deity (*Sukuna-Mi-Kami*), the "Great Gods" of Miwa and of Kadzuraki and the three Water-Deities of Sumi, alone are mentioned as having been specially worshipped. Of these the first and the last appear together, forming a sort of quaternion, while the other five appear singly and have no connection with each other. The deities of the mountains, the deities of the rivers, the deities of the sea, etc., are also mentioned in the aggregate, as are likewise the heavenly deities and the earthly deities; and the Empress Jin-gō is represented as conciliating them all previous to her departure for Korea by "putting into a gourd the ashes" of a *maki* tree,[67] and likewise making a quantity of chopsticks and also "of leaf-platters, and scattering them all on the waves."

This brings us to the subject of religious rites,—a subject on which we long for fuller information than the texts afford.[68] That the conciliatory offerings made to the gods were of a miscellaneous nature will be expected from the quotation just made. Nevertheless, a very

---

67.  *Podocarpus macrophylla.*
68.  The least meagre account will be found in Sects. XVI and XXXII.

natural method was in the main followed; for the people offered the things by which they themselves set most store, as we hear at a later period of the poet Tsurayuki, when in a storm at sea, flinging his mirror into the waves because he had but one. The Early Japanese made offer-
58 ings of two kinds of cloth, one being hempen cloth and the other cloth manufactured from the bark of the paper mulberry,—offerings very precious in their eyes, but which have in modern times been allowed to degenerate into useless strips of paper. They likewise offered shields, spears, and other things. Food was offered both to the gods and to the dead; indeed, the palace or tomb of the dead monarch and the temple of the god cannot always be distinguished from each other, and, as has already been mentioned, the Japanese use the same word *miya* for "palace" and for "temple." Etymologically signify-ing "august house," it is naturally susceptible of what are to us two distinct meanings.

With but one exception,[69] the "Records" do not give us the words of any prayers (or, as the Japanese term *norito* has elsewhere been translated, "rituals.") Conver-sations with the gods are indeed detailed, but no devo-tional utterances. Fortunately, however, a number of very ancient prayers have been preserved in other books, and translations of some of them by Mr. Satow will be found scattered through the volumes of the Transactions of this Society. They consist mostly of declarations of praise and statements of offerings made, either in return for favours received or conditionally on favours being granted. They are all in prose, and hymns do not seem to have been in use. Indeed of the hundred and eleven

69. To be found at the end of Sect. XXXII.

Songs preserved in the "Records," not one has any religious reference.

The sacred rite of which most frequent mention is made is purification by water. Trial by hot water is also alluded to in both histories, but not till a time confessedly posterior to the commencement of intercourse with the mainland. We likewise hear of compacts occasionally entered into with a god, and somewhat resembling our European wager, oath, or curse. Priests are spoken of in a few passages, but without any details. We do not hear of their functions being in any way mediatorial, and the impression conveyed is that they did not exist in very early times as a separate class. When they did come into existence, the profession soon became hereditary, according to the general tendency in Japan towards the hereditability of offices and occupations.

Miscellaneous superstitions crop up in many places. Some of these were evidently obsolescent or unintelligible at the time when the legends crystallized into their present shape, and stories are told purporting to give their origin. Thus we learn either in the "Records" or in the "Chronicles," or in both works, why it is unlucky to use only one light, to break off the teeth of a comb at night-time, and to enter the house with straw hat and rain-coat on. The word-wide dread of going against the sun is connected with the Jim-mu legend, and recurs elsewhere.[70] We also hear of charms,—for instance, of

---

70. In the Jin-mu legend we have the more usual form of the superstition, that, viz., which makes it unlucky to go from West to East, which is the contrary of the course pursued by the sun. In Sect. CLIII, on the other hand, the Emperor Yū-riaku is found fault with for acting in precisely the reverse manner, viz., for going from East to West,

the wondrous "Herb-Quelling Sabre" found by Susa-no-Wo (the "Impetuous Male Deity") inside a serpent's tail, and still preserved as one of the Imperial *regalia*. Other such charms were the "tide-flowing jewel" and "tide-ebbing jewel," that obtained for Jim-mu's grandfather the victory over his elder brother, together with the fish-hook which figures so largely in the same legend.[71] Divination by means of the shoulder-blade of a stag was a favourite means of ascertaining the will of the gods. Sometimes also human beings seem to have been credited in a vague manner with the power of prophetic utterance. Earthenware pots were buried at the point of his departure by an intending traveller. In a fight the initial arrow was regarded with superstitious awe. The great precautions with which the Empress Jin-gō is said to have set out on her expedition to Korea have already been alluded to, and indeed the commencement of any action or enterprise seems to have had special importance attributed to it.

To conclude this survey of the religious beliefs of the Early Japanese by referring, as was done in the case of the arts of life, to certain notable features which are conspicuous by their absence, attention may be called to the fact that there is no tradition of a deluge, no testimony to any effect produced on the imagination by the earthquakes from which the Japanese islanders suffer such constant alarms, no trace of star-worship, no notion

---

*i.e.* with his back to the sun. The idea is the same, though its practical application may thus diametrically differ, the fundamental objection being to going *against* the sun, in whatever manner the word *against*, or some kindred expression, may be interpreted.

71. See Sects. XXXIX to XLI. For the "Herb-Quelling Sabre" see Sects. XVIII and LXXXII, *et. seq.*

of incarnation or of transmigration. This last remark
goes to show that the Japanese mythology had assumed
its present shape before the first echo of Buddhism
reverberated on these shores. But the absence of any
tradition of a deluge or inundation is still more remarkable,
both because such catastrophes are likely to occur occasionally in all lands, and because the imagination of
most nations seems to have been greatly impressed by
their occurrence. Moreover what is specifically known
to us as *the* Deluge has been lately claimed as an
ancient Altaïc myth. Yet here we have the oldest of
the *undoubtedly* Altaïc nations without any legend of the
kind. As for the neglect of the stars, round whose
names the imagination of other races has twined such
fanciful conceits, it is as characteristic of Modern as of
Archaic Japan. The Chinese designations of the con-
stellations, and some few Chinese legends relating to
them, have been borrowed in historic times; but no
Japanese writer has ever thought of looking in the stars
for "the poetry of heaven." Another detail worthy of
mention is that the number seven, which in so many
countries has been considered sacred, is here not prominent
in any way, its place being taken by eight. Thus we
have Eight Great Islands, an Eight-forked Serpent, a
beard Eighty Hand-breadths long, a God named "Eight-
Thousand Spears," Eighty or Eight Hundred Myriads
of Deities, etc., etc. The commentators think it necessary
to tell us that all these eights and eighties need not be
taken literally, as they simply mean a great number.
The fact remains that the number eight had, for some
unknown reason, a special significance attached to it;
and as the documents which mention eight also mention

lxxxii          *Translator's Introduction.*

nine and ten, besides higher numbers, and as in some
test cases, such as that of the Eight Great Islands, each
of the eight is separately enumerated, it is plain that
when the Early Japanese said eight they meant eight,
though they may doubtless have used that number in
a vague manner, as we do a dozen, a hundred, and a
thousand.

How glaringly different all this is from the fanciful
accounts of Shintō that have been given by some recent
60 popular writers calls for no comment. Thus one of
them, whom another quotes as an authority,[72] tells us
that Shintō " consists in the belief that the productive
ethereal spirit being expanded through the whole universe,
every part is in some degree jmpregnated with it, and
therefore every part is in some measure the seat of the
deity ; whence local gods and goddesses are everywhere
worshipped, and consequently multiplied without end.
Like the ancient Romans and the Greeks, they acknowledge a Supreme Being, the first, the supreme, the intel-
lectual, by which men have been reclaimed from rudeness
and barbarism to elegance and refinement, and been
taught through privileged men and women, not only to
live with more comfort, but to die with better hopes."(!)
Truly, when one peruses such utterly groundless assertions,—for that here quoted is but one among many,—
one is tempted to believe that the nineteenth century
must form part of the early mythopœic age.

With regard to the question of government, we learn
little beyond such vague statements as that to so-and-so
was yielded by his eighty brethren the sovereignty of
the land of Idzumo, or that Izanagi divided the dominion

—————————
72. General Le Gendre, quoted by Sir Edward Reed.

over all things between his three children, bestowing on one the "Plain of High Heaven," on another the Dominion of the Night, and on the third the "Sea-Plain." But we do not in the earlier legends see such sovereignty actually administered. The heavenly gods seem rather to have been conceived as forming a sort of commonwealth, who decided things by meeting together in counsel in the stony bed of the "River of Heaven," and taking the advice of the shrewdest of their number. Indeed the various divine assemblies, to which the story in the "Records" and "Chronicles" introduces us, remind us of nothing so much as of the village assemblies of primitive tribes in many parts of the world, where the cleverness of one and the general willingness to follow his suggestions fill the place of the more definite organization of later times.

Descending from heaven to earth, we find little during the so-called "Divine Age" but stories of isolated individuals and families; and it is not till the narrative of the wars of the earlier Emperors commences, that any kind of political organization comes into view. Then at once we hear of chieftains in every locality, who lead 62 their men to battle, and are seemingly the sole depositories of power, each in, his microscopic sphere. The legend of Jim-mu itself, however, is sufficient to show that autocracy, as we understand it, was not characteristic of the government of the Tsukushi tribes; for Jim-mu and his brother, until the latter's death, are represented as joint chieftains of their host. Similarly we find that the "Territorial Owners" of Yamato, and the "Rulers" of Idzumo, whom Jim-mu or his successors are said to have subjugated, are constantly spoken of in the Plural,

as if to intimate that they exerted a divided sovereignty. During the whole of the so-called "Human
Age" we meet, both in parts of the country which were
already subject to the Imperial rule and in others which
were not yet annexed, with local magnates bearing these
same titles of "Territorial Owners," "Rulers," "Chiefs,"
etc.; and the impression left on the mind is that in early
historical times the sovereign's power was not exercised
directly over all parts of Japan, but that in many cases
the local chieftains continued to hold sway though own-
ing some sort of allegiance to the emperor in Yamato,
while in others the emperor was strong enough to depose
these local rulers, and to put in their place his own
kindred or retainers, who however exercised unlimited
authority in their own districts, and used the same titles
as had been borne by the former native rulers,—that, in
fact, the government was feudal rather than centralized.
This characteristic of the political organization of Early
Japan has not altogether escaped the attention of the
native commentators. Indeed the great Shintō scholar
Hirata not only recognizes the fact, but endeavours to
prove that the system of centralization which obtained
during the eighth, ninth, tenth, eleventh, and part of the
twelfth centuries, and which has been revived in our own
day, is nothing but an imitation of the Chinese bureaucratic system; and he asserts that an organized feudalism,
similar to that which existed from the twelfth century
down to the yest 1867, was the sole really ancient and
national Japanese form of government. The translator
cannot follow Hirata to such lengths, as he sees no
evidence in the early histories of the intricate organization of mediæval Japan. But that, beyond the immediate

limits of the Imperial domain, the government *resembled* feudalism rather than centralization seems indisputable. 63 It is also true that the seventh century witnessed a sudden move in the direction of bureaucratic organization, many of the titles which had up till that time denoted actual provincial chieftains being then either suppressed, or else allowed to sink into mere "gentile names." Another remark which is suggested by a careful perusal of the two ancient histories is that the Imperial succession was in early historical times very irregular. Strange gaps occur as late as the sixth century of our era; and even when it was one of the children who inherited his father's throne, that child was rarely the eldest son.

\*　　　\*　　　\*

What now are we to gather from its analysis of the religious and political features revealed to us by a study of the books containing the Early Japanese traditions as to the still remoter history and tribal divisions of Japan, and as to the origin of the Japanese legends? Very little that is certain, perhaps; but, in the opinion of the present writer, two or three interesting probabilities.

In view of the multiplicity of gods and the complications of the so-called historical traditions, he thinks that it would be *a priori* difficult to believe that the development of Japanese civilization should have run on in a single stream broken only in the third century by the commencement of intercourse with the mainland of Asia. We are, however, not left to such a merely theoretical consideration. There are clear indications of there having been three centres of legendary cycles, three streams which mixed together to form the Japan which meets us

at the dawn of authentic history in the fifth century of
our era. One of these centres,—the most important in
the mythology,—is Idzumo; the second is Yamato: the
third is Tsukushi, called in modern times Kiushiu.
Eastern and Northern Japan count for nothing; indeed,
much of the North-East and North was, down to comparatively recent times, occupied by the barbarous Ainos
or, as they are called by the Japanese, Yemishi, Yebisu,
or Yezo. That the legends or traditions derived from the
three parts of the country here mentioned accord but imperfectly together is an opinion which has already been
alluded to, and upon which light may perhaps be thrown
by a more thorough shifting of the myths and beliefs
classified according to this three-fold system. The question of the ancient division of Japan into several independent states is, however, not completely a matter of
64 opinion. For we have in the "*Shan Hai Ching*"[73] a
positive statement concerning a Northern and a Southern
Yamato (倭), and the Chinese annals of both the Han
dynasties tell us of the division of the country into a
much larger number of kingdoms, of which, according to
the annals of .he later Han dynasty, Yamato (邪馬臺) was
the most powerful. A later official Chinese historian also
tells us that *Jih-pên* (日本, our *Japan*) and Yamato had
been two different states, and that *Jih-pên* was reported
to have swallowed up Yamato. By *Jih-pên* the author
evidently meant to speak of the island of Tsukushi or of
part of it. That the Chinese were fairly well acquainted
with Japan is shown by the fact of there being in the
old Chinese literature more than one mention of "the
country of the hairy people beyond the mountains in the

73. 山海經.

East and North."—that is of the Yemishi or Ainos. No
Chinese book would seem to mention Idzumo as having
formed a separate country; and this evidence must be
allowed its whole weight. It is possible, of course, that
Idzumo may have been incorporated with Yamato before
the conquest of the latter by the Tsukushi people, and
in this case some of the inconsistencies of the history
may be traceable to a confusion of the traditions concerning the conquest of Idzumo by Yamato and of those
concerning the conquest of Yamato by Tsukushi. Perhaps
too (for so almost impossible a task is it to reconstruct-
history out of legend) there may not, after all, be sufficient warrant for believing in the former existence of
Idzumo as a separate state, though it certainly seems
hard to account otherwise for the peculiar place that
Idzumo occupies in mythic story. In any case, and whatever light may hereafter be thrown on this very obscure
question, it must be remembered that, so far as clear
native documentary evidence reaches, 400 A.D. is approximately the highest limit of reliable Japanese history.
Beyond that date we are at once confronted with the
miraculous; and if any facts relative to earlier Japan are
to be extracted from the pages of the " Records " and
" Chronicles," it must be by a process very different from
that of simply reading and taking their assertions upon
trust.

  With regard to the origin, or rather to the significance, of the clearly fanciful portions of the Japanese legends, the question here mooted as to the probability 65
of the Japanese mythology being a mixed one warns us to
exercise more than usual caution in endeavouring to
interpret it. In fact, it bids us wait to interpret it until

such time as further research shall have shown which
legends belong together.  For if they are of hetero-
geneous origin, it is hopeless to attempt to establish a
genealogical tree of the gods, and the very phrase so
often heard in discusions on this subject,—"the original
religious beliefs of the Japanese,"—ceases to have any
precise meaning ; for different beliefs may have been
equally ancient and original, but distinguished geo-
grapically by belonging to different parts of the country.
Furthermore it may not be superfluous to call attention
to the fact that the gods who are mentioned in the
opening phrases of the histories as we now have them
are not therefore necessarily the gods that were most
anciently worshipped.  Surely in religions, as in books,
it is not often the preface that is written first.  And yet
this simple consideration has been constantly neglected,
and, one after another, European writers having a tincture
of knowledge of Japanese mythology, tell us of original
Dualities, Trinities, and Supreme Deities, withont so much
as pausing to notice that the only two authorities in the
matter,—viz., the "Records" and the "Chronicles,"—
differ most gravely in the lists they furnish of primary
gods.  If the present writer ventured to throw out a
suggestion where so many random assertions have been
made, it would be to the effect that the various abstrac-
tions which figure at the commencement of the "Records"
and of the "Chronicles" were probably later growths,
and perhaps indeed mere inventions of individuals priests.
There is nothing either in the histories or in the Shintō
Rituals to show that these gods, or some one or more
of them, were in early days, as has been sometimes
supposed, the objects of a pure worship which was

afterwards obscured by the legends of Izanagi, Izanami, and their numerous descendants. On the contrary, with the exception of the deity Taka-Mi-Musu-Bi,[74] they are no sooner mentioned than they vanish into space.

Whether it is intrinsically likely that so rude a race [66] as the Early Japanese, and a race so little given to metaphysical speculation as the Japanese at all times of their history, should have commenced by a highly abstract worship which they afterwards completely abandoned, is a question which may better be left to those whose general knowledge of early peoples and early religious beliefs entitles their decisions to respect. Their assistance likewise, even after the resolution of the Japanese mythology into its several component parts, must be called in by the specialist to help in deciding how much of this mythology should he interpreted according to the " solar " method now so popular in England, how much should be accepted as history more or less perverted, how much should be regarded as embodying attempts at explaining facts in nature, and what residue may be rejected as simple fabrication of the priesthood in comparatively late times.[75] Those who are personally acquainted with the Japanese character will probably incline to enlarge the area of the three later divisions more than would be prudent in the case of the highly imaginative Aryans, and to point out that, though some few Japanese legends

---

74. *I.e.* the High August Producing Wondrous Deity. He is the second divine personage whose birth is mentioned in the " Records " (see Sect. I, Note 5). In the story of the creation given in the " Chronicles " he does not appear except in " One account."

75. Sect. XXXVII is a good instance of the third of these catagories. For an elaborate myth founded on the name of a place see Sect. LXV. Lesser instances occur in Sects. XLIV, LXV, and LXXIII.

or portions of legends can be traced to face etymologies invented to account for names of places, and are therefore true myths in the strict acception of the term, yet the kindred process whereby personality is ascribed to inanimate objects,—a process which lies at the very root of Aryan mythology,—is altogether alien to the Japanese genius, and indeed to the Far-Eastern mind in general. Mythology thus originated has been aptly described as a " disease of language." But all persons are not liable to catch the same disease, neither presumably are all languages ; and it is hard to see how a linguistic disease which consists in mistaking a metaphor for a reality can attack a tongue to which metaphor, even in its tamest shape, is an almost total stranger. Thus not only have Japanese Nouns no Genders and Japanese Verbs no Persons, but the names of inanimate objects cannot even be used as the subjects of Transitive Verbs. Nowhere for instance in Japanese, whether Archaic, Classical, or 67 Modern, do we meet with such metaphorical,—mythological,—phrases at " the hot wind melts the ice," or " his conversation delights me," where the words " wind " and " conversation " are spoken of as if they were personal agents. No, the idea is invariably rendered in some other and impersonal way. Yet what a distance separates such statements, in which the ordinary European reader unacquainted with any Altaïc tongue would scarcely recognize the existence of any personification at all, from the bolder flights of Aryan metaphor ! Indeed, though Altaïc Asia has produced very few wise men, the words of its languages closely correspond to the definition of words as " the wise man's counters ; " for they are colourless and matter-of-fact, and rarely if ever carry him who speaks them above the level of sober reality. At the same time, it is patent that the sun plays *some* part in the Japanese mythology; and even the legend of Prince Yamato-Take, which has hitherto been generally accepted as historical or semi-historical, bears such close resemblance to legends in other countries which have been pronounced to be solar by great authorities that it may at least be worth while to subject it to investigation from that point of view.[76] The present writer has already expressed his conviction that this matter is not one for the specialist to decide alone. He would only, from the Japanese point of view, suggest very particular caution in the application to Japanese legend of a method of interpretation which has elsewhere been fruitful of great results.

A further particular which is deserving of notice is the almost certain fact of a recension of the various traditions at a comparatively late date. This is partly shown by the amount of geographical knowledge displayed in the enumeration of the various islands supposed to have been given birth to by Izanagi and Izanami (the "Male who Invites" and the "Female who Invites"),—an amount and an exactness of knowledge unattainable at a time prior to the union under one rule of all the provinces mentioned, and significantly not extending much beyond those provinces. Such a recension may likewise be inferred,—if the opinion of the manifold origin of the Japanese traditions be accepted,—from the fairly ingenious manner in which their component parts have generally been welded together. The way in which one or two legends,—for instance, that of the curious curse pro-

76. See Sects. LXXIX.-XCI.

nounced by the younger brother Ho-wori on the elder
Ho-deri—are repeated more than once exemplifies a less
intelligent revision.[77] Under this heading may, perhaps,
be included the legends of the conquest of Yamato by
the Emperor Jim-mu and of the conquest of the same
country by the Empress Jin-gō, which certainly bear a
suspicious likeness to each other. Of the subjection of
Korea by this last-named personage it should be observed
that the Chinese and Korean histories, so far as they are
known to us, make no mention, and indeed the dates, as
more specially given in the "Chronicles," clearly show
the inconsistency of the whole story; for Jin-gō's husband,
the Emperor Chiū-ai, is said to have been born in the
19th year of the reign of Sei-mu, *i.e.* in A.D. 149, while
his father, Prince Yamato-Take, is said to have died in
the 43rd year of Kei-kō, *i.e.* in A.D. 113, so that there
is an interval of thirty-six years between the death of
the father and the birth of the son!"[78]

One peculiarly interesting piece of information to be
derived from a careful study of the "Records" and
"Chronicles" (though it is one on which the patriotic
Japanese commentators preserve complete silence) is that,
at the very earliest period to which the twilight of legend
stretches back, Chinese influence had already begun to

---

77. See this legend as first given in Sects. XL and XLI and afterwards in quite another context in Sect. CXVI. The way in which "One
account" of the "Chronicles of Japan" tells the story of the ravages
committed on the fields of the Sun-Goddess by her brother, the "Impetuous Male Deity," might perhaps justify the opinion that that likewise
is but the same tale in another form. The legend is evidently a very
important one.

78. The translator's attention was drawn to the inconsistency of these
dates by Mr. Ernest Satow.

make itself felt in these islands, communicating to the inhabitants both implements and ideas. This is surely a fact of very particular importance, lending, as it does, its weight to the mass of evidence which goes to prove that in almost all known cases culture has been introduced from abroad, and has not been spontaneously developed. The traces of Chinese influence are indeed not numerous, but they are unmistakable. Thus we find chopsticks mentioned both in the Idzumo and in the Kiushu legendary cycle. The legend of the birth of the Sun-Goddess and Moon-God from Izanagi's eyes is a scarcely altered fragment of the Chinese myth of P'an Ku; the superstition that peaches had assisted Izanagi to repel the hosts of Hades can almost certainly be traced to a Chinese source, and the hand-maidens of the Japanese Sun-Goddess are mentioned under the exact title of the Spinning Damsel of Chinese myth (天衣織女), while the River of Heaven (天河), which figures in the same legend, is equally Chinese,—for surely both names cannot be mere coincidences. A like remark applies to the name of the Deity of the Kitchen, and to the way in which that deity is mentioned.[79] The art of making an intoxicating liquor is referred to in the very earliest Japanese legends. Are we to believe that its invention here was independent of its invention on the continent? In this instance moreover the old histories bear witness against themselves; for they mention this same liquor in terms showing that it was a curious rarity in what, according to the accepted chronology, corresponds to the century immediately preceding the Christian era, and again in the third century of that era. The whole story

79. See Sect. XXIX, Note 16.

of the Sea-God's palace has a Chinese ring about it,
and the "cassia-tree" (桂) mentioned in it is certainly
Chinese, as are the crocodiles. That the so-called *maga-
tama*, or "curved jewels," which figure so largely in the
Japanese mythology, and with which the Early Japanese
adorned themselves, were derived from China was already
suspected by Mr. Henry von Siebold; and quite latterly
Mr. Milne has thrown light on this subject from an
altogether unexpected quarter. He has remarked, namely,
that jade or the jade-like stone of which many of the
*maga-tama* are made, is a mineral which has never yet
been met with in Japan. We therefore know that *some*
at least of the "curved jewels" or of the material for
them came from the mainland, and the probability that
the idea of carving these very oddly shaped ornaments
was likewise imported thence gains in probability. The
peculiar kind of arrow called *nari-kabura* (鳴鏑) is another
trace of Chinese influence in the material order, and a
thorough search by a competent Chinese scholar would
perhaps reveal others. But enough at least has been
said to show the indisputable existence of that influence.
70 From other sources we know that the more recent
mythic fancy of Japan has shown itself as little im-
penetrable to such influence as have the manners and
customs of the people. The only difference is that
assimilation has of late proceeded with much greater
rapidity.

In this language is another guide; for, though the
discoverable traces of Chinese influence are comparatively
few in the Archaic Dialect, yet they are there. This is
a subject which has as yet scarcely been touched. Two
Japanese authors of an elder generation, Kahibara and

Arawi Hakuseki, did indeed point out the existence of some such traces. But they drew no inference from them, they did not set to work to discover new ones, and their indications, except in one or two obvious cases, have received little attention from later writers whether native or foreign. But when we compare such words as *kane, kume, kuni, saka, tana, uma,* and many others with the pronunciation now given, or with that which the phonetic laws of the language in its earlier stage would have caused to be given, to their Chinese equivalents 金, 軍, 郡, 尺, 壇, 馬, etc., the idea forces way that such coincidences of sound and sense cannot all be purely accidental; and when moreover we find that the great majority of the words in question denote things or ideas that were almost certainly imported, we perceive that a more thorough sifting of Archaic Japanese (especially of botanical and zoological names and of the names of implements and manufactures) would probably be the best means of discovering at least the negative features of an antiquity remoter than all written documents, remoter even than the crystallization of the legends which these documents have preserved. In dealing with Korean words found in Archaic Japanese we tread on more delicate ground; for there we have a language which, unlike Chinese, stands to Japanese in the closest family relationship, making it plain that many coincidences of sound and sense should be ascribed to radical affinity rather than to later intercourse. At the same time it appears more probable that, for instance, such seemingly indigenous Japanese terms as *Hotoke,* "Buddha," and *tera,* "Buddhist temple," should have been in fact borrowed from the corresponding Korean words *Puchhö* and *chöl* than that both nations should have independently chosen homonyms to denote the same foreign ideas. Indeed, it will perhaps not be too bold to assume that 71 in the case of *Hotoke*, "Buddha," we have before us a word whose journeyings consist of many stages, it having been first brought from India to China, then from China to Korea, and thirdly from Korea to Japan, where finally the ingenuity of philologists has discovered for it a Japanese etymology (*hito ke*, " human spirit ") with which in reality it has nothing whatever to do.

These introductory remarks have already extended to such a length that a reference to the strikingly parallel case of borrowed customs and ideas which is presented by the Ainos in this same archipelago must be left undeveloped. In conclusion, it need only be remarked that a simple translation of one book, such as is here given, does not nearly exhaust the work which might be expended even on the elucidation of that single book, and much less can it fill the gap which still lies between us and a proper knowledge of Japanese antiquity. To do this, the co-operation of the archæologist must be obtained, while even in the field of the critical investigation of documents there is an immense deal still to be done. Not only must all the available Japanese sources be made to yield up the information which they contain, but the assistance of Chinese and Korean records must be called in. A large quantity of Chinese literature has already been ransacked for a similar purpose by Matsu-shita Ken-rin, a translation of part of whose very useful compilation entitled "An Exposition of the Foreign Notices of Japan" (異稱日本傳) would be one of the greatest helps towards the desired knowledge. In fact there still remains to be done for Japanese antiquity from our standpoint what Hirata has done for it from the standpoint of a Japanese Shintoist. Except in some of Mr. Satow's papers published in these " Transactions," the subject has scarcely yet been studied in this spirit, and it is possible that the Japanese members of our Society may be somewhat alarmed at the idea of their national history being treated with so little reverence. Perhaps, however, the discovery, of the interest of the field of study thus only waiting to be investigated may reconcile them to the view here propounded. In any case if the early history of Japan is not all true, no amount of make believe can make it so. What we would like to do is to sift the true from the false. As an eminent writer on anthropology[80] has recently said, " Historical criticism, that is, judgment, is practised 72 not for the purpose of disbelieving, but of believing. Its object is not to find fault with the author, but to ascertain how much of what he says may be reasonably taken as true." Moreover, even in what is not to be accepted as historic fact there is often much that is valuable from other points of view. If, therefore, we lose a thousand years of so-called Japanese history, it must not be forgotten that Japanese mythology remains as the oldest existing product of the Altaïc mind.

\* \* \*

The following is a list of all the Japanese works quoted in this Introduction and in the Notes to the Translation. For the sake of convenience to the English reader all the titles have been translated excepting some

80. Dr. Tylor in his "Anthropology," Chap. XV.

few which, mostly on account of their embodying a recondite allusion, do not admit of translation :—

Catalogue of Family Names, 姓氏錄, by Prince Mata.[81]

Chronicles of Japan (generally quoted as the "Chronicles,") 日本紀 or 日本書紀, by Prince Toneri and others.

Chronicles of Japan Continued, 續日本紀, by Sugano Ason Mamichi, Fujihara no Ason TSUGUNAHA and others.

Chronicles of Japan Explained, 釋日本記, by URABE no Yasukata.

Chronicles of the Old Matters of Former Ages, 先代舊事記, authorship uncertain.

Collection of a Myriad Leaves, 萬葉集, by TACHIBANA NO MORAYE (probably).

Collection of Japanese Songs Ancient and Modern, 古今和歌集, by Ki no TSURAYUKI and others.

Commentary on the Collection of a Myriad Leaves, 萬葉考, by Kamo no MABUCHI.

73 Commentary on the Lyric Dramas, 謠曲拾葉集, by Jinkō.

Commentary on the Ritual of the General Purification, 大祓詞後釋, MOTOWORI Norinaga.

Correct Account of the Divine Age, 神代正語, by MOTOWORI Norinaga.

Dictionary of Pillow-Words, 冠辭考, by Kamo no MABUCHI.

Digest of the Imperial Genealogies, 纂輯御系圖, by Yokoyama Yoshikiyo and Kurokaha Saneyori.

---

81. The names in small capitals are those by which the authors (or compilers) are best known, and are mostly either their surname or personal name. Japanese usage is however very fluctuating, and sanctions moreover the use of a variety of *noms de plume.* Thus Motowori is not only often mentioned by his personal name Norinaga, but also by the designation of *Suzunoya no Ushi*, Mabuchi by the designation of *Agatawi no Ushi*, etc.

Discussion of the Objections to the Inquiry into the True Chronology, 眞歷不審考, by MOTOWORI Norinaga.

Examination of Difficult Words, 難語考, by Tachibana no MORIBE.

Examination of the Synonyms for Japan, 國號考, by MOTOWORI Norinaga.

Explanation of Japanese Names, 日本譯名, by KAHIBARA Tokushin.

Explanation of the Songs in the Chronicles of Japan, 日本紀歌廼解, by Arikida no HISAŌI.

Exposition of the Ancient Histories, 古史傳, by HIRATA Atsutane.

Exposition of the Foreign Notices of Japan, 異稱日本傳 by, Matsushita Ken-rin.

Exposition of the Records of Ancient Matters (usually) quoted simply as "Motowori's Commentary"), 古事記傳, by MOTOWORI Norinaga.

Exposition of tho Record of Ancient Matters Criticized (usually quoted as "Moribe's Critique on Motowori's Commentary,") 難古事記傳, by Tachibana no MORIBE.

Gleanings from Ancient Story, 古語拾遺, by Imibe no HIRONARI.

*Idzu no Chi-Waki*, 稜威道別, by Tachibana no MORIBE.

*Idzu no Koto-waki*, 稜威言別, by

Inquiry into the Signification of the Names of the Provinces (MS.), 諸國名義考, by Fujihara no Hitomaro.

Inquiry into the True Chronology, 眞歷考, by MOTOWORI Norinaga.

Japanese Words Classified and Explained, 和名類聚鈔, by MINAMO NO SHITAGAFU.

*Ko-Chi Tsū*, 古史通, by ARAI Kumbi HAKUSEKI.

*Kō-Gan Shō*, (MS.), 厚顏抄, by KEI-CHIYU.

74 Perpetual Commentary on the Chronicles of Japan (usually
    quoted as "Tanigaha Shisei's Commentary,") 日本書記
    通證, by TANIGAHA SHISEI.

Records of Ancient Matters (often quoted simply as the
    "Records"), 古事記, by Futo no YASUMARO.

Records of Ancient Matters in the Divine Character, 神字
    古事記, by Fujihara no Masaoki.

Records of Ancient Matters in the Syllable Character.
    假名古事記, by Sakata no Kaneyasu.

Records of Ancient Matters Revised, 校正古事記, Anony-
    mous.

Records of Ancient Matters With Marginal Notes (usually
    quoted as "the Edition of 1687"), 鼇頭古事記, by De-
    guchi NOBUYOSHI.

Records of Ancient Matters With the Ancient Reading,
    古訓古事記, by Nagase no Masachi (published with
    Motowori's sanction)

Records of Ancient Matters with Marginal Readings, 標註
    古事記, by Murakami Tadayoshi.

Ritual of the General Purification, 大祓詞, Authorship Un-
    certain.

Shintō Discussed Afresh, 神道新論, by Takahashi Gorō.

Sources of the Ancient Histories, 古史徵, by HIRATA Atsu-
    tane.

Tale of a Bamboo-Cutter, 竹取物語, Authorship Uncertain.

Tama-Katsuma, 玉勝間, by MOTOWORI Norinaga.

Tokihara-Gusa (the full title is *Jin-Dai-Sei-Go Tokiha-Gusa*),
    常盤草, (神代正語常盤草), Hosoda TOMINOBU.

Topography of Yamashiro, 山城風土紀, Authorship Un-
    certain.

*Tō-Ga* (MS.), 東雅, by ARAI Kumbi HAKUSEKI.

*Wa-Kun Shiwori,* 和訓栞, by TANIGAWA SHISEI.

Yamato Tales, 大和物語, Authorship Uncertain.

Besides these two or three standard Chinese works are referred to such as the "*Yi Chin*" or "Book of Changes" (易經), and the "*Shan Hai Ching*" or "Mountain and Sea Classic" (山海經; but they are very few, and so easily recognized that it were unnecessary to enumerate them. All Japanese words properly so called are transliterated according to Mr. Satow's "Orthographic System," which, while representing the native spelling, does not in their case differ very greatly from the modern pronunciation. In the case of Sinico-Japanese words, where the divergence between the "Orthographic" spelling and the pronunciation is often considerable, a phonetic spelling has been preferred. With but two or three exceptions, which have been specially noted, Sinico-Japanese words are found only in proper names mentioned in the Preface and in the translator's Introduction, Footnotes, and Sectional Headings. The few Chinese words that occur in the Introduction and Notes are transliterated according to the method introduced by Sir Thomas Wade, and now so widely used by students of Chisese.

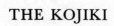

# THE KOJIKI

# RECORDS OF ANCIENT MATTERS.

## VOL. I.[1]

## PREFACE.[2]

I[3] Yasumaro[4] say :[5]

Now when chaos had begun to condense, but force and [4] form were not yet manifest, and there was nought named, nought done, who could know its shape ?[6] Nevertheless Heaven and Earth first parted, and the Three Deities performed the commencement of creation ; the Passive and Active Essences then developed, and the Two Spirits became the ancestors of all things.[7] Therefore[8] did he enter obscurity and emerge into light, and the Sun and Moon were revealed by the washing of his eyes ; he floated on and plunged into the sea-water, and Heavenly and Earthly Deities appeared through the ablutions of his person ?[9] So in the dimness of the great commencement, we, by relying on the original teaching, learn the time of the conception of the earth and of the birth of islands ; in the remoteness of the original beginning, we, by trusting the former sages, perceive the era of the genesis of Deities and of the establishment of men.[10] Truly do we know that a mirror was hung up, that [5] jewels were spat out, and that then an Hundred Kings succeeded each other ; that a blade was bitten, and a serpent cut in pieces, so that a Myriad Deities did flourish.[11] By deliberations in the Tranquil River the

Empire was pacified; by discussions on the Little Shore
the land was purified.[12]    Wherefore His Augustness Ho-
no-ni-ni-gi[13] first descended to the Peak of Takachi,[14] and
the Heavenly Sovereign Kamu-Yamato[15] did traverse the
6 Island of the Dragon-Fly.[16]    A weird bear put forth its
claws, and a heavenly sabre was obtained at Takakura.[17]
They with tails obstructed the path, and a great crow
guided him to Yeshinu.[18]    Dancing in rows they destroyed
the brigands, and listening to a song they vanquished
the foemen.[19]    Being instructed in a dream, he was
reverent to the Heavenly and Earthly Deities, and was
therefore styled the Wise Monarch,[20] having gazed on
the smoke, he was benevolent to the black-haired people,
and is therefore remembered as the Emperor-Sage.[21]
Determining the frontiers and civilising the country, he
issued laws from the Nearer Afumi;[22] reforming the
7 surnames and selecting the gentile names, he held sway
at the Further Asuka.[23]    Though each differed in caution
and in ardour, though all were unlike in accomplishments
and in intrinsic worth, yet was there none who did not
by contemplating antiquity correct manners that had
fallen to ruin, and by illumining modern times repair
laws that were approaching dissolution.[24]

In the august reign of the Heavenly Sovereign who
governed the Eight Great Islands from the Great Palace
of Kiyomihara at Asuka,[25] the Hidden Dragon put on
8 perfection, the Reiterated Thunder came at the appointed
moment.    Having heard a song in a dream, he felt that
he should continue the succession; having reached the
water at night, he knew that he should receive the
inheritance.    Nevertheless Heaven's time was not yet,
and he escaped like the cicada to the Southern Mountains;

both men and matters were favourable, and he marched
like the tiger to the Eastern Land. Suddenly riding
in the Imperial Palanquin, he forced his way across
mountains and rivers: the Six Divisions rolled like
thunder, the Three Hosts sped like lightning. The erect
spears lifted up their might, and the bold warriors arose
like smoke: the crimson flags glistened among the
weapons, and the ill-omened crew were shattered like
tiles. Or ere a day had elapsed, the evil influences
were purified: forthwith were the cattle let loose and
the horses given repose, as with shouts of victory they
returned to the Flowery Summer; the flags were rolled
up and the javelins put away, as with dances and
chants they came to rest in the capital city. The year
was that of the Cock, and it was in the Second Moon.²⁶
At the Great Palace of Kiyomihara did he ascend to ₉
the Heavenly seat: in morality he outstripped Ken-Kō,
in virtue he surpassed Shiū-Ō. Having grasped the
celestial seals, he was paramount over the Six Cardinal
Points; having obtained the heavenly supremacy, he
annexed the Eight Wildernesses. He held the mean
between the Two Essences,²⁷ and regulated the order
of the Five Elements. He established divine reason
wherewith to advance good customs; he disseminated
brilliant usages wherewith to make the land great.
Moreover the ocean of his wisdom, in its vastness, pro-
foundly investigated the highest antiquity; the mirror of
his heart, in its fervour, clearly observed former ages.

Hereupon the Heavenly Sovereign commanded, saying:
"I hear that the chronicles of the emperors and likewise
the original words in the possession of the various families
deviate from exact truth, and are mostly amplified by

empty falsehoods. If at the present time these imperfections be not amended, ere many years shall have elapsed, the purport of this, the great basis[23] of the country, the grand foundation of the monarchy, will be destroyed. So now I desire to have the chronicles of the emperors selected and recorded, and the old words examined and ascertained, falsehoods being erased and the truth determined, in order to transmit [the latter] to after ages."[29] At that time there was a retainer whose surname was Hiyeda and his personal name Are. He was twenty-eight years old, and of so intelligent a disposition that

10 he could repeat with his mouth whatever met his eyes, and record in his heart whatever struck his ears.[30] Forthwith Are was commanded to learn by heart the genealogies of the emperors, and likewise the words of former ages. Nevertheless time elapsed and the age changed, and the thing was not yet carried out.[31]

Prostrate I consider how Her Majesty the Empress, having obtained Unity, illumines the empire,—being versed in the Triad, nourishes the people.[32] Ruling from the Purple Palace, Her virtue reaches to the utmost limits of the horse's hoof-marks: dwelling amid the Sombre Retinue, Her influence illumines the furthest distance attained to by vessels' prows. The sun rises, and the brightness is increased; the clouds disperse, neither is there smoke. Never cease the historiographers from recording the good omens of connected stalks and double rice-ears; never for a single moon is the treasury without the tribute of continuous beacon-fires and repeated interpretations. In fame She must be pronounced superior to Bum-Mei, in virtue more eminent than Ten-Itsu.[33]

11 Hereupon,[34] regretting the errors in the old words, and

wishing to correct the misstatements in the former chronicles, She, on the eighteenth day of the ninth month of the fourth year of Wa-do[35], commanded me Yasumaro to select and record the old words learnt by heart by Hiyeda no Are according to the Imperial Decree, and dutifully to lift them up to Her.[35]

In reverent obedience to the contents of the Decree, I have made a careful choice. But in high antiquity both speech and thought were so simple, that it would be difficult to arrange phrases and compose periods in the characters.[37] To relate everything in an ideographic transcription would entail an inadequate expression of the meaning ; to write altogether according to the phonetic 12 method would make the story of events unduly lengthy.[88] For this reason have I sometimes in the same sentence used the phonetic and ideographic systems conjointly, and have sometimes in one matter used the ideographic record exclusively. Moreover where the drift of the words was obscure, I have by comments elucidated their signification ; but need it be said that I have nowhere commented on what was easy?[89] Again, in such cases as calling the surname 日下 *Kusaka*, and the personal name written with the character 帶 *Tarashi*, I have followed usage without alteration.[40] Altogether the things recorded commence with the separation of Heaven and Earth, and conclude with the august reign at Woharida.[41] So from the 13 Deity Master-of-the-August-Centre-of-Heaven down to His Augustness Prince-Wave-Limit-Brave-Cormorant-Thatch-Meeting-Incompletely makes the First Volume ; from the Heavenly Sovereign Kamu-Yamato-Ihare-Biko down to the august reign of Homuda makes the Second Volume ; from the Emperor Oho-Sazaki down to the great palace of Woharida makes the Third Volume.[42] Altogether I have written Three Volumes, which I reverently and respectfully present.[43] I Yasumaro, with true trembling and true fear, bow my head, bow my head.

Reverently presented by the Court Noble Futo no Yasumaro, an Officer of the Upper Division of the Fifth Rank and of the Fifth Order of Merit, on the 28th day of the first moon of the fifth year of Wa-dō.[44]

---

1. Literally "Upper Volumes," there being three in all, and it being the common Japanese practice (borrowed from the Chinese) to use the words Upper, Middle, and Lower to denote the First, Second and Third Volumes of a work respectively.

2. The peculiar nature of this Preface, which is but a *tour de force* meant to show that the writer could compose in the Chinese style if he chose to do so, has been already hinted at in the Introduction. It is indeed a laboured little composition, and, but for the facts stated in its latter portion, has no value except perhaps as a specimen of the manner in which the legends of one country may be made to change aspect by being presented through the medium of the philosophical terminology and set phrases of another. It may be divided into five parts. In the first the writer, in a succession of brief allusions antithetically balanced, summarizes the most striking of the legends that are detailed in the pages of his "Records," and in a few words paints the exploits of some of the early emperors. In the second the troubles that ushered in the reign of the Emperor Tem-mu and his triumph over Prince Ohotomo are related at greater length in high-flown allusive phrases borrowed from the Chinese historians. The third division gives us the Emperor Temmu's decree ordering the compilation of the "Records," and the fourth tells how the execution of that decree was delayed till the reign of the Empress Gemmiyō (A.D. 708-715), on whom likewise a panegyric is pronounced. In the fifth and last the compiler enters into some details concerning the style and method he has adopted.

3. The First Personal Pronoun is here represented by the humble character 臣, "vassal," used in China by a subject when addressing his sovereign in writing.

4. This is the compiler's personal name. His full name and titles, as given at the end of this preface, were 正五位上勳五等太朝臣安萬侶, *i.e.*, the Court Noble Futo no Yasumaro, an Officer of the Upper Division of the First Class of the Fifth Rank and of the Fifth Order of Merit. The family of Futo claimed to descend from His Augustness Kamu-yawi-mimi, second son of the Emperor Jim-mu. Yasumaro's death is recorded in the " Chronicles of Japan Continued," under date of 30th August, A.D. 723.

5. *I.e.*, I report as follows to Her Majesty the Empress.

\* This number and that in the corner of every succeeding page of the Translation is the number of the Volume of Motowori's Commentary treating of the Section in question.

6. *I.e.*, in the primeval void which preceded all phenomena there was neither form nor movement, and it was therefore unnamed and unknowable.

7. This sentence summarizes the first eight Sections of the text of the " Records." The " three Deities " are the Deity Master-of-the August-Centre-of-Heaven, the High-August-Producing-Wondrous-Deity (see Sect. I, Notes 4, 5, and 6.) The two Spirits representing the " Passive and Active Elements " are the creatrix and creator Izanami and Izanagi (the " Female-Who-Invites " and the " Male-Who-Invites,"—see Sect. II, Note 8), the procreation by whom of the islands of the Japanese archipelago and of a large number of gods and goddesses forms the subject of Sections III-VII.

8. The word " therefore " is not appropriate in this place, and Motowori accordingly warns the reader to lay no stress upon it.

9. This sentence alludes to Izanagi's visit to Hades, and to the purification of his person on his return to the Upper World (see Sects. IX and X). It also refers to the birth of the Sun-Goddess and of the Moon-God from his left and from his right eye respectively, and to that of a large number of lesser gods and goddesses, who were produced from every article of his wearing apparel and from every part of his person on the occasion of his performing those ablutions (see Sect. X.)

10. The " original teaching " here mentioned means the original traditions of Japanese antiquity. The " former sages,"—a term which in China fitly designates such philosophers as Confucius, and Mencius, but which it is difficult to invest with any particular sense here in Japan where no sages have ever arisen,—may be best taken to mean those unknown persons who transmitted the legends of the gods and early emperors. The " establishment of men " probably alludes to the investiture of the

sovereignty of Japan in the human descendants of the Sun-Goddess. The expression is however obscure, and Motowori himself has nothing satisfactory to tell us about it.

11. The mirror here mentioned is that by means of which the Sun-Goddess was allured out of the cave (see Sect. XVI); the jewels are those which Susa-no-Wo (the "Impetuous Male Deity") begged of his sister the Sun-Goddess, and crunched into fragments (see Sect. XIII); the blade that was bitten to pieces by the Sun-Goddess figures in the same legend; the serpent is that slain by Susa-no-Wo after his banishment from Heaven (see Sect. XVIII); the "Myriad Deities" are supposed by Motowori to be this same god's numerous descendants (see Sect. XX), who ruled in Idzumo. There remains the phrase "an Hundred Kings," which is lacking in clearness. The only rational interpretation of it is as designating the Japanese imperial line, and yet the reference seems to have no special appropriateness in this context.

12. For the Tranquil River of Heaven, in whose stony bed the gods were wont to meet in council, see Sect. XIII, Note 12. The divine deliberations here referred to are those which resulted in the investiture of the sovereignty of Japan in the grandson of the Sun-Goddess (see Sects. XXX-XXXIII). The "discussions on the Little Shore" allude to the parleys on the beach of Inasa in Idzumo which preceded the abdication of the Deity who had held sway over that part of the country prior to the descent of the Sun-Goddess's grandson (see Sect. XXXII).

13. The abbreviated form of the name of the Sun-Goddess's grandson (see Sect. XXXIII, Notes 5 and 10).

14. *I.e.,* Mount Takachiho (see Sect. XXXIV, Note 5). The final syllable is here apocopated, in order to preserve the rhythmical balance of the sentence by using only three Chinese characters to write this name, the "Island of the Dragon-Fly" being likewise written with three characters.

15. *I.e.,* the first "human Emperor" Jim-mu, whose full native Japanese name is Kamu-Yamato-Ihare-Biko. For the account of his reign see Sects. XLIV-LII.

16. *I.e.,* Japan. For the traditional origin of this poetical synonym of Japan see Sect. V, Note 26 and also the legend in Sect. CLVI. The word "traverse" in this sentence alludes to the Emperor Jim-mu's victorious progress from Western Japan to Yamato in the centre of the country, which he is said to have subdued, and where it is related that he established his capital (see Sect. XLIV-L).

17. For the mention of the bear, whose appearance caused the Emperor Jim-mu and his army to faint away, see commencement of Sect. XLV. Motowori thinks that the character 爪, "claws," is a copyist's error for 山, "mountain" or 穴, "hole," *Conf.* Sect. XLV, Note 2). For the curious legend of the sabre see the same Section; and for the name of Takakura see more especially Note 3 to that Section.

18. For the Gods with tails who met and conversed with the Emperor Jim-mu in Yamato, see the latter part of Sect. XLVI, a perusal of which will however show that the phrase " obstructed the path," which is here used of them, is not exactly applicable. The miraculous crow which was sent down from Heaven to assist Jim-mu in his conquests, is mentioned at the commencement of the same Section and again at the commencement of Sect. XLVII. For Yeshinu (modern Yoshino) see Sect. XLVI, Note 3.

19. The word " dancing " in this sentence must not be too closely pressed, as it is used simply to balance the word " song " in the parallel clause,—which clause itself does but echo the sense of that which precedes it. The reference is to the song which Jim-mu sang as a signal to his followers to destroy the " earth-spiders " (see Sect. XLVIII), and perhaps also to the songs in Sect. XLIX.

20. " The Emperor Su-jin " must be mentally supplied as the logical subject of this clause. For the story of his dream see Sect. LXIV, and for the origin of the laudatory designation here mentioned see the end of Sect. LXVII, which is however obscure.

21. " The Emperor Nin-toku " must be supplied as the logical subject of this clause. The allusion to the smoke and the laudatory designation here mentioned will be understood by reference to Sect. CXXI. The " black-haired people " is a common Chinese phrase for the peasantry or the people in general.

22. " The Emperor Sei-mu " must be supplied as the logical subject of this clause. His labours are briefly recapitulated in Sect. XCIV. For the province called Nearer Afumi (*Chika-tsu-Afumi*), see Sect. XXIX, Note 20. Its name is here rhythmically balanced against " Further Asuka " in the following clause.

23. " The Emperor In-giyō " must be supplied as the logical subject of this sentence. This Sovereign's rectification of the names forms the subject of Sect. CXXXIX. For Further Asuka (*Toho-tsu-Asuka*) see Sect. CXXXIII, Notes 13 and 11.

24. *I.e.*, though unlike in character, some of the ancient emperors excelling in caution and others in ardour, some being remarkable for their

attainments others for their native worth, yet was there not one without a claim to greatness, not one who did not regard antiquity as the standard by which modern times should be judged, and repair the deviations from antique perfection that successively arose during the lapse of ages.— How marvellously inapplicable is this rodomontade to the early monarchs of Japan the student of Japanese history need scarcely be told, and Motowori himself allows that "it is not completely appropriate." Here the first part of the Preface terminates.

25. Viz., the Emperor Tem-mu, whose struggle for the crown in the latter part of the seventh century of our era against the contending claims of Prince Ohotomo is related at great length in the pages of the "Chronicles," though naturally beyond the scope of these "Records," which close in A.D. 628. The "Eight Great Islands" is one of the synonyms of Japan (see Sect. V, Note 27). The reason for the specially laudatory mention in this place of the Emperor Tem-mu is the fact that it was with him that the idea of compiling these Records originated, as is indeed stated a little further on. He is here alluded to by the expressions Hidden Dragon and Reiterated Thunder, metaphorical names borrowed from the "*Yi Ching*" and denoting the heir apparent, Temmu not having ascended the throne till some time after his predecessor's death, as Prince Ohotomo disputed by force of arms his right to the succession. The phrases "put on perfection" and "came at the appointed moment" are attempts at representing the original 體元 and 應期. The meaning is that the Emperor Tem-mu was the man for the age, and that he took his proper and exalted place in it. In the following sentences we have a flowery *résumé* of the story of the successful war by which he obtained the crown. The reference to the "song in a dream" is indeed obscure; but the "water at night" is the River Yoko, which we read of in the "Chronicles" as having been crossed by him. The characters somewhat freely rendered by the English words "succession" and "inheritance" are 業 and 基, which approximate to that sense in this context. The "Southern Mountains" are the Mountains of Yoshino, whither he escaped for a season as a cicada escapes from its cast-off shell; the "Eastern Land" denotes the eastern provinces of Japan where he organized his army. The "Six Divisions" and the "Three Hosts" are Chinese designations of the Imperial troops, while the "ill-omened crew" of course refers to Tem-mu's enemies.—Prince Ohotomo and his followers. In the ensuing sentence we see peace restored: Tem-mu has returned to the capital (for which the words "Flowery Summer" are a Chinese periphrasis), he has taken in his hands the insignia of office, and reigns

supreme over the Six Cardinal Points (North, South, East, West, Above, and Below) and over the " Eight Wildernesses " (*i.e.*, the barbarous regions on all sides). The writer concludes this divison of his Preface by a glowing panegyric of the Monarch, who was, he says, superior to Hsüan Hou (軒后 Jap. Ken-Kō), and Chou Wang (周王 Jap, Shiū-O), famous Chinese sovereigns of the legendary period. So intelligent were his efforts, so perfect was his conformity with the ways of Heaven as displayed in the workings of the Active and Passive Essences, that the Five Elements (Water Fire, Wood, Metal and Earth) all interacted with due regularity, and laudable usages alone prevailed throughout the land. Up to this point the preface may be said to be purely ornamental.

*I.e.*, March (20th as the " Chronicles " tell us), A. D. 673. The original, to denote the year and the month mentioned, uses the periphrases 歲次大梁 and 月踵夾鍾, but doubtless without any reference to the originat proper meaning of those terms.

27. The text literally reads thus : " He rode in thc exactness of the Two Essences." But the author's intention is to tell us that Tem-mu acted according to the golden mean, keeping the balance even, and not inclining unduly either to the Active or the Passive side.

28. Literally " warp and woof," *i.e.*, cannon, standard, mainspring, first necessity.

29. This is the imperial decree ordering the compilation of the " Records of Ancient matters." The expressions " original words " (本辭) and " old words " (舊辭) are curious, and Motowori is probably right in arguing from the emphatic manner in which they are repeated that the Emperor Tem-mu attached special importance to the actual archaic phraseology in which some at least of the early documents or traditions had been handed down.

30. *Le.*, he could repeat the contents of any document that he had once seen and remember all that he had ever heard.

31. *Le.*, the Emperor Tem-mu died before the plan of the compilation of these " Records " had been carried into execution, viz., it may be presumed, before a selection from the various original documents committed to memory by Are had been reduced to writing.

32. 得一光宅通三亭育. For the phrase " obtaining Unity," which is borrowed from Lao Tzŭ, the student should consult Stanislas Judien's " Livre de la Voie et de la Vertu," pp. 144-149. The " Triad " is the threefold intelligence of Heaven. Earth, and Man. The general meaning of the sentence is that the Empress's perfect virtue, which is in complete

accord with the heavenly ordinances, is spread abroad throughout the empire, and that with her all-penetrating insight she nourishes and sustains her people.

33. In the above four sentences the compiler expresses his respectful admiration of the Empress Gem-miyō, who was on the throne at the time when he wrote, and tells us how wide was her rule and how prosperous her reign. The "Purple Palace" is one of the ornamental names borrowed from the Chinese to denote the imperial residence. The "Sombre Retinue" (if such indeed is the correct rendering of the original expression 玄扈) is a phrase on which no authority consulted by the translator throws any light. The "utmost limits of the horses' hoofmarks" and the "furthest distance attained to by vessels' prows" are favourite phrases in the old literature of Japan to express extreme distance (see, for instance, Mr. Satow's translations of the Ritual of the Praying for Harvest," Vol. VII, Pt. II, p. 111 of these "Transactions" and the present writer's "Classical Poetry of the Japanese," p. 111. Such unusual phenomena as connected stalks, *i.e.*, trunks springing from the same root and uniting again higher up and "joint rice-ears," *i.e.*, two rice-ears growing on a single stem, are considered lucky omens by the Chinese, and their appearance is duly chronicled in those Japanese histories that are composed after the Chinese model. The "continuous beacon-fires" and the "repeated interpretations" are phrases alluding to the foreign lands (*i.e.*, the various small Korean states) speaking strange languages, whence tribute was sent to Japan, The text, as it stands, gives the impression that the arrival of the tribute-ships was announced by beacon-fires being lighted. Motowori however wishes us to understand the author's meaning to be that foreign states which, in the natural course of events, would be . inimical, and the approach of whose ships would be signalized by the lighting of beacon-fires, now peacefully sent gifts to the Japanese monarch. It may be added that the whole sentence is borrowed scarcely without alteration from the "*Wên Hsüan*" (文選). Bum-mei is the Japanese pronunciation of the characters 文命, the original name of Yü (禹) a celebrated legendary emperor of China. Ten-Itsu is the Japanese pronunciation of the characters 天乙, the original name of the ancient emperor T'ang (湯), who is said to have founded the Shang dynasty in the eighteenth century B.C.

34. This word is here used as an initial particle without special significance.

35. *I.e.*, 3rd November A.D. 711. Wa-dō (和銅) is the name of a Japanese "year-period" which lasted from A.D.. 708 to 714.

36. *I.e.*, present them to her. With this sentence ends the fourth division of the preface.

37. *I.e.*, the simplicity of speech and thought in Early Japan renders it too hard a task to rearrange the old documents committed to memory by Are in such a manner as to make them conform to the rules of Chinese style.

38. *I.e.*, if I adopted in its entirety the Chinese ideographic method of writing, I should often fail of giving a true impression of the nature of the original documents (*conf.* the preceding Note). If, on the other hand, I consistently used the Chinese characters, syllable by syllable, as phonetic symbols for Japanese sounds, this work would attain to inordinate proportions, on account of the great length of the polysyllabic Japanese as compared with the monosyllabic Chinese. The author's meaning may be illustrated by referring to the first clause of the "Records," 天地初發 之時 ("when Heaven and Earth began"), which is thus written ideographically with six Chinese characters, whereas it would require no less than eleven to write it phonetically so as to represent the sound of the Japanese words *ame tsuchi no hazhime no toki*, viz., 阿米都知能波士實能登伎. It should be noticed that in this passage the author employs the technical expressions *on* and *kun* (音 and 訓) in a manner which is the precise reverse of that sanctioned by modern usage, *on* being with him the phonetic, and *kun* the ideographic, acceptation of the Chinese characters.

39. It will be seen by perusing the following translation that the author can scarcely be said to have vouchsafed as much exegetical matter as this statement would lead us to expect. Indeed his "comments" are mostly confined to information concerning the pronunciation of certain characters. See however Motowori's remarks on this sentence in Vol. 11, pp. 19-20 of this Commentary.

40. The author here refers to a certain class of Japanese words which offer peculiar difficulties because written neither ideographically nor phonetically, but in a completely arbitrary manner, the result of a freak of usage. His manner of expressing himself is, however, ambiguous. What he meant to say is, as Motowori points out : "Again in such cases as writing the surname *Kusaka*, with the characters 日下, and the personal name *Tarashi* with the character 帶, I have followed usage without alteration." It is his imperfect mastery over the Chinese construction that makes him fall into such errors,—errors easily rectifiable, however, by the more widely read modern Japanese *literati*.

*I.e.*, commence with the creation, and end with the death of the Empress Sui-ko (A. D. 628), who resided at Woharida.

## 14 *Records of Ancient Matters.*

42. For the Deity Master-of-the-August-Centre-of Heaven see Sect.
I, Note 4, and for Prince-Wave-Limit, etc., see Sect. XLII, Note 15.
Kamu-Yamato-Ihare-Biko is the proper native Japanese name of the em-
peror commonly known by the Chinese " canonical name " of Jim-mu.
Homuda is part of the native Japanese name of the Emperor Ojin (see
Sects. XCIV to CXVIII). Oho-Sazaki is the native Japanese name of
the Emperor Nin-toku (see Sects. CXIX to CXXX.)

43. *Q.d.*, to the Empress.

44. *I.e.*, 10th March, A. D. 712.

# RECORDS OF ANCIENT MATTERS. 15

[SECT. I.— THE BEGINNING OF HEAVEN AND EARTH.]

The names of the Deities[1] that were born[2] in the Plain of High Heaven[3] when the Heaven and Earth began were the Deity Master-of-the-August-Centre-of-Heaven,[4] next the High-August-Producing-Wondrous Deity,[5] next the Divine-Producing-Wondrous-Deity.[6] These three Deities were all Deities born alone, and hid their persons.[7] The names of the Deities that were born next from a thing that sprouted up like unto a reed-shoot when the earth,[8] young and like unto floating oil, drifted about medusa-like, were the Pleasant-Reed-Shoot-Prince-Elder Deity,[9] next the Heavenly-Eternally-Standing- 16 Deity.[10] These two Deities were likewise born alone, and hid their persons.

The five Deities in the above list are separate Heavenly Deities.[11]

---

1. For this rendering of the Japanese word *kami* see Introduction, pp. xvii-xviii.

2. Literally, "that became" (成). Such "becoming" is concisely defined by Motowori as "the birth of that which did not exist before."

3. In Japanese *Takama-no-hara*.

4. *Ame-no-mi-naka-nushi-no-kami*.

5. *Taka-mi-musu-bi-no-kami*. It is open to doubt whether the syllable *bi*, instead of signifying "wondrous," may not simply be a verbal termination, in which case the three syllables *musubi* would mean, not "wondrous producing," but simple "producing," *i.e.*, if we adopt the interpretation of the Verb *musubu* as "to produce" in the Active sense of the word, an interpretation as to whose propriety there is some room for doubt. In the absence of certainty the translator has followed the view expressed by Motowori and adopted by Hirata. The same remark applies to the following and other similar names.

6. *Kami-musu-bi-no-kami.* This name reappears in later Sections under the lengthened form of *ami-musu-bi-mi-oya-no-mikoto,* i.e., His Augustness the Deity-Producing-Wondrous-August-Ancestor, and also in abbreviated forms.

7. *I.e.,* they all came into existence without being procreated in the manner usual with both gods and men, and afterwards disappeared, *i.e.,* died.

9. Here and elsewhere the character 國, properly "country" (*regio*), is used where "earth" (*tellus*) better suits the sense. Apparently in the old language the word *kuni* (written 國), which is now restricted to the former meaning, was used ambiguously somewhat like our word "land."

9. *Umashi-ashi-kabi-hiko-ji-no-kami.* For *hiko* here and elsswhere rendered "prince" see Introduction p. xvi ; *ji* is rendered. " elder " in accordance with the opinion expressed by Motowori and Hirata, who say that it is " an Honorific designation of males identical with the *ji* meaning old man."

10. Or, the Deity-Standing-Eternally-in-Heaven, *Ame-no-toko-tachi-no-kami.* The translation of the name here given follows the natural meaning of the characters composing it, and has the sanction of Tanigaha Shisai. Motowori and Hirata take *toko* to stand for *soko,* "bottom," and interpret accordingly ; but this is probably but one of the many instances in which the Japanese philologists allow themselves to be led by the boldness of their etymological speculations into identifying words radically distinct.

11. This is a note in the original, where such notes are indented, as has also been done In the translation. The author's obscure phrase is explained by Motowori to mean that these Heavenly Deities were separate from those who came into existence afterwards, and especially from the Earthly-Eternally-Standing-Deity (*Kuni-no-toko-tachi-no-kami*) who in the "Chronicles" is the first divine being of whom mention is made. These five were, he says, "separate" and had nothing to do with the creation of the world. It should be stated that the sentence will also bear the interpretation "The five Deities in the above list are Deities who divided Heaven" (presumably from Earth ;) but this rendering has against it the authority of all the native editors. As the expressions "Heavenly Deity" and "Earthly Deity" (lit., Country Deity" are of frequent occurrence in these "Records," it may be as well to state that, according to Motowori, the "Heavenly Deities" were such as either dwelt in Heaven or had originally descended to Earth from Heaven, whereas the Earthly Deities were those born and dwelling in Japan.

[SECT. II.—THE SEVEN DIVINE GENERATIONS.]

The names of the Deities that were born next were the Earthly-Eternally-Standing-Deity,[1] next the Luxuriant-Integrating-Master-Deity.[2] These two Deities were likewise Deities born alone, and hid their persons. The names of the Deities that were born next were the Deity Mud-Earth-Lord next his younger sister the Deity Mud-Earth-Lady;[3] next the Germ-Integrating-Deity, next his younger sister the Life-Integrating-Deity;[4] next the Deity Elder-of-the-Great-Place, next his younger sister the Deity Elder-Lady-of-the-Great-Place;[5] next the Deity Perfect-Exterior,[6] next his younger sister the Deity Oh-Awful-Lady;[7] next the Deity the Male-Who-Invites, next his younger sister the Deity the Female-Who-Invites.[8]

From the Earthly-Eternally-Standing Deity down to the Deity the Female-Who-Invites in the previous list are what are termed the Seven Divine Generations. (The two solitary Deities above [-mentioned] are each called one generation. Of the succeeding ten Deities each pair of deities is called a generation.[9]

---

1. Or, the Deity-Standing-Eternally-on-Earth, *Kuni-no-toko-tachi-no-kami*, *Conf.* Note 10 to Sect. 1.

2. *Toyo-kumo-nu-no-kami*. There is much doubt as to the proper interpretation of this name. The characters 雲野 ("cloud-moor"), with which the syllables read *kumo-nu* are written, are almost certainly phonetic, and the translator has followed Motowori's view as corrected by Hirata, according to which *kumo* is taken to stand for *kumu*, "integrating," and *nu* is considered to be an apocopated form of *nushi*, "master" (or more vaguely "the person who presides at or does a thing"). Mabuchi in his "Dictionary of Pillow-words," Article *Sasutake*, argues that the syllables in question should be interpreted in the sense of "coagulated mud"; out this is less satisfactory.

3. *U-hiji-ni-no-kami* and *Su-hiji-ni-no-kami.* The names of this pair lend themseles to a variety of interpretations. Motowori's view of the meaning of the first three syllables in each seems best, if it is founded on the Chinese characters with which they are written in the parallel passage of the "Chronicles," and it has therefore been adopted here. Hirata interprets the names thus: First-Mud-Lord and First-Sand-Lady, and takes *ni* to be an alternative form of the Honorific *ne* found in so many proper names. This view of the meaning of *ni* has been followed by the translator. On the other hand Mabuchi explains the names to mean respectively Floating-Mud-Earth and Sinking-Mud-Earth. The only thing therefore that is granted by all is that the names in question refer to the mud or slime out of which the world was afterwards made. The reader will bear in mind that "younger-sister" and "wife" are convertible names in Archaic Japanese. (See Introduction p. XXXVIII.)

4. *Tsunu-guhi-no-kami* and *Iku-guhi-no-kami.* The interpretation given is one in which the commentators agree, and which has some probability in its favour. It must however only be accepted with reservation.

5. *Oho-to-no ji-no-kami* and *Oho-to-no-be-no-kami.*

6. *Omo-daru-no-kami.* We might also render *omo-daru* by "perfect-face," *i.e.*, perfectly beautiful."

7. *Aya-kashiko-ne-no-kami.* For "awful" we might substitute "venerable." Hirata, commenting on this name and the seven which precede it, says: *U-hiji-ui* and *Su-hiji-ni* are so named from their having contained the germs of what was to become the earth. *Oho-to-no-ji* and *Oho-to-no-be* are so called from the appearance of the incipient earth. *Tsunu-guhi* and *Iku-guhi* are so called from the united appearance of the earth and the Deities as they came into existence. *Omo-daru* and *Kashiko-ne* are so called from the completion of the august persons of the Deities. Thus their names were given to them from the gradual progress [of creation]."

8. *Izana-gi-no-kami* and *Izana-mi-no-kami.* There is some slight diversity of opinion as to the literal signification of the component parts of the names of these the best-known of the Deities hitherto mentioned, though the gist of the meaning remains unchanged. Motowori would prefer to read *Iza-na-gi* and *Iza-na-mi*, taking the syllable *na* as the Second Personal Pronoun "thou," and understanding the names thus: "the Prince-Who-Invites-Thee" and the "Princess-Who-Invites-Thee." It seems however more natural to look on *izana* as forming but one word, viz., the Root of the Verb *Izanafu*, "to invite." The older native com-

mentators mean the same thing when they tell us that *na* is an Expletive.
The syllables *gi* and *mi* are of uncertain etymology, but occur in other
Archaic words to denote the female and male of a pair. The appro-
priateness of the names of these deities will be seen by referring to
Sect. IV.

9. For explanatory notes which are printed in small type in the
original, small type is likewise used in this translation.

---

[SECT. III.—THE ISLAND OF ONOGORO ]

Hereupon all the Heavenly Deities commanded the
two Deities His Augustness' the Male-Who-Invites and
Her Augustness¹ the Female-Who-Invites, ordering them
to "make, consolidate, and give birth to this drifting
land." Granting tō them an heavenly jewelled spear,²
they [thus] deigned to charge them. So the two Deities,
standing upon the Floating Bridge of Heaven,³ pushed 19
down the jewelled spear and stirred with it, whereupon,
when they had stirred the brine till it went curdlecurdle,⁴
and drew [the spear] up, the brine that dripped down
from the end of the spear was piled up and became an
island. This is the Island of Onogoro.⁵

---

1. For this rendering of the Japanese title *Mikoto* see Introduction,
p. xvi, last paragraph.

2. The characters translated "jewelled spear" are 沼矛, whose proper
Chinese signification would be quite different. But the first of the two
almost certainly stands phonetically for 瓊 or 玉,—the syllable *nu*, which
is its sound, having apparently been an ancient word for "jewel" or
"bead," the better-known Japanese term being *tama*. In many places the
word "jewel" (or "jewelled") seems to be used simply as an adjective
expressive of beauty. But Motowori and Hirata credit it in this instance
with its proper signification, and the translator always renders it literally,
leaving the reader to consider it to be used metaphorically if and where
he pleases.

3. *Ama-no-uki-hashi* or *Ame-no-uki-hashi.* The best authorities are at variance as to the nature of this bridge uniting Heaven with Earth. Hirata identifies it with the Heavenly-Rock-Boat (*Ame-no-iha-fune*) mentioned in some ancient writings, whereaa Motowori takes it to have been a real bridge, and finds traces of it and of similar bridges in the so-called "Heavenly Stairs" (*Ama-no-hashi-date*) which are found on several points of the coast, forming a kind of natural breakwater just above water-level.

4. *I.e.,* "till it became thick and glutinous." It is not easy to find in English a word which will aptly render the original Japanese onomatopoeia *koworokoworo.* The meaning may also be "till it made a curdling sound." But though the character 鳴, "to make a noise," sanctions this view, it is not the view approved by the commentators, and 鳴 is probably only written phonetically for a homonymous word signifying "to become," which we find in the parallel passage of the "Chronicles."

5. *I.e.,* "Self-Curdling," "Self-Condensed." It is supposed to have been one of the islets off the coast of the larger island of Ahaji.

---

[SECT. IV.—COURTSHIP OF THE DEITIES THE MALE-WHO-INVITES AND THE FEMALE-WHO-INVITES.]

Having descended from Heaven onto this island, they saw to the erection[1] of an heavenly august pillar, they saw to the erection of an hall of eight fathoms.[2] Tunc quæsivit [Augustus Mas-Qui-Invitat] a minore sorore Augustâ Feminâ-Qui-Invitat: "Tuum corpus quo in modo factum est?" Respondit dicens: "Meum corpus crescens crevit, sed est una pars quæ non crevit continua." Tunc dixit Augustus Mas-Qui-Invitat: "Meum corpus crescens crevit, sed est una pars quæ crevit superflua. Ergo an bonum erit ut hanc corporis mei partem quæ crevit superflua in tui corporis partem quæ non crevit continua inseram, et regiones procreem?" Augusta Femina-Quæ-Invitat respondit dicens: "Bonum erit." Tunc dixit Augustus Mas-Qui-Invitat: "Quod

quum ita sit, ego et tu' hanc cœlestem augustam colum-
nam circumeuntes mutuoque occurrentes, augustarum
[i.e. privatarum] partium augustam coitionem faciemus."[3]
Hâc pactione factâ, dixit [Augustus Mas-Qui-Invitat]:
"Tu a dexterâ circumeuns occurre; ego a sinistrâ oc-
curram." Absolutâ pactione ubi circumierunt, Augusta
Femina-Qui-Invitat primum inquit: "O venuste et amabilis
adolescens!" Deinde Augustus Mas-Qui-Invitat inquit:
"O venusta et amabilis virgo!" Postquam singuli orationi
finem fecerunt, [Augustus Mas-Qui-Invitat] locutus est
sorori, dicens: "Non decet feminam primum verba facere."
Nihilominus in thalamo [opus procreationis] inceperunt,
et filium [nomine] Hirudinem[4] [vel Hirudini similem]
pepererunt. This child they placed in a boat of reeds,
and let it float away. Next they gave birth to the
Island of Aha.[5] This likewise is not reckoned among
their children.[6]

---

1. The original of this quasi-causative phrase, of which there is no
other example in Japanese literature so far as the translator's reading
goes, is interpreted by Motowori in the sense of the English locution to
which it literally corresponds, and it has here been rendered accordingly,
though with considerable hesitation. Hirata does not approve of Motowori's view; but then the different text which he here adopts imposes on
him the necessity of another interpretation. (See his "Exposition of the
Ancient Histories," Vol. II, pp. 39-40).

2. The original word *hiro* (written 尋) is defined as the distance
between the hands when the arms are outstretched. The word rendered
"hall" may also be translated "palace."—The text of the parallel passage
of the "Chronicles" is "they made the Island of Onogoro the central
pillar of the land,"—a statement which seems more rational and more in
accordance with general tradition than that of these "Records."

3. This is Hirata's view of the import of the somewhat obscure
original (see his "Exposition of the Ancient Histories," Vol. II, pp. 61-64).
Motowori's interpretation is: "auguste in thalamo coibimus."

4. The name in the original is Hiru-go, an instance of the fortuitous verbal resemblances occasionally found between unrelated languages.

5. Literary "foam." It is supposed to have been an islet near the island of Ahaji in the province of Sanuki.

6. Hiru-go was not so reckoned, because he was a failure.

———

[SECT. V.—BIRTH OF THE EIGHT ISLANDS.]

Hereupon the two Deities took counsel, saying: "The children to whom we have now given birth are not good. It will be best ,to announce this in the august 21 place¹ of the Heavenly Deities." They ascended forthwith to Heaven and enquired of Their Augustnesses the Heavenly Deities. Then the Heavenly Deities commanded and found out by grand divination,² and ordered them, saying: "They were not good because the woman spoke .first. Descend back again and amend your words." So thereupon descending back, they again went round the heavenly august pillar as before. Thereupon his Augustness the Male-Who-Invites spoke first: "Ah! what a fair and lovely maiden! Afterwards his younger sister Her Augustness the Female-Who-Invites spoke: "Ah! what a fair and lovely youth!" Tali modo quun orationi finem fecerant, auguste coierunt et pepererunt a child the Island of Ahaji, Ho-no-sa-wake.³ Next they 22 gave birth to the Island of Futa-no in Iyo.⁴ This island has one body and four faces, and each face has a name. So the Land of Iyo is called Lovely-Princess;⁵ the Land of Sanuki⁶ is called Prince-Good-Boiled-Rice;⁷ the Land of Aha is called the Princess-of-Great-Food;⁸ the Land of Tosa⁹ is called Brave-Good-Youth.¹⁰ Next they gave birth to the Islands of Mitsu-go¹¹ near Oki,¹² another name for which [islands] is Heavenly-Great-Heart-Youth-¹⁴

This island likewise has one body and four faces[15] and
each face has a name. So the Land of Tsukushi is
called White-Sun-Youth;[16] the Land of Toyo[17] is called 23
Luxuriant-Sun-Youth;[18] the Land of Hi is called Brave
Sun-Confronting - Luxuriant - Wondrous - Lord - Youth;[19] the
Land of Kumaso is called Brave-Sun-Youth.[20] Next they
gave birth to the Island of Iki,[21] another name for which
is Heaven's One-Pillar.[22] Next they gave birth to the
Island of Tsu,[23] another name for which is Heavenly-
Hand-net-Good-Princess.[24] Next they gave birth to the
Island of Sado.[25] Next they gave birth to Great-Yamato-
the - Luxuriant - Island - of - the - Dragon - Fly,[26] another name
for which is Heavenly-August-Sky-Luxuriant-Dragon-fly- 24
Lord - Youth. The name of "Land - of - the - Eight - Great-
Islands "[27] therefore originated in these eight islands
having been born first. After that, when they had
returned,[28] they gave birth to the Island of Ko [-shima][29]
in Kibi,[30] another name for which [island] is Brave-Sun[9]
Direction-Youth. Next they gave birth to the Island of
Adzuki,[31] another name for which is Oho-Nu-De-Hime. 25
Next they gave birth to the Island of Oho [-shima],[32]
another name for which is Oho-Tamaru-Wake. Next
they gave birth to the Island of Hime,[33] another name
for which is Heaven's-One-Root. Next they gave birth
to the Island of Chika,[34] another name for which is
Heavenly-Great-Male. Next they gave birth to the Island
[s] of Futa-go,[35] another name for which is Heaven's-
Two-Houses. (Six islands in all from the Island of Ko in Kibi to
the Island of Heaven's-Two-Houses.

---

1. The characters 御所, here translated "august place" (the proper
Chinese signification is "imperial place") are those still in common use
to denote the Mikado's palace.

2. For an elaborate account of the various methods of divination practised by the Ancient Japanese see Note 5 to Mr. Satow's translation of the "Service of the Gods of Wind at Tatsuta" in the "Transactions of the Asiatic Society of Japan," Vol. VII, Pt. IV, p. 425 *et seq.* "The most important mode of divination practised by the primitive Japanese was that of scorching the shoulder-blade of a deer over a clear fire, and finding, omens in the cracks produced by the heat."

3. *Aha-ji* signifies "foam-way," *i.e*, "the way to Foam (Aha)-Island," on account, it is said, of its intermediate position between the mainland and the province of Aha in what is in modern parlance the Island of Shikoku. The author of the "Chronicles of Old Affairs" fancifully derives the name from *a haji* "my shame." The etymology of Ho-no-sa-wake is disputed; but Hirata, who in the body of Vol. III of his "Exposition of the Ancient Histories" had already expended much ingenuity in discussing it, gives the most satisfactory interpretation that has yet been proposed in a postscript to that volume, where he explains it to signify "Rice-ear-True-Youth." *Wake* (sometimes *wake* or *waku*) is a word of frequent occurrence in the names of gods and heroes. Whether it really signifies "youth," as Hirata believes and as it is most natural to suppose, or whether Motowori's guess that it is an Honorific title corrupted from *waga kimi ye* (lit. "my prince elder brother," more freely "lord") remains undecided. When it is used as a "gentile name," the translator renders it by "lord," as that in such cases is its import apart from the question of derivation. *Sa*, rendered "true," may almost be considered to have dwindled down to a simple Honorific.—It is this little island which is said by the author of the "Chronicles" to have been the caul with which the great island of Yamato was born. Ahaji and Ho-no-sa-wake must be understood to be alternative names, the latter being what in other cases is prefaced by the phrase "another name for whom."

4. *Futa-na* is written with characters signifying "two names," and Motowori's derivation from *futa-narabi*, "two abreast," does not carry conviction. The etymology of Iyo is quite uncertain. It is here taken as the name of the whole island called in modern times Shikoku; but immediately below we find it in its usual modern acceptation of one of the four provinces into which that island is divided. A similar remark applies to Tsukushi a little further on.

5. *Ye-hime.* For the rendering of *hiko* and *hime* as "prince" and "princess" see introduction, p. xvi.

6. Probably derived, as Hirata shows, from *saho-ki*, "pole-trees," a

tribute of poles having anciently been paid by that province. Motowori adopts the unusual reading of the name given in the " Japanese Words Classified and Explained," viz. Sanugi, with the last syllable *nigori*'ed.

7. *Ihi-yori-hiko*. The translator, though with some hesitation, follows Motowori in looking on *yori* as a contraction of *yorishi*, " good." The character used for it in the original is 依.

8. *Oho-ge-tsu-hime.* Remember that *aha* signifies not only " foam " but " millet," so that we need not be astonished to find that the alternative designation of the island so designated is that of a food-goddess.

9. Etymology uncertain, only fanciful derivations being proposed by the native philologists.

10. *Take-yori-wake*

11. *Mitsu-go* signifies " triplets," lit., " three children." The three islets intended are *Ama-na-shima*, *Mukafu-no-shima* and *Chiburi-no-shima.*

12. *Oki* probably here signifies " offing," which is its usual acceptation.

13. *Ame-no-oshi-koro-wake* The syllables *oshi*, which recur in the names of many gods and heroes, are rendered " great " in accordance with Motowori's plausible conjecture that they are an abbreviation of *ohoshi* (" great," not " many " as in the later language). The translation of *koro* by " heart " follows a conjecture of Hirata's (Motowori acknowledged that he could make nothing of the word), according to which it is taken to be an abbreviated form of *kokoro*, " heart."

14. None but fanciful derivations of this word are suggested by the native philologists.

15. A note to the edition of 1687 says : " Should the word 'four ' be changed to 'five ? ' " For most texts enumerate five countries in this passage with slight variations in the names, Himuka, (Hiuga), which it certainly seems strange to omit, being the fourth on the list with the alternative name of Toyokuzhi-hine-wake, while the alternative name of Hi is Haya-hi-wake, Motowori argues that an enumeration of four agrees better with the context, while Moribe in his Critique on Motowori's Commentary decides in favour of the five. There are thus texts and authorities in favour of both views.

16. *Shira-bi-wake.*

17. *Toyo* means " luxuriant " or " fertile." *Hi* appears to signify " fire " or " sun." *Kumaso* is properly a compound, *Kuma-so*, as the district is often mentioned by the simple name of *So- Kuma* signifies " bear," and Motowori suggests that the use of the name of this the fiercest of

beasts as a prefix may be traced to the evil reputation of that part of the country for robbers and outlaws. He quotes similar compounds with *kuma* in support of this view.

18. *Toyo-bi-wake.*

10. *Take-hi-mukahi-toyo-kuzhi-hine-wake.* The interpretation of this name follows Motowori.

20. *Take-bi-wake.*

21. Etymology uncertain, but there seems reason to suppose that the name was originally pronounced Yiki or Yuki.

22. *Ame-hito-tsu-bashira.*

23. *Tsu* (Tsu-shima) means "port," "anchorage," a name probably given to this island on account of its being the midway halting-place for junks plying between Japan and Korea.

24. *Ame-no-sade-yori-hime.* The interpretation of *sade* (rendered "hand-net") is uncertain. The translator has followed that sanctioned by an ode in Vol. I of the "Collection of a Myriad Leaves" and by a passage in the "Japanese Words Classified and Explained." Hirata takes *sa* to be an Honorific and *te* to be the usual word for "hand," while Motowori gives up the name in despair.

25. Etymology uncertain.

26. *Oho-yamato-toyo-aki-dzu-shima* (the original of the alternative personal name is *Ame-no-mi-sora-toyo-aki-dzu-ne-wake*). The etymology of Yamato is much disputed. Mabuchi, in his "Addenda to the Commentray on the Collection of a Myrial Leaves," derives the name from *yama-to*, "mountain-gate." Motowori, in a learned discussion to be found in his "Examination of the Synonyms of Japan," pp. 24.27, proposes three other possible derivations, viz. *yama-to*, "mountain-place," *yama-to* (supposed to stand for *yama-tsubo* and to mean "mountain-secluded"), and *yama-utsu* (*utsu* being a supposititious Archaic form of *uchi*,) "within the mountains." Other derivations are *yama-to* (山外), "without the mountains," *yama-ato*, "mountain-traces" and *yama-todomi*, "mountains stopping," *i.e.* (as Moribe, who proposes it, explains), "far as the mountains can be seen." Another disputed point is whether the name of Yamato which here designates the Main Island of the Archipelago, but which in the common parlance of both ancient and modern times is the denomination on the one hand of the single province of Yamato and on the other of the whole Empire of Japan, originally had the wider application or the more restricted one. Motowori and the author of the "Exposition of the Foreign Notices of Japan" seem to the present writer to make

out the case in favour of the latter view. Motowori supposes the name to have denoted first a village and then a district, before being applied to a large province and finally to the entire country. The "Island of the Dragon-fly" is a favourite name for Japan in the language of the Japanese poets. It is traced to a remark of the Emperor Jim-mu, who is said to have compared the shape of the country round Mountain Hohoma to "a dragon-fly drinking with its tail." *"Conf.* also the tradition forming the subject of Sec. CLVI of the present translation.

27. *Oho-ya-shima-kuni.* A perhaps still more literal English rendering of this name would be "Land of the Grand Eight Islands" or "Grand Land of the Eight Islands," for the word *oho* must be regarded rather as an Honorific than as actually meant to convey an idea of size.

28. "To the Island of Onogoro," says Motowori; but we are not told that the god and goddess had ever left it.

29. *Ko* means "infant" or "small." The original of the alternative personal name is *Take-hi-gata-wake. Gata* (or, without the *nigori, Kata*) here and in other names offers some difficulty. The translator renders it by the equivalent of the usual Japanese signification of the character 方, "direction," with which it is written.

30. Etymology uncertain.

31. *Adzuki* is written with the characters 小豆, which signify a kind of bean (the *Phaseolus radiatus*); but it is possible that they represent the sound, and not the sense, of the name. In the alternative personal name *oho* signifies "great," and *hime* "princess," while the syllables *nu-de* are of altogether uncertain interpretation. Motowori suggests that *nu* may mean "moor" and *de* (for *te*) "clapper-bell."

32. *I.e.,* Great Island. The word *tamaru* in the alternative personal name is so obscure that not even any plausible conjecture concerning it has been ventured and the name is therefore of necessity left untranslated.

33. *Hime* signifies "princess" or "maiden." The original of the alternative personal name is *Ame-hito-tsu-ne.*

34. Etymology uncertain. Motowori would take the name in a plural sense as standing for the modern islands of Hirado and Go-tō (Goto). The original of the alternative personal name is *Ame-no-oshi-wo;* in which as usual, *oshi* is supposed to represent *ohoshi* (大), "great."

35. *Futa-go* means "twins." The original of the alternative personal name is *Ame-futa-ya.*

[SECT. VI.—BIRTH OF THE VARIOUS DEITIES.]

When they had finished giving birth to countries, they began afresh giving birth to Deities. So the name of the Deity they gave birth to was the Deity Great-Male-of-the-Great-Thing;[1] next they gave birth to the Deity Rock-Earth-Prince;[2] next they gave birth to the Deity

26 Rock-Nest-Princess;[3] next they gave birth to the Deity Great-Door-Sun-Youth;[4] next they gave birth to the Deity Heavenly-Blowing-Male;[5] next they gave birth to the Deity Great-House-Prince;[6] next they gave birth to the Deity Youth-of-the-Wind-Breath-the-Great-Male;[7] next they gave birth to the Sea-Deity, whose name is the Deity Great-Ocean-Possessor;[8] next they gave birth to the Deity of the Water-Gates,[9] whose name is the Deity Prince-of-Swift-Autumn;[10] next they gave birth to his younger sister the Deity Princess-of-Swift-Autumn. (Ten Deities in all from the Deity-Great-Male-of-the-Great-Thing to the Deity Princess-of-Autumn.)[11] The names of the Deities given birth to by these two Deities Prince-of-Swift-Autumn and

27 Princess-of-Swift-Autumn from their separate dominions of river and sea were: the Deity Foam-Calm;[12] next the Deity Foam-Waves; next the Deity Bubble-Calm; next the Deity Bubble-Waves; next the Deity Heavenly-Water-Divider;[13] next the Deity Earthly-Water-Divider; next the Deity Heavenly-Water-Drawing-Gourd-Possessor;[14] next the Deity Earthly-Water-Drawing-Gourd-Possessor. (Eight Deities in all from the Deity Foam-Prince to the Deity Earthly-Water-Drawing-Gourd-Possessor.) Next they gave birth to the Deity of Wind, whose name is the Deity Prince-of-Long-Wind.[15] Next they gave birth to the Deity of Trees, whose name is Deity Stem-Elder,[15] next

they gave birth to the Deity of Mountains, whose name is the Deity Great-Mountain-Possessor.[17] Next they gave birth to the Deity of Moors, whose name is the Deity Thatch-Moor-Princess,[18] another name for whom is the Deity Moor-Elder. (Four Deities in all from the Deity Prince-of-Long-Wind to Moor-Elder.) The names of the Deities given 28 birth to by these two Deities, the Deity Great-Mountain-Possessor and the Deity Moor-Elder from their separate dominions of mountain and moor were: the Deity Heavenly-Elder-of-the-Passes; next the Deity Earthly-Elder-of-the-Passes;[19] next the Deity Heavenly-Pass-Boundary, next the Deity Earthly-Pass-Boundary;[20] next the Deity Heavenly-Dark-Door; next the Deity Earthly Dark-Door;[21] next the Deity Great-Vale-Prince; next the Deity Great-Vale-Princess.[22] (Eight Deities in all from the Deity Heavenly-Elder-of-the-Passes to the Deity Great-Vale-Princess.) The name of the Deity they[23] next gave birth to was the Deity Bird's-Rock-Camphor-tree-Boat,[24] another name for whom is the Heavenly-Bird-Boat. Next they gave birth to the Deity Princess-of-Great-Food.[25] Next they gave 29 birth to the Fire-Burning-Swift-Male-Deity,[26] another name for whom is the Deity Fire-Shining-Prince, and another name is the Deity Fire-Shining-Elder.

---

1. *Oho-koto-oshi-wo-no-kami.* "The Male-Enduring-Great-Things" would be a possible, but less good rendering. This god is identified by Motowori with *Koto-toke-no-wo* mentioned in "One account" of the "Chronicles of Japan."

2. The original *Ika-tsuchi-biko-no-kami* (石土毘古神) is identified by Motowori with *Uha-zutsu-no-wo*, (上箇之男) mentioned in Sect. X (Note 18). He would interpret the first *tsu* (*dzu*) as the Genitive particle and the second as identical with the "Honorific appellation *ji* of males," such as *Hikoji*, *Oho-to-no-ji*, etc. If this surmise were correct, the entire name would signify Upper-Lord-Prince; but it is safer to be guided by the characters in the text.

3.  *Iha-zu-bime-no-kami.*  Here too Motowori takes the syllable *zu*
to be "connected with" the syllables *tsu-tsu* interpreted as above, forgetting apparently that the second *tsu* (*ji*) is said to occur only in the
names of males.

4.  *Oho-to-bi-wake-na-kami*, a name which Motowori, by supposing
corruptions of the text and by making a plentiful use of the pliant and
powerful system of derivation with which the Japanese etymologists lay
siege to the difficulties of their language, identifies with *Oho-naho-bi-no-
kami*, "the Great-Rectifying-Wondrous.Deity," mentioned in Sect. X
(Note 16).

5.  *Ame-no-fuki-wo-no-kami*, identified by Motowori with *I-buki-do-
nushi* mentioned in the "Ritual of the General Purification." (See his
Commentary on this Ritual, Vol. II, pp. 29-32.)

6.  *Ohoyabikonokami*, identified by Motowori with *Oho-aya-tsui-bi*
mentioned in "One account" of the Chronicles."

7.  *Kaza-ge-tsu-wake-no-oshi-wo-no-kami.*  Motowori's conjectural interpretation has been followed; but both the reading and the meaning of
the original are encompassed with difficulties. Motowori identifies this
deity with *Soko-sasura-hime* mentioned in the "Ritual of the General
Purification."

8.  *Oho-wata-tsu-mi-no-kami.*  The interpretation of *mochi*, "possessor," though not absolutely sure, has for it the weight both of authority
and of likelihood.

9.  *I.e.*, river-mouths, estuaries, or ports. In the original *Minato-no-
kami.*

10.  *Haya-aki-dzu-hiko.  Aki*, whose proper signification is "autumn,"
might also by metonymy be interpreted to mean "dragon-fly" or "Japan."
Motowori, *àpropos* of this name, launches forth on very bold derivations
and identifications with the names of other gods. The original of the
sister-deity is *Haya-aki-dzu-hime-no-kami.*

11.  The text here omits the word "Swift" from this name.

12.  The original names of this deity and the three that follow are
*Awa-nagi.no-kami, Awa-nami-no-kami, Tsura-nagi-no-kami*, and *Tsura-nami,
no-kami.* The interpretation of the component parts is open to doubt,
but that here adopted has the authority of Motowori and Hirata.

13.  *Ame-no-mi-kumari-no-kami.*  The following deity is *Kuni-nomi-
kumari-no-kami.*

15. This Deity and the next are in the original *Ame-no-ku-hiza-mochi-no-kami* and *Kuni-no-ku-hiza-mochi-no-kami.* The etymology is obtained by comparison with a passage in the "Ritual for Averting Fire" (鎮火察祀詞).

15. *Shina-tsu-hiko-no-kami.* The original of this name is explained by Motowori, who founds his view on two passages in the "Collection of a Myriad Leaves," to signify Prince-of-Long-*Breath.* But the translator feels confident that *shi-na,* by him interpreted in the sense of "long breath" (or rather "long of breath") should be connected with *shi,* an old word for wind which we see in *ara-shi* ("storm-wind"), *ni-shi* ("west-wind"), *hi-gashi* ("east wind"), and perhaps under a slightly altered form in *kaze,* "wind," whereas *shi* nowhere occurs in the sense of "breath." Hirata notices approvingly this etymology of *shi* ("Exposition of the Ancient Histories," Vol. III. p. 63), though without venturing flatly to contradict his precedessor's decision as to the import of the name in question. The difference in the meaning is after all slight. *Na* is to be taken as an apocopated form of *nagaki,* "long." In later times *Shinato* has been used as a name for the north-west wind.

16. Such seems to be the meaning of the original *Kuku-no-chi-no-kam*.

17. *Oho-yama-tsuna-ka-mi.*

18. *Kaya-nu-himi-no-kami.* The etymology of the alternative personal name (in the original *Nu-dzn-chi-no-kami*) is not quite certain.

19. The original of these two names is *Ame-no-sa-dzu-chi-no.kami* and *Kuni-no-sa-dzu-chi-no-kami.* Their signification is obscure, but the translator has, after some hesitation, followed Motowori's interpretation. The words "heavenly" and "earthly" should probably be considered as qualifying "passes." This word "pass," used here and elsewhere to render the Japanese term *saka* (*sa*), must be understood to include lesser ascents than those very arduous ones which are alone denoted by the word "pass" in ordinary English parlance. In the later language of Japan the word *tauge* (*tōge*) generally denotes "passes" properly so called, while *saka* is restricted to the meaning of small ascents or hills. But this distinction is by no means strictly observed.

20. *Ame-no-sa-giri-no-kami* and *Kuni-no-sa-giri-no-kami.* *Sa* seems to be rightly considered, as in the two preceding names, to be an archaic form of *saka* (properly *sa-ka,* "hill-place"), and *giri* as an apocopated form of *kagiri,* (properly *ka-giri,* "place-cutting") "limit" or "boundary." Hirata however, following the Chinese character with which *kiri* is written, interprets it in the sense of "mist."

21. *Ame-no-kura-do-no-kami* and *Kuni-no-kura-do-no-kami.* Moto-wori explains *kura* (闇, dark") by *tani* (谷, " valley "), and *to* " door ") by *tokoro* (處, " place ").

22. Such appears to be the proper interpretation of the originals of these two names, *Oko-tomato-hiko-no-kami* and *Oho-tomato-hime-no-kami,* *tomato* being plausibly referred to *towomaru* and *tawamu.* It is difficult to find an English word to represent exactly the idea, which is rather that of a gentle *fold* in the mountains than of the narrower and steeper hollow which we call a " valley."

23. *I.e.,* the Prince-Who-Invites and the Princess-Who-Invites (*Izanagi* and *Iza-nami*).

24. *Tori-no-iha-kusa-bune-no-kami.* The alternative name is *Ame-no-tori-bune,* from which the title of Deity is omitted. Motowori's Com-mentary, Vol. V, pp. 52-53 should be consulted on the subject of this deity.

25. Homonymous with the alternative personal name of the Island of Aha. (See Sect. V, Note 8).

26. *Hi-no-haya-yagi-wo-no-kami.* If, as seems likely, *yagi,* is an in-correct reading for *kagi,* we should have to translate by " shining " the word here rendered " burning." The alternative names are *Hino-kaga-biko-no-kami* and *Hino-kagu-tsuchi-no-kami.* In " One account " of the " Chroni-cles " and elsewhere in the " Rituals " this fire-god is called *Ho-musubi* i.e. " the Fire-Producer."

---

[SECT. VII.—RETIREMENT OF HER AUGUSTNESS THE
PRINCESS-WHO-INVITES.]

Through giving birth to this child her august private parts were burnt, and she sickened and lay down.[1] The names of the Deities born from her vomit were the Deity Metal-Mountain-Prince and next the Deity Metal-Mountain-Princess.[2] The names of the Deities that were born from her faeces were the Deity Clay-Viscid-Prince and next the Deity Clay-Viscid-Princess.[3] The names of the Deities that were next born from her urine were the Deity Mitsuhanome[4] and next the Young-Wondrous-Producing-Deity.[5] The child of this Deity was called the Deity Luxuriant-Food-Princess.[5] So the Deity [30] the Female-Who-Invites, through giving birth to the Deity-of-Fire, at length divinely retired.[7] (Eight Deities in all from the Heavenly-Bird-Boat to the Deity Luxuriant-Food-Princess.[8])

The total number of islands given birth to jointly by the two Deities the Male-Who-Invites and the Female-Who-Invites was fourteen, and of Deities thirty-five.. (These are such as were given birth to before the Deity Princess-Who-Invites divinely retired. Only the Island of Onogoro was not given birth to,[9] and moreover the Leech-Child[10] and the Island of Aha are not reckoned among the children).

So then His Augustness the Male-Who-Invites said: Oh! Thine Augustness my lovely younger sister! Oh! that I should have exchanged thee for this single child![11] And as he crept round her august pillow, and [31] as he crept round her august feet and wept, there was born from his august tears the Deity that dwells at Konomoto near Unewo on Mount Kagu,[12] and whose name is the Crying-Weeping-Female-Deity.[13] So he buried the divinely retired[14] Deity the Female-Who-Invites on Mount Hiba[15] at the boundary of the Land of Idzumo[16] and the Land of Hahaki.[17]

---

1. "Lying down" (*koyasu*) is a term often used in the Archaic language in the sense of "dying." But here it must be taken literally, the death ("divine retirement") of the goddess being narrated a few lines further on.

2. *Kana-yama-biko-no-kami* and *Kana-yama bime-no-kami*. The translation of this pair of names follows the plain sense of the characters 金山 with which they are written, and which seems appropriate enough, coming as they do between the deity of fire and deities of clay. Motowori however, declaring both characters to be merely phonetic, derives *kana-yama* from *korena-yamasu*, "to cause to wither and suffer," and interprets the names accordingly. This is at any rate ingenious.

3. *Hani-yasu-biko-no-kami* and *Hani-yasu-bime-no kami.*

4. The signification of this name is not to be ascertained. In the text |it is written phonetically 彌都波能賣, and two passages in the "Chronicles," where this deity is mentioned as 爲嚴罔象女 and 水名 水神罔象女 with directions in each case to read the name with the sounds here given to it, do not help us much, except in so far as they show that Mitsuhanome was conceived of as the deity of water and as a female.

5. *Waku-musu-bi-no-kami.*

6. *Toyo-uke-bime-no-kami.*

7. *I.e.,* " died."

8. There is here an error in the computation, as *nine* deities are mentioned. The total of thirty-five deities given immediately below is still more erroneous, as no less than *forty* are named in the preceding passage. Motowori makes an ingenious effort to reconcile arithmetic and revelation by supposing the five pairs of brothers and sisters with parallel names to have been considered as each forming but one day.

9. See Sect. III. This island was not *born*, but arose, spontaneously from drops of brine.

10. *Hiru-go.* See the latter part of Sect. IV for these two names, Hiru-go was not counted among the |children of these Deities for the reason that the latter abandoned him as soon as he was born, he being a failure. The reason for omitting Aha from the computation is not so clear.

11. The text here is very peculiar, the characters rendered "single child" being 子之一木 where we should expect 子之一人 or 子一人. Hirata proposes to consider 木, "tree," while most scholars agree in reading *ke* instead of *ki* in this place, as phonetic for *ke* (毛) "hair," and to interpret the god's words to signify that he values the child no more than a single hair in comparison with the wife whom that child's birth has lost for him. Moribe, in his "Examination of Difficult Words," s.v. *Ko no hito-tsu ki* (Vol. I. p. 8 *et seq.*), ingeniously argues that *ki* was an old native Japanese "Auxiliary Numeral" for animals, afterwards driven out by the somewhat like-sounding Chinese word *hiki* (疋) which is now in common use, and that the god employs this degrading Auxiliary Numeral in speaking of his child on account of the resentment which he feels against him. On the other hand we gather from the "Chronicles of Japan Explained" that 木 was used in its natural sense as an "Auxiliary Numeral" for gods and for men of exalted rank. This seems to the translator the better view to follow, and it is supported by the use of

桂, *hashira*, as the regular " Auxiliary Numeral" for divine personages. The parallel passage in the "Chronicles" has simply 一兒 " one infant."

12. This rendering is but tentative; for it is not certain that Hirata, whose view has been adopted, is right in regarding Konomoto and Unewo as names of places. If we followed the older authorities, we should have to translate thus: " The Deity that dwells at the foot of the trees on the slope of the spur of Mount Kagu." The etymology of the name of this celebrated mountain (known also as *Ame-no-kagu-yama* or *Ama-no-kagu-yama*, i.e. " Heavenly Mount Kagu ") is disputed. But Hirata's view, according to which it should be connected with *kago*, " deer," is the most plausible. If it were established, we should be tempted to follow him in rendering by " deer-possessor " the name of the deity *Kagu-tsu-chi*, of whom were born the eight gods of mountains, and whose slaying forms the title of the next section. That the fire-deity should be connected with the mountain-deities, and thereby with the deer who roam about the mountains and furnish the hunter with a motive for penetrating into their recesses, is of course but natural. The character 香 with which Kagu is written signifies " fragrant "; but it has been suggested that the Japanese word may be connected with an expresion signifying " heaven-descended," in allusion to the supposed origin of the mountain as related in an old geographical work (now lost) treating of the Province of Iyo.

13. *Naki-saha-me-no-kami.* The sense of the second word of the compound is " marsh " or " stream "; but Motowori seems right in considering the character 澤 to be here used phonetically as an abbreviation of *isaha* from *isatsu*, " to weep."

14. *I.e.,* dead.

15. Etymology uncertain.

16. For this name see Sect. XIX, Note 6.

17. Etymology uncertain.

---

[SECT. VIII.—THE SLAYING OF THE FIRE-DEITY.]

Then His Augustness the Male-Who-Invites, drawing the ten-grasp sabre[1] that was augustly girded on him, cut off the head of his child the Deity Shining-Elder. Hereupon the names of the Deities that were born from the blood that stuck to the point of the august sword

and bespattered the multitudinous rock-masses were: the Deity Rock-Splitter,[2] next the Deity Root-Splitter, next the Rock-Possessing-Male-Deity.[3] The names of the Deities that were next born from the blood that stuck to the upper part[4] of the august sword and again bespattered the multitudinous rock-masses were: the Awfully-Swift-Deity,[5] next the Fire-Swift-Deity,[6] next the Brave-Awful-Possessing-Male-Deity,[7] another name for whom is the Brave-Snapping-Deity,[8] and another name is the Luxuriant-Snapping Deity. The names of the Deities that were next born from the blood that collected
33 on the hilt of the august sword and leaked out between his fingers were: the Deity *Kura-okami* and next the Deity *Kura-mitsuha*.[9]

All the eight Deities in the above list, from the Deity Rock-Splitter to the Deity *Kura-mitsuha*, are Deities that were born from the august sword.

The name of the Deity that was born from the head of the Deity Shining-Elder, who had been slain was the Deity Possessor-of-the-True-Pass-Mountains.[10] The name of the Deity that was was next born from his chest was the Deity Possessor-of-Descent-Mountains.[11] The name of the Deity that was next born from his belly was the Deity Possessor-of-the-Innermost Mountains.[12] The name of the Deity that was next born from his private parts was the Deity Possessor-of-the-Dark-Mountains. The name of the Deity that was next born from his left hand[13] was the Deity Possessor-of-the-Dense[ly-Wooded]-Mountains. The name of the Deity that was next born from his right hand[13] was the Deity Possessor-of-the-Outlying-Mountains. The name of the Deity that was next born from his left foot[14] was the Deity Possessor-of-the-

Moorland-Mountains. The name of the Deity that was next born from his right foot[14] was the Deity Possessor-of-the-Outer-Mountains. (Eight Deities in all from the Deity Possessor-of-the-True-Pass-Mountains to the Deity Possessor-of-the-Outer Mountains). So the name of the sword with which [the Male-Who-Invites] cut off [his son's head] was Heavenly-Point-Blade-Extended, and another name was Majestic Point-Blade-Extended.[15]

---

1. One " grasp " is defined as " the breadth of four fingers when the hand is clenched," so that the meaning intended to be conveyed is of a big sabre ten hand-breadths long. The length of sabres and of beards was measured by such " grasps " or " hand-breadths."

2. The original names of this deity and the next are *Iha-saku-no-kami* and *Ne-saki-no-kami*.

3. Or the Rock-Elder, *i.e.*, the Male Deity the Elder of the Rocks, if with Motowori we regard the second *tsu* of the original name *Iha-tsutsu-no-wo-no-kami* as being equivalent to *chi* or *ji*, supposed to be " the honorific appellation of males " elsewhere rendered " elder." The translation in the text proceeds on the assumption that this *tsu* represents *mochi :* The purport of the name remains much the same whichever of these two views be adopted.

4. Explained by reference to the parallel passage of the " Chronicles " through a character signifying " the knob at the end of the guard of the sword."—(Williams' " Syllabic Dictionary."

5. *Mika-haya-bi-no-kami*. Motowori seems to be right in regarding *mika* as equivalent to *ika*, the root of *ikameshiki*, " stern," " awful," and *bi* as the root of *buru*, a verbalising suffix.

6. *Hi-haya-bi-no-kami*.

7. *Take-mika-dzu-chi-no-wo-no-kami*, written with the characters 建御雷之男神. The translator has without much hesitation followed Motowori's interpretation.

8. *Take-futsu-no-kami*. The text name is *Toyo futsu-no-kami*. *Futsu* is interpreted in the sense of " the sound of snapping " by reference to a passage in the " Chronicles " where it occurs written both ideographically and phonetically in the name of the deity *Futsu-no-mi-tama*.

9. The etymology of both these name is obscure. *Kura*, the first element of each compound, signifies " dark."

10. This is the explanation of the original name *Ma-saka-yama-tsu-mi-no-kami* which is given in the "Secret of the Chronicles of Japan," and is approved by the later commentators.

11. *Odo-yama-tsu-mi-no-kami.* The English rendering is uncertain, as it rests only on a conjecture of Motowori's, deriving *odo* from *ori do* (下處), "descending place," "way down."

12. The original names of this and the following five deities are: *Oku-yama-tsumi-no-kami,    Kura-yama-tsu-mi-no-kami,    Shigi-yama-tsu-mi-no-kami,    Ha-yama-tsu-mi-no-kami,    Hayama-tsu-mi-no-kami* and *To-yama-tsumi-no-kami.Shigi,* here translated "dense," seems to be almost certainly a contraction of *Shigeki,* which has that signification. *Ha-yama* is a term for which it is hard to find an exact English equivalent. It denotes the lesser hills or first visibly rising ground forming the approach to an actual mountain-range. The signification of *to* in the last name of the set is disputed. Mabuchi takes it in the sense of "gate." The translator prefers Motowori's view: but after all, the difference in meaning does not amount to much. A third derivation proposed by Motowori is *tawa-yama,* i.e. "mountains with folds."

13. Or "arm."

14. Or "leg."

15. These two names are in the original *Ame-no-wo-ha-bori* and *Itsu-no-wo-ha-bori.* Their import is not absolutely clear, but they seem to designate a weapon broad towards the point, such as is represented in the illustrations given in Vol. I, pp. 19-20 and Vol. II, pp. 4-5 of the "*Tokiha-Gusa.*"

---

[SECT. IX.—THE LAND OF HADES.]

Thereupon [His Augustness the Male Who-Invites], wishing to meet and see his younger sister Her Augustness the Female-Who-Invites, followed after her to the Land of Hades.[1]  So when from the palace she raised the door and came out to meet him,[2] His Augustness the Male-Who-Invites spoke, saying: "Thine Augustness my lovely younger sister! the lands that I and thou made are not yet finished making; so come back!" Then Her Augustness the Female-Who-Invites answered, saying:

"Lamentable indeed that thou camest not sooner! I have eaten of the furnace of Hades.[3] Nevertheless, as I reverence[4] the entry here of Thine Augustness my lovely elder brother, I wish to return.[5] Moreover[6] I will discuss it particularly with the Deities of Hades.[7] Look not at me!" Having thus spoken, she went back inside the palace; and as she tarried there very long, he could not wait. So having taken and broken off one of the end-teeth[8] of the multitudinous and close-toothed comb stuck in the august left bunch [of his hair], he lit one light[9] and went in and looked. Maggots were swarming, and [she was] rotting, and in her head dwelt the Great-Thunder, in her breast dwelt the Fire-Thunder, in her left hand[10] dwelt the Young-Thunder, in her right hand[10] dwelt the Earth-Thunder, in her left foot[11] dwelt the Rumbling-Thunder, in her rightfoot[11] dwelt the Couchant-Thunder:—altogether eight Thunder-Deities had been born and dwelt there.[12] Hereupon His Augustness the Male-Who-Invites, overawed at the sight, fled back, whereupon his younger sister Her Augustness the Female-Who-Invites said: "Thou hast put me to shame," and at once sent the Ugly-Female-of-Hades[13] to pursue him. So His Augustness the Male-Who-Invites took his black august head-dress[14] and cast it down, and it instantly turned into grapes. While she picked them up and ate them, he fled on; but as she still pursued him, he took and broke the multitudinous and close-toothed comb in the right bunch [of his hair] and cast it down, and it instantly turned into bamboo-sprouts. While she pulled them up and ate them, he fled on. Again later [his younger sister] sent the eight Thunder-Deities with a thousand and five hundred warriors of Hades to pursue him. So he, drawing the ten-grasp sabre that was augustly girded on him, fled forward brandishing it in his back hand;[15] and as they still pursued, he took, on reaching the base of the Even Pass of Hades,[16] three peaches that were growing at its base, and waited and smote [his pursuers therewith], so that they all fled back. Then His Augustness the Male-Who-Invites announced to the peaches: "Like as ye have helped me, so must ye help all living people[17] in the Central Land of Reed-Plains[18] when they shall fall into troublous circumstances and be harassed!"—and he gave [to the peaches] the designation of Their Augustnesses Great-Divine-Fruit.[19] Last of all his younger sister Her Augustness the Princess-Who-Invites came out herself in pursuit. So he drew a thousand-draught rock,[20] and [with it] blocked up the Even Pass of Hades, and

38 placed the rock in the middle; and they stood opposite to one another and exchanged leave-takings;[21] and Her Augustness the Female-Who-Invites said: "My lovely elder brother, thine Augustness! If thou do like this, I will in one day strangle to death a thousand of the folks of thy land." Then His Augustness the Male-Who-Invites replied: "My lovely younger sister, Thine Augustness! If *thou* do this, *I* will in one day set up a thousand and five hundred parturition-houses.[22] In this manner each day a thousand people would surely be born." So Her Augustness the Female-Who-Invites is called the Great-Deity-of-Hades.[23] Again it is said that, owing to her having pursued and reached [her elder brother], she is called the Road-Reaching-Great-Deity.[24] Again the rock with which he blocked up the Pass of Hades is called the Great-Deity-of-the-Road-Turning-

back,[25] and again it is called the Blocking-Great-Deity- [39]
of-the-Door-of-Hades.[26]    So what was called the Even-
Pass-of-Hades is now called the Ifuya-Pass[27] in the Land
of Idzumo.

---

1. The characters in the original which are here rendered Hades
are 黄泉, lit. "Yellow Stream," a Chinese name for the Underworld to
which a remark of Mencius and a story in the "*Tso Chuan*" appear to
have given rise. They here represent the Japanese word *Yomo* or *Yomi*,
which we find phonetically written with the characters 豫母 in the name
of *Yomo-tsu-shiko-me* a little further on, and which is defined by Motowori as "an underworld,....the habitation of the dead,....the land
whither, when they die, go all men, whether noble or mean, virtuous or
wicked." The orthodox Japanese derivation of *Yomi* is from *Yoru*,
"night," which would give us for *Yomo-tsu-kuni* some such rendering as
"the Land of Gloom." A suggestion quoted by Arawi Hakuseki ("*Tōga*,"
art. *Idzumi*) that the word may really be but a mispronunciation of *Yama*,
the Sanscrit name of the Buddhist god of hell, is however worthy of
consideration ; but it seems best on the whole to translate *Yomi* or *Yomo*
by "Hades," a term which is itself of uncertain derivation, and the
signification attached to which closely resembles the Japanese *Shintō*
notion of the world beyond, or rather beneath, the grave.

2. The original text 將自殿騰戸出向之時 seems to be corrupt, and
Motowori, unable to make anything of 騰戸, leaves 騰 without any Japanese reading (see the remarks in his Commentary, Vol. VI. pp. 5-6).
Mr. Aston, in the version of this passage given in the Chrestomathy appended
to his "Grammar of the Japanese Written Language," follows Motowori
in not translating 騰, but does not allude to the difficulty.

*I.e.* "of the food of Hades." It would be more obvious (following
the text) to translate "I have eaten in the doors [*i.e.* in the house] of
Hades ;" but the character 戸 in this place stands almost certainly for
竈, "a place for cooking," "a furnace."

4. The word *kashikoshi* (恐), here translated "reverence," exactly
corresponds to the modern polite idiom *osore-iri-mashita*, for which there
is no precise equivalent in English, but which conveys some such sentiment as "I am overpowered by the honour you do me," "I am sorry
you should have taken the trouble.'

5. *Q.d.* "with thee to the land of the living."

6. The original here has the character 且 which signifies "moreover" as in this translation, and Motowori's proposed emendation to 旦 has for it the authority of no manuscript or earlier printed edition. In his "Records of Ancient Matters with the Ancient Reading" he actually substitutes this very *new* reading, accompanying it in *kana* with the Japanese words *ashita ni*, "in the morning." But what is to become of the text if we are at liberty to alter it to suit our convenience,—for there is more than one other passage where 且 is similarly used?

7. *Yomo-tsu-kami.* Both Motowori and Hirata take the word "Deities" in the Plural, and the translator therefore renders it in that number, though the Singular would be at least equally suitable to the text as it stands. Of the Deities of Hades little or nothing is known. Conf. Note 23 to this Section.

8. Literally "the male pillar," *i.e.* the large tooth of which there is one at each end of the comb.

9. The use of the expression "lit *one* light," where it would have been more natural to say simply "lit [a] light," is explained by a gloss in the "Chronicles," which informs us that "at the present day" the lighting of a single light is considered unlucky, as is also the throwing away of a comb at night-time. It is allowed that the gloss is a late addition, and its statement might perhaps be considered a mere invention made to account for the peculiar expression in the text. Motowori tells us however that "it is said by the natives" that these actions are still (latter part of 18th century) considered unlucky in the province of Ihami, and the same superstition also survives, as the translator is assured, in Yedo itself. It is to be understood that it was the large tooth broken off from the comb which the god lighted.

10. Or "arm."

11. Or "leg."

12. The Japanese names of the eight Thunder-Deities are: *Oho-ikadzuchi, Ho-no-ikadzuchi, Kuro-ikadzuchi, Saka-ikadzuchi, Waki-Ikadzuchi, Tsuchi-ikadzuchi, Naru-ikadzuchi,* and *Fushi-ikadzuchi.* Moribe-in his Critique on Motowori's Commentary, has some observation on the appropriateness of each of these names which the student will do well to consult if the work should be published.

13. *Yomo-tsu-shiko-me.*

14. We might perhaps with equal propriety render by "wreath" the word here translated head-dress,—leaves and flowers having been the earliest ornaments for the hair. In later time, however, it has been used

to designate any sort of head-dress, and that is also the dictionary meaning of the Chinese character with which it is written. The Japanese
words for "head-dress" and "creeper" are homonymous, and indeed the
former is probably but a specialised acceptation of the latter.

15. *I.e.*, brandishing it behind him.

16. Or Flat Hill of Hades, *Yomo-tsu-hira-saka*, said by Motowori
to form the frontier-line between Hades and the World of the Living.
See also Note 27 to this Section.

17. The three characters 青人草 here rendered "people" are evidently
(Motowori notwithstanding) meant to be equivalent to the common Chinese expression 蒼生, which has that signification. The word translated
"living" means literally "present," "visible."

18. *Ashi-hara-no-naka-tsu-kuni*, a common periphrastic designation
of Japan. It is better to translate the name thus than to render it by
"the Land in the Middle of the Reed-Plains," a forced interpretation
which Motowori and Hirata would only seem to adopt in order to veil
the fact that one of the most ancient and revered names of their native
land was imitated from that of China,—everything Chinese being an
abomination in the sight of these ardent Shintoists. Yamazaki Suiga, as
quoted by. Tanigaha Shisei, is more sensible when he remarks that each
country naturally considers itself central and foreign countries barbarous,
and that Japan is not peculiar in being looked on by its inhabitants as
the centre of the universe. This is also the view taken by the other
earlier scholars.

19. *Oho-kamu-dzumi-no-mikoto*. The difference between ̄Singular and
Plural is not often present to the Japanese mind, and though there were
three peaches, we might just as well render their name by the words
"His Augustness, etc.," considering the three as forming together but one
divinity. The interpretation of the name here adopted is the simple and
natural one which Motowori borrowed from Tanigaha Shisei.

20. *I.e.*, a rock which it would take a thousand men to lift.

21. That some kind of leave-taking and separation is intended seems
certain; but the precise import of the characters 度事戸 in the text is
not to be ascertained. Motowori's "Commentary, Vol. VI, pp. 29-30 and
Vol. X, pp. 52-55, should be consulted for an elaborate discussion of the
various interpretations which they may be made to bear. Moribe, in his
Critique on this Commentary, argues that "divorced each other" is the
proper signification of the words, and supports his opinion by the
parallel passage of the "Chronicles."

22. *I.e.,* "I will cause fifteen hundred women to bear children." For the custom of erecting a separate hut for a woman about to be delivered see Introduction, p. xxviii.)

23. *Yomo-tsu-oho-kami.* On this rather embarrassing statement Motowori is silent, and Hirata simply says: "It must be supposed that the 'Deities of Hades' previously mentioned had been its 'Great Deities' up to this time, a position which was henceforward assumed by Her Augustness Izana-mi (the Female-Who-Invites"). Conf. Note 7 to this Section.

24. *Chi-shiki-no-oho-kami.* [This is Motowori's reading. We might also read *Michi-shiki-no-oho-kami*]. Motowori conclusively proves that "reaching" is the signification of the word *shiki* which is here so translated. That it was already obscure at the time of the compilation of these "Records" is however shown by the fact that it is written syllabically in the first instance, and with a "borrowed character" (*i.e.,* a homonymous word) in the second,

25. Because the goddess was turned back by it on the road where she was pursuing her brother-husband. The original is *Chi-gaheshi* [or *Michi.gaheshi*]*.no.oho.kami.*

26. *Sayari-masu-yomi-do-no-oho-kami.*

27. *Ifuya-zaka.* Moribe in his "*Idzu-no-chi-waki*" conjectures that Ifuya may be derived from *Yufu-yami,* "evening darkness," an etymology which has at least the merit of suiting the legend.

---

[SECT. X.—THE PURIFICATION OF THE AUGUST PERSON.]

Therefore the Great Deity the Male-Who-Invites said: "Nay! hideous! I have come to a hideous and polluted land,—I have!¹ So I will perform the purification of my august person." So he went out to a plain [covered with] *ahagi*² at a small river-mouth near Tachibana³ in Himuka⁴ in [the island of] Tsukushi, and purified and cleansed himself. So the name of the Deity that was born from the august staff which he threw down was the Deity Thrust-Erect-Come-Not-Place.⁵ The name of 40 the Deity that was born from the august girdle which he next threw down was the Deity Road-Long-Space.

The name of the Deity that was born from the august skirt which he next threw down was the Deity Loosen-Put.[7] The name of the Deity that was born from the august upper garment which he next threw down was the Deity Master-of-Trouble.[8] The name of the Deity that was born from the august trousers which he next threw down was the Road-Fork-Deity.[9] The name of the Deity that was born from the august hat which he next threw down was the Deity Master-of-the-Open-Mouth.[10] The names of the Deities that were born from the bracelet of his august left hand[11] which he next threw down were the Deities Offing-Distant,[12] next the Deity Wash-Prince-of-the-Offing, next the Deity Intermediate-Direction-of-the-Offing. The names of the Deities that were born from the bracelet of his august right hand 41 which he next threw down were: the Deity Shore-Distant, next the Deity Wash-Prince-of-the-Shore, next the Deity Intermediate-Direction-of-the-Shore.

The twelve Deities mentioned in the foregoing[13] list from the Deity Come-Not-Place down to the Deity Intermediate-Direction-of-the-Shore are Deities that were born from his taking off the things that were on his person.

Thereupon saying: " The water in the upper reach is [too] rapid; the water in the lower reach is [too] sluggish," he went down and plunged in the middle reach; and, as he washed, there was first born the Wondrous-Deity-of-Eighty-Evils, and next the Wondrous-Deity-of-Great-Evils.[14] These two Deities are the Deities that were born from the filth [he contracted] when he went to that polluted, hideous land.[15] The names of the Deities that were next born to rectify those evils were:

the Divine-Rectifying-Wondrous Deity, next the Great-Rectifying - Wondrous - Deity,[16] next the Female-Deity-Idzu.[17] The names of the Deities that were next born, as he bathed at the bottom of the water, were : the Deity Possessor - of - the - Ocean - Bottom,[18] and next His
42 Augustness Elder-Male-of-the-Bottom. The names of the Deities that were born as he bathed in the middle [of the water] were : the Deity Possessor-of-the-Ocean-Middle, and next His Augustness Elder-Male-of-the-Middle. The names of the Deities that were born as he bathed at the top of the water were the Deity Possessor-of-the-Ocean-Surface, and next His Augustness Elder-Male-of-the-Surface. These three Ocean-Possessing Deities are the Deities held in reverence as their ancestral Deities by the Chiefs of Adzumi.[19] So the Chiefs of Adzumi are the descendants of His Augustness *Utsushi-hi-gana-saku*,[20] a child of these Ocean-Possessing Deities.[21] These three Deities His Augustness Elder-Male-of-the-Bottom, His Augustness Elder-Male-of-the-Middle, and His Augustness Elder-Male-of-the-Surface are the three Great Deities of the Inlet of Sumi.[22] The name of the Deity that was born as he thereupon washed his left august eye was the Heaven-Shining-Great-August-Deity.[23] The name of the Deity that was next born as he washed his right august
43 eye was His Augustness Moon-Night Possessor.[24] The name of the Deity that was next born as he washed his august nose was His Brave-Swift-Impetuous-Male-Augustness.[25]

> The fourteen Deities in the foregoing list from the Wondrous-Deity-of-Eighty-Evils down to His Swift-Impetuous-Male-Augustness are Deities born from the bathing of his august person.

1. The words "I have" thus repeated are an attempt to render the concluding words *ari keri* of the sentence in the original, by which, though they have no particular sense, the author evidently set great store, as he writes them syllabically. They may be considered to emphasize what goes before and, says Motowori, "convey the idea of lamentation." The idiom occurs some half-dozen times in the course of the present work.

2. This botanical name is identified by Arawi Hakuseki and Hirata with the modern *hagi*, or "bushclover" (*lespedeza* of various species). The received opinion used to be that the *awoki* (*Aucuba Japonica*) was here intended.

3. Tachibana is understood to be the general designation of trees of the orange tribe. (See however Sect. LXXIV, Note 7). Here it is used as a proper name.

4. This name, which signifies "sun-confronting," was not unnaturally bestowed on a province in the eastern part of the westernmost of the larger Japanese islands, as it might well be conceived as lying "opposite the sun." It has, however, been supposd to have originally denoted the whole of the island in question. In any case the name is not inappropriate, as the island has a long eastern sea-board.

5. In our text *Tsuki-tatsu-funa-do*. But *funa* should almost certainly be *ku-na*, and the name (which has here been translated accordingly) is then illustrated by the more extended version of this myth which is given in the "Chronicles," where we read that the god (probably addressing his sister) threw down his staff with the words : "Come no further." "Stand" must be understood in a Transitive sense : the god *stood* his staff up by thrusting it into the sand.

6. This is Moribe's explanation ("*Idzu-no-Chi-waki.*" Vol. IV, p. 44) of the meaning of the original name *Michi-no-naga-chiha-no-kami*, the syllable *ha* of which is considered by him to be an alternative form of *ma* (間, "space"). It is however a great crux, and Motowori confesses his inability to explain it satisfactorily. Other views as to the import of the syllable in question will be found in the "*Jin-dai no maki Mo-shiho-gusa*," Vol. II. p, 29.

7. This seems to be the meaning of the original name, if we retain the reading *Toki-okashi-no-kami*. See however Motowori's remarks *in loco.*

8. *Wadzurahi-no-ushi-no-kami.*

9. *Chi-mata-no-kami.*

10. *Aki-guhi-no-ushi-no-kami.* The English rendering of this obscure name proceeds on the assumption that Motowori is correct when he proposes to consider *kuhi* as equivalent in this place to *kuchi,* "mouth." The gaping trousers no longer filled by the deity's legs would perhaps suggest the idea of an open mouth, though it is true that this is not the deity said to have been actually born from that portion of the attire.

11. Or " arm."

12. The names of this deity and the five who follow are in the original *Oki-zakaru-no-kami, Oki-tsu-nagisa-biko-no-kami, Oki-tsu-kahi-bera-no-kami, He-zakaru-no-kami, He-tsu-nagisa-biko-no-kami* and *He-tsu-kahi-bera-no-kami.* The word "wash," by which for want of a better one the Substantive *nagisa* has been rendered, must be understood to signify the part nearest to the strand o  the sea or of a river,—the boundary of the waves. The third and sixth of this set of names, in which the syllables *kahi-bera* (here represented by "Intermediate Direction") offer a good deal of difficulty, have been translated in accordance with Motowori's explanation of their probable meaning.

13. Lit. "right." In Chinese and Japanese compositions the lines follow each other from right to left instead of from top to bottom as with us. "Right" therefore signifies "foregoing," and "left," "following."

14. The names of these two deities in the original are *Ya-so-maga-tsu-bi-no-hami* and *Oho-maga-tsu-bi-no-kami.*

15. Viv. to Hades.

16. The names of these two deities in the original are *Kamu-naho-bi-no kami* and *Oho-na-ho-bi-no-kami.*

17. *Idzu-no-me-no-kami.* The word *Idzu* is incomprehensible, unless indeed, following Motowori, we identify this goddess with the god and goddess *Haya-aki-dzu-hiko* and *Haya-aki-dsu-hime* mentioned in Sect. VI, Note 10, and consider *idzu* as standing by apheresis for *aki-dsu,*

18. The original names of this deity and the five who follow are *Soko-tsu-wata-tsu-mi-no-kami, Soko-dzutsu-no-wo-no-mi-koto, Naka-tsu-wata-tsu-mi-no-kami, Naka-dzutsu-no-wo-mikoto, Uha-tsu-wata-tsu-mi-no-kami,* and *Uha-dzutsu-no-wo-no-mikoto.* There is the usual doubt as to the signification to be assigned to the syllable *tsu* in the second, fourth and last of these names. If it really means, not "elder" but "possessor," we should be obliged to translate by "the Bottom-*Possesssing*-Male," etc.

19. *Adumi-no-murazhi.* This name is said by Motowori to be taken from that of a place in the province of Shinano. But Moribe shows that

at any rate the etymology of the word may be traced to *ama-tsu-mochi,* "possessors of fishermen."

20. It is impossible to translate this name which, according to Motowori, is derived from those of two districts in Shinano to which the word *utsushi* (for *utsutsu,* "present" or "living") is prefixed.

21. Attention must again be drawn to the vagueness of the Japanese perception of the distinction between Singular and Plural. As three deities are particularly and repeatedly mentioned in the foregoing text, we are forced to translate this passage in the Plural; and yet how could one child have three fathers?

22. *Sumi-no-ye,* also called *Sumi-yoshi, i.e.,* by a play upon words, "pleasant to dwell in." The real etymology of *sumi* is not certain.—Instead of "the three Great Deities," we might translate by "the Great Deities of the Three Shrines."

23. *Ama-terasu-oho-mi-kami* (天照大御神). The reading *terasu,* which is established by the authority of the "Collection of a Myriad Leaves" and by almost universal usage, must not mislead the student into imagining that the Verb, because it is Causative in form, has a Causative meaning which would require some such English translation as "Heaven-Illuminating." The Causative form is simply Honorific, and the two words *ama terasu* signify, as Motowori explains, "shining in heaven."

24. *Tsuki-yomi-no-kami.* There is no doubt as to a moon-god being intended, but the precise import of the name is disputed. The translator has followed Mabuchi's view as quoted by Motowori, and which is supported by the fact that, from classical times down to the present day, *tsuku-yo* or *tsuki-yo* has been a word in common use to denote a fine moonlight night. If we were to take *yomi* as one word, we should have to render it either by "Moon-Hades" or by "Moon-Darkness," which seem less appropriate designations, though still of plain enough intent. The characters 月讀, 月弓, and 月夜見, with which the name is variously written, seem all phonetic unless we might take the second set 月弓 to mean the crescent (lit. "moon-bow).

25. *Take-haya-susa-no-wo-no-mìkoto. Susa,* which is sometimes read *Sosa,* is rendered by the word "impetuous" in accordance with Mabuchi's view as quoted by Motowori. The first member of this compound name is frequently omitted.

[SECT. XI.—INVESTITURE OF THE THREE DEITIES
THE ILLUSTRIOUS AUGUST CHILDREN.]

At this time His Augustness the Male-Who-Invites
greatly rejoiced, saying: "I, begetting child after child,
have at my final begetting gotten three illustrious children," [with which words,] at once jinglingly taking off
and shaking the jewel-string[1] forming his august necklace, he bestowed it on the Heaven-Shining-Great-August-
Deity, saying: "Do Thine Augustness rule the Plain-
of-High-Heaven." With this charge he bestowed it on
her. Now the name of this august necklace was the
August-Store-house-Shelf-Deity.[2] Next he said of His
Augustness Moon-Night-Possessor: "Do Thine Augustness rule the Dominion of the "Night."[3] Thus he
charged him. Next he said to His-Brave-Swift-Impetu-
ous-Male-Augustness: "Do Thine Augustness rule the
Sea-Plain."[4]

1. *I.e.*, "the string of jewels." For these so-called "jewels" see
Introduction, p. xxxi.

2. *Mi-kura-tana-no-kami.* Motowori comments on this name by saying that the necklace was doubtless so precious, that it was carefully kept
by the goddess on a shelf in her store-house.

3. *Yoru-no-wosu-kuni.*

4. *Una-bara.*

[SECT. XII.—THE CRYING AND WEEPING OF HIS
IMPETUOUS-MALE-AUGUSTNESS.]

So while [the other two Deities] each [assumed his
and her] rule according to the command with which
[their father] had deigned to charge them, His-Swift-
Impetuous-Male-Augustness did not [assume the] rule

[of] the dominion with which he had been charged, but cried and wept till his eight-grasp beard[1] reached to the pit of his stomach.[2] The fashion of his weeping was such as by his weeping to wither the green mountains into withered mountains, and by his weeping to dry up all the rivers and seas.[3] For this reason the sound of bad Deities was like unto the flies in the fifth moon[4] as they all swarmed,[5] and in all things[6] every portent of woe arose. So the Great August Deity the Male-Who-Invites said to His Swift-Impetuous-Male-Augustness : " How is it that, instead of ruling the land with which I charged thee, thou dost wail and weep ? " He replied, saying : " I[7] wail because I wish to depart to my deceased mother's[8] land, to the Nether Distant Land."[9] Then the Great August Deity the Male-Who-Invites was very angry and said : " If that be so, thou shall not dwell in this land,"[10] and forthwith expelled him with a divine expulsion. So the Great Deity the Male-Who-Invites dwells at Taga[11] in Afumi.[12]

---

1. See Sect. VIII, Note 1.
2. Lit, " in front of his heart."
3. *Sic* in the original, to the perplexity of commentators.
4. " Flies in the fifth moon " is the received interpretation of the original term *sa-bahe. Conf. sa-tsuki,* the old native name for the fifth moon.
5. The text has here the character 滿, " to be full," for which Motowori somewhat arbitrarily reads 涌, " to bubble up," taking this word in the sense of swarming. The translator has endeavoured to preserve the vagueness of the original Japanese, which leaves it doubtful at first sight whether the flies or the deities should be regarded as the logical subject of the Verb. There is an almost identical passage near the beginning of Sect. XVI.
6. Lit. " a myriad things," a Chinese phrase for totality.
7. The Chinese character for the First-Personal Pronoun used here

and below by this deity is the humble one 僕 signifying literally " servant." The commentators read it simply " I."

8. The Japanese authorities simply read "mother." But the character 妣, which is used in this place, specially designates a mother who is deceased.

9. *I.e.*, Hades. The translation follows Motowori's explanation of the original term *Ne-no-kata-su-kuni*, which is obscure.

10. *I.e.*, say the commentators, "in this realm of ocean which I granted to thee as thy domain." Probably, however, this is reading into the text more than it was meant to contain.

11. Derivation unknown.

12. From *aha-umi*, "fresh sea," *i.e.*, "lake." The province of Afumi was doubtless so called from Lake Biha which occupies a great portion of its surface. It is also known as *Chiku-tsu-Afumi*, *i.e.*, "the Nearer Afumi," in contradistinction to *Toho-tsu-fumi* (in modern pronunciations *Tōtōmi*), *i.e.*, "Distant Afumi," a province further to the East. The modern pronunciation of *Afumi* is *Omi*.

----

[SECT. XIII.—THE AUGUST OATH ]

So thereupon His-Swift-Impetuous-Male-Augustness said : " If that be so, I will take leave[1] of the Heaven-Shining-Great-August-Deity, and depart." [With these words] he forthwith went up to Heaven, whereupon all the mountains and rivers shook, and every land and country quaked. So the Heaven-Shining-Great-August Deity, alarmed at the noise, said : " The reason of the ascent hither of His Augustness my elder brother[2] is surely no good intent.[3] It is only that he wishes to wrest my land from me." And she forthwith, unbinding her august hair, twisted it into august bunches ; and both into the left and into the right august bunch, as likewise into her august head-dress and likewise on to her left and her right august arm,[4] she twisted an augustly complete [string] of curved jewels eight feet

[long],—of five hundred jewels,[5] and slinging on her back a quiver holding a thousand [arrows], and adding [thereto][6] a quiver holding five hundred [arrows], she likewise took and slung at her side a mighty and high [-sounding] elbow-pad,[7] and brandished and stuck her bow upright so that the top[8] shook, and she stamped her feet into the hard ground up to her opposing thighs,[9] kicking away [the earth] like rotten snow,[10] and stood valiantly like unto a mighty man, and waiting, asked: " Wherefore ascendest thou hither ? " Then His-Swift-Impetuous-Male-Augustness replied, saying : " I have no evil intent. It is only that when the Great-August-Deity [our father] spoke, deigning to enquire the cause [47] of my wailing and weeping, I said 'I wail because I wish to go to my deceased mother's land,'—whereupon the Great-August-Deity said : " Thou shalt not dwell in this land,' and deigned to expel me with a divine expulsion. It is therefore solely with the thought of taking leave of thee and departing, that I have ascended hither. I have no strange intentions." Then the Heaven-Shining-Great-August-Deity said : " If that be so, whereby shall I know the sincerity of thine intentions ? " Thereupon His-Swift-Impetuous-Male-Augustness replied, saying : " Let each of us swear," and produce children." So as they then swore to each other from the opposite banks of the Tranquil River of Heaven,[12] the august names of the Deities that were born from the mist [of her breath] when, having first begged His - Swift - Impetuous - Male-Augustness to hand her the ten-grasp sabre which was girded on him and broken it into three fragments, and with the jewels making a jingling sound[13] having brandished and washed them in the True-Pool-Well of

Heaven,[14] and having crunchingly crunched them, the
48 Heaven-Shining-Great-Deity blew them away, were Her
Augustness Torrent-Mist-Princess,[15] another august name
for whom is Her Augustness Princess-of-the-Island-of-the
Offing; next Her Augustness Lovely-Island-Princess,[16]
another august name for whom is Her Augustness Good-
Princess; next Her Augustness Princess-of-the-Torrent.[17]
The august name of the Deity that was born from the mist
[of his breath] when, having begged the Heaven-Shining-
Great-August-Deity to hand him the augustly complete
[string] of curved jewels eight feet [long],—of five hundred
jewels,—that was twisted in the left august bunch [of
her hair], and with the jewels making a jingling sound
having brandished and washed them in the True-Pool-
Well of Heaven, and having crunchingly crunched them,
His-Swift-Impetuous-Male-Augustness blew them away,
was His Augustness Truly - Conquer - I - Conqueror - Conquering - Swift - Heavenly - Great - Great - Ears.[18] The august
name of the Deity that was born from the mist [of his
breath] when again, having begged her to hand him the
49 jewels that were twisted in the right august bunch [of
her hair], and having crunchingly crunched them, he
blew them away, was His Augustness Ame-no-hohi.[19]
The august name of the Deity that was born from the
mist [of his' breath] when again, having begged her to
hand him the jewels that were twisted in her august
head-dress, and having crunchingly crunched them, he
blew them away, was His Augustness Prince-Lord-of-
Heaven.[20] The august name of the Deity that was born
from the mist [of his breath] when again, having begged
her to hand him the jewels that were twisted on her
left august arm,[21] and having crunchingly crunched them.

he blew them away, was His Augustness Prince-Lord-of-Life.[22] The august name of the Deity that was born from the mist [of his breath] when again, having begged her to hand him the jewels that were twisted on her right august arm,[23] and having crunchingly crunched them, he blew them away, was His-Wondrous-August-ness-of-Kumanu.[24] (Five Deities in all).

---

1. The English locution "to take leave" exactly represents the Chinese character here used which, from having the sense of "asking permission," has come to mean "bidding adieu."

2. He was her younger brother. But see what is said on the subject of names expressive of relationship on p. xxxvii of Introduction. The phonetic characters 那勢 are here used to represent 兄, "elder brother."

3. Literally "heart," here and elsewhere.

4. Or "hand."

5. The original is here obscure, but the translator has, as usual, followed the Chinese characters as far as possible, and has been chiefly guided by Moribe's interpretation. According to this, the "eight feet" (which Moribe takes to mean simply "several feet") must be supposed to refer to the length of the necklace which, he says, probably resembled a Buddhist rosary, only that the beads were somewhat larger. For a discussion of the various interpretations to which this phrase descriptive of the Sun-Goddess's ornaments may be subjected, see Note 4 to Mr. Satow's third paper on the "Rituals" in Vol. IX, Pt. II, p. 198 of these "Transactions," and Moribe's "Examination of Difficult Words," Vol. II. pp. 4-5, *s.v. Ya-saka-ni no iho-tsu no mi sumaru no tama.* Mr. Satow, adopting some of the bolder etymologies of the Japanese commentators, translates thus : " the ever-bright curved (or glittering) jewels, the many assembled jewels," and concludes that "a long string of, perhaps, claw-shaped stone beads" was what the author meant to describe.

6. Hirata supposes this additional quiver to have been slung in front.

7. Motowori's long note on the expression *taka-tomo*, to be found in Vol. VII, pp. 39-40 of his "Commentary" seems to prove that "high-sounding elbow-pad" (竹 being written phonetically for 高) is the most likely meaning,—these pads, of which one was worn on the left elbow, having been made of skin, Arawi Hakuseki however takes 竹 in |its

literal sense of "bamboo," and Moribe suggests the (健) which occurs so often in proper names with the signification of "bold," "brave," or "stout."

8. The reading *yu-hara*, here rendered "top of the bow]" is doubtful, and *yu-hadsu*, "bow-notch," has been proposed as an emendation.

9. *I.e.,* "both legs penetrated into the ground up to the thigh," a proof of the vigour with which she used her limbs in stamping.

10. Lit. "bubble-snow."

11. *I.e.,* "pledge our faith," "bind ourselves," in order to show forth the sincerity of our intentions.—Hirata has a long note on the word *ukehi,* here rendered "swear" (elsewhere as a Substantive, "oath,") which the student will do well to consult. It is contained in his "Exposition of the Ancient Histories," Vol. VII, pp. 61-63.

12. *Ame-no-yasu-kaha* (according to Motowori's reading *Ame-no-yasu-no-kaha*), our Milky Way. The "Chronicles of Old Matters of Former Ages" perhaps preserve the true etymology of the word by writing it *Ama-no-ya-se-kaha,* *i.e.,* "the Heavenly River of eight currents (or reaches)." This would mean simply "a broad river." The text literally says: "having placed the Tranquil River of Heaven in the middle," etc.; but the sense of the clause is that given in the translation.

13. These words seem, as Motowori says, to have been erroneously brought in here from the next sentence, where they come in appropriately.

14. *Ame-no-ma-na-wi.* The interpretation adopted is that which has the authority of Motowori and Hirata. Perhaps only "Heavenly Well" is intended. The above authorities warn us that the word *wi,* "well," was not in ancient days restricted to its modern sense, but was used to designate any place at which water could be drawn, and Motowori thinks that Heaven contained several such. That mentioned in the text seems to have been a pool in the bed of the Tranquil River of Heaven.

15. This is the interpretation of the original name *Ta-kiri-bime-no-mikoto* which is proposed by Moribe. It is less far-fetched, and agrees better with the name of the sister deity Princess-of-the-Torrent, than do the other explanations that have been attempted. The alternative name is *Oki-tsu-shima-no-mikoto.*

16. *Ichiki-shima-hime-no-mikoto, ichiki* being an unusual form of *itsuki.* The island, which is in the Inland Sea, is still celebrated, but bears in common parlance the name of *Miya-shima,* i.e., "Temple Island."

The alternative name is *Sa-yori-bime-no-mikoto*, in which *sa* is an Ornamental Prefix not calling for translation.

17. *Tagi-tsu-hime-no-mikoto.*

18. *Masa - ka-a - katsu - kachi - hayabi-ame-no-oshi-ho-mimi-no-mikoto.* The word *mimi* (耳 "ears") forms part of a large number of Ancient Japanese proper names. Motowori, who of conrse passes over in silence the fact that large ears are considered lucky, not only in Japan, *but also in China and Korea*, suggests the etymology *hi hi* or *bi bi* (靈々), *i.e.,* the word "wondrous" or "miraculous" repeated. But there are examples of such names in which the interpretation of *mimi* as "ears" is unavoidable. Thus Prince Umayado (commonly called *Shō-to-ku Tai-shi*) had also the name of *Yatsu-mimi no Tai-shi* 八耳太子 bestowed upon him on account of his extraordinary intelligence. Is it not therefore simpler in all cases to allow to the word this its natural meaning? The proper names in *mi* do however undoubtedly offer some difficulty, and Motowori scarcely seems content with his own derivation of the troublesome syllable. *Oshi*, as in other cases, is taken to represent *ohoshi*, "great"; and after much hesitation the translator has followed Motowori in regarding *ho* likewise as an abbreviated form of that word.

19. *Ame-no* signifies "of Heaven" or "heavenly." The syllables *hoki* are incomprehensible.

20. *Amatsu-hiko-ne-no-mikoto.*

21. Or "hand."

22. *Iku-tsu-hiko-ne-no-mikoto.*

23. This god does not seem to be known by any other name: but is conjectured by Hirata to be identical with *Ame-no-hohi*, the second of these divine brothers. *Kumanu*, or less archaically *Kumano*, is said to be, not the well-known Kumano in the province of Kishiu, but a place in Idzumo near Suga (see Sect. XIX, Notes 1 and 2). The name is written with the characters, 熊野, "bear moor." The native commentators however interpret it as a corruption of *Komori-nu*, 隱野, "the moor of retirement," on account of a tradition preserved in the "Chronicles" of Izanami (the Female-Who-Invites) having been interred at the Kishiu Kumano.

[SECT.—XIV. THE AUGUST DECLARATION OF THE DIVISION OF
THE AUGUST MALE CHILDREN AND THE
AUGUST FEMALE CHILDREN.]

Hereupon the Heavenly Shining-Great-August-Deity
said to His-Swift-Impetuous-Male-Augustness: "As for
the seed[1] of the five male Deities born last, their birth
was from things of mine; so undoubtedly they are my
children. As for the seed of the three female Deities
50 born first, their birth was from a thing of thine; so
doubtless they are thy children." Thus did she declare
the division. So Her Augustness Torrent-Mist-Princess,
the Deity born first, dwells in the Inner temple of
Munakata.[2] The next, Her Augustness Lovely-Island-
Princess, dwells in the middle temple of Munakata. The
next, Her Augustness Princess-of-the-Torrent, dwells in
the outer temple[3] of Munakata. These three Deities are
the three Great Deities[4] held in reverence by the Dukes
of Munakata.[5] So His Augustness Brave-Rustic-Illumi-
nator, child of His Augustness Ame-no-hohi, one of the
five children born afterwards ([6]this is the ancestor of the Rulers
51 of the Land of Idzumo,[7] of the Rulers of the Land of Musashi,[8] of the
Rulers of the Upper Land of Unakami,[9] of the Rulers of the Lower Land
of Unakami,[10] of the Rulers of the Land of Izhimu,[11] of the Departmental
Suzerains of the Island of Tsu[12] and of the Rulers of the Land of Toho-
tsu-Afumi[13]). The next, His Augustness Prince-Lord-of-
Heaven (is the Ancestor of the Rulers of the Land of Ofushi-kafuchi,[14]
of the Chiefs of Nukatabe-no-yuwe,[15] of the Rulers of the Land of Ki,[16]
52 of the Suzerains of Tanaka[17] in Yamato, of the Rulers of the Land of
Yamashiro,[18] of the Rulers of the Land of Umaguta,[19] of the Rulers of
the Land of Kine[20] in Michi-no-Shiri,[21] of the Rulers of the Land of
Suhau,[22] of the Rulers of Amuchi,[23] in Yamato, of the Departmental
Suzerains of Takechi,[24] of the Territorial Lords of Kamafu,[25] and of the
Rulers of Sakikusabe[26]).

1. *I.e.*, the origin.

2. A place in the province of Chikuzen. The name signifies either "breast-shape" or "body-shape."

3. Or "sea-shore temple."

4. Or "the Great Deities of the three shrines."

5. *Munakata-no-kimi*. Remember that all the names in this and similar lists are hereditary "gentile names" (see Introduction, p. xvi), and that "Duke" and the other titles used in this translation to designate them must only be regarded as approximations towards giving the force of the Japanese originals, which are themselves by no means always clear, either etymologically or historically. Indeed Motowori in a chapter entitled "*Kuni no Miyatsuko*" (國造) in his "*Tama-Katsuma*," Vol. VI, p. 25, remarks that the distinctions obtaining between the various titles of *Kimi, Wake, Murazhi*, etc., are no longer to be ascertained, if indeed they were ever sharply drawn, and that *Kuni no Miyatsuko* (here rendered "Rulers of the Land") seems to have been a general term including all the rest, and roughly corresponding to the modern title of *Daimyo.*—It must be well understood that all these names, though properly and originally denoting an office, were inherited as titles, and ended (after the custom of conferring new ones had died out) by being little more than an extra surname appended to the surname proper (*uji*). This kind of quasi-official quasi-titular surname is what is called by the Japanese a *kabane*, which the translator, for want of a better equivalent, renders by "gentile name." Motowori's learned note in Vol. XXXIX, pp. 14-15 of his Commentary, should be consulted for a full exposition of this somewhat intricate subject, on which there has been much misapprehension, chiefly owing to the want of a fitting Chinese character to denote the word *kabane*.

6. Here and throughout the work passages of this nature containing genealogies are in all the editions printed small, and might therefore be supposed to be either intended as foot-notes, or to be later glosses. Motowori however rightly rejects such an inference. To an English reader the word "this" may seem, by disturbing the grammar of the sentence, to support that inference; but in Japanese [construction little importance need be attached to the presence of this double Nominative.—The name in the original of the ancestral deity whose children are here enumerated is *Taka-Hira-Tori-no-mikoto*, and the interpretation thereof in the sense given in the translation is Motowori's *Hira-tori* being supposed by him to stand for *Hina-teri*.

7. *Idzumo-no-kuni-no-miyatsuko.*

8. *Muzashi-no-kuni-no-miyatsuko.* In classical and modern nsage *Mu-sashi* does not take the *nigori*.

9. *Kami-tsu-Unakami-no-kuni-no-miyatsuko.* Unakami was a part of what forms the modern province of Kadzusa. The name probably signifies "on the sea."

10. *Shimo-tsu-Unakami-no-kuni-no-miyatsuko.*

11. *Izhimu-no-kuni-miyatsuko.* Izhimu (given in the "Japanese Words Classified and Explained" as *Izhimi*) was a portion of the modern province of Kadzusa. The etymology of the name is unknown.

12. *Tsushima-no-agata-no-atahe.*

13. *Toho-tsu-afumi-no-kuni-no-miyatsuko.* In modern times *Toho-tsu-afumi* has been contracted te *Tohotafumi* and is pronounced *Tōtōmi*. The name signifies "distant fresh sea" (i.e. "distant lake") the province which bears it being thus designated in reference to a large lagoon which it contains, and in contradistinction to *Chika-tsu-afumi*, "near fresh sea." the name of the province in which lies Lake Biha. In modern times the latter has come to be known simply as Afumi (pronounced Omi), and the original connection of ideas between its name and that of Tōtōmi is lost sight of.

14. *Ohoshi-kafuchi-no-kuni-no-miyatsuko.* *Ohoshi-kafuchi* (in modern times pronounced *Ochikochi*) signifies "within the great rivers."

15. *Nukatabe-no-yuwe-no-murazhi.* The meaning of this name is not certain, but *yuwe* seems to be the word for "bathing woman" mentioned in Sect. LXXI (Note 11). See Motowori's remarks in Vol. XXIV, p. 56 of his "Commentary" and the story of the origin of the name given in the "Catalogue of Family Names," Vol. II, pp. 8-9) edit. of 1834).

16. *Kino-kuni-no-miyatsuko.* *Kĭ* signifies "tree," and the province doubtless received this name from its forests. Motowori supposes the character 芙 to have been lost in this place, and reads *Ubaraki* (the modern *Ibaraki*), a portion of the province of Hitachi. See Vol. VII, pp. 75-76 of his "Commentary."

17. *Tanaka-no-atahe.* The word *tana-ka* signifies "in the middle of rice-fields."

18. *Yamashiro-no-kuni-no-miyatsuko.* *Yama-shiro* signifies "behind the mountains," though it is now, by a play upon words, written with characters signifying "mountain-castle."

19. *Umaguta-no-kuni-no-miyatsuko.* Umaguta is a portion of the modern province of Kadzusa. The etymology of the name is not known.

20. *Kiuhe-no-kuni-no-miyatsuko.* The etymology of the name and the position of the place are equally obscure.

21. The modern province of Echigo, or perhaps any not well defined district in the north of Main Island. (See Section LX, Note 20.)

22. *Suhau-no-kuni-no-miyatsuko.* The etymology of Suhau is not known; but the name sounds Chinese.

23. *Amuchi-no-miyatsubo.* The derivation of Amuchi is unknown.

24. *Takechi-no-agata-nushi.* Takechi means "high market" or "high town."

25. *Kamafu-no-inaki.* Kamafu was a portion of Afumi. Motowori's suggestion that the name may be derived from *kama* (*gama*), "a bull-frog," does not seem a happy one.

26. *Sakikusabe-no-miyatsuko.* *Sakikusa-be* means literally "lily clan," *saki-kusa*, the old name for the lily (or one species of lily) being literally "the luck-plant." The story of the origin of this cognomen is to be found in the "Catalogue of Family Names," Vol. II, p. 9.

---

[SECT XV.—THE AUGUST RAVAGES OF HIS IMPETUOUS-
MALE-AUGUSTNESS]

Then His-Swift-Impetuous-Male-Augustness said to the Heaven-Shining-Great-August-Deity: "Owing to the sincerity of my intentions I have, in begetting children, gotten delicate females. Judging from this,[1] I have undoubtedly gained the victory." With these words, and impetuous with victory, he broke down the divisions of the ricefields[2] laid out by the Heaven-Shining-Great-August-Deity, filled up the ditches, and moreover strewed 53 excrements[3] in the palace where she partook of the great food.[4] So, though he did thus, the Heaven-Shining-Great-August-Deity upbraided him not,[5] but said: "What looks like excrements must be something that His August-ness mine elder brother has vomited through drunkenness. Again, as to his breaking down the divisions of the rice-fields and filling up the ditches, it must be because he grudges the land [they occupy[6]] that His Augustness mine elder brother acts thus." But notwithstanding these apologetic words, he still continued his evil acts, and was more and more [violent]. As the Heaven-Shining-Great-August-Deity sat in her awful[7] weaving-hall[8] seeing to the weaving of the august garments of the Deities, he broke a hole in the top[9] of the weaving-hall, and through it let fall a heavenly piebald horse 54 which he had flayed with a backward flaying,[10] at whose sight the women weaving the heavenly garments were so much alarmed that impegerunt privatas partes adversis radiis et obierunt.[11]

---

1. Literally "if one speak from this."

2. The character used is 田, which in Chinese does not necessarily signify a *rice*-field. But in Japanese it seems to have been always limited to this narrower · meaning, to which likewise the context here clearly points.

3. In the original written 屎麻理, which is partly ideographic and partly phonetic for *kuso-mari*. Motowori interprets it to signify "excrements and urine"; but the parallel passage of the "Chronicles" which he himself quotes goes to prove that *mari* had not the latter meaning, as does also another well-known passage in the "Tale of a Bamboo-Cutter."

4. 大嘗 read *oh-nihe.* The word *nihe* now denotes "a sacrifice," and *oh-nihe no matsuri* is the religious festival of the tasting of the first new rice of the season..

5. We might, following classical usage, translate the Verb *togamezu*, which is written phonetically, by the words "took no heed" or "made no observation"; but in this passage it certainly seems to have the stronger and more specialized signification of "upbraiding," "scolding," which attaches to it in the colloquial dialect.

6. *I.e.*, he thinks that none of the land should be wasted in ditches and embankments, but should all be devoted to the production of food.

7. The character used is 忌, "to shun," which in Japanese has approximately the meaning of "sacred." Thus a certain family of priests

was called by the name of *Imibe*, lit. " the shunning clan," on account of the uncleanness from which they were bound to abstain.

8. Written with characters signifying literally " garment-house," but the meaning, as understood by the native commentators is that given in the text.

9. 項. This character is taken by the native commentators in the sense of 棟, *mune*, " ridge-pole."

10. *I.e.*, it is supposed, beginning at the tail. That this was considered criminal may be seen by comparing Sect. XCVII, Note 3.

11. In the parallel passage of the " Chronicles " it is the goddess who injures herself with her shuttle, but without dying of the effects of the accident.

---

[SECT. XVI.—THE DOOR OF THE HEAVENLY
ROCK-DWELLING.]

So thereupon the Heaven-Shining-Great-August-Deity, terrified at the sight, closed [behind her] the door of the Heavenly Rock-Dwelling,[0] made it fast,[2] and retired. Then the whole Plain of High Heaven was obscured and all the Central Land of Reed-Plains darkened. Owing to this, eternal[3] night prevailed. Hereupon the voices of the myriad[4] Deities were like unto the flies in the fifth moon as they swarmed, and a myriad portents of woe all arose. Therefore did the eight hundred myriad[5] Deities assemble in a divine assembly in the bed[6] of the Tranquil River of Heaven, and bid the Deity Thought-Includer,[7] child of the High-August-Producing-Wondrous-Deity think of a plan, assembling the long-singing birds of eternal night[8] and making them sing, taking the hard rocks of Heaven from the river-bed of the Tranquil River of Heaven, and taking the iron[9] from 55 the Heavenly Metal-Mountains,[10] calling in the smith Ama-tsu-ma-ra,[11] charging Her Augustness I-shi-ko-ri-do-

me[12] to make a mirror, and charging His Augustness
Jewel-Ancestor[13] to make an augustly complete [string]
of curved jewels eight feet [long],—of five hundred
jewels,[14]—and summoning His Augustness Heavenly-
56 Beckoning-Ancestor-Lord[15] and His Augustness Great-
Jewel,[16] and causing them to pull out with a complete
pulling the shoulder [-blade] of a true[17] stag from the
Heavenly Mount Kagu,[18] and take cherrybark[19] from the
Heavenly Mount Kagu, and perform divination,[20] and
pulling up by pulling its roots a true *cleyera japonica*[21]
with five hundred [branches] from the Heavenly Mount
Kagu, and taking and putting upon its upper branches
the augustly complete [string] of curved jewels eight
feet [long],—of five hundred jewels,—and taking and
tying to the middle branches[22] the mirror eight feet
57 [long],[23] and taking and hanging upon its lower branches
the white pacificatory offerings[24] and the blue pacificatory
offerings, His Augustness Grand-Jewel taking these divers
things and holding them together with the grand august
offerings,[25] and His Augustness Heavenly-Beckoning-
Ancestor-Lord prayerfully reciting grand liturgies,[26] and
the Heavenly Hand-Strength-Male-Deity[27] standing hidden
beside the door, and Her Augustness Heavenly-Alarming-
Female[28] hanging [round her] the heavenly clubmoss of the
Heavenly Mount 'Kagu as a sash,[29] and making the
heavenly spindle-tree her head-dress,[30] and binding the
58 leaves of the bamboo-grass of the Heavenly Mount Kagu
in a posy for her hands, and laying a soundingboard[31]
before the door of the Heavenly Rock-Dwelling, and
stamping till she made it resound and doing as if possessed by a Deity,[32] and pulling out the nipples of her
breasts, pushing down her skirt-string usque ad privates

partes.[33] Then the Plain of High Heaven shook, and
the eight hundred myriad Deities laughed together.
Hereupon the Heaven-Shining-Great-August-Deity was
amazed, and, slightly opening the door of the Heavenly
Rock-Dwelling, spoke thus from the inside: "Methought
that owing to my retirement the Plain of Heaven would
be dark, and likewise the Central Land of Reed-Plains
would all be dark: how then is it that the Heavenly-
Alarming-Female makes merry, and that likewise the
eight hundred myriad Deities all laugh?" Then the
Heavenly-Alarming-Female spoke saying: "We rejoice
and are "glad because there is a Deity more illustrious
than Thine Augustness." While she was thus speaking,
His Augustness Heavenly-Beckoning-Ancestor-Lord and
His Augustness Grand-Jewel pushed forward the mirror
and respectfully showed it to the Heaven-Shining-Great-
August-Deity, whereupon the Heaven-Shining-Great-
August-Deity, more and more astonished, gradually came
forth from the door and gazed upon it, whereupon the
Heavenly-Hand-Strength-Male-Deity, who was standing
hidden, took her august hand and drew her out, and then
His Augustness Grand-Jewel drew the bottom-tied rope[34] 59
along at her august back, and spoke, saying: "Thou
must not go back further in than this!" So when the
Heaven-Shining-Great-August-Deity had come forth, both
the Plain of High Heaven and the Central-Land-of-Reed-
Plains of course again became light.[35]

1. Motowori says that the word "rock" need not here be taken
literally. But it is always (and the translator thinks rightly) so understood,
and the compound considered to mean a cave in the rocks, which is also
the expression found in the "Chronicles" (岩窟).

2. The word *sasu*, which is here used, implies that the goddess

made the door fast either by sticking something against it or by bolting it,—perhaps with one of the metal hooks of which mentioned is made in Sect. LXV (Note 7).

3. *Toko-yo*, here properly written 常夜, and a few lines lower down semi-phonetically 常世.

4. Motowori supposes "myriad" to be a copyist's error for "evil." This clause is a repetition of one in Sect. XII.

5. The parallel passage in the "Chronicles" has "eighty myriads."

6. The Japanese word *kohara*, translated "bed," is thus defined in Dr. Hepburn's Dictionary, 2nd Edit. *s.v. Kawara*: "That part of the stony bed of a river which is dry except in high water."

7. *Omohi-kane-no-kami*, "He *included* in his single mind the thoughts and "contrivances of many," says Motowori.

8. *I.e.*, as is generally believed, the barndoor fowl.

9. The text has the character 鐵, "iron," which Hirata reads *magane*, lit. "true metal," the common Japanese term being *kuro-gane*, lit, "black metal," Motowori prefers to read simply *kane*, "metal" in general. The main text of the parallel passage in the "Chronicles" omits to mention the metal of which the mirror was made; but "One account" has the character 金, "metal" in general, often in Chinese, but rarely if ever in old Japanese, with the specific sense of "gold." The "Chronicles of Old Matters" alone, which are of very doubtful authenticity, say that the mirror was made of copper. (Copper was not discovered in Japan till the eighth century of the Christian era, a few years before the discovery of gold). The best and most obvious course is to adhere to the character in the text, which is, as above stated, "iron."

10. *I.e.*, the mines. The original expression is *Ame no kana-yama*.

11. *Ama-tsu* signifies "of Heaven," but the rest of this name is not to be explained. Motowori adopts from the "Chronicles" the reading, *Ama-tsu-ma-ura*, where the character used for *ma* signifies "true," and that for *ura* signifies "sea-shore." (It should be remarked that the forging of a spear by this personage is referred by the author of the "Chronicles," not to the "Divine Age" but to the reign of the Emperor Sui-zei.) Motowori also proposes to supplement after the name the words "to make a spear." Hirata identifies this god with *Ama-no-ma-hito-tsu-no-mikoto*, His Augustness Heavenly-One-Eye, who is however not mentioned in the "Records." Obvius hujus nominis sensus foret "Coelestis Penis," sed nullius commentatoris auctoritate commendatur.

12. This name is written in the "Chronicles" with characters signifying Stone-Coagulating-Old-Woman, which however seem to be as

merely phonetic as those in the present text (伊斯許理度賣). Motowori proposes the interpretation of " Again-Forging-Old-Woman " (鑄重老女, *I-shikiri-tome*) which is supported by a tradition preserved in the " Gleanings of the Ancient Story," where it is related that the mirror, not having given satisfaction at first, was forged a second time. There is a long note on the subjects of this name in Hirata's " Exposition of the Ancient Histories," Vol. IX, p. 56, where that author propounds the novel opinion that I-shi-ko-ri-do-me was not a goddess at all, but a god.

13. *Tama-noya-no-mikoto.* The " Chronicles " write this name with characters signifying " Jewel-House," but such a reading seems less good.

14. See Sect. XIII, Note 5.

15. *Ame-no-ko-ya-ne-no-mikoto,* also reads *Ame-no* etc. and *Ama-tsu* etc. The signification of the syllables *ko-ya,* rendered " beckoning ancestor" in accordance with Motowori's view connecting the name with the share taken by the god who bore it in the legend here narrated, is obscure. Mr. Satow thinks that Koya may be the name of a place (see these " Transactions " Vol. VII, Pt. IV, p. 400).

16. *Futo-tama-no-mikoto.* The name is here rendered in accordance with the import of the Chinese characters with which it is written. Motowori, however, emits a plausible opinion when he proposes to consider *tama* as an abbreviation of *tamuke,* " holding in the hands as an offering," in connection with what we are told below about this deity and *Ame-no-ko-ya-ne* holding the symbolic offerings.

17. The word " true " (*ma*) here and below is not much more than an Honorific.

18. We might also, though less well, translate by " Mount Kagu in Heaven." This would suit the view of Motowori, who is naturally averse to the identification of this Mount Kagu with the well-known mountain of that name in Yamato (see Sect. VII, Note 12). But of course an European scholar cannot allow of such a distinction being drawn.

19. Or perhaps the bark of the common birch is intended. The word in the original is *haha-ka.*

20. See Mr. Satow's already quoted note in Vol. VII, Pt. II, p. 425 *et seq,* and more especially pp. 430-432, of these " Transactions."

21. In Japanese *saka-ki.* It is commonly planted in the precincts of Shintō temples.

22. We might also translate in the Singular " to a middle branch," in order to conform to the rigid distinction which our language draws between Singular and Plural.

23. A note to the edition of 1687 proposes to substitute the characters 八咫 for 八尺, and a note in the original tells us to read them not *ya-ta*, but *ya-ata*. Hereupon Motowori founds his derivation of *ya-ta* from *ya-atama*, "eight heads," and supposes the mirror to have been, not eight feet in length, but octangular, while Moribe, who in the case of the jewels accepts the obvious interpretation "eight feet [long]," thinks that the mirror had "an eightfold flowery pattern" (*yaha-na-gata*) round its border. But both these etymologies are unsupported by the other cases in which the word *ya-ta* occurs, and are rendered specially untenable by the fact of the mirror and curved beads being spoken of together further on as the 八尺勾瓊鏡 (Sect. XXXIII, Note 20).

24. In rendering the original word *nigi-te* (here written phonetically, but elsewhere with the characters 和幣), the explanation given by Tanigaha Shisei, and indeed suggested by the characters, has been followed. Motowori's view does not materially differ, but he considers "pacificatory" or "softening" to be equivalent to "soft" applied to the offerings themselves, which consisted of soft cloth, the syllable *te* of *nigi-te* being believed to be a contraction of *tahe* which signifies cloth. The white cloth in ancient times was made of the paper mulberry (*Broussonetia papyrifera*), and the blue of hemp.

25. The original word is written with the same character as the *te* of *nigi-te* translated "offerings" above.

26. Or in the Singular "a grand liturgy," or "ritual."

27. *Ame-no-ta-jikara-wo-no-kami.*

28. *Ame-no-uzume-no-mikoto.* The translator has followed the best authorities in rendering the obscure syllable *uzu* by the word "alarming." Another interpretation quoted in Tanigaha Shisei's "Perpetual Commentary on the Chronicles of Japan" and adopted by Moribe in his "*Idzu no Chi-waki*," is that *uzu* means head-dress, and that the goddess took her name from the head-dress of spindle-tree leaves which she wore. The character 釵, with which the syllables in question (here written phonetically) are rendered ideographically in the "Chronicles," signifies "metal head-gear," "flowers of gold or silver."

29. *Tasuki*, "a cord or sash passed over the shoulders, round the back of the neck, and attached to the wrists, to strengthen the hands for the support of weights, whence the name, which means 'hand-helper.' It was thus different both in form and use from the modern *tasuki*, a cord with its two ends joined which is worn behind the neck, under the

arms and round the back, to keep the modern loose sleeves out of the way when household duties are being performed." (E. Satow).

30. *I.e.*, making for herself a head-dress of spindle-tree leaves.

31. The original of these words, *uke fusete*, is written phonetically, and the exact meaning of *uke*, here rendered "sounding-board," is open to doubt. The parallel passage in the "Chronicles" has the character, 槽, which signifies a "trough," "manger" or "tub," and the commentators seem therefore right in supposing that the meaning intended to be conveyed in both histories is that of some kind of improvised wooden structure used for the purpose of amplifying sound.

32. Neither the text nor Motowori's Commentary (which Hirata adopts word for word) is absolutely explicit, but the imitation and not the reality of divine possession appears to be here intended. In the parallel passage of the "Chronicles," on the other hand, we seem to be reading of genuine possession.

33. The subject of the Verb is not clear in many of the clauses of this immensely long sentence, which does not properly hang together. Some clauses read as if the different deities who take a part in the action did so of their own free will; but the intention of the author must have been to let a Causative sense be understood throughout, as he begins by telling us that a plan was *devised* by the deity Thought-Includer, which plan must have influenced all the subsequent details.

34. *Shiri-kume-naha*, *i.e.*, rope made of straw drawn up by the roots, which stick out from the end of the rope. Straw-ropes thus manufactured are still used in certain ceremonies and are called *shime-naha*, a corruption of the Archaic term. Motowori's explanation shows that this is more likely to be the proper signification of the word than "back-limiting-rope" (*shiri-ho-kagiri-me-naha*), which had been previously suggested by Mabuchi with reference to its supposed origin at the time of the event narrated in this legend.

35. Motowori plausibly conjectures the character 得 in the concluding words of this passage to be a copyist's error for 復, and the translator has accordingly rendered it by the English word "again." As it stands, the clause 自得照明, though making sense, does not read like the composition of a Japanese.

[SECT. XVII.—THE AUGUST EXPULSION OF HIS-IMPETUOUS-
MALE-AUGUSTNESS.]

Thereupon the eight hundred myriad Deities took
counsel together, and imposed on High-Swift-Impetuous-
Male-Augustness a fine of a thousand tables,[1] and
likewise cut his beard, and even caused the nails
of his fingers and toes to be pulled out, and
expelled him with a divine expulsion. Again he
begged food of the Deity Princess-of-Great-Food.[2]
Then the Princess-of-Great-Food took out all sorts
of dainty things from her nose, her mouth, and
her fundament, and made them up into all sorts [of
dishes], which she offered to him. But His-Swift-Impetuous-
Male-Augustness watched her proceedings, considered that
she was offering up to him filth, and at once killed the
Deity Princess-of-Great-Food. So the things that were
born in the body of the Deity who had been killed were
60 [as follows]: in her head were born silkworms, in her
two eyes were born rice-seeds, in her two ears was born
millet,[3] in her nose were born small beans,[4] in her private
parts was born barley,[5] in her fundament were born
large beans.[6] So His Augustness the Deity-Producing-
Wondrous-Ancestor[7] caused them to be taken and used
as seeds.

---

1. *I.e.,* "an immense fine." The student should consult Motowori's
elaborate note on this passage in Vol. IX, pp. 1-5 of his Commentary.
Tables of gifts are mentioned in Sect. XXXVII, Note 7 and Sect. XL,
Note 13.

2. *Oho-ge-tsu-hime-no-kami.* This personage (but without the title
of "Deity") has already appeared in Section V, (Note 8) as the alternative personal name of the Island of Aha.

3. *Panicum Italicum.*

4. *Phaseolus Radiatus.*

5. Or less probably "wheat."

6. *Soja Glycine.*

7. *Kami-musu-bi-mi-oya-no-mikoto*, the same deity as the one mentioned at the beginning of these "Records" under the shorter title of *Kami-musu-hi-no-kami.* (See Sect. I, Note 6.)

---

[SECL. XVIII.—THE EIGHT-FORKED SERPENT.]

So, having been expelled, [His-Swift-Impetuous-Male-Augustness] descended to a place [called] Tori-kami[1] at the head-waters of the River Hi[2] in the Land of Idzumo. At this time some chopsticks[3]. came floating down the stream. So His-Swift-Impetuous-Male-Augustness, thinking that there must be people at the head-waters of the river, went up it in quest of them, when he came upon an old man and an old woman,—two of them,—who had a young girl between them,[4] and were weeping. Then he deigned to ask: "Who are ye?" So the old man replied, saying: "I[5] am an Earthly Deity,[6] child of the Deity Great-Mountain-Possessor.[7] I am called by the name of Foot-Stroking-Elder,[8] my wife is called by the name of Hand-Stroking Elder, and my daughter is called by the name of Wondrous-Inada-Princess."[9] Again he asked: What is the cause of your crying?" [The old man answered,] saying: "I had originally eight young girls as daughters. But the eight-forked serpent of Koshi[10] has come every year and devoured [one], and it is now its time to come, wherefore we weep." Then he asked him: "What is its form like?" [The old man] answered, saying: "Its eyes are like *akahagachi*,[11] it has one body with eight heads and eight tails. Moreover on

its body grows moss, and also chamaecyparis[12] and cryptomerias. Its length extends over eight valleys and
eight hills, and if one look at its belly, it is all constantly
62 bloody and inflamed."          (What is called here *akakagachi* is the
modern *hohodzuki*.[13])          Then His-Swift-Impetuous-Male-Augustness said to the old man: "If this be thy daughter,
wilt thou offer her to me?" He replied, saying: "With
reverence,[14] but I know not thine august name." Then
he replied, saying: "I am elder brother[15] to the Heaven-
Shining-Great-August-Deity. So I have now descended
from Heaven." Then the Deities Foot-Stroker-Elder and
Hand-Stroking-Elder said: "If that be so, with reverence
will we offer [her to thee]." So His-Swift-Impetuous-
Male-Augustness, at once taking and changing the young
girl into a multitudinous and close-toothed comb which
he stuck into his august hair-bunch, said to the Deities
Foot-Stroking-Elder and Hand-Stroking-Elder: "Do you
distill some eight-fold refined liquor.[16] Also make a
fence round about, in that fence make eight gates, at
each gate tie [together] eight platforms,[17] on each platform
put a liquor-vat, and into each vat pour the eight-fold
refined liquor, and wait." So as they waited after having
thus prepared everything in accordance with his bidding,
63 the eight-forked serpent came truly as [the old man] had
said, and immediately dipped a head into each vat, and
drank the liquor. Thereupon it was intoxicated with
drinking, and all [the heads] lay down and slept. Then
His-Swift-Impetuous-Male-Augustness drew the ten-grasp
sabre,[18] that was augustly girded on him, and cut the
serpent in pieces, so that the River Hi flowed on changed
into a river of blood. So when he cut the middle tail,
the edge of his august sword broke. Then, thinking it

strange, he thrust into and split [the flesh] with the point of his august sword and looked, and there was a great sword [within]. So he took this great sword, and, thinking it a strange thing, he respectfully informed the Heaven-Shining-Great-August-Deity.[19] This is the Herb-Quelling Great Sword.[20].

---

1. Written with the characters 鳥髪, "bird's hairs," but these must surely be phonetic. In the "Chronicles" the same name is written 鳥上.

2. Or Hii, the chief river in Idzumo. The name is supposed by some to have been derived from the name of the god *Hi-hayabi* (see Section VIII, Note 6).

Or in the Singular, "a chopstick."

4. Literally "had placed a young girl between them," a similar construction to that in Section XIII, (Note 11).

5. The humble character 僕 "servant" is used by the old man for the First Personal Pronoun.

6. 國神. Being generally used antithetically to 天神, "Heavenly Deity," it seems better to translate the characters thus than by "Country Deity" or "Deity of the Land." (See Section I, Note 11).

7. *Oho-yama-tsu-mi-no-kami*, first mentioned in Sect. VI, (Note 17).

8. *Ashi-nadzu-chi*, the wife's being *Te-nadzu-chi*. "One account" in the "Chronicles" gives *Ashi nadzu-te-nadzu* (足摩手摩) as the name of the old father alone, while the mother is called *Inada-no-miya-nushi Susa-no-yatsu-mimi*. (*Inada-no-miya-nushi* signifies "Mistress of the Temple of Inada; the signification of the second compound, which forms the name properly so called is not clear, but should probably be interpreted to mean "Impetuous-Eight-Ears," the word *susa*, "impetuous," containing an allusion to the name of her divine visitor, and "eight ears" being Honorific).

9. *Kushi-[I]nada-hime*, Inada (*i.e. ina-da*, "rice-field") being the name of a place. *Kushi* signifies not only "wondrous" but "comb," and is indeed here written with the character for "comb" 櫛, so that there is a play on the word in connection with the incident of her transformation into a comb which is mentioned immediately below, though most authorities agree in considering 櫛 to be here used phonetically for 奇, which is the reading in the "Chronicles." Moribe, however, in his "*Idzu no Chi-waki*" suggests the etymology *Kushi-itadaki-hime* (櫛頂姫) *i.e*, "Princess [used as] a comb [for] the head."

10. Derivation quite obscure. Motowori quotes an absurd etymology given in the " Japanese Words Classified and Explained," which identifies the name of *Koshi* with the Past Tense of the Verb *kuru,* " to come " ! There is a district (*kohori*) named Koshi in the modern province of Echigo ; but Koshi was down to historical times a somewhat vague designation of all the north-western provinces,—Echizen, Kaga, Noto, Etchiu, and Echigo. A tradition preserved in the "Chronicles" tells us that it was meant to denote the Island of Yezo (or rather, perhaps, the land of the Yezo, *i.e.* the Ainos). The expression in the first Song in Sect. XXIV, and other similar ones in the early literature show that it was not looked upon as a part of Japan proper.

11. See Note 13.

12. A coniferous tree, the *Chamæcyparis obtusa,* in Japanese *hi-no-ki.* The cryptomeria is *Cryptomeria japonica.*

13. The winter-cherry, *Physalis Alkekengi.*

14. For the word " reverence " here and a few lines further on. *conf.* Sect. IX, Note 4.

15. He was her younger brother ; but see Introduction, p. xxxvii.

16. In Japanese *sake,* and archaically *ki,* written with the character 酒 and generally translated "rice-beer," but by Dr. Rein "rice-brandy" (*Reis-branntwein*). The modern *sake* resembles the Chinese *huang chiu* (黃酒). If we translated it by "rice-beer," we should of course have to render by " to brew " the Verb *kamu* or *kamosu* (釀) here rendered " to distill." It should be mentioned that Professor Atkinson who, like Dr. Rein, has studied the subject specially, uses the word " brewing ; " but apparently no English term exactly represents the process which the liquor undergoes in the course of preparation. A curious question is suggested by the fact that the old Japanese word for " distilling " or " brewing " liquor is homonymous with the " Verb " to chew," But there is not, beyond this isolated verbal resemblance, any documentary evidence in favour of the Japanese ever having practised a method of making liquor which still obtains in some of the South Sea Islands.—" One account " of the Chronicles of Japan makes *Susa-no-wo* say "Take *all the fruits,* and distill liquor."

17. The author doubtless intended, as Motowori suggests, to speak only of eight platforms,—one at each gate,—and not of sixty-four. But what he actually says is as in the translation.

18. See Section VIII, Note 1.

19. The text is not quite clear, but the above gives the interpretation to which the words most naturally lend themselves. Motowori, influenced by the parallel passage in the "Chronicles," which says explicitly that the sword itself was sent up to the Sun-Goddess, reads the passage thus: "thinking it a strange thing, he sent it up with a message to the Heaven-Shining-Great-August-Deity"; and Mr. Satow follows him in thus translating (see Note 4 to Ritual 8, Vol. IX, Pt. II, 198-200 of these "Transactions," where the whole of this legend is translated with one or two slight verbal differences from the version here given). In the opinion of the present writer, Hirata's arguments in favour of the view here taken are conclusive (see his "Sources of the Ancient Histories," Section LXXII, in the second part of Vol. III, pp. 66-67). That the sword afterwards appears at the temple of the Sun-Goddess in Ise (see end of Section LXXXII), by the high-priestess of which it is bestowed on the legendary hero Yamato-take, is not to the point in this connection, as it is not necessary that all the parts of a myth should be perfectly consistent.

20. *Kusa-nagi no tachi.* For the applicability of this name see Sect. LXXXIII.

---

[SECT. XIX.—THE PALACE OF SUGA.]

So thereupon His Swift-Impetuous-Male-Augustness sought in the land of Idzumo for a place where he might build a palace. Then he arrived at a place [called] Suga,[2] and said: "On coming to this place my august heart is pure,"[1]—and in that place he built a palace to dwell in. So that place is now called Suga.[2] When this Great Deity first built[3] the palace of Suga, clouds rose up thence. Then he made an august song.[4] That song said:[5]

> "Eight clouds arise. The eight-fold fence
> of Idzumo makes an eight-fold fence for
> the spouses to retire [within]. Oh! that
> eight-fold fence."[6]

65    Then he called the Deity Foot-Stroking-Elder and said: "Thee do I appoint Headman[7] of my palace;" and moreover bestowed on him the name of Master-of-the-Temple-of-Inada-Eight-Eared-Deity-of-Suga.[8]

---

1. *I.e.,* "I feel refreshed." The Japanese term used is *suga-sugashi*, whence the origin ascribed to the name of the place Suga. But more probably the name gave rise to this detail of the legend.

2. The real derivation of Suga is unknown, all the native commentators accepting the statement in the text, and Motowori supposing that up to the time of the Deity's arrival it had borne the name of Inada. We may perhaps conjecture some connection between *Suga* and *Susa-no-wo* ("Impetuous Male," see Motowori's Commentary,[1] Vol. IX, p. 49), and it may be mentioned that the "Eight-Eared Deity of Suga" is also mentioned as the "Eight-Eared Deity of Susa."

3. Or "began to build."

4. "Ode" is another rendering of the Japanese term *uta*, which has been used by the present writer and by others. *Uta* being however connected with *utafu*, "to sing," it seems more consistent to translate it by the English word "song."

5. Or perhaps rather "in that song he said."

6. This difficult song has been rather differently rendered by Mr. Aston in the Second Appendix to his "Grammar of the Japanese Written Language" (2nd Edition), and again by Mr. Satow in the note to his translation of the Ritual already quoted. Mr. Aston (premising that he follows Motowori's interpretation) translates it thus:

> "Many clouds arise:
> The clouds which come forth (are) a manifold fence:
> For the husband and wife to retire within
> They have formed a manifold fence:
> Oh! that manifold fence!"

Mr. Satow's translation is as follows:

> "Many clouds arise.
> The manifold fence of the forth-issuing clouds
> Makes a manifold fence
> For the spouses to be within.
> Oh! that manifold fence."

In any case the meaning simply is that the multitudinous clouds rose up like a fence or screen behind which the newly-married deities might retire from public gaze, and Moribe suggests that the repetitions are an after-addition made to bring up to the usual number of thirty-one syllables what were originally but the three lines—

> *Tachi-idzuru kumo mo*
> *Tsuma-gome ni*
> *Yo-he-gahi tsukuru yo!*

*I.e.*—

> " The uprising clouds even, to shut up
> the spouses, make an eight-fold fence."

(See his discussion on this song in the " *Idzu no Kotowaki*," Vol. I, pp. 1-3.)—The present writer has already stated in the Introduction (see p. lx,) his reasons for always rendering the native word for " eight" (*ya*) by " eight" instead of by " many" or " numerous," as is done by the two eminent scholars above quoted. With regard to the word *Idzumo* which they, in deference to the opinions of the native commentators, render by " clouds which come forth" or " forth-issuing clouds" (the Chinese characters 出雲 with which the word is written having that signification), the present writer cannot persuade himself that such a corruption as *idzumo* for *ide-kumo* either retained at the time of the composition of the song, or should now be credited with, the signification which this its supposed etymology assigns to it. The etymology moreover is far from being established, and in this, as in many other cases, the Chinese characters used to write the name of the province of Idzumo may well have rested on nothing more than a vague similarity of sound, and probably no European scholar would endorse the opinion of the native commentators, to whom the " Records " are a sacred book, that the province of Idzumo received its name from this very poem. On the other hand, we need have no difficulty in conceding that the Pillow-Word *ya-kumo-tatsu*, by which Idzumo is preceded in poetical compositions, did probably here originate.—This song is in the " Chronicles " only quoted in a note, for which reason some authorities dispute its antiquity. In the note in question, we find the reading *-gome* (the " Records " have *-gomi*), *i.e.*, the Transitive form instead of the Intransitive. If this were adopted, the translation would have to run thus : .... " The eight-fold fence of Idzumo makes an eight-fold fence to shut up the spouse[s ?] in ;" and probably " spouse " should be understood in the Feminine to mean " wife."

7. *Cbito*, written with the Chinese character 首, while the Japanese word is probably derived from *oho-bito*, "great man." When used, as it often is, as a "gentile name," the translator renders it by "Grandee."

8. *Inada-no-miya-nushi Suga-no ya-tsu-mimi-no-kami.* It should be stated that Motowori, as usual, objects to the view that *mimi* signifies "ears" (its proper meaning) in this name. But he has no better explanation to offer, and the Chinese characters give us *ya-tsu mimi*, "eight ears." The author of the "*Tokiha-gusa*" ingeniously proposes to consider *ya-tsu mimi* as a corruption of *yatsuko mi mi* (奴御身) "[servant august body," but this cannot be seriously entertained (Conf. Sect. XIII, Note 18).

---

[SECT. XX.—THE AUGUST ANCESTORS OF THE DEITY-MASTER-OF-THE-GREAT LAND.]

Quare, quum incepit in thalamo [opus procreationis] cum Mirâ-Herâ-Inadâ, procreavit Deum nomine Eight-Island Ruler.[1] And again, having wedded the Divine-Princess-of-Great-Majesty,[2] daughter of the Deity Great-Mountain-Possessor, he begot children: the Great-Harvest Deity[3] and the August-Spirit-of-Food.[4] The elder brother the Deity Eight-Island-Ruler wedded Princess-Falling-Like-the-Flowers-of-the-Trees,[5] daughter of the Deity Great-Mountain-Possessor, and begot a child: the Deity Fuha-no-moji-Ku-nu-su-nu.[6] This Deity wedded Princess Hikaha,[7] daughter of the Deity Okami,[8] and begot a child: Water-Spoilt-Blossom-of-Fuka-buchi.[9] This Deity wedded the Deity Ame-no-tsudohe-chi-ne,[10] and begot a child: the Deity Great-Water-Master.[11] This Deity wedded the Deity Grand-Ears,[12] daughter of the Deity Funu-dzu-nu,[02] and begot a child: the Deity Heavenly-Brandishing-Prince-Lord.[14] This Deity wedded the Young-Princess-of-the-Small-Country,[15] daughter of the Great-Deity-of-the-Small-Country,[16] and begot a child: the

Deity Master-of-the-Great-Land,[17] another name for whom
is the Deity Great-Name-Possessor,[18] and another name
is the Deity-of-the-Reed-Plains,[19] and another name is the 68
Deity of Eight-Thousand-Spears,[20] and another name is
the Deity-Spirit-of-the-Living-Land.[21] In all there were
five names.[22]

---

1. *Ya-shima-zhi-nu-mi.* *Ya-shima* means "eight islands." The
syllables *zhi-nu-mi* are obscure, but the translator has little doubt "ruler"
fairly represents their import. Motowori takes *zhi* to be an apocopated
and *nigori*'ed form of *shiru,* "to rule," *nu* to be an apocopated form of
*nushi,* "master," and *mi* to be an apocopated form of the "Honorific
termination *mimi.* Tanigaha Shisei considers *zhimu* to stand for *shidzu-
muru,* "to govern," which comes to the same thing so far as the sense
is concerned.

2. *Kamu-oho-ichi-hime.* The rendering of *Oho-ichi* as "Great
Majesty" rests on a plausible conjecture of Hirata's, who proposes to
identify *ichi* with *idzu* (稜威). Motowori thinks that *Oho-ichi* should be
taken as the name of a place; but this seems less good.

3. *Oho-toshi-no-kami,* written 大年神, the obvious rendering of which
would be "great year." But the Japanese term *toshi* is believed to have
originally signified, not "year" in the abstract, but that which was produced each year, viz., the harvest (conf. *toru,* "to take").

4. *Uka-no-mi-tama.*

5. *Ko-no-hana-chiru-hime,* so called, says Motowori, because she
probably died young, as a blossom that falls from the tree. We might
however perhaps take the Verb *chiru* in a Causative sense, and consider
the name to signify "the Princess-Who-Causes-the-Flowers-of-the-Trees-to-
Fall. A sister of this goddess appears in the pretty legend narrated in
Sect. XXXVII under the parallel name of the Princess-Blossoming-Brilliantly-Like-the-Flowers-of-the-Trees. See Note 3 to that Sect.

6. *Fuha-ni-moji-ku-nu-su-nu-no-kami.* The import of this name is
quite uncertain. *Fuha* however seems to be the name of a place.

7. *"Hi-kaha-mime.* *Hi-kaha* (lit. "sun-river") is supposed to stand
for the name of a place in Musashi, which is however written "ice-river"
(冰河, and not 日河), the old Japanese words for "ice" and "sun"
being homonymous.

8. See Sect. VIII. (Note 9), where the name is given as *Kura okami.*

9. *Fuka-buchi-no-midzu-yare-hana.* If Fuka-buchi were sscertained tŏ be not, as is supposed, the name of a place, we should have to render it " deep pool," and the whole would mean in English " Water-Spoilt-Blossom-of-the-Deep-Pool."

10. *Ame-no-tsudohe-chi-ne-no-kami.* In this name nothing is clear but the first three syllables, which signify " heavenly." But if Mabuchi's conjecture as to the meaning of the rest were accepted, we should have to translate the whole by " Heavenly-Assembling-Town-Lady."

11. This is the meaning plausibly assigned by Motowori to the original *O-midzu-nu-no-kami.*

12. *Fute-mimi-no-kami*, plausibly conjectured by Tominobu to stand for *Futo-mimi*, etc., which gives the sense here adopted.

13. *Funu-dzu-nu-no-kami.* Motowori believes Funu to be the name of a place, and interprets the name to signify " Master of Funu." But this seems highly uncertain.

14. *Ame-no-fuyu-kinu-no-kami* (Motowori's reading) or *Ama-no*, etc. (Hirata's reading). The translation of the name follows Hirata's explanation, which is based on Motowori's, and according to which the characters 冬衣 (" winter garments ") in this text, and 葺根 read *Fuki-ne* in the " Chronicles," are merely phonetic, while the meaning is derived from a comparison of the sounds given by each. Though himself believing in the soundness of Hirata's conclusion, the translator must admit that it is not indisputable.

15. *Sasu-kuni-waka-hime*, or *Sashi-kuni*, etc. The former reading, which Hirata's adopts, seems best. The meaning of *sasu*, here rendered " small," is open to doubt.

16. *Sasu-kuni-oho-[no-]kami*, or *Sashi*, etc. The syllable *no* in the Japanese reading seems to be a superfluous addition of the modern commentators.

17. *Oho-kuni-nushi-nc-kami.*

17. *Oho-na-muji-no-kami*, to which Tominobu proposes to give the sense of " Great Hole-Possessor," in connection with the story of the mouse-hole in which he took refuge from the fire lit by the Impetuous-Male-Deity (*Susa-no-wo*) for his destruction (see Sect. XXIII). But the interpretation followed in the translation is the most likely as well as the orthodox one, this Deity being entitled the possessor of a Great Name or of Great Names on account of his renown in Japanese mythic story.

19. *Ashi-hara-shiko-wo-no-kami.* The " reed-plains " are doubtless put by metonymy for Japan.

20. *Yachi-hoko-no-kami.*

21. *Utsushi-kuni-tama-no-kami.* The name must be understood to mean " Spirit of the Land of the Living," and to be antithetical to that of one of his fathers-in-law, the Impetuous Male-Deity (*Susa-no-wo*) who became the god of Hades.

22. Or " he had five names."

---

[SECT. XXI—THE WHITE HARE OF INABA.]

So this Deity Master-of-the-Great-Land had eighty Deities his brethren ; but they all left the land to the Deity Master-of-the-Great-Land. The reason for their leaving it was this : Each of these eighty Deities had in his heart the wish to marry the Princess of Yakami[f] in Inaba,[2] and they went together to Inaba, putting their bag on [the back of] the Deity Great-Name-Possessor, whom they took with them as an attendant. Hereupon, when they arrived at Cape Keta,[3] [they found] a naked hare lying down. Then the eighty Deities spoke to the hare, saying : " What thou shouldest do is to bathe in the sea-water here, and lie on the slope of a high mountain exposed to the blowing of the wind." So the hare followed the instructions of the eighty Deities, and lay down. Then, as the sea-water dried, the skin of its body all split with the blowing of the wind, so that it lay weeping with pain. But the Deity Great-Name-Possessor, who came last of all, saw the hare, and said : " Why liest thou weeping ? " The hare replied, saying : " I was in the Island of Oki,[4] and wished to cross over to this land, but had no means of crossing over. For this reason 69 I deceived the crocodiles[5] of the sea, saying : ' Let you and me compete, and compute the numbers of our [res-pective] tribes. So do you go and fetch every member of your tribe, and make them all lie in a row across from this island to Cape Keta. Then I will tread on them, and count them as I run across. Hereby shall we know whether it or my tribe is the larger.' Upon my speaking thus, they were deceived and lay down in a row, and I trod on them and counted them as I came across, and was just about to get on land, when I said: 'You have been deceived by me.' As soon as I had finished speaking, the crocodile who lay the last of all seized me and stripped off all my clothing. As I was weeping and lamenting for this reason, the eighty Deities who went by before [thee] commanded and exhorted me, saying: 'Bathe in the salt water, and lie down exposed to the wind.' So, on my doing as they had instructed me, my whole body was hurt." Thereupon the Deity Great-Name-Possessor instructed the hare, saying: "Go quickly now to the river-mouth, wash thy body with the fresh water, then take the pollen of the sedges [growing] at the river-mouth, spread it about, and roll about upon it, whereupon thy body will certainly be restored to its original state."[6] So [the hare] did as it was instructed, and its body became as it had been originally. This was the White Hare of Inaba.[7] It is now called the Hare Deity. So the hare said to the Deity Great-Name-Pos-sessor: "These eighty Deities shall certainly not get the Princess of Yakami. Though thou bearest the bag, Thine Augustness shall obtain her."

---

1. *Yakami-hime.* The etymology is uncertain.

2. The name of a province not far from that of Idzumo. The word may possibly, as Motowori suggests, be derived from *ina-ba,* " rice-leaves."

3. *Kita-no-saki.* The etymology of the name seems uncertain. The meaning of the word *keta* is "the-beams of a roof, the yards of a sail." But perhaps *Keta* and *keta* may be nothing more than homonyms of independent origin.

4. Not far from the coast of Iduzmo and of Inaba.

5. See Translator's Introduction, p. xxxiii, Note 41.

6. Literally "to its original skin"; that is to say that its skin would again be covered with fur.

7; Motowori and Moribe agree in considering that the word "white" means "bare" in this place, and the latter in his Critique of the former's Commentary quotes examples which show that their view is probably correct.

---

## [SECT. XXII.—MOUNT TEMA.]

Thereupon the Princess of Yakami answered[1] the eighty Deities, saying: " I will not listen to your words. I mean to marry the " Deity Great-Name-Possessor." So the eighty Deities, being enraged, and wishing to slay the Deity Great-Name-Possessor, took counsel together, on arriving at the foot of Tema[2] in the land of Hahaki, and said [to him] : " On this mountain there is a red boar. So when we drive it down, do thou wait and catch it. If thou do not wait and catch it, we will certainly slay thee." Having [thus] spoken, they took fire, and burnt a large stone like unto a boar, and rolled it down. Then, as [they] drove it down and [he] caught it,[2] he got stuck to and burnt by the stone, and died. Thereupon Her Augustness his august parent[4] cried and lamented, and went up to Heaven, and entreated His Divine-Producing-Wondrous-Augustness,[5] who at once sent Princess Cockle-Shell[6] and Prince Clam[7] to bring him to life. Then Princess Cockle-Shell triturated and scorched[8] [her shell], and Princess Clam carried water and

smeared [him] as with mother's[9] milk, whereupon he
became a beautiful young man, and wandered off. Hereupon the eighty Deities, seeing [this], again deceived him,
71 taking him with them into the mountains, where they
cut down a large tree, inserted a wedge in the tree,[1J] and
made him stand in the middle, whereupon they took
away the wedge and tortured him to death.[11] Then on
Her Augustness his august parent again seeking him
with cries, she perceived him, and at once cleaving the
tree, took him out and brought him to life, and said to
him :[13]  " If  thou  remain  here,  thou  wilt  at  last  be
" destroyed by the eighty Deities." Then she sent him
swiftly off to the august place of the Deity Great-House-
Prince[13] in the land of Ki.[14] Then when the eighty
Deities searched and pursued till they came up to him,
and fixed their arrows [in their bows], he escaped by
dipping under the fork of a tree, and disappeared.

---

1. It must be understood that in the meantime they had arrived at
her dwelling and begun to court her.

2. Etymology unknown.

3. The text is here concise to obscurity, but yet there ought not to
be much doubt as to the author's intention.

4. The text has the character 祖, signifying properly " grand-parent,"
but frequently used in Archaic Japanese writings in the sense of " mother."
It is then read *oya*, which the English word " parent " exactly represents.

5. *Kami-musu-bi-no-mikoto.* See Sect. I, Note 6.

6. *Kisa-gahi-hime.* The *kiga-gahi* here mentioned is the modern
*aka-gahi*, a cockle, the *Arca inflata.*

7. *Umugi-hime.* The *umugi* here mentioned is the modern *hama-
guri*, a clam of the family *Mactridæ*, the *Cytherea Mereirix.*

8. The character used is 集, " collected," " gathered together." But
the combined authority of Mabuchi, Motowori and Hirata obliges us either
to consider it a copyist's error for 焦, " scorched," or else to believe that
in early time in Japan the two characters were used interchangeably.[

9. Or "nurse's." The meaning is that a paste like milk was made of the triturated and calcined shell mixed with water. There is in this passage a play upon words which it is impossible to reproduce in English, the Japanese term for "triturating," *kisage* (which the author has taken care to write phonetically) resembling the name of Princess *Kisa-gahi* (Cockle-Shell), while *omo*, "mother" or "nurse," similarly recalls that of Princess *Umugi* (Clam). Motowori traces the names of the shell-fish in question to this exploit of the two goddesses. We shall be justified in applying an inverse interpretation to the legend.

10. The original of this clause. 茹矢打立其木, or according to another reading 茹矢, etc. is a great crux to the native commentators, who can make sure neither of the exact sense nor of the Japanese reading of the first two characters, which seem to be ideographic for three others occurring immediately below, 氷目矢, which are themselves of doubtful import. An elaborate discussion of the question will be found in Hirata's "Exposition of the Ancient Histories," Vol. XVII, pp. 25-27. The general sense at all events is that here given.

11. The characters 拷殺也, here rendered "tortured him to death." are by the modern commentators read *uchi-koroshiki*, which simply means "killed [him]."

12. Literally "to her child."

13. *Oha-ya-biko-no-kami.* This Deity is identified with the Deity *I-dakeru* mentioned in the "Chronicle" as a son of *Susa-no-wo* (the "Impetuous-Male-Deity"), and as the introducer into the Island of Tsukushi in particular and into all the "Eight Great Islands" of Japan of the seeds of plants and trees. Motowori's note on this name in Vol. X, pp. 28-29, is worth consulting, though his idea of connecting the agricultural and arboricultural renown of the Deity bearing it with the name of the province of Ki is doubtless quite fanciful.

14. *I.e.*, "the land of tree" (木國). Later the character 木 was replaced by 紀, which in Sinico-Japanese has the same sound *ki*, while a second one, 伊, was added in order to conform to an edict of the Empress Gem-miyō (A. D. 713) to the effect that all names of places were to be written with two Chinese characters, as was usual in China and Korea. The second character in this case simply carried on the *i* sound with which the first ends, so that the name became *Kii*.

---

[SECT. XXIII.——THE NETHER-DISTANT-LAND.]

[The Deity Great-House-Prince spoke to him[1]] saying:
"Thou must set off to the Nether-Distant-Land where
72 dwells His Impetuous-Male-Augustness.     That   Great
Deity will certainly counsel thee." So on his obeying
her command and arriving at the august place[2] of His
Impetuous-Male-Augustness,   the   latter's   daughter   the
Forward-Princess[3] . came   out   and   saw   him,   and   they
exchanged glances and were married, and [she] went in
again, and told her father, saying: "A very beautiful
Deity has come." Then the Great Deity went out and
looked, and said: "This is the Ugly-Male-Deity-of-the-
Reed-Plain,"[4] and at once calling him in, made him
sleep in the snake-house. Hereupon his wife, Her Augustness the Forward-Princess, gave her husband a snake-
scarf,[5] saying: "When the snakes are about to bite
thee, drive them away "by waving this scarf thrice."
So, on his doing as she had instructed, the snakes became
quiet, so that he came forth after calm slumbers. Again
on the night of the next day [the Impetuous-Male-Deity]
put him into the centipede and wasp-house;[6] but as she
again gave him a centipede and wasp-scarf, and instructed
him as before, he came forth calmly. Again [the Im-
petuous-Male-Deity] shot a whizzing barb[7] into the
middle of a large moor, and sent him to fetch the arrow,
73 and, when he had entered the moor, at once set fire to
the moor all round. Thereupon, while he [stood] knowing no place of exit, a mouse[8] came and said: "The
inside is hollow-hollow; the outside is narrow-narrow."[9]
Owing to its speaking thus, he trod on the place, whereupon he fell in and hid himself, during which time the

fire burnt past. Then the mouse brought out in its
mouth and presented to him the whizzing barb. The
feathers of the arrow were brought in their mouths by
all the mouse's children. Hereupon his wife the Forward-
Princess came bearing mourning-implements,[10] and crying.
Her father the Great Deity, thinking that [the Deity-
Great-Name-Possessor] was already dead and done for,
went out and stood on the moor, whereupon [the Deity
Great-Name-Possessor] brought the arrow and presented
it to him, upon which [the Great Deity], taking him into
the house and calling him into an eight-foot spaced large
room,[11] made him take the lice off his ¦head. So, on
looking at the head [he saw that] there were many
centipedes [there]. ˙Thereupon, as his wife gave to her
husband berries of the *muku* tree[12] and red earth, he
chewed the berries to pieces, and spat them out with
the red earth which he held in his mouth, so that the
Great Deity believed him to be chewing up and spitting
out the centipedes, and, feeling fond [of him] in his
heart, fell asleep. Then [the Deity Great-Name-Possessor],
grasping the Great Deity's hair, tied it fast to the various
rafters of the house, and, blocking up the floor of the
house with a five hundred draught rock,[13] and taking his
wife the Forward Princess on his back, then carried off 74
the Great Deity's great life-sword[14] and life-bow-and-
arrows,[15] as also his heavenly speaking-lute, and ran out.
But the heavenly speaking-lute brushed against a tree,
and the earth resounded. So the Great Deity, who was
sleeping, started at the sound, and pulled down the house.
But while he was disentangling his hair which was tied
to the rafters, [the Deity Great-Name-Possessor[ fled a
long way. So then, pursuing after him to the Even Pass

of Hades,[17]. and gazing on him from afar, he called out
to the Deity Great-Name-Possessor, saying : "With the
great life-sword and the life-bow-and-arrows which thou
carriest, pursue thy half-brethren[18] till they crouch on the
august slopes of the passes,[19] and pursue them till they
are swept into the reaches of the rivers, and do thou,
wretch![20] become the Deity Master-of-the-Great-Land;[21]
and moreover, becoming the Deity Spirit-of-the-Living-
Land, and making my daughter the Forward-Princess thy
75 consort,[21] do thou make stout the temple-pillars at the
foot of Mount Uka[23] in the nethermost rock-bottom, and
make high the cross-beams to the Plain-of-High-Heaven,
and dwell [there], thou villain!"[24] So when, bearing the
great sword and bow, he pursued and scattered the eighty
Deities, he did pursue them till they crouched on the
august slope of every pass,[25] he did pursue them till
they were swept into every river, and then he began to
make the land.[26] Quamobrem Hera Yamaki, secundum
anterius pactum, [cum eo] in thalamo coivit.  So he
brought her with him ; but, fearing his consort the Forward Princess, she stuck into the fork of a tree the child
that she had borne, and went back.[27] So the child was
called by the name of the Tree-Fork-Deity,[28] and another
name was the Deity-of-August-Wells.[29]

---

1. Literally, " to the child." The words placed in brackets, and
which are not to be found in either of the early printed editions, are
supplied in accordance with a suggestion of Moribe's contained in his
Critique of Motowori's Commentary. Motowori himself had supplied the
words "Her Augustness his august parent spoke to him," which seem
less appropriate. It is true that one MS. is quoted by Motowori as
favouring his view ; but such authority is insufficient, and the mistake,
moreover, peculiarly easy for a copyist to make (*mi oya* for *oho-ya*).

2. *I.e.*, the Palace.

3. This is Motowori's view of the import of the original name *Suseri-bime*, which he connects with *susumu*, "to advance," "to press forward," and explains by reference to the bold, forward conduct of the young goddess.

4. One of the alternative names of this Deity, who is mostly mentioned by one of his other four designations, for a list of which see Sect. XX, (Notes 17 to 21).

5. *I.e.*, "a scarf by waving which he might keep off the snakes." Similarly the "centipede and wasp-scarf" mentioned a little farther on must be understood to mean "a scarf to ward off centipedes and wasps with."

6. The word *hachi*, translated "wasp," is a general name including other insects of the family of *Vespidæ*.

7. *I.e.*, "arrow." The original expression is *nari-kabura* (鳴鏑), which has survived in the modern language under the modified form of *kabura-ya*, defined in Dr. Hepburn's Dictionary as "an arrow with a head shaped like a turnip, having a hole in it, which causes it to hum as it flies." It was used in China in the time of the Han dynasty.

8. Or "rat."

9. The translator cannot think of any better English equivalents for the child-like onomatopoeias *hora-hora* and *subu-subu* of the Japanese original.

10. The edition of 1687 reads the two characters 喪貝 (here translated "mourning implements,") *mo-gari no sonahe*, *i.e.*, "preparations for the funeral." Such preparations are detailed in the latter part of Sect. XXXI.

11. This is Mabuchi's interpretation, as quoted by Motowori, of the expression *ya-ta-ma no oho-muro-ya*. Motowori's own view is that *ya-ta* stands for *ya-tzu*, which give us in English "an eight-spaced large room." The character 間, "space" has been in later times used as a measure of length (six Japanese feet.) Altogether the precise meaning of the expression is not quite clear, but the general sense is a "large spacious room."

12. *Aphananthe Aspera*, also sometimes called *Celtis Muku*.

13. *I.e.*, "a rock which it would require five hundred men to lift."

14. *Iku-tachi* (生大刀), supposed by Motowori to be "a sword having the virtue of conferring long life upon its possessor."

15. *Iku-yumi-ya* (生弓矢).

16. *Ame no nori-goto* (天詔琴), so called because, as will be seen in Sect. XCVI, divine messages were conveyed through a person playing

on the lute. Hirata, in his "Exposition of the Ancient Histories," invents the reading *ame no nu-goto* (天詔琴), "heavenly jewelled lute."

17. See Sect. IX, (Note 16).

18. They were not born of the same mother. The Chinese characters in the text (庶兄弟) imply, properly speaking, that the eighty brethren of the Great-Name-Possessor were the sons of concubines. But Motowori denies that such is the Japanese usage with regard to the characters in question.

19. Or "hills."

20. The word in the text is *ore*, an insulting equivalent Second Personal Pronoun. If we were translating into German, we might perhaps approximately represent its force by "*er.*"

21. Thus according to this legend, "Master-of-the-Great-Land" (*Oho-kuni-nushi*) was not the original name of the Deity commonly designated by it, and his sovereignty over the Land of the Living (whence the appropriateness of the second name in this context) was derived by investiture from the god of the Land of the Dead.

22. The characters 嫡妻, which are here used, designate specifically the chief or legitimate wife, as opposed to the lesser wives or concubines.

23. *Uka-no-yama*. No satisfactory etymology of *Uka* is forthcoming.

24. "*I.e.*, "Firmly planting in the rock the pillars forming the foundation of thy palace, and rearing its fabric to the skies, do thou rule therefrom the Land of the Living, thou powerful wretch, who hast so successfully braved me!"

25. Or "hill."

26. This is taken to mean that he continued the act of creation which had been] interrupted by the death of *Izanami* (the "Female-Who-Invites"). See Sect. IX, p. 35, where her husband Izanagi says to her: "The lands that I and thou made are not yet finished making." The words "*Kuni tsukuri* (國作), here used for "making the land," became a title for "Ruler-of-the-Land" and finally a "gentile name" (*kabane*).

27. *Q.d.*, to Inaba.

28. *Ki-no-mata-no-kami.*

29. *Mi-wi-no-kami.* He is supposed to have benefitted the country by digging wells in many places.

[SECT. XXIV.—THE WOOING OF THE DEITY-OF-EIGHT-THOUSAND-SPEARS.]

This Deity-of-Eight-Thousand-Spears,[1] when he went forth[2] to woo the Princess of Nuna-kaha,[3] in the land of Koshi, on arriving at the house of the Princess of Nuna-kaha sang, saying:

" [I] His Augustness the Deity-of-Eight Thousand-Spears, having been unable to find a spouse in the Land of the Eight Islands, and having heard that in the far-off Land of Koshi there is a wise maiden, having heard that there is a beauteous maiden, I am standing [here] to truly woo her, I am going backwards and forwards to woo her. Without having yet untied even the cord of my sword, without having yet untied even my veil, I push back the plank-door shut by the maiden; while I am standing [here], I pull it forward. While I am standing [here], the *nuye* sings upon the green mountain, and [the voice of] the true bird of the moor, the pheasant, resounds; the bird of the yard, the cock, crows. Oh! the pity that [the] birds should sing! Oh! these birds! Would that I could beat them till they were sick! Oh! swiftly-flying heaven-racing messenger, the tradition of the thing, too, this!"[4]

76

Then the Princess of Nuna-kaha, without yet opening the door, sang from the inside saying:—

77

" Thine Augustness the Deity-of-Eight-Thousand-Spears ! Being a maiden like a drooping
plant, my heart is just a bird on a
sand-bank by the shore ; it will now indeed
be a dotterel. Afterwards it will be a gentle
bird ; so as for thy life, do not deign to die.
Oh ! swiftly-flying heaven-racing messenger ! the tradition of the thing, too, this !"[5]

78                    [*Second Song of the Princess.*[6]]

" When the sun shall hide behind the green
mountains, in the night [black as] the
true jewels of the moor will I come forth.
Coming radiant with smiles like the morning sun, [thine] arms white as rope of
paper-mulberry-bark shall softly pat [my]
breast soft as the melting snow ; and patting [each other] interlaced, stretching out
and pillowing [ourselves] on [each other's]
jewel-arms,—true jewel-arms,—and with
outstretched legs, will we sleep. So speak
not too lovingly, Thine Augustness the
Deity-of-Eight-Thousand-Spears ! The tradition of the thing, too, this !"[7]

Quamobrem eâ nocte non coierunt, sed sequentis diei
nocte auguste coierunt.

---

1. In this Section, the Deity Master-of-the-Great-Land is spoken of
under this *alias*. See Sect. XX, Note 20).

2. The characters 幸行 here, in accordance with the reading of the
commentators, rendered by the words "went forth," as Honorific, being
only properly applied to the progresses of a sovereign.

3. *Nuna-kawa-hime. Nuna-kaha* or *Nu-na-kaha* ("lagoon-river") is
supposed to be the name of a place in the province of Echigo.

4. The drift of this poem needs but little elucidation :—After giving his reasons for coming to woo the Princess ot Nuna-kaha, the god declares that he is in such haste to penetrate to her chamber, that he does not even stay to ungird his sword or take off his veil, but tries to push or pull open the door at once. During these vain endeavours, the mountain-side begins to re-echo with the cries of the birds announcing the dawn, when lovers must slink away. Would that he could kill these unwelcome harbingers of day, and bring back the darkness !—The Land of the Eight Islands (*i.e.* Japan proper, beyond whose boundaries lay the barbarous northern country of Koshi) is in the original *Ya-shima-kuni* (Conf. Sect. V, Note 27).—The *nuye* is a bird which must be fabulous if most of the accounts given of it are accepted. The "Commentary on the Lyric Dramas" tells us (with variations) that "it has the head of a monkey, the body of a racoon-faced "dog, the tail of a serpent, and the hands (*sic*) and feet of a tiger," adding, as the reader will make no difficulty in allowing, that "it is a strange and peculiar creature." The *Wa-Kun Shiwori* says that "it is a bird much larger than a pigeon, and having a loud and mournful cry." It is likewise said to come out at night-time and retire during the day, for which reason doubtless Mabuchi likens it to the owl. A very ancient and curious Chinese book entitled the "Mountain and Sea Classic" (山海經), the modern editions of which contain extremely droll illustrations of fabulous creatures, tells us of a bird called the "white *nuye* (白鵺), which is "like a pheasant, with markings on its head, white wings, and yellow feet, and whose flesh is a certain cure for the hiccough." The character 發 and て, with which, as well as with ス, the word *nuye* is variously written, seem to be unauthorized— The line here (following Motowori and Moribe's view) rendered "Would that I could beat them till they were sick !" will also bear the interpretation formerly proposed by Keichiyu, "Would that I could beat them till they left off !"—The last five lines, here rendered "Oh ! swiftly-flying heaven-racing messenger," etc., are extremely obscure. It is possible that *ishi tafu ya* (rendered "Oh ! swiftly flying," in deference to Moto-wori's and Moribe's view) may be but a meaningless *refrain*. "Heaven-racing messenger" is tolerably certain. Of the rest it is not easy to make sense. Motowori proposes to credit the five lines in question with the following general meaning : "May this song, like a messenger, "run down to future ages, preserving for them the tradition of this event !" Moribe, in his Critique of Motowori's Commentary, supposes the lines in question to be an addition made by the official singers, who in later

times sang these songs as an accompaniment to dances. Whatever their origin and proper signification, it is plain that they had come to be used as a *refrain,* from which the first two lines were sometimes omitted, as we see in some of the songs further on.

5. The drift of the poem is this : " Being a tender maiden, my heart flutters like the birds on the sandy islets by the beach, and I cannot yet be thine. Yet do not die of despair ; for I will soon comply with thy desires."—The word *nuye-kusa* (here rendered " drooping plant," in accordance with the views of the commentators) is a Pillow-Word of somewhat obscure derivation.—The word *chidori* (rendered " dotterel" throughout this translation) denotes in its modern acceptation, according to Messrs. Blakiston and Pryer, " any kind of sandpiper, plover or dotterel." Its proper and original signification is, however, greatly debated by the commentators, and some think that it is not the specific name of any kind of bird, but stands simply by apocope for *tachi-dori,* " rising bird," thus designating any kind of small bird that rises and flies along near the beach.—The word *na-dori* (here, in accordance with Moribe's view, rendered " gentle bird") is taken by Motowori to mean simply " gentle," " compliant." But both the construction and the context seem to impose on us the interpretation here given. Keichiyu, in his 'Kōgan-Shō,' interprets the whole passage differently ; but in order to do so he, without sufficient authority, changes the readings of the text into *wa tori*, " my bird," and *na tori* " thy bird."—The *refrain* is the same as in the previous song.

6. There is no break in the text ; but the commentators rightly consider the following to be a separate poem.

7. The import of this very plain-spoken poem needs no elucidation.— *Nubatama* (here rendered " true jewels of the moor ") is the Pillow-Word for things black or related to darkness. The " true jewels of the moor " are supposed to be the jet-black berries of the *hiafugi* (pron. *hiōgi, Ixia chinensis*). The whole etymology is, however, not absolutely certain.—Of which of the two lovers the words "coming radiant " with " smiles " are spoken, is not clear ; but they probably refer to the male deity, as do the white arms, strange though such an expression may appear as applied to a man. The goddess represents herself and her lover as using each other's arms for pillows. The word " jewel-arms " means simply " beautiful arms."

[SECT. XXV.—THE CUP PLEDGE.]    79

Again this Deity's Chief Empress,[1] Her Augustness
the Forward-Princess, was very jealous. So the Deity
her husband, being distressed, was about to go up from
Idzumo to the Land of Yamato ; and as he stood attired,
with one august hand on the saddle of his august horse
and one august foot in the august stirrup, he sang,
saying :

> " When I take and attire myself so carefully
> in my august garments black as the true
> jewels of the moor, and, like the birds of
> the offing, look at my breast,—though I
> raise my fins, [I say that] these are not
> good, and cast them off on the waves on
> the beach. When I take and attire myself
> so carefully in my august garments green
> as the kingfisher, and, like the birds of the
> offing, look at my breast,—though I raise
> my fins, [I say that] these, too, are not
> good, and cast them off on the waves on
> the beach. When I take and attire myself
> so carefully in my raiment dyed in the sap
> of the dye-tree, the pounded madder sought
> in the mountain fields, and, like the birds
> of the offing, look at my breast,—though
> I raise my fins, [I say that] they are good.
> My dear young sister, Thine Augustness !
> Though thou say that thou wilt not weep,—
> if like the flocking birds, I flock and depart,
> if, like the led birds, I am led away and
> depart, thou wilt hang down thy head like

a single eulalia upon the mountain and thy
weeping shall indeed rise as the mist of
80      the morning shower. Thine Augustness
[my] spouse like the young herbs! The
tradition of the thing, too, this!"[2]

Then his Empress, taking a great august liquor-cup,
and drawing near and offering it to him, sang, saying:—

" Oh! Thine Augustness the Deity-of-Eight-
Thousand-Spears! [Thou], my [dear] Master-of-the-Great-Land indeed, being a man,
probably hast on the various island-head-
81      lands that thou seest, and on every beach-
headland that thou lookest on, a wife like
the young herbs. But as for me alas! being
a woman, I have no man except thee; I
have no spouse except thee. Beneath the
fluttering of the ornamented fence, beneath
the softness of the warm coverlet, beneath
the rustling of the cloth coverlet, [thine]
arms white as rope of paper-mulberry bark
softly patting [my] breast soft as the melting snow, and patting [each other] interlaced, stretching out and pillowing [our-
selves] on [each other's arms],—true jewel-
arms, and with outstretched legs, will we
sleep. Lift up the luxuriant august liquor!"[3]

She having thus sung, they at once pledged [each
other] by the cup with [their hands] on [each other's]
necks,[4] and are at rest till the present time. These are
called divine words.[5]

1. *I.e.*, chief wife.

2. The meaning of this poem is:—"I start for Yamato, there to search for a better wife, and I carefully array myself for the journey. Black,—the colour of mourning,—is not fair enough, and red is more beautiful than green; so it is on my red garments that my choice rests. And thou, jealous and imperious woman! for all that thou sayest that thou wilt not heed my going, thou wilt weep when I depart with my retainers as departs a flock of birds, and thou wilt bury thy head in thy hands, and thy tears shall be as the misty drops of the morning shower."—The words *hata tagi* (rendered in accordance with Motowori's view by " raise my fins ") are supposed to signify " raise my sleeve." If the last syllable were found in any text written with a character not requiring the use of the *nigori* in the Japancse transcription, we should get the more satisfactory reading *ha tataki*, i.e. " beat my wings ; " but the syllable in question does not seem to be anywhere so written:—The " madder " is in the original *akane*, here written (but doubtless only through the error of some copyist) *atane*. The words rendered "sought in the mountain fields " might also be translated " sown in the mountain fields," *magashi*, "sought," and *makishi*, "sowed " being thought to be convertible.—The words "my beloved" represent the Japanese *itokoya no*, whose meaning is obscure and much disputed.—The words "when I am led away " must be understood as if they were Active instead of Passive, signifying as they do " when I lead away my retinue of followers."—The eulalia (*Eulalia japonica*) is a long king of grass very often alluded to in the later classical poetry.—The words " on the mountain " represent the Japanese words *yama-to no*, in accordance with Motowori's and Hirata's view of the meaning of the latter (山處 or 山本). The *primá f..cie* interpretation of " in the province of Yamato," which Keichiyu adopts, will not bear investigation.—It is not quite clear whether "the mist of the morning shower " means mist separate from the rain, or is simply a phrase for the rain-drops themselves. Motowori adopts the former opinion.—" Young herbs," *waka-kusa*, is the Pillow-Word for "spouse,"—newly married youths and maidens being likened to the fresh-grown grass. The *refrain* is an abbreviated form of that found in the two previous poems.

3. The import of this poem needs little explanation :—The goddess says to her husband, " Come back and live with me, and quaff this goblet as a sign of reconciliation; for though thou, as a man, mayest have a wife on every shore, I shall be left solitary if thou depart."—

The "ornamented fence" is supposed to mean "a curtain round the sleeping place."—The latter part to the poem (excepting the concluding phrase) is a repetition of lines that have already occurred in the last one of Sect. XXIV (note 7). The word *tate-matsurase* (here rendered "lift up") occasions some difficulty. It properly signifies "present to a superior;" but here it must be taken to mean "partake of," as the goddess is speaking to her spouse himself, unless indeed we suppose the final words of the song to be a command addressed to one of her attendants to present the cup to their common lord and master.

4. This is the probable and generally accepted meaning of the original of this clause, which is written phonetically.

5. Explained by Moribe to mean, with reference to the whole story, "conversation about divine events." Motowori proposes to supplement the character 歌, "song," to the two (神語) in the text, and to take the three together as designating the nature of the preceding songs, in accordance with the usage in other cases,—"Rustic Songs," "Courtier's Songs," etc. If this view were adopted, we should have to translate by "Divine Converse Songs."

---

82    [SECT. XXVI.—THE DEITIES THE AUGUST DESCENDANTS
OF THE DEITY MASTER-OF-THE-GREAT-LAND.

So this Deity Master-of-the-Great-Land wedded Her Augustness Torrent-Mist-Princess, the Deity dwelling in the inner temple of Munakata,[1] and begot children: the Deity Aji-shiki-taka-hiko-ne,[2] next his younger sister Her Augustness High-Princess,[3] another name for whom is Her Augustness Princess Under-Shining.[4] This Deity Aji-shiki-taka-hiko-ne is he who is now called the Great August Deity of Kamo.[5] Again the Deity Master-of-the-Great-Land wedded Her Augustness Princess Divine-House·Shield[6] and begot a child: the Deity Thing-Sign-Master.[7] Again he wedded the Deity Bird-Ears,[8]
83 daughter of the Deity Eight-Island-Possessor, and begot

a child: the Deity Bird-Growing-Ears.[10] This Deity wedded Hina-teri'nakata'bichi'wo'ikochini[1],[1] and begot a child: the Deity Land-Great-Wealth.[02] This Deity wedded the Deity Ashi-nadaka,[13] another name for whom is Princess-Eight-Rivers-and-Inlets,[14] and begot a child: the Deity Swift-Awful-Brave-Sahaya-Land-Ruler.[15] This Deity wedded Princess Luck-Spirit,[16] daughter of the 84 Deity Heavenly-Awful-Master,[17] and begot a child: the Deity Awful-Master-Prince.[18] This Deity wedded Princess Hina-rashi,[19] daughter of the Deity Okami,[20] and begot a child: the Deity Tahiri-kishi-marumi.[21] This Deity wedded the Deity Princess-Life-Spirit-Luck-Spirit,[22] daughter of the Deity Waiting-to-See-the-Flowers-of-the-Holly,[23] and begot a child: the Deity Miro-na-mi.[24] This Deity wedded Princess Awo-numa-oshi,[25] daughter of the Master-of-Shiki-yama,[26] and begot a child: the Deity Nunoshi-tomi-tori-naru-mi.[27] This Deity wedded the Young-Day-Female-Deity,[29] and begot a child: the Deity Heavenly-Hibara-Great-Long-Wind-Wealth.[29] This Deity wedded 85 the Deity Toho-tsu-ma-chi-ne,[30] daughter of the Deity Heavenly'Pass Boundary,[31] and begot a child: the Deity Toho-tsu-yama-zaki-tarashi.[32]

From the above-mentioned Deity Eight-Island-Ruler down to the Deity Toho-tsu-yama-zaki-tarashi are called the Deities of seventeen generations.[33]

---

1. See Sect. XIII, Note 15 and Sect. XIV, Note 2.

2. *Aji-shiki taka-hiko-ne no-kami.* The meaning of the first two members of this compound name is altogether obscure. *Taka-hiko-ne* signifies "high-prince lord."

3. *Taka-hime-no-mikoto.* *Taka-hime* is supposed by Hirata to be a mutilated form of *Taka-teru-hime*, "High-Shining-Princess," which would make the two names of this personage properly complementary.

4. *Shita-teru-hime-no-mikoto.* This goddess is popularly supposed to have been extremely beautiful, whence perhaps the name, which might be taken to imply that her beauty shone forth from under her garments as in the case of *So-towori-hime* (see Sect. CXXXVII, Note 9).

5. Because there worshipped. The etymology of K<sub>1</sub>mo is not clear.

6. *Kamu-ya-tate-hime-no-mikoto.* The translation here follows the Chinese characters. Another proposal of Motowori's is to regard the syllables *ya-tate* as a corruption of *iya-taka-teri,* "more and more high shining," which would give us for the whole name in English "Divine-More-and-More-High-Shining-Princess."

7. *I.e.,* "the Deity who gave a sign of the thing he did." The Japanese original is *Koto-shiro-nushi-no-kami.* The translation of the name here given follows Motowori's interpretation, which takes it to contain an allusion to the act by which its bearer symbolized his surrender of the sovereignty of the land to the descendant of the Sun-Goddess. Lengthened forms of the name are *Ya-he-koto-shiro-nushi-no-kami* ("the Deity Eight-Fold-Thing-Sign-Master") and *Tsumi-ba-ya-he-koto-shiro-nushi-no-kami,* the first three syllables of which latter are obscure. Both of the lengthened forms are supposed to contain a reference to the manifold "green branches" mentioned in the legend referred to,—that, viz., which forms the subject-matter of Sect. XXXII.

8. *Tori-mimi-no-kami.* "Motowori suggests that *tori,* "bird," may be but the name of a place in Yamato."

*Ya-shima-muji-no-kami.* "Possessor" is the probable meaning of *muji,* regarded here and elsewhere as an alternative form of *mochi.* Motowori suggests that Yashima may be meant for the name of a district in Yamato, in which case both this god and his daughter would have been named from the places of their birth or residence, which are near each other in the same province.

10. *Tori-naru-mi-no-kami.* The above interpretation, which is proposed by Motowori, seems more acceptable than "Bird-Sounding-Sea," which the Chinese characters yield. *Tori* "bird," if taken above to be the name of a place, must be likewise so considered here.—Motowori reasonably conjectures that a clause to the following effect is here omitted: "He wedded such and such a princess, daughter "of such and such a Deity, and begot a child: the Deity *Take-mina-gata*" [i.e. probably Brave-August-Name-Firm] (See Sect. XXXII, Note 21). Hirata's text, in his "Exposition of the Ancient Histories," is 娶高志之沼河北賣命而令生給之子謂御穗須美命亦名健御名方神.

11. The text is here evidently corrupt, and Motowori proposes to read either *Hina-teri-nukata-bichi-wo-no-kami no musume Iko-chi-ni-no-kami,* which would give us in English "the Deity Ikochini, daughter of the male Deity Hina-teri-nukata-bichi," or else to take the whole as the father's name, and to suppose that the name of the daughter has been accidentally omitted. *Hina-teri* means "Rustic Illuminator," and the name resembles that of a deity mentioned in Sect. XIV, Note 6. *Nukata* and *Bichi* (or *Hiji,* reversing the position of the *nigori*) are supposed to be names of places. *Ikochini* is altogether obscure.

12. *Kuni-oshi-tomi-no-kami, oshi,* as in other instances, being considered a contraction of *ohoshi,* "great."

13. *Ashi-nakada-no-kami.* It is not clear whether this is a personal name or, as Motowori supposes, the name of the place where tha goddess resided. He quotes places named Ashidaka and Ashida; but this hardly seems satisfactory. In any case the name remains obscure.

14. *Ya-kaha-ye-hime.* The translation follows the meaning of the Chinese characters with which the name is written. It is, however, also open to us to consider *Yaka-ha-ye* as a corruption of *iya-ko-haye,* "more flourishing."

15. *Haya-mika-no-take sahaya-ji-nu-mi-no-kami.* The syllables *sahaya* are obscure, and Motowori's proposal to consider them as the name of a place has only been followed in the translation for want of something more satisfactory,

16. *Saki-tama-bime.*

17. *Ame-no-mika-nushi-no-kami.*

18. *uika-nushi-hiko-no kami.*

19. *Hina-rashi-bime.* Motowori takes Hina to be the name of a place, and *rashi,* to be an apocopated form of *tarashi* or some such word. But this is mere guess-work.

20. *Okami-no-kami.* See Sect. VIII, Note 9.

21. *Tahiri-kishi-marumi-no-kami.* The meaning of this name is quite obscure. Motowori throws out the suggestion that *Tahiri* may stand for *Tari-hiri* and *Kishi-marumi* for *Kizhima-tsu-mi,—Tarihi* and *Kizhiwa* being names of places, and *tsu-mi,* as usual, being credited with the signification of "possessor."

22. *Iku-tama-saki-tama-hime.*

23. *Hihira gi-no-sono-hana-madzu-mi-no-kami.* The interpretation of the name here given is conjectural as far as the words "waiting to see" (taken on Tominobu's authority to be the most likely meaning of *madzu-mi*)

are concerned. Motowori suggests that *hihira-gɩ-no* may be but a sort of Pillow-Word, and not part of the actual name at all, and the remaining characters corrupted. *Hihira-gi* rendered "holly," is properly the *Olea Aquifolia.*

24. *Miro-nami-no-kami.* Meaning obscure. *Miro* is supposed by Motowori to be the name of a place, and *na* and *mi* to be Honorific appellations.

35. *Awo-numa-nu-oshi-hime.* Meaning obscure.

26. *Shiki-yama-nushi-no-kami.* *Shiki-yama* is supposed to be the name of a place in Echizen.

27. *Nunoshi-tomi-tori-nara-mi-no-kami.* *Nunoshi* is supposed to be the name of a place, and identical with *Nunoshi*, which forms part of the mother's name. Motowori takes *tomi* to be an Honorific, and *Tori* (as previously in the case of the deities *Tori-mimi* and *Tori-naru-mi* (See Notes 8 and 10) to be the name of another place. The translator would prefer to take both words in their common signification, and (leaving *nunoshi* aside as incomprehensible) to render the rest of the name thus : "Wealth-Bird-Growing-Ears."

28. *Waka-hiru-me-na-kami.*

29. *Ame-no-hibara-oho-shi-na-domi-no-kami.* Motowori supposes Hibara to be the name of a place, a view which the translator has adopted for want of a better.

30. *Toho-tsu-ma-chi-ne-no-kami.* Motowori supposes Tohotsu to be the name of a place, and the remaining syllables to be Honorific.

32. *Toho-tsu-yama-zaki-tarashi-no-kami.* *Toho-tsu* (lit. "distant") and *yamazaki* ("mountain-cape" are both considered by Motowori to be names of places. *Tarashi* signifies "perfect" or "perfection." We might perhaps render the name thus : "Perfection-of-the-Distant-Mountain-Cape."

33. *I.e.* "seventeen generations of Deities." But the construction is curious. Motowori points out that there is here an error in the computation, as the text enumerates but fifteen generations. The names of the gods and goddess mentioned in this section offer unusual difficulties Motowori says that it is with hesitation that he proposes many of his interpretations, and it is with still greater hesitation that the translator has accepted them.

### SECT. XXVII.—THE LITTLE-PRINCE-THE-
### RENOWNED-DEITY.

So when the Deity Master-of-the-Great-Land dwelt at
the august cape of Miho[1] in Idzumo, there came riding
on the crest[2] of the waves in a boat of heavenly *Kagami*[3]
a Deity dressed in skins of geese[4] flayed with a complete 85
flaying, who, when asked his name, replied not ; moreover
the Deities who accompanied him, though asked, all said
that they knew not. Then the toad[5] spoke, saying :
"As for this, the Crumbling Prince[6] will surely know
it." Thereupon [the Deity Master - of - the - Great - Land]
summoned and asked the Crumbling-Prince, who replied.
saying : "This is the Little-Prince-the-Renowned-Deity,[7]
the august child of the Deity - Producing - Wondrous-
Deity."[8] So on their then respectfully informing[9] His
Augustness the Deity - Producing - Wondrous - August - Ancestor, he replied, saying : "This is truly my child.
He among my children is the child who dipped between
the fork of my hand.[10] So do he and thou become 87
brethren, and make and consolidate this land."[11] So
from that time forward the two Deities the Great-Name-
Possessor and the Little-Prince-the-Renowned-Deity made
and consolidated this land conjointly. But afterwards
the Little-Prince-the-Renowned-Deity crossed over to the
Eternal Land.[12] So [the Deity here] called the Crumbling
Prince, who revealed the Little-Prince-the-Renowned-Deity,
is what is now [called] the scarecrow in the mountain
fields. This Deity, though his legs do not walk, is a
Deity who knows everything in the Empire.[13]

---

1. Not to be confounded with the better known Miho in Suruga.
derivation of the name seems uncertain.

2. The character used is 穗, which properly denotes an ear of rice or other grain.

3. What plant the author intends by this name is not quite certain. The characters 薢茩 and 荄 are variously used to write it in the native work of reference, where also we learn that it probably corresponds to the plant known in different provinces of modern Japan as *chichi-gusa, tombo-no-chichi, kagarahi and gaga-imo,* We may best understand the *Ampelopsis serianæfolia* to have been intended, as the plant is described as having a berry three or four inches long shaped like a towel-gourd, (*hechima*), so that, if scooped out, it would fairly resemble a boat in miniature.

4. All the authorities are agreed in considering the character 鳫, "goose," to be a copyist's error; but there is no agreement as to the character which should be substituted for it. Hirata reads 鶺, "wren," changing the phonetic. "Wren" also is the reading in "One account" of the "Chronicles," and Moribe, commenting thereon in his "*Idzu no Chi-Waki*," thinks that "wren" must have been the bird originally intended by the framers of the tradition. Motowori, following a suggestion of the editor of 1687, prefers to consider the radical for "bird" to have been put by mistake for the radical for "insect," and reads 蛾 which signifies "moth," especially the "silkworm moth." Motowori, however, proceeds to give to the character in question the Japanese reading of *hi mushi* (lit. "fire-insect," i.e. "ephemera"), which is not warranted. The proper Japanese reading is *hihiru.* The best would seem to be to adopt the reading 蛾 "moth."

5. The original word is *tani-guku.* Its derivation and the name of the species which it denoted are alike unknown. Indeed we might equally well translate by "frog."

6. *Kuye-biko.* The interpretation of the name here adopted is Motowori's. Tominobu takes *Kuye* to be the name of a place, and the personage in question to have been the inventor of scarecrows, whence the tradition connected with his name.

7. *Sukuna-biko-na-no-kami,* or without the *nigori, Sukuna-hiko-na-no-kami.* The interpretation of the name here followed is that proposed by Motowori, but not followed by Hirata and Moribe, who prefer to consider it antithetical to that of *Oho-na-muji,* "the Great-name-Possessor."

8. First mentioned in Sect. 1, Note 6. Immediately below, his name is given in the lengthened form.

9. Motowori (who, strange to say, is followed by Hirata, - conf. Sect. XVIII, Note 18) interprets the two characters 白上 (here in accordance

with general usage taken to signify "respectfully informed") as "informed and took up," thus making it appear that the diminutive deity was
personally taken up to Heaven. Surely a recollection of the parallel
passage in the "Chronicles," which says that "a messenger was sent up
to inform the Heavenly Deities," should have preserved the commentators
from thus offending against both grammar and common sense.

10. *I.e.*, "slipped away between my fingers." In the legend as
given in the "Chronicles," the father explains more particularly that the
Little-Prince-the-Renowned-Deity had been a bad boy who ran away.

11. For an explanation of this expression see Sect. XXIII, Note 26.

12. *Toko-yo-no-kuai* (常世國). Some kind of Paradise or Hades is
meant, as is proved by innumerable references in the early literature of
Japan: and we may suppose the idea to have been borrowed from the
Chinese or through them from Buddhism, and to have been afterwards
vaguely located in some distant country. In Sect. LXXIV we are told
of the orange having been brought from the "Eternal Land" by Tajima-
mori, who is said to have been of Korean extraction. Korea, which is to
the west of Japan, and the Buddhist paradise in the west might well he
confounded by tradition, though it is equally open to discussion whether
Southern China or even the Loochoo Islands might not have been thus
vaguely designated. In any case it was a distant place, imperfectly known,
though specifically named. In the "Chronicles," Tajima-mori is made to
say that it is "the retreat of Gods and Fairies, and not to be reached by
common men."—Motowori's immense note on this word (see Vol. XXI,
pp. 10-13 of his Commentary) is a specimen of the specious
arguments by which he endeavours to ward off from the Early
Japanese the imputation of ever having borrowed any ideas from their
neighbours. He would have us believe that *Toko-yo* is derived from *soko
yori*, "thence" (!) and that the name simply denotes foreign countries in
general. This is on a par with the opinion emitted by Arawi Hakuseki
in his "*Ko-shi Tsū*," to the effect that the "Eternal Land" was simply
a place in the province of Hitachi. The latter good old commentator
apparently founded himself on no better reasons than his general rejec-
tion of supernatural or otherwise perplexing details, and the fact that one
of the characters with which the name of the province in question
written is 常, which also forms part of the name of *Toko-yo-no-kuni.*

13. Literally "everything beneath Heaven." "Beneath Heaven" (天
下), i.e. "all that is beneath the Heavens," is a common Chinese phrase
for the Chinese Empire, which was in ancient days not unnaturally

supposed by its inhabitants to form the whole civilized world. The expression was borrowed by the Japanese to designate their own country. But its use by them had not the same plea of ignorance of other civilized l ands, as they were acquainted with China and Korea, and had hence obtained nearly all the arts of life.

---

88 [SECT. XXVIII.—THE AUGUST-LUCK-SPIRIT-THE-AUGUST-
WONDROUS-SPIRIT.][1]

Thereupon the Deity Master-of-the-Great-Land lamented himself, and said : "How shall I alone be able to make this land ?[2] Together with what Deity can I make this land?" At this time there came a Deity illuminating the sea. This Deity said : "If thou wilt lay me to rest[3] well, I can make it together with thee. If not, the land cannot be made." Then the Deity Master-of-the-Great-Land said : "If that be so, what is the manner of reverently laying thee to rest ?" He replied, saying : "Reverently worship me on Yamato's green fence, the eastern mountain's top."[4] This is the Deity who dwells on the top of Mount Mimoro.[5]

---

1. In the " Chronicles," this is given as the designation of the Deity who came over the sea, aad Motowori therefore adopts it as the heading of this Section.

2, For an explanation|of this expression see Sect. XXIII, Note 26.

3. *I.e.* "if thou wilt build me a temple." The original might also be rendered "if thou wilt worship before me," or "at my shrine," or "if thou wilt establish a temple to me."

4. *I.e,* on Mount Mimoro which stands as a protecting fence in the eastern part of the province of Yamato. *Awo-kaki-yama,* "green fence mountain," became a proper name used alternatively for Mount Mimoro (or, according to the later pronunciation, Mimuro). In like manner *Himukashi-yama* (in the later language *Higashi-yama*) "eastern mountain," has by some been considered to be a proper name.

5. *I.e.* "august house;" so called probably from the temple of the deity.

[SECT. XXIX.—THE AUGUST CHILDREN OF THE GREAT-
HARVEST-DEITY AND OF THE SWIFT-
MOUNTAIN-DEITY.]

So the Great-Harvest-Deity wedded the Princess [ of ? ]
Inu,[1] daughter of the Divine-Life-Producing-Wondrous-
Deity,[2] and begot children: the Deity August-Spirit-of- 8
the-Great-Land;[3] next the Deity of Kara;[4] next the Deity
Sohori;[5] next the Deity White-Sun;[6] next the Sage-Deity.[7]
(Five Deities[8]). Again he wedded the Refulgent-Princess,[9]
and begot children: the Deity Great-Refulgent-Mountain-
Dwelling-Grandee,[10] next the August-Harvest-Deity.[11]
Again he wedded Princess Ame-shiru-karu-midzu,[12] and
begot children: the Deity Oki-tsu-hiko,[13] next Her
Augustness Oki-tsu-hime,[14] another name for whom is 90
the Deity Great Furnace-Princess[15]—this is the Deity
of the Furnace[16] held in reverence by all people—next
the Deity Great-Mountain-Integrator,[17] another name for
whom is the Deity-Great-Master-of-the-Mountain-End:[18]
this Deity dwells on Mount Hiye[19] in the land of Chika-
tsu-Afumi,[20] and is likewise the Deity dwelling at Matsu-
no-wo[21] in Kadzunu,[22] who uses the whizzing barb.[23]
Next the Deity-of-the-Fire-in-the-Yard;[24] next the Deity
Asahi;[26] next the Deity Hahigi;[25] next the Deity 91
Refulgent-Mountain-Dwelling-Grandee;[27] next the Deity
Swift-Mountain-Dwelling;[28] next the High Deity-of-the-
Fire-in-the-Yard;[29] next the Great-Earth-Deity,[30] another
name for whom is the Deity August-Ancestor-of-Earth.[31]
(Nine Deities.[32])

In the above paragraph the children of the Great- 92
Harvest-Deity, from the Deity August-Spirit-of-the-
Great-Land down to the Great-Earth-Deity, are
altogether sixteen Deities.

The Deity Swift-Mountain-Dwelling[33] wedded the Deity
Princess-of-Great-Food,[34] and begot children : the Deity
Young - Mountain - Integrator ; [35]   next  the  Young - Harvest-
Deity ; [36]  next  his  younger  sister  the  Young-Rice-Trans-
planting - Female - Deity, ;[37]  next   the   Water - Sprinkling-
Deity ; [38]  next  the  Deity - of - the - High - Sun - of - Summer,[39]
another name for whom is the Female-Deity-of-Summer ;[40]
next  the  Autumn - Princess ;[41]  next   the   Deity   Stem-
Harvest ;[42]  next  the  Deity  Lord-Stem-Tree-Young-House-
Rope.[43]

In the above paragraph the children of the Deity
Swift-Mountain-Dwelling, from the Deity Young-
Mountain-Integrator down to the Deity Lord-Young-
House-Rope,[44] are altogether eight Deities.

---

1. *Inu-hime.* Motowori supposes *Inu* to be the name of a place.
The word properly signifies " dog."

2. *Kamu-iku-musu-bi-no-kami.*

3. *Oho-kuni-mi-tama-no-kami.*

4. *Kara-no-kami,* 韓神. *Kara* signifies Korea and China, and the
Deity thus named appears in the "Chronicle" under the name of *I-so-
takeru* ("Fifty-fold-Valiant), of whom it is related that he was taken
over to Korea by his father *Susa-no-wo* (the "Impetuous-Male).

5. *Sohori-no-kami.* The etymology is not clecr. Hirata derives the
name from a Verb *soru,* "to ride," "to go in a boat," in connection
with the story (mentioned in the preceding note) of I-so-takeru having
been taken over to Korea. According to this view, *Sohori,* like *Kara-
no-kami,* would be an alternative name of *I-so-takeru.* But the derivation
is hazardous, to say the least.

6. *Shira-hi-no-kami.* Motowori supposes *shira hi* (白日) to be a
copyist's error for *makahi* (向日). The latter, however, does not make
satisfactory sense, and Tomonobu proposes to invert the characters, thus :
日向, which means " sun-confronting." Motowori suggests that the word
tmay, after all, be but the name of a place.

7. *Hizhiri-no-kami,* written with the characters 聖神. The first of
hese is defined as signifying him who is intuitively wise and good, i.e.

the perfect sage. But perhaps we should in Archaic Japanese take the term *hizhiri* in what is its probable native etymological sense, viz. "sun-governing" (*hizhiri*, 日知), a title properly applied to the Japanese Emperors as descendants of the Sun-God, and of which the character 聖, which is used of the Chinese Monarchs, is only an equivalent in so far as it, too, is employed as an Honorific title.

8. Viz. from the August-Spirit-of-the-Great-Land to the Sage-Deity inclusive.

9. *Kagaya-hime.*

10. *Oho-kaga-yama-to-omi-no-kami.* The translation follows Hirata's interpretation, which nearly agrees with that proposed by Mabuchi.

11. *Mi-toshi-no-kami.* For the meaning of "harvest" attributed to the word *toshi* see Sect. XX, Note 3.

12. *Ame-shiru-karu-midzu-hime.* The name might tentatively be translated thus : Heaven-Governing-Fresh-Princess-of-Karu. Motowori suggests that *amerishiru* may be but a sort of Pillow-Word for the rest of the name. *Ama-tobu* is, however, the only Pillow-word for Karu found in the poems. After all, Karu may not here be the name of a place at all.

13. *Oki-tsu-hiko-no-kami.* The translator ventures to think that the names of this deity and the next might simply be rendered (in accordance with the first character, 奥, entering into their composing) "Inner Prince" and "Inner Princess" or "Prince of the Interior" and "Princess of the Interior." Motowor however suggests that *Okitsu* may be the name of a place, while Hirata derives the names from *oki-tsuchi*, "laid earth," finding therein a reference to the furnace (made of clay) mentioned immediately below.

14. *Oki-tsu-hime-no-mikoto.*

15. *Oho-be-hime-no-kami.*

16. *Kama-no-kami* (竈神). The "furnace" means the "kitchen." Neither Motowori nor Hirata informs us that the immense popularity of this Goddess, as well as her name, can clearly be traced to China.

17. *Oho-yama-kuni-no-kami.* The meaning of *kuhi*, here (as in the case of *Tsumu-guhi* and *Iku-guhi* (see Sect. II, Note 4) rendered by the word "interior," is open to doubt.

18. *Yama-suwe-no-oko-mushi-no-kami.* Motowori supposes the word *suwe*, "end," to have the signification of "top."

19. As it stands, the etymology of this name is not clear. In later times the mountain was called *Hiyei* (比叡). But whether the, to outward appearance, native *Hiye* is but a corruption of this Chinese one, or

whether it be true that the latter (on this hypothesis bestowed on account of its likeness in sound to the native designation) was not used till the end of the eighth or beginning of the ninth century, as is commonly stated, is difficult to decide.

20. *I.e.* "Close-Fresh-Sea." *Afumi* (modern pron. *Omi*, for *aha-umi*) alone signifies "fresh sea," *i e.* "lake." This province contains the large lake commonly known as Lake Biha (Biwa), but anciently simply called "the Fresh Sea," as being the lake *par excellence* of Japan. When one of the eastern provinces received, on account of a large lagoon or inlet which it contains, the name of *Toho-tsu-Afumi* (in modern pronunciation *Tō-tōmi*), *i.e.* "Distant-Fresh-Sea," the epithet Close was prefixed to the name of the province nearer to the ancient centre of government.

21. *I.e.* Pine-tree-Declivity.

22. *I.e.* Pueraria-Moor.

33. This passage (用鴨鏑神者也) must be corrupt. Mabuchi proposes to insert the character 祭 before 神, and to understand the author to have meant to tell us that the deity was worshipped with arrows, that is to say, that arrows were offered at his shrine. Motowori's proposal to consider 用 as an error for 成 or 化, and to interpret the clause thus: "the Deity who was changed into an arrow" is also worthy of notice. But a further suggestion of his to read 丹 for 用 and to interpret thus: "the Deity of the Red Arrow." seems best of all when taken in connection with the tradition, which he quotes from the "Topography of Yamashiro," to the effect that this god took the shape of a red arrow to gain access to his mistress *Tama-yori hime*, such a transformation being one of the common-places of Japanese myth.

24. *Niha-tsu-hi-nc-kami.* The interpretation of this name here adopted is not Motowori's, who takes *hi* in the sense of "wondrous," but Hirata's. The latter author makes it clear that this deity (for whom *Niha-taka-tsu-hi-no-kami*, i.e. "The High-Deity-of-the-Fire-in-the-Yard," is but a slightly amplified designation) was none other than the above-mentioned Deity of the Kitchen, and his name an inclusive one for the pair of deities *Oki-tsu-hiko* and *Oki-tsu-hime.*

25. *Asuha-ho-kami.* The signification of this name is obscure, and Motowori's proposal to derive it from *ashi-niha*, "foot-place," because the god in question may be supposed to protect the place on which people stand, is not altogether convincing. In fact he himself only advances it with hesitation. It should be added, however, that Hirata stamps it with his special approval, as he does also Motowori's derivation of the following name, *Hahigi.*

26. *Hahi-gino-kami*. Obscure, but ingeniously derived by Motowori from *hachi-iri-gimi*, i.e. "entering prince," the deity in question being supposed to have been the special protcetor of the entrances to houses, and to have thence received his name. Mr. Satow has translated it in the Rituals as "Entrance Limit."

27. *Kaga-yama-to-omi-no-kami*. The name is almost identical with that in Note 10.

28. *Ha-yama-to-no-kami*. The interpretation of the name is that proposed by Motowori, and which seems tolerably satisfactory.

29. *Niha-taka-tsu-hi-no kami*. See note 24.

30. *Oho-tsuchi-no-kami*.

31. *Tsuchi-no-mi-oya-kami*.

32. This number is obtained if (as is perhaps permissible from a Japanese point of view) we consider *Oki-tsu-hiko* and *Oki-tsu-hime* as forming a single deity. Otherwise there are ten. A similar remark applies to the number sixteen mentioned immediately below.

33. See Note 28.

34. See Sect. V, Note 8. The fact that this goddess is related to have been previously killed (see Sect. XVII) causes Motowori some embarassmeut.

35. *Waka-yama-kuhi-no-kami*.

36. *Waka-toshi-no-kami*. Motowori proposes (considering this name in connection with the four that follow) to take *waka-toshi* in this place in the signification of the "the first sprouting" of the young rice. The five deities whose birth is here mentioned seem collectively to represent the natural succession of agricultural operations throughout the year.

37. *Waka-sa-name-no-kami*.

38. *Midzu-maki-no-kami*.

39. *Natsu-taka-tsu-hi-no-kami*. Motowori's interpretation of *hi* as "wondrous" is perhaps as good as that here adopted, according to which it signifies "sun." His view would give us in English "the Summer-High-Wondrous-Deity."

40. *Natsu-no-me-no-kami*.

41. *Aki-bime no-kami*.

42. *Kuku-toshi-no-kami*. The word *kuku*, "stem," seems to allude to the length of the well-grown rice.

43. *Kuku-ki-waka-muro-tsunane-no-kami.* Motowori supposes this god to have been the protector of houses, and interprets the name to denote the beams, and the ropes with which the beams were bound together. The word here read *tsuna*, "rope;" is written with the character, and might perhaps be rendered "pueraria." But as in early times the tendrils of such creeping plants formed the only substitute for rope, the two renderings come to have very nearly the same signification.

44. The name is here abbreviated in the original to *Waka-muro-tsuna-ne no-kami.*

---

93            [SECT. XXX.—THE AUGUST DELIBERATION FOR
                         PACIFYING THE LAND.]

The Heaven-Shining-Great-August-Deity commanded, saying : "The Luxuriant-Reed-Plains-the-Land-of-Fresh. Rice-ears-of-a-Thous-and-Autumns, — of Long-Five-Hund, red-Autumns[1] is the land which my august child His Augustness Truly - Conqueror-I-Conquer - Conquering - Swift-Heavenly-Great-Great-Ears[2] shall govern." Having [thus] deigned to charge him, she sent him down from Heaven.[3] Hereupon His Augustness Heavenly - Great - Great - Ears, standing on the Floating Bridge of Heaven,[4] said: " The Luxuriant - Reed - Plains - the - Land - of - Fresh - Rice-ears-of-a-Thousand-Autumns, — of Long-Five-Hundred-Autumns is painfully uproarious,—it is."[5] With this announcement, he immediately re-ascended, and informed the Heaven-Shining - Great - August - Deity. Then the High - August-Producing - Wondrous - Deity[6] and the Heaven - Shining-Great-August-Deity commanded the eight hundred myriad Deities to assemble in a divine assembly in the bed of the Tranquil River of Heaven,[7] and caused the Deity Thought-Includer[8] to think [of a plan], and said :[9] " This Central Land of Reed-Plains is the land with which we have deigned to charge our august child as the land which he shall govern. So as he deems that violent and savage Earthly Deities[10] are numerous in this land, 69 which Deity shall we send to subdue them?" Then the Deity Thought-Includer and likewise the eight hundred myriad Deities took counsel and said: "The Deity Ame-no-ho-hi[11] is the one that should be sent." So they sent the Deity Ame-no-ho-hi; but he at once curried favour with the Deity Master-of-the-Great-Land, and for three years brought back no report.

---

1. *Toyo - ashi - hara - no - chi-aki-no-naga-i-ho-aki-no-midzu-ho-no-kuni*, i.e., freely rendered, " ever fruitful Japan with its reed-covered plains and its luxuriant rice-fields."

2, See Sect. XIII, Note 18. Henceforward this tremendous name is mostly abbreviated to *Ame-no-oshi-ho-mimi* (probably signifying " Heavenly-Great-Great-Ears.")

3. So in the original. The sense, however, is rather "told him to descend from Heaven;" for he did not actually go further than the top of the "Floating Bridge," and never came down to earth.

4. See Sect. III, Note 3.

5. The words "it is" stand for *ari keri* in the original. *Conf.* Sect. X, Note 1.

6. *Taka-mi-musu-bi-no-kami*, first mentioned at the very commencement of the work. In this legend this god's name is constantly coupled with that of the Sun-Goddess, who alone, up to this point, had appeared as the ruler of Heaven.

7. See Sect. XIII, Note 12.

8. See Sect. XVI, Note 7.

6. The meaning must be, as Motowori suggests, that the story was told first, and the Deity Thought-Includer asked for his advice after he had heard it.

10. See Sect. I, Note 11.

11. See Sect. XIII, Note 19.

[SECT. XXXI.—THE HEAVENLY-YOUNG-PRINCE.]

Therefore the High-August-Producing-Wondrous-Deity and the Heaven-Shining-Great-August-Deity again asked all the Deities, saying. "The Deity Ame-no-ho-hi, whom we sent down to the Central Land of Reed-Plains, is long of bringing back a report.[1] Which Deity were it best to send on a fresh mission?"[2] Then the Deity Thought-Includer replied, saying: "The Heavenly-Young-Prince,[3] son of the Deity Heaven's-Earth-Spirit[4] should be sent." So they bestowed on him the Heavenly feathered arrows,[5] and sent him. Thereupon the Heavenly-Young-Prince, descending to that land, at once wedded Princess Under-Shining,[6] daughter of the Deity Master-of-the-Great-Land,[7] and moreover, planning how he might gain [possession of] the land, for eight years brought back no report. So then the High-August-Producing-Wondrous-Deity and the Heaven-Shining-Great-August-Deity again asked all the Deities, [saying]: "The Heavenly-Young-Prince is long of bringing back a report.[8] Which Deity shall we send on a fresh mission to enquire the cause of the Heavenly-Young-Prince's long tarrying?" Thereupon all the Deities and likewise the Deity Thought-Includer replied, saying: "The pheasant the Name-Crying-Female[9] should be sent," upon which [the High-August-Producing-Wondrous-Deity and the Heaven-Shining-Great-August-Deity] charged [the pheasant], saying: "What thou shalt go and ask the Heavenly-Young-Prince is this: 'The reason for which thou wast sent to the Central Land of Reed-Plains was to subdue and pacify the savage Deities of that land. Why for eight years bringest thou back no report?'" So then the Crying-

Female, descending from Heaven, and perching on the
multitudinous [-ly-branching] cassia-tree[10] at the Heavenly-
Young-Prince's gate, told him everything according to the
mandate of the Heavenly Deities. Then the Heavenly-
Spying-Woman,[11] having heard the bird's words, spoke
to the Heavenly-Young-Prince, saying : "The sound of
this bird's cry is very bad. So thou shouldest shoot it
to earth." On her [thus] urging him, the Heavenly-
Young-Prince at once took the heavenly vegetable wax- 96
tree bow and the heavenly deer-arrows bestowed on him
by the Heavenly Deities, and shot the pheasant to death.
Then the arrow, being shot up upside down[12] through
the pheasant's breast, reached the august place where
the Heaven-Shining-Great-August-Deity and the High-
Integrating-Deity[18] were sitting in the bed of the Tranquil
River of Heaven. This "High-Integrating-Deity" is
another name for the High-August-Producing-Wondrous-
Deity. So, on the High-Integrating-Deity taking up the
arrow and looking at it [he saw that] there was blood
adhering to the feathers of the arrow. Thereupon the
High-Integrating-Deity, saying : "This arrow is the
arrow that was bestowed on the Heavenly-Young-Prince,"
showed it to all the Deities, and said : "If this be an
arrow shot at the evil Deities by the Heavenly-Young-
Prince in obedience to our command, let it not hit him.
If he has a foul heart, let the Heavenly-Young-Prince
perish[14] by this arrow." With these words, the took the
arrow and thrust it back down through the arrow's hole,[15]
so that it hit the Heavenly-Young-Prince on the top of his
breast[16] as he was sleeping on his couch, so that he died.
(This is the origin of [the saying] Beware of a returning arrow.'[17])
Moreover the pheasant returned not. So this is the 97

origin of the modern proverb which speaks of ' the
pheasant as sole messenger.'[18]   So the sound of the
wailings of the Heavenly-Young-Prince's wife Princess
Under-Shining, re-echoing in the wind, reached Heaven.
So the Heavenly-Young-Prince's father, the Deity Heaven's-Earth-Spirit, and his wife and children[09] who were
in heaven, hearing it, came down with cries and lamentations, and at once built a mourning-house there,[20] and
made the wild goose of the river[20] the head-hanging
bearer,[22] the heron the broom-bearer, the kingfisher the
person of the august food, the sparrow the pounding-
98 woman,[20] the pheasant the weeping woman ; and, having
thus arranged matters, they disported themselves[24] for
eight days and eight nights, At this time the Deity
Ajishiki-taka-hiko-ne[25] came and condoled on the mourning for the Heavenly-Young-Prince, whereupon the
Heavenly-Young-Prince's father and wife who had come
down from Heaven bewailed themselves,[23] saying :  " My
child is not dead, no ! My lord is not dead, no !" and
with these words clung to his hands and feet, and
bewailed themselves and lamented. The cause of their
mistake was that the two Deities closely resembled each
other in countenance : so therefore they made the mistake.
Thereupon the Deity Ajishi-ki-taka-hiko-ne was very
angry, and said :  " It was only because he was my dear
friend that I came to condole. Why should I be likened
to an unclean dead person ?"—and with these words he
drew the ten-grasp sabre[27] that was augustly girded on
him, and cut down the mourning-house, and kicked away
[the pieces] with his feet. This was on what is called
Mount Mourning[23] at the source of the River Awimi[29] in
the land of Minu.[30] The great sword with which he cut

[the mourning-house to pieces] was called by the name of Great-Blade-Mower,[00] another name by which it was called being the Divine-Keen-Sabre.[32] So when the 99 Deity Aji-shiki-toba-hiko-ne flew away in his anger, his younger sister Her Augustness the High-Princess in order to reveal his august name, sang, saying :

" Oh ! 'tis the Deity Aji-shiki-Taka-Hiko-Ne traversing two august valleys with the refulgence of august assembled hole-jewels, of the august assembled jewels worn round her neck by the Weaving Maiden in Heaven !"[83]

This Song is of a Rustic Style.[34]

1. Literally, " long brings back no report."
2. Literally, " to send again." The same expression occurs below.
3. *Ame-waka-hiko.* All the commentators agree that it is in order to express disapprobation of this god's wickedness that the title of Deity or Augustness is never coupled with his name.
4. *Ama-tsu-kuni-tama-no-kami.*
5. *Ame-no-koko-yumi* and *ame-no-haha-ya.* In Sect. XXXIV these weapons are mentioned under the slightly altered names of *ama-no-hazhi-yumi* (" heavenly vegetable wax-tree bow ") and *ama no-kaku-ya* (" heavenly deer-arrows.") A large bow made of vegetable wax-tree (*Rhus succedanea*) wood, and arrows with broad feathers, are supposed to be intended.
6. *Shita-teru-hime.* See Sect. XXVI, Note 4.
7. *Oho-kuni-nushi-no-kami.* See Sect. XX, Note 17.
8. Literally, " long brings back no report."
9. *Na-naki-me.* If the view here taken of the meaning of the Japanese expression be correct (it is that preferred by Motowori and Hirata), the pheasant would seem to have been supposed to cry out its own name,—in Archaic Japanese *kigishi.* The syllables *na naki me*, however, lend themselves equally well to the interpretation of " nameless female," and are in the " Chronicles " found written with characters having that signification. Another reasonable opinion is that the name should be connected with the tradition mentioned further on of the

pheasant having been the mourner (lit. "crying female," *naki-me*) at the funeral of the Heavenly-Young-Prince. In this case the word *na*, "name," would have to be considered redundant, and it will be observed thar, the next time the name is mentioned, we find simply *naki-me*, "crying female," without the syllable in question.

10. *Katsura-no-ki*, variously written 桂, 楓, 香木, 杜木, and phonetically 加都羅. Though it is not absolutely certain what tree is intended, the weight of authority and of probability is in favour of its being the cassia, which plays a part in Chinese mythology. In modern parlance the *katsura* is a tree whose Latin name is *Cercidiphyllum japonicum.*

11. *Ama-no-sagu-me.*

12. This expression, as Motowori explains, signifies only that, as the arrow was shot from below straight up at a pheasant perching on a branch overhead, the feathers, which are properly considered to form the top part of the arrow, were naturally underneath.

13. *Taka-gi-no-kami.* The name is written with the characters 高木神, which, taken ideographically, would give us in English "High-Tree-Deity." But the translator has little doubt but that Motowori is correct in considerinx 木 to be here used phonetically, and the syllable *gi*, which it represents, to be a contraction of *guhi* (for *kuhi*), itself derived from *kumu*, and best rendered by the Verb "to integrate."

14. In Japanese *magare*, lit. "turn aside," "become crooked," i.e., "come to a bad end."

15. *I.e.*, through the hole in the bottom of the sky through which the arrow had entered, or which the arrow had made for itself.

16. Literally "high breast-hill."

17. The sentence placed between brackets is supposed by Motowori to be an addition to the text made by some copyist who had in his mind the parallel passage of the "Chronicles." In the "Records of Ancient Matters Revised" the two characters answering to our word "beware" are omitted, and the resulting meaning is: "This was the origin of the practice of sending back arrows," *i.e.*, of shooting an enemy with the arrow he had himself just used.

18. The import of the proverb seems to be that an embassy should always consist of more than one person. This is Motowori's view, based on his interpretation of the character 頓 as *hita*, which he identifies with *hito*, "one"; and it agrees well with the story in the text. Hirata, who, in his "Exposition of the Ancient Histories," following the version

of the legend given in the " Chronicles." narrates two pheasant embassies, —the male bird being sent first and (as it did not return) the female afterwards,—takes the character in the proper sense belonging to it in Chinese, and interprets the words of the proverb to mean " the pheasant's hurried embassy."

19. *I.e.*, the wife and children of the Heavenly-Young-Prince, who had been left behind by him in Heaven when he went on his embassy to Idzumo.

20. *I.e.*, in the place where he died. The " mourning house " was used to keep the corpse in till it was finally buried.

21. Some of the commentators believe this bird to be a separate species, and Moribe, who says that he saw one at the estuary near Kuhana in Ise, describes it as " rather slenderer than an ordinary wild goose, with longer legs and a higher back." If we accepted this, the better English translation wou·d be " river wild goose."

22. The original of this expression (*kisari-mochi*) is very obscure even in the "Chronicles," by whose ideographic reading the translator has been guided, and being here written phonetically becomes more conjectural still. The most likely opinion is that it signifies one bearing on his head the food to be offered to the corpse, though if this view be adopted, the office of the mourner in question may seem to resemble too closely that of the kingfisher. The latter has however been supposed to have brought fish, while the goose may have brought rice. Another proposal is that the goose brought the food and the kingfisher cooked it, while the sparrow, as mentioned below, performed the intermediate operation of pounding the rice. (See Motowori's elaborate note on this word in Vol. XIII, pp. 47-48 of his Commentary).

23. Or simply, " the pounder."

24. The parallel passage of the " Chronicles " tells us that " they wept and wailed and sang for eight days and eight nights."

25. See Sect. XXVI, Note 2. He was brother to the Heavenly-Young-Prince's wife.

26. The author of the "Perpetual Commentary on the Chronicles of Japan " tells us that these tears were tears of joy. Doubtless such is the meaning of the text; yet the repetition of the words " bewailing " and " lamenting " is curious.

27. See Sect. VIII. Note 4.

28. *Mo-yama*. No such mountain is now known.

29. *Awimi-gaha.* No such river is now known. According to the characters with which it is written the name signifies "Knot-grass-Seeing River."

30. Afterwards called Mino. This province probably received its name, as the author of the "Explanation of Japanese Names" suggests, from *mi nu, i.e.,* "three moors," from the large moors of Kagami, Awo, and Seki-ga-hara which it contains. The modern commentators prefer to derive it from *ma nu*, "true moor."

31. *Oho-ha-kari.* The name might also be rendered "Great Leaf-Mower." The translator has followed Hirata in omitting the *nigori* from the syllable *ka.*

32. *Kamudo-tsurugi.*

33. The meaning of the Song is: "Oh! this is *Aji-shihi-taka-hiko-ne*, whose refulgence, similar to that of the jewels worn by the Weaving Maiden in Heaven, shines afar across hills and valleys."—The translator does not follow those commentators who emend *ana-dama*, "hole-jewels" to *aka-dama*, "red," *i.e.* "resplendent jewels," as the frequent reference in this and the other ancient books to the string on which beads were strung, and the presence in ancient tombs, etc. of numbers of such beads with holes drilled through them (they are now known by the name of *kuda-dama, i.e.* "tube-jewels") renders such an emendation unnecessary The "Weaving Maiden in Heaven" is evidently, notwithstanding Motowori's endeavour to disprove the fact, the Chinese *Chih Nü*, a personification of *a* Lyrae, to whom there are countless allusions in Chinese literature, and who also became a frequent theme of the later Japanese poets.

34. Or, "barbarous style" Motowori endeavours to explain away the various names of styles of Songs found in the early literature by asserting that they are simply derived from the initial words of the Song in question, and that, for instance, in the present case, the title of Rustic Song was bestowed on the poem only because in the "Chronicles" it is coupled with another which lends itself to such an interpretation. Moribe gives his sanction to this view; but, though it is difficult to explain many of the titles on any other theory, the translator thinks that it cannot be accepted as generally satisfactory in the face of the numerous cases which contradict it, and of which its supporters can give no satisfactory explanation. The whole subject of the titles, of the manner of singing, etc., of the ancient poems is indeed involved in obscurity.

[SECT. XXXII.—ABDICATION OF THE DEITY
MASTER-OF-THE-GREAT-LAND.]

Hereupon the Heaven-Shining-Great-August-Deity said :
" Which Deity were it best to send on a fresh mission ?"[1]
Then the Deity Thought-Includer and likewise all the
Deities said : " He who is named the Deity Majestic-
Point-Blade-Extended[2] and dwells in the Heavenly Rock-
Dwelling by the source of the Tranquil River of Heaven,
is the one that should be sent : or if not this Deity,
then this Deity's child, the Brave-Awful-Possessing-Male-
Deity,[3] might be sent. Moreover,[4] owing to this Deity
Heavenly-Point-Blade-Extended having blocked up and
turned back the waters of the Tranquil River of Heaven,
and to his dwelling with the road blocked up, other
Deities cannot go [thither]. So the Heavenly-Deer-
Deity[5] should be sent specially to ask him." So then
the Heavenly-Deer-Deity was sent to ask the Deity
Heaven-Point-Blade-Extended, who replied, saying : " I
will obey, and will respectfully serve you. Nevertheless
on this errand[6] ye should send my[7] child, the Brave-
Awful-Possessing-Male-Deity,"[8]— [and with these words]
immediately offered [his son to Heaven-Shining-Great-
August-Deity]. So the Deity Heavenly-Bird-Boat[9] was
attached to the Brave-Awful-Possessing-Male-Deity, and
they were sent off. Therefore these two Deities, descending to the little shore[10] of Inasa[11] in the land of Idzumo, 101
drew their swords ten hand'breadths long,[12] stuck them
upside down[13] on the crest of a wave, seated themselves
cross-legged[14] on the points of the swords, and asked the
Deity Master-of-the-Great-Land,     saying :     " The Heaven-
Shining-Great-August-Deity     and     the     High-Integrating-

Deity have charged us and sent us to ask, [saying] : 'We have deigned to charge our august child with thy dominion, the Central Land of Reed-Plains, as the land which he should govern. So how is thy heart ?' "[15] He replied, saying : "I[16] am unable to say. My child the Deity Eight-Fold-Thing-Sign-Master[17] will be the one to tell you ; but he is gone to Cape Miho[18] to pursue birds and catch fish, and has not yet returned." So then the Deity Bird-Boat was sent to summon the Deity Eight-Fold-Thing-Sign-Master, who, on being graciously asked, spoke to the Great Deity his father, saying : "I will obey. [Do thou][19] respectfully present this land to the august child of the Heavenly Deity ;"—and thereupon he trod on [the edge of] his boat so as to capsize it, clapped his heavenly departing hands in the fence of green branches, and disappeared.[20] So then they asked 102 the Deity Master-of-the-Great-Land, saying : "Thy son the Deity Thing-Sign-Master has now spoken thus. Hast thou other sons who should speak ?" Hereupon he spoke again, saying : "There is my other son, the Deity Brave-August-Name-Firm.[21] There is none beside him." While he was thus speaking, the Deity Brave-August-Name-Firm came up, bearing on the tips of his fingers a thousand-draught rock,[22] and said : "Who is it that has come to our land, and thus secretly talks ? If that be so,[23] I should like to have a trial of strength. So I should like to begin by taking thine august hand." So on his letting him take his august hand, his touch at once turned it into an icicle, and again his touch turned it into a sword-blade.[24] So then he was frightened and drew back. Then on the Brave-Awful-Possessing-Male-Deity wishing to take the hand of the Deity

Brave-August-Name-Firm, and asking permission to take
it in return, he grasped and crushed it as if it were
taking a young reed, and cast it aside, upon which [the
Deity Brave-August-Name-Firm] fled away.  So when
[the Brave-Awful-Possessing-Male-Deity] pursuing after
him, came up with him at the Sea of Suha[25] in the
land of Shinanu,[26] and was about to slay him, the Deity 103
Brave-August-Name-Firm said : "I will obey.  Slay me
not.  I will go to no other place but this, neither will I
go against the command of my father the Deity Master-
of-the-Great-Land.  I will not go against the words of
the Deity Eight-Fold-Thing-Sign-Master.  I will yield up
this Central Land of Reed-Plains according to the command of the august child of the Heavenly Deities." So
they returned again, and asked the Deity Master-of-the-
Great-Land [saying] : "Thy children the two Deities the
Deity Thing-Sign-Master and the Deity Brave-August-
Name-Firm have said that they will follow and not go
against the commands of the august child of the Heavenly
Deities.  So how is thy heart ?" Then he replied, saying :
According as the two Deities my children have said, I
too will not go against them.  In accordance with the
[heavenly] command, I will at once yield up this Central
Land of Reed-Plains.  But as to my place of residence,
if ye will make stout the temple pillars on the nethermost rock-bottom, and make high the cross-beams to
the Plain of High Heaven like the rich and perfect
august nest where the august child of the Heavenly
Deities rules the succession of Heaven's sun, and will
deign to establish me, I will hide in the eighty (less
than a hundred) road-windings, and wait on him.  Again,
as for my children the hundred and eighty Deities, if the

124        *Records of Ancient Matters.*

Deity Eight-Fold-Thing-Sign-Master will be the Deities,
august rear and van and will respectfully serve them.
104 there will be no disobedient Deities."[27]    Having thus
spoken [he hid himself.[28]    So in accordance with his
word,[29]] they built a heavenly august abode on ·the
shore[30] of Tagishi[31] in the land of Idzumo ; and the
Deity Wondrous-Eight-Spirits,[32] grandson of the Deity of
Water-Gates,[33] was made butler to offer up the heavenly
august banquet, when,[34] having said prayers, the Deity
Wondrous-Eight-Spirits turned into a cormorant, went
down to the bottom of the sea, took in his mouth red
earth from the bottom, made eighty heavenly platters,
and, cutting sea-weed[35] stalks, made a fire-drill mortar,
and made a fire-drill pestle out of stalks of *komo*,[36] and
drilled out fire, saying :  " This fire which I have drilled
105 will I burn until, in the Plain of High Heaven, the soot
on the heavenly new lattice of the gable of His Augustness  the  Wondrous-Divine-Producer-the-August-Ancestor[37]
hang down eight hand-breadths ;  and as for what is
below the earth, I will bake down to the nethermost
rock-bottom, and,—the fishing sailors, who spread their
thousand-fathom ropes of paper-mulberry and angle,
having with many shouts drawn in and landed the
large-mouthed small-finned perch,—I will offer up the
heavenly true fish-food so that the split bamboos bend."[38]
So  the  Brave-Awful-Possessing-Male-Deity  re-ascended
[to Heaven], and reported how he had subdued and
pacified the Central Land of Reed-Plains.

1.  Literally, " to send again."
2.  *Itsu-no-wo-ha-bari no kami.* We have already seen (Sect. VIII,
Note 15) this name (*minus* the title of Deity) as the appellation of the
sword with which Izanagi (" the-Male-Who-Invites ") decapitated his son

Kagu-tsu-chi ("Shining Elder") for having by his birth caused the death of Izanami ("the Female-Who-Invites.") This sword's alternative name appears immediately below as the alternative name of this deity,—*Ame-no-wo-ha-bari-no-kami*, i.e., "the Deity Heavenly-Point-Blade-Extended." Motowori's gloss to the effect that the deity was the *spirit* of the sword has no warrant from the text.

3. *Take-mika-dzu-chi-no-wo-no-kami.* See Sect. VIII, Note 7.

4. Here, as in Sect. IX, (Note 6) the character 且, "moreover," occurs where some other Conjunction would seem more appropriate both in Japanese and in English. We may here understand it to be used for "but."

5. *Ame-no-kaku-no-kami.* The interpretation of *kaku* as "deer" is Hirata's. See his "Exposition of the Ancient Histories," Vol. XXII, p. 6, and *conf.* the remarks on Mount Kagu in Sect. VII, Note 12 of this translation.

6. Literally, "in this road."

7. The First Personal Pronoun is here represented by the humble character 僕, "servant."

8. See Sect. VIII, Note 7.

9. *Tori-bune-no-kami.* See Sect. VI, Note 24.

10. The word "little" is merely a sort of Honorific Expletive.

11. The true etymology of this word is doubtful; for Motowori's proposal to derive it from *ina se*, supposed to mean "no or yes" (諾否), in allusion to the question here put to the Deity Master-of-the-Great-Land is a mere fancy, and does not provide for the alternative forms *Itasa* and *Isasa*, which occur in other documents.

12. See Sect. VIII, Note 1.

13. *I.e.*, as Motowori explains, hilt downwards.

14. The "Chronicles" say that they "squatted."

15. *I.e.*, "What sayest thou to this our decree?"

16. Here and below the humble character 僕, "servant," is used for the First Personal Pronoun.

17. *Ya-he-koto-shiro-nu-shi-no-kami.* For this difficult name see Sect. XXVI, Note 7.

18. See Sect. XXVII, Note 1.

19. Or, "We will."

20. *I.e.*, He capsized his boat and himself into the sea,—the place being one where (as is still done in Japan) a large space of shallow water had been fenced in with posts, and stuck over with branches of

trees, a single opening being left for fish to enter by,—then clapped his hands in token of departure, and sank to the bottom.—This is Hirata's interpretation of the passage, which is a difficult one, and is differently understood by Motowori, whom Mr. Satow has followed in one of his notes to the Rituals (see Vol. VII, Pt. II, p. 122 of these "Transactions"), rendering it thus : "He then trod upon the edge of his boat so as to overturn it, and with his hands crossed back to back (in token of consent), transformed his boat into a green fence of branches, and disappeared." A careful comparison of the remarks in Motowori's Commentary (Vol. XIV, pp. 16-19) with those in Hirata's "Exposition of the Ancient Histories" (Vol. XXII, pp. 50-55) and with the text itself, as also with the text of the parallel passage in the "Chronicles," has however left no doubt in the mind of the translator that Hirata's view is the correct one.

21.  *Take-mi-gata-no-kami.*  The interpretation of the name is that proposed by Motowori.

22.  *I.e.,* a rock which it would take a thousand men to lift.

23.  This expression seems here, as Motowori says, to be used in the sense of "Come on !" It has survived in the modern word *saraba*, which sometimes has that meaning.

24.  *I.e.,* the Brave-Awful-Male-Deity's hand turned first into an icicle and next into a sword-blade on being touched by the Deity Brave-August-Name-Firm, to the alarm and hurt of the latter.

25.  *I.e.,* the Lake of Suha. No satisfactory etymology of the name is forthcoming.

26.  In later times called *Shinano.* The usual derivation of the word is that which connects it with *shina-zaka;* "mountainous ascents,"—an appropriate enough name for the province in question. It is, however, more probably derived from *shina,* the name of a tree resembling the lime (*Tilia cordata*) and *nu* or *no,* "moor."

27.  *I.e.* "If ye will build me a temple founded on the nethermost rocks and reaching up to Heaven like unto the august residence of the Heavenly Deity who is coming to replace me as sovereign upon earth, I will vanish to Hades, and serve him there; and as for the Gods my children, none of them will rebel against their new Lord, if the Deity Thing-Sign-Master be accepted as the protector of his escort."—Some of the expressions in the original stand in need of explanation. *Su,* here rendered "nest " in accordance with the character 巣 employed in writing it, may mean "lattice" (簀), and refer to the lattice-work over the hole

in the chimney of the roof. The "succession of Heaven's sun" (in Japa-nese *ama-tsu-hi-tsugi*) means the inheritance of the sovereignty of Japan, or of Idzumo. *Momotaradzu* (" less than a hundred ") is the Pillow-Word for *va se*, "eighty," and for some other words; it must be disregarded in making sense of any sentence in which it occurs. The "eighty road-windings" signify, says Motowori, an immensely long way," and are here meant for the long road leading to Hades or for Hades itself (Conf. Sect. XCVI, Note 7). In rendering the last sentence of the passage (that commencing "Again, as for my children," etc.), which is particularly vague, the translator has been guided by Motowori's opinion, which seems the most satisfactory one. It must be understood that the deities whose rear and van the Deity Thing-Sign-Master is to become, are those who are about to escort the new sovereign down from heaven.

28. *I.e.*, disappeared.

29. The passage placed within brackets is supplied by Motowori to fill up an evident omission in the text.

30. Literally " little shore." See Note 10 to this Section.

31. The derivation of *Tagishi* is doubtful; but *conf.* Sect. LXXIX, Note 2. Motowori remarks that we seem to have here the old name of the place now known only, on account of the temple which it contains, as *Kidzuki no Oho-yashiro*, *i.e.* " the pestle-hardened great shrine."

32. *Kushi-ya-tama-no-kami*. Motowori proposes to consider *tama* as a contraction of *tamuke*, " offering," and to take the name to signify " the Deity of Wondrous Increasing Offerings." Hirata's interpretation, which is followed in the translation, seems better, as the term "eight spirits " or "eight [fold] spirit " accords with the religious role attributed to this Deity without necessitating any hazardous philological conjectures. The actual character used to write the disputed word is 玉, "jewel."

33. See Sect. VI, Note 9.

34. The word "when" must be understood resumptively, as signify-ing that the way in which he carried out his task was by turning into a cormorant, making platters, etc.

35. It is uncertain whether the word *me* (海布), here rendered sea-weed, is a general designation or the name of the particular species.

36. Supposed to be the same as, or similar to, the modern *hon-dahara* (*Halochola macrantha*).

37. *Kamu-musu-bi-mi-oya-no-kami*.

38. The translator has followed Moribe in the interpretation of the first part and Hirata in the interpretation of the latter part of this ex-tremely difficult passage, which is a crux to all the commentators, but

whose general sense at least is this: "I will continue drilling fire for the｜God's kitchen, until the soot hangs down from the roof of the temple of the Ancestral Deity in Heaven above, and until the earth below is baked down to its nethermost rocks; and with the fire thus drilled will I cook for him the fish brought in by the fishermen, and present them to him in baskets woven of split bamboos which will bend beneath their weight."—Another plausible interpretation of the original expression rendered by these last two words is that they are simply the Pillow-Word for *towowo-towowo ni,* "bending." The rope with which the fishermen are supposed to have angled is described in detail by Hirata ("Exposition of the Ancient Histories," Vol. XXIV, p. 21) as a long rope from which other strings, each with a hook attached, depended, and is said by him to be still in use in the provinces of Shimofusa (Shimōsa) and Hitachi. The "lattice of the gable" must be understood to mean bamboo lattice covering a hole beneath the gable, which served as a chimney. Moto-wori's｜remarks on this passage will be found in Vol. XIV, pp. 39-42 of his Commentary, and Moribe's on the words *to-daru ama no nihi-su* (rendered " on the heavenly new lattice of the gable ") in his "Exami-nation of Difficult Words," Vol. II, pp. 26-29; the latter especially are well worth perusal by the student. Mr. Satow, in one of the notes to his｜translation of the Rituals, (See Vol. IX, Pt. II, p. 209 of these "Transactions "), gives a somewhat divergent rendering of this passage, following, as he does, the interpretation given by Motowori. It is as follows: "The fire which I have drilled will I burn until the soot of the rich and sufficing heavenly new nest of the PARENT Kami-musubi in heaven hangs down many hand-breadths long, and the earth below will I bake down to its bottom-most rocks, and stretching a thousand fathoms of paper-mulberry rope, will draw together and bring ashore the fisher-man's large-mouthed small-finned *suzuki,* [and] will offer up the heavenly fish-food on bending split bamboos."

----

[SECT. XXXIII.—THE AUGUST DESCENT FROM HEAVEN OF
HIS AUGUSTNESS THE AUGUST GRANDCHILD.]

Then the Heaven-Shining-Great-August-Deity and the High-Integrity-Deity[1] commanded and charged the Heir Apparent[2] His Augustness Truly-Conqueror-I-Conquer-

Swift Heavenly-Great-Great-Ears[3] [saying : " The Brave.
Awful-Possessing-Male-Deity] says that he has now
finished-pacifying the Central Land of Reed-Plaius. So
do thou, in accordance with our gracious charge, descend
to and dwell in and rule over it." Then the Heir
Apparent His Augustness Truly-Conqueror-I-Conquer-
Conquering-Swift-Heavenly-Great-Ears replied, saying :
" While I[4] have been getting ready to descend, there has
been born [to me] a child whose name is His Augustness Heaven-Plenty - Earth - Plenty - Heaven's - Sun - Height-
Prince-Rice-ear-Ruddy-Plenty.[5] This child should be sent
down." [[6]As for this august child,[7] he was augustly 107
joined to Her Augustness Myriad-Looms-Luxuriant-
Dragon-fly-Island-Princess,[8] daughter of the High-Integrating-Deity, and begot children : His Augustness-Heavenly
Rice-ear-Ruddy[9] and next His Augustness Prince-Rice-
ear-Ruddy-Plenty.[10]] Therefore, in accordance with these
words, they laid their command on His Augustness
Prince Rice-ear-Ruddy-Plenty, deigning to charge him
with these words : " This Luxuriant Reed-Plain-Land.
of-Fresh-Rice-ears[11] is the land over which thou shalt
rule." So [he replied] : " I will descend from Heaven
according to your commands." So when His Augustness
Prince-Rice-ear-Ruddy-Plenty was about to descend from
Heaven, there was at the eight-forking road of Heaven
a Deity whose refulgence reached upwards to the Plain
of High Heaven and downwards to the Central Land of 108
Reed-Plains. So then the Heaven-Shining-Great-August-
Deity and the High-Integrating Deity commanded and
charged the Heavenly-Alarming-Female-Deity[12] [saying] :
Though thou art but a delicate female, thou art a
Deity who conquers in facing Deities.[13] So be thou the

one to go and ask thus : ' This being the road by which our august child is about to descend from Heaven, who is it that is thus there ?' [14] So to this gracious question he replied, saying "I[15] am an Earthly Deity named the Deity Prince of Saruta.[16] The reason for my coming here is that, having heard of the [intended] descent of the august child of the Heavenly Deities, I have come humbly to meet him and respectfully offer myself as His Augustness's vanguard."[7] Then joining to him His Augustness Heavenly-Beckoning-Ancestor-Lord, His Augustness Grand-Jewel, Her Augustness Heavenly-Alarming-Female, Her Augustness I-shi-ko-ri-do-me, and His Augustness Jewel-Ancestor,[18] in all five chiefs of companies,[19] they sent him down from Heaven. Thereupon they 109 joined to him the eight-foot [long] curved jewels and mirror that had allured [the Heaven-Shining-Great-August-Deity from the Rock-Dwelling,[20]] and also the Herb-Quelling-Great-Sword,[21] and likewise the Deity Thought-Includer, the Hand-Strength-Male-Deity, and the Deity Heavenly-Rock-Door-Opener[22] of Eternal Night,[23] and charged him thus : "Regard this mirror exactly as if it were our august spirit, and reverence it as if reverencing us."[24] Next did they say : "Let the Deity Thought-Includer take in hand our affairs, and carry on the government." These two Deities are worshipped at the temple of Isuzu.[25] The next, the Deity of Luxuriant-110 Food,[26] is the Deity dwelling in the outer temple of Watarahi.[27] The next, the Deity Heavenly-Rock-Door Opener, another name for whom is the Wondrous-Rock-True-Gate-Deity, and another name for whom is the Luxuriant-Rock-True-Gate-Deity,[28]—this Deity of the August Gate.[29] The next, the Deity Hand-Strength-Male, dwells in Sanagata.[30] Now His Augustness the Heavenly-Beckoning-Ancestor-Lord (is the ancestor of the Nakatomi Chieftains); [31] His Augustness Grand Jewel (is the ancestor of the Imibe Headmen); [32] Her Augustness the Heavenly-Alarming-Female (is the ancestress of the Duchesses of Saru[33]); Her Augustness I-shi-ko-ri-do-me (is the ancestress of the Mirror-Making Chieftains); [34] His Augustness-Jewel-Ancestor (is the ancestor of the Jewel-Ancestor Chieftains).[35]

---

1. *Taka-no kami.* See Sect. XXXI, Note 13.

2. It will be remembered that this god was son of the Sun-goddess (or of her brother *Susa-no-wo*, "the Impetuous Male";—see Sect. XII, Note 18, and also the first two sentences of Sect. XIV and the first sentence of Sect. XV). The characters rendered "Heir Apparent are 太子, which form the usual Chinese equivalent of that term, and were borrowed by the Japanese. Motowori's reading of them as *Hi-tsugi-no-miko*, "Prince of the Sun's Succession," has no authority but his own patriotic fancy.

3. For this tremendous name see Sect. XIII, Note 18.

4. The humble character 僕, "servant" is used for the First Personal Pronoun.

5. *Ame-nigishi-kuni-nigishi-ama-tsu-hi-daka-hiko-ho-no-ni-nigi-no-mi-koto.* Excepting as regards the final *gi* of *ni-nigi*, which it is surely better with Hirata to consider as helping to form the word *nigi*, "plenty," than to take it as a separate word signifying "lord," as Motowori does, the translation follows Motowori's interpretation of the various component parts of this tremendous name, which is mostly abbreviated to its latter portion. It is precisely to this latter portion (the syllables *hiko ho-no nigi*) that considerable doubt attaches. *Ho* might mean "fire" rather than "rice-ears," and Motowori himself suggests that *ni-nigi* should perhaps be regarded as a corruption of *nigi-kahi*, "plentiful spikes of grain," rather than as "ruddy plenty." About the meaning of the rest of the name there cannot be much doubt. "Heaven's Sun Height" must be understood as an honorific designation signifying "high as the sun in heaven."

6. The translator puts this sentence between brackets because it is an evident interruption of the main story. Indeed the edition of 1688 prints it as a note to the text. The grammar of it is curious, as, on a first

reading, one would be tempted to suppose that "this child," i.e., His August *Ame-nigishi-kuni-nigishi-amatsu-hi-doka-hiko-ho ni-nigi*, was the father of *Hiko-ho-no-ni-nigi*. But the latter name is but an abbreviated form of the former, and the god could not be his own father. The meaning rather is (and such a construction is not so forced in Japanese as it sounds in English): "As for the parentage of this child, he was born of the marriage [of His Augustness Truly-Conqueror-etc.] with Her Augustness Myriad-Looms-etc. Princess. There is, however, real confusion in the traditional genealogy, as the "Chronicles" make the deity in question father to His Augustness Heavenly-Rice-ear-Ruddy, instead of younger brother.

7. Viz. His Augustness Truly-Conqueror-etc.

8. *Yorodzu-hata-toyo-aki-dzu-shi-hime-no-mikoto.* Mabuchi, as quoted by Motowori, suggests that *yorodzu*, "myriad," should be connected with the word *yoroshi* "good," as signifying an extreme degree, the *ne plus ultra*. But, though perhaps a good guess at the origin in the word, it need not affect our estimate of its actual signification. The translator has, however, followed Mabuchi in considering the syllable *shi* as an apocopated form of *shima*, "island," and *Aki-dzu-shi*[ma] as having its usual signification of "Dragon-fly Island" (more literally "Island of the Autumn Insect) rather than accept Motowori's explanation of *shi* as representing the Verb *chijimu*, "to be puckered," and of the whole compound *aki-dzu-shi* as signifying "crape like dragon-flies' wings." Not only is there no mention of crape in other passages of these "Records," but the derivation does not, to say the least, recommend itself on philogical grounds.

9. *Ame-no-ho-akari-no-Mikoto.* The word rendered "ripe" will bear equally well the interpretation "red."

10. *Hiko-ho-no-ni-nigi*, the abbreviated form of the name in Note 6.

11. *Toyo-ashi-hara-no-midzu-hono-kuni.* This periphrastic synonym of Japan has appeared under a slightly shorter form in Sect. IX (Note 18).

12. *Ame-no-udzu-me-no-kami*, the goddess whose loud, bold merriment was the chief cause of the Sun-Goddess emerging from her retreat in the cavern (see Sect. XVI, Note 28).

13. *I.e.*, "The brazen-facedness allows thee to stare others out of countenance, and make them uneasy."

14. Between this sentence and the next, the Alarming-Female-Deity must be supposed to have gone on her embassy and to have delivered the message with which she had been entrusted.

15. Written 僕, literally "servant."

16. *Saruta-biko-no-kami.* This is Motowori's reading. The more usual reading is *Saruda-hiko*, transposing the *nigori*. Hirata prefers to read *Sada-biko*, and takes *Saruda* or *Sada* to be the name of a place, which indeed seems the most acceptable view. The name actually signifies " monkey field." Motowori's interpretation of its import is a marvellous example of Japanese etymological gymnastics (see Vol. XV, p. 16 of his Commentary). Moribe's derivation from *sari-hate-hiko* 避果彦) is no better.

17. Or "guide."

18. For these five names and for the Deity Thought-Includer and the [Heavenly] Hand-Strength-Male-Deity mentioned a few lines further on, see Sect. XVI, Notes 15, 16, 28, 12, 13, 7, and 27 respectively.

19. *Tomo-no-wo.* This expression is here taken to refer to the various offices assumed by the five deities in question at the time of the withdrawal of the Sun-Goddess into the cave. It signifies properly the head of a company.

20. The allusion is to the story in Sect. XVI. Moribe, in his Critique on Motowori's Commentary, points out that it was only the mirror which allured the goddess from the cave. In the Japanese original of this passage, however, even more than in the English translation, the expression "that had allured" is made to both objects.

21. Obtained from the tail of the Serpent of Koshi. See the story in Sect. XVIII.

22. *Ame-no-iha-to-wake-no-kami.* Hirata observes that this must not be considered as the name of an independent Deity, but be taken simply as an alternative name of *Ame-no-ta-jikara-wo-no-kami* (the " Heavenly-Hand-Strength-Male-Deity "). The part taken by this Deity in the legend narrated in Sect. XVI. seems a sufficient warrant for such an opinion, though a little lower down in this Section the two are again mentioned separately.

23. *Toko-yo.* These words, which, according to the rules of Japanese construction, are placed at the commencement of the clause, must be understood to apply either to the three gods collectively or to the first-mentioned (the Deity Thought-Includer) alone.

24. Or "worshipping before us," or "in our presence." ·The strictly logical concordance of an English sentence makes it appear as if the mirror were to be taken to represent the spirit of both Deities whose names are subjects of the first clause. In Japanese, however, all such concordances are much more loosely observed, and it is only the spirit of the Sun-Goddess that we must understand to be here intended.

25. *Isuzu* (literally "fifty bells," or else perhaps the name of a kind of grass with which the neighbourhood may originally have been overgrown) is the name of the site of the "Inner Temple" of Ise. It is in the Japanese text preceded by the Pillow-Word *saku-kushiro*, literally "rent bracelet." See Mabuchi's "Dictionary of Pillow-Words" *s. v.*

26. *Toyo-uke-no-kami*, the same as *Toyo-uke-bime* (see Sect. VII, Note 6). The mention of this goddess in this place is curious, as she would not seem to be connected with the legend. Motowori, however, supposes that it is through some accidental omission that she does not figure in the list of deities said to have accompanied the heaven-descended Sovereign.

27. This name signifies "meeting when crossing" or "crossing to meet," and is connected by the commentators with an unimportant tradition, for which see Motowori's Commentary, Vol. XV, p. 48.

28. These two names are in the original *Kushi-iha-ma-do-no-kami* and *Toyo-iha-mado-no-kami*. The tradition in the "Gleanings of Ancient Story" makes them two separate deities.

29. Viz. of the gate or gates of the Imperial Palace.

30. Etymology obscure.

31. *Nakatomi no murazhi*. *Nakatomi* is taken by Motowori to be a contraction of *naka-tori-omi*, and by Mabuchi to be a contraction of *naka-tsu-ami*, either of which may be freely rendered "middemen," "intercessors," referring to the religious functions which were hereditary in this family. See "Commentary on the Ritual of the General Purification," Vol. II, pp. 2-3.)

32. *Imibe no obito*. *Imibe* is derived from *imu*, "to avoid," *i.e.* "to abstain from," and *mure*, "a flock" or "collection of persons," "a clan," and refers to the religious duties of this hereditary class of priests, which naturally required their avoidance of all ceremonial uncleanness. The word "priest" would fairly, though freely, represent the meaning of the compound.

33. *Saru me no kimi*. For the traditional origin of this name see Sect. XXXV. These "duchesses" were priestesses : but it is a matter of dispute between the commentators whether the title was simply an official one, or hereditary in the female line.

34. *Kagami-tsukuri no murazhi*. Of this family nothing would seem to be known.

35. *Tama-no-ya* (or *Tama n'Oya*) *no murazhi*. But the name should probably be *Tama-tsukuri no murazhi, i.e.* " Jewel-Making Chieftains," a " gentile name" which is found in the later literature. Perhaps, however, we should understand both this means and the previous one to be simple inventions by names of which divine ancestry was claimed for the hereditary guilds of jewellers and mirror-makers.

---

[SECT. XXXIV.—THE AUGUST REIGN IN HIMUKA OF HIS
AUGUSTNESS PRINCE RICE-EAR-RUDDY-PLENTY.]¹

111

So then [the Heaven-Shining-Great-August-Deity and the High-Integrating-Deity] commanded² His Augustness Heaven's-Prince-Rice-ear-Ruddy-Plenty; and he, leaving the Heavenly Rock-Seat,³ pushing asunder the eight-fold heavenly spreading clouds, and dividing a road with a mighty road-dividing, set off floating shut up in the Floating Bridge of Heaven,⁴ and descended from Heaven onto the peak of Kuzhifuru which is Takachiho in Tsu- 112 kushi.⁵ So His Heavenly Great Wondrous Augustness⁶ and His Augustness Heaven's-Round-Eyes,⁷ both⁸ taking on their backs the Heavenly rock-quivers,⁹ taking at their side the large mallet-headed swords,¹⁰ taking in their hands the Heavenly vegetable-wax-tree bow,¹¹ and clasping under their arms the Heavenly true deer-arrows, stood in his august van in respectful attendance. So His Heavenly-Great-Wondrous-Augustness¹² (is the ancestor of the Kume Lords).¹³ Thereupon he said : " This place is opposite to the "land of Kara.¹⁴ One comes straight across to the august Cape of Kasasa ;¹⁵ and it is a land whereon 113 the morning sun shines straight, a land which the evening sun's sunlight illumines. So this place is an exceedingly good place."¹⁶ Having thus spoken, he made stout the temple-pillars on the nethermost rock-bottom, and made high the cross-beams to the Plain of High Heaven,[17] and dwelt there.

1. Motowori makes Sect. XXXIV commence here, and it seems on the whole best to follow him in so doing, as the entire period of the reign on earth of the first of the heaven-descended gods is thus included in one Section. On the other hand, the " Descent from Heaven," which gives its name to the preceding Sect., cannot properly be said to be accomplished until the end of this first sentence of Sect. XXXIV. It will be remembered that the Japanese name of this first deity-king is (in its abbreviated and most commonly used form) *Hiko-ho-no-ni-nigi.*

2. Motowori proposes to suppress the character 詔, " commanded," in this clause, and the character 而, " and," at the beginning of the next, and to take the Prince as the subject of the whole sentence. This would be convenient ; but the characters 詔 and 而 are in all the texts.

3. *I.e.,* his place in Heaven. The original Japanese of the term is *ama-no-ihakura.*

4. The translator has adopted the interpretation proposed by Hirata, the only commentator who gives an acceptable view of this extremely difficult clause, which Motowori admitted that he did not understand. It must be remembered that Hirata identifies the " Floating Bridge of Heaven " with the " Heavenly Rock-Boat." (For details see his " Exposition of the Ancient Histories," Vol. XXVII, pp. 31-32).

5. Tsukushi, anciently the name of the whole of the large island forming the South-Western corner of Japan, and Himuka (in modern pronunciation Hiuga), one of the provinces into which that island is divided, have already been mentioned in Sect. V, Note 14 and Sect. X, Note 4 respectively. It is uncertain whether the mountain here named is the modern Takachiho-yama or Kirishima-yama, but the latter view is generally preferred. *Kuzhifuru* is explained (perhaps somewhat hazardously) as meaning " wondrous," while *Taka-chi-ho* signifies " high-thousand-rice-ears."

6. *Ame-no-oshi-hi no mikoto.* The interpretation is only conjectural.

7. *Ama-tsu-kume no mikoto.* The traditional origin of this curious name will be found below in the third and fourth Songs of Sect. LI (see Notes 21 and 22 to that Section), where the " sharp slit eyes " of this worthy are specially referred to. But Moribe seems to prove that *kume* is in reality not a personal name at all, but simply the old term for

"army," through a misconception of the original import of which has arisen the idea that *Oho-kume* and *Oho-tomo* were two distinct personages. The elaborate and interesting note on this subject in his "Examination of Difficult Words," Vol. II., pp. 46-55 is well worth consulting. The only point in which the present writer differs from him is with regard to the etymology of the word *kume*, which Moribe connects with *kumi*, "a company," and *kuma*, "a bravo," whereas in the opinion of the former it is probably nothing more nor less than an ancient mispronunciation of the Chinese word *chun* (軍) modern Japanese *gun*, "army," "troops."

8. The Auxiliary Numeral here used is that properly denoting human beings, not deities,—*futari* (二人), instead of *futa-hashira* (二柱).

9. In Japanese *ama no iha-yugi*.

10. This is the generally received interpretation of the obscure original term *kabu-tsuchi* (or *kabu-tsutsui*) *no tachi*, the parallel term *ishi-tsutsui* being understood to mean "a mallet-headed sword made of stone." (Both names appear below in the Song at the end of Sect. XLVIII, Note 4). Moribe, however, in his "*Idzu no Chi-waki*," rejecting the opinion that any part of the swords were made of stone, explains *kabu-tsutsui* in the sense of "broad-tempered" and *ishi-tsutsui* in that of "hard-tempered."

11. For the bows and arrows here mentioned see XXXI. Note 5.

12. *Ohotomo no murazhi*, a common "gentile name" down to historical times. *Oho-tomo* means "numerous companies" or "large tribe," in allusion, as Moribe supposes, to the force of which the personage here mentioned was the general.

13. *Kume no atahe*. *Conf*. Note 7.

14. Or *Kan* according to the Sinico-Japanese reading. We might render it in English by Korea. The Chinese character is 韓.

15. Etymology uncertain. An alternative form of this name, which is preserved in the "Chronicle," is *Nagasa*, which Hirata thinks may stand for *Nagasaki*.

16. This is the sense of the original Japanese text of this passage as literally as it can be rendered, and so the older editors understood it. Motowori however, though not daring actually to alter the characters, assumes that they are corrupt, and in his *kana* rendering gives us this instead: "Thereupon, passing searchingly through a bare-backed empty country, he arrived at the august cape of Kasasa, and said: "This land is a land whereon the morning sun shines straight, etc.'" His evident reason for wishing to alter the reading is simply and solely to conceal

the fact that Korea is mentioned in a not unfriendly manner, in the traditional account of the divine age, *i.e.* long before the epoch of its so-called revelation and conquest by the Empress Jin-gō (see Sect. XCVI to XCVIII). That the parallel passage of the " Chronicles " lends some sanction to his view is no excuse for so dishonest a treatment of the text he undertakes to commentate ; for the " Records " and the " Chronicles " often differ greatly in the accounts they have preserved. One of Moto-wori's arguments is that, as Kasasa is said to have been in the province of Hiuga, it could not have been opposite to Korea, seeing that Hiuga faces east and not west. He here forgets that a little later on in his own same Commentary (Vol. XVII, p. 86) he asserts that Hiuga in ancient times included the provinces of Ohosumi and Satsuma, the latter of which does face west.

17. *I.e.*, he built himself a palace to dwell in (Conf. Sect. XXXII, Note 27).

———

[SECT. XXXV.—THE DUCHESS OF SARU.]

So then he charged Her Augustness the Heavenly-Alarming-Female [saying] : "Do thou, who wast the one to make known this Great Deity Prince of Saruta who respectfully served as my august vanguard,[1] respectfully escort him [back] ; and do thou likewise bear the august name of that Deity, and respectfully serve me." Wherefore the Duchesses of Saru bear the name of the Male Deity the Prince of Saruta, and the women are Duchesses of Saru.[2]

———

1. See Sect. XXXIII from a little before Note 11 to Note 17.
2. *Q.d.*, instead of the men being Dukes, as would be more natural. The title was confined to females (see Sect. XXXIII, Note 33).

———

[SECT. XXXVI.—THE DEITY PRINCE OF SARUTA     114
AT AZAKA.]

Now when this Deity Prince of Saruta dwelt at Azaka,[1]
he went out fishing, and had his hand caught by a *hirabu*
shell-fish,[2] and was drowned in the brine of the sea. So
the name by which he was called when he sank to the
bottom was the Bottom-Touching-August-Spirit ;[3] the name
by which he was called when the sea-water gurgled up
was the Gurgling-up-August-Spirit ;[4] the name by which
he was called when the bubbles formed was the Bubble-
Bursting-August-Spirit.[5]     Thereupon [Her Augustness the
Heavenly-Alarming-Female], having escorted [back] the
Deity Prince of Saruta, came back,[6] and at once drove
together all the things broad of fin and the things narrow
of fin,[7] and asked them, saying : "Will ye respectfully
serve the august son of the "Heavenly Deities ? "—upon
which all the fishes declared that they would respectfully
serve him.   Only the bèche-de-mer said nothing.   Then
Her Augustness the Heavenly-Alarming-Female spoke to
the bèche-de-mer, saying : "Ah ! this mouth is a mouth
that gives no reply !"—and [with these words] slit the
mouth with her stiletto.[8]   So at the present day the 115
bèche-de-mer has a slit mouth.   Wherefore [from august
reign to] august reign, when the offerings of the first-
fruits of Shima[9] are presented [to the Emperor], a portion
of them is granted to the Duchesses of Saru.

---

1. Etymology unknown.
2. What species was denoted by this ancient name is not clear ; but
one of Motowori's suggestion, to the effect that it may have been identical
with the modern *sarubo-yahi* (a shell of a family *Arcadæ*, probably *Arca
subcrenata*), the origin of whose name would thus be traced up to the
mythological age, is at least ingenious.

3. *Soko-daku-mi-tama.*

4. *Tsubu-tatsu-mi-tama.*

5. *Aha-saku-mi-tama.* *Saku* might be translated by "opening," "forming," etc. It is the same word as that used to express the blossoming of a flower.

6. The characters rendered "came back" are 還到. Motowori and Hirata believe 還 to be put erroneously for 罷, which would give the sense of "arrived there," and would thus enable us to locate the episode of the fishes at Ise instead of in Hiuga, which would better suit the concluding clause of this Section narrating the participation of the Duchesses of Saru in the first-fruits of the province of Shima. If the word Shima however here means, not the province of that name, but simply "islands" in general, there is nothing to be gained by the proposed emendation, which has moreover no sanction from any text; and it may be added that no notice is to be found in any history of the custom here said to have existed.

7. *I.e.* all the fishes both great and small.

8. Literally, "small string-sword," supposed to have been so called from its having been carried inside the garments, attached to the under-belt.

The smallest of the Japanese provinces, situated to the East of Ise. The name signifies "island," and it is possible that it ought here to be taken in that sense as a common noun.

---

[SECT. XXXVII.—THE CURSE OF THE DEITY GREAT-MOUNTAIN-POSSESSOR.]

Hereupon His Augustness Heaven's-Sun-Height-Prince-Rice-ear-Ruddy-Plenty met a beautiful person at the august cape of Kasasa, and asked her whose daughter she was. She replied, saying: " I am a daughter of the Deity-Great-Mountain-Possessor,[9] and my name is the Divine-Princess-of-Ata,[2] another name by which I am called being Princess - Blossoming - Brilliantly - Like - the - Flowers-of-the-Trees."[3] Again he asked: " Hast thou any brethren ?"[4]   She replied, saying :   " There is my elder sister, Princess - Long - as - the - Rocks."[5]   Then he charged her, [saying] :   " Ego sum cupidus coiendi tecum. Tibi quomodo videtur ?"   She replied, saying :   " I[6] am not able to say. My father the Deity Great-Mountain-Possessor will say."   So he sent a request [for her] to her father the Deity Great-Mountain-Possessor, who, great-ly delighted, respectfully sent her off, joining to her her [116] elder sister Princess Long-as-the-Rocks, and causing mer-chandise to be carried on tables holding an hundred.[7] So then, owing to the elder sister being very hideous, [His Augustness Prince - Rice - ear - Ruddy - Plenty] was alarmed at the sight of her, and sent her back, only keeping the younger sister Princess-Blossoming-Brilliantly-Like-the-Flowers-of-the-Trees, whom he wedded for one night.   Then the Deity-Great-Mountain-Possessor was covered with shame at Princess Long-as-the-Rocks being sent back, and sent a message [to His Augustness Prince-Rice-ear-Ruddy-Plenty], saying :   " My reason for res-pectfully presenting both my daughters together was that, by sending Princess-Long-as-the-Rocks, the august off-spring[8] of the Heavenly Deity,[9] though the snow[10] fall and the wind blow, might live eternally immovable like unto the enduring rocks, and again that by sending Princess - Blossoming - Brilliantly - Like-the - Flowers - of - the-Trees, [they] might live flourishingly like unto the flow-ering of the blossoms of the trees : to insure this,[11] I offered[12] them.   But owing to thy thus sending back[13] Princess Long-as-the-Rocks, and keeping only Princess-Blossoming - Brilliantly - Like - the - Flowers - of - the-Trees, the august offspring of the Heavenly Deity shall be but as frail[14] as the flowers of the trees."   So it is for this [117] reason that down to the present day the august lives of Their Augustnesses the Heavenly Sovereigns[15] are not long.

---

1. See Sect. VI. Note 17.

2. *Kamu-ata-tsu-hime*. *Ata* is a place in Satsuma.

3. Or "Tree." *Ko-no-hama-saku-ya-hime*. Perhaps (though there is no native authority for doing so) we might rather understand *saku* as a Causative in intention, though not in form, and render the name thus: "Princess-Causing-the-Flowers-of-the-Trees-to-Blossom." The tree alluded to is doubtless the cherry. This deity is now worshipped as the goddess of Mount Fuzhi (Fusiyama), and in common parlance the last member of the compound forming her name does not receive the *nigori*, — *hime* instead of *bime*. The syllable *ya* has no signification in this and similar names. It will be remembered that there was another sister named "Princess-Falling-like-the-Flowers-of-the-Trees. (See Sect. XX, Note 5).

4. Or perhaps, so written 兄弟, the original expression were here better rendered by "sisters."

5. *I.e.*, as enduring as the rocks. The original name is *Iha-naga-hime*.

6. The character used here and immediately below for the First Personal Pronoun is 僕, "servant."

7. *I.e.*, every kind of goods as a dowry for his daughters.

8. The usual word child (子) is employed in the text; but it here almost certainly has, as Motowori suggests, a more extended meaning, and signifies the posterity of the Sun-Goddess or of Prince-Rice-ear-Ruddy-Plenty generally, i.e. the Emperors of Japan. The vaguer term "offspring" is therefore nearer to the author's intention.

9. *I.e.*, either of the Sun-Goddess or of Prince-Rice-ear-Ruddy-Plenty, There is no difference in the sense, whichever of these two deities we take the speaker to refer to. The Sun-Goddess was his ancestress, and he was ancestor of the Japanese Emperors.

10. Or "snow and rain," the reading being uncertain.

11. Or "having sworn this," or "pledged [myself to the accomplishment of] this."

12. The Chinese characters used are those properly denoting the presenting of tribute.

13. Motowori proposes an emendation in this passage of 此令 to 朋令, which would not materially alter the sense.

14. The precise meaning of the syllables *a-ma-hi-no-mi*, here rendered by the words " but as frail " in accordance with Motowori's and Moribe's tentative interpretation, is extremely obscure. The parallel passage in the " Chronicles " is 木華之移落, i.e. " fading and falling like the flowers of the trees."

15. The characters rendered " Heavenly Sovereign " are 天皇, a common Japanese designation of the Emperor. It would, especially in the later volumes of this work where the expression is repeated on almost every page, be more convenient to translate by the single word " Emperor." But the commentators lay great stress on the high significance of the component portions of the title, which, they contend, was not borrowed from China, but was first used in Japan. It is first met with in Chinese history in the middle of the seventh century of our era, just early enough indeed for it to have been borrowed before the time of the compilation of these " Records." But as there was no difficulty in putting together the two component parts " Heavenly, Sovereign," it is possible that the contention of the Japanese commentators is correct. The ancient pure native term seems to have been *Sumera-mikoto*, for which Mr. Satow has proposed the rendering of " Sovereign Augustness."

---

[SECT. XXXVIII.—THE AUGUST CHILD-BEARING OF PRINCESS-
BLOSSOMING BRILLIANTLY-LIKE-THE-FLOWERS-
OF-THE-TREES.]

So later on Princess-Blossoming-Brilliantly-Like-the-Flowers-of-the-Trees waited on[1] [His Augustness Prince Rice-ear-Ruddy-Plenty. and said : " I[2] am pregnant, and now the time for my delivery approaches. " It is not fit for me to be delivered of the august offspring of Heaven privately ;[3] so I tell thee." Then [His Augustness Prince Rice - ear - Ruddy - Plenty] said : " Princess-Blossoming-Brilliantly ![4] what ! pregnant after one night ![5] It cannot be my child. It must surely be the child of an Earthly Deity."[6] Then she replied, saying : " If the child with 118 which I am pregnant be the child of an Earthly Deity,

my delivery will not be fortunate. If it be the august
child of the Heavenly Deity,[7] it will be fortunate;"—
and thereupon she built a hall eight fathoms [long] without doors.[8] went inside the hall and plastered up [the
entrance] with earth; and when the time came for her
delivery, she set fire to the hall and was delivered.[9] So
the name of the child that was born when the fire was
burning most fiercely was His Augustness Fire-Shine[10]
(this is the ancestor of the Hayabito, Dukes of Ata;[11] the name of
the child born next was His Augustness Fire-Climax;[12]
the august[13] name of the child born next was His August-
119 ness Fire-Subside,[14] another name for whom is His
Augustness Heaven's-Sun-Height-Prince-Great-Rice-ears-
Lord-Ears[15] (three Deities in all).

1. More literally "came to"; but the character which is employed
implies that her visit was to a superior.

2. Written with the character 妾, a "concubine" or "handmaid
a common self-depreciatory equivalent of the First Personal Pronoun in
Chinese, when the speaker is a woman.

3. *I.e.* "secretly," "without telling thee."

4. In this one instance only is the name thus abbreviated. Moto
wori supposes it to be on account of the scorn implied in the god's words

5. Literally, "one sojourn."

6. See Sect. I, Note II. Here of course one of the gods of the
same country-side is meant.

7. *I.e.* "thy child and the Sun-Goddess descendant."

8. That is to say that it remained doorless after she had, as stated
immediately below, plastered up the entrance.

9. Viz. of child, not from the flames. There is no ambiguity in the
Japanese expression.

10. *Ho-deri-na-mikoto.*

11. *Hayabito-ata-no-kimi.* Ata is, as has been already stated in
Note 2 to Sect. XXXVII, the name of a place in Satsuma. *Haya-bito*
("swift men," "bold men," literally, if we follow the Chinese characters
"falcon men") was an ancient designation of the inhabitants of the south-
western corner of Japan which was subsequently divided into the provinces

of Satsuma and Ohosumi, and came by metonymy to be used to denote the province of Satsuma itself, for which reason it remained as the Pillow-Word for the word Satsuma even after the exclusive use of this latter name had been established. In after times the *hayabito* (also contracted to *hayato* and *haito*) were chiefly known as forming the Infantry of the Imperial Guard, a curious choice of provincials for which mythological sanction was invoked. They are also said to have furnished the performers of a symbolic dance mentioned at the end of Sect. XLI (see Note 3 to that Sect.) In later Sections of this work, the translator has ventured to render *hayabito* by "man-at-arms."

12. *Ho-suseri-no-mikoto.*

13. The Honorific is doubtless prefixed in this case and not in the others, because it was to this prince or deity that the Imperial House traced its descent. Motowori's *kana* reading, which prefixes Honorifics to all such names indifferently, obliterates this delicate distinction.

14. *Ho-wori-no-mikoto.* The derivation of this name is less clear than that of his elder brothers. Motowori's proposal to consider it as a corruption of *ho-yohari*, "fire weakening," is however plausible; and as this triad of names is evidently intended to paint the stages in the progress of the conflagration, the import of the third must be something very like what Motowori suggests, even if his guess at the original form of the word be not quite correct. The names of all three brethren differ more or less in the parallel passage of the "Chronicles".

15. *Ama-tsu-hi-daka-hiko-ho-ho-de-mi-no-mikoto.* The interpretation of the last four members of this compound name is extremely doubtful.

16. The actual word in the text is not *kami*, "deity," but its Auxiliary Numeral *hashira*.

---

[SECT. XXXIX.—THE AUGUST EXCHANGE OF LUCK.]

So His Augustness Fire-Shine was a prince who got his luck[1] on the sea, and caught things broad of fin and things narrow of fin. His Augustness Fire-Subside was a prince who got his luck on the mountains, and caught things rough of hair and things soft of hair. Then His Augustness Fire-Subside said to his elder brother His Augustness Fire-Shine:   "Let us mutually exchange, and use each other's luck." [Nevertheless], though he thrice made the request, [his elder brother] would not accede [to it]; but at last with difficulty the mutual exchange was obtained. Then His Augustness Fire-Subside, undertaking the sea-luck, angled for fish, but never got a single fish; and moreover he lost the fish-hook in the sea. Thereupon his elder brother His Augustness Fire-Shine asked him for the fish-hook, saying: "A mountain-luck is a luck of its own, and a sea-luck is a luck of its own. Let each of us now restore [to the other] his luck."[2] To which the younger brother His Augustness Fire-Subside replied, saying: "As for thy fish-hook, I did not get a single fish by angling with it; and at last I lost it in the sea." But the elder brother required it of him [the more] urgently. So the younger brother, breaking his ten grasp sabre[3] that was augustly girded on him, made [of the fragments] five hundred fish-hooks as compensation; but he would not take them. Again he made a thousand fish-hooks as compensation; but he would not receive them, saying: "I still want the real original fish-hook.

120

---

1. For the archaic Japanese work *sachi*, here rendered "luck," there is no satisfactory English equivalent. Its original and most usual signification is "luck," "happiness;" then that which a man is lucky in or skilful at,—his " *"forte;"* " and finally that which he procures by his luck or skill and the implements which he uses in procuring it. The exchange negociated below was doubtless that of the bow and arrows of one deity for the other deity's fish-hook.

2. *I.e.,* "Some men are naturally good hunters, and others naturally good fishermen. Let us therefore restore to each other the implements necessary to the successful following of our respective avocations."—The clause rendered "Let each of us now restore to the other his luck" is a little confused in the original; but the *kana* readings both old and new agree in interpreting it as has here been done.

3. See Sect. VIII, Note 1.

[SECT. XL.—THE PALACE OF THE OCEAN-POSSESSOR.]

Hereupon, as the younger brother was weeping and lamenting by the sea-shore, the Deity Salt-Possessor[1] came and asked him, saying: "What is the cause of the Sky's-Sun-Height's[2] weeping and lamentation?" He replied, saying: "I had exchanged a fish-hook with my elder brother,[3] and have lost that fish-hook; and as he asks me for it, I have given him many fish-hooks as compensation; but he will not receive them, saying, 'I still want the original fish-hook.' So I weep and lament for this." Then the Deity Salt-Possessor said: "I will give good counsel to Thine Augustness;"—and therewith built a stout little boat without interstices,[4] and set him in the boat, and instructed him, saying: "When I shall have pushed the boat off, go on for some time. There will be a savoury august road;[5] and if thou goest in the boat along that road, there will appear a palace built like fishes' scales,—which is the palace of the Deity, Ocean-Possessor.[6] When thou reachest the august gate of that deity['s palace], there will be a multitudinous[-ly branching] cassia-tree[7] above the well at its side. So if thou sit on the top of that tree, the Sea-Deity's daughter will see thee, and counsel thee." So following [these] instructions, [His Augustness Fire-Subside] went a little [way], and everything happened as [the Deity Salt-Possessor] had said; and he forthwith climbed the cassia-tree, and sat [there]. Then when the hand-maidens of the Sea-Deity's daughter Luxuriant-Jewel-Princess,[8] bearing jewelled vessels, were about to draw water, there was a light in the well.[9] On looking up, there was a beautiful young man. They thought it very strange.

121

122

Then His Augustness Fire-Subside saw the handmaidens, and begged to be given some water. The handmaidens at once drew some water, put it into a jewelled vessel, and respectfully presented it to him.    Then, without drinking the water, he loosened the jewel at his august neck, took it in his mouth, and spat it into the jewelled vessel.    Thereupon the jewel adhered to the vessel, and the handmaidens could not separate the jewel [from the vessel].    So they took it with the jewel adhering to it, and presented it to Her Augustness Luxuriant-Jewel-Princess.    Then, seeing the jewel, she asked her hand-maidens, saying:   "Is there perhaps some one outside the gate?"    They replied, saying:   "There is some one sitting on the top of the cassia-tree above our well.   It is a very beautiful young man.    He is more illustrious even than our king.   Lo, as he begged for water, we respectfully gave him water;  but, without drinking the water, he spat this jewel into [the vessel].    As we were not able to separate this [from the other],[10] we have brought [the vessel] with [the jewel] in it to present to thee."    Then Her Augustness Luxuriant-Jewel-Princess, thinking it strange, went out to look, and was forthwith delighted at the sight.    They exchanged glances, after which she spoke to her father, saying:   "There is a beautiful person at our gate."    Then the Sea-Deity himself went out to look, and saying:  "This person is the Sky's-Sun-Height, the august child of the Heaven's-Sun-Height,"[11] led him into the interior [of the palace], and spreading eight layers of rugs of sea-asses[12] skins, and spreading on the top other eight layers of silk rugs, and setting him on the top of them, arranged merchandise on tables holding an hundred,[13] made an august banquet,

and forthwith gave him his daughter Luxuriant-Jewel-
Princess in marriage. So he dwelt in that land for
three years. Hereupon His Augustness Fire-Subside 123
thought of what had gone before,[14] and heaved one[15]
deep sigh. So Her Augustness Luxuriant-Jewel-Princess,
hearing the sigh, informed her father, saying: "Though
he has dwelt three years [with us], he had never sighed;
but this night he heaved one deep sigh. What may be
the cause of it?" The Great Deity her father asked his
son-in-law saying: "This morning I heard my daughter
speak, saying: 'Though he has dwelt three years [with
us], he had never sighed; but this night he heaved one
deep sigh.' What may the cause be? Moreover what
was the cause of thy coming here?" Then [His Augustness Fire-Subside] told the Great Deity exactly how his
elder brother had pressed him for the lost fish-hook.
Thereupon the Sea-Deity summoned together all the
fishes of the sea, great and small, and asked them, saying: "Is there perchance any fish that has taken this
fish-hook?" So all the fishes replied: "Lately the *tahi*[16]
has complained of something sticking in its throat[17] pre-
venting it from eating|; so it doubtless has taken [the
hook]." On the throat of the *tahi* being thereupon
examined, there was the fish-hook [in it]. Being forthwith taken, it was washed and respectfully presented to
His Augustness Fire-Subside, whom the Deity Great-
Ocean-Possessor then instructed, saying: "What thou
shalt say when thou grantest this fish-hook to thine
elder brother [is as follows]: 'This fish-hook is a big
hook, an eager hook, 'a poor hook, a silly hook.'[18] Having [thus] spoken, bestow it with thy back hand.[19] 124
Having done thus,—if thine elder brother make high

fields,[20] do Thine Augustness make low fields; and if thine elder brother make low fields, do Thine Augustness make high fields. If thou do thus, thine elder brother will certainly be impoverished in the space of three years, owing to my ruling the water. If thine elder brother, incensed at thy doing thus, should attack thee, put forth the tide-flowing jewel[21] to drown him. If he express grief, put forth the tide-ebbing jewel to let him live. Thus shalt thou harass him." With these words, [the Sea-Deity] gave [to His Augustness Fire-Subside] the tide-flowing jewel and the tide-ebbing jewel,—two in all, —and forthwith summoned together all the crocodiles,[22] and asked them, saying: "The Sky's-Sun-Height, august child of the Heaven's-Sun-Height, is now about to proceed out to the Upper-Land.[23] Who will in how many days respectfully escort him, and bring back a report?"[24] So each according to the length of his body in fathoms spoke, fixing [a certain number of] days,—one of them, a crocodile one fathom [long], saying: "I[25] will escort him, and come back in one day." So then [the Sea-Deity] said to the crocodile one fathom [long]: "If that be so, do thou respectfully escort him. While crossing the middle of the sea, do not alarm him."[26] Forthwith he seated him upon the crocodile's head, and saw him off. So [the crocodile] respectfully escorted him home in one day, as he had promised. When the crocodile was about to return, [His Augustness Fire-Subside] untied the stiletto[27] which was girded on him, and, setting it on the crocodile's neck,[28] sent [the latter] back. So the crocodile one fathom [long] is now called the Deity Blade-Possessor.[29]

125

1. *Shiho-tsuchi no kami.* The view of the meaning of this name which has here been taken is founded on the persistent use in all documents of the character 監, "salt," to write the first element of the compound, and of varying characters to write the syllables *tsu* and *chi*, an indication that the latter are to be taken phonetically and may therefore be interpreted to signify *tsu mochi*, "possessor of," as in numerous other instances. The fact that this god is known as the god of salt-manufacturers (see Tanigaha Shinsei's "Perpetual Commentary on the Chronicles of Japan" Vol. VII, p. 3) adds another reason for rejecting both Motowori's far-fetched derivation of the name for *Shiri-oho-tsu-mochi*, "Great Possessor of Knowledge," and his assertion that it denotes no indiviual deity, but any one gifted with superior wisdom.

2. *Sora-tsu-hi-dɐka.* It will be remembered that *Ama-tsu-hi-daka*, "Heaven's-Sun-Height," was the first part of Prince Fire-Subsides's alternative name (see Sect. XXXVIII, Note 15). The distinction between these two almost identical appellations would seem to be that the former is used of the Heir Apparent, the latter of the reigning sovereign. Both were therefore equally applicable to Prince Fire-Subside; and while that which he eventually bore is mentioned where his names are first given he is naturally spoken of in this place, when his father may be supposed to have been still living, by that variation of the name properly marking the Heir Apparent. These names, *Ama-tsu-hi-daka* and *Sora-tsu-hi-daka*, will be met with again below applied to other personages.

3. *I.e.*, "I had received a fish-hook from my elder brother in exchange for a "bow." The text is here concise to obscurity.

4. *I.e.*, as is supposed, a punt or tub made of strips of bamboo plaited so tightly that no water could find its way in between them.

5. *I.e.*, simply "a pleasant road." *Michi*, "a road" is properly a compound,—*mi-chi*, "august road,"—the single syllable *chi* being the most archaic Japanese word for "road." It is in this place written 御路, showing that the etymology was not yet quite forgotten at the time of the compilation of these "Records." Generally, however, throughout the work we have 路 or .. alone.

6. See Sect. VI, Note 8, where the Adjective "Great" is prefixed to the name.

7. See Sect. XXXI, Note 10.

8. *Toyo-tama-hime.*

9. The character 光 properly "light," "refulgence," is here taken by Motowori in the precisely opposite sense of "shadow" (the parallel

passage in the "Chronicles" having 人影 "human shadow"), and his view is absolved from unreasonableness by the fact of the confusion between light and shade which has always existed in Japanese phraseology. Thus *hi-kage* may signify either "sunlight" or "a shadow cast by the sun." It is safest, however, to adhere to the Chinese characters employed by the author; and in this special instance we may well suppose him to have intended to say that a celestial light shone from the body of the god in question. Such an idea is not foreign to classical Japanese ways of thought and expression. See also Sect. XLVI, Note 9-10.

10. Or, taking the character 是 as an initial Particle, "So, as we were not able to separate [one from the other]."

11. See Note 2 to this Section.

12. This is a literal translation of the Chinese characters 海驢, by which the Archaic word *michi*, here written phonetically, is elsewhere represented. Perhaps the sea-lion (*Otaria arsina*) or a species of seal may be intended.

13. See Sect. XXXVII, Note 7.

14. Literally, "thought of the first things."

15. As the character for "one" is thrice repeated in this passage, Motowori is probably right in saying that it should be given its proper signification, and the translator therefore renders it by the Numeral "one" rather than by the Indefinite Article "a."

16. Pronounced *tai* in modern parlance. Perhaps we should rather add *aka-dahi*, "red *tahi*," as in the parallel passage of the "Chronicles." Both these fishes belong to the family *Sparoidei*, the former being the *Pagrus cardinalis*, the latter probably the P. *major,*

17. Or, "of a fish-bone in its throat."

18. Tanigaha Shisei, quoting from Urabe no Kaneyoshi, comments thus on the parallel passage in the "Chronicles," where the whole of this legend is given several times in slightly varying forms: "By *big* hook is meant one that will not serve its purpose [because too big]; *eager* signifies that which [endeavours to, but] cannot advance; *silly* means unintelligent; hence we have a hook which, not serving its purpose, will be of no use whatever, but rather a road to lead [him who possesses it] to poverty. Poor outwardly, and inwardly silly, he will be the most useless creature in the Empire." It should be noted, however, that Motowori interprets in the sense of "gloomy," and Moribe in the sense of "drowning," the phonetically written and obscure word *obo*, here rendered "great-"

19. *I.e.*, " with thy hand behind thy back." This is supposed by the commentators to have been a sort of charm by which evil was averted from the person of him who practised it, and they point out that Izanagi (the " Male-Who-Invites ") brandished his sword behind him when he was pursued by the hosts of Hades (see Sect. IX, Note 15).

20. By " high fields " and " low fields " are meant respective upland rice-fields where the rice is planted in the dry, and " paddy-fields" properly so called, where the rice perpetually stands in the water. Different varieties of rice are used for these different methods of culture.

21. *Shiho mitsu tama.* The " tide-ebbing jewel " mentioned in the next sentence is in the Japanese *shiho hiru tama.*

22. See Introduction, p. xxxiii, Note 41.

23. *Uha tsu kuni,* 國上.

24. *I.e.*, " Which of you will most speedily escort him home to the upper world, and bring back news of his safe arrival there ?"

25. Written with the respectful 僕, " servant."

26. There is in this sentence a character 若, which is hard to explain if read *moshi*, " if," as usual in Japanese. Probably, however, it simply stands for 汝, " thou," and we might translate thus : " While thou art crossing," etc.

27. See Sect. XXXVI, Note 8.

28. *I.e.*, probably, tying it round the crocodile's neck.

29. *Sahi-mochi-no-kami.* " Blade " is the probable signification of *sahi* or *sabi*, though this particular proper name is written in the " Chronicles " with the Chinese character 鋤, " hoe " or " mattock." Here the syllables *sa hi* are written phonetically.

---

[SECT. XLI.—SUBMISSION OF HIS AUGUSTNESS FIRE-SHINE]. 125

Hereupon [His Augustness Fire-Subside] gave the fish-hook [to his elder brother], exactly according to the Sea-Deity's words of instruction. So thenceforward [the elder brother] became poorer, and poorer, and, with re-newed savage intentions, came to attack him. When he was about to attack [His Augustness Fire-Subside, the latter] put forth the tide-flowing jewel to drown him ; on his expressing grief, he put forth the tide-ebbing jewel to save him. When he had thus been harassed, he bowed his head,[1] saying: "I[2] henceforward will be Thine Augustness's guard by day and night, and respectfully serve thee." So down to the present day his various posturings when drowning are ceaselessly served up.[3]

---

1. *I.e.*, "did humble obeisance by prostrating himself on the ground." The Old Printed Edition has 稽白 instead of 稽首白, and the *kana* gloss *kamugahemausu, i.e.* "reflected and said": but this reading, though interesting, is less good.

2. Written with the humble character 僕, "servant."

3. *I.e.*, "Prince Fire-Shine's descendants the *Hayabito* (see Sect. XXXVIII, Note 11) still constantly perform before the Court dances and posturings symbolical of the antics which their divine ancestor went through for the amusement of his younger brother, after the latter had saved him from drowning. "One account" in the "Chronicles" relates these antics at full, telling us that they represented the straits to which he was put as the waters gradually rose higher and higher; and we learn from other passages in the same work and in the "Chronicles of Japan Continued" that the *Hayabito* did really down to historical times combine the office of Court Jesters with that of Imperial Guardsmen.

---

126    [SECT. XLII.—THE PARTURITION-HOUSE OF CORMORANTS' FEATHERS]

Hereupon the Sea-Deity's daughter Her Augustness Luxuriant-Jewel-Princess herself waited on[1] [His Augustness Fire-Subside], and said: "I[2] am already with child, and the time for my delivery now approaches. But methought that the august child of an Heavenly Deity[3] ought not to be born in the Sea-Plain.[4] So I have waited on thee here."[5] Then forthwith on the limit of the waves upon the sea-shore she built a parturition-hall,[6] using cormorants' feathers for thatch. Hereupon, before the thatch was completed,[7] she was unable to restrain the urgency of her august womb. So she entered the parturition-hall. Then, when she was about to be delivered, she spoke to her husband[8] [saying]: "Whenever a foreigner is about to be delivered, she takes the shape of her native land to be delivered.[9] So I now will take my native " shape to be delivered. Pray look not upon 127 me!" Hereupon [His Augustness Fire-Subside], thinking these words strange, stealthily peeped at the very moment of delivery, when she turned into a crocodile[10] eight fathoms [long], and crawled and writhed about; and he forthwith, terrified at the sight, fled away. Then Her Augustness Luxuriant-Jewel-Princess knew that he had peeped; and she felt ashamed, and, straightway leaving the august child which she had borne, she said: "I had wished always to come and go across the sea-path.[11] But thy having peeped at my [real] shape [makes me] very shame-faced,"[12]—and she forthwith closed the sea-boundary,[13] and went down again.[14] Therefore the name by which the august child whom she had borne was called was his Augustness Heaven's-Sun-Height - Prince - Wave-limit - Brave - Cormorant - Thatch - Meeting - Incompletely.[15] Nevertheless afterwards, although angry at his having wished to peep, she could not restrain her loving heart, and she entrusted to her younger sister Jewel-Good-Princess,[16] on the occasion of her nursing the august child,[17] a Song to be presented [to His 128 Augustness Fire-Subside]. The Song said:

> "As for red jewels, though even the
> string [they are strung on] shines, the
> aspect of [my] lord [who is] like unto
> white jewels is [more] illustrious."[18]

Then her husband replied by a Song, which said:

" As for my younger sister, whom I took
to sleep [with me] on the island where
light the wild-duck, the birds of the
offing, I shall not forget her till the
end of my life."[19]

So His Augustness-Prince-Great-Rice-ears-Lord-Ears[20]
dwelt in the palace of Takachiho for five hundred and
eighty years.[21] His august mausoleum[22] is likewise on
the west of Mount Takachiho.

---

1. For "waited on" see Sect. XXXVIII, Note 1. The word "herself" (自 *midzukara*) has no particular force or meaning in the Japanese original, where it is simply placed in imitation of the Chinese style.

2. See Sect. XXXVIII, Note 2.

3. Or "of *the* Heavenly Deity," *i.e.*, "thyself." But it seems better to understand the speaker to intimate that it would be unfitting for one who properly belonged to Heaven to be born in the sea, which was another country or kingdom.

4. *I.e.*, in the sea.

5. Literally "come out and arrived."

6. It has been noticed in the Introduction, p. xxviii, that in early Japan a parturient woman was expected to build for herself a special hut in which to give birth to her child.

7. Or, completely put on; literally, "thatched [so as] to meet."

8. The text here has 日子. "prince," literally "sun-child," and so the older editors understood the expression. The translator, however, prefers Motowori's view, according to which the character 遅 should be supplied, and the whole read phonetically as *hikoi*, "husband," a word which occurs again a few lines further on.

9. *I.e.*, she assumes the shape proper to her in her native land.

10. According to the parallel passage of the "Chronicles," she turned into a dragon. "One account" however agrees with our text.

11. The original of this passage is rather confused; but the interpretation here adopted from the Old Printed Edition is more natural than Motowori's according to which the Verbs are to be taken in a Causative sense, to the following effect: "I had always wished to let people come

and go across the sea-path." Probably it was only in order to make this clause fit in better with the following sentence, in which we are told that the crocodile-princess "closed the sea-boundary," and with the fact that there is at present no path leading to the Sea-God's palace, that Motowori was induced to sanction such a view of the grammar of this passage.

12. This is Motowori's interpretation of the clause, he having emended 作, "action," "doing," which is found in the older editions, to 怍, "shame-faced." (The edition of 1687 mentions 恠, "strange," as an alternative reading). If we followed the older reading, we should have to translate thus : "Thy having peeped at my [real] shape is an outrageous action."

13. *I.e.*, the boundary dividing the dominions of the Sea-God from the world of men.

14. Viz., to the Sea-God's palace.

15. *Ama-tsu-hi-daka-hiko-nagisa-take-u-gaya-fuki-ahezu no mikoto.* The older editors read *ahasezu* for *ahezu*, i.e. "causing to meet," instead of "meeting." Moribe, in his Critique on Motowori's Commentary, would have us believe that the name comes from *umi-ga kayohi fuki-ahezu* (海陸往來乳養不得), i.e. "going and coming on sea and land and being unable to suckle"!

16. *Tama-yori-bime.*

17. *I.e.*, of Jewel-Good-Princess nursing the child. The mother did not return to the upper world, and so sent this poetic message by her sister, who had consented to act as the child's nurse.

18. "The meaning of the Song," says Motowori, "is this : Although red jewels are so charming that the very string [whereon they are strung] doth shine, the august aspect of my lord, who is like unto white jewels, is still more lovely. Thus does she express her loving feeling."—Moribe supposed the "red jewels" (or "jewel" in the Singular) to be meant for the child, than whom her husband is yet dearer to her heart. The word *kimi*, here etymologically rendered "[my] lord," is commonly used in the sense of "thou," especially in poetry.

19. *I.e.*, "I shall never forget thee who wast my wife in the realm of the Sea-God. The " birds of the offing " are a description of the wild duck, used as a Pillow-Word for their name. In the same manner the whole phrase, "where light the wild-duck, the birds of the offing," may be taken simply as a "Preface " to the word " island." The Sea-God's dwelling is called an island because it is beyond the sea. The words

*yo no koto-goto ni,* here in deference to the views of the best commentators rendered by "till the end of my life," will also bear the interpretation of "night by night."

20. The alternative name of the deity Fire-Subside.

21. Probably the writer means us to understand that the total age reached by this deity was five hundred and eighty years. This is the first mention in these "Records" of anything approaching a date. The way in which it is recorded resembles that in which the chronicle of each Emperor's reign is brought to a close in the later volumes of the work.

22. The character 陵 might also be rendered by the simple word "grave." But neither it nor its Japanese reading *misasaki* are ever used except honorifically of the Imperial tombs, and "mausoleum" seems therefore a more suitable English equivalent.

---

129 [SECT. XLIII.—THE AUGUST CHILDREN OF HIS AUGUSTNESS
CORMORANT-THATCH-MEETING-INCOMPLETELY.]

His Augustness Heaven's - Sun - Height - Prince - Wave-limit - Brave - Cormorant - Thatch-Meeting-Incompletely wedded his maternal aunt Her Augustness Jewel - Good-Princess, and begot august children named : His Augustness Five-Reaches ;[1] next His Augustness Boiled-Rice ;[2] next His Augustness August - Food - Master ;[3] next His Augustness Young - August - Food - Master,[4] another name for whom is His Augustness Luxuriant - August-Food-Master,[5] and another name is His Augustness Divine-Yamato-Ihare-Prince.[6] So His Augustness August-Food-Master, treading on the crest of the waves, crossed over to the Eternal Land.[7] His Augustness Boiled-Rice went into the Sea-Plain, it being his deceased mother's[8] land.

---

1. *Itsu-se-no-mikoto.* The "reaches" are the reaches of a river : at least this seems the most natural view to take of the meaning of the name. Motowori and Moribe, however, consider it to be a corruption of *idzu-shine,* to which they assign the signification of "powerful rice."

Excepting for the fact of its bringing this name into harmony with the three that follow, and which all relate to food, [there seems little to recommend so far-fetched a derivation.

2. *Inu-hi-na-mikoto.* If Motowori's derivatiou of the name from *ina-ihi* is correct, it might be rendered with greater exactness "Rice-boiled-rice," *ine* denoting rice in the husk and *ihi* the same when boiled.

3. *Mi-ke-nu-no-mikoto.* This name has heen translated in accordance with Motowori's interpretation of the syllables that compose it.

4. *Waka-mi-ke-nu-no-mikoto. Conf.* preceding Note.

5. *Toyo-mi-ke-nu-no-mikoto. Conf.* Note 3.

6, *Kamu-yamato-ihare-biko-no-mikoto. Yamato* being the name of the province where this prince, the first Emperor of the so-called "human age," fixed his capital, it appropriately forms part of his name. For a discussion of the etymology of the word Yamato, see Sect. V, Note 26. *Ihare,* a word which is said to signify "assembling," is the name of a village in that province.

7. See Sect. XXVII, Note 12.

8. See Sect. XII, Note 8.

---

# VOL. II.[1]

[SECT. XLIV.——REIGN OF THE EMPEROR JIM-MU[2] (PART 130
I.——HIS PROGRESS EASTWARD, AND DEATH OF
HIS ELDER BROTHER).]

The two Deities His Augustness Kamu-yamato-ihare-biko[2] and his elder brother His Augustness Itsu-se, dwelling in the palace of Takachiho.[4] took counsel, saying : "By dwelling in what place shall we [most] quietly carry on the government of the Empire?[5] It were probably best to go east." Forthwith they left Himuka[6] on their progress[7] to Tsukushi.[8] So when they arrived at Usa[9] in the Land of Toyo,[10] two of the natives, whose names were Usa-tsu-hiko and Usa-tsu-hime[11] built a

palace raised on one foot,[12] and offered them a great august banquet. Removing thence, they dwelt for one
131 year at the palace of Wokoda[13] in Tsukushi. Again making a progress up[14] from that land, they dwelt seven years at the palace of Takeri[15] in the land of Agi.[16] Again removing, and making a progress up from that land, they dwelt eight years at the palace of Takashima[17] in Kibi.[18] So when they made their progress up from that land, they met in the Hayasuhi[19] Channel a person riding towards them on the carapace of a tortoise, and raising his wings[20] as he angled. Then they called to him to approach, and asked him, saying: "Who art thou?" He replied, saying: "I[21] am an Earthly Deity."[22] Again they asked him, saying: "Knowest thou the sea-path?" He replied, saying: "I know it well." Again they asked him, saying: "Wilt thou follow and respectfully serve us?" He replied, saying: "I will respectfully serve you." So they pushed a pole[23] across to him, drew him into the august vessel, and forthwith conferred
132 on him the designation of Sawa-ne-tsu-hiko.[24] (This is the ancestor of the Rulers of the land of Yamato.)[25] So when they went up from that land they passed the Namihaya[26] Crossing, and brought up at the haven of Shirakata.[27] At this time Nagasune-biko[28] of Tomi[29] raised an army, and waited to go out to fight [against them]. Then they took the shields that had been put in the august vessel, and disembarked. So they called that place by the name of Tate-dzu.[30] It is what is now called the Tadetsu of Kusaka.[31] Therefore when fighting with the Prince of Tomi,[32] His Augustness Itsu-se was pierced in his august hand by the Prince of Tomi's hurtful arrow.[33] So then he said: "It is not right for me, an august

child of the Sun-Deity, to fight facing the sun. It is for this reason that I am stricken by the wretched villain's[34] hurtful hand. I will henceforward turn round, and smite him with my back to the sun." Having [thus] decided, he, on making a progress round from the southern side, reached the sea of Chinu,[35] and washed the blood on his august hand: so it is called the sea of Chinu.[36] Making a progress round from thence, and arriving at the river-mouth of Wo[37] in the land of Ki,[38] he said: "Ah! that I should die stricken by the wretched villain's hand!" and expired[39] as a valiant man.[40] So that river-mouth was called the river mouth of Wo.[41] The Mausoleum, too, is on Mount Kama[42] in the land of Ki.

---

1. Literally, "Middle Volume," there being three in all. See Author's Preface, Note 1.

2. . *Jim-mu* signifies "divine valour." It is the "canonical name" of the Emperor *Kamu-yamato-ihare-biko* (see Introduction, p. xiv).

3. In the preceding Section this name was rendered "Divine-Yamato-Ihare-Prince." But in the translation of Vols. II and III of this work, the Japanese proper names are not Englished, unless there be a special reason for so doing. (See Introduction, pp. xviii and xix.)

4. See Sect. XXXIV, Note 5.

5. See Sect. XXVII, Note 13.

6. See Sect. X, Note 4.

7. The Japanese expression here used is one which exclusively denotes an Imperial Progress, and not the movements of lesser people. It recurs perpetually in this and the following Volume.

8. See Sect. V, Note 14.

9. Etymology uncertain.

10. See Sect. V, Note 17.

11. *I.e.*, Prince of Usa and Princess of Usa.

12. In the original 足一騰宮, read *ashi hito-tsu agari no miya*. The parallel passage of the "Chronicles" has 一柱騰宮 which is directed to be read in the same manner. 柱 (*hashira*) however means, not "foot," but "pillar"; and the commentators understand both passages to allude

to a single pillar, which supported the weight of the entire building,—either as being in the middle of it, or (as Motowori opines) by standing in the water, the edifice, according to this view, being built on a river-bank overhanging the stream.

13. This name signifies " hillock rice-field."

14. *Q.d.* towards Yamato, the province where the capital was eventually fixed. In Japanese, as in English, people are said to go *up* to the capital and *down* to the country.

15. Etymology uncertain.

16. Etymology uncertain. This name is better known (without the *nigori* of the second syllable) as Aki. Aki is one of the provinces on the northern shore of the Inland Sea.

17. This name signifies " high island."

18. Etymology uncertain. Kibi is the name of a province.

19. This name signifies " quick sucking."

20. *I.e.*, as Motowori supposes, beckoning by waving his sleeve.

21. The First Personal Pronoun is represented by the humble character 僕, " servant."

22. See Sect. I, Note 11. Motowori wishes us here to understand this expression to mean " I am a Deity (i.e. a person) of the country-side." But there is no sufficient reason for departing from the precedent of rendering the characters 國神, which are constantly used antithetically to 天神, by " Earthly Deity " (as opposed to " Heavenly Deity.") Motowori likewise proposes to append to this sentence the clause " and my name is Udzu-biko," which is found in the " Chronicles." The name may be taken to signify " precious prince."

23. The characters 槁機 are evidently, as Motowori says, meant to represent the Japanese word *sawo*, " pole," though they do not properly convey that meaning. Probably they are corrupt.

24. *I.e.*, if we suppress the syllable *ne*, which seems to be either Expletive or Honorific, the " prince of the pole."

25. *Yamato no kuni no Miyadzuko.*

26. This is the reading of the name preferred by Mabuchi and Motowori; but the usual form *Naniha* seems to be at least as well supported by early documentary evidence. The " Chronicles " tell us that the place was called *Nani-haya* 浪速, i.e. " wave swift," in allusion to the strong current which the Emperor Jim-mu here encountered ; and at the present day it is still a dangerous place for navigation. The name properly denotes the water at the mouth of the River Yodo, on

which stands the modern town of Ohosaka (Ōzaka), for whose name
Naniha is still often used as a poetical synonym. 浪華, "wave flowers,"
and 難波, "dangerous waves," are alternative ways of writing it.

27. Motowori says that he cannot explain the etymology of this
word; but "white sandbank" would seem a simple and obvious derivation. The Shirakata here mentioned is, according to Motowori, that
situated in the province of Idzumo.

28. *I.e.*, the Prince of Nagasune. A plausible interpretation of *nagasune* would be "long-shank," which would give us Prince Long-Shank
as the name of the worthy here mentioned; but the "Chronicles" states
that Nagasune was properly the name of a place. The characters with
which it is written, moreover, signify not exactly "long *shank*," but
"long *marrow*," a designation which would have no evident personal
applicability.

29. A legend in the "Chronicles" connects the name of this place
with the word *tobi*, "a kite," it being there related that a miraculous
gold-coloured kite came and perched on the Emperor Jim-mu's bow, and
helped him to the victory. Probably the legend grew out of the name
of *Tobi*, which is obscure and may have had had nothing to do with a
"kite" originally.

30. *I.e.*, "shield-haven." But *conf.* next Note.

31. The real etymology of *Tada-tsu* seems to be "knot-grass-haven,"
nad probably *Taka-tsu* (for *Takatsu*), which is mentioned in Sect. LXIX,
Note 29, is but another form of the same name. Kusaka is a well-
known name in the annals of early Japan. Its signification is obscure,
and the characters (日下), with which it is written, are particularly
curious. There were two Kusaka, one in the province of Kahachi and
the other in Idzumi.

32. Viz., *Nagasune-biko*.

33. The wording of the original 負登美毗古之痛矢串 is very
curious. Motowori reads it *Tomi-biko ga ita-ya wo ohashite*. Immediately
below we have 負賤奴之痛手.

34. The character is 奴, properly "slave."

35. The most likely derivation of this name is from *chi-numa*,
"eulalia lagoon," the fact that it will also bear the interpretation of
"blood-lagoon" being probably but a coincidence of which the mythopoeic
faculty took advantage.

36. Here written with characters signifying "blood-lagoon."

37. The characters rendered " river-mouth " are 水門, literally " water-gate ; but here, as elsewhere, " river-mouth " seems to be the signification meant to be conveyed. Rivers in Jagan, even at the present day, do not bear one continuous name along their entire course, and there would be nothing unnatural in the fact of the water at the mouth of the river having a special designation. One of the significations of *wo* is " man," and the legendary etymology of the name given immediately below rests on the assumption that such is the meaning of *wo* in this place. Even Motowori, however, is not satisfied with it, and it is probably erroneous.

38. See Sect. XXII, Note 14.

39. The Chinese character 崩, which is here used, is one that specially denotes the demise of an Emperor.

40. Probably the sense meant to be conveyed is that he expired with a gest of anger and defiance.

41. Here written 男, " man." *Conf.* Note 37.

42. *Kama-yama,* i.e. furnace-mountain."

---

134 [SECT. XLV.—EMPEROR JIM-MU (PART II.—THE CROSS-SWORD
SENT DOWN FROM HEAVEN).]

So when His Augustness Kamu-yamato-ihare-biko made a progress round from thence, and reached the village of Kumanu,[1] a large bear came out of the mountain,[2] and forthwith disappeared into it. Then His Augustness Kamu-yamato-ihare-biko suddenly fainted away, and his august army likewise all fainted and fell prostrate. At this time Takakurazhi[3] (this is the name of a person)[4] of Kuma-nu came bearing one cross-sword[5] to the place where the august-child of the Deity was lying prostrate, and pre-sented it to him, upon which the august child of the Heavenly Deity forthwith rose up, and said :   "How long I have slept !"   So when he accepted the cross-sword, the savage Deities of the mountains of Kumanu all spontaneously fell cut down.[6]   Then the whole august

army, that had been bewildered and had fallen prostrate,
awoke and rose up. So the august child of the Heavenly
Deity asked him how he had got the cross-sword. Taka- 135
kurazhi replied, saying: "I was told in a dream that
the two Deities the Heaven-Shining-Great-Deity[7] and the
High Integrating Deity[8] commanded and summoned the
Brave-Awful-Possessing-Male-Deity,[9]       and       charged him
[thus]: 'The Central Land of Reed-Plains[10] is painfully
uproarious,—it is.[11] Our august children must be ill at
ease. As [therefore] the Central Land of Reed-Plains is
a land which thou specially subduedst, thou the Brave-
Awful-Possessing-Male-Deity        shalt      descend     [thither].'
Then he replied, saying: 'I[12] will not descend [myself],
but I have the cross-sword wherewith I specially subdued
the land. (The name by which this sword is called is the Deity
Thrust-Snap;[13] another name by which it is called is the Deity Awful-
Snap,[14] and another name for it is the August-Snap-Spirit,[15] This sword
dwells in the temple of the Deity of Isonokami).[16]   The manner in
which I will send this sword down will be to perforate
the ridge of [the roof of] Takakurazhi's stone-house,[17]
and drop it through!' (So the Brave-Awful-Possessing-
Male-Deity instructed me, saying: 'I will perforate the
ridge of [the roof of] thy store-house, and drop this
sword through.[18]) So do thou, with the good eyes of 136
morning,[19] take it and present it to the august child of
the Heavenly Deity.' So, on my searching my store-
house early next morning in accordance with the instructions of the dream, there really was a cross-sword there.
So I just present this cross-sword to thee."

---

1. This name signifies "bear-moor." The name is now generally
pronounced *Kumano*.

2. Motowori ingeniously conjectures the text of this passage 大熊髪
出, which makes no sense, to be a copyist's error for 大熊従山出, which

gives the meaning rendered in the translation. The running hand form of 從山 might well be mistaken for that of the single character 髪. The editor of 1687 is less happy in his conjecture that the character intended may be 鰐, "crocodile." This incident of the bear was thought important by the compiler for a mention of it to be inserted in his Preface. (See p. 5).

3. The signification of this name is not clear. Taking *zhi* as an apocopated *nigori*'ed form of the Postposition *shita*, we might suppose *taka-kura-zhi* to signify "under the high store house" in allusion to the legend which forms the subject of this section. There are, however, reasons for doubting this etymology. (See Motowori's Commentary, Vol. XVIII, p. 48). In the Preface we have simply *Takahura*, without the final syllable *zhi;* but the omission of *zhi* in that place is almost certainly to be accounted for on euphonic grounds.

4. This note to the original is believed to be an interpolation,

5. 橫力. Motowori avers that the character 橫, "cross," has no importance, and should be neglected in reading. But this assertion seems gratuitous in the face of, for instance, such a Chinese locution as 橫磨劍. We may be justified, perhaps, in paying no special heed to the Numeral "one" in this place, which Motowori neglects in his *kana* reading of the text.

6. *I.e.*, they fell down cut to pieces before they had even been cut at with this wonderful sword.

7. The character 御, "august," which should form the penultimate member of this compound name, is here omitted.

8. See Sect. I, Note 5.

9. See Sect. VIII, Note 7.

10. See Sect. IX, Note 18.

11. Conf. Sect. X, Note 1.

12. The humble character 僕, "servant," is here used.

13. *Sazhi-futsu no kami.* The translator follows Tanigaha Shisei in considering *sazhi* (Tanigaha Shisei in his "Perpetual Commentary" reads *sashi* without the *nigori*) to mean "thrust." For the rendering of *futsu* as "snap" in this and the two following names *conf.* Sect. VIII, Note 8. Moribe, however, in his "*Ikzu no Chi-waki,*" asserts that *futsu* is but an alternative form of *futo,* "broad," "thick," or "vast," as shown by the existence of the phrase *ma-futsu no kagami,* "a true vast mirror."

14. *Mika-futsu no kami.*

15. *Futsu no mi tama.*

16. The name of this place, which is in the province of Yamato, seems to signify "above the rock." It is well known as the Pillow-Word for the syllables *furu*.

17. Properly what is known to Anglo-Orientals as a "godown."

18. The sentence here placed between braces is proposed by Motowori to supplement an evident lacuna in the text.

19. Or, "luckily with morning eyes." Motowori remarks that even in modern times, special joy is felt at a good discovery made in the morning.

----

[SECT. XLVI.—EMPEROR JIM-MU (PART III.—THE GIGANTIC CROW AND GODS WITH TAILS).]

"Then His[1] Augustness the Great-High-Integrating-Deity again commanded and taught, saying: "August son of the Heavenly Deity! make no progress hence into the interior. The savage Deities are very numerous. I will now send from Heaven a crow eight feet [long].[2] So that crow eight feet [long] shall guide thee. Thou must make thy progress following after it as it goes." So on [His Augustness Kamu-yamato-ihare-biko] making his progress following after the crow eight feet [long] in obedience to the Deity's instructions, he reached the lower course of the Yeshinu[3] river, where there was a 137 person catching fish in a weir.[4] Then the august child of the Heavenly Deity asked, saying: "Who art thou?" He replied, saying: "I[5] am an Earthly Deity[6] and am called by the name of Nihe-motsu no Ko."[7] This is the ancestor of the Cormorant-Keepers of Aha.)[8] On [His Augustness Kamu-yamato-ihare-biko] making his progress thence, a person with a tail[9] came out of a well. The well shone. Then [His Augustness] asked: "Who art thou?" He replied, saying: "I am an Earthly Deity, and my name is Wi-hika."[10]   This is the ancestor of the Headmen of Yeshinu).[11] On his forthwith entering the mountains,[12] His Augustness Kamu-yamato-ihare-biko again met a person with a tail. This person came forth pushing the cliffs apart.   Then [His Augustness Kamu-yamato-ihare-biko] asked: "Who art thou?" He replied, saying; "I am an Earthly Deity, and my name is Iha-oshi-waku no Ko. I heard [just] now that the august son of the Heavenly Deity was making his progress. So it is for that that I have come to meet thee."   (This is the ancestor of the Territorial

138 Owners of Yeshinu).[13]   Thence [His Augustness Kamu-yamato-ihare-biko] penetrated over on foot to Uda.[14]   So they say: "The Ugachi of Uda."[15]

---

1. The intention of' the writer is here obscure, but he probably meant the following passage to form part of the dream, as is the case in the parallel passage of the "Chronicles." The inverted commas are therefore continued in the translation.

2. The characters 八咫烏 (*ya ta-garasu*), with which the original of this expression is written, combined with the mention in the Preface of the "great crow," have determined the translator to adopt the interpretation favoured by Tanigaha Shisei, vix., a "crow eight feet [long]." Motowori understands the expression to mean "an eight-headed crow." For the arguments on both sides see the "Perpetual Commentary on the Chronicles of Japan," Vol. VII, p. 16, and Motowori's Commentary, Vol. XVIII, pp. 60-62, and Vol. VIII, pp. 34-58. See also for the translation of a parallel passage Sect. XVI, Note 23.

3. Better known by the classical and modern form of the name, *Yoshino*. It seems to signify "good moor." Yoshino, which is in the province of Yamato, has from the earliest times been renowned for the beauty of its cherry-blossoms, and also figures largely in the early and mediaeval history. Motowori points out geographical difficulties in the Imperial progress as here detailed. In the "Chronicles," the verisimilitudes of the journey are better observed.

4. The character 筌, here rendered "weir" for want of a better word, is defined as signifying "a bamboo trap for catching fish."

5. The First Personal Pronoun is here represented by the humble character 僕, "servant." The other tailed deity mentioned immediately below uses the same expression.

6. See Sect. I, Note 11, and Sect. XLIV, Note 22, for the considerations that make it better to translate thus than to render by "I am a Deity of the Land."

7. *I.e.*, "Offering-Bearing Child." Here and elsewhere the word *ko*, "child," as part of a proper name, should be understood as a kind of Honorific, employed probably in imitation of Chinese usage.

8. *Ada No U-kahi.* This must be understood to be a "gentile name" (*kabane*). The etymology of Ada is uncertain. The practice of fishing with the help of cormorants, though now almost obsolete, seems to have been very common in Japan down to the Middle ages.

9. Commenting on a similar passage a little further on, Motowori, naïvely remarks: "It appears that in very ancient times such persons were occasionally "to be met with." It should be added that they are also mentioned in Chinese literature.

10. *I.e.*, "Well-Shine."

11. *Yeshinu no obito.* For Yeshinu see Note 3.

12. *I.e.*, disappearing among the mountains.

13. *Yeshinu no kuzu. Kuzu* is a contraction of *kuni-nushi* (properly 國主, with which characters the name is found written at the commencement of Sect. CVIII, though elsewhere the semi-phonetic rendering 國巢 or 國栖 is employed.

14. Etymologyy obscure.

15. *Uda no ugachi.* The meaning of the sentence is: "Hence the name of the Ugachi of Uda." *Ugachi* signifies "to penetrate." But the etymology seems a forced one, and Motowori is probably correct in identifying this "gentile name" with that of Ukashi, mentioned in the next sentence.

---

[SECT. XLVII.—EMPEROR JIM-MU (ART IV.—THE UKASHI BRETHREN).]

So then there were in Uda two persons, Ukashi the Elder Brother and Ukashi the Younger Brother.[1] So

[His Augustness Kamu-yamato-ihare-biko] sent the crow
eight feet [long] in advance to ask these persons, saying :
" The august child of the Heavenly Deity has made a
progress [hither].    Will ye respectfully serve him ? "
Hereupon Ukashi the Elder Brother waited for and shot
at the messenger with a whizzing barb to make him turn
back.  So the place where the whizzing barb fell is called
Kabura-zaki.[2]  Saying that he intended to wait for and
smite  [His  Augustness  Kamu-yamato-ihare-biko],  he
[tried to] collect an army.  But being unable to collect
an army he said deceitfully that he would respectfully
serve [His Augustness Kamu-yamato-ihare-biko], and built
a great palace,[3] and in that palace set a pitfall, and waited.
Then Ukashi the Younger Brother came out to[4] [His
Augustness  Kamu-yamato-ihare-biko]  beforehand,  and
made obeisance, saying :    " Mine[5] elder brother Ukashi
the Elder Brother has shot at and turned back the mes-
139 senger of the august child of the Heavenly Deity, and,
intending to wait for and attack thee, has [tried to] collect
an army ; but, being unable to collect it, he has built a
great palace, and set[6] a gin within it, intending to wait
for and catch thee.  So I have come out to inform [thee
of this]."   Then the two persons His Augustness Michi-
no-Omi,[7] ancestor of the Ohotomo Chieftains,[8] and His
Augustness Ohokume,[9] ancestor of the Kume Lords,[10]
summoned Ukashi the Elder Brother and reviled him,
saying :  " Into the great palace which thou[11] hast built
to respectfully serve [His Augustness Kamu-yamato-ihare-
biko], be thou[12] the first to enter, and declare plainly the
manner in which thou intendest respectfully to serve
him ; "—and forthwith grasping the hilts of their cross-
swords, playing with their spears,[13] and fixing arrows [in

their bows], they drove him in, whereupon he was caught in[14] the gin which he himself had set, and died. So they forthwith pulled him out, and cut him in pieces. So the place is called Uda-no-Chihara.[15] Having done thus, [His Augustness Kamu-yamato-ihare-biko] bestowed on his august army the whole of the great banquet presented [to him] by Ukashi the Younger Brother. At this time he sang, saying:

> " The woodcock, for which I laid a wood-     140
> cock-snare and waited in the high castle
> of Uda, strikes not against it; but a
> valiant whale strikes against it. If the
> elder wife ask for fish, slice off a little
> like the berries of the stand *soba ;* if
> the younger wife ask for fish, slice off
> a quantity like the berries of the vigo-
> rous *sasaki.*" [16]

> " Ugh ! [17] pfui ! dolt ! This is saying thou     141
> rascal. Ah ! pfui ! dolt ! This is laugh-
> ing [him] to scorn."

So Ukashi the Younger Brother (he is the ancestor of the Water Directors of Uda).[18]

---

1. *Ye-ukashi* and *Oto-ukashi*. *Ukashi*, as in the other¹ compounds where it occurs, is probably in reality the name of a place. Its etymology is doubtful.

2. *I.e.*, Barb Point or Cape.

3. Or, hall.

4. The original has a respectful expression, which is elsewhere translated "waited on."

5. The First Personal Pronoun is represented by the respectful character 僕 "servant."

6. Literally, "spread." This gin is supposed to have been of the kind whose top closes down after the man or animal has fallen into it.

7. *I.e.*, "Grandee of the Way." This gentile name is said in the "Chronicles" to have been bestowed on this worthy in consideration of the services as a guide to his master the Emperor on the occasion of the latter's progress eastward.

8. See Sect. XXXIV, Note 12.

9. *I.e.*, perhaps "Great Round Eyes," supposed to be a descendant of His Augustness *Ama-tsu-kume* (see however Sect. XXXIV, Note 7 for a discussion of the etymology of *Kume*).

10. See Sect. XXXIV, Note 13.

11. The expression *i ga*, here rendered "thou," is, as Motowori remarks, "extremely hard to understand," and its interpretation as an insulting form of the Second Personal Pronoun is merely tentative. Perhaps the text is corrupt.

12. The insulting Second Pronoun *ore* is here employed.

13. Here again we have an expression written phonetically and of uncertain import. The translator has followed Motowori in tentatively rendering it according to the ideographic reading of the parallel passage of the "Chronicles."

14. Literally "struck by."

15. *I.e.*, Uda's Blood-Plain.

16. This Song is unusually difficult of comprehension : and the latest important commentator, Moribe, seems to show satisfactorily that all his predecessors, Motowori included, more or less misunderstood it. He had at least the advantage of coming after them, and the translator has followed his interpretation excepting with regard to *isukuhashi*, the Pillow-Word for "whale," which is here rendered "valiant," in accordance with the traditional view of its signification. The *soba* tree is identified by Motowori with the *Kaname-mochi*, " *Photinia glabra*." Ths *saka-ki*, taken together with its Prefix *ichi* (here rendered "vigorous") is supposed in this place to signify, not the usual *Cleyera japonica*, but another species popularly known as the *bishiya-gaki*, whose English or Latin name the translator has failed to ascertain. It has a large berry, whereas the *soba* has a small one…The following is the gist of Moribe's exposition of the general signification of the Song : "If for Ukashi's mean design to kill the Emperor in a gin there be sought a term of comparison in the whales and woodcock forming the Imperial banquet, then in lieu of the woodcock that he expected to catch in the trap that he set, that great whale, the Imperial host, has rushed up "against it. Again if, as the fishermen's wives might do, your (*i.e.*, you soldiers') wives ask you

for fish, then let each of you give to his elder wife, of whom he must
have grown weary, only a small and bony portion, and to his younger
wife, who is doubtless his heart's favourite, a good fleshy piece. So
jocular a guess at the "*penchants* of the young warriors excites their
ardour, which they give vent to in the following shouts."

17. Some of the Japanese originals of this string of Interjections
are of uncertain import. The translator has been guided by Motowori's
conjectures, with which Moribe mostly agrees. The exclamations are
supposed not to form part of the actual Song, but to proceed from the
mouths of the Imperial soldiers. The words rendered "this is saying
thou rascal" (such is apparently their meaning) and those rendered "this
is laughing [him] to scorn" seem to be glosses as old as the text, which
had already been obscure in the eighth century. They are not written
altogether phonetically.

18. *Uda na Mohitori.* This tribe or guild of "water-directors" was
entrusted with the charge of the water, the ice, and the gruel used in
the Imperial household. In later times the word *Mohitori* was corrupted
to *Mondo,*

---

[SECT. XLVIII.—EMPEROR JIM-MU (PART V.—THE EARTH-
SPIDER OF THE CAVE OF OSAKA).]

When [His Augustness Kamu-yamato-ihare-biko] made
his progress, and reached the great cave of Osaka,¹ earth-
spiders² with tails, [namely] eighty bravoes,³ were in the
cave awaiting him. So then the august son of the
Heavenly Deity commanded that a banquet be bestowed
on the eighty bravoes. Thereupon he set eighty butlers,
one for each of the eighty bravoes, and girded each of
them with a sword, and instructed the butlers, saying: 142
"When ye hear me sing, cut [them down] simultaneously." So the Song by which he made clear to them to
set about smiting the earth-spiders said:

 " Into the great cave uf Osaka people
       have entered in abundance, and are

[there]. Though people have entered
in abundance, and are [there], the
children of the augustly powerful warriors will smite and finish them with
[their] mallet-headed [swords], [their]
stone-mallet [swords] : the children of
the augustly powerful warriors, with
[their] mallet-headed [swords], [their]
stone-mallet [swords], would now do
well to smite."[4]

Having thus sung, they drew their swords, and simultaneously smote them to death.

---

1. The etymology of this name is not clear, but readers will of
course not confound it with that of the modern town of Ohosaka (Ozaka).
The character rendered " cave," 室, signifies simply " apartment ;"
but the traditional reading is *muro*, which means a cave or pit dug in
the earth. That the latter is the idea which the author wishes to convey
becomes clear by comparison with a greater number of passages in the
older literature. For a more particular discussion of this subject see Mr.
Milne's paper entitled " Notes on Stone Implements from Otaru and
Hakodate," published in Vol. VIII, part I of these " Transactions," p·
76 *et seq.*, where a number of passages relative to the " earth-spiders "
are likewise brought together.

2. *Tsuchi-gumo*, generally written 土蜘蛛, but here semi-phonetically
土雲, There is little doubt that by this well-known name, which has
given rise to much conjecture, a race of cave-dwelling savages or a class
of cave-dwelling robbers is intended. Motowori supposes that their name
had its origin in a comparison ·of their habits with those of the spider.
But it were surely more rational to regard it as a corruption of *tsuchi-
gomori*, " earth-*hiders*," a designation as obvious as it is appropriate. The
" Chronicles " describe one tribe of them as " being short in stature, and
having long arms and legs like pigmies." For a further discussion of
the subject see Motowori's Commentary, Vol. XIX, pp. 30-31, the " Perpetual Commentary on the Chronicles of Japan," Vol. VIII, p. 35, the
" *Tou-ya*," Vol. XX, *s. v. kumo* and the " Examination of Difficult Words,"
Vol. II, pp. 55 *et seq.*

3. The original term is *takeru* (梟師), which might also be rendered "bandit," or "robber chief."

4. The import of this poem is too clear to stand in need of explanation. The word *mitsumitsushi*, here rendered "augustly powerful" in accordance with Moribe's view, is understood by Motowori to mean "perfectly full," in allusion to the fully or perfectly round eyes of the deity Kume, to whose name he supposes there to be a reference. Mabuchi, on the other hand, explains the word to signify "young and flourishing." But Moribe's view both of this and of the import of *kume* as "warriors" seems so greatly preferable to any other, that the translator has not hesitated to follow him (*conf.* Sect. XXXIV, Note 7). The "*children* of the warriors" are of course the warriors themselves. With regard to the signification of the two kinds of swords here mentioned it has, however, been thought best to adhere to the usual view, and Note 10 to Sect. XXXIV should be referred to.

———

[SECT. XLIX.—EMPEROR JIM-MU (PART. VI.—THE PRINCE OF TOMI AND THE SHIKI BRETHREN).]

After this, when about to smite the Prince of Tomi,[1] he sang, saying:                                           143

> " The children of the augustly powerful
> army will smite and finish the one stem
> of smelly chive in the millet-field,—the
> stem of its root, both its root and
> shoots."[2]

Again he sang :

> " The ginger, which the children of the
> augustly powerful army planted near
> the hedge, resounds in the mouth. I
> shall not forget it. I will smite and
> finish it."[3]

144  Again he sang, saying:

> " Like the *turbinidœ* creeping round the
> great rock in the sea of Ise [on which
> blows] the divine wind, [so] will we
> creep round, and smite and finish them."[4]

Again when he smote Shiki the Elder Brother and
Shiki the Younger Brother,[5] the august army was temporarily exhausted. Then he sang, saying:

> " As we fight placing our shields in a
> row, going and watching from between
> the trees on Mount Inasa, oh! we are
> famished.  Ye keepers of cormorants,
> the birds of the island, come now to
> our rescue ! "[6]

---

1. See Sect. XLIV, Notes 28 *et seq.* The apparent want of sequence
in this portion of the narrative is not noticed by Motowori. We might
endeavour to harmonize it by supposing that after having slain the
" earth-spiders," etc., the Emperor Jim-mu turned round again to fight
with the Prince of Tomi, who had harassed him in the earlier portion
of his career as conqueror of Central Japan.

2. The wild chive growing among the millet is of course the enemy,
the Prince of Tomi and his host; and the gist of the Song is that the
Imperial troops will smite and destroy them root and branch. The commentators suppose the simile to have been taken from the fields of millet
which Jim-mu's troops planted for their subsistenee during the long drawn
out campaigns of early days.—The " stem of its root," *so ne ga moto,* is
a curious expression, which is perhaps best accounted for by Moribe's
supposition that we have here a pun on *Sune ga moto,* "Sune's house,"
*Sune* being a natural abbreviation of *Nagasune,* the name of the Prince
of Tomi (see Sect. XLIV, Note 28).

3. The sense of this Song is: ":I shall not forget the bitterness of
seeing my brother slain by Prince Nagasune's arrow (see the latter part
of Sect. XLIV). The word *hazhikami,* here rendered ginger in accordance
with Motowori's dictum, is taken by Moribe to signify the xanthoxylon.

"Resounding in the mouth" is a curious phrase here used to express bitterness.

4. Motowori thus paraphrases this Song: "As the innumerable *turbinidæ* [-shells] creep round the great rock, so will I with the myriads of the Imperial host encompass the Prince of Tomi on every side, that there may be no outlet whereby he can escape." The shell here mentioned is a kind of small conch. *Kamu-kazo no*, lit. "of divine wind," is the Pillow-Word for Ise, and is of disputed derivation, as is the word Ise itself. The curious reader should refer to Fujihara no Hikomaro's "Inquiry into the Meaning of the Names of All the Provinces" *s.v.* for the legend to which the name of Ise and its Pillow-Word were anciently traced and other conjectures on the point. The "great rock" here mentioned is not otherwise known.

5. *Ye-shiki* and *Otoshiki*. Shiki is the name of a district in the province of Yamato.

6. This Song is a request for provisions made by the Emperor to some fishermen, who were working their cormorants along the mountain-streams. Moribe refers it to an incident, not in the war, but in the hunt, and interprets differently the word here, in accordance with its usual meaning and with older authority, rendered " as we fight." He attributes to it the sense of "as we put our shields together," and thinks that the poet may have compared to shields the trunks of the trees. According to this view, the Song should be viewed rather as a joke. It may be mentioned that there is good authority for considering the word *tata namete*, " placing shields in a row," as a Punning Preface or Pillow-Word for words commencing with *i* (*i* being the Root of *iru*, to shoot"), so that Moribe's explanation need not involve any tautology. It seems however somewhat far-fetched.—The position of Mount Inasa is uncertain, and the name itself of obscure derivation.

---

[SECT. L.—EMPEROR JIM-MU (PART VII.—THE EMPIRE PACIFIED).]

So then His Augustness Nigi-hayabi[1] waited on and said to the august child of the Heavenly Deity : "As I heard that [thou], the august child of the Heavenly Deity, hadst descended from Heaven, I have followed

down to wait on thee."  Forthwith presenting to him the
heavenly symbols,[2] he respectfully served him.  So His
Augustness Nigi-hayabi wedded the Princess of Tomi,[3]
145 sister of the Prince of Tomi, and begot a child, His
Augustness Umashi-ma-ji.[4]  (He was the ancestor of the Chiefs of
the Warrior-Clan,[5] of the Grandees of Hodzumi,[6] and of the Grandees of
the Neck-Clan).[7]  So having thus subdued and pacified the
savage Deities, and extirpated the unsubmissive people,
[His Augustness Kamu-yamato-ihare-biko] dwelt at the
palace of Kashibara[8] near Unebi[9] and ruled the Empire.[10]

---

1.  The component parts of this name, rendered according to the
analogy of that in Sect. XXXIII, Note 5, may be interpreted to signify
"Plenty-Swift."  The genealogy of this god is not known.

2.  *I.e.,* the swords, quivers, bow, and arrows mentioned in Sect.
XXXIII, as having been brought down from Heaven by the divine
attendants of the Emperor Jim-mu's grandfather.

3.  *Tomi-ya-bime.*  The syllable *ya* is inexplicable, but perhaps merely
an Expletive.

4.  The signification of this name is by no means clear; but, rendered
according to the characters with which it is written in the "Chronicles,"
it would mean "Savoury-True-Hand."

5.  *Mononobe no murazhi.*  This and the two following are of course
"gentile names."

6.  *Hodzumi no omi.*  Hodzumi, which is the name of a place, signifies
"rice-ears piled up."

7.  *Une-be no omi.*  The interpretation of this name is given according to Motowori, who explains that the members of this family,—in
particular the female members,—waited at the Emperor's table, and wore
veils over their necks when so employed.  The name is commonly
corrupted to *uneme.*

8.  Better known as Kashihabara.  The name signifies "oak-moor,"
or rather "a place planted with oaks."  This is usually, though without
sufficient foundation, reckoned the earliest of the historical capitals of
Japan.  It is in Yamato.

9.  Unebi is the name of a hill in Yamato.  The etymology of the
word is obscure.

10. *I.e.*, "ruled the Empire from his palace of Kashibara near Unebi. For the expression 天下 (literally "[all] beneath Heaven"), here rendered "Empire," see Sect. XXVII, Note 13.

---

[SECT. LI.—EMPEROR JIM-MU (PART. VIII.—HE WEDS I-SURE-YORI-HIME).]

So when he dwelt in Himuka, [His Augustness Kamu-yamato-ihare-biko] wedded[1] Princess Ahira,[2] younger sister of the Duke of Wobashi[3] in Ata,[4] and begot children: there were two,[5]—His Augustness Tagishi-mimi,[6] next His Augustness Kisu-mimi.[7] But when he sought for a beautiful maiden to make her his Chief Empress," His Augustness Oho-kume said: " There is here a beauteous maiden who is called the august child of a Deity. The reason why she is called the august child of a Deity is that the Princess Seya-datara,[9] daughter of Mizokuhi[10] of Mishima,[11] was admired on account of her beauty by the Great-Master-of-Things the Deity of Miwa,[12] qui, quum pulchra puella oletum fecit, in sagittam rubro [colore] fucatam se convertit, et ab inferiori parte cloacae [ad usum] faciendi oleti virginis privatas partes transfixit. Tunc pulchra virgo consternata est, et surrexit, et trepide fugit. Statim sagittam attulit, et juxta thalamum posuit. Subito [sagitta] formosus adolescens facta est, qui cito pulchram puellam sibi in matrimonio junxit, et filiam procreavit nomine Hoto-tarara-i-susugi-hime;[13] et est nomen alternativum Hime-tatara-i-suke-yori-hime.[14] (Id est posterior mutatio nominis, quoniam abhorruit facere mentionem privatarum partium). So therefore she is called the august child of a Deity. Hereupon seven beauteous maidens were out playing on the moor of Takasazhi,[15] and I-suke-yori-hime[16] was among them. His Augustness Ohokume, seeing I-suke-yori-hime, spoke to the Heavenly Sovereign in a Song, saying:

> " Seven maidens on the moor of Taka-
> sazhi in Yamato :—which shall be in-
> terlaced ? [17]

Then I-suke-yori-hime was standing first among the beauteous maidens. Forthwith the Heavenly Sovereign, having looked at the beauteous maidens, and knowing in his august heart[18] that I-suke-yori-hime was standing in the very front, replied by a Song, saying:

> " Even [after nought but] a fragment[ary
> glimpse], I will intertwine the lovely
> [one] standing in the very front.[19]

148 Then His Augustness Ohokume informed I-suke-yori-hime of the Heavenly Sovereign's decree, whereupon she, seeing the slit sharp eyes[20] of His Augustness Ohokume, sang in her astonishment, saying:

> "        ?        ?
> "        ?        ?
> " Wherefore the slit sharp eye ? [21]

Then His Augustness Ohokume replied by a Song, saying:

> " My slit sharp eyes [are] in order to
> find the maiden immediately." [22]

So the maiden said that she would respectfully serve [the Heavenly Sovereign].[23] Hereupon[24] the house of Her Augustness[25] I-suke-yori-hime was on [the back of] the River Sawi.[26] The Heavenly Sovereign made a progress to the abode of I-suke-yori-hime, and augustly slept 149 [there] one night.[27] (The reason why that river was called the River Sawi was that on the River's banks the mountain-lily-plant grew in abundance. So the name of the mountain-lily-plant was taken, and the designation of River Sawi [bestowed]. The name by which the mountain-lily-plant was originally called was *sawi*). **Afterwards, when I-suke-yori-hime came and entered into the palace, the Heavenly Sovereign sang augustly saying:**

> "In a damp hut on the reed-moor hav-
> ing spread layer upon layer of sedge
> mats, we two slept!"[26]

The names of the august children thus born were: His Augustness Hiko-ya-wi,[29] next His Augustness Kamu-ya-wi-mimi,[30] next His Augustness Kamu-nuna-kaha-mimi[31] (Three Deities.)[32]

---

1. Or. "*had* wedded; for the episode here related must be supposed to have taken place before Jim-mu and his army started eastward on their career of conquest.

2. *Ahira-hime.* Ahira is supposed by Motowori to be the name of a place in Satsuma. Its etymology is quite obscure.

3. *Wobashi no kimi.* Wobashi is supposed by Motowori to be the name of a place in Satsuma. The characters with which it is generally written mean "small bridge."

4. Ata is a place in Satsuma.

5. Or, "there were two Deities." The character employed is not that which itself actually signifies "deity," but is the Auxiliary Numeral for divine beings.

6. *I.e.*, perhaps "rudder-ears."

7. Motowori adduces good reasons for believing this name to be but a slightly altered form of the preceding one, and for holding that in the original form of the tradition there was but one child mentioned.

8. See Motowori's Commentary, Vol. XX, pp. 10-15, for the reasons for thus interpreting the characters 大后 in the text. Elsewhere it has generally, for the sake of convenience, been simply rendered "Empress."

9. *Seya-dotara-hime.* The signification of the name is obscure. Motowori supposes *Seya* to be a place and *tatara* (*nigori*'ed to *datara*) perhaps a plant written with the Chinese character 葦, said by Dr. Williams in his "Syllabic Dictionary" to be possibly a species of *Heteroiropa*.

10. It is uncertain whether this name should, or should not, be

regarded as properly that of a place. The meaning is equally obscure. The Chinese characters with which it is here written signify "ditch-eater," whereas those employed in the "Chronicles" signify "ditch-stake." Perhaps both transcriptions are simply phonetic.

11. A district in the province of Tsu (Settsu). The name signifies "three islands."

12. *Miwa-no-oho-mono-mushi-no-kami.* This god is supposed to be identical with Oho-kuni-nushi (the "Master of the Great Land," see end of Sect. XX and following Sects). The rigidly literal rendering of the name as here given would be "the Deity Great Master of Things of Miwa"; but the more intelligible version here given represents the Japanese author's meaning. For the traditional etymology of Miwa see the story related in Sect LXV.

13. *Hoto* significat partes privatas. Verbi *tatara* sensum supra s. v. *Seya-datara-hime* pertractavimus. *I* est vox expletiva. *Susugi* sensus est "trepide fugiens." Hime indicat regiam puellam.

14. *I.e.*, Princess Tatara-Startled-Good-Princess.

15. Etymology obscure.

16. An abbreviated form of the princess's alternative name.

17. The meaning of this Song is: "To which of the seven maidens now disporting themselves on the moor of Takasazhi shall I convey the Emperor's command to come that he may make her his consort, and sleep with his arms intertwined in hers?"—Motowori, overlooking the difference between *maku*, which is the word in the text, and the *nigori*'ed form *magu* met with in some other passages, misinterprets the last clause thus: "Which shall be sought?" He makes the same mistake in his explanation of the next Song.

18. *I.e.*, "having a presentiment."

19. The translation of this Song follows Moribe's exegesis. Motowori interprets it thus; "Well, well! I will seek the lovely one standing in the very front." As here rendered, the little poem is quite clear,—simply a declaration on the Emperor's part that he will make the girl standing in front his wife.

20. *Sakeru-to-me*, the original of the phrase here rendered "slit sharp eyes," is obscure and variously understood by the commentators. Moribe supposes the god to have worn a casque with a vizor, and the slit to have been made in the latter, and not actually in, or rather near, the eyes. It should however be observed that, though the Japanese word *saku* means "to slit," the Chinese character in the text properly signifies

" to tattoo (or brand) with ink," and is used with that meaning at the end of Sect. CXLIX, and elsewhere in the ancient books. The present writer, after comparing various passages in which the term occurs, thinks that we may understand a tattooiug of the outer corners of the eyes, which would give to the latter the appearance of being long and sharp, or, if the tattooing were very dark, of being actually slit.

21. The first lines of this short poem are so hopelessly unintelligible that the commentators are not even agreed as to how the syllables composing them should be divided into words. For the straits to which Motowori and his predecessors were driven in their efforts to obtain some plausible signification, see his Commentary, Vol. XX, pp. 27-29, and for Moribe's totally divergent interpretation see " *Idzu no Koto-waki*," Vol. II, pp. 30-31. It is not worth while to quote here more such conjectures.—For the doubt attaching to the precise signification of the words rendered by " slit sharp eyes," see the preceding Note.

22. The signification of this Song is as plain as that of the preceding one is obscure.

23. *Q.d.*, as his wife.

24. This initial expression is meaningless.

25. Having become the Emperor's consort, this Honorific title is now prefixed for the first time to her name.

26. *Sawi-gaha. Sawi*, as we learn from the compiler's note below, was the name of a kind of lily.

27. Literally, " one sojourn."

28. The signification of this Song is: " Now indeed thou comest to share the majesty of the palace. But the beginning of our intimacy was on that night when I came to thy humble dwelling on the reed-grown moor where, when we slept together, we had to pile mat upon mat to keep out the damp."—The translator has followed Moribe's interpretation throughout. Motowori takes in the sense of " ugly " the word here rendered ," damp," and all the previous commentators give a different explanation of the words *iya saya shikite*, here translated by " spreading layer upon layer." They take them to mean " spreading more and more cleanlily."

29. This name may signify " prince eight-wells." But the interpretation of *ya wi* as " eight wells " in his and the following name is doubtful.

30. This name may signify " divine-eight-wells-ears." But see preceding Note.

31. This name may signify " divine-lagoon-river-ears." But perhaps *Nuna-kaha* is the name of a place.

32. The character in the text is not actually " Deity," but 柱, *hashira*, the Auxiliary Numeral for Deities, which is constantly throughout these " Records" used in speaking of members of the Imperial family.

---

[SECT. LII.—EMPEROR JIM-MU (PART. IX—TROUBLES WHICH
FOLLOWED HIS DECEASE).]

So when, after the decease of the Heavenly Sovereign,[1]
150 the elder half-brother, His Augustness Tagishi-mimi,[2]
wedded[3] the Empress I-suke-yori-hime, he plotted how
he might slay his three younger brethren, pending which
their august[4] parent I-suke-yori-hime lamented, and made
[the plot] known to her august children by a Song.
The song said :

> " From the River Sawi the clouds have
> risen across, and the leaves of the trees
> have rustled on Mount Unebi : the wind
> is about to blow."[5]

Again she sang, saying :

> " Ah ! What rest on Mount Unebi as
> clouds in the day-time, will surely blow
> as wind at night-fall, [whence] the
> rustling of the leaves ! "[6]

When hereupon her august children, hearing and knowing [of the danger], were alarmed and forthwith were
about to slay Tagishi-mimi, His Augustness Kamu-nuna-
kaha-mimi said to his elder brother His Augustness
Kamu-ya-wi-mimi : " Thy dear Augustness, [do thou]
take a weapon, and go in and slay Tagishi-mimi." So
he took a weapon and went in, and was about to slay
him. But his arms and legs trembled so, that he was

unable to slay him. So then the younger brother His Augustness Kamu-nuna-kaha-mimi begged [to be allowed] to take the weapon which his elder brother held, and 151 went in and slew Tagishi-mimi. So again, in praise of his august name, he was called His Augustness Take-nuna-kaha-mimi.[7] Then His Augustness Kamu-ya-wi-mimi resigned [in favour of] the younger brother His Augustness Take-nuha-kaha-mimi, saying: "I could not slay the foeman; but Thine Augustness was at once able to slay him. So, though I be the elder brother, it is not right that I should be the superior.[8] Wherefore do Thine Augustness be the superior, and rule [all] beneath the Heaven. I[9] will assist Thine Augustness, becoming a priest,[10] and respectfully serving thee."

---

1. *I.e.*, the Emperor Jim-mu. His decease is not otherwise specially mentioned; but a formula at the end of the Section, which is repeated *mutatis mutandis* in the case of each Emperor, tells us the number of years he lived or reigned, and the place of his sepulture. Throughout these "Records," much matter is often placed in the reign of a Monarch already deceased, and which, according to our ideas, would more naturally be narrated under the heading of his successor.

2. Who was the deceased Emperor's son by Princess Ahira (see Sect. LI, Note 6,) and consequently step-son to the Empress and half-brother to her three sons.

3. This is the meaning of the Chinese character in the text. Motowori tries to save the Empress-Dowager's reputation for conjugal fidelity by rendering it in his *kana* reading by a word signifying "raped."

4. See Sect. XXII, Note 4.

5. The import of this metaphorical poem, taken in its context, is too clear to need much comment. The rising of the clouds and the rustling of the leaves may be supposed to represent the murderer's preparations, and the blowing of the wind his actual onslaught.

6. The meaning of this Song is: "The would-be murderer remains quiet during the day-time like the clouds hanging to the mountain-side; but at night he will burst upon you like the storm-wind. Already I

hear the leaves begin to rustle; already he is gathering his men together."

7. The word *take* prefixed to the name of this prince signifies "brave."

8. *I.e.*, either "superior to thee," or as Motowori understands the phrase, "*the* superior of all," *scil.* the Emperor.

9. Though the elder brother, he here uses the humble character 僕 "servant," to show his respect aud deference.

10. Literally, "a person who shuns," *q.d.* who shuns all pollution, and avoids certain food at certain seasons. *Conf.* the gentile name *Imi-be* commented on in Sect. XXXIII, Note 32.

---

[SECT. LIII.—EMPEROR JIM-MU (PART X.—GENEALOGIES).]

So His Augustness Hiko-ya-wi (is the ancestor of the Chieftains of Mamuta,[1] and of the Chieftains of Teshima.)[2] His Augustness Kamu-ya-wi-mimi (is the ancestor of the Grandees of Oho,[3] of the Chieftains of the Tribe of Chihisako,[4] of the chieftains of 152 the Tribe of Sahahi,[5] of the Dukes ol Hi,[6] of the Dukes of Ohokida,[7] of the Dukes of Aso,[7] of the Chieftains of the Granaries of Tsukushi,[9] of the Grandees of the Sazaki Tribe,[10] of the Rulers of the Tribe of Sazaki,[11] of the Rulers of Wo-Hatsuse,[12] of the Suzerains of Tsuke,[13] of the Rulers of the land of Iyo,[14] of the Rulers of the land of Shinanu,[15] of the Rulers of the land of Ihaki in Michinoku,[16] of the Rulers of the Land of Naka 153 in Hitachi,[17] of the Rulers of the land of Nagasa,[18] of the Suzerains of Funaki in Ise,[19] of the Grandees of Niha in Wohari,[20] and of the Grandees of Shimada.)[21]

---

1. *Mamuta no murazhi.* Mamuta is said to have been a place in the province of Kahachi. The etymology of the name is obscure.

2. *Teshima no murazhi.* Teshima is said to have been a place in the province of Tsu (Settsu). The name may signify "luxuriant island."

3. *Oho no omi.* Oho is said to have been a place in the province of Yamato. The name is mostly written with characters signifying "vast" or "numerous.'

4. *Chihisako-be no murazhi.* Chihisako is said to have been a place in the province of Etchiū. But the name of this family has also been traced to an incident mentioned in the "Newly Selected Catalogue of Family Names" as having occurred in the reign of the Emperor Yū-

riyaku, when, owing to a verbal error, a tax was collected in children instead of in cocoons. The monarch, amused at the mistake, is said to have granted to the tax-collector the " gentile name " of *Chihisako*, i.e, " Little Child."

5. *Sakahi-be no muhazhi.* *Sakahi* signifies " boundary," and this " gentile name " is traced to the fact, mentioned in the " Newly Selected Catalogue of Family Names," that the founder of the family distinguished himself by setting up boundary-marks on the frontiers of different provinces in the reign of the Emperor In-giyō (first half of the fifth century of the Christian era).

6. *Hi no kimi.* Hi (肥) is the name of a province (now two provinces) in the south-western island of Tsukushi. It is first mentioned in Sect. V, Note 17.

7. *Ohokida no kimi* Ohokida is the name of a district in the province of Toyo.

8. *Aso no himi.* Aso is the name of a district in Higo, containing a celebrated volcano.

9. *Tsukushi no miyake no murazhi.*

10. *Sazaki-be no omi.* This name is connected by the compiler of the " Newly Selected Catalogue of Family Names " with that of the Emperor Nin-toku (Oho-sazaki no Mikoto), for which see Sect. CIV, Note 18.

11. *Sazaki-be no miyatsuko.*

12. *Wo hatsuse no miyatsuko.* This name is connected with that of the Emperor Mu-retsu, whose name was Wo-Hatsuse no Waka-Sazaki.

13. *Tsuke no atahe.* Tsuke is the name of a place in Yamato.

14. *Iyo no kuni no miyatsuko.* For the province of Iyo see Sect. V, Note 26.

15. *Shinanu no kuni no miyatsuko.* For the province of *Shinanu* (*Shinano*) see Sect. XXXII, Note 26.

16. *Michinoku no Ihaki no kuni no miyatsuko.* A popular derivation of *Michinoku* is from *michi no kuni,* " the country of the road ;" but a more likely one, sanctioned by Motowori, is from *michi no oku,* the furthest or more distant part of the road." (For the word " road," as here used, *conf.* Sect. LXV, Note 2.). It was for many centuries, and is still in poetry, a vague name for the entire north of Japan. *Ihaki,* sometimes considered a province, and at others only ranking as a district, formed its south-eastern portion along the Pacific sea-board. The name seems to signify " rock (or hard) castle."

17. *Hitachi no naka no huni no miyatzuko.* Hitachi is a province to the south of Ihaki. Motowori quotes more than one traditional derivation of its name, the best of which, taken from the old Topography of the province, is *hita-michi*, "plain road," referring to the level nature of that part of the country. *Naka* is the name of a district. The word signifies "middle," and may have arisen from the fact of the district bearing it being situated between two considerable rivers.

18. *Nagasa no kuni no miyatzuko.* Nagasa is a district in that portion of the old province of Kadzusa which was in very early historical times cut off from the little province of Aha. The import of the name is not clear.

19. *Ise no Funaki no atahe.* For Ise see Sect. XLIX, Note 4. Of Funaki nothing is known. The characters with which the name is written signify "boat-tree."

20. *Ohari no Niha no omi.* Wohari is one of the central provinces of Japan. The name is of uncertain origin. Niha is the name of a district, and is of uncertain origin.

21. *Shimada no omi.* Shimada is the name of a district in Wohari, and signifies "island rice-fields."

---

[SECT. LIV.—EMPEROR JIM-MU (PART XI.—HIS AGE AND
PLACE OF BURIAL).]

His Augustness Kamu-nuna-kaha-mimi ruled the Empire. Altogether the august years of this Heavenly Sovereign Kamu-yamato-ihare-biko were one hundred and thirty-seven.[1] His august mausoleum is on the top of the Kashi Spur on the northern side of Mount Unebi.[2]

---

1. The author's confused style must not here mislead the student. It is *after* the decease of the Emperor Jim-mu (Kamu-yamato-ihare-biko), who attains to the age of a hundred and thirty-seven, that the Emperor Suwi-zei (Kamu-nuna-kaha-mimi begins to rule.

2. For *Unebi* see Sect. LI, Note 9. *Kashi* signifies "oak." The word rendered "spur" is *wo*.

[SECT. LV.—EMPEROR SUI-ZEI.]

His Augustness Kamu-nuna-kaha-mimi dwelt at the
palace of Takawoka in Kadzuraki,[1] and ruled the Empire.
This Heavenly Sovereign wedded Kaha-mata-bime,[2] ancestress of the Departmental Lords of Shiki,[3] and begot 154
an august child: His Augustness Shiki-tsu-hiko-tama-de-
mi[4] (one Deity). The Heavenly Sovereign's august years
were forty-five. His august mausoleum is on the Mound
of Tsukida.[5]

---

1. In the province of Yamato. *Taka-woka* signifies "high mound."
*Kadzuraki* means "pueraria castle," a name accounted for by a legend in
the "Chronicles," which relates how an earth-spider was caught in this
place by means of a net made of pueraria tendrils. Kadzuraki was the
name, not only of a town, but of a district.

2. *I.e.*, the Princess of Kahamata, a place in Kahachi. The name
signifies "river-fork." For the omission in this and a few other places
of the words "daughter of," etc., which might be expected instead of
"ancestress," see Motowori's Commentary, Vol. XXI, p. 4.

3. *Shiki na agata-nushi*. Shiki is in Yamato. The signification
of the name seems to be "stone castle."

4. *Shiki-tsu-hiko* signifies "Prince of Shiki." Motowori believes
Tamade to be in like manner the name of a place, while he interprets *mi*
as the common abbreviation of the Honorific (?) *mimi*.

5. A place in Yamato. Motowori derives the name from *tsuki*
modern *toki*), the "ibis," and *ta*, "rice-field."

---

[SECT. LVI.—EMPEROR AN-NEI.]

His Augustness Shiki-tsu-hiko-tama-de-mi dwelt in the
palace of Ukiana at Kata-shiha,[1] and ruled the Empire.
This Heavenly Sovereign wedded Akuto-hime,[2] daughter
of the Departmental Lord Haye,[3] elder brother of Kaha-
mata-bime, and begot august children: His Augustness

Toko-ne-tsu-hiko-irone,[4] next His Augustness Oho-yamato-hiko-suki-tomo,[5] next His Augustness Shiki-tsu-hiko.[6] Of the august children[6] of this Heavenly Sovereign,—three Deities, — His Augustness Oho-yamato-hiko-suki-tomo [was he who afterwards] ruled the Empire. There were two Kings,[7] children of the next [brother], His August-155 ness Shiki-tsu-hiko. One child[8] (was the ancestor of the Territorial Lords of Suchi in Iga,[9] of the Territorial Lords of Nabari,[10] and of the Territorial Lords of Minu);[11] one child,[12] His Augustness Wa-chi-tsumi,[13] dwelt in the palace of Miwi in Ahaji.[14] So this King had two daughters : the name of the elder was Hahe-irone,[15] and another name for her was Her Augustness Princess Oho-yamato-kuni-are :[16] the name of the younger was Hahe-irodo.[17] The Heavenly Sovereign's august years were forty-nine. Augustness mausoleum est in privatis partibus Montis Unebi.[18]

---

1. In Kahachi : *uki-ana* signifies " floating hole," *Kata-shiha* is said to signify " hard rock " (*kata-iha*) ; but this seems doubtful, and the reading given by the characters in the text is not *Kata-shiha*, but *Kata-shiho*.

2. *I.e.,* Princess of Akuto, or Akuta,—for the latter form of the name is more common. There exists a place thus called in Settsu. The derivation of the word is obscure.

3. *Agata-nushi-Haye.* The reading of this name is obscure, and its derivation uncertain.

4. *Irone* signifies " elder brother " or " elder sister." The rest of the compound is obscure.

5. The first three elements of the compound signify " Great Yamato Prince." The last two are obscure, but Motowori identifies *suki* (see Note 3 to preceding Sect.)

6. *I.e.,* " Prince of Shiki "; so called, it is supposed, with reference to the place of residence of his grandfather.

7. The character thus translated is 王, of which " King " is the original and proper signification. To judge by some other passages in the ancient histories, it had not yet in the 8th century altogether paled to

the lesser meaning of "prince," which has belonged to it in later times when denoting Japanese personages. It is still, as far as possible, used to denote the rulers of all countries excepting Japan, the zealous admirers of the native literature and institutions even designating by it the Emperor of China, who, one would have thought, had a special right to the more Honorific title of Emperor, which his own subjects were the first to invent. On the whole, therefore, "King" seems to be the most appropriate readering. The characters 王女 are, by analogy, rendered "Queen."

8. The text has "descendant"; but it must here be corrupt or at least faulty, as may be seen by the omission of the proper name.

9. *Iga no Suchi no inaki.* The etymology of *Iga* and that of *Suchi* are alike obscure. See however Motowori's Commentary, Vol. XXI, p. 13, for the traditional derivation of the former. It is the name of a small province which in very ancient times formed part of the province of Ise.

10. *Nabari no inaki.* Nabari is in Iga. The name signifies, "hiding."

11. *Minu no inaki.* Minu, not to be confounded with the province of the same name, is a place in Iga. The name probably signifies "three moors."

12. *I.e*, the other child.

13. Motowori reads *Chichitsumi.* In any case, the name remains obscure.

14. For Ahaji see Sect. VI, Note 3. *Mi-wi* signifies "august well," and the name is traced to the custom of bringing water from the Island of Ahaji for use in the Imperial Palace, as mentioned in Sect. CXXIX of the present work, and elsewhere in the early literature.

15. *Irone* means "elder sister." *Hahe* is of uncertain import, it being written with completely different characters in the two histories.

16. *Oho - yamato - kuni - are - hime- no-mikoto.* Ono-yamato-kuni signifies "the land of Great Yamato," and *hime* slgnifies "princess" or "maiden." Motowori suggests that *are*, which is an obscure word, may signify "pure."

17. *Irodo* signifies "younger sister." For *hahe conf.* Note 15.

18. *Scil.* in interiori parte montis, *e.g.* in spelunca. Motowori explains the use of the term by reference to such words as *foot*, where the name of a portion of the human body is applied to a mountain. In Japanese there are others besides *ashi* ("foot"), such as *itadaki, hara* and *koshi.*

His Augustness Oho-yamato-hiko-suki-tomo dwelt in the palace of Sakahiwo at Karu,[1] and ruled the Empire. This Heavenly Sovereign wedded her Augustness Princess Futo-ma-waka,[2] another name for whom was Her Augustness Princess Ihi-bi,[3] ancestress of the Departmental Lords of Shiki,[4] and begot august children : His Augustness Mi-ma-tsu-hiko-wake-shine,[5] next His Augustness Tagishi-hiko[6] (two Deities). So His Augustness Mi-ma-tsu-hiko-kawe-shine [was he who afterwards] ruled the Empire. The next His Augustness Tagishi-hiko (was the ancestor of the Lords of Chinu,[7] of the Lords of Take in Tajima,[8] and of the Territorial Lords of Ashiwi).[9] The Heavenly Sovereign's august years were forty-five. His august mausoleum is above the Vale of Manago by Mount Unebi.[10]

---

1. Karu, which still remains as a village in the province of Yamato, was famous down to the early historical days of Japan, being often mentioned by the poets. The derivation of the name is quite uncertain. *Sakahi-wo* probably signifies "boundary mound."

2. *Futo-ma-waka-hime-no-mikoto.* The compound signifies "vast, true, and young princess."

3. *Ihibi-hime-no-mikoto.* The name seems to signify "rice-sun-princess."

4. See Sect. LV, Note 3.

5. The import of this name is obscure.

6. *I.e.*, perhaps "rudder prince."

7. *Chinu no wake.* For Chinu see Sect. XLIV, Notes 35 and 36.

8. *Tajima no Take no wake.* Motowori tells us that no mention of any place called Take in the province of Tajima is to be found in any other book.

9. *Ashiwi no inaki.* The same remark applies to this name as to the last. The two "gentile names" here mentioned are equally unknown except from this passage.

10. *Unebi-yama no Manago-dani.* It is in Yamato, and is now called *Masago*. The name signifies "a sandy place, or desert."

[SECT. LVIII.—EMPEROR KO-SHO.]

His Augustness Mi-ma-tsu-hiko-kawe-shine dwelt at
the palace of Waki-no-kami in Kadzuraki,[1] and ruled the
Empire. This Heavenly Sovereign wedded Her August-157
ness Princess Yoso-taho,[2] younger sister of Oki-tsu-yoso[3]
ancestor of the Chiefs of Wohari,[4] and begot august
children: His Augustness Ame-oshi-tarashi-hiko,[5] and
next His Augustness Oho-yamato-tarashi-hiko-kuni-oshi-
bito[6] (two Deities). Now the younger brother, His Augustness Tarashi-hiko-kuni-oshi-bito [was he who afterwards]
ruled the Empire. The elder brother His Augustnsss
Ame-oshi-tarashi-hiko (was the ancestor of the Grandees of Kasuga,[7]
the Grandees of Ohoyake,[8] the Grandees of Ahata,[9] the Grandees of
Wonu,[10] the Grandees of Kaki-no-moto,[11] the Grandees of Ichihiwi,[12] the
Grandees of Ohosaka,[13] the Grandees of Ana,[14] the Grandees of Taki,[45] 158
the Grandees of Haguri,[16] the Grandees of Chita,[17] the Grandees of Muza,[18]
the Grandees of Tsunuyama,[19] the Dukes of Ihitaka in Ise,[20] the Dukes
of Ichishi,[21] and the Rulers of the Land of Chika-tsu-Afumi).[22]

The Heavenly Sovereign's august years were ninety-
three. His August mausoleum is on Mount Hakata[22] at
Waki-no-kami.

---

1. In Yamato. The name of Waki-no-kami is of uncertain derivation. In the "Chronicles" the Emperor Kō-shō is said to have "dwelt
at the palace of Ikegokoro at Waki-no-kami." For Kadzuraki see Sect.
LV, Note 1.

2. *Yoso-taho-bime-no-mikoto.* Here written phonetically, this name
appears in the "Chronicles" written with characters to which the signification of "perfectly ornamented princess" should be attributed.

3. The signification of this name is obscure, but it seems to be connected in some way with that of the other sister.

4. *Wohari no murazhi.*

5. *I.e.,* heavenly great perfect prince."

6. *I.e.,* "great Yamato perfect prince, country great man." This
name appears in an abbreviated form in the next sentence.

7. *Kasuga na omi.* Kasuga is a celebrated place in the province of Yamato. The name is of uncertain origin, though the "Catalogue of Family Names" gives a story referring it to *Kasu gaki* (糟垣), *i.e.*, "lees fence." The curious combination of characters with which Kasuga is written,—一春日,—may be traced to the Pillow-Word *haru-hi no* (春日之) which was not unnaturally prefixed to a name which so much resembled the Verb *kasumu*, "to be misty."

8. *Ohoyake no omi.* Ohoyake is a place in Yamato. The name signifies "great granary."

9. *Ahata no omi.* Ahata is a place in Yamashiro. The name signifies "millet-field."

10. *Wonu no omi.* Wonu is a place in Afumi. The name signifies "little moor."

11. *Kakinnomoto-uo-omi.* Kaki-no-moto signifies "at the bottom of the persimmon-tree," and the name is said by the compiler of the "Catalogue of Family Names" to have been granted to this family in allusion to a persimmon-tree which grew near their gate. This name was rendered illustrious in the eighth century by the poet Kakinomoto Hitomaro (See the present writer's "Classical Poetry of the Japanese," p. 217 *et seq.*).

12. *Ichihiwi no omi.* Ichihiwi is in Yamato. The name may signify "oak-well."

13. *Ohosaka no omi.* Ohosaka is a place in Bingo. The name signifies "great hill, or pass,"

14. *Ana no omi.* Ana is a department in Bingo. The name signifies "hole" or "cave."

15. *Taki no omi.* Taki is a district in Tamba. The name, which is a common one in Japan, means "water-falls."

16. *Haguri no omi.* Haguri is a district in Wohari. The signification of the name is obscure.

17. *Chita no omi.* Chita is a district in Wohari. The signification of the name is obscure.

18. *Muza no omi.* Mudza is a district in Kadzusa. The name seems to be a corruption of the Chinese words 武射. "warlike archer."

19. *Tsunuyama no omi.* The family, the place, and the signification of the name are alike obscure.

20. *Ise no Ihitaka no kimi.* Ihitaka is the name of a district, and is traced to the signification of "abundant rice."

21. *Ichishi no kimi.* Ichishi is a district in Ise. The signification of the name is obscure.

22. *Chika tsu Afumi no kuni-no-miyatsuko.* For Chika-tsu-Afumi
see Sect. XXIX, Note 20.

23. In Yamato. The signification of the name is obscure.

---

[SECT. LIX.—EMPEROR KOAN.]

His Augustness Oho-yamato-tarashi-hiko-kuni-oshi-bito
dwelt in the palace of Akidzushima at Muro[1] in Kadzuraki, and ruled the Empire. This Heavenly Sovereign
wedded his niece Her Augustness Princess Oshika,[2] and
begot august children : His Augustness Oho-kibi-no-moro-
susumi,[3] next His Augustness, Oho-yamato-ne-ko-hiko-
futo-ni[4] (two Deities). So His Augustness Oho-yamato-ne- 159
ko-hiko-futo-ni [was he who afterwards] ruled the
Empire. The heavenly Sovereign's august years were
one hundred and twenty-three. His august mausoleum
is on the Mound of Tamade.[5]

---

1. In Yamato. *Muro* signifies "cave" or "pit." *Aki-dzu-shima*,
"the Island of the Dragon-Fly," is frequently used as an alternative name
of Japan (see Sect. V, Note 26). See also the Emperor Yū-riyaku's song
given in Sect. CLVI.

2. *Oshika-hime-no-mikoto.* The name *Oshika*, which is obscure,
appears in the "Chronicles" under the form of *Oshi*, which has generally
been interpreted by Motowori (whom the translator follows) as a corruption of *ohoshi*, "great." This version of the name makes it harmonize
with that of the Princess's father.

3. See Sect. LX, Note 11.

4. This name seems to signify "Great Yamato's Lord Prince, the
Vast Jewel."

5. *Tamade no woka.* In Yamato. For this name see Motowori's
Commentary, Vol. XXI, pp. 37-38,

---

[SECT. LX.—EMPEROR KŌ-REI.]

His Augustness Oho-yamato-ne-ko-hiko-futo-ni dwelt at the Palace of Ihodo at Kuruda,[1] and ruled the Empire. This Heavenly Sovereign wedded Her Augustness Princess Kuhashi,[2] daughter of Ohome,[3] ancestor of the Departmental Lords of Tohochi,[4] and begot an august child: His Augustness Oho-yamato-ne-ko-hiko-kuni-kuru[5] (one Deity). Again he wedded Princess Chiji-haya-ma-waka of Kasuga,[6] and begot an august child: Her Augustness Princess Chiji-haya[7] (one Deity). Again wedding Her Augustness Princess Oho-yamato-kuni-are,[8] he begot august children: Her Augustness Yamato-to-mo-so-bime,[9] next His Augustness Hiko-sashi-kata-wake;[10] next His Augustness Hiko-isa-seri-biko,[11] another name for whom is His Augustness Oho-biki-tsu-hiko: next Yamato-to-bi-haya-waka-ya-hime[12] (four Deities). Again he wedded Haheirodo,[13] younger sister of Her Augustness Princess Are, and begot august children,—His Augustness Hiko-same-ma,[14] next His Augustness Waka-hiko-take-kibi-tsu-hiko[15] (two Deities). The august children of this Heavenly Sovereign [numbered] in all eleven Deities (five kings and three queens). So His Augustness Oho-yamato-ne-ko-hiko-kuni-kuru [was he who afterwards] ruled the Empire. The two Deities His Augustness Oho-kibi-tsu-hiko and His Augustness Waka-take-kibi-tsu-hiko together set sacred jars[16] at the front[17] of the River Hi[18] in Harima;[19] and, making Harima the mouth of the road,[20] subdued and pacified the Land of Kibi. So His Augustness Oho-kibi-tsu-hiko (was the ancestor of the Grandees of Kamu-tsu-michi in Kibi).[21] The next, His Augustness Waka-hiko-take-kiki-tsu-hiko (was the ancestor of the Grandees of Shimo-tsu-michi in

Kibi[22] and of the Grandees of Kasa[23]).  The next His Augustness
Hiko-same-ma (was the ancestor of the Grandees of Uzhika in Harima[42]).
The next, His Augustness Hiko-sashi-kata-wake (was the
ancestor of the Grandees of Tonami in Koshi,[25] of the Grandees of Kunisaki in the Land of Toyo,[26] of the Dukes of Ihobara,[27] and of the Maritime Suzerains of Tsunuga).[28]  The Heavenly Sovereign's august
years were one hundred and six.  His august mausoleum
is at Umasaka at Kotawoka.

---

1.  In Yamato.    *Iho-do* signifies "hut door."    *Kuru-da* (*Kuroda*
would be the more natural reading) signifies "black rice-field."

2.  *Kuhashi-hime-no-mikoto.*    The name signifies "beautiful princess."

3.  This seems to have been originally not a personal name, but the
name of a place in Wohari.

4.  *To-hochi no agata-mushi.*    Tohochi is a district in Yamato.  The
name seems to signify "ten marts."

5.  This name signifies "great Yamato's lord prince who rules the
land."

6.  *Kasuga no-chiji-haya-ma-waka-hime.*  This name probably signifies
"the thousand-fold brilliant truly young princess of Kasuga."  For Kasuga
see Sect, LVIII, Note 7.

7.  *Chiji-haya-hime-no-mikoto, i.e.,* probably "thousand-fold brilliant
princess."

8.  *Oho-yamato-kuni-are-hime-no-mikoto.*  See Sect. LVI, Note 16.

9.  Motowori assigns to this name the signification of "Yamato's
hundred thousand-fold illustrious princess," and has a very long note on
the subject in Vol. XXI, p. 42, *et. seq.*

10.  The signification of this name is not clear.

11.  *I.e.,* "prince valorously advancing prince."  The alternative
name signifies "Great Prince of Kibi," and both refer to his conquest of
the province of Kibi as related a little further on in this Section.  Motowori gives good reasons for supposing that *Oho-kibi-no-moro-susumi*, i.e.
"He Who Completely Advances in Great Kibi," is but another form of
the same name, erroneously inserted in the account of the preceding
reign (see Sect, LIX, Note 3).

12.  *I.e.,* perhaps "Yamato's hundred-fold wondrous brilliant young
ornamental Princess."  The name resembles that of the elder sister.

13.  For this and the next following names see Sect. LVI, Notes 17
and 16 respectively.

14. This name is obscure, and differs from that given in the parallel passage of the "Chronicles," where we read Sashima. The latter sounds more authentic.

15. *I.e.,* "the young prince the brave prince of Kibi." This name refers to his conquest of Kibi, as related a few lines further on.

16. *I.e.,* earthenware jars of a moderate size, probably intended to hold the rice-liquor offered to the gods. Being easily broken, they were planted in the ground up to a certain height.

17. The probable meaning of this peculiar expression is "a bend in the river."

18. Written with the character 氷, "ice," which may however be only phonetic. No river of this name is anywhere else mentioned as flowing through the province of Harima, aud one is tempted to suppose that there is some confusion with the celebrated river Hi, which figures so frequently in the Idzumo cycle of legends.

19. One of the central provinces of Japan, on the northern shores of the Inland Sea. Some derive the name from *hagi-hara*, "lespedeza moor," while others, connect it with *hari*, a "needle." Neither etymology has much to recommend it.

20. *I.e.,* "their point of departure." It must also be remembered that "road" came to have the sense of "circuit" or "province," so that we might translate this phrase by "the commencement of the circuit." *Conf.* such denominations as *Koshi no michi no kuchi*, *Koshi no michi no naka*, and *Koshi no michi no shiri* for what are in modern parlance the provinces of Echizen, Etchiu and Echigo. The region nearest to the capital was called the mouth, while equally graphic designations were bestowed on the more remote districts. It was, as we learn by comparison with a passage in the history of the reign of the Emperor Su-jin (see Sect. LXVI, Note 13), customary thus to plant earthenware jars in the earth at the point whence an army started on an expedition, this being considered a means of invoking upon it the blessing of the gods. Not only so, but down to the Middle Ages travellers in general were in the habit of worshipping at the shrine of the god of roads. For "road" in the sense of "circuit," "province," or "administrative division" see Sect. LXVI, Note 2.

21. *Kibi no kamu-tsu-michi no omi.* *Kamu-tsu-michi i.e.,* "the Upper Road" or "Circuit," was the ancient name of the province of Bizen (or of a portion of it), which formerly was a part of the Land of Kibi.

22. *Kibi no shimo-tsu-michi no omi. Shimo-tsu-michi* means "the lower road," and was the ancient name of a portion of the province of Bitchiū, which formerly was a part of the land of Kibi.

23. *Kasa no omi, i.e.,* "Grandees of the Hat," a "gentile name" which is referred by the compiler of the "Catalogue of Family Names" to an incident in the reign of the Emperor O-jin, which he however by no means clearly relates (See Motowori's Commentary, Vol. XXI; p.p. 57-58).

24. *Harima no Uzhika no omi.* Uzhika is the name of a place. It is written with characters signifying "cow and deer," but the true derivation is quite uncertain.

25. *Koshi no Tonami no omi.* Tonami is a district in Etchiū. he signification of the name is uncertain.

26. *Toyo-kuni no Kunisaki no omi.* Kunisaki is a district in Bungo. The name seems to signify "land's end."

27. *Ihobara no kimi.* Ihobara is a district in Suruga. The signification of the name is obscure.

28. *Tsunuga no ama no atahe.* For Tsunuga see Sect. CI, Notes 3 and 12. Perhaps the name should rather be rendered "the Suzerains of Ama in Tsunuga," as Ama may, after all, as Motowori suggests, be here the name of a place.

29. In the Province of Yamato. *Kata-woka* signifies "side-mound" or "incomplete mound." *Uma-saka* signifies "horse-hill" or "horse-pass." Umasaka should perhaps be understood as the particular designation of a portion of the ascent of Katawoka, which is mentioned in the "Chronicles" as the name of a mountain.

———

[SECT. XLI.—EMPEROR KŌ-GEN.  162

His Augustness Oho-yamato-ne-ko-hiko-kuni-kuru dwelt in the palace of Sakaki-bara at Karu,[1] and ruled the Empire. This heavenly Sovereign wedded Her Augustness Utsu-shiko-me,[2] younger sister of His Augustness Utsu-shiko-wo,[3] ancestor of the Grandees of Hodzumi,[4] and begot august children: His Augustness Oho-biko,[5] next His Augustness Sukuna-biko-take-wi-goro;[6] next His Augustness Waka-yamato-ne-ko-hiko-oho-bibi[7] (three Deities).

Again, wedding Her Augustness I-gaka-shiko-me,[8] daughter
of His Augustness Utsu-shiko-wo, he begot an august
child : His Augustness Hiko-futu-oshi-no-makoto.[9] Again,
wedding Princess Haniyasu,[10] daughter of Awotama[11] of
Kafuchi, he begot an august child : His Augustness Take-
hani-yasu-biko[12] (one Deity). The august children of this
Heavenly Sovereign [numbered in all five Deities]. So
His Augustness Waka-yamato-ne-ko-hiko-oho-bibi [was
he who afterwards] ruled the Empire. The children of
163 his elder brother, His Augustness Oho-biko, were His
Augustness Take-numa-kaha-wake[13] (ancestor of the Grandees of
Abe);[14] next His Augustness Hiko-inakoshi-wake.[15] (This
was the ancestor of the Butler Grandees.)[16] His Augustness Hiko-
futu-oshi-no-mikoto wedded Princess Takachina of Kadzuraki,[17] young sister of Cho-nabi,[18] ancestor of the Chiefs
of Wohari,[19] and begot a child : the Noble Umashi Uchi.[20]
(This was the ancestor of the Grandees of Uchi in Yamashiro.)[21]
Again, wedding Princess Yama-shita-kage,[22] younger sister
of Udzu-hiko,[23] ancestor of the Rulers of the Lord of
Ki,[24] he begot a child, the Noble Take-Uchi.[24] The
children of this Noble Take-Uchi [numbered] in all nine
(seven males and two females),— namely] the Noble of Hata-
no-Yashiro,[25] [who] (was the ancestor of the Grandees of Hata,[27]
of the Grandees of Hayashi,[28] of the Grandees of Hami,[29] of the Grandee s
of Hoshikaha,[30] of the Grandees of Afumi,[31] and of the Dukes of
Hatsuse Tribe);[32] next the Noble Kose-no-Wo-Kara[33] [who]
(was the ancestor of the Grandees of Kose,[34] of the Grandees of the
Sazaki Tribe,[35] and of the Grandees of the Karu Tribe);[36] next the
Noble Soga no Ishikaha[37] [who] (was the ancestor of the
Grandees of Soga,[38] of the Grandees of Kahanobe,[39] of the Grandees of Tanaka,[40] of the Grandees of Takamuko,[41] of the Grandees
of Woharida,[42] of the Grandees of Sakurawi,[43] and of the
Grandees of Kishida);[44] next the Noble Heguri-no-Tsuku,[45]

[who] (was the ancestor of the Grandees of Heguri,[46] of the Grandees of Sawara,[47] and of the Uma-mi-kuhi Chiefs);[48] next the Noble Ki-no-Tsunu[49] [who] (was the ancestor of the Grandees of Ki,[50] of the Grandees of Tsumu,[51] and of the Grandees of Sakamoto);[52] next Princess Mato of Kume;[53] next Princess Nu-no-iro;[54] next Kadzuraki-no-Nagaye-no-sotsu-biko[55] [who] (was the ancestor of the Grandees of Tamade,[56] of the Grandees of Ikuha,[57] of the Grandees of Ikuye[58] and of the Grandees of Agina),[59] moreover [there was] the Noble Waku-go[60] (the ancestor of the Grandees of Yenuma).[61] This Heavenly Sovereign's august years were fifty-seven. His august mausoleum is on the mound in the middle of the Pool of Tsurugi.[62]

---

1. In Yamato. For Karu see Sect. LVII, Note 1. *Sakahi-bara* signifies " boundary moor,"

2. *I.e.*, perhaps, " the beautiful but alarming female."

3. *I.e.*, perhaps, " the beautiful but alarming male."

4. *Hodzumi no omi.* There are several places called Hodzumi in various provinces. The name appears to signify " piling up rice-ears."

5. *I.e.*, " great prince."

6. *I.e.*, " little prince-fierce-boar-heart," the boar being known for its savage disposition.

7. Excluding the last member of the compound, this name signifies " young-Yamato-lord-prince-great." *Bibi* is identified by Motowori with the word *mimi*, which so often recurs in proper names (see Sect. XIII, Note 18).

8. Motowori explains this name in the sense of " brilliant-alarming-female," but some doubt must attach to it.

9. *I.e.*, perhaps, " prince vast-great-truth."

10. *Hani-yasu-bime.* This name has already been met with in Sect. VII, Note 3. Motowori however supposes that in this place Haniyasu should be considered to be the name of a place in Yamato.

11. *I.e.*, a man called " green jewel" who lived in the province of Kafuchi.

12. *Take* signifies " brave." For the rest of the name see Note 10.

13. *Take* signifies " brave." *Wake* is either " young" or " lord." For *Nuna-kaha* see Sect. LI, Note 31.

14. *Abe no omi.* There are several places called Abe, and it is doubtful to which of them the text here refers.

15. The signification of *inakoshi* seems to be "rice-chariot". *Hiko* is "prince," and *wake* either "young" or "lord."

16. *Kashihade no omi.* This name is traditionally referred to an incident in the reign of the Emperor Kei-kō, who is said to have bestowed it on one of his attendants who served up to him a particularly savoury dish of shell-fish. "Butlers" (perhaps the word might also be rendered "cooks") have been mentioned towards the end of Sect. XXXII, and again in the legend of Jim-mu's slaughter of the "earth-spiders" related in Sect. XLVIII.

17. *Katsuraki-no-takachina-bime-no-mikoto.* The signification of *Taka-china* is obscure.

18. By aphaeresis for *Oho-inabi*, the form of the name given in the "Chronicles of Old Matters of Former Ages," itself perhaps standing by apocope for *Oho-ina-biko*, which would signify "great rice-prince."

19. *Wohari no Murazhi.*

20. *Umashi Uchi no sukune. Umashi* signifies "sweet," and *Uchi* is the name of a place in Yamashiro.

21. *Yamashiro no Uchi no omi.*

22. This name may be rendered literally "the shade beneath the mountains," but the signification is "the glow from the autumn leaves on the mountain-side."

23. *I.e.*, probably "wonderful (or precious) prince."

24. *Ki no kuni no miyatsuko no aya.*

25. *Take-Uchi no sukune. Take* signifies "brave," and *Uchi* is the name of a district in Yamato. The common, but erroneous, reading of this name is *Take no Uchi no sukune.* The celebrated personage, who may be styled the Methuselah of Japan, is said to have lived during the reigns of five Emperors, who themselves averaged over a hundred years of life each. His own age is variously given as 255, 260, etc. up to 360 years.

26. *Hata no Yashiro no sukune. Hata* and *Yashiro* are supposed by Motowori to be the names of places in Yamato. *Yashiro* signifies "shrine." *Hata* is of uncertain derivation.

27. *Hata no omi.*

28. *Hayashi no omi.* Hayashi is the name of a place in Kawachi, and signifies "forest."

29. *Hami no omi.* There is a Hami in Afumi and another in Tamba. The signification of the name is obscure.

30. *Hoshikaha no omi.* Hoshikaha is a place in Yamato. The name signifies " star river."

31. *Afumi no omi.* For Afumi see Sect. XXIX, Note 20.

32. *Hatsuse-be no Kimi.* For Hatsuse see Sect. CXLIII, Note 8.

33. *Kose no Wo-kara no sukune.* Kose is the name of a place in Yamato. The meaning of Wo-kara is obscure.

34. *Kose no omi.*

35. *Sazakibe no omi.* See Sect. LIII, Note 10.

36. *Kurube no omi.*

37. *Soga no Ishikaha no sukune.* Soga is a place in Yamato, and Ishikaha a district in Kahachi. In cases like this it must generally be presumed that the family had two seats, or was divided into two branches residing in different places. Sometimes, however, the original seat and that to which the family afterwards removed are meant to be indicated.

38. *Soga no omi.* The signification of Soga is obscure.

39. *Kahanobe no omi.* Kahanobe is the name of a district in Settsu, and signifies " river-bank."

40. *Tanaka no omi.* Tanaka is the name of a place in Yamato and signifies " among the rice-fields."

41. *Takamuko no omi.* Takamuko seems to be the name of a place in Echizen. Its signification is uncertain.

42. *Woharida no omi.* Woharida is a place in Yamato. The name seems to mean " little ploughed field."

43. *Sakurawi no omi.* Sakurawi is the name of a place in Kahachi and signifies " cherry-tree well."

44. *Kishida no omi.* Kishida is a place in Yamato. The signification of the name is not clear.

45. *Heguri no Tsuku no sukune.* Heguri is the name of a district in Yamato, and is of uncertain signification. *Tsuku* (modern *dzuku*), " owl," is a name which is referred to a tradition that will be found in Motowori's Commentary, Vol. XXII, p. 29.

46. *Heguri no omi.*

47. *Sawara no omi.* Sawara was perhaps a district in Chikuzen. The signification of the name is obscure.

48. *Uma mi-kuhi no murazhi.* The literal significance of the characters with which *Uma-mi-kuhi* is written is " horse august post." But whether this name had any relation to horses, or whether it should simply be regarded as the name of a place is quite uncertain.

49. *Ki no Tsunu no sukune.* Ki is the name of a province, and

Tsunu that of a district in another province,—the province of Suhau (Suwō). *Conf.* Note 37.

50. *Kĭ no omi.*

51. *Tsunu no omi.*

52. *Sakamoto no omi.* Sakamoto is the name of a place in Idzumi, and signifies " base of the hill."

53. *Kume no Ma-ito-hime.* *Kume* may be, as Motowori says, the name of a place. But see Sect. XXXIV, Note 7. In any case the place, if it existed, was probably called after some person of the name of Kume. The signification of Ma-iro is obscure.

54. *Nu-no-iro-hime.* The meaning of this name is obscure.

55. *Kadzuraki* is the already frequently mentioned name of a district in Yamato, and Nagaye is likewise the name of a place,—whether in Yamato or in Kahachi is not certain. It signifies " long inlet." Motowori thinks that the syllable *so* in this place is the same as the of *kuma-so*, and signifies " valiant " or " fierce."

56. *Tamade no omi.* There is a Tamade in Yamato and another in Kahachi. The signification of the name is uncertain.

57. *Ikuha no omi.* The " Chronicles of Japan " tell us that the original form of this name *Ikuha* was *uki-ha*, *i.e.,* " floating leaf," and give a story to account for it. See Motowori's Commentary, Vol. XXII, pp. 36-37, where the reason traditionally given to explain the fact of the name Ikuha being written with the character 的 is also mentioned at length.

58. *Ikuye no omi.* Ikúye must have been the name of a place; but nothing is known of it.

59. *Agina no omi.* The same observation applies to this as to the preceding name.

60. *Waku-go no sukune.* Waku-go signifies " young child " or " youth," an Honorific designation.

61. *Yenuma no omi.* Yenuma is the name of a district in Kaga, and signifies " inlet-lagoon."

62. In Yamato. This pool or lake is often mentioned in the poems of the " Collection of a Myriad Leaves " and was celebrated for its lotus-flowers. We hear of it in the " Chronicles of Japan," as having been dug in the reign of the Emperor O-jin, but it was probably, like many others, a natural pool or marsh, which was afterwards improved. The name signifies " sabre."

[SECT. LXII.—EMPEROR KAI-KUWA.]

His Augustness Waka - yamato - ne - ko - hiko - ōho-bibi dwelt in the palace of Izakaha at Kasuga,[1] and ruled the Empire. This Heavenly Sovereign wedded the Princess of Takanu,[2] daughter of Yugori[3] the Gréat Departmental Lord of Taniha,[4] and begot an august child: His 167 Augustness Hiko-yumusumi,[5] (one Deity). Again he wedded his step-mother, Her Augustness I-gaka-shiko-me,[6] and begot august children: His Augustness Mima-kiri-biko-iniwe;[7] next Her Augustness Mima-tsuhime[8] (two Deities). Again he wedded Her Augustness Oke-tsu-hime,[9] younger sister of His Augustness Hiko-kuni-oketsu,[10] ancestor of the Grandees of Wani,[11] and begot an august child: King Hiko-imasu[12] (one Deity). Again, wedding Princess Washi,[13] daughter of the Noble Kadzuraki-no-tarumi,[14] he begot an august child,—King Take-tayo-hadzura-wake[15] (one Deity); The august children of this Heavenly Sovereign [numbered] in all five Deities (four Kings and one Queen). So His Augustness Mi-maki-iri-biko-iniwe [was he who afterwards] ruled the Empire. The children of his elder brother, King Hiko-yumusumi were: King Oho-tsutsuki-tari-ne;[16] next King Sanugi-tari-ne[17] (two Kings). There 168 were five Deities daughters of these two Kings. Next King Hiko-imasu wedded the Princess of Yena in Yama-shiro,[18] another name for whom was Kari-bata-tobe,[19] and begot children: King Ohô-mata;[20] next King Wo-mata;[21] next King Noble [of ?] Shibumi[22] (three Deities). Again, wedding Saho-no-oho-kurami-tome,[23] daughter of Take-kuni-katsu-tome, of Kasuga,[24] he begot children: King Saho-biko;[25] next King Wo-zaho;[26] next Her Augustness Saho-bime,[27] another name for whom is Sahaji-hime[28]

(Her Augustness Saho-bime here mentioned was consort of the Heavenly Sovereign Ikume);[29] and King Muro-biko,[30] (four Deities). Again, wedding Okinaga-no-midzu-yori-hime,[31] daughter of the 169 Heavenly Deity Mikage,[32] who is held in reverence by the deacons of Mikami in Chika-tsu-Afumi,[33] he begot children : King Tatatsu-michi-no-ushi, Prince of Taniha ;[34] next King Midzuho-no-ma-wa-ka ;[35] next King Kamu-oho-ne,[36] another name for whom is King Yatsuri-iri-biko ;[37] next Midzuho-no-i-ho-yori-hime ;[38] next Mimi-tsu-hime ;[39] (three Deities). Again, wedding his mother's younger sister Her Augustness Woke-tsu-hime,[40] he begot children : King Ma-wata of Oho-tsutsuki in Yamashiro ;[41] next King Hiko-osu ;[42] next king Iri-ne[43] (two Deities). Altogether the children of King Hiko-imasu [numbered] in all eleven Kings. So the children of the elder brother King Oho-mata were : King Ake - tatsu ;[44] next King Unakami[45] 170 (two Deities). This King Ake-tatsu (was the ancestor of the Dukes of the Homuji Tribe in Ise[46] and of the Rulers of Sana in Ise).[47] King Una-kami (was the ancestor of the Dukes of Himeda.).[48] The next King Wo-mata (was the ancestor of the Dukes of Magari in Tagima).[49] The next King Noble Shibumi (was the ancestor of the Dukes of Sasa).[50] The next King Saho-biko (was the ancestor of the Chiefs of the Kusaka Tribe[51] and of the Rulers of the Land of Kahi).[52] The next, King Wo-zaho (was the ancestor of the Lords of Kadzunu[53] and the Lords of Kanu in Chika-tsu-Afumi.)[54] The next King Muro-biko (was the ancestor of the Lords of Mimi in Wakasa).[55] King Michi-no-ushi wedded the Lady Masu of Kahakami in Taniha,[56] and begot children : Her Augustness Princess Hibasu ;[57] next Her Augustness Princess Matonu ;[58] next Her Augustness Oto-hime ;[59] next King Mi-kado-wake[60] (four Deities). This King Mikado-171 wake (was the ancestor of the Lords of Ho in Mikaha).[61] Prince Midzuho-no-ma-waka, younger brother of this King Michi-no-ushi, (was the ancestor of the Suzerains of Yasu in Chika-tsu-Afumi).[62] The next, King Kamu-oho-be (was the ancestor of the [Rulers of] the Land of Minu,[63] of the Rulers of the land of Motosu,[64] and of the Chiefs of the Nagahata Tribe).[65] The next, King Mawaka of Oho-tsutsuki in Yama-shiro wedded Princess Ajisaha of Mone,[66] daughter of his younger brother Irine, and begot a child: King Kami-me-ikadzuchi.[67] This King wedded Princess Takaki,[68] daughter of the Grandee Tohotsu of Taniha,[69] and begot a child: King Noble Okinaga.[70] This king wedded the Princess of Takanuka in Kadzuraki,[71] and begot children: Her Augustness Princess Okinaga-tarashi;[72] next Her Augustness Soratsu-hime;[73] next King Prince Okinaga[74] (three Deities. This King was the ancestor of the Dukes of Homuji in Kibi,[75] and of the Dukes of Aso in Harima).[76] Again King Noble Okinaga wedded Princess ·Inayori of Kahamata,[77] and begot a child: King Oho-tama-saka.[78] (This was the ancestor of the Rulers of the land of Tajima).[79] The above-mentioned Take-toyo-hadzura-wake (was the ancestor of the Grandees of Chimori,[80] of the Rulers of the Oshinumi Tribe,[81] of the Rulers of the Mima Tribe,[82] of the Oshinumi Tribe in Inaba,[83] of the Lords of Takanu in Taniba,[84] and of the Abiko of Yosami).[85] The Heavenly Sovereign's august years were sixty-three. His august mausoleum is at the top of the hill of Izakaha.[86]

---

1. For Kasuga see Sect. LVIII, Note 7. Izakaha is a place in Yamato. The signification of the name is uncertain.

2, *Takanu-hime.* Takanu is the name of a district in Tango, and signifies "bamboo moor."

3. The signification of this name is quite obscure.

4. *Taniha no oho-agata-nushi. Taniha* (modern *Tamba*) is the name of a province (formerly including the province of Tango) in Central Japan. It is supposed to mean "the place of rice-fields," the rice offered at the shrine of the Sun-Goddess in Ise being brought thence.

5. *Hiko* signifies "prince." The other syllables of the name are obscure.

6. See Sect. LXI, Note 8.

7. *Biko* (*hiko*) signifies "prince." The other elements of this compound are obscure.

8. One is tempted to render this name by Princess of Mima. But there is no authority for regarding Mima either in this or in the preceding personal name as originally the name of a place.

9. Motowori has no explanation to offer of the syllables Oke-tsu. *Hime* means "princess."

10. *Hiko* means "prince" and *kuni* means "country."

11. *Wani no omi.* *Wani* is a place in Yamato, and there is a pass or hill of that name (*Wani-zaka*). The only signification belonging to the word *wani* is "crocodile."

12. *Hiko-imasu no miko.* Signification obscure.

13. Or "the Princess of Washi" or "the Eagle Princess." In Japanese *Washihime.*

14. *Kadzuraki* is the name of a district in Yamato, and Motowori believes Tarumi to be the name of a place in Settsu.

15. *Take-toyo-hadzura-wake no miko.* The first two elements of the compound signify respectively "brave" and "luxuriant" while the last probably means "lord." The signification of *hadzura* is obscure.

16. *Oho-tsutsuki-tari-ne- no miko.* Tsutsuki being the name of a district in Yamashiro, the whole compound signifies "prince great sufficing lord of great Tsutsuki."

17. *Sanugi-tari-ne no miko,* i.e., "prince sufficing lord of Sanugi," (Sanuki,—see Sect. V, Note 6).

18. *Yamashiro no Yena tsu Hime.* Yamashiro is the name of a province, and Yena that of a place in Settsu. The signification of the latter name is obscure.

19. Motowori believes *Karibata* to be the name of a place, and *tobe* (*to-me*) to signify "old woman," as in the name *Ishi-ko-ri-do-me,* which latter is however extremely obscure (see Sect. XVI, Note 12).

20. *Oho-mata no miko.* The signification of this name and of the parallel name of the younger brother is obscure.

21. *Wo-mata no miko.*

22. *Shibumi no Sukune no miko.* Shibumi is probably the name of a place, there being a Shibumi in Ise.

23. *Saho* is the name of a well-known place in Yamato, and *Kurami*

is supposed by Motowori to be the name of a place in Wakasa. *Oho* means "great," and *tome*, according to Motowori, means "old woman" or simply "female." Conf. Note 19.

24. *Kasuga no Take-kuni-katsu-tome.* Motowori supposes this to be the name, not of the father, but the mother of the princess just mentioned. *Take* signifies "brave," and *kuni* "land." The meaning of *katsu* is obscure.

25. *Saho-biko no miko*, i.e., "Prince of Saho."

26. *Wō-zaho no miko*, i.e., "little (*q.d.* 'younger') prince of Saho."

27. *I.e.*, the princess of Saho.

28. It is uncertain whether we should understand this name to signify "princess Sahaji" or "the princess of Sahaji," but the latter seems the more probable.

29. *I.e.*, the Emperor Sui-nin.

30. *Muro-biko no miko.* *Muro-biko* signifies "Prince of Muro." Muro being a place in Yamato. It signifies "dwelling" and specially "cave."

31. *I.e.*, "flourishing and good princess of Okinaga," the latter being the name of a place in Afumi (Omi). Its signification is not clear.

32. *Ame no Mikaga no kami.* The signification of Mikaga is obscure, as is also the connection between this deity and the deacons of Mikami.

33. The signification of the name Mikami is obscure. The word rendered "deacon" is *hufuri*, the name of an inferior class of Shintō priests. See for a discussion of the etymology of the word, etc., Mr. Satow's remarks on p. 112 of Vol. VII of these Transactions. For Chika-tsu-Afumi see Sect. XXIX, Note 20.

34. *Taniha no hiko Tatatsu-michi-no-ushi no miko.* The signification of *Tatatsu* is obscure, but we may accept it as the personal name of the worthy here mentioned. *Michi-no-ushi* means "master of the road," i.e. "lord of the province."

35. *Midzuho no ma-waka no miko*, i.e. "the True Young King of Midzuho," Midzuho being the name of a place in Afumi. It probably means "fresh young rice-ears."

36. *Kamu-oho-ne no miko*, i.e., probably, "prince divine great lord."

37. *Yatsuri-iri-biko no miko.* Yatsuri is the name of a village in Yamato, and is of uncertain origin. The signification of *iri* is obscure.

38. *I-ho* signifies "five hundred" and *yori* probably signifies "good." The compound may therefore be taken to mean "manifoldly excellent princess of Midzuho."

39. *I.e.*, probably " the Princess Miwi " (Miwi-dera in Afumi). *Mi-wi* signifies " three wells."

40. This name is parallel to that which has been commented on in Note 9 to this Section.

41. *Yamashiro-no-oho-Tsutsuki no ma-waka no miko.* All the elements of this compound have already appeared in this Section.

42. *Hiko-osu no miko.* The signification of *osu* is obscure,

43. *Iri-ne no miko.* Signification obscure.

44. *Ake-tatsu no miko.* See Sect. LXXII, Note 20.

45. *Unakami no miko.* See Sect. LXXII, Note 19.

46. *Ise no Homuji-be no kimi.* See the mention of the establishment of this Clan at the end of Sect. LXXII.

47. *Ise no Sana no miyatsuko.* The etymology of Sana is obscure.

48. *Himeda no kimi.* Himeda is a place in Afumi. The signification of the name is obscure.

49. *Tagima no Magari no kimi.* Tagima is the name of a district in Yamato, and is of uncertain origin. Magari is the name of a place, and means " crook " or " bend."

50. *Sasa no kimi.* Sasa is the name of a place in Iga, and is of uncertain signification.

51. *Kusakabe no murazhi.*

52. *Kahi no kuni no miyatsuko.* For Kahi see Sect. LXXXVI, Note 1.

53. *Kadzunu no wake.* Kadzunu is the name of a district in Yamashiro, and signifies " pueraria moor."

54. *Chika-tsu-Afumi no Kanu no wake.* Kanu is a village in Afumi. The name is written with characters signifying " mosquito moor."

55. *Wakasa no Mimi no wake.* Mimi is the name of a village, and is of uncertain signification.

56. *Taniha no Kahakami no Masu no iratsume.* Masu is of uncertain derivation. Kahakami is the name of a village, now comprised in the province of Tango. It signifies " river-land."

57. *Hibasu-hime.* The signification of this name is obscure.

58. *Matonu-hime.* The signification of this name is obscure.

59. *I.e.*, " the younger princess."

60. This name, which is written 朝廷別王, is curious, and Motoworf has no suggestion to make touching its interpretation.

61. *Mikaha no Ho no wake.* Ho is the name of a district, and is of obscure derivation. Mikaha is the name of a maritime province. It

signifies "three rivers," with reference to two large rivers which flow through it and to another which forms the boundary between it and the province of Wohari.

62. *Chika-tsu-Afumi no Yasu no atahe.* Yasu is the name of a district, and is of uncertain origin.

63. *Minu no kuni no [miyatsuko].* The word *miyatsuko*, which is not in the text, is supplied in Motowori's *kana* reading.

64. *Motosu no kuni no miyatsuko.* Motosu is the name of a district in Mino, and seems to signify "original dwelling-place."

65. *Nagahata-be no murazhi.* Nagahata is the name of a place in Hitachi, and seems to signify "long loom."

66. *Mone no Ajisaha-bime.* This name is particularly obscure, and Mone probably corrupt.

67. *Kani-me-ikadzuchi no miko.* Motowori thinks that this name signifies "fierce like a crab's eye," with reference perhaps to some personal peculiarity of the prince who bore it.

68. *Takaki-hime.* This name is obscure and perhaps corrupt.

69. *Taniha no Tohotsu omi.* This name is obscure.

70. *Okinaga no sukune no miko.* For Okinaga see Note 31 to this Section.

71. *Kadzuraki no Takanuka-hime.* Takanuka is the name of a place in Yamato. It is written with characters signifying "high brow."

72. *Okinaga-tarashi-hime.* Okinaga is the name of a place (see Note 31). *Tarashi* is an honorific designation, signifying literally "sufficient," *i.e.*, "perfect," and is supposed by Motowori to have been bestowed after death on this princess, who was the celebrated conqueror of Korea, and is better known to fame by her "canonical name" of Jingō Kōgō.

73. *I.e.,* "the princess of the sky."

74. *Okinaga-hiko no miko.*

75. *Kibi no Homuji no kimi.* Homuji is the name of a district in the modern province of Bingo, and may perhaps be of Chinese origin.

76. *Harima no Aso no kimi.* Aso is the name of a place, and is of uncertain origin.

77. *Kahamata no Ina-yori-bime.* Kahamata ("river-fork") is the name of a place in Kohachi. *Ina* signifies "rice," and *yori* probably signifies "good" in this and numerous other proper names.

78. *Oho-tamu-saka no miko.* This name is obscure. Motowori thinks that *Tamu-saka* may be the name of a place, and signifying "winding ascent."

79. *Tajima no kuni no miyatsuko.* For *Tajima* see Sect. LXXIV, Note 1.

80. *Chi-mori no omi.* *Chi-mori* signifies "road-keeper," and perhaps we should translate this "gentile name," by "road-keeping grandees," and suppose that anciently they may have performed some functions in which the bestowal of it originated.

81. *Oshinumi-be no miyatsuko.* Oshinumi is the name of a district in Yamato, and is of uncertain import.

82. *Mina-be no miyatsuko.* Perhaps we should rather translate thus, "the Rulers of Minabe," for the name is altogether obscure.

83. *Inaba no Oshinumi-be.* Motowori supposes a branch of this family, which was originally established in Yamato, to have removed to the province of Inaba.

84. *Taniha no Takanu no wake.* Takanu is the name of a district in the modern province of Tango. It signifies "high moor."

85. *Yosami no obiko.* Yosami is the name of a place in Kahachi and is of uncertain origin, though the legends connect with the word *ami,* "a net" (see Motowori's Commentary, Vol. XXII, p. 81). It is chiefly known on account of its lake or pool, which is often mentioned in the early poetry. *Abiko* is a very rare "gentile name," which in the "Catalogue of Family Names" is written with the characters 我孫, but is derived by Motowori from 吾彦, *i.e.,* "my grandchildren."

86. In Yamato. The name is of uncertain origin.

---

173    [(SECT. LXIII.—EMPEROR SŪ-JIN (PART I.—GENEALOGIES).]

His Augustness Mima-ki-iri-biko-iniwe dwelt at the Palace of Midzu-gaki at Shiki,[1] and ruled the Empire. This Heavenly Sovereign wedded Tohotsu-no-ayu-me-me-kuhashi,[2] daughter of Arakaha-to-be,[3] Ruler of the land of Ki,[4] and begot august children: His Augustness Toyo-ki-iri-biko,[5] and next Her Augustness Toyo-suki-iri-bime[6] (two Deities). Again, wedding the Great Princess of Ama, ancestress of the Chiefs of Wohori,[8] he begot august children: His Augustness Oho-iri-ki;[9] next His August-

ness Ya-saka-no-iri-biko; next Her Augustness Nuna-ki-
no-iri-bime; next Her Augustness Towochi-no-iri-bime[10]
(four Deities). Again, wedding Her Augustness Princess
Mimatsu,[11] daughter of His Augustness Oho-biko, he
begot august children: His Augustness Ikume-iri-biko-
isachi[12] next His Augustness Iza-no-ma-waka;[13] next
Her Augustness Princess Kuni-kata;[14] next Her August- 159
ness Princess Chiji-tsuku-yamato;[15] next Her Augustness
Princess Iga;[16] next His Augustness Yamato-Hiko[17] (six
Deities). The august children of this Heavenly Sovereign
[numbered] in all twelve Deities (seven Kings and Queens).
So His Augustness Ikume-iri-biko-isachi [was he who
afterwards] ruled the Empire. The next, His August-
ness Toyo-ki-iri-biko (was the ancestor [of the Dukes] of Kami-
tsu ke-nu,[18] and the Dukes of Shimo-tsu-ke-nu).[19] The younger sister,
Her Augustness Princess Toyo-Suki (was high-priestess of[20]
the temple of the Great Deity of Ise.)[21] The next brother, His
Augustness Oho-iri-ki (was ancestor of the Grandees of Noto).[22]
The next, His Augustness Yamato-hiko,—(in the time of this
King a hedge of men was the first time set in the mausoleum).[23]

---

1, In Yamato. *Shiki* probably signifies "stone castle" (*ishi-ki*).
*Midzugaki*-signifies "fresh young hedge,"—an Honorific designation of the
hedge round the Emperor's abode, which passed into a Proper Name.

2. According to Motowori's exegesis, this name is a rather remarkable instance of verbal usage, *ayu-me* ("trout-eyes") being not properly
part of the name at all, but only a Pillow-Word for what follows, viz.,
*Me-kakushi-hime, i.e.* "Princess Beautiful Eyes." *Tohotsu* is the name of
a place in the province of Ki, signifying "far harbour."

3. *Arakaha* is the name of a place in Ki, and signifies "rough (*i.e.*
impetuous and dangerous) river." The syllables *to-be* are of uncertain
import.

4. *Ki no kuni no miyatsuko.*

5. *Toyo* signifies "luxuriant" and *biko* (*hiko*) "prince." The other
elements of the compound are obscure.

6. *Bime* (*hime*) signifies "princess," and *suki* is identified by Motowori with Shiki, the name of the residence of the monarch whose daughter this princess was.

7. *Oho-ama-hime.* Ama is the name of a district in Wohari, and probably signifies "fisherman."

8. *Wohari no murazhi.*

9. The signification of this and the two following names is uncertain.

10. *Towochi* is the name of a district in Yamato.

11. *Mimatsu-hime.* Signification uncertain.

12. Signification uncertain.

13. The syllables *ma* and *waka*, literally "true and young" or "truly young" are honorific. *Iza* is of doubtful signification.

14. *Kuni-kata-hime.* Kuni means "country," and kata here probably signifies "hard" or "firm."

15. *Chiji-tsuku-yamato-hime.* Ohiji probably means "a thousand," and *Yamato* is the name of a province. *Tsuku* is obscure.

16. *Iga-hime.* Iga is the name of a district and of a province (see Sect. LVI, Note 9).

17. *I.e.*, "Yamato Prince."

18. *Kami-tsu-ke-nu* [*no kimi*]. The character 君 (Dukes) is supplied by Motowori. This is the ancient form of the name now pronounced *Kō-dzuke* (*conf. Shimo-tsu-ke-nu* corrupted to *Shimotsuke*). The author of the "Inquiry into the Meaning of the Names of All the Provinces" draws attention to the curious fact that, whereas the final syllable *nu* of the original word is dropped in speaking, it is the *ke* which is dropped in writing—the original form of the name, as written. being 上毛野, whereas now only the first two of these three characters are used. Its signification is supposed to be "upper vegetation-moor," *ke* (毛) being regarded as the Archaic general term for trees and grasses, identical with *ke* that means "hairs," vegetation having struck the early speakers of the language as being similar to the hairs on the bodies of men and beasts.

19. *Shimo-tsu-ke-nu no kimi.* Shimo means "lower." For the rest of the name see preceding Note. Both names are those of provinces in Eastern Japan.

20. Or more literally, "worshipped and celebrated the festivals at," etc.

21. *Viz.*, of the Sun-Goddess (*Ama-terasu*).

22. *Noto no omi.* Noto, formerly a part of the province of Echizen,

is the name of the peninsula that juts out into the Sea of Japan on the western coast of the Main Island. The etymology of the name is obscure.

23. The meaning of this imperfectly formed sentence is: On the occasion of "the interment of the next prince, His Augustness Yamato-hiko, the custom of setting a row of the deceased prince's retainers round his grave and burying them alive was first introduced." For a further notice of this custom see Sect. LXXV, Note 4. According to the "Chronicles," the "ancient" custom of burying retainers up to their necks in the neighbourhood of their lord's grave was abolished after this very same interment. Motowori endeavours to reconcile the two state-ments by supposing that the custom was really an old one, but that on the occasion here mentioned the number of victims was increased to an unprecedented degree, so that, as related in the "Chronicles," their cries, while their heads were being pulled to pieces by the crows and dogs, filled the Emperor with commiseration.

---

[SECT. LXIV.—EMPEROR SŪ-JIN (PART II.—A PESTILENCE IS     175
STAID BY OHO-TATA-NE-KO).]

In the reign of this Heavenly Sovereign a great pestilence arose, and the people died as if none were to be left.[1] Then the Heavenly Sovereign grieved and lamented, and at night, while on his divine couch,[2] there appeared [to him] in an august dream the Great Deity the Great-Master-of-Things,[3] and said: "This is my august doing.[4] So if thou wilt cause me to be worship-ped[5] by Oho-tata-ne-ko,[6] the divine spirit shall not arise,[7] and the land will be tranquillized." When, therefore, couriers[8] were dispatched in every direction[9] to search for the person [named] Oho-tata-ne-ko, he was discovered in the village of Minu[10] in Kafuchi, and was respectfully sent [to the Heavenly Sovereign].[11] Then the Heavenly Sovereign deigned to ask: "Whose child art thou?" He replied, saying: "I[12] am Oho-tata-ne-ko, child of

His Augustness Take-mika-dzu-chi[13] [who was] child of His Augustness Ihi-gata-sumi, [14] [who was] child of His Augustness Kushi-mi-gata,[15] [who was] child of the Great Deity the Great-Master-of-Things by his wife Iku-tama-yori-bime,[16] daughter of His Augustness Suwe-tsu-mimi."[17] Hereupon the Heavenly Sovereign, being greatly rejoiced, commanded that the Empire should be tranquil, and the people flourish, and forthwith made His Augustness Oho-tata-ne-ko high priest[18] to worship[19] the Great Deity of Great Miwa[20] on Mount Mimoro.[21] Again he ordered His Augustness Igaka-shiko-wo[22] to make eighty heavenly platters, and reverently to establish the shrines of the Earthly Deities;[23] likewise to worship with a red-coloured shield and spear the Deity of Sumi-saka[24] at Uda, and with a black-coloured shield and spear the Deity of Oho-saka;[25] likewise to present august offerings of cloth to all the Deities of the august declivities of the hills and to all the Deities of the reaches of the rivers, without neglecting any.[26] [27] In consequence of this the pestilential vapour ceased altogether, and the country was tranquillized.

---

1. Literally, "about to be exhausted."

2. This expression, which recurs at the commencement of Sect. CXLV, is difficult to explain. See Motowori's remarks in Vol. XXIII, pp. 24-25, and again in Vol. XL, pp. 14-15, of his Commentary.

3. See Sect. LI, Note 12.

4. Literally, "my august heart."

5. Or. "cause my shrine to be worshipped at." The import of the god's words is that he wishes Oho-tata-ne-ko to be appointed chief priest of his temple. For the origin of this latter see the second half of Sect. XXXII (pp. 103-105).

6. *Oho* signifies "great," *Tata* (or *Tada*) is taken to be the name of a place, and the syllables *ne* and *ko* are regarded as Honorifics. The

whole name may therefore, though with some hesitation, be interpreted to mean " the Lord of the Great [Shrine of] Tata."

7. *I.e.*, " the divine anger shall no longer be kindled."

8. Mounted couriers are almost certainly intended.

9. Literally, " distributed to the four sides,"—" four sides " being a Chinese phrase for every direction.

10. This name may signify either " three moors " or " august moor." The village of Minu must not be confounded with the province of Minu.

11. The characters used are those which properly denote the pre-senting of tribute to the Monarch.

12. Here and below the First Personal Pronoun is represented by the respectful character 僕, " servant."

13. See Sect. VIII, Note 7, for the explanation of this name. But probably the deity here intended is another.

14. The etymology and signification of this name are alike obscure.

15. Motowori interprets *kushi* in the sense of " wondrous," and *Migata* as the name of a place, which also occurs under the form of Higata.

16. *I.e.*, " life-jewel-good-princess."

17. The precise signification of this name is obscure. Motowori supposes *Suwe* to be the name of a place ; *tsu* is the Genitive Particle, and *mimi* the Honorific of doubtful import, whose meaning has been discussed in Note 18 to Sect. XIII.

18. The exact meaning of the characters used to write the word *kamu-nushi* (modern *kamushi*), here rendered " high-priest," is " owner of the Deity." Though commonly used in modern parlance to denote any Shintō priest, it properly signifies only the chief priest in charge of a temple, whence the odd-sounding name.

19. Or, " conduct the worship at the shrine of."

20. Viz., the Deity Master-of-the-Great-Land. For the traditional etymology of Miwa see the legend in Sect. LXV.

21. See Sect. XXVIII, Notes 4 and 5.

22. Or, *Ikaga-shiko-wo*. The probable meaning of this name, pro-posed by Motowori, is (neglecting the initial letter *i* as expletive) " the refulgent ugly male. '

23. See Sect. I, Note 11 .

24. *Sumisaka* probably signifies " charcoal-hill." Uda, which has already been mentioned in Sect. XLVI, is in Yamato. This passage may equally well be rendered thus: " to present a red-coloured shield and

spear to the Deity of Sumisaka," and similarly in the following clause. The meaning comes nearly to the same.

25. Literally, " great hill," or " great pass." It is at the boundary of the province of Yamato and Kahachi. Neither Motowori nor Tani-gaha Shisei sanctions the view of the elder scholars, who fancied they saw in the distinction of red and black some mysterious import connected with the four cardinal points.

26. In the Old Printed Edition the text of this passage differs slightly from that adopted by Motowori; but the meaning is exactly the same.

27. A large lacuna here occurs in the " Old Printed Edition," in which the four hundred and forty-five Chinese characters forming the original of the following part of the translation, from the words, " In consequence of this" down to the words immediately preceding ' Methinks this is a sign" on p. 180 are missing. Both the editor of 1687 and Motowori are silent as to the manner in which they supplied the deficiency ; but it may be presumed from their silence that the MS. authorities furnished them with what had accidentally been omitted from the printed text.

---

[SECT. LXV.—EMPEROR SŪ-JIN (PART III.—STORY OF OHO-TATA-NE-KO'S BIRTH).]

The reason why this person called Oho-tata-ne-ko was known to be a Deity's child, was that the above-mention-ed Iku-tama-yori-bime was regularly beautiful,[1] whereupon a [divine[2]] youth [who thought] the majesty of her appear-ance without comparison in the world,[3] came suddenly to her in the middle of the night. So, as they loved each other and lived in matrimony together, the maiden ere long was pregnant. Then the father and mother, astonish-ed at their daughter being pregnant, asked her,[4] saying : "Thou art pregnant by thyself. How art thou with child without [having known] a man ?" She replied, saying : "I have naturally conceived through a beautiful young man, whose name[5] I know not, coming here every evening and staying with me." Therefore the father and mother, wishing to know the man, instructed their daughter, saying: "Sprinkle red earth in front of the couch,[6] and pass a skein of hemp through a needle, and pierce [therewith] the skirt of his garment." So she did as they had instructed, and, on looking in the morning, the hemp that had been put in the needle went out through the hole of the door-hook,[7] and all the hemp that remained was three twists[8] only. Then forthwith, knowing how he had gone out by the hook-hole, they went on their quest following the thread, which, reaching Mount Miwa, stopped at the shrine of the Deity. So they knew [that Oho-tata-neko was] the child of the Deity [residing] there. So the place was called by the name of Miwa on account of the three twists of hemp that had remained. (His Augustness Oho-tata-ne-ko, here referred to, was the ancestor of the Dukes of Miwa[9] and of the Dukes of Kamo.)[10]

---

1. It is not easy to render literally into English the force of the characters 容姿端正, containing this description of the maiden's beauty, and of 形姿威儀 in the next clause. But it is hoped that at least the translation represents them better than do Motowori's readings *kaho yokariki* and *kaho sugata*.

2. This word, which is not in most texts, was supplied by the editor of 1687, and is adopted by Motowori on apparently satisfactory grounds.

3. Literally, "in the time."

4. The text places the word "daughter" here, instead of in the preceding clause. For the sake of clearness, the translator has taken the liberty of transposing it.

5. The Chinese characters are 姓名, *i.e.*, "surname and personal (what we should call 'Christian') name." But Motowori's simple reading *na*, "name," approves itself as probably near to the author's intention.

6. Motowori indulges in several conjectures as to the meaning of

this detail, which, it will be seen, is not referred to in the sequel, and is therefore pointless.

7. The same Japanese word *kagi*, which is used as the equivalent of the Chinese character 釣, "hook," came in latter times to denote a key.

8. "Three threads" are in Japanese *mi wa*, whence the etymology of the name of Miwa given below in the text. The real derivation is altogether doubtful. The shrine of Miwa was in very early times regarded with such extraordinary reverence, that the term *Oho-gami*, "Great Deity," unless otherwise qualified, was commonly understood to refer to the god of Miwa.

9. *Miwa no kimi*, written simply 神君 (literally, "Divine Dukes,") another sign of the estimation in which the shrine of Miwa was held.

10. *Kama no kimi*.

---

179  [SECT. LXVI.—EMPEROR SŪ-JIN (PART IV.—WAR WITH KING TAKE-HANI-YASU).]

Again in this august reign His Augustness Oho-biko[1] was sent to the circuit of Koshi,[2] and his son, His Augustness Take-nuna-kaha-wake,[3] was sent to the twelve circuits to the eastward to quiet the unsubmissive people. Again Hiko-imasu was sent to the land of Taniha[4] to slay Kugamimi-no-mikasa[5] (this is the name of a person). So when His Augustness Oho-biko was going away to the land of Koshi, a young girl wearing a loin-skirt[6] stood on the Pass of Hera[7] in Yamashiro, and sang, saying:

180        "Now then! Oh Prince Mima-ki-iri! Oh
        Prince Mi-ma-ki-iri! Ignorant that they,
        to steal and slay one's life, cross back-
        wards and forwards by the back-door,
        cross backwards and forwards by the front
        door and spy,—Oh, Prince Mima-ki-iri!"[8]

Hereupon His Augustness Oho-kiko, thinking it strange, turned his horse back, and asked the young girl, saying: "These words that thou speakest, what are they?" The young girl replied, saying: "I said nothing; I was only singing a song,"—and thereupon she suddenly vanished, none could see whither. So his Augustness Oho-biko returned up again [to the capital] and made a report [of the matter] to the Heavenly Sovereign, who replied and charged him [saying]: "Methinks this is a sign that my half-brother, King Take-hani-yasu,[9] who dwells in the land of Yamashiro, is planning some foul plot.[10] [Do thou,] uncle, raise an army, and go [after him]." When he forthwith sent him off, joining to him his Augustness Hiko-kuni-buku,[11] ancestor of the Grandees of Wani,[12] they set sacred jars on the Pass of Wani,[13] and went away. Thereupon, when they reached the River Wakara[14] 181 in Yamashiro, King Take-hani-yasu, who had raised an army, was waiting to intercept [their passage], and [the two hosts] stood confronting and challenging each other with the river between them.[15] So the place was called by the name of Idomi,[16]—what is now called Idzumi. Then His Augustness Hiko-kuni-buku spoke, begging the other side[17] to let fly the first arrow.[18] Then King Take-hani-yasu shot, but could not strike. Thereupon, on his Augustness Kuni-buku shooting an arrow, it forthwith struck King Take-hani-yasu dead. So the whole army was routed, and fled in confusion. Then the ]Imperial troops pursued] after the fugitive army as far as the ferry of Kusuba, when harassed by the pursuit, exterunt [hostium] excrementa. quae bracis adhaeserunt. Quare isti loco impositum est nomen Kuso-bakama. In proesenti nominatur Kusu-ba.[19] Again, on being intercepted in their flight and cut down, [their bodies] floated like cormorants in the river. So the river was called by the name of U-kaha.[20] Again, because the warriors were cut to pieces, the place was called by the name of Hafuri-sono.[21] Having thus finished [the work of] pacification, they went up [to the capital] to make their report [to the Heavenly Sovereign].

---

1. See Sect. LXI, Note 5.

2. Literally, "to the Lord of Koshi," *i.e.*, "to the land of Koshi;" which provinces are intended by the "twelve circuits to the eastward" mentioned immediately below is uncertain ; but Motowori hazards the guess that we should understand Ise (including Iga and Shima), Wohari, Mikaha, Tohotafumi (pron, Tōtōmi), Suruga, Kahi, Idzu, Sagami Musashi, Fusa (the modern Kadzusa, Shimofusa, and Aha), Hitachi, and Michinoku (a vague name for the north-eastern portions of the Main Island of the whole east and north-east of the country. He likewise supposes the use of the word " road " for circuit or province to have had its origin in the " road " along which the Imperial officers despatched to the outlying provinces had to travel to reach their post, and remarks very pertinently in another passage of his commentary that the term "road" denotes a province more especially from the point of view of its subjugation or government. His explanation is, however, rendered untenable by the fact that the division of the country into such "roads" or "circuits" was an idea evidently borrowed from the neighbouring peninsula of Korea. At first, as in this passage, somewhat vaguely used in the sense of province," it settled down into the designation of "a set of adjacent provinces." Thus the Tō-kai-dō, or "Eastern Maritime Circuit," includes fifteen provinces, the Hoku-roku-dō or "Northern Land Circuit," includes seven provinces, and so on. *Conf.* Sect. LXII, Note 20.

3. *I.e.*, "brave-lagoon-river-youth."

4. Sec Sect. LXII, Note 4.

5. Motowori is unable to help us to any understanding of this name.—or names,—for he suggests that the character 之, *no*, may be an error for 又, *mata* ("also"), and that two individuals may be intended. The note in the original telling us that "this is the name of a person" might equally well be translated in the Plural,—"these are the names of persons."

6. The nature of this garment is not known. One would suppose, from the way it is mentioned in the text, that there was perhaps something contrary to custom in its use by a young girl. The parallel passage in the "Chronicles" does not mention it.

7. Or, "Hill of Hera,"—*Hera-zaka*. The "Chronicles" write this name with the characters 平坂 *Hira-zaka, i.e.,* "Even Pass" or "Hill."

8. The meaning of this poem, which must be considered as one prolonged exclamation, is: "Oh my sovereign! Oh my sovereign! Heedless or ignorant of "the plots hatched against thy life near the very precincts of thy palace. thou "sendest away thy soldiers to fight in distant parts. Oh my sovereign!"—It will be remembered that Prince Mima-ki-ri was the (abbreviated) native name of the reigning monarch, commonly known to posterity by his "canonical name" of Sūjin. The word rendered "life" is literally "thread" and the Impersonal Pronoun "one's" used in the translation, must be understood to refer to the Emperor.

9. See Sect. LXI, Notes 12 and 10.

10. Literally, "foul heart."

11. *I.e.,* probably. "prince land-pacifi ." The first ele ent of the compound is sometimes omitted.

12. *Wani no omi.* Wani ("crocodile") is the name of a place in the province of Yamato.

13. *Wani-zaka.* For the setting of jars *conf.* Sect LX, Note 20.

14. *Wakara gaha.* It is what is now called the Idzumi-gaha. Of Wakara we have nothing but an altogether untenable etymology given in the parallel passage of the "Chronicles."

15. More literally, "each having put the river in the middle, and mutually challenging."

16. *I.e.,* "challenging." The more likely etymology of *Idzumi,* which is written with the character 泉, is "source" or "spring."

17. The original has the very curious expressions 廂人, literally," people of the side-building," which was a great crux to the early editors, Motowori is probably right in interpreting it in the sense of "the other side," i.e., "the enemy."

18. 忌矢; literally "the arrow to be shunned, or avoided,"—but rather, in accordance with Archaic Japanese parlance, "the sacred arrow." Motowori says: "At the commencement of a battle it was the custom for each side to let fly an "initial arrow." Being the commencement of

the affair, the arrow was considered "specially important and was shot off reverently with prayers to the Gods,—"whence its name."

19. *I.e.,* "excrements [fœdatœ] bracæ." But it is not at all probable that this is the correct etymology of the name. The stream is a small one in the eastern part of the province of Kahachi.

20. *I.e.,* "cormorant-river."

21. *I.e.,* "the garden of cutting-to-pieces."

---

182　SECT. LXVII.—EMPEROR SŪ-JIN (PART V.—PEACE RESTORED AND TRIBUTE LEVIED).]

So His Augustness Oho-biko went away to Koshi in accordance with the previous [Imperial] commands. Then Take-nuna-kaha-wake, who had been sent round by the east, and his father Oho-biko met together in Ahidzu. So the place was called by the name of Ahidzu.[1] Wherefore, each of them, having settled the government of the land to which he had been sent, made his report [to the Heavenly Sovereign]. Then the Empire was at peace and the people prosperous. Thereupon tribute on the arrow-notches of the men and tribute on the finger-tips of the women was first levied.[2] So in praise of this august reign they said: "The Heavenly Sovereign Mima-ki, who ruled the first land."[3] Again, in this reign the Pool of Yosami[4] was made; moreover the Pool of Saka-wori at Karu[5] was made.

---

1. A district forming the southern part of the modern province of Ihashiro in north-eastern Japan. The derivation here given, from *ahi-dzu* "meeting port," seems fanciful.

2. *I.e.,* taxes levied on the produce of the chase, by which the men gained their livelihood, and on the domestic handwork of the women.

3. Motowori has a not particularly satisfactory note, in which he endeavours to explain this obscure phrase. The word "first" should evidently qualify the Verb "ruled," and not the Substantive "land," and the applicability of the saying to a sovereign, of whom it is not recorded that he initiated anything save the taxes, is not apparent. The author of the "Chronicles" observes the verisimilitudes better by applying a synonymous designation to the first "Earthly Emperor" Jim-mu.

4. See Sect. LXII, Note 85.

5. Reference to the parallel passage of¹ the "Chronicles" shows that probably a couple of words are here omitted from the text, which should read "the Pool of Karu and the Pool of Sakawori" (*Karu no ike, Sakawori no ike*). Karu is the celebrated ancient capital mentioned in Sect. LVII, Note 1, Sakawori is quite unknown except from this notice of it, and the derivation of the name is uncertain.

---

[SECT. LXVIII.—EMPEROR SŪ-JIN (PART VI.—HIS AGE AND PLACE OF BURIAL.).]

The Heavenly Sovereign's august years were one hundred and sixty-eight. His august mausoleum is on the mound at the corner of the Yamanobe road.¹

---

1. This place, where the Emperor Kei-kō is likewise said to have been interred, was in the province of Yamato, and the road mentioned is supposed by Motowori to have been the highway from Hatsuse into the province of Yamashiro. The word Yamanobe signifies "in the neighbourhood of the mountain" (*yama no he*).

---

[SECT. LXIX.—EMPEROR SUI-NIN (PART I.—GENEALOGIES).] 183

His Augustness Ikume-iri-biko-isachi dwelt at the palace of Tama-kaki in Shiki,¹ and ruled the Empire. This Heavenly Sovereign wedded Her Augustness the

Princess Sahaji,[2] younger sister of His Augustness Saho-biko, and begot an august child: His Augustness Homo-tsu-wake[3] (one Deity). Again, wedding Her Augustness the Princess Hibasu, daughter of King Tatsu-michi-no-ushi, Prince of Taniha, he begot august children: His Augustness ·Ini-shiki-no-iri-biko;[4] next His Augustness Oho-tarashi-hiko-oshiro-wake;[5] next His Augustness Oho-naka-tsu-hiko;[6] next His Augustness Yamato-hime;[7] next His Augustness Waka-ki-iri-biko[8] (five Deities). Again, wedding Her Augustness Nubata-no-iri-bika,[9] younger sister of Her Augustness Princess Hibasu, he begot august children: His Augustness Nu-tarashi-wake;[10] next His Augustness Iga-tarashi-hiko[11] (two Deities). Again, wedding Her Augustness Azami-no-iri-bime,[12] younger
184 sister of His Augustness Nubata-no-iri-bime,[13] he begot august children: His Augustness Ikobaya-wake;[14] next Her Augustness the Princess of Azami[15] (two Deities). Again, wedding Her Augustness Kagu-ya-hime.[16] daughter of King Oho-tsutsuki-tari-ne, he begot an august child: King Wozabe[17] (one Deity). Again, wedding Karibata-tobe daughter of Fuchi Ohokuni in Yamashiro,[18] he begot august children: King Ochi-wake;[19] next King Ika-tarashi-hiko;[20] next King Itoshi-wake.[21] Again, wedding Oto-karibata-tobe,[22] daughter of Fuchi of Otokuni, he begot august children: King Iha-tsuku-wake;[23] next Her August-ness Iha-tsuku-bime, another name for whom was Her Augustness Futaji-no-iri-bime[24] (two Deities). The august children of this Heavenly Sovereign [numbered] alto-gether sixteen (thirteen Kings and three Queens). So His Augustness Oho-tarashi-hiko-oshiro-wake [was he who afterwards] ruled the Empire. (His august stature was ten feet[25]
185 two inches: the length of his august shank was four feet one inch),

The next, His Augustness Inishi-no-iri-biko made the
pool of Chinu;[26] again he made the pool of Sayama, [27]
again he made the pool of Takatsu at Kusaka.[28] Again
he dwelt at the palace of Kahakami at Totori,[29] and
caused a thousand cross-swords[30] to be made, and presented them to the temple of the Deity of Iso-no-kami.[31]
Forthwith he dwelt at that palace,[32] and established the
Kahakami Tribe.[33]     The next, His Augustness Oho-naka-
tsu-hiko, (was the ancestor of the Lords of Yamanobe,[34] of the Saki-
kusa,[35] of the Lords of Inaki,[36] Lords of the Ada,[37] of the Lords of
Minui in the Land of Wohari :[38] of the Lords of Ihanashi in Kibi,[39] of
the Lords of Koromo,[40] of the Lords of Takasuka,[41] of the Dukes of 186
Asuka,[42] and of the Lords of Mure).[43]     The next, Her Augustness
Yamato-hime, (was the high-priestess of [44] the temple of the Great
Deity of Ise).     The next, King Ikobaya-wake (was the ancestor
of the Lords Anahobe at Saho).[45]     The next, Her Augustness
the Princess of Azami (was married to King Inase-biko).     The
next, King Ochi-wake (was the ancestor of the Mountain Dukes of
Wotsuki[46] and of the Duke of Koromo in Mikaha).[47]     The next,
King Ika-tarashi-hiko (was the ancestor of the Mountain Dukes
Kasuga,[48] of the Dukes of Ike in Koshi,[49] and of the Dukes of Kasugahe).[50]
The next, King Itoshi-wake (owing to his having no children,
made the Itoshi Tribe[51] his proxy).     The next, King Iha-tsuku-
wake, (was the ancestor of the Dukes of Haguchi[52] and of the Dukes
of Miwo).[53]     The next, Her Augustness Futaji-no-Iri-bime
(became the empress of His Augustness Yamato-take).

1. For Shiki see Sect. LXIII, Note 1. *Tama-kaki* signifies "jewel
(i.e,, beautiful) hedge."

2. This name and the next have already been met with in Sect.
LXI, as have those of Princess Hibasu, King Tatasu-mechi, King Oho-
tsutsuki-ne, Princess Kari-bata-tobe, and King Inase-biko-

3. See Sect. LXXI, Note 8.

4. The signification of this name is not clear, but Motowori
identifies Shiki with the place of the same name.

5. This name seems to be a string of Honorifics signiying " great perfect prince ruling lord."

6. *I.e.,* " great middle prince," he being third of five children•

7. *I.e.,* " Yamato princess." She is a very celebrated personage in Japanese legendary story,—high priestess of Ise and aunt of the hero Yamato-take. A miraculous tale is related of her birth, and she is supposed to have lived several hundreds of years.

8. The signification of this name is obscure.

9. The signification of this name is obscure.

10. Motowori's conjectural interpretation of this name is " jewel-perfect-lord."

11. The signification of *iga* is obscure. The other two elements of the compound signify " perfect prince."

12. Signification obscure.

13. Signification obscure.

14. Signification obscure. The " Chronicles " read this name *Ike-baya*.

15. *Azami-tsu-hime.* Signification obscure.

16. *I.e.,* probably " the refulgent princess," the syllable *ya* being void of signification as in *Ka-no-hana-saku-ya-hime* (see Sect. XXXVII, Note 3). This name is celebrated as that of the heroine of the fairy-tale entitled " Tale of a Bamboo-Cutter." though there is no reason for identifying the two personages.

17. This name is obscure, and Motowori suspects it of being corrupt.

18. *Yamashiro no ohokunino fuchi.* Yamashiro is the name of a province, and Ohokuni (" great land " that of a village, while Fuchi is a personal name written with a character signifying " deep pool."

19. *Ochiwake no miko.* Motowori derives *ochi* from *oho*, " great," and *chi*, supposed to be an Honorific, while *wake* is taken to mean " lord." After all, the signification of the name remains obscure.

20. *Ika-tarashi-hiko no miko.* The name probably signifies " severe (or dignified) perfect prince."

21. This name is obscure.

22. *I.e.,* Karibata-tobe, the younger sister.

23. This name and the next are obscure. The first of the two is not in the older editions, but Motowori supplies what appears to be a lacuna in the text by adding the five characters 石衝別王次.

24. Signification obscure.

25. The actual word " feet " is not in the original, but an equivalent Chinese measure is used.

26. *Chinu no ike.* The "Sea of Chinu" in the province of Idzumi, which is the same as the "Pool" here mentioned, has been mentioned in Sect. XLIV, Note 36.

27. *Sayama no ike,* in the province of Kahachi. The name probably signifies a "gorge" or "defile."

28. See above Sect. XLIV, Note 31.

29. *Totori* (lit. "bird-catching") was in the province of Idzumi, and the name is said to have been derived from the place having been one of those through which Ohotaka of Yamanobe passed when pursuing the bird whose sight was to make Prince Homachi-wake obtain the power of speech. (See the story as given at the beginning of the next Section). The name of Kaha-kami ("head-waters of the river"), as we learn by comparison with the parallel yassage of the "Chronicles," is to be traced to the River Udo, near whose head waters the palace in question is said to have been situated.

30. See Sect. XLV, Note 5.

31. See Sect. XLV, Note 16.

32. Or, "in that temple."

33. *Kahakami-be.*

34. *Yamanobe no wake.* Yamanobe (or Yamabe) is the name of a district in Yamato and signifies "mountain-slope."

35. *Sakikusa no wake.* Of Sakikusa nothing is known. The word means "lily."

36. *Inaki no wake.* Which Inaki is meant| is not known, there being several places of that name in Japan. The name is connected with the word *ine*, "rice."

37. *Ada no wake.* Of Ada nothing is known.

38. *Wohari no kuni no Minu no wake.* Minu is the name of a village, and signifies "three moors."

59. *Kibi no Ihanashi no wake.* Ihanashi is the name of a district. forming part of the modern province of Bizen, and seems to signify "rockless."

40. *Koromo no wake.* Motowori supposes this name to be corrupt. Koromo is the name of a village in Mikaha.

41. *Takasuka no wake.* Nothing is known either of the place or of the family.

42. *Asuka no kimi.* It is not known where was this Asuka, which must not be confounded with the famous Asuka mentioned in Sect. CXXXIII, Note 11.

43. *Mure no wake* There are several places called Mure. The signification of the name is obscure.

44. Or more literally, "worshipped and celebrated the festivals at," etc.

45. *Saho no Anahobe-wake.* The name Anahobe is derived from Anahobe, the name of the Emperor Yu-riyaku, and *be* "a tribe," it being related in the "Chronicles" that the tribe which was established as his "name-proxy" was so called.

46. *Wotsuki no yama no kimi.* Wotsuki is the name of a place in Afumi (Omi). The family name must be interpreted to signify that they were wardens of the mountain.

47. *Mikaha no Koromo no kimi. Conf.* the name in Note 40, with which this is probably identical. Motowori suspects an error in the text.

48. *Kazuga no yama no kimi. Conf.* the name in Note 46.

49. *Koshi no ike no kimi.* Nothing is known of the place or of the family; Koshi may or may not be the northern province of that name.

50. *Kasugabe no kimi.* There were two places of the name of Kasugabe (i.e. "Kasuga Clan," so called perhaps after a family that had resided there). It is not known which is here alluded to.

51. *Itoshi-be.* The name, which is thus restored by Motowori, is variously mutilated in the older editions. This is the first mention of adoption, lit. in Japanese "child-proxy making." The custom is perpetually referred to in the later portion of these "Records."

52. *Haguhi no kimi.* Haguhi is the name of a district in Noto. The derivation is obscure.

53. *Miwo no kimi.* Miwo is the name of a place in Afumi. It probably means "three mountain-folds."

---

[SECT. LXX.—EMPEROR SUI-NIN (PART II.—CONSPIRACY OF KING SAHO-BIKO AND THE EMPRESS SAHO-BIME).]

When this Heavenly Sovereign made Saho-bime his Empress, Her Augustness Saho-bime's elder brother, King Saho-biko, asked his younger sister, saying: "Which is dearer [to thee], thine elder brother or thy

husband ?" She replied, saying "Mine elder brother is
dearer." Then King Saho-biko conspired, saying : "If
I be truly the dearer to thee, let me and thee rule the
empire," and forthwith he made an eight times tempered
stiletto,[1] and handed it to his younger sister, saying :
"Slay the Heavenly Sovereign in his sleep with this
small knife." So the Heavenly Sovereign, not knowing
of this conspiracy, was augustly sleeping, with the
Empress' august knees as his pillow. Then the Empress
tried to cut his august throat with the stiletto ; but though
she lifted it thrice, she could not cut the throat for an
irrepressible feeling ot sadness, and she wept tears, which
fell overflowing[2] onto [the Heavenly Sovereign's] august
face. Straightway the Heavenly Sovereign started up,
and asked the Empress, saying : "I have had a strange
dream : A violent shower came from the direction of
Saho and suddenly wetted my face ; again a small
damask-coloured snake coiled itself round my neck. Of
what may such a dream be the omen ?" Then the Empress, thinking it improper to dispute,[3] forthwith informed
the Heavenly Sovereign, saying : "Mine elder brother
King Saho-biko asked me,[4] saying : 'Which is dearer
[to thee], thy husband or thine elder brother ?' So, as
I was embarrassed by [this] direct question, I replied,
saying : 'Oh ! mine elder brother is the dearer.' Then he
charged[5] me, saying : 'I and thou will together rule the 188
Empire ; so the Heavenly Sovereign must be slain ;'—
and so saying, he made an eight times tempered stiletto,
and handed it to me. Therefore I wanted to cut thine
august throat ; but though I thrice lifted [the weapon], a
feeling of regret suddenly arose, so that I could not cut
thy throat, and the tears that I wept fell and wetted

thine august face. [The dream] was surely the omen of
this." Then the Heavenly Sovereign said: "How nearly
have I been destroyed!" and forthwith he raised an army
to smite King Saho-biko, whereupon the King made a
rice-castle[6] to await the fray. At this time Her Augustness Saho-bime, unable to forget her elder brother, fled
out through the back-gate [of the palace], and came into
the rice-castle.

1. For stiletto see above, Sect. XXXVI, Note 8. The curious word
*ya-shio-wori* (八塩折) in the text seems to have the sense of "eight
times tempered," i.e., tempered over and over again, which Motowori
assigns to it. The same expression is used in Sect. XVIII (Note 16) to
denote the refining of rice-liquor.

2. This word "overflowing" is more appropriately placed in the
version of the story given in the "Chronicles," where the author makes
her tears first fill her sleeve (a common Japanese figure of speech), and
thence "overflow" on to the sleeping Monarch's face.

3. *I.e.*, seeing that it would be vain in deny the truth.

4. The First Personal Pronoun is written with the self-depreciatory
character 妾, " concubine."

5. Or "enticed."

6. This expression, which is repeated elsewhere, is one which has
given rise to a considerable amount of discussion. The "Chronicles"
tell us expressly that "rice [stalks] were piled up to make a castle,"—
an assertion which, as Motowori remarks, is simply incredible. He therefore adopts Mabuchi's suggestion that a castle *like* a rice-castle is what
is intended,—" rice-castle " being taken " to mean rice-store " or " granary,"
such granaries having probably been stoutly built in order to protect
them from thieves. The historian of the Tang dynasty quoted in the
"Exposition of the Foreign Notices of Japan" says that the Japanese
had no castles, but only palisades of timber. The latter might well
however have been called castles by the Japanese, though they wonld
not have been accounted such by the Chinese, who already built theirs
of stone.

[SECT. LXXI.—EMPEROR SUI-NIN (PART III.—BIRTH OF
PRINCE HOMU-CHI-WAKE AND DEATH OF
THE CONSPIRATORS).]

At this time the Empress[1] was pregnant. Thereupon
the Heavenly Sovereign could not restrain [his pity for]
the Empress, who was pregnant and whom he had loved
for now three years. So he turned his army aside, and
did not hasten the attack. During this delay, the august
child that she had conceived was born. So having put
out the august child and set it outside the rice-castle,
she caused [these words[ to be said to the Heavenly
Sovereign : "If this august child be considered to be 189
the Heavenly Sovereign's august child, let him[2] deign
to undertake it." Hereupon the Heavenly Sovereign
said :[3] "Although detesting the elder brother, I yet
cannot repress my love for the Empress," and forthwith
planned to secure the Empress. Wherefore, choosing
from among his warriors a band of the strongest and
deftest, he charged [them, saying]: "When ye take the
august child, likewise abduct the queen its mother.
Whether by the hair or by the hands, or wherever ye
may best lay hold of her, clutch her and drag her out."
Then the Empress, knowing his intention beforehand,
shaved off all her hair and covered her head with her
hair, and likewise made her jewel-string rotten and wound
it thrice round her arm, and moreover made her august
garments rotten by means of rice-liquor and put on the garments as if they were whole. Having made these preparations, she took the august child in her arms and pushed
it outside the castle. Then the strong men, taking the
august child, forthwith clutched at the august parent.
Then, on their clutching her august hair, the august hair

fell off of itself; on their clutching her august arms, the jewel-string likewise snapped; on their clutching her august garments, the august garments at once tore. Therefore they obtained the august child, but did not get the august parent. So the warriors came back [to the Sovereign], and reported, saying: "On account of her august hair falling off of itself, of her august garments easily tearing, and moreover of the jewel-string which was wound round her august hand at once snapping, we have not got the august parent; but we have obtained the august child." Then the Heavenly Sovereign, sorry and angry, hated the people who made the jewels, 190 and deprived them all of their lands.[4] So the proverb says: "Landless jewels-makers."[5] Again did the Heavenly Sovereign cause[6] the Empress to be told, saying; "A child's name must be given by the mother; by what august name shall this child be called?" Then she replied, saying: "As he was born now at the time of the castle being burnt with fire and in the midst of the fire, it were proper to call him by the august name of Prince[7] Homu-chi-wake."[8] And again he caused her to be asked: "How shall he be reared?"[9] She replied, saying: "He must be reared by taking an august mother[10] and fixing on old bathing-women and young bathing-women."[11] So he was respectfully reared in accordance with the Empress's instructions. Again he asked the Empress, saying: "Who shall loosen the fresh small pendant[12] which thou didst make fast?" She replied, 191 saying: "It were proper that Ye-hime and Oto-hime,[13] daughters of King Tatasu-michi-no-ushi[14] prince of Taniha, should serve thee, for these two queens are of unsullied parentage."[15] So at last [the Heavenly Sovereign] slew King Saho-biko, and his younger sister followed him.[16]

1. *I.e.,* Her Augustness Saho-bime, who was the subject of the preceding sentence.

2. *I.e.,* the Sovereign. The import of this passage is, according to Motowori, that the Empress imagined that her own conduct might perhaps influence the Emperor to refuse to give the child she bore him its proper rank,—not from doubts as to its legitimacy, but as having a rebel mother. By "undertaking" the child is of course meant undertaking the care and education of it.

3. Motowori supposes the Chinese character rendered "said" to be an error, and prefers to consider this clause as containing not the words. but the thought of the Monarch. It would certainly be more convenient to adopt this view. if it were sanctioned by any text.

4. Or, as Motowori prefers to read, "deprived them of all their lands."

5. There is nowhere else any reference to this saying. Motowori supposes it to point to those who, hoping for reward, get punishment instead, these jewellers having doubtless rotted the string on which the beads were strung by special desire of the Empress, whereas they ended by getting nothing but confiscation for their pains.

6. Motowori (following Mabuchi) is evidently correct in supposing the character 命 in this place, and again a little further on, to be a copyist's error for 令, "caused," and the translator has rendered it accordingly.

7. "Prince" is here written 御子.

8. This name may also be read *Ho-muchi-wake,* and is in the "Chronicles" given as *Ho-muchi-wake* while it appears as *Homuchi-wake* at the commencement of Sect. LXIX. The first two elements apparently signify "fire-possessing," while *wake* is the frequently recurring Honorific signifying either "lord" or "young and flourishing."

9. Lit., "his days be reverently prolonged." The same expression is repeated thrice below.

10. *I.e.,* foster-mother.

11. The characters 大湯坐若湯坐 used in the original of this passage would, if they stood alone, be of difficult interpretation. But a comparison with the passage in "One account" of "Chronicles," which relates the nursing of Fuki-ahez-no-mikoto, the father of the first "Earthly Emperor" Jim-mu, leaves no doubt that the author intended to speak of bathing-women attached to the service of the Imperial infant.

12. The words *midzu no wo-himo,* literally rendered "fresh small pendant," call for some explanation. *Midzu.* which includes in a single

term the ideas of youth, freshness, and beauty, is here used as an Honorific. The " small pendant " is interpreted by Mabuchi and Motowori to signify the " inner, girdle " which held together the under-garment of either sex. The old literature of Japan teems with allusions to the custom of lovers or spouses making fast each other's inner girdle, which might not be untied till they met again, and the poets perpetually make a lover ask some such question as " When I am far from thee, who shall loosen my girdle ? " The translator cannot refrain from here quoting, for the benefit of the lover of Japanese verse (though he will not attempt to translate them), the two most graceful of the many stanzas from the " Collection of a Myriad Leaves " brought together by Motowori to illustrate this passage :

> *Wagimoko ga*
> *Yuhiteshi himo wo*
> *Tokame ya mo :*
> *Toyeba tayu to mo*
> *Tada ni afu made ni.*
> *Unabara wo*
> *Tohoku watarite*
> *Toshi-fu to mo :*
> *Ko-ra ga musuberu*
> *Himo toku na yume.*

Tanigaha Shisei also appropriately quotes the following :

> *Futari shite*
> *Musubishi himo wo*
> *Hitori shite*
> *Ware ha toki-mizhi*
> *Tada ni afu made ha.*

a literal rendering of which would run thus : " I will not, till we meet face to face, loosen alone the girdle which we two tied together."

13. *I.e.,* the " Elder Princess and the Younger Princess."

14. Motowori is probably right in explaining *tatasu* as the Honorific Causative of *tatsu,* " to stand " and *michi no ushi* as *michi-nushi* or *kuni-nushi, i.e.,* " owner of the province," " ruler."

15. Lit., " are pure subjects."

16. *I.e.,* was slain with him.

192

So the way they led about and amused the august
child was by making a two-forked boat[1] out of a two-
forked cryptomeria from Ahidzu in Wohari,[2] bringing it
up and floating it on the Pool of Ichishi and on the
Pool of Karu[3] in Yamato, [thus] leading about and
amusing the august child. Nevertheless the august child
spoke never a word, though his eight-grasp beard reached
to the pit of his stomach.[4] So[5] it was on hearing the
cry of a high-flying swan[6] that he made his first utterance.[7]
Then [the Heavenly Sovereign] sent Yamanobe-no-Oho-
taka[8] (this is a name of a person) to catch the bird. So this
person, pursuing the swan, arrived in the Land of Harima
from the Land of Ki, and again in his pursuit crossed
over to the Land of Inaba, then reaching the Land of
Taniba and the Land of Tajima; [thence] pursuing round 193
to the eastward, he reached the Land of Afumi. and
thereupon crossed over into the Land of Minu; and,
passing along by the Land of Wohari, pursued it into
the Land of Shinanu, and at length, reaching in his
pursuit the Land of Koshi, spread a net in the Estuary
of Wanami,[9] and, having caught the bird, brought it up
[to the capital] and presented it [to the Sovereign]. So
that estuary is called the Estuary of Wanami. It had
been thought that, on seeing the bird again, he would
speak; but he did not speak, as had been thought.[10]
Hereupon the Heavenly Sovereign, deigning to be grieved,
augustly fell asleep, when, in an august dream, he was
instructed, saying: "If thou wilt build my temple like
unto thine august abode, the august child shall surely
speak." When he had been thus instructed, [the Heaven-

ly Sovereign] made grand divination to seek what Deity's
desire[11] this might be. Then [it was discovered that]
the curse was the august doing of the Great Deity of
Idzumo.[12] So when about to send the august child to
worship [at] that Great Deity's temple, [he made divination to discover[13]] by whom it were well to have him
attended. Then the lot fell on King Ake-tatsu.[14] So he
194 made King Ake-tatsu swear,[15] saying : " If there is
truly to be an answer[16] to our adoration of this Great
Deity, may the heron dwelling on the tree by the Pool
of Sagisu[17] here fall [through my] oath." When he thus
spoke, the heron that had been sworn by fell to the
ground dead. Again on his commanding it to come to
life] in answer to his] oath, it then came to life again.[18]
Moreover he caused to wither by an oath and again
brought to life again by an oath a broad-foliaged bear-
oak on Cape Amakashi.[19] Then [the Heavenly Sovereign]
granted to Prince Ake-tatsu the name of Prince Yamato-
oyu-shiki-tomi-tomi-toyo-asakura-ake-tatsu.[20] So when the
august child was sent off with the two Princes, Prince
Ake-tatsu and Prince Una-kami,[21] as his attendants, it
was divined[22] that [if they went out[ by the Nara gate,[23]
195 they would meet a lame person and a blind person ;[24] [if
they went out] by the Ohosaka[25] gate, they would likewise meet a lame person and a blind person, and that
only the Ki gate,—a side gate,[26]—would be the lucky gate ;
and when they started off, they established the Homuji
clan[27] in every place they arrived at. So when they had
reached Idzumo and had finished worshipping the Great
Deity, and weré returning up [to the capital], they made
in the middle of the River Hi[28] a black plaited bridge and
respectfully offered a temporary palace [for the august

child] to dwell in.[29]   Then when the ancestor of the
rulers of the Land of Idzumo, whose name was Kihisa- 196
tsu-mi,[30] having made an imitation green-leafed mountain,[31]
placed [it] in the lower reach of the river, and was about
to present the great august food the august child spoke,
saying : " What here resembles a green-leafed mountain
in the lower [reach of the] river; looks like a mountain,
but is not a mountain.   Is it perchance the great court[33]
of the deacon[34] who holds in reverence the Great Deity
Ugly-Male-of-the-Reed-Plains[35] that dwells in the temple
of So at Ihakuma in Idzumo ?"[36]   [Thus] he deigned to
ask.   Then the Kings, who had been sent in august
attendance [on him], hearing with joy and seeing with
delight,[37] set the august child to dwell in the palace of
Nagaho at Ajimasa,[38] and despatched a courier [to inform
the Heavenly Sovereign].   Then the august child wedded 197
Princess Hinaga[39] for one night.   So, on looking privately
at the beautiful maiden, [he found her] to be a serpent,
at the sight of which he fled away alarmed.   Then
Princess Hinaga was vexed, and, illuminating the sea-
plain,[40] pursued after them in a ship ; and they, more
and more alarmed at the sight, pulled the august vessel
across the mountain-folds,[41] and went fleeing up [to the
capital].   Thereupon they made a report, saying : " We
have come up [to the capital] because thy great and
august child has become able to speak through worshipping the Great Deity."   So the Heavenly Sovereign,
delighted, forthwith sent King Unakami back to build
the Deity's temple.   Thereupon the Heavenly Sovereign,
on account of this august child, established the Totori
Clan, the Torikahi Clan, the Homuji Clan, the Ohoyuwe
and the Wakayuwe.[42]

1. From a comparison with a passage in the "Chronicles," where the same expression occurs, one is led to suppose that the craft here mentioned was a sort of double boat, in each half of which passengers could sit.

2. Nothing is known of any place called Ahidzu in the province of Wohari.

3. Karu has been mentioned in Sect. LVII, Note 1. The Pool of Ihare.

4. Lit., "in front of his heart." This phrase descriptive of a long beard has already occurred at the commencement of Sect. XII.

5. Motowori reasonably supposes the character 今 in this sentence to be a copyist's error for the emphatic 尓, and the translation has been made accordingly.

6. The original has the character 鵠, which is now applied to a small species of swan (*Cignus minor*, Pallas; *Cygnus Bewickii*, Yarrell). But it is uncertain what bird is intended by the author.

7. A more or less inarticulate utterance is probably meant: but the expression in the original is obscure.

8. Motowori supposes the Note in the original to refer only to the word Ohotaka, while he takes Yamamobe to be the name of a place (already mentioned in Sect. LXVIII, Note 1). The surname of Ohotaka, signifying "great hawk," was, according to the same commentator, given to the worthy here mentioned in consequence of the incident related in the text. As the bird was not a hawk, this does not seem very convincing, and Motowori's apparent idea that the man was likened to a hawk because he pursued the other bird as a hawk would do, is extremely far-fetched. It is moreover doubtful whether the name should not be read *Oho-washi* (this is Mabuchi's reading). "great." The "Chronicles" give an altogether different name, viz., *Ame-no-yukaha-tana*.

9. No such place is now known. The name may be interpreted to mean "snare-net" in allusion to this story, as stated in the next sentence of the text.

10. The various texts and printed editions all differ slightly in their reading of this passage, and from some it might be gathered that the prince did indeed speak as it had been thought that he would do, but could not speak freely. The translation follows Motowori's emended text.

11. Literally, "heart."

12. *I.e.*, *Oho-kuni-nushi* (the Master of the Great Land), the aboriginal monarch of Idzumo, the descendant of the Sun Goddess, whose

abdication of the sovereignty of Japan in favour of the descendant of the Sun Goddess forms the subject-matter of Sect. XXXII. The word *tatari*, here written with the Chinese character 祟 and rendered "curse," signifies properly the vengeance of a spirit, *i.e.*, either of a deity or of the ghost of a dead man. The word translated "doing" is literally "heart."

13. That some such words must be supplied is evident, and the translator has followed Mabuchi and Motowori in supplying them.

14. Lit., "King Ake-tatsu at the divination."

15. Remember that the original word *ukehi* combines the meanings of our words "wager," "oath," "pledge," "curse," etc.,—being in fact a general name for all words to which any mysterious importance attaches.

16. Lit., a "sign," a "proof."

17. *Sagisu no ike*, a pool in Yamato. *Sagi-su*, signifies "heron's nest."

18. The reading of the characters 爾者 (rendered "then") in this passage has been a crux to all the editors. Fortunately they make no fdifference to the sense.

19. *Amakashi no saki*. Perhaps "Amakashi Point" would be a better rendering if, as Motowori supposes, an inland place in the province of Yamato is meant. It might be the point or extremity of a hill or bluff. *Ame-kashi* signifies literally "sweet oak." The "broad-foliaged bear-oak" mentioned immediately above is supposed by Motowori to be the usual evergreen oak, and not any special kind. The epithet "broad-oliaged" is not, as he remarks, specially appropriate, and he moreover supposes the word *kuma*, "bear," to be a corruption of *kumi* or *kumori*, words which would refer to the thick luxuriance of the foliage. The dictionaries do not help us much to a decision on the point.

20. The component parts of this tremendous name, which is happily abbreviated to Ake-tatsu in the subsequent portions |of the te , are somewhat obscure, especially the word *oyu*, whose reading rests only on a conjecture of Motowori's, who emends the evidently erroneous character 者 to 老 (*oyu*,) "old." *Toyo.* "luxuriant," is an Honorific, *ake* and *tatsu* signify respectively "dawn" and "rise," while the rest seem to be names of places of which this Prince may be supposed to have been the possessor.

21. Or, the Prince of Unakami, as Unakami is the name of a place in Kadzusa.

22. *I.e.*, shown by divination.

23. Nara in Yamato, which is here mentioned for the first time, was the capital, of Japan from A.D. 710 to 784, and has always been famous in Japanese history and literature. The name is derived by the author of the "Chronicles" from the verb *narasu*, "to cause to resound," the hosts of the Emperor Su-jin having, it is said, caused the earth to resound with their trampling when they went out to do battle with Hani-yasu. A more probable derivation is from *nara*, the name of a kind of deciduous oak, the *Quercus glandulifera*. The word rendered "gate" should possibly be taken simply in the sense of "exit" or "approach."

24. Or, "lame people and blind people," a peculiarly unlucky omen for travellers, to whom, as Motowori remarks, sound feet and good eye-sight are indispensable to carry them on their way.

25. See Sect. LXIV, Note 25.

26. In the text the word "gate" is here, by a copyist's error written "moon." When the author says that the Ki gate, *i.e.*, gate or exit leading to the province of Ki, as a "side-gate," he means that it was; not the one by which travellers would naturally have left the town :— the province of Ki, indeed, is to the South of Yamato where the capital was, whereas the province of Idzumo, whither they were bound, was to the north-west. This road into Ki over Matsuchi-yama is one famous in the classical poetry of Japan.

27. *Homuji-be.* The meaning of the clause is that they granted the surname of Homuji to persons in every important locality through which they passed on their journey.

28. See Sect. XVIII, Note 2.

29. The signification of this passage is : "They built as a temporary abode for the prince a house in the River Hi (whether with its foun a-tions actually in the water or on an island is left undetermined), connect-ing it with the main land by a bridge made of branches of trees twisted together and with their bark left on them" (this is here the import of the word "black"). Such bridges have been met with by the translator in the remote northern province of Deha, where the country people call them *shiba-bashi* (or, rather, in their patois *suba-bashi*, i.e., "twig-bridge"). The traveller is so likely to fall through interstices into the stream below, that it is not to be wondered at that they should now be confined to the rudest localities.

30. Motowori supposes *Kihisa* to be the name of a place, and *tsu-mi* to stand as usual for *tsu mochi*, "possessor," according to which view the name would mean "lord" or "possessor of Kihisa."

31. No book of reference with which the translator is acquainted throws any light cn this curious expression, and there is no parallel passage in the "Chronicles" to look for help.

32. Viz., to the Prince ("the august child"). The preparations which *Kihisa-tsu-mi* is here said to have made are supposed by Motowori to have been prompted by a desire to add beauty to the feast. But the whole passage is very obscure.

33. Viz., the court in front of, or the approach to, the shrine, which would naturally be planted with the sacred tree, the *saka-ki* (*Cleyera japonica*), and thus justly the prince's comparison to it of the artificial grove at which he was looking.

34. *I.e.*, the priest attached to the worship of, etc. For "deacon" see Note 33 to Sect. LXII.

35. *Ashihara-shiko-wo*, one of the many names of the Deity *Oho-kuni-nushi* ("Master of the Great Land," see Sect. XX, Note 19), the Deity whom the Prince and his followers had just been worshipping.

36. These names cannot now be identified, and are of uncertain etymology. Ikakuma seems, however, to mean "curve in the rock." One would have expected in this place, instead of these unknown names, to find a reference to the main temple of the Deity, which was styled *Kidzuki no oho-yashiro*, i.e., "the great shrine of Kidzuki."

37. Some such words as "the changed and more intelligent appearance of the Prince, and his attainment of the power of speech" must be mentally supplied in order to bring out the sense which the author intends to convey.

38. These names cannot be identified. *Nagaho* signifies "long-rice-ear," while *ajimasa* in modern usage is the name of a palm (the *Levistona Sinensis*); but Motowori supposes that it formerly designated the palmetto or some cognate tree.

39. *Hi-naga-hime.* The signification of the name is obscure, but it would seem most natural to suppose it connected with the River Hi which figures in the Idzumo cycle of legends. A proposal of Motowori's to read *Koye-naga* instead of the traditional *Hi-naga* seems scarcely to be meant in earnest. If accepted, it would give us the meaning of "fat and long princess," with reference to the story of her being a serpent.

40. It will be remembered that the Province of Idzumo is a maritime one, and that the fugitives might be supposed to reach the sea-shore in their flight. It is true that this is exactly the reverse of the direction which they would be obliged to take in travelling up to the capital, which was in Yamato.

41. *I.e.*, the depressions or valleys separating one mountain from another.

42. In the original *Totori-be, Torikahi-be, Homuji-be, Oho-yuwe and Waka-yuwe.* All these "gentile names" have a meaning connecting them either really or apparently with the story above related,—*to-tori* signifying "bird-catcher" and *tohi-kahi* "bird-feeder," while the name of the *Homuji* Clan is of course derived from that of the Prince (Homuchi or Homuji), and *Oho-yuwe* and *Waka-yuwe* signify respectively "elder bather" and "younger bather."

[SECT. LXXIII.—EMPEROR SUI-NIN (PART. V.—HIS
LATER WIVES.)]

Again, in accordance with the Emperor's words, he summoned Her Augustness Princess Hibasu, next Her Augustness Princess Oto, next Her Augustness Princess Utakori, next Her Augustness Princess Matonu,[1] daughters of Prince Michi-no-ushi—four Deities in all. Now he kept the two Deities Her Augustness Princess Hibasu and Her Augustness Princess Oto; but as for the two Deities the younger queens, he sent them back to their native place on account of their extreme hideousness. Thereupon Princess Matonu said with mortification: "When it is known in the neighbouring villages that, among sisters of the same family, we have been sent back on account of our ugliness, it will be extremely mortifying;" and, on reaching Sagaraka[2] in the Land of Yamashiro, she tried to kill herself[3] by hanging herself from a branch of a tree. So that place was called by the name of Sagariki. It is now called Sagaraka. Again, on reaching Otokuni,[4] she at last killed herself by jumping[5] into a deep pool. So that place was called by the name of Ochikuni. It is now called Otokuni.

1. *Hibasu-hime, Oto-hime, Utakori-hime* and *Matonu-hime.* The first two of these names have already appeared above, where the etymology of *Hibasu* was said to be doubtful, while *Oto* signifies "younger sister." *Matonu* has likewise already appeared, and is of uncertain derivation. Motowori supposes this last name to be in this place but an alias for *Utakori,* which he explains in the sense of "sad heart" with reference to the story of this princess as here told. In any case there is confusion in the legend, for in the parallel passage of the "Chronicles" five princesses are mentioned, whereas at the end of Sect. LXXI of these "Records" the Empress is made to speak of only two. The father's name has been already there explained.

2. The real derivation of this name is obscure. The ancient (perhaps here and elsewhere suppositious ancient) form *Sagari-ki* signifies "hanging-*tree.*" *Saga-raka* is written 相樂, a good example of the free manner in which some Chinese characters were anciently used for phonetic purposes. *Sau-raku, Sa-raku* or *Sa-gara* would be the only readings possible in the modern tongue.

3. Literally, "wished to die." Motowori supposes that her design was frustrated by her attendants.

4. Written with characters signifying "*younger country,*" but here supposed by the author to be derived from *ochi-kuni,* falling country," in connection with this legend.

5. Lit. "died by falling."

---

[SECT. LXXIV.—EMPEROR SUI-NIN (PART VI.—TAJI-MORI
BRINGS BACK THE ORANGE FROM THE
ETERNAL LAND.)]

Again the Heavenly Sovereign sent Tajima-mori,[1] ancestor of the Chiefs of Miyake,[2] to the Eternal Land[3] to fetch the fruit of the everlasting[4] fragrant tree. So Tajima-mori at last reached that country, plucked the fruit of the tree, and brought of clubmoss eight and of spears eight; but meanwhile the Heavenly Sovereign had died. Then Tajima-mori set apart of clubmoss four and of spears four, which he presented to the Great Empress,[5] and set up of clubmoss four and of spears four as an offering at the door of the Heavenly Sovereign's august mausoleum, and, raising on high the fruit of the tree, wailed and wept, saying : "Bringing the fruit of the everlasting fragrant tree from the Eternal Land, I have cóme to serve thee ;" and at last he wailed and wept himself to death. This fruit of the everlasting fragrant tree is what is now called the orange.[6]

---

1. The meaning of this name, which is written phonetically both here and in the " Chronicles," has given rise to differences of opinion, some deriving it from the name of the province of Tajima (itself of obscure origin) and from the word *mori* " keeper," while others think it comes from *tachibana*, the Japanese word for orange, with reference to the story here told. The supporters of the former view, on the other hand, derive the *tachibana* from *Tajima-mori*.

2. *Miyake no murazhi.* Whether *miyake* is simply the name of a place or whether it should be taken in the sense of " granary," is uncertain. If the latter view be adopted, it would be natural to suppose that this family had originally furnished the superintendents of the Imperial Granaries. In any case it traced its origin to a Korean source (see the " Catalogue of Family Names," and the genealogies in Sect. CXV).

3. See Sect. XXV).

4. Written in the parallel passage of the " Chronicles " with characters signifying literally " timeless." The whole of this circumlocution for the orange has indeed to be interpreted by the help of the " Chronicles." it being here written phonetically and offering some difficulties as it stands.

5. This corrupt and obscure passage seems to be well restored by Motowori, whose explanation of it is likewise as convincing as it is ingenious. The expression " clubmoss-oranges " signifies oranges as they grow on the branch surrounded by leaves, while " spear-oranges " are the same divested of leaves, and hanging to the bare twig. Thus the words " clubmoss " and " spear " come to be used as " Auxiliary Numerals " for oranges plucked in these two different manners.

6. Viz., says Motowori, Princess Hibasu, who however, according to the account in the " Chronicles," was already dead at this time.

7. The word *tachibana* (written 橘) in the text should probably be taken as a specific and not as a general term. In modern usage it designates the *Citrus japonica*. But it is a matter of dispute whether the application of the term has not altered since ancient times, and whether we should not understand by it one of the other kinds of orange now to be found in Japan,—perhaps the *Citrus nobilis*.

---

SECT. LXXV.—EMPEROR SUI-NIN (PART VII.—HIS DEATH AND THAT OF THE EMPRESS HIBASU.)] 200

This Heavenly Sovereign's august years were one hundred and fifty-three. His august mausoleum is in the middle of the moor of Mitachi at Sugahara.[1] Again in the time of the Great Empress Her Augustness Princess Hibasu,[2] the Stone-Coffin-Makers[13] were established, and also the Earthenware-Masters' Clan[4] was established. This Empress was buried in the mausoleum of Terama near Saki.[5]

---

1. Both the locality and the etymology of *Mitachi* are obscure. *Sugahara* (" sedge-moor ") is known to be in the province of Yamato.

2. *I.e.*, at the time of the burial of the great Empress, etc.

3. The character 祝 (" to pray ") in the text is indubitably a copyist's error for "棺, coffin." These stone coffins are described by Mr. Henry von Siebold in his " Note on Japanese Archaeology " p.5. It must be understood that, from being the name of an office, Stone-Coffin-Maker (*Ishi-ki-tsukuri*) became a " gentile name."

4. *Hanishi-be.* The meaning of this expression becomes clear by reference to the parallel passage of the " Chronicles," which it may be worth while to quote at length from Mr. Satow's translation in pp. 229-330 of Vol. VIII, Pt. III, of these Transactions : " In the autumn of 32nd year, on the *tsuchi no to u* day of the moon, which rose on the *ki no ye inu* day, the empress Hi ba su hime no Mikoto (in another source called Hi-ba-su ne no Mikoto) died, and they were several days going to bury her. The Mikado commanded all his high officers, saying : " We knew

before that the practice of following the dead is not good. In the
case of the present burying what shall be done? Thereupon Nomi no
Sukune advanced and said: "It is not good to bury living men standing at the sepulchre of a prince, and this cannot be handed down to
posterity. I pray leave now to propose a convenient plan. and to lay
this before the sovereign." And he sent messengers to summon up a
hundred of the clay-workers' tribe of the country of Izumo, and he
himself directed the men of the clay-workers' tribe in taking clay and
forming shapes of men, horses and various things, and presented them
to the Mikado, saying: 'From now and henceforward let it be the law
for posterity to exchange things of clay for living men, and set them up
at sepulchres.' Thereupon the Mikado rejoiced, and commanded Nomi no
Sukune, saying: 'Thy expedient plan has truly pleased Our heart;' and
the things of clay were for the first time set up at the tomb of Hi-ba-su
hime no Mikoto. Wherefore these things were *haniwa* (a circle of clay).
Then he sent down an order, saying: 'From now and henceforward, be
sure to set up these things of clay at sepulchres, and let not men be
slain.' Mikado bountifully praised Nomi no Sukune, bestowed on
him a kneading-place, and appointed him to the charge of the clay-
workers' tribe."

5. In the province of Yamato. In the old poetry there are many
plays on this word *Saki*, which is homonymous with the Verb "to blossom." But whether that be its real derivation, it were hard to say.
*Terama* appears to signify "Buddhist temple-space," an etymology which
is embarrassing to the Shinto commentators who, accepting every word
of our text as authentic history, are hard-driven to explain how Buddhist
temples could have existed in Japan before the date assigned for the
introduction of Buddhism.

---

201　[SECT. LXXVI.—EMPRESS KEI-KŌ (PART I,—GENEALOGIES.)]

The Heavenly Sovereign Oho-tarashi-hiko-oshiro-wake
dwelt in the palace of Hishiro at Makimuku,[1] and ruled
the Empire. This Heavenly Sovereign wedded the Elder
Lady of Inabi in Harima,[2] daughter of Waka-take, Prince
of Kibi,[3] ancestor of the Grandees of Kibi,[4] and begot

august children : King Kushi-tsunu-wake ;[5]. next His Augustness Ohousu ;[6] next His Augustness Wo-usu, another name for whom is His Augustness Yamato wo-guna ;[7] next His Augustness Yamato-ne-ko ;[8] next King Kamukushi.[9] Again wedding Her Augustness Princess Yasaka-202 no-iri,[10] daughter of His Augustness Prince Yasaka-no-iri, he begot august children : His Augustness Prince Waka-rarashi ;[11] next His Augustness Prince Iho-ki-no-iri ;[12] next His Augustness Oshi-no-wake ;[13] next Her Augustness Princess Iho-ki-no-iri.[14] Children by another concubine were : King Toyo-to-wake ;[15] next the Lady Nunoshiro.[16] Children by another concubine were : the Lady Nunaki ;[17] next Her Augustness Princess Kago-yori ;[13] next King Prince Waka-ki-no-iri ;[19] next King the Elder Prince of Kibi-no-ye ;[20] next Her Augustness Princess Takaki ;[21] next Her Augustness Princess Oto.[23] Again wedding Princess Mi-hakashi of Himuku,[23] he begot an august child : King Toyo-kuni-wake.[24] Again wedding the Younger Lady of Inabi,[25] younger sister of the Elder Lady of Inabi,[26] he begot august children : King Ma-waka ; next King Hiko-hito-no-oho-ye.[27] Again wedding Princess 203 Ka-guro,[28] daughter of King Princess Sume-iro-oho-naka-tsu-hiko,[29] great-grand-child of His Augustness Yamato-take,[30] he begot an august child : King Oho-ye.[31] The august children of this Heavenly Sovereign Oho-tarashi-hiko numbered in all twenty-one kings and queens[32] of whom there is a register. and fifty-nine kings and queens of whom there is no record,—eighty kings and queens altogether, out of whom His Augustness Waka-tarashi-hiko and also His Augustness Yamato-take, and also His Augustness Prince I-ho - ki - no-iri,—these three Kings,— bore the name of Heirs Apparent.[33] The seventy-seven

kings and queens beside these[31] were all granted Ruler-
ships in the various lands, or else [posts as] Lords,
Territorial Lords or Departmental Chiefs.[35]   So His Augustness Waka-tarashi-hiko [was he who afterward] ruled
the Empire.   His Augustness Wo-usu subdued the savage
deities and likewise the unsubmissive people in the East
204 and West.   The next, King Kushi-tsunu-wake (was the ancestor of the chiefs of Mamuta).[36]   The next, His Augustness
Oho-Usu, (was the ancestor of the Dukes of Mori,[37] of the Dukes of
Ohota[38] and of the Dukes of Shimada.)[39]   The next, King Kamukushi, (was the ancestor of the Sakabe Abiko in the Land of Ki,[40] and
of the Sakabe of Uda).[41]   The next, King Toyo-kuni-wake
(was the ancestor of the Rulers of the Land of Himuka.)[42]

---

1.   In the province of Yamato.   The etymology of *Makimuku* is
obscure.   *Hishiro* is tentatively derived by Motowori from *hi*, the *Chamaecyparis obtusa* (a kind of conifer), and *shiro*, "an enclosure."

2.   *Harima no inabi no oho-iratsume.*   Inabi is also known under the
alternative form of *Inami*: etymology uncertain.

3.   *Waka-take Kibi tsu hiko*,   *Waka-take* signifies "young brave."

4.   *Kibi no omi.*

5.   *Kushi* signifies "wondrous," and *wake* either "young," or "lord."
The meaning of *tsunu* is obscure.

6.   The names of this prince and the next signify respectively "great-
foot-pestle" and "little foot-pestle," the origin of the bestowal of which
singular designations is thus related in the parallel passage of the
"Chronicles:"   "The Imperial child Oho-usu and His Augustness Wo-
usu were born together the same day as twins.   The Heavenly Sovereign,
astonished, informed the foot-pestle.   So the two Kings were called
Great Foot-pestle and Liitle Foot-pestle."   What the import of this
paasage may be is, however, a mystery both to Tanigaha Shisei and to
Motowori.

7.   Motowori supposes *wo-guna* to have been an archaic word for
"boy," "me-guna" signifying "girl."   *Yamato wo-guna* would thus signify
"*the* boy of Japan." a not inappropriate designation for this prince, who
under his later name of Yamato-take (Japan Brave," i.e. *the* brave man of
Japan ") has remained as the chief legendary type of the martial prowess
of his native land.

8. *I.e.*, Yamato Prince.

9. *Komu-kushi no miko, i.e.*, " divine wondrous."

10. *Yamasaka no iri-bime no mikoto*. The signification of this name and of the next (*Ya-saka no iri-biko no mikoto*) is obscure.

11. *Waka-tarashi-hiko no mikoto, i.e.*, " young and perfect prince."

12. *I-ho-ki no iri-biko no mikoto*. Signification obscure.

13. Or, *Oshi-wake, i.e.*, perhaps " Great Lord."

14. *I-ho-ki no iri-bime no mikoto*. Signification obscure.

15. *Toyo-to-wake no mikoto, i.e.*, perhaps " luxuriant swift prince."

16. *Nunoshiro no iratsumo*. Signification obscure.

17. *Nunaki no iratsume*. Signification obscure.

18. *Kago-yori-hime no mikoto*. *Yori ime* probably means " good princess." The sense of *kago* is very doubtful, for it may either be the name of a place, or else identical with the Verb *kagayaku* " to shine," or with *kago*, " a stag."

19. *Waka-ki no iri-biko no mikoto*. The signification of this name is obscure.

20. *Kibi no ye-hiko no mikoto*.

21. *Takaki-hime no mikoto*. The meaning of *takaki* in this place is not certain.

22. *Oto-hime no mikoto, i.e.*, " the younger princes."

23. *Himuka no Mi-hakashi-bime*. *Mi hakashi* signifies " august sabre." See Motowori's Commentary, Vol. XXVI, p. 11, for a gloss on this curious name.

24. *Toyo-kuni-wake no miko, i.e.*, perhaps " lord of the luxuriant land," or else " lord of the land of Toyo," the Emperor Kei-kō having, according to the account in the " Chronicles," spent some years fighting in South-Western Japan, where the province of Toyo is situated.

25. *Inabi no waki-iratsume*. See Note 2 to this Section.

26. *Ma-waka no miko, i.e.*, " truly young prince."

27. *Hiko-hito no oho-ye no miko*. *Hiko* signifies " prince," *hito* is " person " (or here, according to Motowori, " headman "), and *oho-ye* is " great elder brother."

28. *Ka-guro-hime, i.e.*, probably " the black-haired princess."

29. *Sume-iro-oho-naka-tsu-hiko-no-mikoto*. The signification of this name is not clear. Motowori identifies *sume* with the like-sounding Verb signifying " to be supreme." *Oho-naka-tsu-hiko* may signify " great middle prince," referring to the comparative ages of this prince and his brethren.

30. There is here an evident error in the genealogy, as it would make the emperor marry his own great-great-grand daughter! A guess of the editor of 1687 that for Yamato-take we should read Waka-take (a son of the Emperor Kō-rei) is approved by Motowori, and may be adopted as probably correct,—i.e. (what is but little likely) if this portion of the "Records" should eventually be proved to be historically trustworthy. The question is discussed by Motowori in Vol. XXVI, pp. 12-14. of his Commentary.

31. *Oho-ye no miko.* This name would, as Motowori remarks, appear to have erroneously crept in here through the influence of the name mentioned in Note 27, the whole account of this union with Princess Ka-guro being corrupt.

32. The Japanese term (王 *miko*) includes both males and females.

33. 子太.

34. As above remarked, the Japanese term includes both males and females, and moreover some of the female children are specially mentioned. The difficulty as to how females could have been appointed to the offices here mentioned is not solved by Motowori, whose note on this passage is evasive.

35. The four names of offices (also used as "gentile names") here mentioned are in the original Japanese *Kuni no Miyatsuko, Wake, Inaki,* and *Agata-nushi.* (See Introduction, p. xvi.)

36. *Mamuta no murazhi.* (See Sect. LIII, Note 1.)

37. *Mori no kimi. Mori* seems to be the name of a place (perhaps in Mino); but nothing is known of this family.

38. *Ohota no kimi. Ohota* is the name of a place in Mino, and signifies "great rice-field."

39. *Shimada no kimi. Shimada* is perhaps the name of a place in Wohari. It signifies "island rice-fields."

40. *Ki no kuni no sakabe no abiko.* For *abiko* see Sect. LXXII, Note 85. *Sakabe* seems to signify "liquor tribe," this family and the next having been entrusted with the management of the Imperial feasts.

41. *Uda no sakabe,* i.e., the "Liquor Tribe of Uda." (in Yamato).

42. *Himuka no kuni no miyatsuko.*

[SECT. LXXVII.—EMPEROR KEI-KŌ (PART II.—THE MAIDENS
YE-HIME AND OTO-HIME).]

Hereupon the Heavenly Sovereign, to assure himself
of what he had heard of the beauty of the two maidens
Ye-hime and Oto-hime,[1] daughters of King Kamu-oho-
ne,[2] ancestor of the Rulers of the Land of Minu,[3] sent
his august child, His Augustness Oho-usu, to summon
them up [to the Capital]. So His Augustness Oho-usu
who had been sent, instead of summoning them up,
forthwith wedded both the maidens himself, and then
sought other women, to whom he falsely gave the maidens'
names, and sent them up [to his father]. Hereupon the
Heavenly Sovereign, knowing them to be other women,
frequently subjected them to his long glances;[4] but, never
wedding them, caused them to sorrow. So the child
that His Augustness Oho-usu begot on wedding Ye-[205]
hime, was King Oshi-kuro-no-ye-hiko[5] (he was the ancestor of
the Lords of Unesu in Minu.)[6] Again, the child that he begot
on wedding Oto-hime, was King Oshi-kuro-no-oto-hiko
(he was the ancestor of the Dukes of Mugetsu.)[7]

---

1. *I.e.*, the elder princess and the younger princess.
2. See Sect. LXII, Note 36.
3. *Minu no kuni no miyatsuko.*
4. *I.e.*, "gazed at them intently." The Classical word *nagamuru*,
"to gaze," is properly a compound of *naga*, "long," and *miru*, "to see"
5. The meaning of the syllables *oshi* in this name and the com-
panion one (*Oshi-kuro no oto hiko*) immediately below is probably "great;"
*kuro* is obscure; *ye-hiko* signifies "elder prince" and *oto-hiko* "younger
prince."
6. *Minu no Unesu no wako.* Of Unesu nothing is known.
7. *Mugetsu no kimi.* Mugetsu or Muge was in the province of
Minu (Mino).

[SECT. LXXVIII.—EMPEROR KEI-KŌ (PART III.—VARIOUS DEEDS.)]

In this august reign the Labourers' Tribe[1] was established; again, the port of Aha in the East was established; again, the Great Butlers' Tribe[2] was established; again, the granaries of Yamato were established; again, the Pool of Sakate was made, and bamboos planted on the bank.[3]

---

1. Such is the reasonable explanation of the original term *tabe* (田部) given by Motowori. It seems to have become a "gentile-name."

2. *Kashikade no oho-tomo-be.* This "gentile name" originally denoted one who was butler, steward, or cook, in the Emperor's household. The tradition of its origin is preserved in the "Chronicles."

3. Motowori supposes that the mention both in his history and in the "Chronicles of Japan" of the planting of bamboos on the banks of this pool or lake should be attributed to the rarity of such a proceeding in ancient times.

[SECT. LXXIX.—EMPEROR KEI-KŌ (PART IV.—YAMATO-TAKE SLAYS HIS ELDER BROTHER).]

The Heavenly Sovereign said to His Augustness Wo-usu: "Why does not thine elder brother come forth to the morning and evening great august repasts?[1] Be thou the one to take the trouble to teach him [his duty]." Thus he commanded; but for five days after, still [the prince] came not forth. Then the Heavenly Sovereign deigned to ask His Augustness Wo-usu [saying]: "Why is thine elder brother so long of coming? Hast thou perchance not yet taught him [his duty]?" He replied, saying: "I have been at that trouble." Again [the Heavenly Sovereign] said: "How didst thou take the trouble ?"[2]    He replied, saying :   "In the early morning when he went into the privy, I grasped hold of him and crushed him, and, pulling off his limbs,[3] wrapped them in matting and flung them away."

---

1.  Viz., to attend on his Imperial father.
2.  *I.e.*, "How didst thou do it ? "
3.  Literally, " branches."

---

[SECT. LXXX.—EMPEROR KEI-KŌ (PART V.—YAMATO-TAKE
SLAYS THE KUMASO BRAVOES).]

Thereupon the Heavenly Sovereign, alarmed at the valour and ferocity of his august child's disposition, commanded him, saying : " In the West there are two Kumaso bravoes,[1]—unsubmissive and disrespectful men. So take[2] them,"—and [with this command] he sent him off.    It happened that at this time his august hair was bound at the brow.[3]    Then His Augustness Wo-usu was granted by his aunt Her Augustness Yamato-hime[4] her august [upper] garment and august skirt ; and, with a sabre hidden in his august bosom, he went forth.[5]    So, on reaching the house of the Kumaso bravoes, he saw that near the house there was a three-fold belt of warriors, who had made a cave[6] to dwell in.    Hereupon they, noisily discussing a rejoicing for the august cave,[7] were getting food ready.    So [Prince Wo-usu sauntered about the neighbourhood, waiting for the day of the rejoicing.    Then when the day of the rejoicing came, having combed down after the manner of girls his august hair which was bound up,[8] and having put on his aunt's august [upper] garment and august skirt, he looked quite like a young girl, and, standing amidst the women,[9] went inside the cave. Then the elder brother and the younger brother, the two Kumaso bravoes, delighted at the sight of the maiden, set her between them, and rejoiced exuberantly. So, when [the feast was] at its height, [His Augustness Wo-usu], drawing the sabre from his bosom, and catching Kumaso[10] by the collar of his garment. thrust the sabre through his chest, whereupon, alarmed at the sight, the younger bravo ran out. But pursuing after and reaching him at the bottom of the[2] steps[11] of the cave, and catching him by the back,[12] [Prince Wo-usu] thrust the sabre through his buttock. Then the Kumaso bravo spoke, saying: "Do not move the sword; I[13] have something to say." Then [His Augustness Wo-usu], respited him for a moment, holding him down [as he lay] prostrate. Hereupon [the bravo] said: "Who is Thine Augustness?" Then he said: "I am the august child of Oho-tarashi-hiko-oshiro-wake, the Heavenly Sovereign who, dwelling in the palace of Hishiro at Makimuku, rules the Land of the Eight Great Islands; and my name is King Yamato-wo-guna. Hearing that you two [fellows[14]], the Kumaso bravoes, were unsubmissive and disrespectful, [the Heavenly Sovereign] sent me with the command to take and slay you." Then the Kumaso bravo said: "That must 208 be true. There are no persons in the West so brave and strong as we two.[15] Yet in the Land of Great Yamato there is a man braver than we two,—there is.[16] Therefore will I offer thee an august name. From this time forward it is right that thou be praised as the August Child Yamato-take.[17] As soon as he had finished saying this, [the Prince] ripped him up[18] like a ripe

melon,[19] and slew him.[20] So thenceforward he was praised
by being called by the august name of[21] his Augustness
Yamato-take. When he returned up [to the capital]
after doing this, he subdued and pacified every one of
the Deities of the mountains and of the Deities of the
rivers and likewise of the Deities of Anado,[22] and then
went up to [the capital].

---

1. *I.e.*, presumably "bravoes at Kumaso;" but it is to be remarked
that in this and like compounds with *takeru* ("bravo") the Japanese
language uses no Postposition. For Kumaso see Sect. V, Note 17.

2. Motowori seems right in interpreting "take" here and elsewhere
in the sense of "slay." But "take" is in the text.

3. *I.e.*, caught up from the brow and tied together on the crown
of the head. This being the way in which the hair of boys was dressed,
the author thus intimates that His Augustness was still a youth.

4. Who was high-priestess of the temple of the Great Deity of
Ise, as mentioned in Sect. LXIX (Note 44).

5. The characters used for these last two words are those properly
restricted to the mention of an Imperial progress, but Yamato-take is
constantly spoken of as if he had actually sat on the throne.

6. The character used is 室, which simply means apartment; but
see Sect. XLVIII, Note 1.

7. Motowori reads "*New* cave," but the word   August" is in the
text. At the same time we see that this feast was intended as¹a house-
warming. *Conf.* the commencement of Sect. CLXIV.

8. The parallel passage of the "Chronicles" puts the same meaning
into plainer words. It says: "undid his hair, and made it ɪappear
like a girl's."

9. Or, according to the old reading, "mixing with the concubines."

10. *I.e.*, the elder bravo of Kumaso.

11. The word rendered "steps" is of doubtful interpretation.

12. Or perhaps "the skin of his back" or the (beast's?) skin on
his back." But Motowori is probably right in supposing the character
皮, "skin" to be an error for 以, "with," to be construed with the
word "sabre." (In the English idiom this Particle falls away.)

13. Written with the humble character 僕, "servant."

14. The contemptuous Second Personal Pronoun *ore* is used here and in the next clause.

15. There is Motowori's authority for thus understanding the bravo's words. Taken still more literally, they would seem to imply that there were no brave and strong men in the West *excepting* himself and his brother.

16. The words "there is" are an attempt at rendering the termination *keri* of the original. See X, Note 1.

17. *I.e.*, "Yamato-Brave," *q.d.*, "the Bravest in Yamato." It is by this name that the hero is commonly spoken of. Remember that "august child" signifies prince.

18. 折, "broke," in the text is, as the commentators observe, an evident error for 栃, "ripped."

19. Or specifically, the "musk melon."

20. The translator has followed Motowori's restoration of this passage, in which, by the transposition of the characters 也 and 故, the end of this sentence and the beginning of the next were mixed together in the older editions.

21. Lit., "[they] praised the august name, calling him," etc.

22. Or, "of the Ana passage" (lit. door), the modern Strait of Shimonoseki. The word *ana* signifies "hole," and there is a tradition (which Motowori quotes in his note on this name in Vol. XXVII, pp. 26-29 of his Commentary) to the effect that formerly the Main Island and the island of Kiushiu were continuous at this point, there being only a sort of natural tunnel, through which junks could pass.

---

[SECT. LXXXI.—EMPEROR KEI-KŌ (PART VI.—YAMATO-TAKE SLAYS THE IDZUMO BRAVO).]

Forthwith entering the Land of Idzumo, and wishing to slay the Idzumo bravo, he on arriving, forthwith bound [himself to him in] friendship. So, having secret-
209 ly made [the wood of] an oak [-tree[1][ into a false sword and augustly girded it, he went with the bravo to bathe the River Hi.[2] Then, His Augustness Yamato-take

getting out of the river first, and taking and girding on the sword that the Idzumo bravo had taken off and laid down, said: "Let us exchange swords!" So afterwards the Idzumo bravo, getting out of the river, girded on His Augustness Yamato-take's false sword. Hereupon His Augustness Yamato-take, suggested, saying: "Come on! let us cross[3] swords." Then on drawing his sword, the Idzumo bravo could not draw the false sword. Forthwith His Augustness Yamato-take drew his sword and slew the Idzumo bravo. Then he sang augustly, saying:

> "Alas that the sword girded on the Idzumo
> bravo, and wound round with many a
> creeper, should have had no true blade![4]

So having thus extirpated the [bravoes] and made [the land] orderly, he went up [to the capital], and made his report [to the Heavenly Sovereign].

---

1. The species mentioned (*ichihi*) is the *Quercus gilva*.

2. See Sect. XVIII, Note 2.

3. Lit., "let us join swords." The word "suggested" (誂) in this sentence is an emendation of Motowori's, the text having 誹, "slandered." The older printed editions, while retaining the character 誹, read it *azamukite*, "deceived."

4. In its position in the present text, this Song must be taken as an ironical lament of the Prince for the dead bravo. In the "Chronicle" the time and the heroes of the episode, and the singers of the Song are all different, and in that context the lament sounds like a genuine one. The reader will remember what was said in the Introduction as to the use of creepers for string. That mentioned in the text is supposed to be the *Cocculus thunbergi*.

[SECT. LXXXII.—EMPEROR KEI-KŌ (PART VII.—YAMATO-TAKE
IS SENT TO SUBDUE THE EAST, AND VISITS HIS
AUNT AT ISE).]

Then the Heavenly Sovereign again urged a command
on His Augustness Yamato-take, saying: "Subdue and
pacify the savage Deities and likewise the unsubmissive
people of the twelve roads of the East;"[1] and when he
sent him off, joining to him Prince Mi-suki-tomo-mimi-
take,[2] ancestor of the Grandees of Kibi,[3] he bestowed on
210 him a holly-wood[4] spear eight fathoms [long]. So when
he had received the [Imperial] command and started off,
he went into the temple of the Great August Deity of
Ise, and worshipped the Deity's court,[5] forthwith speaking to his aunt, Her Augustness Yamato-hime, saying:
"It must surely be that the Heavenly Sovereign thinks[6]
I may die quickly; for after sending me to smite the
wicked people of the West, I am no sooner come up
again [to the capital] than, without bestowing on me an
army, he now sends me off afresh to pacify the wicked
people of the twelve circuits of the East. Consequently
I think that he certainly thinks I shall die quickly."
When he departed with lamentations and tears, Her
Augustness Yamato-hime bestowed on him the "Herb-
Quelling-Sabre,"[7] and likewise bestowed on him an august
bag,[8] and said: "If there should be an emergency, open
the mouth of the bag."

1. See Sect. LXVI. Note 2.
2. *Mi-suki-tomo-mimi-take-hiko.* *Mi* is an Honorific, *mimi* probably
signifies "ears," and *take* means "bravo." The words *suki* and *tomo* are
obscure.
3. *Kibi na omi.*
4. Properly the *Olea aquifolium*, which resembles holly. Motowori

supposes that an entirely wooden spear or stick is here meant to be spoken of, and not the weapon with a metal point which is commonly understood by the word "spear" (*hoko*).

5. Perhaps we should write "august court," for the characters 朝廷 in the text are evidently intended for the homonymous 朝門. The court in front of the Deity's temple is what is here alluded to, and it would perhaps be a not unpardonable departure from the text to insert the Preposition "at," or "in," and translate thus: "worshipped *in* the Deity's court."

6. Here and below, the word "thinks," may be understood to mean "wishes."

7. *Kusa-nagi no tsurugi*. The discovery of this sword by the deity Susa-no wo ("Impetuous Male") inside one of the tails of the eight-headed serpent which he had slain, is narrated at the end of Sect. XVIII.

8. The use of the contents of this bag will be seen in the next Section.

---

[SECT. LXXXIII.—EMPEROR KEI-KŌ (PART VIII.—YAMATO-TAKE SLAYS THE RULERS OF SAGAMU.)]　　211

So reaching the Land of Wohari, he went into the house of Princess Miyadzu,[1] ancestress of the Rulers of Wohari,[2] and forthwith thought to wed her; but thinking again that he would wed her when he should return up [toward the capital], and having plighted his troth, he went [on] into the Eastern Lands, and subdued and pacified all the savage Deities and unsubmissive people of the mountains and rivers. So then, when he reached the Land of Sagamu,[3] the Ruler of the land lied, saying: "In the middle of this moor is a great lagoon, and the Deity that dwells in the middle of the lagoon is a very violent Deity." Hereupon [Yamato-take] entered the moor to see the Deity. Then the Ruler of the land set fire to the moor. So, knowing that he had been deceived, he opened the mouth of the bag which his aunt, Her Augustness Yamato-hime had bestowed on him, and saw that inside of it there was a fire-striker.[4] Hereupon he first mowed away the herbage with his august sword, took the fire-striker and struck out fire, and, kindling a counter-fire, burnt [the herbage] and drove back [the other fire], and returned forth, and killed and destroyed all the Rulers[5] of that Land, and forthwith set fire to and burnt them. So [that place] is now called Yakidzu.[6]

1. *Miyazu-hime* (in the "Chronicles" and in the printed editions of these "Records" previous to Motowori's written *Miyasu-hime* without the *nigori*). Neither Motowori nor Tanigaha Shisei makes any suggestion as to the signification of this name.

2. *Wohari no miyatsuko.*

3. In the present time *Sagami.* No authority great or small has given a satisfactory etymology of this name, though numerous and elaborate attempts have been made to explain it.

4. In the original *hi-uchi* (火打). Mr. Satow, who has given a translation of this passage in a note to his third paper on the "Rituals" to be found in Vol. IX, Pt. II. p. 202 of these "Transaction," renders this word by "steel." The present writer prefers not to prejudge the question as to whether the fire-striker" intended by the author was a steel, or a wooden fire-drill. Motowori would seem to have held the latter view, as in his gloss on this passage he refers to the previous passage near the end of Sect. XXXII, where the fire-drill is explicitly mentioned. He also quotes an ancient one in which "a fire-striker of metal" is specially referred to, so that it would seem that all fire-strikers were not of that material.

5. Remember that this word "Ruler" (*Miyatsuko*) had the acceptation of a "gentile name" as well as of the name of an office, so that we may understand the author to mean that Yamato-take destroyed the whole Ruling Family of [Sagami. Parallel passage of the "Chronicles" has "he burnt all that rebel band, and destroyed them."

6. The words rendered "that place" are supplied by Motowori, their omission being evidently a copyist's error. *Yaki-dzu* signifies "the port of burning."

[SECT. LXXXIV.—EMPEROR KE[I]-KŌ (PART [1]X.—YAMATO-          212
TAKE'S EMPRESS STILLS THE WAVES.)]

When he thence penetrated on, and crossed the sea of
Hashiri-midzu,[1] the Deity of that crossing raised the
waves, tossing the ship so that it could not proceed
across. Then [Yamato-take's] Empress,[2] whose name
was Her Augustness Princess Oto-tachibana[2] said: "I[4]
will enter the sea instead of the august child.[5] The
august child must complete the service[6] on which he
has been sent, and take back a report [to the Heavenly
Sovereign]." When she was about to enter the sea, she
spread eight thicknesses of sedge rugs,[7] eight thicknesses
of skin rugs and eight thicknesses of silk rugs on the
top of the waves, and sat down on the top [of them]
Thereupon the violent waves at once went down, and
the august ship was able to proceed. Then the Empress
sang, saying:

> "Ah! thou [whom I] enquired of, standing
> in the midst of the flames of the fire burn-
> ing on the little moor of Sagamu, where
> the true peak pierces![8]

So seven days afterwards the Empress's august comb 213
drifted onto the sea-beach,—Which comb was forthwith
taken and placed in an august mausoleum which was made.

---

1. *I.e.*, "running water."
2. *I.e.*, his consort. Conf. Sect. KXXX, Note 5.
3. *Oto-tachibana-hime no mikoto.* (See Sect. XCII, Note 3.)
4. Written with the humble character 妾, literally "concubine."
5. *I.e.*, instead of thee, the Prince."
6. More literally, "finish the government."
7. Or "mats." But the same word is used as that which must be
ranslated "rugs" immediately below.

8. This Song gives much trouble to the commentators, whose remarks (to be found in Motowori's "Commentary." Vol. XXVII, pp. 67-9, and Moribe's "*Idzu no Koto-Waki*" Vol. III, pp. 6-9,) should be consulted by the student desirous of forming an opinion of his own. The general purport of the poem is of course to allude to Yamato-take's adventure on the burning moor, and at the same time to the love which bound him and his consort together; almost each individual line offers matter for doubt. Thus it is not certain whether the Verb *tohishi*, here rendered "enquired of" (*i.e.*, attended upon *q.d.*, by the Empress). should not rather be given the word "thou" as subject, in which case the signification would be "thou who enquiredst of [*i.e.*, wooedst]." The word used for "thou," is the Honorific equivalent of that Pronoun signifying literally "prince." Moribe disputes the propriety of considering Sagamu in this place as the name of a province, and the word *sanesashi*, here translated "where the true peak pierces" (Mt. Fuji being by some supposed to be thus alluded to) is of very doubtful interpretation. Motowori tells us that the final Particles *ha mo*, rendered by the initial Interjection "Oh," should here be understood as an exclamation more forcible than that which usually belongs to him. Finally Moribe points out that the Song does not suit the context in which it is found, and has probably been erroneously inserted here instead of in an earlier portion of the text.

---

[SECT. LXXXV.—EMPEROR KEɪ-KŌ (PART X.—YAMATO-TAKE SLAYS THE DEITY OF THE ASHIGARA PASS.)]

When, having thence penetrated on and subdued all the savage Yemishi[1] and likewise pacified all the savage Deities of the mountains and rivers, he was returning up [to the capital], he, on reaching the foot of the Ashigara Pass,[2] was eating his august provisions, when the Deity of the pass, transformed into a white deer, came and stood [before him]. Then forthwith, on his waiting[3] and striking [the deer] with a scrap of wild chive,[4] [the deer] was hit in the eye and struck dead. So, mounting to the top of the pass, he sighed three times and spoke, saying:  "*Adzuma ha ya!*"[5]  So that land is called by the name of Adzuma.

---

1. This is the traditional ancient reading of what is according to the modern pronunciation *Yezo*, while the Chinese characters 蝦夷, with which the name is written, signify "Prawn Barbarians," in allusion (if Motowori may be trusted) to the long beards which make their faces resemble a prawn's head. The hairy barbarians known to English readers as *Ainos*, and whose name of *Yezo* is applied by the Japanese to the northernmost large island of the Japanese Archipelago, which is still chiefly tenanted by them, are almost certainly here referred to. In ancient times they inhabited a great part of the Main Island of Japan. The translator may add that the genuiness of the so-called ancient reading " *Yemishi* " appears to him doubtful. The name known to the people themselves, and which apparently can be traced as far as Kamschatka, is *Yezo*.

2. *Ashigara-zaka*, one of the passes from Sagami into Suruga leading towards Mount Fuji.

3. *I.e.*, lying in ambush.

4. *Nira*, the *Allium odorum*.

5. *I.e.*, "my wife!" *Adzuma* is still used as a poetical designation of Eastern Japan. The translator doubts the correctness of the derivation of it given in the text, although it is universally accepted and certainly fits in well with the graceful legend by which it is here accounted for.

---

[SECT. LXXXVI.—EMPEROR KEI-KŌ (PART XI.—YAMATO-TAKE 214 DWELLS IN THE PALACE OF SAKAWORI.)]

When, forthwith crossing over from that land out into Kahi,[1] he dwelt in the palace of Sakawori,[2] he sang, saying:

> " How many nights have I slept since passing
> Nihibari and Tsukuha ?"[3]

Then the old man, who was the lighter of the august fire,[4] completed the august Song, and sang, saying:

> "Oh! having put the days in a row, there
> are of nights nine nights, and of days ten
> days!"[5]

Therefore [Yamato-take] praised the old man, and forthwith bestowed [on him] the Rulership of the Eastern Land [s].[6]

---

1. This name is identified by the native etymology with an homonymous Substantive signifying "a place between mountains.',

2. The etymology of this name is uncertain. But the most likely opinion is that it signifies "a zigzag road down a pass."

3. *I.e.*, since leaving the province of Hitachi, of which Tsukuha (in modern parlance *Tsukuba*, with the last syllable *nigori*ed) and Nihibari (modern *Nihiharu*) are two districts. In the later poetry *Nihibari no* is often used as a Pillow-Word for the name of Mount Tsukuba. The etymology of both names is uncertain, but "newly tilled" seems to be the most probable etymology of the first of the two.

4. Not necessarily a fire kindled for the sake of obtaining warmth, but fire in general, including, as Motowori suggests, torches and fires lit to drive away mosquitoes. There are frequent mentions in the classical literature of this latter sort of fire, which may indeed still be met with in some districts where mosquito-nets are not yet in common use.

5. The meaning is: "On counting up, I find that we have been ten days and nine nights."—Previous to Motowori the expression *ka-ga nabette*, "having put in a row (*i.e.* counted) the days" was curiously misunderstood, and subjected to various far-fetched interpretations. There can however be no doubt but that Motowori is right.—The reason why the old man is said to have "completed" the Prince's song is that the former taken alone is of incomplete rhythm.

6. Or, as Motowori would prefer to consider it, "the Rulership of *an* Eastern Land," viz., one out of the twelve Eastern provinces.

[SECT. LXXXVII.—EMPEROR KEI-KŌ (PART XII.—YAMATO-
TAKE WOOES PRINCESS MIYAZU).]

Having crossed over from that land [into the land of
Shinanu[1] and subdued the Deity of the Shinanu pass,[2]
he came back to the land of Wohari, and went to dwell
in the house of Princess Miyazu, to whom he had before
plighted his troth. Hereupon, when presenting to him
the great august food, Princess Miyazu lifted up a great
liquor-cup and presented it to him. Tunc Heræ Miyazu
veli oræ adhæserunt menstrua.    Quare ]Augustus Yamato-
take] illa menstrua vidit, et auguste cecinit, dicens:

> " Ego volui reclinare [caput] in fragili,
>    molli brachiolo [tuo, quod est simile] vallo
>    impingenti acutæ falci in Monte Kagu in
>    cœlo formato quasi cucurbita ;—ego de-
>    sideravi dormire [tecum]. Sed in orâ veli
>    quod induis luna surrexit."[3]

Tunc Heræ Miyazu augusto cantui respondit, dicens:        216

> " Altè resplendentis solis auguste puer!
>    Placidè administrationem faciens mi magne
>    domine! Renovatis annis venientibus et
>    effluentibus, renovatæ lunæ eunt veniendo
>    patienter expecto, luna suàpte surgit in
>    orâ veli quod ego induo !"[4]

Quare tunc [ille] coivit [cum illâ], after which, placing
in Princess Miyazu's house his august sword "the Grass-
Quelling Sabre," he went forth[5] to take the Deity of
[Mount] Ibuki.[6]

---

1. See Sect. XXXIII, Note 26.
2. *Shinanu no saka*, a pass between the provinces of Shinano and
Mino which is no longer used.

3. Even taken apart from its immediate context, the import of this Song is plain, notwithstanding Moribe's efforts to explain away its inde-licacy. The details of the first part, however, require some comment in order to make them comprehensible to the European reader, the words in question being these which might in English be rendered " thy fragile, slender, delicate arm [which resembles] a post striking against the sharp sickle on Mount Kagu of the gourd-shaped heaven." In Japanese they run thus:

*Hisa-kata no*
*· Ame no Kagu-yamo*
*To-kama ni*
*Sa-wataru kuhi :—*
*Hiha-boso*
*Ta-waya-gahina wo* etc.

It will be remarked that the first four lines form a "Punning Preface" to the fifth. Such Punning Prefaces have not necessarily any logical connection with what follows, as has been explained by the present writer in a paper "On the Use of Pillow Words and Plays upon Words in Japanese Poetry," to be found in Vol. V, Pt. I, pp. 79 *et seq.* of these "Transactions." In this particular case, however, there is sufficient continuity of sense to warrant the continuous translation above given. The word "post," though such a use of it is very curious, must be understood to denote not a dead, but a living trunk, or rather the stem of some delicate plant or grass whic. falls beneath the sickle of the mower on Mount Kagu in Heaven, or, as it may better be under-stood, on the Heavenly Mount Kagu [in Yamato]. "Gourd-shaped" is the translation of *hisa-kata no* or *hisa-gata no*, the Pillow-Word for "heaven." Its meaning is disputed, but Mabuchi in his "Dictionary of Pillow-Words" and Motowori agree in giving to it the sense here adopted (see the above-mentioned paper "On the Use of Pillow-Words, etc.," p. 81).

4. The total sense of this Song is quite plain.—In the first lines of it the Prince is addressed as if he were the reigning sovereign. The words *placidè administrationem faciens* represent the Japanese *yasumishishi,* the Pillow-Word for *wa ga oho-kimi,* "my great lord." Elsewhere the English rendering "who tranquilly carries on the government" has been adopted. The word *aratama no,* rendered by the Adjective *renovatis,* is the Pillow-Word for "sun," "moon" and "year," and is of not quite certain import. The interpretation here adopted has, however, for it the weight of probability and of native authority, Mabuchi in his "Dictionary of Pillow-Words" deriving it from the Verb *aratamaru,* "to be renewed."

5. The characters in the text might also be rendered " he made a progress," as they are those only properly applied to the movements of a reigning sovereign. Here and elsewhere, they are used in speaking of Yamato-take. (Conf. Sect. LXXX, Note 5.)

6. On the frontier of Afumi (Omi) and Mino. *Ibuki* seems to signify "blowing,' in allusion, it is said, to the pestilential breath or influence of the god by whom the place was tenanted. The word rendered "Mount" is supplied by the editor of 1687.

———

[SECT. LXXXVIII.—EMPEROR KEI-KŌ (PART XIII.—YAMATO-TAKE MEETS THE DEITY OF MOUNT IBUKI).]

Hereupon he said : " As for the Deity of this mountain, I will simply take him empty-handed."[1]—and was ascending the mountain, when there met him on the mountain-side a white boar whose size was like unto that of a bull,[2] Then he lifted up words,[3] and said : " This creature that is transformed into a white boar must be a messenger from the Deity.[4] Though I slay it not now, I will slay it when I return,"—and [so saying.] ascended. Thereupon the Deity caused heavy ice-rain[5] to fall, striking and perplexing His Augustness Yamato-take. (This creature transformed into a white boar was not a messenger from the Deity,[6] but the very Deity in person. Owing to the lifting up of words, he appeared and misled [Yamato-take.[6]]) So when, on descending back, he reached the fresh spring of Tama-kuro-be[7] and rested there, his august heart awoke some-what.[8] So that fresh spring is called by the name of the fresh spring of Wi-same.

———

1. *I.e.*, without weapons, and specially without the magic sword which he had left behind in Princess Miyazu's house.

2. Or " ox," or " cow," the original word not distinguishing between the sexes.

3. The Japanese expression *koto-age shite*, here rendered "lifted up words," very frequently has the signification of "lifting up a prayer" to some superhuman being. In this passage, however, it conveys no more than its proper etymological meaning.

4. Viz., the god of Mount Ibuki.

5. Perhaps "hail" may be intended by this expression, and so Motowori decides. But this interpretation of the term seems to agree well with the Song in Sect. CXLII.

6. The commentators disagree as to whether this note should or should not be considered to form part of the original text. Motowori so considers it. He however, in the opinion of the translator, is not happy in his alteration of the *kana* reading given by the editor of 1687, which latter has accordingly been followed in the English version.

7. The literal meaning of this name is "jewel-store-tribe;" but complete uncertainty attaches both to the etymology of the word and to the position of the place. The first printed edition has *Tama-kuhi-be*.

8. He had been misled and dazed, but now came to himself again. Thence, according to the etymology of our author, the name of *Wi-same*, which signifies "dwelling (resting) and awaking," given to the spring,

———

When he departed thence and reached the moor of 218 Tagi[1] he said: "Whereas my heart always felt like flying through the sky, my legs are now unable to walk. They have become rudder-shaped."[2] So that place was called by the name of Tagi. Owing to his being very weary with progressing a little further beyond that place. he leant upon an august staff to walk a little. So that place is called by the name of the Tsuwetsuki pass.[3] On arriving at the single pine-tree on Cape Wotsu,[4] an august sword, which he had forgotten at that place before when augustly eating,[5] was still [there] not lost. Then he augustly sang, saying:

"O mine elder brother, the single pine-tree
that art on Cape Wotsu which directly
faces Mohari! If thou, single pine-tree!
wert a person, I would gird [my] sword
[upon thee], I would clothe thee with
[my] garments,—O mine elder brother, the
single pine-tree!"

When he departed thence and reached the village of
Mihe,[7] he again said: "My legs are like three-fold
crooks,[8] and very weary." So that place was called by
the name of Mihe. When he departed thence and reached
the moor of Nobe,[9] he, regretting[10] [his native] land,[11]
sang, saying:

"As for Yamato, the most secluded of lands
— Yamato, retired behind Mount Awogaki
encompassing it with its folds is delightful."[12]

Again he sang, saying:

"Let those whose life may be complete stick
[in their hair] as a head-dress the leaves
of the bear-oak from Mount Heguri,—those
children!"

This song is a Land-Regretting Song.[13] Again he
sang, saying:

"How sweet! ah! from the direction of
home clouds are rising and coming!"

This is an Incomplete Song.[14] At this time, his august
sickness was very urgent. Then, he sang augustly, saying:

"The sabre-sword which I placed at the
maiden's bed-side, alas! that sword!"[15]

As soon as he had finished singing, he died, Then a
courier was despatched [to the Heavenly Sovereign.]

219

1. *Tagi-nu.* We might, following the Chinese characters, translate thus: "and arrived on the Moor of Tagi." But the character 上 has in this context scarcely any meaning. The real etymology of *Tagi* (in classical and modern parlance *taki* without the *nigori*) is "rapid" or "waterfall," the cascade formed by the river Vo-ro in Mino being alluded to. The derivation in the next sentence of the text from *tagishi* supposed to mean "a rudder" is a mere fancy.

2. The word here rendered "rudder" is *tagishi*, which is written phonetically and does not occur elsewhere, except in a few Proper Names of doubtful import. There is however some probability in favour of the meaning assigned to it by the native commentators.

3. *Tsuwe-tsuki-zaka, i.e.,* "the pass of leaning on a staff." It is in the province of Ise between Yokaichi and Ishi-yakushi.

4. *Wotsu-no-saki,* in the province of Ise. The name probably signifies "harbour of the mountain declivity."

5. The former portion of the text tells us nothing either of the meal or of the sword here mentioned.

6. This quaintly simple and apparently very ancient poem needs no elucidation.

7. In Ise. *Mihe* signifies "three fold."

8. This is the literal rendering of the text. Motowori thinks, however, that we should understand that there were various swellings on his legs, such as would be produced if the limb were tightly tied round with cord in three places.

9. *Nobo-un* in the province of Ise. The name seems to signify "the moor of mounting."

10. The Chinese character here used signifies simply "thinking of;" but in such a context its common Japanese interpretation is "loving" or "regretting," and so Motowori means us to understand it when he reads *shinuhashite.*

11. Viz., Yamato.

12. This Song and the two following form but one in the pages of the "Chronicles," where they appear with several verbal differences, and are attributed, not to the Prince, but to his father the Emperor. Moribe decides that in the latter particular the text of these "Records" gives the preferable account, but that the "Chronicles" are right in making the three Songs one continuous poem. The expression "this Song is a Land-Regretting Song" strongly supports this view; for, though we might also render in the Plural "these Songs are, etc.," such a translation would be less natural, as in similar cases the numeral is used, thus

" these *two* Songs are, etc." The expression "this is an Incomplete Song" points as decidelly to some mutilation of the original document, from which the compiler of the "Records" copied this passage. Taking then the three Songs as one, the entire drift is that of a paean on Yamato, the poet's native land, which he could not hope ever to see again :—Commencing by praising its still seclusion as it lies there behind its barrier of protecting mountains, he goes on to mention the rural pleasures enjoyed by those who, wandering over the hill-sides, deck their hair with garlands of leaves and flowers. For himself indeed these delights are no more ; " but," says he, " do you, ye children full of health and happiness, pursue your innocent enjoyment !" In conclusion he lovingly apostrophises the clouds which, rising up from the south-west, are, as it were, messengers from home. The word *mahoroha*, rendered " secluded," is a great crux to the commentators, and Motowori's "Examination of the Synonyms of Japan," pp. 17-18. and Moribe's " *Idzu no Koto Waki*," Vol. III, p. 31, should be consulted by the student desirous of forming his own opinion on the point. Another apparent difficulty is the word *gomoreru*, whose position in the sentence Motowori seems to have misunderstood. By following Moribe, and taking it as a compound with the word *Awogaki-yama* into *Awogaki-yama-gomoreru* the difficulty vanishes, and we are likewise relieved from the necessity of supposing anything so highly improbable as that the Verb *komoreru* when not compounded, should have commenced with a *nigori*'ed syllable "Complete" signifies "healthy." Mount Heguri is preceded in the original by *tatamikomo* (Moribe reads *tatamigomo* with the *nigori*) a Pillow-Word whose import is disputed. In any case, being a punning one, it cannot be translated. For the " bear-oak " see Sect. LXXII, Note 19. Moribe labours, but without success, to prove that " come," the last word of the translation, signifies " go," and imagines that the prince is expressing his envy of the clouds which are rising and going off in the direction of the home which he will never revisit.

13. *I.e.,* a Song of loving regret for his native land.

14. "Incomplete Song" mnst be understood as the designation of a poem of a certain number of lines, viz, three, and was probably given by comparison with the greater length of poetical compositions in general.

15. This poem is an exclamation of distress at the thought of the sword which he had left with his mistress Princess Miyazu and which, if he had had it with him, would doubtless have preserved him from the evil influences of the god of Mount Ibuki, which were the beginning of

his end.—" Sabre-sword " (*tsnrugi no tachi*) is a curious expression, which Moribe thinks means " double-edged sword."

---

[SECT. XC.—EMPEROR KEI-KŌ (PART XV.—YAMATO-TAKE
TURNS INTO A WHITE BIRD)]

Thereupon [his] Empresses[1] and likewise [his] august
221 children, who dwelt in Yamato, all went down[2] and
built an august mausoleum, and, forthwith crawling
hither and thither in the rice-fields encompassing [the
mausoleum]. sobbed out a Song, saying:

" The *Dioscorea quinqueloba* crawling hither
and thither among the rice-stubble, among
the rice-stubble in the rice-fields encompassing [the mausoleum] . . . ."[3]

Thereupon [the dead prince], turning into a white
dotterel[4] eight fathoms [long], and soaring up to Heaven,
flew off towards the shore. Then the Empress and likewise the august children, though they tore their feet
treading on the stubble of the bamboo-grass, forgot the
pain, and pursued him with lamentations. At that time
they sang, saying:

" Our loins are impeded in the plain [over-
grown with] short bamboo-grass. We are
not going through the sky, but oh! we
are on foot."[5]

222 Again when they entered the salt sea,[6] and suffered
as they went, they sang, saying.

" As we go through thé sea, our loins are
·impeded,—tottering in the sea like herbs
growing in a great river-bed."[7]

Again when [the bird] flew and perched on the sea-side, they sang, saying:

> "The dotterel of the beach goes not on the
> beach, but follows the seaside."[8]

These four Songs were all sung at [Yamato-take's] august interment. So to the present day these Songs are sung at the great interment of a Heavenly Sovereign. So [the bird] flew off from that country,[9] and stopped at Shiki in the land of Kafuchi.[10] So they made an august mausoleum there, and laid [Yamato-take] to rest.[11] Forthwtth that august mausoleum was called by the name of the "August-Mausoleum of the White-Bird.[12] Nevertheless the bird soared up thence to heaven again, and flew away.

223

---

1. *I.e.*, wives. It will be remembered that the historian habitually mentions Yamato-take as if he had been Emperor.

2. *Q.d.*, to the land of Ise.

3. The drift of the Song is a comparison of the helpless wanderings of the mourners in the neighbourhood of the tomb to the convolutions of the *Dioscorea quinqueloba* (a creeping plant) growing among the rice in the adjacent fields. But there are evidently some lines omitted. If we were to adopt the elegant verses conjecturally supplied by Moribe, the entire translation would run thus: "The *Dioscorea quinqueloba* crawl hither and thither among the rice-stubble, among the rice-stubble in the rice-fields encompassing [the mausoleum]; but though like it, we crawl hither and thither, and weep and speak to thee, thou answerest not a word."—Moribe supposes this poem to be the Empress's composition, and the following three to have proceeded from the children.

4. As usual when the word *chidori* (defined as "any kind of dotterel, plover or sandpiper") is used, it is doubtful what bird is really intended. At the end of this Section we are told that the Mausoleum was called the Mausoleum of the White Bird (白鳥)." Specifically, however, these characters are used with their Sinico-Japanese pronunciation of *haku-cho* as the name of the swan. But as swans are nowhere else mentioned in these "Records" and as moreover their habits are not

such as to accord with the legend here narrated, it will perhaps be safer to retain " dotterel " in the translation. " Heron " also has been suggested.

5. The signification of this Song is : " It is easy enough for thee, thou bird-spirit! to fly through the air. [But remember that we are on foot, and that our feet are getting torn by the short stubble of the bamboo-grass (*Bambusa shino*)."

6. When the bird flew over the sea, they too waded after it through the waves.

7. The signification of the Song is: " As we pursue thee through the sea, we sink in the waves up to our middles, and totter like the water-plants against " which strikes the current of a great river."—The word *uwe-gusa*, lit. " herbs planted," is curious ; but it simply means " herbs growing," as in the translation (*conf.* our word " plant "). The latter part of the poem is in the original highly elliptical.

8. The point of the Song seems to rest on a delicate distinction between the words *hama*, " beach " and *iso*, " seaside," which does not obtain in the later Japanese language any more than it does in English. Both *hama* and *iso*, " beach " and " seaside," denote the boundary-line between sea and land ; but we must suppose with the commentators that while the former was used with special reference to the land, the latter considered the idea (so to speak) from the point of view of the sea. The import of the song is therefore to upbraid the bird for flying over the waves instead of flying along the adjacent shore.

9. *I.e.*, says Motowori, from Ise.

10. Not to be confounded with the Shiki in Yamato, which is written with different phonetic character.

11. The Verb used in the original is *shizumeru*, " to repress," "to quiet," "to lay," "to establish," hence "to build a temple to a god," "to worship." The grammatical vagueness of the Japanese language helps in all this passage to preserve the connection of ideas in a manner which it is difficult to render in an English translation. Using no pronouns, it does not require to specialise in each instance whether it is the bird that is meant, or Yamato-take, but the two are confounded together in language as they were in thought.

12. *Shira-tori no misasaki.* According to the parallel passage of the " Chronicles," it was not only this tomb in Kafuchi, but the previously mentioned tomb at Nobonu, and also another in Yamato, which were severally known by this designation.

[SECT. XCI.—EMPEROR KEI-KŌ (PART XVI.—YAMATO-TAKE'S BUTLER).]

During all the time that this [Prince] His Augustness Yamato-take went about pacifying countries, Nana-tsuka-hagi,[1] ancestor of the Suzerains of Kuna,[2] always followed and respectfully served him as butler.

---

1. The name signifies "seven-grasp shins," implying that the worthy here mentioned was so big and strong as to have shins seven handbreadths in length. For the use of the word "grasp" as a measure of length, see Sect. VIII, Note 1.

2. This family has already been mentioned at the end of Sect. XXXIV, as descended from Ama-tsu-kume no Mikoto, one of the companions of the Emperor Jim-mu's grandfather on the occasion of his descent from Heaven. But see Note 7 to that Sect. for the probable mistake with regard to the origin of the name.

---

[SECT. XCII.—EMPEROR KEI-KŌ (PART XVII.—YAMATO-TAKE'S DESCENDANTS).]

This [Prince] His Augustness Yamato-take wedded Her Augustness Princess Futaji-no-iri,[1] daughter of the Heavenly Sovereign Ikume, and begot an august child: His Augustness Tarashi-naka-tsu-hiko[2] (one Deity). Again, wedding Her Augustness Princess Oto-tachibana[3] who [afterwards] entered the sea,[4] he begot an august child: King Waka-take[5] (one Deity). Again, wedding Princess Futaji,[6] daughter of Oho-tamu-wake,[7] ancestor of the Rulers of the Land of Yasu in Chika-tsu-Afumi,[8] he begot an august child: King Ine-yori-wake[2] (one Deity). Again, wedding Princess Oho-kibi-take,[10] younger sister of Take-hiko [ancestor of the] Grandees of Kiki,[11] he begot an august child: King Take-kahiko[12] (one Deity). Again, wedding Princess Kukuma-mori of Yamashiro,[13] he begot an august child, King Ashi-kagami-wake[14] (one Deity). A child by another wife was King Okinaga-ta-wake.[15] Altogether the entire [number] of the august children of His Augustness Yamato-take was six Deities. So His Augustness Tarashi-naka-tsu-hiko [was he who afterwards] ruled the Empire. The next, King Ine-yori-wake (was the ancestor of the Dukes of Inukami[16] and of the Dukes of Takebe.)[17]

225 The next, King Take-kahiko (was the ancestor of the Dukes of Aya in Sanugi,[18] the Dukes of Wake in Iyo,[19] the Lords of Towo,[20] the Headmen of Masa[21] and the Lords of Miyaji.)[22] King Ashi-kagami-wake (was the ancestor of the Lords of Kamakura,[23] the Dukes of Wodzu,[24] the Lords of Ihashiro[25] and ths Lords of Fukita.)[25] The child of the next, King Okinaga-ta-wake was King Kuhi-mata-naga-hiko.[27] This King's children were: Her Augustness Princess Ihinu-ma-guro,[28] next Okinaga-ma-waka-naka-tsu-hime,[29] next Oto-hime[30] (three Deities). So the above mentioned King Waka-take wedded Princess Ihinu-

226 ma-guro, and begot King Sume-iro-oho-naka-tsu-hiko.[31] This King wedded Princess Shibanu,[32] daughter of Shibanu-iri-ki[33] of Afumi, and begot a child, Her Augustness Princess Kaguro.[34] So the Heavenly Sovereign Oho-tarashi-hiko wedded this [lady] Her Augustness Princess Kaguro, and begot King Oho-ye[35] (one Deity). This King wedded his younger half-sister Queen Shiro-kane,[36] and begot children: King Oho-na-gata,[37] and next Her Augustness Oho-naka-tsu-hime[38] (two Deities). So this [Lady] Her Augustness Oho-naka-tsu-hime was the august mother[39] of King Kagosaka[40] and King Oshikuma.[41]

---

1. For this name see Sect. LXIX, Note 24.
2. *I.e.*, "the perfect middle prince," a name which is justified by

the genealogy as given in the "Chronicles," where he is mentioned as the second of three sons borne by this princess.

3. *Oto-tachibana-hime no mikoto.* Oto signifies "younger [sister]," and *Oto-tachibana* is the name of the orange.

4. See the story in Sect. LXXXIV.

5. *Waka-ṭate no miko.* This name signifies "young brave."

6. *Futaji-hime.* Signification [obscure. Futaji may be the name of a place.

7. If *Tamu* is, as Motowori surmises, the name of a place, this personal name signifies "Great Lord of Tamu."

8. *Chika-tsu-Afumi no Yasu no kuni no miyatsuko.* For *Yasu* see Sect. LXII, Note 62.

9. *Ine-yori-wake no miko.* This name probably signifies "rice-good-lord."

10. *Oho-kibi-take-hime.* Oho signifies "great." For the other two elements of the compound see next Note.

11. The text has *Kibi no omi Take-hiko,* as if this worthy had been himself the "Grandee of Kibi." Motowori however compares the commencement of Sect. LXXXII (Notes 2 and 3), and supplies the words "ancestor of." *Kibi* is of course the province of that name (the modern, Bizen, Bitchiū, and Bingo), and *take* signifies "brave."

12. *Take-kahiko no miko.* Take signifies "brave," *kahiko* is either "egg" or "cocoon," or else perhaps a corruption of some other word.

13. *Yamashiro no Kukuma mori-hime.* This name is obscure. Motowori identifies *Kukuma* with a place called *Kurihuma,* and *mori* is probably the Verb "to guard."

14. *Ashi-kagami-wake no miko.* This name is written with characters signifying "foot-mirror-[lord]."

15. *Okinaga-ta-wake no miko.* This name is obscure. Motowori believes Okinaga to be the name of a place in Afumi, but has no explanation to offer of *ta.*

16. *Inukami no kimi.* Inukami is the name of a district in Afumi, Its signification is not clear.

17. *Takebi no kimi.* Takebe became the name of a place in Idzumo, but it originally signified "brave tribe," the family having, as in so many other cases, given its name to the place of its residence, instead of being called after the latter. See the origin of the name, given in Motowori's Commentary, Vol. XXIV, pp. 35-36.

18. *Sanugi no Aya no kimi.* For *Sanugi* see Sect. V, Note 6. *Aya* is a district in the province; the name is of doubtful origin.

19. *Iyo no wake no kami.* For *Iyo* see Sect. V, Note 4. (The text here has *Ise* for Iyo, and the word *wake* is missing, but Motowori's emendation may be accepted). *Wake* is the name of a district in Iyo.

20. *Towo no wake.* Of *Towo* nothing is known.

21. *Masa no obito.* Of *Masa* nothing is known.

22. *Miyagi* (宮道) *no wake.* This is Motowori's ingenious emendation of the characters in the text, 官首, out of which it is impossible to make a famiy name. *Miyagi* is the name of a place in the province of Mikaha, and signifies "temple road."

23. *Kamakura no wake.* Kamakura is the name of a district in the province of Sagami, which became famous during the Middle Ages as the site of an immense town,—the capital of the Shōgun, and the centre of the feudalism which then ruled Japan. The import of the name (literally "sickle-store") is not clear. though it has been fancifully explained by native etymologists.

24. *Wodzu no kimi.* The words *no kimi* are supplied by Motowori, this name and the next being in the text run into one. Wodzu seems to be the name of a place in Afumi, and signifies "little mart."

25. *Ihashiro no wake.* Motowori says that this Ihashiro is not the province of that name, but a place in Kishiu. The meaning of the name is obscure.

26. *Fukita no wake.* This is but Motowori's conjectural restoration (founded on a statement in the "Chronicles of Old Matters of Former Ages") of the name as given in the text, 漁田.

27. *Kuhimata-naga-hiko no miko.* *Kuhimata* (modern *Kumata*) is the name of a place in Settsu. The signification is obscure. *Naga-hiko* means "long prince."

28. *Ihinu-ma-guro-hime,* i.e., "quite black princess of Ihinu," the blackness being doubtless predicated of her hair. *Ihinu* is the name of a district in Ise, and is written with characters signifying "boiled-rice-moor."

29. For *Okinaga* see Note 15. *Ma-waka* means "truly young." *Naka-tsu-hime* means "middle princess," referring to her being the second of three.

30. *I.e.,* "younger princess."

31. See Sect. LXXVI, Note 29.

32. *Shibanu-hime.* This name is obscure.

33. *Shibunu iri-ko.* This name is obscure.

34. *Ka-gara hime,* see Sect. LXXVI, Note 28.

35. For the confusion in this portion of the genealogy see Sect. LXXVI, Note 30.

36. *Shiro-kane no miko. Shiro-kane* means "silver," but Motowori suspects corruption in the text.

37. *Oho-nagata no miko,* i.e., "great prince of Nagata," the latter being the name of a place in Settsu, signifying "long rice-field."

38. *Ie.,* "great middle princess."

39. Literally, "ancestress."

40. Or, "the King of Kagosaka," for it is uncertain whether Kagosaka should or should not be regarded as the name of a place. The etymology of the name may be *kago,* "a stag" and *saka,* "an ascent." The original form of the name and title is *Kagosaka|no miko.*

41. Or, "the King of Oshikuma," *Oshikuma no miko. Oshikuma* is a word of doubtful etymology.

———

[SECT. XCIII.—EMPEROR KEI-KŌ (PART XVIII.—HIS AGE AND PLACE OF BURIAL).]

This Heavenly Sovereign's august years were one hundred and thirty-seven, and his august mausoleum is above the Yamanobe road.[1]

———

1. See Sect. LXVIII, Note 1.

———

[SECT. XCIV.—EMPEROR SEI-MU.]

The Heavenly Sovereign Wata-tarashi-hiko dwelt at the palace of Taka-anaho at Shiga[1] in Chika-tsu-Afumi and ruled the empire. This Heavenly Sovereign wedded 227 the Lady Oho-takara,[2] daughter of Take-oshiyama-tari-ne,[3] ancestor of the Grandees of Hodzumi,[4] and begot an august child: King Wata-nuke[5] (one Deity). So [the

Heavenly Sovereign] raised the Noble Take-uchi[6] [to the office of] Prince Minister,[7] deigned to settle the Rulers of the Great Countries and Small Countries,[8] and likewise deigned to settle the boundaries of the various countries, as also the Department Lords of the Great Departments and Small Departments.[9] The Heavenly Sovereign's august years were ninety-five, and his august mausoleum is at Tatanami near Saki.[10]

---

1. *Shiga no Taka-anaho. Shiga* is the name of a well known district, and is of uncertain, signification, as is also *Taka-anaho.* For *Chika-tsu-Afumi* see Sect. XXIX, Note 20.

2. *Oto-takara no iratsume. Oto* signifies " younger [sister]," and *takara* is " treasure."

3. *Oshiyama* is the name of a place in Ise, *take* signifies " brave " and *tari* and *ne* are Honorifics of frequent occurrence.

4. *Hodzumi no omi.* See Sect. LXI, Note 4.

5. *Waka-nuke no miko.* This name is of doubtful signification, and Motowori suspects that it is corrupt, and that the true reading would be *Waka-take,* " young-brave."

6. See Sect. LXI, Note 25.

7. 大臣. Motowori tries to prove that in the earliest times this official title was simply an Honorific surname formed by prefixing the Adjective 大, " great " to 臣, a surname read " *Omi* " (the character signifies properly " attendant," " subject.") Probably like other " gentile names " it combined both characters, and had a tendency to become hereditary.

8. *Oho-kuni wo-kuni no kuni no miyatsuko.*

9. *Oho-agata wo-agata no agata nushi* (大 縣 小 縣 縣 主). Their duties are supposed to have consisted in supervising the government farms.

10. For *Saki* see Sect. LXXV, Note 5. *Tatanami* may perhaps signify " putting shields in a row."

---

[SECT. XCV.—EMPEROR CHIU-AI (PART I.—GENEALOGIES).]

The Heavenly Sovereign Tarashi-naka-tsu-hiko dwelt at the palace of Toyora at Anado,[1] and likewise at the palace cf Kashihi[2] in Tsukushi, and ruled the Empire. 328 This Heavenly Sovereign wedded Her Augustness Oho-naka-tsu-hime,[3] daughter of King Oho-ye, and begot august children: King Kagosaka and King Oshikuma (two Deities). Again he wedded Her Augustness Princess Okinaga-tarashi. This Empress[4] gave birth to august children: His Augustness Homu-ya-wake,[5] and next His Augustness Oho-tomo-wake,[6] another name for whom was His Augustness Homuda-wake.[7] The reason why this Heir Apparent[8] was given the august name of His Augustness Oho-tomo-wake was that when first[9] born, he had on his august arm [a protuberance of] flesh resembling an elbow-pad,[10] whence the august name bestowed on him. By this it was known while he was in the womb that he would rule countries.[11] In this august reign the granaries of Ahaji were established.

---

1. For *Anado* see Sect. LXXX (Note 22). *Toyora* (for *Toyo-ura*) signifies "fertile shore."

2. This name seems to be derived from that of the evergreen oak. It will be noticed that both these capitals are in the South-Western Island of Kiushiu, whereas, from Jim-mu downwards, the capitals of all the Emperors previously mentioned are either in Yamato or in one of the adjacent central provinces.

3. For this and the three following names see Sect. XCII, and for *Okinaga tarashi* Sect. LXII, Note 72.

4. Written 大后. It is she who is celebrated in Japanese history under the name of Jin-gō Kōgō, and in the "Chronicles" her reign is counted separately. In these "Records," however, the period of her rule is forming part of the reign of her son O-jin.

5. The signification of this name is obscure.

6. *I.e.,* " great elbow-paid lord," *tomo* signifying " elbow pad." The next sentence of the text gives the traditional origin of this curious name.

7. *I.e.,* lord of Homuda. *Homuda* is supposed by Motowori and Moribe to be the name of a place, they (apparently with reason) rejecting as a late addition a note to the " Chronicles," which states that *homuda* was synonymous with *tomo* " elbow-pad,"

8. For " heir apparent " see Sect. XXXIII, Note 2.

9. This word,¡says Motowori, is redundant.

10. For the use of elbow-pads in war see Sect XIII, Note 7.

11. The word rendered " rule " (*shiru,* 知) is supplied by the editor of 1687. Motowori supplies the evident lacuna in the text by the word " establish " (*sadamarn* 定); but this seems less good. Motowori's reasons for taking the word *kuni* (" country ") in the Plural are, however, convincing,—the three countries into which Korea was anciently divided, and which are appropriately designated by the title of *San Kan* (三韓), being evidently designated by the expression in the text, as may be seen both by reference to the parallel passage in the " Chronicles," and also by considering that in this manner that warlike implement the elbow-pad, with the semblance of which the young Emperor was born, obtains its proper significance. This Emperor (for it is he who is known as Ō-jin Ten-nō) is sometimes designated by the name of the " Emperor in the Womb " (胎中天皇).

---

229 [SECT. XCVI.—EMPEROR CHIŪ-AI (PART II.—THE POSSESSION OF KOREA DIVINELY PROMISED).]

This Empress, Her Augustness Princess Okinaga-tarashi, was at that time,[1] divinely possessed. So when the Heavenly Sovereign, dwelling at the palace of Kashihi in Tsukushi, was about to smite the Land of Kumaso.[2] the Heavenly Sovereign played on his august lute, and the Prime Miinster the Noble Take-uchi, being in the pure court,[3] requested the divine orders. Hereupon the Empress, divinely possessed, charged him with this instruction and counsel: " There is a land to the Westward, and in that land is abundance of various treasures dazzling to the eye, from gold and silver downwards.[4] I will now bestow this land upon thee." Then the Heavenly Sovereign replied, saying: "If one ascend to a high place and look Westward, no country is to be seen. There is only the great sea;" and saying,[5] "They are lying Deities,"[6] he pushed away his august lute, did not play on it, and sat silent. Then the Deities were very angry, and said: "Altogether as for this empire, it is not a land over which thou oughtest to rule. Do thou go to the one road!"[7] Hereupon the Prince Minister the Noble Take-uchi said; "[I am filled with] awe, my Heavenly Sovereign![8] Continue playing thy great august lute." Then he slowly drew his august lute to him, and languidly played on it. So almost immediately the sound of the august lute became inaudible. On their forthwith lifting a light and looking, [the Heavenly Sovereign] was dead.

230

---

1. At what time, we are not told.

2. See Sect. V, Note 17.

3. This is Motowori's interpretation of the obscure original word *sa-niha*, which is written phonetically. He supposes it to have heen so called as being a place used for enquiring the will of the gods, and therefore kept clean and held in reverence. "Place" would perhaps represent the Japanese word *niha* as well as "court," though "court" has been its usual acceptation in later times.

4. Literally, "making gold and silver the origin."

5. Motowori tells us to understand "saying" in the sense of thinking."

6. As already frequently remarked, the Japanese mind does not occupy itself much with the distinction (to us all-important) of Singular and Plural. The reason why the translator renders the word *kami* by the Plural "Deities" throughout this passage is because we learn later on that four divine personages were intended by the author.

7. With the commentators we must accept this as an alternative name of Hades, without being able satisfactorily to explain it. The expression "eighty road-windings" (*yaso kumado*) in Sect. XXXII (Note 27) may be compared with this one.

8. *I.e.*, "I tremble Sire, for the consequences of thine impiety."

------------

[SECT. XCVII.—EMPEROR CHIŪ-AI (PART III.—PREPARATIONS FOR THE CONQUEST OF KOREA).]

Then, astonished and alarmed, they set him in a mortuary palace,[1] and again taking the country's great offerings,[2] seeking out all sorts of crimes, such as flaying alive and flaying backwards,[3] breaking down the divisions of rice-fields, filling up ditches, evacuating excrements and urine, marriages between superiors and inferiors,[4] marriages with horses, marriages with cattle, marriages with fowls, and marriages with dogs, and having made a great purification of the land,[5] the Noble Takeuchi again stood in the pure court and requested the Deities' commands. Thereupon the manner of their instruction and counsel was exactly the same as on the former day: "Altogether this land is a land to be ruled over by the august child in Thine Augutness's august womb."[6] Then the Noble Take-uchi said, "[I am filled with] awe, my Great Deities! The august child in this Deity's womb,[7] what [sort of] child may it be?" [The Deities] replied, saying: "It is a male child." Then [the Noble Take-uchi] requested more particularly, [saying]: "I wish to know the august names of the Great Deities whose words have now thus instructed us." Forthwith [the Deities] replied, saying: "It is the august doing[8] of

the Great - August - Heaven - Shining - Deity, likewise it is
the three great Deities Bottom-Possessing-Male, Middle-
Possessing Male and Surface-Possessing-Male.[9] (At this time
the august names of these three great Deities were revealed.[10]) If now
thou truly thinkest to seek that land, thou must, after
presenting the offerings[11] to every one of the Heavenly
Deities and Earthly Deities,[12] and likewise of the Deities
of the mountains and also of all the Deities of the river
and of the sea, and setting our august spirits[13] on the
top of thy vessel, put into gourds[14] the ashes of the
*podocarpus macrophylla* tree,[15] and likewise make a quantity
of chopsticks and also of leaf platters,[16] and must scatter 232
them all on the waves of the great sea, that thou mayest
cross over." So when [she] punctually fulfilled these
instructions, equipped an army, marshalled her vessels,
and crossed over, the fishes of the sea-plain, both great
and small, all bore the august vessels[17] across their
backs, and a strong favourable wind arose, and the
august vessel followed the billows.

1. A temporary resting-place for the corpse before interment. (See
Sect. XXXI, Note 20.)

2. Or, if, with Motowori, we take country in the Plural, "the great
offerings of the countries," i.e., of the various countries or provinces of
Japan or of Kiushiu. These "offerings" (*nusa*) are the same as those
mentioned in Sect. XVI (Notes 24 and 25) under the names *nigi-te*
and *mitegura*. They consisted of cloth, for which in later times paper
has been substituted.

3. There are different views as to the exact bearing of this curious
expression. Conf. Sect. XV, Note 10.

4. *I.e.*, incest between parents and children.

5. *I.e.*, a general purification.

6. The Deities now speak to, as well as through, the Empress.
Before the quotation marks announcing their words we must understand
some such clause as "and they added this divine charge." It would

also be possible to translate the whole passage thus: "Thereupon the manner of their instruction and counsel. was '[Things] being exactly as on the former day, altogether this land,'" etc., etc.

7. *I.e.*, in the Empress's womb. Motowori supposes that she is thus spoken of as a Deity on account of her being at that moment divinely possessed.

8. Literally, "heart."

9. *Soko-dzu-tsu-no-wo, Naka-dzu-tsu-no wo,* and *Uha-dzu-tsu-no-wo* three of the deities born at the time of the purification of Izanagi (the "Male-Who-Invites") on his return from Hades, and known collectively as the Deities of the Inlet of Sumi. (See Sect. X, Notes 18 and 22). The grammar of this sentence is, as Motowori remarks, not lucid. One would expect the author to say that it was "the august doing" of all the four deities mentioned.

10. *I.e.*, says Motowori, they then first informed Take-uchi who they were. Up in that time, it had not been known by what Deities the Empress was possessed. Mabuchi, however, rejected this gloss as a later additions.

11. *I.e.*, the sacred offerings of white and blue cloth.

12. Here witten writh the Chinese locution 天神地祇, by some rendered "the Spirit of Heaven and Earth." *Conf.* Sect. I. Note II.

13. Here, as before, the Singular would be at least as natural an interpretation as the Plural. The three ocean-deities are supposed to be specially referred to, and in that case, the three being easily conceived as one (like the deified peaches mentioned in Sect. IX, Note 19) owing to the want of discrimination in Japanese between Singular and Plural, we might retain the Singular in English. Altogether the Sun-goddess seems out of place in this passage, and it would be satisfactory to have some authority for expunging from it the mention of her name.

14. Or, "into a gourd."

15. In the original *maki* (眞木). In modern *ma-ki* signifies the *P. macrophylla*, as in the translation. It is however uncertain whether that or the *Chamæcyparis obtusa* (both being conifers), or simply any "true (*i.e.*, good) tree is here intended by the author.

16. *I.e.*, broad shallow platters made of the oak-tree, and used for placing food on.

17. Viz., that in which the Empress herself took passage,

[SECT. XCVIII.—EMPEROR CHIŪ-AI (PART IV.—THE EMPRESS
JIN-GŌ CONQUERS KOREA).]

So the wave[1] of the august vessel pushed up onto the
land of Shiragi[2] reaching to the middle of the country.
Thereupon the chieftain[3] of the country, alarmed and
trembling. petitioned[4] [the Empress], saying : "From
this time forward obedient to the Heavenly Sovereign's
commands, I will feed his august horses and will marshal
vessels every year, nor ever let the vessels' keels[5] dry
or their poles and oars dry, and will respectfully serve
him without drawing back while heaven and earth shall
last."[6] So therefore the Land of Shirai was constituted
the feeder of the august horses, and the Land of Kudara 233
was constituted the crossing store.[8] Then the Empress
stuck her august staff on the gate of the chieftain of
Shiragi, and having made the Rough August Spirits[9] of
the Great Deities of the Inlet of Sumi[10] the guardian
Deities of the land, she laid them to rest,[11] and crossed
back. So while this business[12] was yet unconcluded,
[the child] with which she was pregnant was about to
be born. Forthwith, in order to restrain her august
womb, she took a stone and wound it round the waist
of her august skirt,[13] and the august child was born after
she had crossed [back] to the Land of Tsukushi.[14] So
the name by which the place was called where the 234
august child was born was Umi.[15] Again the stone
which she wound round her august skirt is at the village
of Ito[16] in the Land of Tsukushi.

---

1. *I.e.,* "the wave on which the august vessel was riding."

2. In Sinico-Japanese *Shin ra* (新羅), one of the three states into
which Korea was anciently divided, the other two being known i n pur

Japanese as *Kudara* and *Koma* (in Sinico-Japanese *Hiyaku-sai* 百濟 and Kōrai 高麗).   *Shiragi* is evidently a mere corruption of the Sinico-Japanese form, which closely resembles the native Korean *Shin-la*. The origin of the pure Japanese forms of the other two names is obscure.

3.   The editions previous to Motowori's have " King" (王 instead of 主); but as the latter character is used in all parallel passages of this work, we must attribute the occurrence of the former in this single place to a copyist's error, and accuse the author rather than his commentator of the ill-natured degradation of the Korean King into a mere chieftain (more literally a " master ").

4.   The character 奏, which is here used, is that employed in speaking of a subject's addressing his sovereign.

5.   Literally " bellies."

6.   Literally, " with heaven and earth."

7.   See Note 2.

8.   *I.e.*, the sea-store." The author means to say that from the Land of Kudara tribute was to be paid with the regularity implied by the King's asseveration to the effect that the keels, poles, and oars of the [tribute-bearing] vessels should never remain dry.

9.   *Ara-mi-tama*, the antithetical term to which is *Nigi-mi-tama*, " Gentle August Spirit." We also find *Saki-mi-tama* and *Kushi-mi-tama*, which signify respectively " August Luck-Spirit " and " Wondrous August Spirit." In this passage it must be understood that the spirits which floated above the Imperial junk to protect it were the " Gentle August Spirits," while the "Rough August Spirits" presided at the Empress's feats of arms and kept the enemy in subjection. Motowori warns us not to fall into the mistake of supposing that the Rough and Gentle Spirits of a god were separate individualities, they being only, according to him, various manifestations of the same individuality. The student is advised to consult his beautifully written note on the subject of these spirits in Vol. XXX, pp. 72-76 of his Commentary.

10,   See Sect. X Note 22.

11.   Literally "established and worshipped." Motowori says that this mention of their being laid to rest is made with an implied reference to the journey on which the deities in question had accompanied the Imperial army.   He also tries to prove that this laying to rest of the deities must have occurred after the return of the Empress to Japan, as it is not possible to suppose that the gods could find a home in a foreign land (!).   But the wording of the text is against him

12. Literally "government."

13. *I.e.,* as Motowori suggests, "she wrapped the stone up, and tied it into the waist of her skirt in something resembling a sash."

14. In South-Western Japan.

15. *I.e.,* "bearing." The word, however, also signifies "sea." According to the "Chronicles" the original name of the village was Kada.

16. This word signifies "thread," and would therefore, one might think, find a more appropriate place in the legend next narrated, where the "threads" of the Empress's garment are specially mentioned.

---

[SECT. XCIX.—EMPEROR CHIŪ-AI (PART V.—THE EMPRESS JIN-GŌ FISHES IN TSUKUSHI).]

Again when, having reached the village of Tamashima[1] in the Department of Matsura[2] in Tsukushi, she partook of an august meal on the bank of the river, it being then the first decade of the fourth moon, she then sat on a shoal[3] in the middle of the river, picked out threads from her august skirt, used grains of rice as bait, and hooked the trout[4] in the river. The name by which the river is called is the Wo-gaha;[5] again the name by which the shoal is called is Kachi-do-hime.[6]) So down to the present time it is an uninterrupted [custom] for women in the first decade of the fourth moon to pick out threads from their skirts, use grains as bait, and hook trout.

---

1. *I.e.,* "jewel-island."

2. *Matsura-gata.* The "Chronicles" give an absurd derivation of Matsura from the Adjective *medzurashi,* "astonishing," which the Empress is supposed to have ejaculated on finding a trout hooked to her line! The obvious etymology is *matsu-ura,* "pine-beach."

3. The character in the original is 磯 (for 礒), in Japanese *iso,* which may or may not be connected with the word *ishi,* "stone." In any case Motowori is not justified in saying that it must be understood to mean

"stone" in this place, as *iso* means rather a sandy than a stony place, rising above the water level.

4. In Japanese *ayu*, a small species of the salmon family (*Plecoglossus altivelis*).

5. *I.e.*, "little river."

6. *I.e.*, "princess of the gate of victory." But though the words lend themselves to this interpretation, it can hardly be supposed that such is their real etymology, and indeed the editor of 1687 draws attention in a Note to the difficulty of accepting the statement in the text.

235   [SECT. C.—EMPEROR CHIŪ-AI (PART VI.—THE EMPRESS
JIN-GO SUBDUES YAMATO).]

Hereupon, when Her Augustness Princess Okinaga-tarashi was returning up to Yamato, she, owing to doubts concerning the disposition[1] of the people, prepared a mourning-vessel,[2] set the august child in that mourning-vessel, and let a report ooze out that the august child was already dead. While she went up thus, King Kagosaka and King Oshikuma,[3] having heard [of the circumstance], thought to waylay[4] her, went forth to the moor of Toga,[5] and hunted for an omen. Then King Kagosaka climbed up an oak-tree,[6] and then[7] a large and angry boar came forth, dug up the oak-tree, and forthwith devoured King Kagosaka. His younger brother, King Oshikuma, undaunted by this circumstance, raised an army and lay in wait [for the Empress], to close with the mourning-vessel as being an empty[8] vessel. Then an army was landed from the mourning-vessel,[9] and joined in combat [with the opposing forces]. At this time King Oshikuma made the Noble Isahi,[10] ancestor of
236 the Kishi Clan of Naniha,[11] his generalissimo;[12] and on

the august side of the Heir Apparent His Augustness Naniha-ne-ko-take-furu-kuma,[13] ancestor of the Grandees of Wani,[14] was made generalissimo. So when [the Empress's troops] had driven [King Oshikuma's troops] as far as Yamashiro, [the latter] turned and made a stand, and both [sides] fought together without retreating. Then His Augustness Take-furu-kuma planned, and caused it to be said that, as Her Augustness Okinaga-tarashi was already dead, there was no need for further fighting,— forthwith snapping his bowstrings and feigning submission. Therefore King Oshikuma's generalissimo, believing the falsehood, unbent his bows and put away his arms. Then [the Empress's troops] picked out of their topknots some prepared bowstrings one [name [of [the bowstrings] [was *usa-yu-dzuru*,[15] stretched [their bows] again, and pursued and smote [the enemy]. So [these] fled away to Afusaka,[16] rallied, and fought again. Then [the Empress's troops] pursued on, and defeated them, and cut to pieces that army at Sasanami.[17] Thereupon King Oshikuma, together with the Noble Isahi, being pursued and pressed, got on board a vessel and floated on the sea, and sang, saying :

> "Come on, my lord ! rather than be stricken        237
> by Furu-kuma's hurtful hand, I will plunge
> like the grebe into the Sea of Afumi,—I
> will !"[18]

Forthwith they plunged into the sea, and died together.

---

1. Literally, " the hearts."

2. *I.e.*, a boat or junk containing a coffin. We might also (adopting the interpretation given by the older editors to the character in this passage) translate by " specially prepared a mourning-vessel."

3. These two princes, who are first mentioned at the end of Sect.

XCII (Notes 40 and 41), were. according to the story, elder sons of the late monarch Chiū-ai, and therefore step-sons of tbe Empress Jingō and half-brothers to the young Emperor Ō-jin.

4. Literally, "wait for and catch." This "catch" is always taken by Motowori to mean "slay."

5. *Taga-nu.* It was in the province of Settsu. The etymology of the name is obscure.

6. The species mentioned in the text the *Quercus serrata.*

7. Motowori's conjecture that the character 是, "then," is a copyist's error for 見, "saw" or "looked," seems hardly called for, and the translator has therefore not departed from the traditional reading.

8. *I.e.,* defenceless, not filled with troops.

9. Which of course was in reality no mourning-vessel, but full of the soldiers who had just returned from conquering Korea.

10. *Isahi no [Sakune.* Isahi or Isachi is supposed to mean "leading elder."

11. *Naniha no Kishi-be.* Naniha is the old name of the sea and river-shore on which now stands the town of Ohosaka. The name Kishi is said by Motowori to be properly a Korean official designation (吉士), but it is one whose origin is to be sought in China.

12. 將軍, *Shōgun.* This is the earliest mention of this office, which, passing from the [military to the political sphere, played such a great part in the mediaeval and modern history of Japan.

13. The signification of all the elements of this compound name is not clear, but it is partly Honorific and descriptive of the bravery of its bearer.

14. *Wani no omi* (see Sect. LXII, Note 11).

15. The text is here somewhat obscure, and the note in small print is of doubtful authenticity. If we retain it, we must understand it to mean that *usa-yu-dzuru,* a term whose derivation is by no means clear, was an alternative name of the *make dzuru, i.e.,* "prepared bowstrings," such as they had brought witch them concealed in their top-knots.

16. *I.e.,* "the pass [or hill] of meeting." It was on the boundaries of the provinces of Yamashiro and Afumi. The modern pronunciation is *Osaka* (not to be confounded with the like-sounding name of a well-known town in Central Japan).

17. *I.e.,* in Afumi. Mabuchi, in his "Dictionary of Pillow-Words," explains this name to mean "bamboo-grass bending." Motowori, following the *Shim-puku-ji* MS., alters the character 於 before the word *Sasanami* to 出, but without sufficient warrant.

18. The meaning of the poem is · "Rather than fall beneath the attacks of the enemy, let us drown ourselves in the Sea of Afumi" (Lake Biwa).—For the expression "stricken by a hurtful hand" see Sect. XLIV, Note 33.

———

[SECT. CI.—EMPEROR CHIŪ-AI (PART VIII.—THE HEIR APPARENT EXCHANGES NAMES WITH THE GREAT DEITY IZASA-WAKE).]

So when His Augustness the Noble Take-uchi, taking with him the Heir Apparent for the purpose of purification,[1] passed through the lands of Afumi and Wakasa,[2] he built a temporary palace at Tsunuga[3] at the mouth of the Road of Koshi[4] [for the Heir Apparent] to dwell in. Then His Augustness the Great Deity Izasa-wake,[5] who dwelt in that place, appeared at night in a dream,[6] and said: "I wish to exchange my name for the august name of the august child." Then [the dreamer of the dream] prayed, saying: "[I] am filled with awe!"[7] The name shall be respectfully exchanged according to thy command." Again the ·Deity charged [him, saying]: "To-morrow morning [the Heir Apparent] must go out on the beach; I will present my [thank] offering for the name [given me] in exchange." So when [the Heir Apparent] went out in the morning to the beach, the whole shore was lined with broken-nosed dolphin-fishes.[8] Thereupon the august child caused the Deity to be addressed, saying: "Thou bestowest on me fish of thine august food."[9] So again his august name was hououred by his being called the Great Deity of August Food.[10] So he is now styled the Food-Wondrous-Great-Deity.[11]

Again the blood from the noses of the dolphin-fishes stank. So the strand was called by the name of Chiura.[12] it is now styled Tsunuga.

---

1. Viz., by water, as described in Sect. X.

2. Etymology obscure.

3. The marvellous etymology of this name which the author seems to adopt will be found at the end of the Section (Note 12). The compiler of the "Chronicles" is probably nearer the truth when he derives it from *tsunu-ga*, "horned stag."

4. For the meaning of this curious expression see Sect. LX, Note 20.

5. The commentators give no explanation of this one of the three names of the deity in question. It would appear to be made up of a word expressive of solicitation and of a portion of the Heir Apparent's name, thus signifying perhaps "Come on, Wake, [give me thy name]" with reference to the legend here narrated.

6. To which of the two personages of the legend is not clear. Motowori, however, prefers to suppose that it was to Take-uchi, as, if the prince himself were intended, the word "dream" would probably receive the Honorific 御.

7. Or, "I reverence [thy commands]."

8. Motowori supposes that they were caught by being speared in the nose.

9. *I.e.,* "fish that would naturally have formed part of thine august food." Is less good to translate by "fish for *mine* august food." As usual, the original Japanese text has no Personal Pronouns to guide the reader; but, though Emperors are sometimes made to use the Honorific in speaking of themselves, this is not the custom in the case of princes' and Ō-jin is supposed to have not yet assumed the Imperial dignity.

10. *Mi-ke-tsu-oho-kami.* Motowori mentions several Deities of this name, who were, according to him, separate beings.

11. *Kehi no oho-kami.* The meaning of the syllable *hi*, rendered by "wondrous" in accordance with Motowori's suggestion, is not certain.

12. *I.e.,* "the strand of blood." From *chi-ura* Motowori is obliged to derive Tsunuga as well as he can in order not to throw discredit on the implied assertion of the author: hat the latter is but a mispronunciation of the former. The true derivation of Tsunuga is probably from *tsunuga* "horned stag," as already stated in Note 3.

[SECT. CII.—EMPEROR CHIŪ-AI (PART VIII.—THE EMPRESS
JIN-GŌ PRESENTS LIQUOR TO THE HEIR APPARENT).

Hereupon, when the [Heir Apparent] returned up [to
the Capital], his august parent, Her Augustness Princess
Okinaga-tarashi. distilled some waiting-liquor,[1] and presented it to him.    Then his august parent sang augustly,
saying :

> " This august liquor is not my august
> liquor ; — oh ! it is august liquor respect-
> fully brought as a divine congratulation, a
> repeated congratulation, a bountiful con-
> gratulation, a reiterated congratulation by
> the Small August Deity, who dwells eternal-
> ly, firmly standing.    Partake not shallow-
> ly !   Go on ! go on !"[2]

Having thus sung, she presented to him the great
august liquor.    Then His Augustness the Noble Take-
uchi replied for the august child and sang, saying :

> " Whatever person distilled this august liquor
> must surely have distilled it singing the
> while with that drum on the mortar, —
> must surely have distilled it dancing the
> while, for this august liquor, august liquor,
> to be ever more and more joyful.  Go on !
> go on !"[3]

These are Drinking Songs.[4]

---

1.  *Machi-sake.* This expression, which recurs in the poems of the
" Collection of a Myriad Leaves," signifies liquor distilled for an absent
friend by those who are awaiting his return.

2.  The General signification of the Song is : " Think not that this
liquor was made by me.  'Tis a present from the small August Deity
(*Suku-na-biko-no*), who dwells forever in unshaken power and who sends

239

it to thee with endless congratulation. Come on! come on! drink deeply!"—Some of the expressions in this Song are a subject of debate among the commentators. Excepting the clause "partake not shallowly," in which the translator has adopted the opinion of the author of the "Explanation of the Songs in the Chronicles of Japan," Moribe's interpretation has been followed throughout. The latter critic would identify *asazu* ("not slowly") with *amasazu* ("without leaving anything"). But there seems no warrant for supposing such an elision of the syllable *sa*. The use of the expression *kuruhoshi* and *motohoshi* to express reiteration is worthy of notice. It will be remembered that the Deity mentioned was the microscopic personage who came riding over the waves to share the sovereignty of Idzumo with the Deity Master-of-the-Great-Land (see Sect. XXVII).

3. This Song signifies; "Such a joyful feast must surely have been preceded by a joyful distilling of the liquor for it. Continue to drink, oh Prince!"—The commentators disagree on the subject of one or two of the words of this Song, in which the translator has followed Motowori's interpretation throughout. The words "that drum" are the chief difficulty. Motowori supposes that drums, being originally unknown in Japan, were first seen by the Japanese on the occasion of the conquest of Korea in this very reign, and he thinks that the drum would be placed by the side of the mortar during the pounding of the rice out of which the liquor was to be made. "That drum" means the drum belonging to the pounder of the rice. The original words *so no*, "that," might also be rendered by "his."

4. Literally, "liquor-rejoicing songs."

---

240　　[SECT. CIII.—EMPEROR OHIŪ-AI (PART IX.—HIS DEATH AND THAT OF THE EMPRESS JIN-GŌ).]

Altogether the august years of this Heavenly Sovereign Tarashi-naka-tsu-hiko[1] were fifty-two. His august mausoleum is at Nagaye,[2] near Wega.[3] in Kafuchi. (The Empress died at the august age of one hundred. She was buried in the mausoleum of Tatanami in Saki.[4]

---

1. The Emperor Chiū-ai. The author of these "Records" not re-

cognizing, as does the author of the "Chronicles," the time during which
the Empress Jin-go held sway as a separate reign, Chiū-ai is by fiction
supposed to have reigned down to the moment his posthumous son
Ō-jin mounted the throne after the conquest of Korea and of Yamato.

2. *I.e.* "long branch," or perhaps "long inlet."

3. Etymology obscure,

4. Mabuchi and Motowori seem right in supposing the sentence in
small type to be an addition to the text, copied from the "Chronicles."
But as all the MSS. and printed editions previous to Motowori's contain
it, it has been retained in the translation.

———

[SECT. CIV.—EMPEROR Ō-JIN[1] (PART I.—GENEALOGIES).]

His Augustness Homuda-wake dwelt at the palace of
Akira at Karushima,[2] and ruled the Empire. This Heaven-
ly Sovereign wedded three[3] queens, daughters : of King
Homuda-no-Ma-waka,[4] the name of one of whom was
Her Augustness Princess Takagi-no-iri;[5] of the next,
Her Augustness Naka-tsu-hime;[6] and of the next, Her
Augustness Oto-hime.[7] (The father of these Queens, King Homuda-
no-ma-Waka, was the son of His Augustness Prince Iho-ki-noiri[8] by his 241
wife Shiritsuki-tome,[9] daughter of the Noble Take-inada.[10] ancestor of the
Chiefs of Wohari.)[11] So the august children of Her Augustness Princess Takagi-no-iri were : His Augustness Nakuta-
no-oho-waka-tsu-hiko;[12] next His Augustness Oho-yama-
mori;[13] next His Augustness Iza-no-ma-waka;[14] next
his younger sister the Lady of Ohohara;[15] next the
Lady of Komuku.[16] (Five Deities). The august children
of Her Augustness Naka-tsu-hime were : the Lady of
Arata in Ki;[17] next His Augustness Oho-sazaki;[17]
next His Augustness Netori.[19] (Three Deities). The august 242
children of Her Augustness Oto-hime were : the Lady
Abe;[20] next the Lady of Mihara in Ahaji;[21] next

the Lady of Unu in Ki;[22] next the Lady of Minu[23] (five Deities).[24] Again he wedded the Princess Miya-nushi-ya-kaha-ye,[25] daughter of the Grandee Wani-no-Hifure, and begot august children: Uji-no-waki-iratsuko;[26] next his younger sister Yata-no-waki-iratsume;[27] next Queen Medori.[28] (Three Deiites). Again he wedded Wo-nabe-no-iratsume,[29] younger sister of Yakaha-ye-hime, and begot an august child: Uji-no-iratsume.[30] (one Deity). Again he wedded Okinaga-ma-waka-naka-tsu-hima,[31] daughter of King Kuhimata-naga-hiko,[32] and begot an august child: King Waka-nuke-futa-mata[33] (one Deity). Again he wedded the Princess of Itowi,[34] daughter of Shima-tari-ne,[35] ancestor of the Agricultural Chiefs of Sakurawi,[36] and begot an august child; His Augustness Hayabusa-wake[37] (one Deity). Again, he wedded Naga-hime of Idzumi in Himuka,[38] and begot august children: King Oho-haye,[39] next King Wo-haye;[40] next Hata-bi-no-waki-iratsume[41] (three Deiti s). Again he wedded Princess Ka-guro,[42] and begot august children: Kaha-rada-no-iratsume;[43] next, Tama-no-ira-tsume,[44] next, Osaka-no-oho-naka-tsu-hime;[45] next, Toho-hi-no-iratsume;[46] next, King Kataji[47] (five Deities). Again, he wedded Nu-iro-me of Kadzuraki,[48] and begot an august child: King Iza-no-ma-waka,[49] (one Deity). The august children of this Heavenly Sovereign [numbered] alto-gether twenty-six (eleven Kings and fifteen Queens). Of these His Augustness Oho-sazaki [was he who afterwards] ruled the Empire.

---

1. Son of the Emperor Chiū-ai and the Empress Jin-gō.
2. In Yamato. *Akira* Signifies "brilliant." *Krushima* seems to mean "the neighbourhood of Karu, Karu being the often mentioned place of that name in Yamato.
3. The Auxiliary Numeral for deities is here used.

4. *Homuda-no-ma-waka no miko. Homuda* has already been met with as the name of a place in Kahachi. *Ma-waka* signifies "truly young." The name might therefore be rendered "truly young king of Homuda."

5. *Takagi no iri-bime no mikoto.* Motowori identifies this princess with the *Takaki-hime* of Sect. LXXVI, Note 21.

6. *I.e.,* "middle princess," she being the second of three sisters.

7. *I.e.,* "younger princess," she being the youngest of the sisters.

8. *I-ho-ki-no-iri-biko no mikoto.* See Sect. LXXVI, Note 12.

9. *I.e.,* probably "old woman of Shiritsuki." But it is not certain that Shiritsuki is the name of a place.

10. *Take-inada no sukune.* In the "Chronicles of Old Matters of Former Ages" the name is written *Take-ina-dane*, and it may therefore mean "brave-rice-seed."

11. *Wohari no murazhi.*

12. *I.e.,* "great middle Prince of Nukata," the latter being the name of a place in Yamato. It is of uncertain signification.

13. *I.e.,* "great mountain-warden." For the appropriateness of this name *conf.* Sect. CV.

14. The same name has appeared in Sect. LXIII, Note 13.

15. *Ohohara no iratsume.* Ohohara is the name of a place in Yamato It signifies "great moor."

16. *Komuku no iratsume.* This name is written 高目, and its reading as *Komuku* is somewhat hypohtetical. It is the name of a place in Kahachi, and probably signifies "an overflowing pool of water."

17. *Ki no Arata no iratsume. Ki* is the provinoe of that name, and *Arata* is a place in it. The latter name probably means "uncultivated fields."

18. This name signifies "Great Wren," and is thus accounted for by the author of the "Chronicles": "On the day when the Emperor [this Prince became the Emperor Nin-toku] was born, an owl flew into the parturition-hall. Next morning early, the Heavenly Sovereign Homuda (*i.e.,* the Emperor O-jin) sent for the Prime Minister, the Noble Take-uchi, and asked him whereof this might be a sign. The Prime Minister replied, saying: 'It is a good omen. Moreover yesterday, when thy servant's wife was delivered of a child, a wren flew into the parturition-house, likewise a strange thing.' Then the Heavenly Sovereign said: 'It is a portent from heaven that my child and thine should be born on the same day, and both be attended by a good omen. So let the names of the birds be taken,' and each used for the name of the other (*i.e.,*

the name of the owl for him into whose parturition-house the wren flew, and *vice-versâ*], as a covenant for the future.' So the wren's name was bestowed on the Heir Apparent, who was called Great-Wren Prince, and the owl's name was given to the Prime Minister's child. who was called the Noble Owl."

19. This name is obscure.

20. *Abe no iratsume.* Abe is the name of several places in different provinces, and is of obscure derivation and import.

21. *Ahaji no Mikara no iratsume.* The text properly has *Ayuchi*, but Motowori emends this to *Ahaji* on the authority of the "Chronicles."' Mihara is the name of a district in the island of Ahaji, and probably signifies "three moors."

22. *Ki no Unu uo iratsume.* *Ki* is the province of that name, and *Unu* a place in it. The latter name is of uncertain import.

23. *Minu no iratsume.* *Minu (Mino)* is the province of that name.

24. "Five" must here be a mistake for "four."

25. For this name and the next see Sect. CVI, Notes 5 and 4.

26. *I.e.,* "the young lord of Uji." Uji is the name of a district in Yamashiro, famous in classical and modern times for its tea. The etymology is obscure.

27. *I.e.,* "the young lady of Yata." Yata is the name of a place in Yamato. The etymology is obscure.

28. *Medori no miko.* *Medori* signifies "hen-bird:" but the reason for the application of so strange a name to this princess, whose fortunes are related at some length in Sect. CXXVI and CXXVII, does not appear. A similar remark applies to the next name.

29. *I.e.,* probably "the lady of the little kettle."

30. *I.e.,* "the young lady of Uji."

31. *I.e.,* "the truly young middle princess of Okinaga."

32. See Sect. XCII, Note 27.

33. *Waka-muke-futa-mata no miko.* This name is obscure.

34. *Itowi-hime.* Itowi is the name of a place in Yamato, and is of uncertain origin.

35. *Shima* is probably the name of a place, while *tari* and *ne* are the frequently recurring Honorifics rendered respectively "perfect" and "lord" in former parts of this translation.

36. *Sakurawi no ta-be no murazhi.* *Ta-be*, rendered "agricultural,' is literally "rice-field tribe." *Sakurawi* ("cherry well") is the name of a place in Kahachi.

37. *I.e.,* falcon-lord.

38, *Himuka no Idzumi no Naga-hime.* Himuka is the name of a province, and Idzumi that of a district now comprised within the limits of Satsuma. *Nagahime*, literally "long princess," probably signifies "elder princess."

39. *Oho-haye no miko.* Signification obscure.

40. *Wo-haye no miko.* Signification obscure. The antithesis of the Adjectives *oho* and *wo* ("great" and "small") shows however that the names partly served to distinguish the elder from the younger brother.

41. *Waki-iratsume* is "younger lady." *Hata-bi* is incomprehensible.

42. See Sect. LXXVI, Note 28.

43. *I.e.,* probably "the lady of Kaharada." The latter name (literally "rice-field on the border of a river") is often met with.

44. *I.e.,* "the jewel lady."

45. *I.e.,* "the great middle lady of Osaka," the latter being the name of a place in Yamato (see Sect. XLVIII, Note 1).

46. Motowori identifies this name with that *Koto-fushi no iratsume* in Sect. CXVII, *q.v.,* and thinks that both this and the preceding name have only crept into this Section by mistake.

47. *Kataji no miko.* Signification obscure,

48. *Kadzuraki no Nu-iro-me.* All the elements of this name have already been met with several times.

49. This child has already appeared early in this Section, and the name is here doubtless only repeated through some copyist's error.

---

[SECT. CV.—EMPEROR Ō-JIN (PART II.—HE DIVIDES THE INHERITANCE BETWEEN HIS THREE SONS)]

Hereupon the Heavenly Sovereign asked His August-ness Oho-yama-mori and His Augustness Oho-sazaki, saying: "Which think ye the dearer, an elder child or a younger child?" (The reason why the Heavenly Sovereign propounded this question was because it was his intention[1] to make Uji-no-waki-iratsuko rule the Empire). Then His Augustness Oho-yama-mori said: "The elder child is the dearer." Next His Augustness Oho-sazaki, knowing the august feeling which made the Heavenly Sovereign deign to ask [the question], said: "The elder child, having already become a man, gives no trouble; but the younger child, not being yet a man, is the dearer." Then the Heavenly Sovereign said: "My lord Sazaki's words agree with my thoughts," and forthwith ordained the division [of the inheritance] thus: His Augustness Oho-yama-mori to administer the government of the mountains and the sea,[2] His Augustness Oho-sazaki to take and deign to report on the government of the realm,[3] and Uji-no waki-iratsuko to rule the succession of Heaven's sun.[4] So His Augustness Oho-sazaki was not disobedient to the Heavenly Sovereign's commands.[5]

---

1. Literally, "heart."

2. *I.e.*, Motowori thinks, to have control over the guilds of foresters and fishermen.

3. *I.e.*, to act as regent or minister.

4. *I.e.*, to inherit the empire.—It will be remembered that the Japanese Emperors claim to descend from the Sun-Goddess.

5. This statement refers proleptically to the contrary course which was taken by the elder Oho-yama-mori.

---

SECT. CVI.—EMPEROR Ō-JIN (PART III.—HE WOOES PRINCESS MIYA-NUSHI-YA-KAHA-YE).]

One day[1] the Heavenly Sovereign, when he had crossed over into the land of Afumi, augustly stood on the moor of Uji, gazed on the moor of Kadzu, and sang, saying:

245. "As I look on the Moor of Kadzu in Chiba.
both the hundred thousand-fold abundant
house-places are visible, and the land's
acme is visible."[2]

So when he reached the village of Kohara,[3] a beautiful
maiden met him at a fork in the road, Then the Heavenly Sovereign asked the maiden, saying : "Whose child
art thou ?" She replied, saying : "I am the daughter of
the Grandee Wani-no-Hifure,[4] and my name is Princess
Miya-nushi-ya-kaha-ye. "[5] The Heavenly Sovereign forthwith said to the maiden : "When I return on my progress
to-morrow, I will enter into thy house." So Princess
Ya-kaha-ye told her father all that [had happened].
Thereupon her father replied, saying : "Ah ! it was the
Heavenly Sovereign ! [His commands are] to be respect
ed. My child, respectfully serve him !"—and so saying
he grandly decorated the house, and awaited [the Heaven
ly Sovereign's return], whereupon he came in on the
next day.[6] So when [the father] served [the Heavenly
Sovereign] a great august feast, he made his daughter
Her Augustness[7] Princess Ya-kaha take the great august [246]
liquor-cup and present it. Thereupon, while taking the
great liquor-cup, the Heavenly Sovereign augustly sang,
saying :

> "Oh this crab ! whence this crab ? [It is]
> a crab from far-distant Tsunuga. Whither
> reaches its sideward motion ? [It has]
> come towards Ichiji-shima and Mi-shima.
> It must be because, plunging and breathless
> like the grebe, I went without stopping
> along the up and down road by the wavelets,
> that the maiden I met on the Kohata road
> has a back oh ! like a small shield, a row
> of teeth like acorns. Oh ! the earth of the
> Wani pass àt Ichihiwi ! Owing to the skin
> of the first earth being ruddy, to the last

> earth being of a reddish black, she, without
> exposing to the actual sun that makes one
> bend one's head the middle earth like
> three chestnuts, draws thickly down her
> drawn eye-brows;—the women I met, the
> child I saw and wanted in this way, the
> child I saw and wanted in that way, oh!
> she is opposite to me at the height of
> the feast! oh! she is at my side!"[118]

247    Ita auguste coivit [cum illâ], et procreavit filium Uji-
no-waki-iratsuko.

---

1. Literally, "one time."

2. According to Moribe, whose interpretation has been followed
throughout, this Song signifies: "As I gaze across from Uji to the Moor
of Toba, I see the numerous and prosperous homesteads of the people, I
see the most fertile portion of the country."—On this view Chiba is
identified with Toba, the name of a district; and the word *ho*, rendered
"acme," is taken to mean the best, highest, most showy part of anything.
For Motowori's opinion, which is that of the older commentators as well,
that *chi-ba* is a Pillow-Word, there is much to be said, and if we followed
it, we should have to render the first two lines thus: "As I look on
the thousand-leafed pueraria-moor," etc. (*kadzu* signifying "pueraria.")
Motowori's explanation of *momo-chi-daru* (here rendered by "hundred
thousand-fold abundant") as referring to the soot of the peasant's roofs,
and of *ho* as signifying "a plain surrounded by mountains" seems much
less good than Moribe's interpretation of those difficult expressions.

3. In the district of Uji in the province of Yamashiro. The characters with which the name is written signify "tree-flag."

4. *Wani no Hifure no omi.* For *Wani no omi* see Sect. LXII,
Note 11. The meaning of *Hifure* is obscure.

5. *Miya-nushi-ya-kata-hime.* *Miya-nushi* is "priestess," or more
literally "temple-guardian." For the rest of the name see Sect. XXVI,
Note 14, though the personages are! of course meant to be different.

6. *I.e.,* that day having passed by, the Emperor came on the next
day according to his promise.

7. Motowori supposes with apparent reason that the character 命,

" Augustness," has only crept into the text through the attraction of the following character 令, "made," which it resembles in appearance.

8. It must be understood that in this Song the Imperial singer commences by referring to what doubtless formed part of the feast,—a crab, —and thence passes on by an imperceptible transition to allude to his own adventure with the maiden. As the crab when alive walked sideways, so was the Emperor zigzagging up and down the road that lines the shore of Lake Biwa, pursuing his breathless course like that of the busy grebe that perpetually plunges into the water, when the maiden met him near Kohata. Beautiful indeed was she : her back straight as a shield, her teeth like a row of acorns, and the artificial eye-brows painted a dark colour on her forehead drawn low down in a perfect crescent-shape. She had been careful in selecting the clay to make the paint, rejecting the upper layer of earth, for that was of too bright a red, rejecting likewise the lower layer, for that was too dark, but taking the middle, which was of the correct blue tint, and drying it, not in the fierce, but in a mildly tempered, sun-light. And now this maiden, for whom his heart had been panting and turning this way and that ever since the previous day, is actually seated opposite to him, nay ! at his very side, and he is feasting in her sweet company.—Tsunuga is the name of a place in the province of Echizen. " Far-distant " is an imperfect attempt at rendering the force of the Pillow-Word *momo-dzutafu*, which implies that the traveller must pass through a hundred other places before reaching his destination. " Whither reaches its sideward motion ? " signifies " whither is it going with its sideward motion ? " Ichiji-shima and Mishima are places of which nothing is known, so that the allusion to them is obscure. At this point Motowori's interpretation diverges from that of Moribe, which has been followed throughout. *Sasanami*, here rendered " wavelets," is taken by him, as by the older commentators, as the name of a place, and the description of the maiden's teeth is misunderstood to signify that she had a beak filled with a row of teeth like the water-caltrop ! Motowori also would here divide the Song in two, a proceeding for which there is not sufficient warrant. On other minor points, too, his decisions do not seem so happy as Moribe's. The view of both commentators will be found at length in Motowori's Commentary, Vol. XXXII, pp. 33.51, and in Moribe's "*Idzu no Koto-Waki*," *in loco*. Three chestnuts " (*mitsu-guri no*) is a common Pillow-Word for *naka*, " middle," founded on the fact, real or supposed, that one burr always contains three nuts, whereof one of course is in the middle, between the other two.

[SECT. CVII.—EMPEROR Ō-JIN (PART IV.—HE GRANTS PRINCESS
KAMINAGA TO HIS SON OHO-SAZAKI),]

The Heavenly Sovereign, hearing of the beauty of
Princess Kaminaga,[1] daughter of the Duke of Muragata[2]
in the land of Himuka, and thinking to employ her,[3] sent
down for her,[4] whereupon the Heir Apparent[5] His
Augustness Oho-sazaki, having seen the maiden land at
248 the port of Naniha, and being charmed with the grace
of her appearance, forthwith directed the Prince Minister
the Noble Taka-uchi, to intercede for him in the august
presence of the Heavenly Sovereign, and make [the lat-
ter] grant to him Princess Kami-naga, whom he had
sent down for. Then on the Prime Minister the Noble
Take-uchi requesting the great commands,[6] the Heavenly
Sovereign forthwith granted Princess Kami-naga to his
august child. The way he granted her was this:—the
Heavenly Sovereign, on a day when he partook of a
copious feast,[7] gave Princess Kami-naga the great august
liquor oak-[leaf[8]] to present to the Heir Apparent. Then
he augustly sang, saying:

> "Come on, children! oh! the fragrant flower-
> ing orange-tree on my way as I go to pluck
> the wild garlic,—to pluck the garlic,—has
> its uppermost 'branches withered by birds
> perching on them, and its lowest branches
> withered through people plucking from them.
> But the budding fruit on the middle branch,
> like three chestnuts,—the ruddy maiden, oh!
> if thou lead her off with thee, it will be
> good, oh!"[9]

249     Again he augustly sang, saying:

> "Driving the dyke-piles into Lake Yosami

where the water collects, my heart (ignorant
of the pricking of the stumps of the water-
caltrop, ignorant of the creeping: of the roots
of the *Brasenia peltata*), being more and
more laughable, is now indeed repentant "[10]

Having thus sung, he bestowed [ her on the Heir Apparent ]. So after having been granted the maiden, the
Heir Apparent sang, saying:

"Oh! the maiden of Kohada in the back of
the road! though I heard of her like the
thunder, we mutually intertwine [ our arms ]
as pillows. "[11]

Again he sang saying:

"I think lovingly ah! of how the maiden
of Kohada in the back of the road sleeps
[ with me ] without disputing. "[12]

250

---

1. *Kami-naga-hime.* The name signifies " the long-haired princess."
2. *Murakata no kami. Murakata* seems to signify " many towns."
3. *I.e.*, wed her.
4. Literally, " summoned her up." The same phrase occurs immediately below.
5. 太子. Mabuchi thinks that 御子, "august child," should be
substituted for the reading in the text. But Motowori insists that the
title translated Heir Apparent was anciently borne by all the sons of an
Emperor, and that consequently no emendation is called for.
6. *I.e*, the Emperor's orders.
7. The native term translated " copious feast]" is *toyo no akari*,
variously written with the characters 豊明, 豊樂, 宴樂, etc., etc. It literally signifies "copious brightness." in allusion to the ruddy glow which
wine gives to the faces of the revellers, and henceforward perpetually
recurs in this history. In later times it specifically denoted the festival
of. the tasting of the first rice, but anciently its meaning was not thus
limited. Motowori's note on the subject, in Vol. XXXII, pp. 57-59 of
his Commentary, may be consulted with advantage.
8. *I.e.*, an oak-leaf which was used as a cup to sip out of. Leaf-

platters for food have already been mentioned. Motowori says that the word *kashika* (properly the name of a deciduous oak, the *Quercus dentata*) was employed to denote any kind of leaf thus used.

9. The whole gist of this Song is contained in the last three lines. "The ruddy maiden, oh if thou lead her off with thee, it will be good," —i.e. "thou and the maiden, will form a fitting couple." All that goes before is what is technically called a "Preface," though its bearing is so clear as to admit of translation, and even in English to form an appropriate introduction to the Song:—It is not the stinking garlic, but the fragrant orange that the singer has met by the way, and it is the choicest young fruit in the very middle of the tree that forms a suitable comparison for the lovely young girl.—With the favourite allusion to upper, middle, and lower the reader is already familiar, and the Pillow-Word "three chestnuts" was explained in the note on the proceding Song (Sect. CVI, Note 8).

10. The gist of the Song is: "I knew not that thou, my son, hadst conceived a secret passion for the maiden; but I am now conscious of my own mistake, and my foolish old heart is ashamed of itself." With this explanation the elaborate comparison between the state of the monarch's mind and the condition of the peasant driving piles for the foundation of a dyke, and having his feet either lacerated by the stumps of the water-caltrop, or made slimy by brushing against the roots of the *Brasenia peltata* at the bottom of the water, becomes intelligible and appropriate.—The word *kuri*, rendered "roots," perplexed Motowori, who suggests that it may be but a second name of the *Brasenia*, appended to the first; but Moribe's suggestion that it is to be identified with *kori*, and taken in the signification of "roots" though not quite convincing, is at least more plausible. The text of this Song is corrupt in these "Records" and has to be corrected by a comparison with that of the "Chronicles." Moribe goes into an amusing ecstasy over the picture of ancient manners which it presents, and lauds the simplicity of days when a father and son could so peacefully woo the same maiden without mutual concealment or disastrous consequences!

11. The meaning of this Song is: "At first I heard of the maiden of Kohada in the furthest parts of Himuka as one hears the distant thunder; but now she is mine, and we sleep locked in each other's arms."—This Kohada in Himuka must not be confounded with the Kohata in Yamashiro mentioned in the preceding Section. The "back of the road" means the remotest portion (conf. Sect. LX, Note 20). The thunder must be understood to refer to a very faint and distant

sound: the Prince had first heard of the maiden vaguely, but now she is his and has been his for some time; for this Song must be supposed to have been composed after the occasion of the feast with the story of which it is here connected.

12. The meaning of this Song is: "I love this maiden of Kohada in Himuka, who disputed not my desire and my father's grant, but willingly became my wife."—It is hard to render into English the force of the string of Particles *wo shi zo mo* in the penultimate line.

---

[SECT. CVIII.—EMPEROR Ō-JIN (PART V.—SONGS OF THE
TERRITORIAL OWNERS OF YESHINU).]

Again, the Territorial Owners of Yeshinu,[1] seeing the august sword which was girded on His Augustness Oho sazaki, sang, saying:

" Sharp is the beginning, freezing is the end
of the sword girded on Oho-sazaki, Oho-
sazaki, the solar august child of Homuda,—
[it is] chilly, chilly like the trees beneath
the trunks of the winter trees."[2]

Again, having made a cross-mortar[3] at Kashifu[3] in 251 Yeshinu, and having in that cross-mortar distilled[5] some great august liquor, they, when they presented the great august liquor [to the Heavenly Sovereign], sang as follows, drumming with their mouths:

" We have made a side-mortar at Kashinofu,
and in the side-mortar we have distilled
some great august liquor, which do thou
sweetly partake of, oh our lord !"[6]

This Song is one which it is the custom to chant down to the present day when, from time to time, the Territorial Owners present a great feast [to the Sovereign].

1. Yeshinu is the modern Yoshino, in the province of Yamato (see Sect. XLVI, Note 3). For the title of *kudzu* see Sect. XLVI, Note 13, where it also occurs in connection with Yeshinu.

2. According to Moribe, whose interpretation seems best to the translator. the signification of this difficult poem is: "The sword worn by Prince Oho-sazaki, son of the Emperor Homuda (O-jin) is double-edged at its upper part, and like glistening ice towards its point;—oh! 'tis like the icicles on the plants that cluster about the trunks of the dead trees in winter!" Almost every line, however (excepting those giving the name and title of the Prince), is a subject of controversy, and the " *Gō-Gan Shō*" *in loco* and Motowori's Commentary, Vol. XXXIII, pp. 2-5, should be consulted for Keichiū's, Mabuchi's and Motowori's views on the disputed /point.—The expression " solar august child " signifies "sun-descended prince," in allusion to the supposed descent of the Japanese monarchs from the Sun-Goddess.

3. *Yoko-usu* or *yokusu* (横臼). It is not plain what sort of mortar the author intended to designate by this term. Motowori supposes it to mean a broad flat mortar in contradistinction to a high and narrow one. Keichiū's view, which he quotes, to the effect that it was a mortar that had been carved out of the block against the grain of the wood, seems an equally good guess, where all is guess-work.

4. In the Song this same name is read *Kashinafu*; but the commentators tell us that the Genitive Particle *no* (" of ") is simply inserted for the sake of rhythm, and it is not unlikely that they are right. The name seems to signify " [a place where] oak-trees grow."

5. See Sect. XVIII, Note 16. The character 醸, rendered by " distil " or " brew," according to the view which one may take of the resulting liquor, would seem to be here used in the sense of " to pound."

6. In this simple Song the Territorial Owners of Yoshino beg the Monarch to deign to partake of the *sake* which they have made.

---

[SECT. CIX.—EMPEROR Ō-JIN (PART VI.—VARIOUS DEEDS)]

In this august reign were graciously established the Fisher Tribe,[1] the Mountain Tribe,[2] the Mountain Warden Tribe,[3] and the Ise Tribe.[4] Again the Pool of Tsurugi was made. Again there came over [to Japan] some

people from Shiragi, Therefore His Augustness the
Noble Take-uchi, having taken them with him and set
them to labour on pools and embankments, made the
Pool of Kudara.[5]

---

1. *Ama-be* (written 海部 and read *Una-be* in the Old Printed Edition
and in the edition of 1687, and perhaps better rendered "Sea-Tribe.")
The name of this guild or clan does not seem to have remained, like the
tw mentioned together with it, as a "gentile name."

2. *Yama-be.* Motowori thinks that this word has crept into the
text erroneously through the influence of that next mentioned, as the
functions of the tribes or guilds thus separately named were identical
The differentiation may have taken place after the terms had come to be
used as "gentile names."

3. *Yama-moribe.*

4. *Ise-be.* Nothing is known of this tribe or guild.

5. Doubtless so named after the Korean labourers employed upon
it,—Kudara and Shiragi, as different parts of the same peninsula, being
confounded in thought.

---

[SECT. CX.—EMPEROR Ō-JIN (PART VIII.—TRIBUTE
FROM KOREA).]

252

Again King Shō-ko,[1] the Chieftain of the land of
Kudara, sent as tribute by Achi-kishi[2] one stallion and
one mare. (This Achi-kishi was the ancestor of the Achiki Scribes.[3])
Again he sent as tribute a cross-sword,[4] and likewise
a large mirror. Again he was graciously bidden[5] to
send as tribute a wise man, if there were any such in
the land of Kudara. Therefore receiving the [Imperial]
commands, he sent as tribute a man named Wani-kishi,[6]
and likewise by this man he sent as tribute the Confucian Analects[7] in ten volumes and the Thousand Character Essay[8] in one volume,—altogether eleven volumes.

253 (This Wani-kishi was the ancestor of the Fumi Grandees.)⁹   Again he
sent as tribute two artisans,—a smith from Kara named
Taku-so¹⁰ and a weaver from Go¹¹ named Sai-so.¹⁴

---

1. 照古王, according to the Japanese *kana* spelling, *Sen-ko.*

2. 阿知吉師. Other forms of the name are *Ajiki* and *Atogi*, and
all three are but attempts at transcribing phonetically into Japanese a
Korean name, the proper characters for which are not given. 吉師 is
not properly part of the name, but is simply an official title (帥 here
stands for 士).

3. *Achiki no fumi-bito. Fumi-bito* (abbreviated to *Fubito*) became a
"gentile name."

4. See Sect. XLV, Note 5.

5. *Q.d.*, by the Japanese Emperor.

6. Here written phonetically 和邇吉師, but properly, 王仁吉士, *i.e.*
"the Official Wang In." He is generally spoken of simply as *Wani.*

7. 論語. ("*Lun Yu,*" or according to the Japanese pronunciation
"*Rongo.*")

8. 千文字. ("*Chien Tzu Wen,*" or according to the Japanese
pronunciation "*Sen-ji-mun.*") See the translator's remarks on this subject
in the Introduction, p. xliii. The "Chronicles" more prudently mention
only "various classics"

9. *Fumi no obito. Fumi* signifies "any written document," so that
this "gentile name" is equivalent to our word "scribe."

10. 卓素. The transliteration of this, as of all other such names
here occurring, is the Sinico-Japanese transliteration. *Kara* (Korea) is
written 韓.

11. 吳 (*Wu*, Jap. *Go*), one of the states into which China was
divided during the third century of our era. A draper's shop is still
called *go-fuku-ya*, *i.e.*, "Wu-garment-house" in memory of the introduction
of wearing apparel from that country.

12. 西素,

[SECT. CXI.—EMPEROR Ō-JIN (PART VIII.—THE EMPEROR
INTOXICATED).]

Again there came over [to Japan] the ancestor of the
Hada Rulers,[1] the ancestor of the Aya Suzerains,[2] and
likewise a man who knew how to distil liquor, and
whose name was Nim-pan,[3] while another name for him
was Susukori.[4] So this [man] Susukori distilled some
great august liquor, and presented it to the Heavenly
Sovereign, who, excited with the great august liquor
that had been presented to him augustly sang, saying:

"I have become intoxicated with the august
  liquor distilled by Susukori. I have become intoxicated with the soothing liquor,
  with the smiling liquor."[5]

On his walking out singing thus, he hit with his 254
august staff a large stone in the middle of the Ohosaka[5] road, upon which the stone ran away. So the
proverb says: "Hard stones get out of a drunkard's
way."

---

1. *Hada na miyatsuko*, 秦造, a " gentile name." *Hada* is the native
Japanese word used as the equivalent of the Chinese name 秦, *Ch'in*.
Its origin is uncertain.

2. *Aya no ataha* 漢直. a " gentile name." The use of Aya to
represent the Chinese name 漢, *Han*, is as difficult' to account for as is
that of Hada mentioned in the preceding Note.

3. 仁番. Another and more Japanese-like reading, *Niho*, is invented
by Motowori; but the older editors read *Nim-pan* according to the usual
Sinico-Japanese sound of the characters. The modern Korean reading
would be In-pon.

4, Written phonetically 須須許理.

5. Thus translated, this Song is too clear to need any explanation.
The lines, however, which are rendered by " with the soothing liquor,
with the smiling liquor."—in Japanese *koto nagu shi we-guzhi-ni,*—are in
reality extremely obscure, and Moribe understands them to signify, " Oh !

how difficult it is for me to speak! Oh! how ill at ease I am!" In order to do so he has, however, to change and add to the text; and the translator, though not sure of being in the right path, has preferred to follow Motowori,'whose interpretation, without requiring any such extreme measures, yet gives a very p ausible sense.

6. See Sect. LXIV, Note 25.

---

[SECT. CXII.—EMPEROR Ō-JIN (PART IX.—TROUBLES WHICH FOLLOWED HIS DECEASE).]

So after the decease of the Heavenly Sovereign, His Augustness Ohosazaki, in conformity with the Heavenly Sovereign's commands, ceded the Empire to Uji-no-waki-iratsuko. Thereupon His Augustness Ohoyama-mori, disobeying the Heavenly Sovereign's commands, and anxious in spite thereof to obtain the Empire, had the design to slay the Prince[1] his younger brother, secretly raised an army, and prepared to attack him. Then His Augustness Oho-sazaki, hearing that his elder brother had prepared an army, forthwith despatched a messenger to apprise Uji-no-waki-iratsuko. So, startled at the news, [the latter] set troops in ambush by the river-bank, and likewise, after having drawn a fence of curtains and raised a tent on the top of the hill, placed there publicly on a throne[2] one of his retainers to pretend that he was the King.[3] the manner in which all the officials[4] reverentially went and came being just like that [usual] in the King's presence. And moreover, preparing for the time 255 when the King his elder brother[5] should cross the river, he arranged and decorated a boat and oars, and moreover[6] ground [in a mortar] the root of the *Kadzura japonica*, and having taken the slime of its juice, rubbed

therewith the grating[7] inside the boat, so as to make
any who should tread on it fall down, and then himself[8]
put on a cloth coat and trowsers, and having assumed
the appearance of a common fellow, stood in the boat
holding the oar. Hereupon, when the King his elder
brother, having hid his troops in ambush and put on
armour beneath his clothes, reached the river-bank and
was about to get into the boat, he gazed at the grandly
decorated place [on the hill], thought the King his
younger brother was sitting on the throne, being altogether ignorant [of the fact] that he was standing in
the boat holding the oar, and forthwith asked the fellow
who was holding the oar, saying: "It has been reported
to me that on this mountain there is a large and angry
boar. I wish to take that boar. Shall I peradventure
get that boar?" Then the fellow holding the oar replied,
saying: "Thou canst not." Again he asked, saying:
"For what reason?" [The boat-man] answered, saying:
"He is not to be got, however often and in however
many places he be chased. Wherefore I say that thou
canst not [catch him either]." When they had crossed
as far as the middle of the river, [Prince Uji-no-waki-
iratsuko] caused the boat to be tilted over, and [his
elder brother] to fall into the water.[9] Then forthwith
he rose to the surface, and floated down with the
current. Forthwith, as he floated, he sang, saying:

"Whoever is swiftest among the boatmen
of the Uji ferry will come to me."[10]

Thereupon the troops that had been hidden on the 256
river-bank rose up simultaneously on this side and on
that side, and fixing their arrows [in their bows], let
him go floating down. So he sank on reaching Kawara

Point.[11] So on their searching with hooks[12] the place
where he had sunk, [the hooks] struck on the armour
inside his clothes, and made a rattling sound.[13] So the
place was called by the name of Kawara Point. Then
when they hooked up[14] his bones, the younger King
sang saying:

" *Catalpa* bow, *Evonymus* standing by the
ferry-bank of Uji! My heart had thought
to cut [you], my heart had thought to
take [you]; but at the base methought of
the lord, at the extremity methought of the
younger sister; grievously methought of
this, sorrowfully methought of, that; and
I came [back] without cutting it,—the
*Catalpa* bow, the *Evonymus*.[15]

257        So the bones of His Augustness Oho-yama-mori were
buried on the Nara[16] mountain. His Augustness Oho-
yama-mori ( was the ancestor of the Dukes of Hijikata,[17] the Dukes
of Heki,[18] and the Dukes of Harihara.[19])

---

1. 皇子. This is the only passage in the work where this expression
occurs. *Uji-no-waki-iratsuko* is the personage thus designated.

2. The same expression has been in Sect. XXXI (near Note 16)
rendered "couch." The characters in the original are 吳床 or 胡床.

3. *I.e., Uji-na-maki-iraisuko.*

4. The Chinese phrase 百官, "the hundred officials," is here used.

5. *Q.d.,* his Augustness Oho-yama-mori.

6. The text has the character 者, which, in combination with the
preceding words "oars," gives the sense of "oarsman," boatman." But
Motowori reasonably suggests that it is an error for 亦, the grass hand
forms of the two characters closely resembling each other, and 亦 making
much better sense; for who would talk of "decorating an oarsman"?

7. A bamboo grating.

8. Literally "that king's son."

9. It must be understood that Uji-no-waki-iratsuko and his men

having planned to act thus, were on their guard, and did not fall into the water as did Oho-yama-mori, who was taken unawares.

10. This is Motowori's view of the meaning of the Song, which he interprets as a request for help to some friendly boatman. Moribe adopts quite a different view, and thinks that the drowning prince is rather giving vent to sentiments of pride and defiance. He says (speaking in the Prince's name): " It is not that I have been capsized out of the boat into the river, but that I am swimming off after a pole which has fallen into the water. If there be any strong and willing fellows among my partizans, let them swim after me." It must be explained that the word rendered " boatmen " in the translation is literally " pole-takers " (or, according to Moribe's view, " to take a pole.") Motowori's interpretation seems to do less violence to the wording of the original, and Moribe's has not even the merit of accounting for the use of the Future *komu* where the Imperative *kone* would be what we should naturally expect.— *Uji* is preceded by the, in this context, untranslatable Pillow-Word *chihayaburu* (see " Dictionary of Pillow-Words," *s.v.*).

11. *Kawara no saki*. The author, in the next sentence, derives this name from the rattling sound made by the books as they struck on the armour. But there seems a great deal to be said in favour of Arawi Hakuseki's view that *kawara* is an old word itself signifying " armour."

12. The word *kagi* here used occurs elsewhere to denote the hooks employed for fastening doors, and in later times took the specific meaning of " key."

13. Literally, " sounded *kawara*."

14. The text has the characters 掛出. But Motowori says that 掛 stands for 搔, and that we must interpret the passage to mean that they scratched [about to find] and take out [his corpse].

15. The signification of this Song is : " I came here meaning to kill thee as I might cut down and kill that *Catalpa* tree, that *Evonymus*, growing on the river-bank. But the thought of our father and of thy sister (or wife) touched me with pity, and I return without having drawn my bow at thee."—Uji is preceded by the untranslatable Pillow-Word *chihayahito* (see Dictionary of Pillow-Words " *s.v.*;—Motowori reads it *chihaya-hito* without the *nigori*).—The words *adzusa-yumi ma-yumi*, here respectively rendered " *Catalpa* bow " and " *Evonymus*," are difficult, and the doubt as to whether we should understand the prince to be speaking simply of the trees, or to intend likewise to allude to his bow which was made of the wood of one of those trees, is probably not to be settled, as the words in question have always oscillated between the two

meanings, and here evidently contain a double allusion. Motowori thinks
that the first of the two forms only a sort of Pillow-Word for the
second.—The word rendered " bank," in accordance with Moribe's suggestion, is literally " reach."—No special importance must be attached to
the expressions " base " (or ｜ " main part ") and " extremity," though they
may doubtless be thought to allude to the father and sister, the recollection of whom softened the victorious younger brother's heart. The word
*iranakeku*, rendered " grievously," is of not quite certain interpretation.—
It must be understood that though, by overturning the boat, Uji-no-waki-
iratsuko did constructively cause Oho-yama-mori's death, he did not
actually shoot at and slay him when in the water, but followed down
the river-side lamenting over what had happened.—This Song is singled
out by Moribe for special praise.

　　16. See Sect. LXXII, Note 23.
　　17. Tohotafumi (Tōtōmi). In the original *Hijikata no kimi*.
　　18. *Heki na kimi.* Of Heki nothing is known,
　　19. *Harihara no kimi.* In Tohotafumi. *Harihara* signifies " alder
plantation."

--------

[SECT. CXIII.—EMPEROR Ō-JIN (PART X.—PRINCES OHO-SAZAKI
AND UJI-NO-WAKI-IRATSUKO CEDE THE EMPIRE
TO EACH OTHER).]

Thereupon while the two Deities[1] His Augustness
Oho-sazaki and Uji-no-waki-iratsuko were, each of them,
ceding the Empire to the other,[2] a fisherman[3] came with
a great feast as tribute.[4] So they each resigned it to
the other. So the elder brother refused it, and caused
258 it to be offered to the younger brother, and the younger
brother refused it, and caused it to be offered to the
elder brother, during which mutual cedings many days
elapsed. As such mutual ceding took place not [ only ]
once or twice, the fisherman wept from the fatigue of
going backwards and forwards. So the proverb says:

"Ah ! the fisherman weeps on account of his own things. "[5] Meanwhile Uji-no-waki-iratsuko died early.[6] So His Augustness Oho-sazaki did rule the Empire.

---

1. It is not actually the word *kami*, " deity," that is here used in the original, but *hashira*, which is the Auxiliary Numeral for Deities.

2. Neither being willing to accept the Imperial dignity.

3. Or, " some fishermen," and similarly in the Plural throughout.

4. *I.e.*, came to present fish to His Majesty.

5. Motowori is probably right in saying that[1] the point of this proverb lies in the consideration that, whereas people in general weep for that which they have not, this fisherman wept on account of the trouble which was caused to him by the fish which he had.

6. Or, " died first." The use in this place of the character 崩, properly confined to the meaning of the " death of an Emperor," is remarkable. See Motowori's observations on the point in Vol. XXXIII, pp. 78-80.

---

[SECT. CXIV.—EMPEROR Ō-JIN (PART XI.—AMA-NO-HI-BOKO CROSSES OVER TO JAPAN )]

Moreover of old there had been [ a man ] called by the name of Ama-no-hi-boko, child of the ruler of the land of Shiragi. This person crossed over here [ to Japan ]. The reason of his crossing over here was [ this ]: In the land of Shiragi there was a certain lagoon,[2] called by the name of the Agu Lagoon.[3] On the bank of this lagoon[4] a certain poor girl was [ taking her ] midday sleep. Tunc solis radii, coelesti arcui similes, in privatas partes impegerunt. Again there was a certain poor man, 259 who, thinking this occurrence[5] strange, constantly watched the woman's behaviour. So the woman, having conceived from the time of that midday sleep, gave birth to a red jewel. Then the poor man who had watched her begged [ to be allowed ] to take the jewel, and kept it constantly wrapped up by his side.[6] This person, having planted a rice-field in a valley,[7] had loaded a cow[8] with food for the labourers, and was getting into the middle of the valley, when he met the ruler's son, Ama-no-hi-boko, who thereupon asked him, saying : " Why enterest thou the valley with a load of food upon a cow ? Thou wilt surely kill this cow and eat her. " Forthwith he seized the man and was about to put him into prison, when the man replied, saying : " I was not going to kill the cow. I was simply taking food to the people in the fields. " But still [ the ruler's child ] would not let him go. Then he undid the jewel [ which hung ] at his side, and [ therewith ] bribed [ the ruler's child ]. So [ the latter ] let the poor man go, brought the jewel [ home ], and placed it beside his couch. Forthwith it was transformed into a beautiful maiden, whom he straightway wedded, and made his chief wife. Then the maiden perpetually prepared all sorts of dainties with which she constantly fed her husband. So the ruler's child [ grew ] proud in his heart, and reviled his wife. But the woman said : " I am not a woman who ought to be the wife of such as thou. I will go to the land of my ancestors ; "— and forthwith she secretly embarked in a boat, and fled away across here [ to Japan ], and landed[9] at Naniha.[10] (This is the deity called Princess Akaru,[11] who dwells in the shrine of Hime-goso[12] at Naniha.) Thereupon Ame-no-hi-boko, hearing 260 of his wife's flight, forthwith pursued her across hither, and was about to arrive at Naniha, when the Deity of the passage[13] prevented his entrance. So he went back again, and landed in the country of Tajima.[14]

1. Or, according to Motowori's reading, *Ame no-hi-boko.* The characters in the next, 大之日矛一 signify "heavenly sun-spear." But the homonymous characters 海檜槍, with which the name is written in the "Gleanings from Ancient Story," and which are approved of both by Motowori and by Tanigaha Shisei. signify "fisherman's chamaecyparis spear."

2. Apparently nothing more is meant than that there was "*a* lagoon;" but still the *one* (一) in this context is curious, and Motowori retains it as *hito-tsu no* in the Japanese reading. "A certain" seems best to render its force in English, as again in the following sentences, where Motowori interprets it by the character 或. It is of strangely frequent recurrence in the opening sentences of this Section, which are altogether peculiar in style.

3. *Agu-numa.* The meaning of this name is unknown.

4. The Old Printed Edition has the word "mud" instead of "lagoon."

5. Literally, "this appearance."

6. Literally, "attached to his loins."

7. The words rendered "in a valley" are in the text 山谷之間, of which the commentators find it difficult to make proper Japanese. The translator has followed them in neglecting the character 山, mountain."

8. Or bull, or bullock; for Japanese does not distinguish Genders.

9. Literally, "stopped."

10. See Sect. XLIV, Note 26.

11. *Akaru-hime, i.e.,* "Brilliant Princess."

12. The signification of this name is obscure. Motowori identifies the place with the modern Kodzu (高津).

13. *I.e.,* the water-god of the sea near Naniha.

14. See Sect. LXXIV, Note 1.

---

[SECT. CXV.—EMPEROR Ō-JIN (PART XII.—DESCENDANTS OF AMA-NO-HI-BOKO, AND TREASURES BROUGHT BY HIM.)]

Forthwith staying in that country, he wedded Saki-tsu-mi,[1] daughter of Tajima-no-matawo,[2] and begot a child: Tajima-morosuku.[3] The latter's child was Tajima-hi-ne.[4] The latter's child was Tajima-hinaraki.[5] The latter's children were Tajima-mori,[6] next Tajima-hitaka,[7] next Kiyo-hiko[8] (three Deities).[9] This Kiyo-hiko wedded Tagima-no-mehi,[10] and begot children: Suga-no-morowo,[11] next his younger sister Suga-kama-yura-domi.[12] So the above mentioned Tajima-hitaka wedded his niece Yura-domi, and begot a child: Her Augustness Princess Takanuka of Kadzuraki.[13] (This was the august parent[14] of Her Augustness Princess Okinaga-tarashi.) So the things which Ama-no-hi-boko brought over here, and which were called the " precious treasures,"[15] were: two strings of pearls;[16] likewise a wave-shaking scarf, a wave-cutting scarf, a wind-shaking scarf, and a wind-cutting scarf;[17] likewise a mirror of the offing and a mirror of the shore,[18]—eight articles in all. (These are the Eight Great Deities of Idzushi.)

---

1. This name may mean "lucky ears," or "possessor of luck;" but it is obscure, and is moreover in the " Chronicles " (where it is given as the name, not of the daughter, but of the father) read *Mahe-tsu-mi,*—a reading which will not bear either of these interpretations.

2. *Matawo* seems to signify "complete (*i.e.*, healthy or vigorous) male." Observe that the word Tajima enters into the designations of most of his descendants.

3. In the " Chronicles" *Morosuke*, and elsewhere *Morosugi*. The etymology of these names is obscure except that of the last-mentioned, which signifies "many cryptomerias."

4. *Hi-ne* may perhaps signify "wondrous lord."

5. The meaning of this name is obscure, but that of *Hina-rashi-hime* in Sect. XXVI (Note 19) may be compared.

6. See Sect. LXXIV, Note 1.

7. *Hi-taka* may signifiy either "sun-height " or "wondrous height."

8. This name signifies "pure prince."

9. As usual, it is not the actual word Deity that is used, but the Auxiliary Numeral for Deities.

10. *Tagima* is the name of a place, not to be confounded with the province of Tajima. The signification of *mehi* is quite obscure.

11. *Suga* may either be the name of place in Tajima, as proposed

by Motowori, or identical with the Suga of Sect. XIX. The meaning of *Morowo* is obscure.

12. The signification of this name is obscure. But Suga, Kama, and Yura are apparently the names of places.

13. *Kadzuraki no Taka-nuka-hime.* Kadzuraki is the name of a department, and Takanuka that of a place in that department, in the province of Yamato.

14. Literally, "ancestress." But see Sect. XXII, Note 4. It will be remembered that *Okinaga-tarashi-hime* was the Empress Jin-go.

15. Literally, "treasures of jewels."

16. Or, "beads."

17. *I.e.*, a scarf to raise the waves and a scarf to still the waves, a scarf to raise the wind and a scarf to still the wind. *Conf.* the magic scarfs mentioned near the beginning of Sect. XXIII, by waving which the Deity Master-of-the-Great-Land (*Oho-kuni-nushi*) kept off the snakes, the wasps and the centipedes.

18. This seems to be the signification of the original terms *oki tsu kagami* and *hi tsu kagami*, but we are not hereby helped to a very clear understanding of the nature of the articles which the author ment to describe. The parallel passage of the "Chronicles" tells us of a "sun, mirror." Indeed it enumerates the "eight precious treasures" in a manner that diverges a great deal from the account given in these "Records."

19. Or, the "Eight-fold Great Deity." As has already frequently been remarked, the distinction which we so rigorously draw between Singular and Plural does not occupy the Japanese mind, and "eight" and "eight-fold" are taken to mean much the same thing. In the following sentence we find these eight deities (or this eight-fold deity) spoken of in such a manner as to necessitate the use of the Singular Number in the translation. Motowori supposes that they (or he) took the form of a young man (as in several other legends) to become the father of the Goddess mentioned in the text.···*Idzushi* seems to signify "wonderful stone."

So this Deity had a daughter whose name was the Deity Maiden-of-Idzushi.[1] So eighty Deities wished to 262 obtain this Maiden-of-Idzushi in marriage, but none of them could do so.[2] Hereupon there were two Deities, brothers, of whom the elder was called the Youth-of-the-Glow-on-the-Autumn-Mountains,[3] and the younger was named the Youth-of-the-Haze-on-the-Spring-Mountains.[4] So the elder brother said to the younger brother: "Though I beg for[5] the Maiden of Idzushi, I cannot obtain her in marriage. Wilt thou [be able] to obtain her?" He answered, saying: "I will easily obtain her." Then the elder brother said: "If thou shalt obtain this maiden, I will take off my upper and lower garments, and distil liquor in a jar of my own height,[6] and prepare all the things of the mountains and of the rivers[7] [and give them to thee] in payment of the wager." Then the younger brother told his mother everything that the elder brother had said. Forthwith the mother, having taken wistaria-fibre, wove and sewed in the space of a single night an upper garment and trowsers, and also socks and boots, and likewise made a bow and arrows, and clothed him in this upper garment, trowsers, 263 etc., made him take the bow and arrows, and sent him to the maiden's house, where both his apparel and the bow and arrows all turned into wistaria-blossoms. Thereupon the Youth-of-the-Haze-on-the-Spring-Mountains hung up the bow and arrows in the maiden's privy. Then, when the Maiden-of-Idzushi, thinking the blossoms strange, brought them [home, the Youth-of-the-Haze-on-

the-Spring-Mountains ] followed behind the maiden into
the house, and forthwith wedded her. So she gave birth
to a child.[8]  Then he spoke to his elder brother, saying:
"I have obtained the Mayden-of-Idzushi." Thereupon
the elder brother, vexed that the younger brother should
have wedded her, did not pay the things he had wager-
ed.  Then when [the younger brother] complained to his
mother, his august parent replied, saying: "During my
august life the Deities indeed are to be well imitated;
moreover it must be because he imitates mortal men[9]
that he does not pay those things." Forthwith, in her
anger with her elder child, she took a jointed bamboo[10]
from an island in the River Idzushi, and made a coarse
basket with eight holes,[11] and took stones from the
river, and mixing them with brine, wrapped them in the
leaves of the bamboo[12] and caused this curse to be
spoken:[13]   "Like unto the becoming green of these
bamboo-leaves, [do thou] become green and wither! 264
Again, like unto the flowing and ebbing of this brine,[14]
[do thou] flow and ebb! Again, like unto the sinking
of these stones, [do thou] sink and be prostrate!"
Having caused this curse to be spoken, she placed [the
basket] over the smoke.[15] Therefore the elder brother
dried up, withered, sickened, and lay prostrate[16] for the
space of eight years. So on the elder brother entreating
his august parent with lamentations and fears, she forthwith caused the curse to be reversed.[17] Thereupon his
body became sound[18] as it had been before. (This is the
origin of the term "a divine wager.payment.")[19]

---

1. *Idzushi-wotome no kami.*
2. Literally "eighty Deities wished to obtain this Maiden of Idzushi,
but none could wed (her)." But the sense is that given in the translation.

3. *Aki-yama no shita-bi-wotoko.* The explanation of the name is that given by Motowori (following Mabuchi), who sees in it a reference to the ruddy brilliance of the leaves, which is so marked a feature of the Japanese woods in autumn. The Chinese characters used have, indeed, the signification of the lower ice of the autumn mountains; but "lower ice" may well be simply phonetic in this case.

4. *Haru-yama no kasumi-wotoko.*

5. In Japanese *kohedomo*, written with the characters 雖乞. Perhaps Motowori is right in supposing this Verb to have been originally identical with *kofuru*, "to love" (戀) whose corresponding form is *kofuredomo*. If so, the author may have meant to make his hero say, though I love the maiden, etc." But it is better to be guided by the characters, and to suppose that he referred to the request made to her mother to grant her to him.

6. Literally, "compute the height of my person and distil liquor in a jar."

7. *I.e.,* all the valuable produce of the chase and of the fisheries, such as are perpetually mentioned in the Shinto "Rituals" as being presented to the gods, Thus in the "Service of the Goddess of Food" (see Mr. Satow's translation in Vol. VII, Pt. IV, p. 414 of these "Transactions,") we read that the worshipper offered: "as to things which dwell in the mountains—things soft of hair and things rough of hair; as to things which grow in the great-field-plain—sweet herbs and bitter herbs; as to things which dwell in the blue-sea-plain—things wide of fin and things narrow of fin, down to weeds of the offing and weeds of the shore."

8. Literally, "one child."

9. The·Japanese original of the words here unavoidably rendered by "mortal men" in order to mark the antithesis to the word "Deities," has been more literally translated by "living people" in an earlier passage of the work (see Sect. IX, Note 17). The signification of the entire sentence is: "During my lifetime, thy brother should be careful to imitate the upright conduct of the gods. For if, instead of doing so, he be dishonest and untruthful as are the sons of men, it will be at his own peril."

10. Or, according to the more usual reading, "a one-jointed bamboo;" but in either case the meaning is obscure. Motowori, who adopts the reading that has been followed in the translation, suggests that the expression may simply be a periphrasis for the bamboo in general.

11. 八目荒籠. Motowori remarks that the word "eight" in this

place (where, to indicate a considerable number we should rather expect "eighty") is curious, and he surmises that 八 may be an error for 大. "large." The word "coarse" itself is sufficient to show that the apertures left in the plaiting of the basket were large.

12. *Scil.* of which the basket was woven.

13. *Scil.* by her younger son.

14. In this case, as Motowori remarks, it is the sea-water that is intended to be spoken of, whereas the allusion in the previous sentence is to hard salt. But the Japanese language uses the same word for both, and the same Chinese character is here also used in both contexts. For this curse *conf.* Sect. XL (Note 18 *et. seq.*) and Sect. XLI.

15. *Scil.* of the furnace (kitchen) in the younger brother's house, as Motowori suggests.

16. The text has the character 枯, which signifies "to wither" or "dry up" (spoken of trees). But the translator agrees with Motowori in considering it to be in all probability an error for 臥, "to be prostrate; and in any case it could not here be rendered by either of the verbs "dry up" or "wither" without introducing into the English version a tautology which does not exist in the Japanese original.

17. Such seems to be the meaning of the obscure original *sono tokohi-do wo kahesashimeki* (令返其詛戸). Motowori would understand it in a rather more specialized sense to signify that "she caused the implement of the curse (*i.e.*, the basket) to be taken away,"

18. Literally, "was pacified."

19. Or, if we take 言 in the text as equivalent to 事, "this is the origin of "divine water-payments."

---

[SECT. CXVII.—EMPEROR Ō-JIN (PART XVI.—GENEALOGIES).]

Again this Heavenly Sovereign Homuda's[1] august child King Wake-nuke-futa-mata wedded his mother's younger sister Momo-shiki-iro-be,[2] another name for whom was Her Augustness Oto-hime-ma-wake-hime,[3] and begot children: Oho-iratsuko,[4] another name for whom 265 was King Ohohodo;[5] next her Augustness Osaka-no-oho-naka-tsu-hime: next Tawi-no-naka-tsu-hime;[7] next Tamiya-no-naka-tsu-hime;[8] next Fujihara-no-koto-fushi-no-ira-tsume;[9] next Queen Torime;[10] next King Sane.[11] (Seven Kings [and Queens].[12]) So King Oho-hodo (was the ancestor of the Dukes of Mikuni,[13] the Dukes of Hata,[14] the Dukes ef Okinaga,[15] the Dukes of Sakahito of Sakata,[16] the Dukes of Yamaji,[17] the Dukes of 266 Meta in Tsukushi,[18] and the Dukes of Fuse )[19] Again King Netori wedded his younger half-sister the Lady Mihara, and begot children: King Naka-tsu-hiko;[20] next King Iwa-shiha.[21] (Two Kings.) Again the child of King Kata-shiha[22] was King Kuni.[23]

---

1. *I.e.*, the Emperor O-jin's.

2. The import of this compound is not clear.

3. *I.e.*, "the younger princess, the truly young princess."

4. *I.e.*, "the great lord."

5. *Oho-hodo no miko.* The signification of *Oho-hodo* is obscure. Motowori surmises it to have been originally the name of a place.

6. *I.e.*, "the great middle princess of Osaka. Osaka is the name of a place in Yamato. The word "middle" should by the analogy of other such genealogies indicate the fact that this princess was the fourth child out of seven. Here however she is mentioned second, and the same designation is applied to the two next daughters. There is evidently some confusion in the tradition.

7. *I.e.*, "the middle princess of Tawi,"—a place in Kahachi.

8. *I.e.*, the middle princess of Tamiya.

9. *I.e.*, "the lady Koto-fushi of Fuji-hara." But the meaning of *Koto-fushi* is obscure, and Motowori surmises it to be an alternative or corrupt form of *Sotohoshi*. (For the celebrated princess of the latter name see Sect. CXXXVII, Note 9.) Fujihara is the name of a place in Yamato, and signifies "wistaria-moor."

10. *Torime no miko.* This name is obscure.

11. *Sane no miko.* Motowori believes *sane* to stand erroneously for *sami*; but both forms are obscure.

12. The Japanese word includes both genders,

13. *Mikuni no kimi.*  *Mikuni* is the name of a well-known place in the province of Echizen.  It signifies "three countries."

14. *Hata no kimi.*  There are several places called Hata, and it is not known which of them is here intended.  The signification of the name is also uncertain.

15. *Okinaga no kimi.*  See Sect. LXII, Note 31.

16. *Sakata no Saka-bito no kimi.*  This is Motowori's restoration of an apparently corrupt text.  Sakata and Sakabito are both taken to be names of places, the first of a district in Afumi, the second of a place in Settsu.  *Sakabito* (酒人) seems a very curious compound for the name of a place.  Moreover the double title is unusual, and it may be thought that the word "Dukes" has fallen out of the text, and that in reality two families were intended to be spoken of.

17. *Yamaji no kimi.*  *Yamaji* ("mountain road") is supposed by Motowori to be the name of a place,—perhaps in the province of Higo.

18. *Tsukushi no Meta no kimi.*  Tsukushi is the old name of the whole of the South-Western island of the Japanese archipelago and Meta the name of a place in the province of Hizen in that island.  The etymology of Meta is uncertain.

19. *Fuse no kimi.*  Fuse is the name of uncertain import found in several provinces.  It is not known which is meant to be here designated.

20. *Naka-tsu-hiko no miko,* i.e., "the middle prince," a designation which would lead one to expect to find mention of an elder brother.

21. *Iwashima no miko.*  Iwashima seems to be the name of a place, but the signification of *Iha* (not to be confounded with *iha* "stone" or "rock") is altogether obscure.

22. *Katashiha no miko.*  This prince has not been mentioned in the previous genealogies, which is curious.  Katashiha is the name of a place in Chikuzen, and signifies "hard rock."

23. *Kunu no miko.*  Kunu is altogether obscure.

[SECT. CXVIII.—EMPEROR Ō-JIN (PART XV.—HIS AGE AND

PLACE OF BURIAL).]

The august years of this Heavenly Sovereign Homuda
were altogether one hundred and thirty. His august
mausoleum is on the mound of Mofusu[1] at Wega in
Kafuchi.

---

1. Or, as Motowori reads it, *Mofushi.* The etymology is uncertain.
*Wega* has already appeared in Sect. CIII (Note 3). The Old Printed
Edition and some Manuscripts have at the conclusion of this volume
the following note: 百舌鳥陵也. "It is the mausoleum of Mozu." But
Mozu is in the province of Idzumi, and all the later editions discard this
note as an interpolation.

# VOL. III.[1]

His Augustness Oho-sazaki dwelt in the palace of Takatsu[2] at Naniha, and ruled the Empire. This Heavenly Sovereign wedded (the Empress[3]) Her Augustness Iha-no-hime,[4] daughter of Kadzuraki-no-sotsu-biko,[5] and begot august children : His Augustness Ohoye-no-izaho-wake ;[6] next the Middle King of the Inlet of Sumi ;[7] next His Augustness Midzu-ha-wake of Tajihi ;[8] next His August-ness the Noble Wo-asadzuma-no-waku-go[9] (four Deities.) Again he wedded Princess Kami-naga, daughter of the Duke of Muragata in Himuka, as mentioned above,[10] and begot august children : Hatabi-no-oho-iratsuko,[11] another 268 name for whom was the King of Great Kusaka ;[12] next Hatabi-no-waki-iratsume,[13] another name for whom was Her Augustness Princess Nagahi,[14] and another name was Her Augustness Waka-kusaka-be.[15] (Two Deities.) Again he wedded his younger half-sister Yata-no-waki-iratsume.[16] Again he wedded his younger half-sister Uji-no-waki-iratsume. These two Deities had no august children. Altogether the august children of this Heavenly Sovereign Oho-sakaki [ numbered ] in all six Deities, (Five Kings and one Queen). So His Augustness Izaho-wake [ was he who afterwards ] ruled the Empire. Next His Augustness Tajihi-no midzu-ha-wake likewise ruled the Empire. Next His Augustness the Noble Oh-asadzuma-no-waku-go like-wise ruled the Empire.[17]

---

1. Literally, " lower volume " (there being three in all). See Author's Preface, Note 1.

2. *I.e.*, " high port."

3. Motowori surmises that the reason why the characters signifiying "Empress" are in all the text here written in small characters is on account of this personage not having been of Imperial birth.

4. *I.e.,* "the rock princess." Motowori supposes the name to be indicative of prosperity and long life.

5. See Sect. LXI, Note 55.

6. *I.e.,* "the elder brother lord Izaho," the latter name being of uncertain import.

7. *Sumi-no-ye-no-naka-tsu-miko.* Both the phrase "middle king" and the Inlet of Sumi have been already commented on.

8. *Tajihi no midzu-ha-wake.* Tajihi is the name of a place in Kahachi. The traditional origin of its application to this will be found in Motowori's Commentary, Vol. XXXV, p. 6. *Midzu-ha-wake* probably means "the lord with the beautiful teeth."

9. *Wo-asadzuma-no-waku-go no sukune.* Asadzuma is the name of a place in Yamato, and *wo* (though written 男) seems to be the slightly Honorific Prefix *wo* (小) whose proper signification is "small." *Waku-go* means "younger child."

10. See Sect. CVII.

11. *I.e.,* "the great lord of Hatabi." *Hatabi* is altogether obscure.

12. *Oho-kusaka no miko.* For *Kusaka* see Sect. CI, Note 2.

13. *I.e.,* "the young lady of Hatabi." Conf. Note 11.

14. *Nagahi-hime.* This name is obscure.

15. *Kusaka-be* is an alternative form of *Kusaka.* The compound therefore signifies "young princess of Kusaka."

16. This name and the following have already appeared in the genealogies of the preceding reign (Sect. CIV.)

17. These were the Emperors Ri-chiu, Han-zei, and In-giyo.

---

[SECT. CXX.—EMPEROR NIN-TOKU (PART II.—VARIOUS DEEDS).]

In the august reign of this Heavenly Sovereign the Kadzuraki Tribe[1] was established as the august proxy of the Empress, Her Augustness Iha-no-hime. Again the Mibu

Tribe[2] was established as the august proxy of the Heir Apparent, His Augustness Izaho-wake. Again the Tajihi Tribe[3] was established as the august proxy of His Augustness Midzuna-wake. Again the Oho-kusaka Tribe[4] was 269 established as the august proxy of King Oho-kusaka, and the Waka-kusaka Tribe[5] was established as the august proxy of King Waga-kusake-be. Again people from Hada were set to labour, and the embankment at Mamuta[6] and also the granaries of Manuta were made. Again the Pool of Wani[7] and the Pool of Yosemi were made. Again the Naniha Channel[8] was dug, and [the waters of the rivers] led to the sea. Again the Wobashi Channel[9] was dug. Again the port of the inlet of Sumi[10] was established.

---

1. *Kadzuraki be.* For Kadzuraki see Sect. LV, Note 1.

2. *Mibu-be.* Motowori quotes approvingly a derivation of the "gentile name" of Mibu from *Bi-fuku-mon* (美福門), the name of a gate which the first bearer of the name is related to have constructed. Taking into account the letter-changes which occurred in older times in the passage of words from Chinese into Japanese, the etymology is plausible enough.

3. *Tajihi-be.* Tajihi is the name of a place in Kahachi, and is of uncertain origin.

4. *Oho-kusaka-be.* This tribe of course took its name simply from that of Prince Oho-kusaka.

5. *Waka-kusaka-be.* A similar observation to that in the last applies to this name.

6. See Sect. LIII, Note 1.

7. *Wani no ike*, in the province ef Kahachi. *Wani* signifies "crocodile," and it was also the name of the Korean personage mentioned in Sect. CX (Note 6). But the reason why the Pool here spoken of was so called does not appear. The Pool of Yosami has already been mentioned in Sect. LXII (Note 85). Motowori supposes that it must have dried up during the interim.

8. *Naniha no hori-ye.* Motowori tells us that the regularization of

the channels of the Yodo and Yamato Rivers, whose mouths nearly meet at this point with various intersecting†branches, is what is here intended to be referred to.

9. *Wobashi no ye.* *Wo-bashi* (" little bridge ") is the name of a village in the†province of Settsu.

10. *Suminoye no tsu.* Close of Naniha; it is the modern *Sumiyoshi.* Conf. Sect. X, Note 22.

---

[SECT. CXXI.—EMPEROR NIN-TOKU [PART III.—HE REMITS
THE TAXES).]

Thereupon the Heavenly Sovereign, ascending a lofty mountain and looking on the land all round, spoke, saying : " In the whole land there rises no smoke ; the land is all poverty-stricken. So I remit[1] all people's taxes and[ [forced labour] from now till three years [ hence. ] " Therefore the great palace became dilapidated, and the rain leaked in everywhere ; but no repairs were made. The rain that leaked in was caught in troughs,[2] and [the inmates] removed from [its reach] to places where there was no leakage. When later [the Heavenly Sovereign]] looked on all the land, the smoke was abundant in the land. So finding the people rich, he now exacted taxes and forced labour. Therefore the peasantry[3] ¡prospered, and did not suffer from forced labour. So in praise of that august reign, it was called the reign of the Emperor-Sage.[4]

---

1. Motowori's reading of this Verb in the Imperative Mood (as if containing an order addressed by the monarch to his ministers) seems less natural than the order reading in the Indicative, which accordingly the translator has followed.

2. There is uncertainty as to the exact character in the original.

But the older editions read it as the Japanese word *hako*, "boxes." while Motowori prefers *hi*, "tubes." "Troughs" seems to conciliate both views, and to be also appropriate to the use mentioned in the text.

3. Or simply, "the people." But the expression 百姓 is generally used in Japanese of the peasantry only.

4. 聖帝; If, following most texts, we omitted the final character 世, "reign," the English translation would be "in praise of that august reign, [the Heavenly Sovereign] was called the Emperor-Sage."

---

[SECT. CXXXII.—EMPEROR NIN-TOKU (PART IV.—HE LOVES PRINCESS KURO).]

His Empress, Her Augustness Iha-no-hime, was exceedingly jealous. So the concubines employed by the Heavenly Sovereign could not even peep inside the palace; and if anything happened,[1] [the Empress] stamped with jealousy. Then the Heavenly Sovereign, hearing of the regular beauty of Princess Kuro,[2] daughter of the Suzerain of Ama in Kibi,[3] and having sent for her, employed her. But she, afraid of the Empress's jealousy, fled down to her native land. The Heavenly Sovereign, gazing from an upper story upon Princess Kuro's departure by boat upon the sea, sang saying:

"In the offing there are rows of small boats. My wife Masadzuko of Kurozaki goes down towards her [native] land."[4]

So the Empress was very angry on hearing this august Song, and sent people to the great strand[5] to drive Princess Kuro ashore, and chase her away on foot.[6] Thereupon the Heavenly Sovereign, for love of Princess Kuro, deceived the Empress, saying that he wanted to see the Island of Ahaji.[7] And when he made his progress and was in the Island of Ahaji, he, gazing afar, sang saying:

> "When, having departed from the point
> of wave-beaten Naniha, I look at the
> country,—the Island of Aha, the Is-
> land of Onogoro, and also the Island
> of Ajimasa are visible. The Island of
> Saketsu is visible."[8]

Forthwith passing on from that island, he made a progress to the land of Kibi. Then Her Augustness Princess Kuro made him grandly reside at a place among the mountain-fields,[9] and presented to him great august food, When for this [purpose] she plucked cabbage in that place to boil into great august soup, the Heavenly Sovereign went to the place where the maiden was plucking the cabbage, and sang, saying:

> "Oh! how delightful it is to pluck
> with a person of Kibi the cabbage
> sown in the mountain fields!"[10]

When the Heavenly Sovereign made his progress up,[11] Princess Kuro presented an august[12] Song saying:

> "Even though the west wind blow up
> towards Yamato, and the clouds part,
> and we be separated, shall I forget
> [thee]?"[13]

273  Again she sang, saying:

> "Whose spouse is it that goes towards
> Yamato? Whose spouse is it that
> creeps from beneath like hidden water?"[14]

---

1. Motowori shows by collating various passages in other ancient works that this is the probable signification of the curious expression in

the original, *kotodateba* (言立者 for 事立者). The reference of course is to the occurrence of anything noteworthy among the concubines, such as the birth of a son, etc.

2. *Kuro-hime*, i.e, "black princess," probably meaning "black-haired princess."

3. *Kibi no Ama no atahe*. Of this family nothing is known. *Ama* signifies "fisherman." *Kibi* is the name of a province.

4. Thus interpreted (according to Moribe), the general sense of the Song is quite clear. The word *Masadzuko*, considered by Moribe to be one of the names of Princess Kuro, is however not so understood by Motowori, who is inclined to see in it rather an Honorific description of her. *Kurozaki* likewise (*i.e.*, "black cape," the word *kuro* seemingly containing an allusion to the name of the Princess) is but the best of many emendations of the name as it stands in the text, viz., *Furozaya*. See Motowori's Commentary, Vol. XXXV. p. 33, for all the possible emendations proposed by him or his predecessors.

5. *Scil*, of the neighbourhood of Naniha. Or possible *Oho-ura* ("Great Strand") should be taken as the name of a place, though Motowori does not suggest such a view.

6. *I.e.*, to make her perform the journey on foot.

7. See Sect. V, Note 3.

8. Moribe, commenting on the import of this Song, says: Though the alleged reason was a tour of inspection, it was truly out of love for Princess Kuro that the Monarch had undertaken the journey. When her vessel could no longer be descried, he could still alas! see the islands that remained behind,—the Island of Aha and the Island of Ajimasa; he could still, alas! see the Islands of Onogoro and Saketsu. Alas for him left alone, parted from his love! Though he spoke not openly, those around him understood the under-current of his "words." —"Wave-beaten" is the accepted interpretation of *oshiteru ya* (or *oshi-teru*), the Pillow-Word for Naniha. For the Islands of Aha and Ono-goro see respectively Sect. IV, Note 5 and Sect. iii, Note 5. Of the Islands of Ajimasa and Saketsu nothing is known. *Ajimasa* is the name of a species of palm, the *Livistona sinensis*, and Motowori supposes that one of the islands in that neighbourhood may anciently have received its name from the palm-trees growing on it. Palms of any kind are, however, not very common in Japan, and seem only to grow when specially cultivated.

9. Motowori thinks we should in this place understand the word *yamagata* (for *yama-agata*) as the name of a place. But in the Song

which immediately follows, it must certainly be taken in its etymological sense of "mountain-fields," and it seems therefore quite inconsistent to translate it differently here. Moreover it is allowed that no such place as Yamagata in Kibi is anywhere made mention of.

10. The import of this Song is perfectly clear, "the person of Kibi" being of course the Imperial poet's lady-love.

11. *I.e.*, was about to start back to the capital, which was in the province of Settsu.

12. This Honorific seems so out of place (seeing that it is not applied to the Emperor's own Songs given in this Section), that it is supposed by the commentators to be an erroneous addition to the text.

13. We might also translate thus: "Even though we be separated, as the clouds that part owing to the west wind blowing up towards Yamato, etc.;"—for the initial lines of the poem which contain the allusion to the wind and to the clouds are simply a Preface, and their import may therefore at will be either considered separately, or else made continuous with that of the rest of the poem.

14. The meaning of this Song1 is: "Whose spouse is it that returns to Yamato? Whose spouse is it that comes thus secretly to make love to me, like a stream flowing underground?"—The allusion contained in the twice repeated words "whose spouse" is of course to the Empress. The poetess, full of tenderness or the Emperor, regrets for his sake, as well as for her own, that he should be the husband of so jealous a wife. "Hidden water" is the accepted interpretation of the Pillow-Word *kontoridzu no*, which is with apparent reason supposed to be a contraction of *komori-midzu no*.

-----

[SECT. CXXIII.—EMPEROR NIN-TOKU (PART V.—THE EMPRESS RETIRES TO YAMASHIRO).]

After this time the Empress made a progress to the land of Ki in order to pluck aralia-leaves for a copious feast;[1] and in the mean while the Heavenly Sovereign wedded Yata-no-waki-iratsume. Hereupon, when the Empress was returning in her august vessel loaded full of aralia-leaves, a coolie from Kozhima[2] in the land of Kibi, who was in the service of the Superintendent of the Water-Directors,[3] being on his way off to his own country, met at the great passage[4] of Naniha the vessel of a lady of the train[5] who had got behind, and forthwith told her, saying: "The Heavenly Sovereign has 274 recently[6] wedded Yata-no-waki-iratsume, and plays with her day and night. It must probably be because the Empress has not heard of this thing, that she quietly makes progress for pleasure." Then the lady of the train, having heard this narrative, forthwith pursued and reached the august vessel, and reported everything exactly as the coolie had told it. Hereupon the Empress, greatly vexed and angry, threw away into the sea all the aralia-leaves which she had put on board the august vessel. So the place [ where she did so ] is called by the name of Cape Mitsu.[7] Forthwith without entering the palace, but taking her august vessel [ from it ][8] and ascending the channel[9] against the current, she made a progress up into Yamashiro by the river.[10] At this time she sang, saying:

"Oh! the river of Yamashiro where the seedlings grow in succession! As I ascend, ascend the river, oh! on the bank of the river [ there ] stands growing a *sashibu*!— a *sashibu*-tree; below it stands growing a broad-foliaged five hundred [ -fold branching ] true camellia-tree; oh! he who is brilliant like its blossoms, widely powerful like its foliage, is the great lord.[11]

Forthwith going round by Yamashiro,[12] and arriving at 275 the entrance of the Nsra Mountajn,[13] she sang, saying:

"Oh! the river of Yamashiro where the
seedlings grow in succession! As I ascend,
ascend to Miya, I pass Nara, I pass
Yamato with its shield of mountains; and
the country I fain would see is Takamiya
in Kadzuraki, the [neighbourhood of my
home."[14]

276    Having sung thus, she returned and entered for some
time into the house of a person from Kara[15] named
Nurinomi[16] at Tsutsuki.[17]

---

1. See Sect. CVII, Note 7.

2. *I.e.*, " small island." It is first mentioned in Sect V (Note 29).

3. See Sect. XLVII, Note 18.

4. *Oho watari.* The mouth of the River Yedo is meant to be designated by this name.

5. The original expression *kuru-bito-me* (倉人女) is obscure, being
met with nowhere else in Japanese literature. Motowori conjectures that
the function exercised by this lady was one connected with the Emperor's
privy purse.

6. The text has the character 皆, "all," which make no sense;
and Motowori (following Mabuchi) reasonably emends it to 比日, recently," " just now."

7. *Mitsu no saki.* *Mitsu,* signifying "three," is supposed by the
author to refer to the three-cornered leaves of the aralia (the name of
the latter being *mitsuna gashiha*)*;* but a more likely opinion is that
which would have us take mitzu as two words, in the sense of "august
harbour." In the parallel passage of the "Chronicles," we are told that
the place was called *Kashiha no watari, i.e.,* " Oak passage."

8. *I.e.,* going on up the river without stopping at Naniha where the
palace was.

9. *I.e.,* the artificial bed of the river mentioned in Sect. CXX,
Note, 8.

10. *I.e.,* the river Yodo.

11. The meaning of this Song is: "As I make my way up the river
by boat, I see a *sashibu* (the name of a tree which cannot now be identified), below which,—that is to say nearer to the water,—there grows a

camellia-tree, wide-spreading and full of blossoms. Ah! how the sight of the sturdy brilliant beauty of this camellia-tree brings back my lord and master to my mind!"—It must be remembered that in Japan the camellia-trees grow to a size far superior to that reached by their representatives in Europe. *Tsuginefu*, rendered according to the view taken by Motowori and Moribe by the phrase "where the seedlings grow in succession," is the Pillow-Word for Yamashiro, and its import is disputed. The interpretation here adopted considers it to refer to the regular succession of young trees planted on a mountain's side when a tract of older timber has been cut down. Mabuchi, in his "Dictionary of Pillow-Words," sees in it, on the contrary, a reference to the rising of peak upon peak in a mountainous district (*tsugi-ne fu*—次巓經). Both interpretations rest on the connection between this term and *yama*, the first half of the name of the province of Yamashiro, which it qualifies. "Five handred [-fold-branching]" and "true" are ornamental epithets applied by the poetess to the camellia-tree. Moribe would take the syllable *ma*, "true," in the sense of *ha*, "leaf;" but this seems less good.

12. For the straight road from Naniha in Settsu-to Nara in Yamato would have taken her through the province of Kafuchi, and not through Yamashiro.

13. *I.e.*, the pass or hill leading from the district of Sagara in Yamashiro to Nara in Yamato. For Nara see Sect. LXXII, Note 23.

14. This Song expresses the Empress's desire to return to her parental house at Takamiya in the district of Kadzuraki,—a desire which, however, her restless frame of mind did not allow her to fulfil.—The Pillow-Word for Yamashiro, which here recurs, has already been discussed in Note 11. There are two other Pillow-Words in this Song,—*awoniyoshi*, which is prefixed to Nara, and *wo-date* (or *wo-date-yama* according to the old reading, or *wo-date tatsu* according to another reading), which is prefixed to Yamato. The former of these is so obscure that, rather than attempt to render it into English, ths translator prefers to refer the student to the remarks of the various commentators,—Mabuchi *s.v.* in his "Dictionary of Pillow-Words," Motowori in his Commentary, Vol. XXXVI, pp. 22-24, and Moribe *in loco*. *Wodate* [*-yama*] seems to refer undoubtedly to the circle of mountains that guard the approach to the province of Yamato, and it has been rendered accordingly. The great difficulty of the Song lies in the line rendered "ascend to Miya," and the commentators from Keichiu downwards make all sorts of efforts to explain it. Moribe's view, according to which the word should be re-

garded as a familiar abbreviation of Takamiya, naturally used by one whose native place it was, seems the most acceptable. Motowori takes the line to signify: "When I ascend past the palace [of Naniha.]"

15. 韓, *i.e.*, Korea.

16. For *Nuri no omi*, i.e., "the Grandee of Nuri." Nuri is probably a corrupt form of some Korean name.

17. Or Tsudzuki, in Yamashiro. Etymology obscure.

---

[SECT. CXXIV.—EMPEROR NIN-TOKU (PART VI.—HE FOLLOWS THE EMPRESS INTO YAMASHIRO).]

The Heavenly Sovereign, having heard that the Empress had made a progress up by Yamashiro, made a person,— a retainer called by the name of Toriyama,[1]—give an august Song,[2] which said:

" Reach [ her ] in Yamashiro, Toriyama !
　　Reach [ her ] ! reach [ her ] ! Ah ! wilt thou
　　reach and meet my beloved spouse ?"[3]

Again he continued by despatching Kuchiko, Grandee of Wani,[4] and sang, saying:

" Wilt thou be without thinking even of the
　　Heart that is in the moor of Ohowiko, the
　　moor of Ohowiko, that is by Takaki at
　　Mimoro ?"[5]

Again he sang, saying:

" If indeed I had pillowed [ my head ] on the
　　white arm like the whiteness of the roots,
　　the great roots, that were beaten with
　　wooden hoes by the women of Yamashiro
　　where the seedlings grow in succession,
　　[ then ] mightest thou say, ' I know [ thee ]
　　not'. "[6]

So when the Grandee of Kuchiko was repeating this 278 august Song [to the Empress,] it was raining heavily. Then upon his, without avoiding the rain, coming and prostrating himself at the front door of the palace,[7] she on the contrary went out at the back door; and on his coming and prostrating himself at the back door of the palace, she on the contrary went out at the front door. Then, as he crept backwards and forwards on his knees in the middle of the court, the streams of water[8] reached to his loins. Owing to the grandee being clad in a garment dyed[9] green and with a red cord, the streams of water brushed against the red cord, and the green all changed to red colour. Now the Grandee of Kuchiko's younger sister Princess Kuchi[10] was in the service of the Empress.[11] So Princess Kuchi sang saying:

"Oh! how tearful is my lord-elder brother, saying things in the palace of Tsutsuki in Yamashiro!"[12]

Then when the Empress asked the reason,[13] she replied, saying: "He is my brother the Grandee of Kuchiko." Thereupon the Grandee of Kuchiko and also his younger sister Princess Kuchi and likewise Nurinomi [all] three took counsel [together,] and sent to report to the Heavenly 279 Sovereign, saying: "The reason of the Empress's progress is that there are [some] insects reared by Nurinomi,— strange insects changing in three ways,[14] once becoming creeping insects, once becoming cocoons,[15] and once becoming flying birds[16]—and it is only to go and look at them that she has entered into [Nurinomi's house.] She has no strange intentions."[17] When they had thus reported, the Heavenly Sovereign said: "That being so, I want to go and see [these insects,] as

I think [ they must be ] strange ; " [ and with these words ] he made a progress up from the great palace. When he entered into Nurinomi's house, Nurinomi, had already presented to the Empress the three-fold insects reared by him. Then the Heavenly Sovereign augustly stood at the door of the palace where the Empress dwelt, and sang, saying :

> "Pure as the great roots that were beaten
> with their wooden hoes by the women of
> Yamashiro where the seedings grow in
> succession : — it is because thou spokest
> tumultuously that I come in here [ with
> my retainers numerous ] as the more and
> more flourishing trees that I look across
> at. "[18]

280	These six Songs by the Heavenly Sovereign and by the Empress are Changing Songs which are Quiet Songs.[19]

---

1. This name signifies "bird-mountain." The commentators presume that it contains an allusion to the fact of its bearer being an Imperial courier.

2. This is the actual sense conveyed by the original 使舍人名謂鳥山人送御歌, and we naturally infer that Toriyama was made the bearer to the Empress of the following Song. The Song itself, however, is addressed not to her, but to Toriyama on his departure. On the other hand, the two poems which follow are evidently for the Empress, and it is impossible to suppose that the first messenger was not likewise intended to convey to her some poetic missive. All that we can do is to render the text as it stands, and to suppose it corrupt.

3. The meaning of this Song is:	"O Toriyama! pursue her into Yamashiro! I tremble at the thought of the possibility of thy not finding her."

4. *Wani no omi Kuchiko* (further on he is mentioned as *Kuchiko no omi*, i.e., "the Grandee [of] Kuchiko.") *Kuchi-ko* may be interpreted

to mean "mouth child" and Moribe thinks that this personage was so called on account of the verbal messages of which he was made the bearer. The translator would prefer to consider *ko* as an abbreviation of *hiko*, "prince," especially as the sister's name is *Kuchi-hime*, where the word *hime* must mean "princess."

5. This Song is so obscure that Motowori and Moribe differ completely as to its interpretation. The translator has followed Moribe, though by no means persuaded that the latter has hit on the proper signification. According to this view, the Emperor makes a pun on the word "heart," which is supposed to have been the name of a pool situated on the moor of Ohowiko near Takaki at Mimoro,—all names of places with which the Empress was familiar,—and reproaches her for having no thought of *his* heart which beats so lovingly for her. Motowori, on the other hand, thinks that the poem proper consists only of its last two lines (in the English translation they necessarily come first): "Wilt thou be without thinking even of the heart?"—and that all the rest is a "Preface" to the Pillow-Word *kimo-mukafu* by which the word *kokoro*, "heart," is preceded. As for *oho-wi-ko* and *takaki*, they are taken, not as names of places, but as common Nouns. According to this view of the structure of the Song, it ceases (with the exception of its last two lines) to have any rational signification, and it is needless to attempt to translate it for the English reader. Persons familiar with Japanese are therefore referred to Motowori's Commentary, Vol. XXXVI, pp. 34-36.

6. The meaning of this Song is: "If thou and I had not so long been spouses, then indeed mightest thou break with me, and declare that thou knowest me not. But how canst thou so far forget our wedded life as to desert me now?"···The "great root," *oho-ne*, is the modern *dai-kon* (*Raphanus sativus*), a kind of radish which is a favourite vegetable with the Japanese and is distinguished by its brilliantly white appearance. "Beaten" here signifies "dug up." The use of the Past Tense is curious. *Ko-guha*, here in accordance with Motowori's view rendered "wooden hoes," is interpreted by Moribe to mean "little hoes." "Where the seedlings grow in succession" is the English rendering of *tsugi-ne fu*, the Pillow-Word for Yamashiro (see Sect. CXXIII Note 11).

7. The Empress was lodging with a private individual, but her presence warrants the application of the term "palace" to his house.

8. It was raining too hard for the water to stop on the surface in the shape of puddles, so it streamed off in little rivulets.

9. Literally, "rubbed." See Introduction p. xxx. Instead of "green,"

we might equally well translate by "blue." The garment intended must be the upper garment or coat.

10. *Kuchi-hime.*

11. Literally, "respectfully served the Empress."

12. The meaning of these lines, which can only be called poetry because they are in metre, is plain: in them the speaker draws the Empress's attention to the pitiful condition of the messenger who is doing his best to deliver to her the Emperor's message. Probably the reading in our text has been corrupted; for that in the "Chronicles," which may be translated thus; "Oh! how tearful am I when I see my lord elder brother," etc,, is much preferable.

13. *Scil.* of her attendant thus taking the messenger's part.

14. Literally, "colours."

15. This is Motowori's conjectural restoration of the reading of this word, which in all the texts is hopelessly corrupt.

16. According to another reading, "flying insects."

17. *I.e.*, "she is not meditating any evil conduct."

18. The Song consists of two divisions, the first of which is but a Preface for the second, the pivot being formed by the word *sawa-sawa ni*, which has the meaning of "pure" "cool," or "refreshing," with reference to what precedes it, and the meaning of "tumultuously" (*sawa-sawa ni—sawagashiku*) when taken together with what follows. The difficulties which present themselves in the first division have all been explained in Note 11 to the last and and Note 6 to the present Section. The general sense of the second division is plain enough; but the precise application of the comparison to the "more and more flourishing tree" is obscure. Motowori's view has been adopted by the translator, and the words in brackets supplemented accordingly. Moribe prefers to consider that the reference is to the repeated visits first of the Emperor's messengers and afterwards of the Emperor himself The words "look across at" must be explained by supposing that the trees were in the neighbourhood of Nurinomi's house; they were shoots springing up from roots that had been cut down close to the ground.

19. The commentators thus explain these obscure expressions: "A Quiet Song is one which is sung to a tranquil tune. A Changing Song is one temporarily sung while the tone (mode ?) is changing." The six Songs in question must be supposed to have combined both characteristics.

[SECT. CXXV.—EMPEROR NIN-TOKU (PART VIII.—HE LOVES
YATA-NO-WAKI-IRATSUME).]

The Heavenly Sovereign, loving Yata-no-waki-iratsume,
deigned to send her an august Song. That Song said:

" Will the one sedge-stem of Yata, having
no children, wither as it stands? Poor
sedge-moor! Sedge-moor indeed is what
I may *say*—poor pure girl!"[1]

Then Yata-no-waki-iratsume replied in a Song, saying:

" Even though the one sedge stem of Yata
be alone, if the Great Lord say it is right
even though it be alone [it is right.]"[2]

So the Yata Tribe[3] was established as the august
proxy of Yata-no-waki-iratsume.

---

1. In this Song the Emperor condoles with his mistress on her
childlessness: " Will the single sedge on the moor of Yata die without
leaving any offspring? Sedge, indeed! Yes, sedge is the term I use for
my metaphor, but what is in my thoughts is the girl I love."—There is
in the original a *jeu-de-mots*, not capable of translation into English, between *suge* or *suga*, " sedge, and *sugashi* pure."

2. The girl replies: " Even though I be childless, I care not if
my lord cares not."

3. *Yata-be.*

---

[SECT. CXXVI.—EMPEROR NIN-TOKU (PART VIII.—DEATH OF
KING HAYABUSA-WAKE AND QUEEN MEDORI).]

Again the Heavenly Sovereign begged for his younger
half-sister Queen Medori, using as middle-man his younger
brother King Haya-busa-wake. Then Queen Medori[281]
spoke to King Hayabusa-wake, saying: " Owing to the

violence of the Empress, [ the Heavenly Sovereign ] has
not deigned to take Yata-no-waki-iratsume [ into the
Palace. ]    So I will not respectfully serve him.    I will
become the wife of Thine Augustness. " Forthwith they
wedded each other, wherefore King Hayabusa-wake made
no report [ to the Heavenly Sovereig.n[1] ]    Then the
Heavenly Sovereign, going straight to the place where
Queen Medori dwelt, stood on the door-sill of the palace.
Hereupon, Queen Medori being at her loom, was weaving
garments.    Then the Heavenly Sovereign sang saying :

> " Oh !  for whom may be the garments that
> my Great Lady Medori weaves ? "[2]

Queen Medori replied in a Song saying :

> " For an august veil for the high-going
> Falcon-Lord. "[3]

So the Heavenly Sovereign, perceiving her feelings,
returned into the palace.    At this time[4] when her husband
King Hayabusa-wake came, his wife Queen Medori sang,
saying :

> " The lark flies to heaven.  Oh ! high-going
> Falcon-Lord, catch the wren. "[5]

282    The Heavenly Sovereign, hearing this Song,[6] forthwith
raised an army, wishing to slay King Hayabusa and
Queen Medori, who then fled away together, and ascended
Mount Kurahashi.[7]    Thereupon King Hayabusa-wake sang,
saying :

> " Owing to the steepness of ladder-like
> Mount Kurahashi, being unable to clamber
> [ up ] the rocks, oh ! she takes my hand ! "[8]

Again he sang, saying :

> " Though ladder-like Mount Kurahashi be

> steep, it is not steep when I ascend it
> with my younger sister. "

So when they fled thence, and reached Soni in Uda,[9] the Imperial[10] army pursued, overtook, and slew them.

---

1. *Scil.* of the success of his mediation.

2. Or, "for whom is the loom [employed], with which my Great Lady Medori weaves?—The word *hata* in Archaic Japanese signifies both "garment" and the instrument which is used to weave a garment, i.e. a "loom" (服 and 機). In later times the second meaning has prevailed to the exclusion of the first.

3. There is here a play on the name of the Queen's paramour Hayabusa-wake, which signifies "Falcon-Lord" as in the translation— The parallel passage of the "Chronicles" gives these two Songs as a single one which is put into the mouth of Queen Medori's handmaidens, —is a more acceptable version of the incident.

4. Motowori suspects that there is here an error in the text, which should, according to him, read: "After this."

5. The gist of this Song is an instigation to murder the Emperor (whose name was *Oho-sazaki, i.e.,* "Great Wren." Conf. Sect. CIV, Note 18), addressed to the singer's husband (whose name was *Hayabusa-wake, i.e.,* "Falcon Lord"). But the allusion to the lake remains obscure. Keichiu suggests that it is simply mentioned as a term of comparison for the falcon's power of flight, while Motowori opines that the meaning rather is: "The lark flies so high up to heaven that it would be hard to catch it; but the wren is an easy prey."

6. Viz., as may be supposed, repeated by some fourth person.

7. *Kurahashi-yama,* in Yamato.

8. The Song, like the next, is too clear to stand in need of explanation. "Ladder-like" is an attempt to render the force of the Pillow-Word *hashi-tate.* See Mabuchi's "Dictionary of Pillow-Words," *s.v.,* for the exact force attributed to it by Mabuchi.

9. For Uda see Sect. XLVI, Note, 14. The etymology of Soni is equally obscure.

10. The character 御, though read by the commentators with the usual Japanese Honorific *mi,* "august," has here its proper Chinese signification of "Imperial."

[SECT. CXXVII.—EMPEROR NIN-TOKU (PART VIII.—QUEEN
MEDORI'S ARMLET).]

Chief Ohotate of Yamabe,[1] who was the generalissimo
of that army, took the jewelled armlet which was wound
round Queen Medori's august arm, and gave it to his
own wife.    After this time, when a copious feast[2] was
to be held, the women of the various families all went
to court.    Then the wife of Chief Ohotate came with
that Queen's jewelled armlet wound round her own arm.
283 Thereupon the Empress, Her Augustness Iha-no-hime,
herself took the oak-leaves[3] [full] of great august liquor
and graciously gave them to the women of the various
families.    Then the Empress, recognizing the jewelled
armlet, gave [the wearer] no oak-leaf [-full] of great
august liquor, but forthwith sent her away;[4] and sending
for the husband, Chief Ohotate, said: "Owing to that
King and Queen's impropriety, [the Emperor] deigned
to send them away.    This was nothing strange.    And a
slave such as thou despoils of the jewelled armlet that
was wound round her august arm the body of his lady
[that was still] warm, and gives it to his own wife!"—
and forthwith he was condemned to death.[5]

---

1.    *Yamabe no Ohotate no murazhi.*    The "gentile name" was
*Yamabe no murazhi,* and the personal name *Ohotate,* though the confused
wording of this passage does not make it appear so.    *Yama-be* signifies
mountain (*i.e.,* hunters') tribe.    *Oho-tate* is "big shield."

2.    See Sect. CVII, Note 7.

3.    Or, perhaps rather "aralia-leaves" (*Conf.* Sect. CXXIII).

4.    Or, "had her dragged away."

5.    Literally, "was granted the punishment of death," or "[the
Emperor] deigned to condemn him to death."

[SECT. CXXVIII.—EMPEROR NIN-TOKU (PART IX.—A WILD-
GOOSE LAYS AN EGG).]

Another time, the Heavenly Sovereign, when about to
hold a copious feast,[1] made a progress to the Island of
Hime,[2] just when a wild-goóse had laid an egg on that
island. Then, sending for His Augustness the Noble Take-
uchi, he asked him in a Song about the laying of an egg by
a wild goose. This Song said :

> " Court Noble of Uchi ! thou indeed art a
> long-lived person. Hast thou [ever] heard
> of a wild-goose laying an egg in the land
> of Yamato ?"[3]

Hereupon the Noble Take-uchi spoke in a song, saying : 284

> " August Child of the high-shining Sun, it
> is indeed natural that thou shouldest
> deign to ask, it is indeed right that thou
> shouldest ask. I indeed am a long-lived
> person, [but] have not yet heard of a
> wild goose laying an egg in the land of
> Yamato."[4]

Having thus spoken, he was granted the august[5] lute
and sang saying :

> " Oh thou prince ! the wild goose must have
> laid the egg because thou wilt at last rule."[6]

This is a Congratulatory Incomplete Song.[7]

---

1. See Sect. CVII, 7.
2. *Hime-shima*, *i.e.*, " Princess Island." The name is supposed to
be connected with that of the goddess of Himegoso mentioned near the
end of Sect. CXIV, and first occurs in Sect. V (Note 33).
3. The wild-goose goes far north at the approach of spring, and the
translator is informed by Capt. Blakiston that the latter has not known

of any breeding even on the island of Yezo. The Emperor was therefore naturally astonished at so strange an occurrence as that of a wild-goose laying an egg in Yamato, and asks the Noble Take-uchi whether he had ever heard of the like of it before, Take-uchi being at that time more than two hundred years old (!) according to the chronology of the "Chronicles," and therefore the oldest and most experienced man in the Empire.—"Court Noble" represents the Japanese word *Aso* (for *Asomi*, believed by Motowori and Moribe to be derived from *a se omi* 吾兄臣, lit. "my elder brother minister" but used simply as a title). The words *Uchi* and *Yamato* are preceded in the original by their respective Pillow-Words *tamaki-haru* and *soramitsu*, whose force it is impossible to render in English, and whose origin indeed is obscure. The words rendered "laying an egg" are literally "giving birth to a child."

4. This Song is too clear to need explanation. As in the preceding one, Yamato is accompanied by the Pillow-Word *sora-mitsu*.

5. Or, "Imperial."

6. *I.e.*, say Motowori and Moribe, who refer this episode to a time previous to Nin-toku's accession, "The wild-goose has laid an egg in token of the future accession to the throne." The translator prefers the view expressed by Keichiu in his *Kō-Gan Shō*, and adopted in the "Explanation of the Songs in the Chronicles of Japan," that the words *tsuhi ni* "at last," must here be taken in the sense of "long," and the Song interpreted to mean "The wild-goose lays an egg as an omen that thy reign will be a long one." This view is supported by the story in the "Chronicles," which places the Song in the Emperor's fiftieth year and gives him thirty-six years of subsequent existence, thus making the prophecy amply fulfil itself, as one would expect that it should do in the pages of such a work. According to the other view, the text of the "Chronicles" calls for emendation.

7. *Hogi-uta no kata-uta.* For "Incomplete Song" see Sect. LXXXIX, Note 14.

[SECT. CXXIX.—EMPEROR NIN-TOKU (PART X.—A VESSEL IS
MADE INTO A LUTE).]

In this august reign there was a tall tree on the west
of the river Tsuki.[1] The shadow of this tree, on its
being struck by the morning sun, reached to the Island
o Ahaji:[2] and on its being struck by the evening sun,
it crossed Mount Takayasu.[3] So the tree was cut down
and made into a vessel, and a very swift-going vessel
it was. At the time, this vessel was called by the name
of Karanu.[4] So with this vessel the water of the Island
of Ahaji was drawn morning and evening, and presented
as the great august water.[5] The broken [pieces] of this
vessel were used [as fuel] to burn salt and the pieces
of wood that remained over from the burning were made
into a lute, whose sound re-echoed seven miles[6] [off]. So
[some one[7]] sang, saying:

> " Karanu was burnt [as fuel] for salt; the
> remainder was made into a lute; oh!
> when struck, it sounds like the wet
> plants standing rocked on the reefs in the
> middle of the harbour, the harbour of
> Yura."[8]

This is a Changing Song which is a Quiet song.[9]

1. This is Moribe's reading (given without any comment) of the
original characters 兔寸. Motowori pronounces them corrupt; but, having
no emendation to propose, simply leaves them without any *kana* reading.

2. See Sect. V, Note 3.

3. *Takayasu no yama*, in the province of Kahachi. The characters
with which the name is written signify " high and easy."

4. The significance of this name, written 枯野, remains obscure notwithstanding the efforts of the commentators to explain it.

5. *I.e.*, this vessel was used to bring over every morning and evening

the water for the Imperial household, which was drawn on the Island of Ahaji.

6. 里, the Chinese *li* Japanese *ri*. The length of the *ri* has varied greatly at different times and in different parts of the country. The modern standard Japanese *ri* is equivalent to about 2.44 English statute miles ; but Motowori supposes the *ri* of the epoch mentioned in our text to have been less than one-seventh of that distance.

7. In the " Chronicles " this story is placed in the reign of the Emperor O-jin, and the Song is attributed to that monarch.

8. In this Song the sound of the twanging of the lute that had been made from the remnant of the boat Karanu is compared to the rustling of the plants standing half out of water on the reefs in the harbour of Yura.—The compound word *kaki-hiku*, rendered by " struck," signifies literally " scratched and struck," the lute being struck with the nail. The onomatopoetic word *saya-saya*, of which " sound " is but a colourless equivalent, represents both the delightful ring of the lute and the rustling of the sea-plants. What plants are intended by the expression " wet plants " (*nadzu no ki*) is a point that has been much disputed. Moribe even thinks that the term is meant for the name of a particular species of (apparently) coral now found in the island of Hachijo. Yura is in the Island of Ahaji.

9. See Sect. CXXIV, Note 19.

---

[SECT. CXXX.—EMPEROR NIN-TOKU (PART XI.—HIS AGE AND

PLACE OF BURIAL.]

The august years of this Heavenly Sovereign were eighty-three. His august mausoleum is on the Ear-Moor of Mozu.[1]

---

1. *Mozu no mimi-hara.* The origin of this singular name is thus explained in the " Chronicle " (Emperor Nin-toku, 67th year, Winter, 10th Moon): " [The Emperor] made a progress to the moor of Ishidzu in Kafuchi to fix the site of his mausoleum. On the day when the construction of his mausoleum was begun, a deer suddenly ran out from the middle of the moor, rushed into the midst of the coolies, fell down, and

died. The suddenness of its death causing astonishment, its wound was looked for, whereupon a shrike came out of its ear, and flew away. So on looking into the ear, it was found to be all eaten away. So that is the reason why the place is called *Mozu no mimi-hara* (the Shrike's Ear-Moor.')"

---

[SECT. CXXXI.—EMPEROR RI-CHIU (PART I.—GENEALOGIES).]

His Augustness Iza-ho-wake dwelt in the palace of Wakasakura at Ihare,[1] and ruled the Empire. This Heavenly Sovereign wedded Her Augustness Princess Kuro,[2] daughter of the Noble of Ashida,[3] child of So- 287 tsu-biko of Kadzuraki.[4] and begot august children : King Oshiha of Ichinobe ;[5] next King Mima :[6] next his younger sister Awomi-no-iratsume,[7] another name for whom was Ichi-toyo-no-iratsume.[8]

---

1. For *Ihare* see Sect. XLIII, Note 26. *Waka-sakura* signifies "young cherry-tree." The origin of the name is traced, rightly or wrongly, to an incident mentioned in the "Chronicles" under the reign of this Emperor, 3rd year.

2. *Kuro-hime i.e.*, "black princess." The same name occurs several times, and has reference to the black hair of the person so designated.

3. *Ashida no sukune. Ashi-da* signifies "reed-moor." It is the name of a place in Yamato.

4. *Kadzuraki no So-tsu-biko.* For this name, which is here abbreviated, see Sect. LXI, Note 55.

5. *Ichinobe no Oshiha no miko.* Ichinobe is in the province of Yamashiro, and the name seems to mean "near the market." The name of *Oshiha* refers to the "uneven teeth" of this personage which are mentioned in Sect. CLXVII (near Note 5).

6. *Mima no miko.* The signification of this name is quite obscure.

7. *Awomi no iratsume. Awomi* is supposed by Motowori to be the name of a place.

8. *Ihitoyo no iratsume. Ihitoyo* is supposed by Motowori to be the name of a bird, perhaps a kind of owl.

[SECT. CXXXII.—EMPEROR RI-CHIU (PART II.—HE IS TAKEN
TO ISO-NO-KAMI).]

Originally, when dwelling at the palace of Naniha,
[the Heavenly Sovereign] on holding a copious feast
when at the great tasting,[1] was intoxicated with the
great august liquor, and fell greatly and augustly asleep.
Then his younger brother, King Sumi-no-ye-naka-tsu,
wishing to take the Heavenly Sovereign, set fire to the
great palace. Thereupon the Suzerain of Achi,[2] ancestor
of the Suzerains of Aya[3] in Yamato, having taken him
away by stealth, set him on an august horse, and caused
him to make a progress into Yamato. So [the Heavenly
Sovereign] awoke on reaching the moor of Tajihi,[4] and
said: "What place is this?" Then the Suzerain of
Achi said: "King Sumi-no-ye-no-naka-tsu set fire to the
great palace; so I am fleeing with thee into Yamato." Then
the Sovereign sang, saying:

257        "Had I known that I should sleep on the
               Moor of Tajihi, oh! I would have brought
               my dividing matting, had I known that
               I should sleep!"[5]

On reaching the Pass of Hanifu[6] and gazing at the
palace of Naniha, the fire was still bright. Then the
Heavenly Sovereign sang again, saying:

               "The group of houses sparklingly burning,
               as I stand and look from the Pass of
               Hanifu, is in the direction of the house
               of my spouse."

So when they reached the entrance of the Ohosaka
mountain,[8] they met one woman. This woman said:
"A number of men bearing weapons are barring [the

way across] the mountain. Thou shouldst cross it going round by way of Tagima.["9] Then the Heavenly Sovereign sang, saying :

> " Oh ! on asking the way of the maiden
> we met at Ohosaka, she tells not [the]
> direct [way], but tells of the Tagima
> way."[10]

So making his progress up, he dwelt in the temple of 289 the Deity of Isonokami.[11]

---

1. *I.e.*, on the occasion of his performing the religious ceremony of tasting the first rice of the season.

2. *Achi no atahe*, supposed to be of Korean origin, and to be a descendant of 阿知, great grandson of the Chinese Emperor 靈帝.

3. *Aya no atahe*. This family was of continental origin, *Aya* being the Japanese reading of the character 漢 ; see Sect. CXI, Note 2.

4. *Tajihi no nu*, in the provinces of Kahachi. The signification of the name is obscure.

5. This Song expresses the Monarch's regret at not having brought his mats with him.—From the expression used in the text (*tatsu gomo*), the commentators suppose that such mats were used as a sort of screen to avert draughts. One proposal is to consider *tatsu* as the Verb *tatsuru*, " to set up," because these mats must have been " set up " round the room. But it agrees better with grammatical usage to take it in its other sense of " cutting," or " dividing," and to suppose that the mats were so called because they " cut off " the draught from the person sitting behind them.

6. Or " Hill of Hanifu," *Hanifu-zaka*, in the province of Kahachi.

7. The meaning of this Song is perfectly clear.

8. See Sect. LXIV, Note 25. The word rendered " entrance " here and below in the same context is literally " mouth."

9. See Sect. LXII, Note 49.

10. Moribe thus paraphrases this Song: " If the maiden whom I met at Ohosaka and whom I sought direction of had been a common mortal, she would have simply told me the shortest road. But now I see why it was that she bid me go round by way of Tagima : it was to preserve me from danger. Ah ! she must have been a Goddess."—The

words *tada ni* generally have the sense of "directly," "immediately," and are indeed here so understood by Motowori. Moribe's interpretation, which has been followed by the translator, does but little violence to the text, and suits the general meaning better.

11. See Sect. XLV, Note 16.

———————

[SECT. CXXXIII.—EMPEROR.—RI-CHIU (PART III.—HIS
REBELLIOUS BROTHER AND THE LATTER'S
RETAINER SOBAKARI ARE SLAIN).]

Thereupon his younger brother His Augustness Midzu-ha-wake came, and and sent [to ask for] an audience.[1] Then the Heavenly Sovereign caused him to be told [these words]: "As I am in doubt whether perhaps Thine Augustness may [not] be of like mind[2] with King Sumi-no-ye-no-naka-tsu, I will not meet and speak with thee." [His Augustness Midzu-ha-wake] replied, saying: "I have no evil intent. I am not of like mind with King Sumi-no-ye-no-naka-tsu." [The Heavenly Sovereign] again caused him to be told [these words]: "If that be so, [do thou] now return down, and slay King Sumi-no-ye-no-naka-tsu, and come up [again hither]. At that time I will surely meet and speak with thee." So he forthwith returned down to Naniha, and deceived [a man] named Sobakari,[3] a man-at-arms[2] in the personal service of[4] King Sumi-no-ye-no-naka-tsu, saying: "If thou wilt obey my words, I shall become Heavenly Sovereign, and will make thee prime Minister, to rule the Empire.[5] How [would this be]?" Sobakari replied, saying " "[I will do] according to thy command." Then plenteously endowing that man-at-arms, he said: "If that be so, slay the King." Thereupon Sobakari watched for the time when his King went into the privy, and thrust him to death with a spear. So when [His Augustness Midzu-ha-wake] was making his progress to Yamato taking Sobakari with him, he, on reaching the entrance of the Ohosaka mountain, thought [thus]: "Although Sobakari deserves very well of me, he has truly[6] slain his lord. This is unrighteous. Nevertheless if I reward not his deed, I may be called untruthful; and if I quite carry out my promise, his intentions are on the contrary to be feared. So, though recompensing his deed, I will destroy his actual person." Therefore he said to Sobakari: "I will halt here to-day and bestow on thee the rank of Prime Minister, and to-morrow will [continue my] progress up." So a halt was made at the entrance to the mountain, a temporary palace forthwith built, a copious feast[7] suddenly held, the rank of Prime Minister forthwith bestowed on the man-at-arms, and all the officials[8] made to do obeisance [to him]. The man-at-arms, delighted, thought that he had accomplished his design. Then [His Augustness Midzu-ha-wake] said to the man-at-arms: "To-day I will drink liquor from the same cup as the Prime Minister." And when they drank together, a bowl[9] large [enough] to hide the face was filled with the liquor presented.[10] Hereupon the King's child drank first, and the man-at-arms drank afterwards. So when the man-at-arms was drinking, the great cup covered his face. Then [His Augustness Midzu-ha-wake] drew forth a sabre which he had laid under the matting, and cut off the head of the man-at-arms. Forthwith on the morrow he made his progress up. So the place was called by the name of Chika-tsu-Asuka.[11]

291 Going up and reaching Yamato, he said: " I will halt here to-day and, having purified myself, will go forth to-morrow and worship at the temple of the Deity."[12] So that place is called by the name of Toho-tsu-Asuka.[13] So going forth to the temple of the Deity of Iso-no-kami, he sent to report to the Heavenly Sovereign that he had come up to serve him after accomplishing the work [with which he had been entrusted].[14] So [the Heavenly Sovereign] sent for, and met, and spoke with him.

---

1. The original of this clause is very elliptical, consisting only of the two characters 令詔. The old reading joins thereto the characters 爾天皇, which according to Motowori form the commencement of the next sentence. The meaning is not affected by the change.

2. Literally, "heart." Similarly below, where the word "intent" is used in the translation.

3. The signification of this name is quite obscure.

4. *Hayabito.* The reader should compare Section XXXVIII. Note 11.

5. Literally, "closely accustomed to."

6. The original leaves it uncertain whether the words "to rule the Empire" should be applied to the speaker, to Sobakari, or to both; and the ambiguous application has therefore been preserved in the translation.

7. Literally, "already."

8. See Sect. CVII, Note 7.

9. Literally, "the hundred officials," a Chinese phrase, which has been met with before.

10. The character ‥ used in the text implies by its radical that the bowl was of metal. It is an unauthorized form of 椀 or 盌

11. *Scil.* by the prince to the man-at-arms.

12. *I.e.*, Nearer Asuka. The name is written 近飛鳥. The student should consult Motowori's note on this passage in Vol. XXXVIII, pp. 38-39 of his Commentary, to see what can be done towards reconciling the name, the characters it is written with, and the origin ascribed to it, all of which are so apparently incongruous.

13. *Scil.* of Isonokami. This deity was the sword forming the subject of the legend narrated in Sect. XLV.

13. 遠飛鳥, i.e., Further Asuka. *Conf.* Note.

14. This is the gist of the original phrase, which will not bear literal translation into English: 政既平訖參上侍之.

---

[SECT. CXXXIV.—EMPEROR RI-CHIU (PART IV.— VARIOUS DEEDS).]

The Heavenly Sovereign thereupon first appointed the Suzerain of Achi to the office of Treasurer,[1] and likewise bestowed on him domains.[2] Again in this august reign the name of Waka-sakura Tribe[3] was granted to the Grandees of the Waka-sakura Tribe.[4] Again the gentile name[5] of Dukes of Himeda[6] was granted to the Dukes of Himeda. Again the Ihare Clan[7] was established.

---

1. In Japanese the same word is used for a "store-house" and for the "treasury." But the appointment here mentioned would seem really to correspond to what we should call Lord of the Treasury or Minister of Finance. The characters in the original are 藏官.

2. Literally, "ration grounds."

3. *Waka-sakura-be.*

4. *Waka-sakura-be no omi. Conf.* Sect. CXXXI, Note 1.

5. All the editors agree in here reading as *kabane* ("gentile name," see Sect. XIV, Note 5) the character 姓, which signifies properly "family name."

6. *Himeda no kimi.* Nothing is known of this family.

7. *Ihare-be.* For Ihare see Sect. XLIII, Note 6. It will be remembered that the Emperor of whose reign the present Section forms part held his court at Ihare.

---

292   [SECT. CXXXV.—EMPEROR RI-CHIU (PART V.—HIS AGE AND
PLACE OF BURIAL).]

The Heavenly Sovereign's august years were sixty-four.
His august mausoleum is at Mozu.[1]

---

1. See Sect. CXXX, Note 1.

[SECT. CXXXV.—EMPEROR HAN-ZEI.]

His Augustness Midzu-ha-wake dwelt in the palace of
Shibakaki at Tajihi,[1] and ruled the Empire. The length
of this Heavenly sovereign's august person was nine feet
two inches and a half.[2] The length of his august teeth
was one inch, and their breadth two lines, and the upper
and lower [row] corresponded exactly, like jewels strung
together]. The Heavenly Sovereign wedded the Lady
of Tsunu,[3] daughter of Kogoto, Grandee of Wani,[4] and
begot august children : the Lady of Kahi ;[5] next the
Lady of Tsubura[6] (two Deities). Again he wedded Oto-
hime,[7] daughter of the same Grandee, and begot august
children :   King Takara ;[8] next the Lady of Takabe.[9]—
altogether four Kings [and Queens].[10] The Heavenly
Sovereign's august years were sixty. His august mausoleum
is on the Moor of Mozu.[11]

---

1. For Tajihi see Sect. CXXXII, Note 4.  *Shiba-kaki* (or *Shiba-gaki*)
signifies " a fence of brushwood."

2. As to the ancient Japanese measures we have no accurate information, and the English equivalents used in this passage correspond but
approximately to the modern Japanese standards. The character rendered
" line " is 分, which denotes the tenth part of a 寸 or " inch." Motowori remarks that the dimensions of the teeth are not anything extra-

ordinary judged by the present standard, and suppose that anciently the measures of length must have been smaller than at present.

3. *Tsunu no iratsume.* The signification of this name is obscure.

4. *Wani no kogoto no omi.* The meaning of Kogoto is obscure. Wani has already often appeared.

5. *Kahi no iratsume.* Kahi is the name of a province, but it cannot be said for certain that it is from it that this Princess derived her name.

6. *Tsubura no iratsume.* The meaning of *Tsubura* is obscure.

7. *I.e.*, " the younger princess."

8. *Takara no miko. Takara* signifies " treasure."

9. *Takabe no iratsume. Takabe* seems to be the name of a place unless it be considered to be connected with the word *taka*, " hawk."

10. Remember that the single character 王 includes both sexes.

11. See Sect. CXXX. Note 1.

---

[SECT. CXXXVII.—EMPEROR IN-GIYŌ[1] (PART I —GENE-
ALOGIES).]

His Augustness Wo-asa-dzu-ma-waku-go-no-sukune dwelt in the Palace of Toho-tsu-Asuka,[2] and ruled the Empire. This Heavenly Sovereign wedded Her Augustness Osaka-no-oho-naka-tsu-hime,[3] younger sister of King Oho-hodo, and begot august children : King Karu of Kinashi ;[4] next Nagata-no-oho-iratsume ;[5] next King Kurohiko of Sakahi ;[6] next His Augustness Anaho ;[7] next Karu-no-oho-iratsume,[8] another name for whom is Sotohoshi-no-iratsume[9] (the reason for her being given the august name of Queen So-tohoshi was that the refulgence of her person passed through her garments); next King Shiro-biko of Yatsuri ;[10] next His August- ness Oho-hatsuse :[11] (nine Deities). Altogether the Heaven-ly Sovereign's august children [numbered] nine Deities-(five Kings and four Queens). Of these nine Kings and

Queens, His Augustness Anaho [was he who afterwards] ruled the Empire. Next his Augustness Oho-hatsuse ruled the Empire.

---

1. Also pronounced *In-kiyo.*

2. See Sect. CXXXIII, Note 13.

3. This name and the next have already appeared in Sect. CXVII.

4. *Kinashi no Karu no miko.* Karu is properly the name of a place in Yamato which has already often appeared in the text. It is uncertain whether *kinashi* is likewise the name of a place or of a particular kind of pear; but Motowori inclines to the former view.

5. *I.e.,* "the great lord of Nagata." There are many places of this name (lit. "long rice-field"), and it is not known which is here intended.

6. *I.e.,* "the black prince of Sakahi." The latter word signifies "frontier." It is not known where Sakahi is, neither is the reason for the name of "black prince" applied to this personage known (*Conf.* the "white prince" mentioned a little further on).

7. Or, "of Anaho," for Anaho is properly the name of a place in Yamato. Its import is not clear.

8. *I.e.,* "the great lady of Karu."

9. Written 衣通郎女, i.e., "the garment-passing lady." *So-tohoshi* is Motowori's reading of the characters, the usual reading being *So-tohori* (the Intransitive instead of the Transitive form of the Verb). He likewise identifies Koto-fushi (see Sect. CXVII, Note 9) with this celebrated princess, who is commonly worshipped as Goddess of Poetry. There is much confusion in the traditions concerning her, and Motowori's notes on the subject in Vol. XXXIV, pp. 53-54 and in Vol. XXXIX of his Commentary, p. 3, should be consulted.

10 *Yatsurino shiro-biko no miko, i.e.,* "the white prince of Yatsuri." Yatsuri is the name of a place in Yamato. It is written with characters signifying "eight melons."

11. *I.e.,* "great Hatsuse," so called from Hatsuse, a celebrated place in Yamato, which has already been mentioned.

12. *I.e.* "the great lady of Tachibana," the latter being the name of a place in Yamato. The word signifies "orange."

13. *I.e.,* "the lady of Sakami," the latter being apparently the name of a place either in Harima or in Wohari. Its derivation is not clear.

[SECT. CXXXVIII.—EMPEROR IN-GIYŌ (PART II.—HIS SICKNESS
IS CURED BY A KOREAN PHYSICIAN).]

The Heavenly Sovereign, when first about to rule the
succession of Heaven's Sun,[1] declined, saying: " I have
a long sickness; I cannot rule the sun's succession. "
Nevertheless, as from the Empress downwards all the
magnates strongly urged him, he forthwith ruled the
Empire. At this time the ruler of Shiragi[2] dutifully sent
eighty-one vessels with august tribute. Then the chief
envoy[3] sent with the august tribute, whose name was
Komu-ha-chimu-kamu-ki-mu,[4] was a man deeply versed
in the medical art. So he cured the Heavenly Sovereign's
august sickness.

1. For this expression see Sect. XXXIII, Note 27. The story of
the refusal of this monarch to accept the crown which was offered to
him by the magnates of the nation is told at considerable length in the
parallel passage of the " Chronicles." According to the same authority
he belonged to a collateral branch of the Imperial family, and was therefore not in the regular line of succession.

2. See Sect. XCVIII, Note 2,

3. Literally, " great messenger.'

4. 金波鎮漢紀武. Motowori decides that 金 is the surname, 波鎮
an official title, 漢紀 an official designation of the kinsmen of the Korean
King, and 武 the personal name.

———

[SECT. CXXXIX.—EMPEROR IN-GIYŌ (PART III. HE RECTIFIES
THE PEOPLE'S NAMES).]

Thereupon the Heavenly Sovereign, lamenting the
transgressions in the surnames and gentile names of the
people of all the surnames and names in the Empire[1]
placed jars [for trial by] hot water[2] at the Wondrous

Cape of Eighty Evils in Words at Amakashi,[3] and
deigned to establish the surnames and gentile names of
the eighty heads of companies.[4] Again the Karu Tribe[5]
was established as the august proxy of King Karu of
Ki-nashi; the Osaka Tribe[6] was established as the Empress's august proxy; and the Kaha Tribe[7] was established
as the august proxy of the Empress's younger sister
Ta-wi no Naka-tsu-hime.[8]

---

1. The original is; 天下氏氏名名人等之氏姓, which Motowori
reads *ame no shita no uji-uji na-na no hito domo no uji kabane.*

2. We learn from the " Chronicles " that he whose hand was injured
in the process of dipping it into the jar of boiling water was pronounced
a deceiver, while those who stood the trial unhurt were considered to be
telling the truth.

3. *Amakashi no koio-yo-maga-tsu-hi no saki.* Motowori truly observes
that this does not sound like an actual geographical name, but was rather,
it may be supposed, a new designation given to Cape Amakashi (see
Sect. LXXII, Note 10) on account of the incident here mentioned. The
name reminds us of that of one of the deities born from the purification
of the person of the creator Izanagi after his return from Hades (see
X, Note 14 .

4. *Ya-sotomo-no-wo.* See Sect. XXXIII, Note 19.

5. *arube.*

6. *Osaka-be*, so called after the Empress's native place (See Sect.
CXXXVII, Note 3, and Sect. CXVII, Note 6). The reading of *Osaka-be*
is given in all the editions to the characters in the text, 刑武, where we
should expect 忍坂部. Motowori's explanation of the reason why the
name was thus written will be found in Vol. XXXIX, p. 19, of his Commentary.

7. *Kaha-be* Motowori supposes that there is here some corruption
of the text, as no connection can be discovered between the name of this
Tribe and that of the Princess whose proxy the tribe became.

8. See Sect. CXVII, Note 7.

[SECT. CXL.—EMPEROR IN-GIYŌ (PART IV.—HIS AGE AND
PLACE OF BURIAL,]

The Heavenly Sovereign's august years were seventy-eight. His august mausoleum is at Naga-ye near Wega in Kafuchi.[1]

---

1. See Sect. CIII, Note 2 and 3.

---

[SCCT. CXLI.—EMPEROR IN-GIYŌ (PART V.—PRINCE KARU       296
LOVES HIS SISTER PRINCESS SO-TOHOSHI)]

After the decease of the Heavenly Sovereign, it was settled that King Karu of Ki-nashi should rule the Sun's succession.[1]   But in the interval before his accession, he debauched his younger sister the Great Lady of Karu, and sang, saying:

" Making rice-fields on the mountain, making
    hidden conduits run on account of the
    mountain's height:—to-day indeed [my]
    body easily touches the younger sister
    whom I wooed with a hidden wooing, the
    spouse for whom I wept with a hidden
    weeping. "[2]

This is a Hind-Lifting Song.[3]   Again he sang, saying:
" The rattle-rattle of the hail against the
    bamboo-grass:—After I shall have certainly
    slept, what though I be plotted against by
    people!   When I shall have slept delight-
    fully, if there is the disorder of the cut
    *Hydropyrum latifolium*, let there be dis-
    order,—when I shall have slept a good            297
    sleep! "[4]

This is a Rustic Lifting Song.[5]

1. See Sect. XXXII. Note 27. The wording of this sentence would make it appear that it was only *after* the Emperor In-giyo's death that King Karu was chosen to succeed him. But probably King Karu had been appointed Heir Apparent (皇太子) during his Father's life time, as is indeed expressly stated in the "Chronicles," and is implied in later passages of this work; and what our author meant to say was: "It was settled that King Karu should rule the "Empire after the former Sovereign's decease," etc.

2. The meaning of the Song is: "The sister, the mistress, whom I wooed with such difficulty, is now easily mine."—The first phrase, down to "mountain's height," is but a "Preface" to the poem properly so called, serving to introduce by a *jeu-de-mots* the word *shita-dohi*, which means not only "hidden conduit," but "hidden wooing." At the same time the implied comparion of the poet's secret love of one so difficult to obtain as his own sister, to the course of the water in hidden conduits which is carried up the mountain's side to irrigate a field perched in a spot almost inaccessible, is by no means devoid of aptness. The word "mountain" (*yama*) is in the original preceded by the Pillow-Word *ashihiki* (or *ashiki*) *no*, whose signification is obscure and much disputed.

3. *Shirage-uta* (written phonetically). The interpretation of the term here adopted is that which has the sanction of Motowori and Moribe. They explain it to signify that the voice rose gradually toward the latter part of the Song.

4. As in the case of the preceding Song, the first phrase is but a Preface, which plays on the coincidence in sound between the words *tashi-dashi*, "rattling," and *tashika*, "certainly," i.e. "undisturbedly." The signification of the Song proper is: "If I shall but have gratified my passion, what care I however men may plot against me? If I can but press my beloved to my bosom, let all things go to rack and ruin, like the *Hydropyrum latifolium*, a grass which, when cut, falls into disorder!" —Of the sentiment of the Song, the less said the better; but viewed simply from a literary point of view, it is certainly one of the most fascinating little productions of the early Japanese muse, and the literal rendering of it into English does it woful injustice. Moribe rightly rejects Motowori's proposal to divide the poem in two after the words *hito hakayu to mo*, "plotted against by people." *Kari-komo no*, "of the *Hydropyrum latifolium*," is a Pillow-Word.

5. *Hinaburi no ageuta*. The commentators have nothing more precise to tell us concerning the expression "Lifting-Song" than that "it refers to the lifting of the voice in singing."

[SECT. CXLII.—EMPEROR IN-GIYŌ (PART VI.—WAR BETWEEN PRINCE KARU AND PRINCE ANAHO).]

Therefore all the officials[1] and likewise the people of the Empire turned against the Heir Apparent Karu, and towards the August Child Anaho. Then the Heir Apparent Karu, being alarmed, fled into the house of the Grandee the Noble Oho-mahe Wo-mahe,[2] and made a provision of implements of war. (The arrows made at this 298 time[3] were provided with copper arrow-insides;[4] so those arrows are called by the name of Karu arrows.) Prince Anaho likewise made implements of war. (The arrows made by this Prince were just the arrows of the present time;[5] they are called Anaho arrows.) Thereupon Anaho raised an army, and beleaguered the house of the noble Oho-mahe Wo-mahe. Then, when he reached the gate, heavy ice-rain[6] was falling. So he sang, saying:

" Come thus under cover of the metal gate
    of the Noble Oho-mahe Wo-mahe! We
    will stand till the rain stops. "[7]

Then the Noble Oho-mahe came singing, lifting his hands, striking his knees, dancing, and waving his arms. The Song said:

" The courtiers are tumultuous, [ saying ] that
    the small bell of the garter of the courtiers
    has fallen off. Country-people, too, be-
    ware ! "[8]

This Song is of a Courtier's Style[9] Singing thus, he 299 came near and said: " August Child of our Heavenly Sovereign ! Come not with arms against the King thine elder brother. If thou shouldst come against him with arms, people will surely laugh. I[10] will secure him and

present him to thee. [11]    The Prince Anaho disbanded
his troops and went away.    So the Noble Oho-mahe
Wo-mahe secured Prince Karu, and led him forth, and
presented him [to Prince Anaho].    The captive Prince
sang, saying:

> "Maiden of heaven-soaring Karu! if thou cry
> violently, people will know.    Cry quietly
> like the doves on Mount Hasa. [12]

Again he sang:

> "Maiden of heaven-soaring Karu! Come and
> sleep, and [then] pass on, oh maiden of
> Karu! [13]

---

1.   See Sect. CXII, Note 4.

2.   *Oho-mahe Wo-make sukune no omi* (according to the old reading
*Oho-saki Wo-saki*, etc.. Motowori considers this double name to denote
two brothers, the words *oho* and *wo* ("great" and "small") naturally
lending themselves to the interpretation of "elder" and "younger."
Moribe, on the contrary, thinks that there was but one, and is supported
both by the authority of the "Chronicles of Japan" and by the fact
that, except in the "Chronicles of Old Matters of Former Ages," which
is believed to be a forgery, no second brother is anywhere mentioned.
He explains the use of the double name in the prose text as having crept
in through the influence of the text of the following Song (see Note 7
below). This seems to the translator the better view.

3.   *I.e.,* "on this occasion."

4.   There is here an evident corruption of the text, and Motowori
aptly conjectures that arrow-*heads*, or, as they are called in Japanese,
arrow-*points*, are intended. He adds that up till then arrow-heads had
always been made of iron.

5.   The author's style is here rather at fault; for he apparently
wishes to say that the arrows employed by Prince Anaho were those
which had been used in anci nt t mes and were still the most universally
employed—that, in fact, they were the usual style of arrow in contradistinction to those of Prince Karu's invention.

6.   See Sect. LXXXVIII, Note 5.

7. The prince, in this Song, bids his troops follow his example, and take refuge from the rain under cover of the gate of Oho-mahe's house. Such, at least, is the actual sense of the words used; but Motowori sees in them nothing less than a slightly veiled exhortation to his followers to attack the castle, while Moribe, on the other hand, thinks they were meant to convey to Oho-mahe a hint of his presence, and enable the beleaguered prince, for whom (as being his elder brother) Prince Anaho retained a great affection and respect, to devise some method of escape. This seems extremely far-fetched.—The word "metal" probably refers only to the fastenings of the gate, and not to its whole structure.

8. The exact purport and application of this Song is disputed, but this much seems clear: that the composer of it seeks to quiet both the besieging army (out of politeness called courtiers), and the peasants who had joined the fray, by making light of the whole occurrence, which he compares to so trivial an accident as the falling of a bell from a man's "garter" or "leggings." The custom of ornamenting this article of dress with a small bell is, however, not mentioned elsewhere. The word *yume*, which concludes the Song and is here rendered "beware," is identified by Motowori and Moribe with the Imperative of the Verb *iuu* "to avoid," "to shun," "not to do."

9. *Miya-hito-buri.* This is one of the cases which lend support to Motowori's view that the names of the so called styles of Songs are derived from their initial words.

10. Written with the humble character 僕, "servant."

11. The word used in the text, here and also in the next sentence, is that which properly denotes the presenting of tribute.

12. Another reading gives this sense:

> "As, if the maiden of heaven-soaring Karu cried
> violently, people would know, she cries quietly
> like the doves on Mount Hasa."

According to this reading, the poet simply explains the reason of the undemonstrativeness of his mistress's grief; according to that in the text, he implores her not to weep too passionately.—*Amadamu* or *amadamu ya*, "heaven-soaring," is the Pillow-Word for Karu, applied to it punningly on account of its similarity in sound to the word *kari*, "a wild-goose," which well deserves the epithet "heaven-soaring." Of Mount Hasa nothing is known.

13.　Rendered thus according to Moribe's exegesis, which quite approves itself to the translator's mind, this Song signifies: "Oh! maiden of Karu! come and sleep with me but once, before my impending banishment renders it hard for us to meet again." Motowori chooses to interpret *nete* as a crasis of *nayete*, "bending," and sees in the Song an invitation to the maiden to come quietly so as not to attract observation.—The final word, translated "maiden," is *wotome-domo*, properly a Plural, but here used in a Singular sense, as *watakushi-domo*, "I" (properly "we"), so constantly is in the modern Colloquial Dialect. For the Pillow-Word "heaven-soaring" see preceding Note.

---

300　[SECT. CXLIII.—EMPEROR IN-GIYŌ (PART VII.—DEATH OF PRINCE KARU AND PRINCESS SO-TOHOSHI).]

So Prince Karu was banished to the hot waters of Iyo.[1] Again when about to be banished, he sang saying:

"The heaven-soaring birds, too, are indeed messengers. When thou hearest the voice of the crane, ask my name."[2]

These three songs are of a Heaven-Soaring style.[3] Again he sang, saying:

"If they banish the Great Lord to an island, he will indeed make the remaining return voyage. Beware of my mat! Mat indeed in words,—beware of my spouse!"[4]

301　This Song is of a Partly Lowered Rustic style.[5] Queen So-tohoshi presented a Song [to him]. That Song said:

"Let not thy feet tread on the oyster-shells of the shore of Ahine with its summer herbs! Pass there [after] having made clear!"[6]

So when afterwards again, being unable to restrain her love, she went after him, she sang, saying :

> " Thy going has become long past. I will go,
> oh ! to meet thee. Wait ! I can not wait. "
> (What is here called *yama-tadzu* is [what is] now
> [known by the name of] *tatsuge*.)[7]

So when in her pursuit she reached [ the place where Prince Karu was, he, who had been ] pensively waiting, sang, saying :

> " Alas ! beloved spouse, who settledst the   302
> whereabouts of our grave, setting up flags
> in the great vale, setting up flags in the
> little vale of Hatsuse the hidden castle !
> Alas ! beloved spouse, whom I see after
> [ our many troubles ], prostrate like a *tsuki*
> bow, standing like an *adzusa* bow ! "[8]

Again he sang, saying :

> " Driving sacred piles in the upper reach,
> driving true piles in the lower reach of the
> river of secluded Hatsuse, and hanging on   303
> the sacrificial piles a mirror, hunging on
> the true piles true jewels :—if they said
> that the younger sister whom I love like a
> true jewel, that the spouse whom I love
> like a mirror were [ there ], I would go
> home, I would long for my country. "[9]

Having thus sung, they forthwith killed themselves together.[10] So these two songs are Reading Songs.[11]

---

1. For Iyo see Sect. V, Note 4. Its hot springs are often mentioned in early documents. Motowori identifies them with a place now called Dō-go (道後).

2. The meaning of this Song is : " I go where perchance no messengers will reach me. But thou must ask tidings of me from the birds."

3. *Ama-da-buri.* The title seems to be derived from the initial Pillow-Word of these three Songs.

4. The meaning of this Song seems to the translator to be: "Even if they dare to banish me now, I shall some day return again. Respect my mat during my absence. Mat, indeed! It is my wife that must be respected." The commentators consider the concluding words to be a command addressed to the wife, and interpret the phrase to mean, "My spouse, beware!" But surely this makes less good sense, and moreover fails to suit the exactly parallel passage in the first Song of Sect. CXXV. By the words "Great Lord" the princely poet denotes himself, —perhaps with a touch of anger at the indignity to which he is subjected. The difficult expression *funa-amari* is here, in accordance with Moribe's view rendered by the words "remaining voyage," i.e., "the voyage homeward," which is that part of a voyage that may be said to remain over for an outward-bound vessel when she has reached her destination. Motowori's Commentary, Vol. XXXIX, pp. 50 51, should be consulted for older views of the meaning of the term. The expression "beware of my mat" reminds us that in early days the entire floor of a Japanese room was not matted according to the modern custom, but that each individual had his own mat on which to sit and sleep. Great care was always taken not to defile another's mat, *Conf.* an elegy from the "Collection of a Myriad Leaves" translated by the present writer in his "Classical Poetry of the Japanese," p. 79.

5. *Hina-buri no kata-oroshi.* Like most of the names of styles of Songs, this one is extremely obscure. The commentators suppose that one part was sung in a lower voice than the rest. But they are merely guessing.

6. The actual words of the Song signify: "Lacerate not thy feet by walking on the unseen oyster-shells of the shore of Ahine that is covered with the summer herbs; but walk there after dawn." (This is Keichiü's interpretation of the word *akashite,* "having made clear," and is the best in the present writer's opinion; the latter commentators see in it a recommendation to the exiled prince to clear the grass away on either side.) The word *Ahine* calls, however, for special explanation in order that the full import of the poem may be brought out. It properly signifies "sleeping together" or "lying on each other," and is therefore applicable either to the two spouses or to the summer grass. Indeed it is doubtful if it be the name of any real place at all. The word *natsu-kusa* may also be taken simply as a Pillow-Word for Ahine.—The total gist of the Song is in any case a warning from the maiden to her lover to guard himself against the perils of the journey.

7. The meaning of this Song is : " It is too long since thy departure. I can wait no longer, but will go and meet thee."—The Verb "to meet" (*mukahe*) is in the original preceded by the Pillow-Word *yama-tadzu*, which forms the subject of the note appended to the poem by the compiler. The commentators are not agreed as to the precise nature of the instrument intended ; but it seems to have been some kind of axe. The cause of its use as a Pillow-Word for " meeting " is equally disputed. It only occurs written phonetically. The term *tatsu-ge*, by which it is explained in the text, is there written 造木, which does not help us much towards understanding what is meant to be designated.

8. So obscure is this Song in the original, that Motowori confesses himself unable to make any sense of it. The translator has adopted Moribe's interpretation, according to which the gist of it is this : " Alas ! my dear wife, who wast so willing to be for ever united to me that thou didst even fix on the spot in the funereal vale of Hatsusé where we should one day be buried togethr! Alas for thee, whom at last I now see again "—In order to arrive at this meaning, Moribe is obliged to prove more less satisfactorily that the thrice repeated word *wo* signifies " vale " or " mountain-fold " the first two times that it occurs, and " grave " the third, and that *komoriku no hatsuse*, usually interpreted as secluded " Hatsuse, means " the hidden csstle," the " final place, *i.e.,* " the tomb." It is also necessary to suppose, without authority, that the flags mentioned by the poet are meant for funeral flags, and that the words " prostrate like a *tsuki* bow," etc., which, according to the laws of Japanese construction, precede instead of following the phrase " alas ! beloved spouse," etc., are but a Preface for the latter.—It will be seen that the foundation on which Moribe's interpretation rests is slight, and that Motowori was scarcely to be blamed for pronouncing the Song incomprehensible. At the same time the translator has thought it better, by following Moribe, to give *some* translation of it than to leave the passage blank. With this warning, the student may search for other possible meanings if he pleases.—Hatsuse is a still existent and celebrated place among the mountains of Yamato. The etymology of the name, unless we accept Moribe's mentioned above, is obscure. It is now usually pronounced *Hase*. The *tsuki* is said to be almost indistinguishable from the *keyaki* tree (*Zelkowa keaki*). The *adzusa* seems to be the *Catalpa kaempferi*, but some believe it to be the cherry-tree.

9. The first half of this Song down to the words " hanging on the true piles true jewels " is a Preface for what follows. The signification

of the rest is: "If my dearly loved sister-wife were still at Hatsuse in Yamato, I would fly to her either in thought or deed; but now that she has followed me into exile, the land of exile is good enough."
—Moribe, while allowing the first half of the Song to be a Preface for the rest, contends that it also should be credited with a signification bearing on the subject-matter of the main part of the Song. He supposes, namely, the religious ceremony, whatever it was, of driving piles into the bed or bank of the river and of decorating them with beads and a mirror, to have been one really performed by Princess So-tohoshi to compass her lover's return. In the translator's opinion, it is more elegant and more in accordance with Archaic usage to consider the Preface as having no special significance or connection (otherwise than verbal) with the rest of the poem. The word *i-kuhi* or *i-guhi*, rendered "sacred piles," occasions some difficulty; for it is not certain whether Motowori is right in giving to the initial syllable *i* the meaning of "sacred." It may be simply what has been termed an "Ornamental Prefix," devoid of meaning. Motowori however points out that this usage of it is restricted to Verbs, and does not occur with Substantives. *Komoriku no*, the Pillow-Word for Hatsuse, is rendered by "secluded" in accordance with Mabuchi's usually accepted derivation from *komori-kuni*, "retired land." Moribe, notwithstanding what he has said in his exegesis of the preceding poem (Note 8), is willing to allow that, though perhaps not its original, this was its common, meaning even in ancient times.

10.  *I.c.*, committed suicide together.

11.  This expression is interpreted to mean that these Songs were recited in monotone, as one would read a book or tell a tale.

---

[SECT, CXLIV.—EMPEROR AN-KŌ (PART I.—HE SLAYS KING OHO-KUSAKA).]

The august child[1] Anaho dwelt at the palace of Anaho at Isonokami,[2] and ruled the Empire. The Heavenly Sovereign sent the Grandee of Ne,[3] ancestor of the Grandees of Sakamoto, to the residence of King Oho-kusaka, on behalf of his younger brother Prince Oho-hatsuse to command thus: "I wish Thine Augustness's younger sister

Queen Waka-kusaka to wed Prince Oho-hatsuse. So do thou present her." Then King Oho-kusaka did obeisance four times, and said: "Owing to a supposition that there might be some such Great Commands, I have kept her always indoor.[5] With reverence[6] will I respectfully offer her according to the Great Commands." Nevertheless, thinking it disrespectful [merely] to send a message,[7] he forthwith, as a ceremonial gift[8] from his younger sister, made [the Grandee of Ne] take a pushwood jewel head-dress[9] to present [to the Heavenly Sovereign]. The Grandee of Ne forthwith stole the jewel headdress meant as a ceremonial gift, and slandered King Oho-kusaka, say-ing: "King Oho-kusaka would not receive the Imperial Commands, but said: "An soror mea fiet ejusdem stirpis [viri] inferior storea?'[10] and, grasping the hilt of his cross-sword,[11] was angry." So the Heavenly Sovereign, having in his great anger slain King Oho-kusaka, took that King's chief wife Nagata-no-oho-iratsume,[12] and made her Empress.

---

1. *I. e.*, Prince. In all other cases we find the word *mikoto,* "August-ness," as the title by which the Sovereign is mentioned at the commence-ment of his reign.

2. See Sect. XLV, Note 16.

3. *Ne no omi.* The etymology of *ne* is obscure.

4. Literally, as "tribute."

5. More literally, "I have kept her without putting her out of doors."

6. *Conf.* Sect. IX, Note 4 and Sect. XVIII, Note 14.

7. Motowori surmises that 其 may be an error for 者 in the original of this clause 然言以白事其思无禮.

8. 禮物. This term corresponds to the modern 結納, the name by which the presents which are exchanged at the time of betrothal are designated.

9. The original term *oshi-ki no tam-akadzura* is extremely obscure. One of Motowori's conjectures is that the "push-wood" was a kind of frame by which the jewels or beads, strung on an erect stem of some hard material, were kept firmly attached to the head. Perhaps some notion of the *coiffure* intended may be gathered from the plate opposite p. 354 of Part III of Vol. VIII of these "Transactions" (Mr. J. Conder's paper on "The History of Japanese Costume").

10. *I.e.*, "An scror mea, cujus pater Imperator Nin-toku, fiet uxor præsentis Imperatoris ?"—Hujus similitudinis rusticitas et ipsis Japonicis commentatoribus pudori est.

11. See Sect. XLV, Note 5.

12. See Sect, CXXXVII, Note 5.

---

305    [SECT. CXLV.—EMPEROR AN-KŌ (PART II.—HE IS SLAIN
BY KING MA-YOWA).]

After this, the Heavenly Sovereign, being on [ his ] divine couch,[1] was sleeping at midday. Then he spoke to his Empress, saying : "Is there anything on thy mind ?[2] She replied, saying : "Being the object of the Heavenly Sovereign's generous favour, what can there be on my mind ?" Hereupon the Empress's former child,[3] King Ma-yowa, who was seven years old that year, happened to be just then playing outside the apartment.[4] Then the Heavenly Sovereign, not Knowing that the young King was playing outside the apartment, spoke to the Empress, saying : "I have constantly something upon my mind, namely [ the fear ] that thy child King Ma-yowa, when he comes to man's estate, may, on learning that I slew the King his father, requite me with a foul heart.[5] Thereupon King Ma-yowa, who had been playing outside the apartment, and whose ear had caught these words, forthwith watched for the Heavenly Sovereign to be augustly asleep, and, taking the great sword [that lay] by his side,[6] forthwith struck off the Heavenly Sovereign's head, and fled into the house of the Grandee Tsubura.[7] The Heavenly Sovereign's august years were fifty-six, His august masoleum is on the mound of Fushimi at Sugahara[8]

---

1. *Conf.* Sect. LXIV, Note 2.

2. Literally, "Hast thou anything to think about?" The same construction is used in the next sentence.

3. *I.e.*, her son by her former husband King Oho-kusaka.

4. Literally, "below the palace." The same expression recurs further on. The parallel passage in the "Chronicles" has "below the upper storey," *i.e.*, in the court or garden of a two-storeyed house. With the small proportions assumed by Japanese architecture, conversation could well be overheard under these conditions.

5. *I.e.*, "take vengeance upon me.

6. *Scil.* by the Emperor's side.

7. *Tsubura omi.* The etymology of Tsubura is obscure.

8. For Sugahara see Sect. LXXV, Note 1. The Fushimi here mentioned, which is in Yamato, must not be confounded with the better known Fushimi in Yamashiro. The popular etymology of this name and it is to be found in many books) traces it to *Fushi mi*, *i.e.*, "lying three," in connection with the story of a man who "lay on the mound for three years." Probably *fuse-midzu*, "water laid on," a name perhaps given on account of an aqueduct or of water-pipes, was the original designation, which has been corrupted.

306 [SECT. CXLVI.—EMPEROR AN-KŌ (PART III.—PRINCE OHO HATSUSE SLAYS PRINCES KURO-BIKO AND SHIRO--BIRO).]

Then Prince Oho-hatsuse,[1] who at that time was a lad, was forthwith grieved and furious on hearing of this event, and went forthwith to his elder brother King Kurobiko,[2] and said: "They have slain[3] the Heavenly Sovereign. What shall be done?" But King Kurobiko was not startled, and was of unconcerned heart.[4] Thereupon King Oho-hatsuse reviled his elder brother, saying: "For one thing it being the Heavenly Sovereign, for another thing it being thy brother, how is thy heart without concern?[5] What! not startled, but unconcerned on hearing that they have slain thine elder brother!"—and forthwith he clutched him by the collar; dragged him out, drew his sword, and slew him. Again, going to his elder brother King Shiro-biko, he told him the circumstances as before. The unconcernedness again was like [that shown by] King Kuro-biko. [So King Oho-hatsuse,] having forthwith clutched him by the collar, pulled him along, and dug a pit on reaching Woharida,[6] buried him as he stood,[7] so that by the time he had been buried up to the loins, both his eyes burst out, and he died.[8]

---

1. See Sect. CXXXOIJ, Note 11.

2. See Sect. CXXXVII, Note 6.

3. Literally, "taken."

4. *I.e.*, treated the matter with indifference.

5. Literally, "withot relying," as if the speaker meant to say that the dead man could not rely on him for vengeance.

6. In Yamato. The name seems to mean "new tilled field."

7. Written 隨立 in the text followed by Motowori. The other reading 墮立 is untenable.

8. In order to account for such an effect from so apparently insufficient a cause, Motowori supposes that after the prince had been made
to stand up to the height of his loins in the pit, the latter was filled
by having stones thrown into it, whereby his feet and legs would be
crushed.

---

[SECT. CXLVII.—EMPEROR A-NKŌ (PART IV.—DEATH OF
PRINCE MA-YOWA-AND OF THE GRANDEE TSUBURA)]

Again he raised an army and beleaguered the house
of the Grandee Tsubura. Then [the other side also]
raised an army to resist the attack,[1] and the arrows that
were shot forth were like unto the falling down of the
[ears of the] reeds.[2] Thereupon King Oho-hatsuse, using
his spear as a staff, peeped in,[3] and said: "Is perchance
the maiden, with whom I spoke, in this house?"[4] Then
the Grandee Tsubura, hearing these commands,[5] came
forth himself, and having taken off the weapons with
which he was girded, did obeisance eight times, and
said: "The maiden Princess Kara, whom anon thou
deignedst to woo, is at thy service. Again in addition
I will present to thee five granaries. (What are called the
five granaries are now the gardeners of the five villages of Kadzuraki:[6])
Meanwhile the reason why she does not come out to
meet thee in person is that from of old down to the
present time grandees and chiefs have been known to
hide in the palaces of Kings, but Kings have not yet
been known to hide in the houses of grandees.[7] Therefore I think that, though a vile slave of a grandees[8] exert-
ing his utmost striength in the fight can scarcely conquer,
yet must he die rather than desert a Prince who, trusting
in him, has entered into his house."[9] Having thus

spoken, he again took his weapons and went in again to
fight.[1] Then, their strength being exhausted and their
arrows finished, he said to the Prince: "My[10] hands are
wounded, and our arrows likewise are finished. We cannot now fight. What shall be done?" The Prince
266 replied, saying: "If that be so, there is nothing more to
do. [Do thou] now slay me." So [the Grandee Tsubura]
thrust the Prince to death with his sword, and forthwith
killed himself by cutting off his own head.

---

1. Literally, "to wait and fight."

2. The character 來, "to come" (here in accordance with English
idiom rendered by "down") is supposed to be an error. One conjectural
emendation of it, viz., 盛, would suggest the "plentiful" falling of the
flowers of the reeds.

3. *I.e.,* he lifted himself on tiptoe by leaning on his spear, so as to
be able to peep in.

4. The maiden thus suddenly introduced into the story is Tsubura's
daughter Kara, whom it must be supposed that the Prince had previously
been wooing.

5. Or rather, "Imperial words." The application of the characters
詔命 to the words of one who was not yet actually Emperor is curious.

6. *I.e.,* the places where the five granaries originally were are now
the five villages inhabited by the men who cultivate the Imperial gardens.
For Kadzuraki see Sect. LV, Note 1.

7. Or we may, following Motowori's proposal, take the character 臣
in this clause in its slightly different acceptation of "subject," which
better suits the sense. The partly phonetic wording of the next sentence
賤奴意富美者 shows how the writer was perplexed by the double use of
the term.

8. *Q.d.,* in comparison with a prince of the Imperial family, even a
grandee was but a vile slave.

9. The character 隨 in the original of this passage 入坐于隨家 is
corrupt. But the sense remains clear, and it is scarcely worth while
looking about for a probable emendation. Motowori has no satisfactory
proposal to make.

10. The humble character 僕, "servant" here used for the First

Personal pronoun. The expression 僕者手悉傷, here literally rendered "my hands are all wounded," is very curious. Motowori reads it *ita-te ohinu, i.e.,* "I have received (or suffered from) hurtful hands," and compares two somewhat similar expressions found in Sect. XLIV (see Note 33 to that Sect). The translator may however point out that the similarity is much more apparent in Motowori's *kana* reading than it is in the Chinese text itself. May not the sense of the present passage rather be: "All our men are wounded?" for the word *te* (手) "hand," is frequently used in Japanese,—in compounds at least,—in the sense of "man," somewhat as it is in English naval, mining, and other technical parlance.

---

[SECT. CXLVIII.—EMPEROR AN-KŌ (PART V.—PRINCE OHO-HATSUSE SLAYS PRINCE OSHIHA).]

After this Karu-fukuro,[1] ancestor of the Dukes of Yama of Sasaki in Afumi,[2] said [ to King Oho-hatsuse ]: " At Kuta[3] [and ?] on the moor of Kaya at Wata in Afumi, boars and deer are abundant. Their legs as they stand are like a moor [covered] with *wogi* ;[4] the horns they point up are like withered trees." At this time time [King Oho-hatsuse], taking with him King Ichi-no-be-no-oshiha, made a progress to Afumi, and on reaching this moor, each of them built a separate temporary palace to lodge in. Then next morning, before the sun had risen, King Oshiha with a tranquil heart rode along on his august horse, and, reaching and standing beside King Oho-hatsuse's temporary Palace, said to King Oho-hatsuse's attendants: " Is he not awake yet ? He must be told quickly [that I am come]. It is already daylight.[5] He must come to the hunting-ground, "— and forthwith urging his horse, he went forth. Then the people who served the august person of King Oho-hatsuse said: "As [King Oshiha] is a violent-spoken[6] Prince, thou shouldst be on thy guard, and likewise it were well to arm thine august person." Forthwith he put on armour underneath his clothes, took and girded on him his bow and arrows, rode off on horseback, and in a sudden interval setting his horse by the side [of the other King's], took out an arrow, shot King Oshiha down, forthwith moreover cut his body [to pieces], pu[them] into a horse's manger, and buried them leve[l] with the earth.

1. This name has the curious signification of "Korean (or Chinese) bag."

2. *Afumi no Sasaki no yama no kimi.* Conf. Sect. LXIX, Note 46.

3. This and the following names are altogether obscure, neither is it evident whether two places are meant, or only one. The present passage reads as if two were intended, but a little further down the author seems to be speaking of but one.

4. *The Hedysarum esculentum.*

5. Literally "the night has already finished dawning."

6. Motowori endeavours, not every successfully, to explain the use of this epithet by Prince Oho-Hatsuse's attendants. As the sequel shows, the violence was all on the other side.

[SECT. CXLIX.—EMPEROR AN-KŌ (PART VI.—FLIGHT OF PRINCES OHOKE AND WOKE)].

Hereupon King Ichi-no-be's children[1] King Ohoke and King Woke (two Deities), having heard of this affray, fled away. So when they reached Karibawi[2] in Yamashiro and were eating their august provisions, an old man with a tattooed face came and seized the provisions. Then the two Kings said: "We do not grudge the provisions. But who art thou?" He replied, saying: "I am a boar-herd in Yamashiro." So they fled across the River Kusuba,[3] reached the land of Harima,[4] entered the house of a native of that country named Shizhimu,[5] hid their persons, and worked as grooms and cow-herds.

---

1, Literally "prince" (王子). Their names apparently signify "big basket" and "little basket."

2. Known in later times as Kaniha and Kabawi. The name signifies (if the characters with which it is written may be relied on) "the well where the leaves were cut."

3. See Sect. LXVI. Note 19.

4. See Sect. LX, Note 19.

5. Or Shizhimi. Properly the name of a village, it is here used as the name of a man. The etymology is obscure.

---

[SECT. CL.—EMPEROR YŪ-RIYAKU, (I.—GENEALOGIES).]     310

His Augustness Oho-hatsuse-no-waka-take dwelt in the palace of Asakura at Hatsuse,[1] and ruled the Empire. The Heavenly Sovereign wedded Queen Wake-kusaka-be, younger sister of King Oho-kusaka (no children). Again he wedded Princess Karu, daughter of the Grandee Tsubura, and begot august children: His Augustness Shiraka; next his younger sister Her Augustness Princess Waka-tarashi (two Deities).

---

1. For Hatsuse see Sect. CXLIII, Note 8. Several Asakuras are named in the pages of these "Records." That here named is in Yamato. The name seems to mean "morning store-house."

[SECT. CLL.—EMPEROR YŪ-RIYAKU (PART
II.—VARIOUS DEEDS).]

So the Shiraka Clan[1] was established as the august
proxy of Prince Shiraka. Again the Hatsuse-Clan-
Retainers[2] were established. At this time there came
over people from Kure. Again the Kahase Retainers[3]
were established. These people from Kure[4] were lodged[5]
at Kure-hara. So the place was called by the name of
Kure-hara.[6]

---

1. *Shiraka-be.*

2. *Hatuse-be no tomire.* This clan was called after the reigning
Emperor. Remember that the word "Retainers" is here a "gentile
name."

3. *Kahase no toneri. Kaha-se* signifies "river-reach," and the
"Chronicles," under date of the eleventh year of this reign, tell a story
of the appearance of a white cormorant, to commemorate which this
family was established. Cormorants, it will be remembered, were used
for catching fish in rivers; hence the appropriateness of the name bestowed
on the family in question.

4. The name given by the early Japanese to Wu (吳), an ancient
state in Eastern China to the South of the Yang-tzo River. In Japanese
it however, like other names of portions of China, often denotes the whole
of that country in a somewhat vague manner. The derivotion the word
*Kura* is obscure. The most acceptable proposition is that which would
see in it corruption of the original Chinese term *Wu*, of which *Go* is
the Sinico-Japanese pronunciation. But what of the second syllable *re?*

5. The phrase 安置 is in this place used for "lodged."

6. *I.e.,* Kure Moor. It is in Yamato. According to the "Chronicles," the former name of the place had been *Himokuma-nu.*

[SECT CLII.—EMPEROR YŪ-RIYAKU (PART III.—THE ROOF   311
OF THE HOUSE OF THE GREAT DEPARTMENTAL
LORD OF SHIKI.

In the beginning, when the Empress[1] dwelt at Kusaka,[2] [the Heavenly Sovereign] made a progress in Kafuchi by way of the Tadagoye[3] road at Kusaka. Then, on climbing to the top of the mountain and gazing on the interior of the country, [he perceived that] there was a house built with a raised roof-frame.[4] The Heavenly Sovereign sent to ask [concerning] that house, saying: " Whose roof with a raised frame is that ? " The answer was : " It is the house of the great Departmental Lord of Shiki. "[5] Then the Heavenly Sovereign said : " What ! a slave builds his own house in imitation of the august abode of the Heavenly Sovereign !" ....and forthwith he sent men to burn the house [down], when the Great Departmental Lord, with trembling and dread, bowed his head,[6] saying : " Being a slave, I like a slave did not understand, and have built overmuch. I am in great dread. "[7] So the thing that he presented as an august offering [ in token ] of his entreaty was a white dog 312 clothed in cloth,[8] and with a bell hung [ round its neck ] ; and he made a kinsman of his own, named Koshihaki,[9] lead it by a string and present it [ to the Heavenly Sovereign ]. So the Heavenly Sovereign ordered them to desist from burning [ the house ].

1. *I.e.,* Waka-kusaka-be.

2. See Sect· XLIV, Note 31. The Kusaka here mentioned is that in Kafuchi.

3. From *tada*, "straight" and *koyuru* "to cross," this being a short cut over the mountains.

4. The original of this clause is 有上堅魚作舍屋之家, which is read *katsuwo wo agete ya wo tsukureru ihe ari.* The *katsuwo* (properly

*katsuwo-gi* 堅魚木) is the name of the uppermost portion of the roof in modern Shintō temples, and apparently in ancient times also in houses that were not devoted to religious purposes. The difficulty is not with the sense, but with the derivation of the word *katsuwo-gi.* Following the characters with which it is here and elsewhere written, Motowori sees in it a reference to the shape of the blocks of wood resembling "dried bonitoes," which is the modern signification of *katsuwo.* But Moribe, in his "Examination of Difficult Words," proposes a derivation which approves itself more to the present writer's mind, viz., *kadzuku wo-gi* (戴小木), "small timbers atop" (see "Examination of Difficult Words," *s.v.*). Motowori's Commentary, Vol. XLI, pp. 11-14, should be consulted for a discussion of the whole question of the use of these frames in ancient times, and for the special force to be attributed to the word "raised" (上) in this passage.

5. *Shiki no oho-agata-nushi.* For Shiki see Sect. LXIII, Note 1.

6. *i.e.*, did humble obeisance by prostrating himself on the ground.

7. Or, according to the older reading, "This *i.e.*, thy command) [is to be received with] awe."

8. Or, "tied with [a string of] cloth." The translation follows Motowori's interpretation.

9. The name signifies "loin-girded," *i.e.*, as may be presumed, "wearing a sword."

---

[SECT. CLIII.—EMPEROR YŪ-RIYAKU (PART IV.—HE WOOES PRINCESS WAKA-KUSAKA-BE).]

Forthwith making a progress to the residence of Queen Wakakusaka-be the Heavenly Sovereign sent the dog as a message, saying : "This thing is a strange thing which I got to day on the road. So it is a thing to woo with,"—and so saying, sent it in as a present. Thereupon Queen Waka-kusaka-be sent to say to the Heavenly Sovereign : "It is very alarming that thou shouldst make a progress with thy back to the sun.[1] So I will come up straight [ to the capital ], and respectfully serve thee.[2] When therefore he returned up and dwelt in the palace, he went and stood on the ascent[3] of that mountain, and sang, saying:

> "In the hollow between the nearer and the further mountain, this Mount Kusakabe and Mount Heguri, [ is ] growing the flourishing broad-leafed boar-oak; at the base grow intertwining bamboos; on the top grow luxuriant bamboos:—we sleep not [ now ] intertwined like the intertwining bamboos, we sleep not certainly like the luxuriant bamboos: [ but ] oh! my beloved spouse, with whom [ I ] shall afterwards sleep intertwined![4]

313

And he forthwith sent back a messenger with this Song.[5]

---

1. For he had come from Yamato in the East to Kafuchi in the West.

2. The meaning is: "Thy Majesty must not come to woo me here, as the direction is unlucky. But I will myself come up straightway to the palace to be "thine Empress."

3. The ascent or way up here mentioned is, says Motowori, the Tadagoye Road, and the mountain is Mount Kusaka. See Sect. CLII, Notes 2 and 3.

4. In this Song the Emperor consoles himself for the delay in his union with Princess Waka-kusaka-be by reflecting that after all she will soon be his.—The first half of the poem down to the colon and dash is a Preface to the rest. Most of the difficult words occurring in it have been explained in previous notes; for the "broad-leafed bear-oak" see Sect. LXXII, Note, 19; for *tatami-komo*, the Pillow-Word by which Heguri is preceded in the Japanese text, see Sect. LXXXIX, Note 12. *Kusaka-be* is curious, for whereas it properly signifies Kusaka-Tribe,—this tribe or family being called after the place where they resided,—the place itself came to be renamed after them when the fact of the posterior origin of the family designation had been forgotten. The reason (or the

mention in the Preface of the oak-tree, which is not referred to in the main text of the poem, is difficult to ascertain. Moribe thinks, however that it is on account of the luxuriance of its foliage which, as if it were a Preface within the Preface, paves the way for the mention of the thick-growing bamboos. The punning connection between *tashimi-dake*, "luxuriant bamboos," and *tashi ni ha wi-nezu*, "we sleep not certainly," is necessarily obliterated in the English translation. "Certainly" must be taken in the sense of "undisturbedly."

5. *I.e.*, as may be conjectured, a messenger dispatched to him by his mistress. It seems best to suppose the author to represent the Emperor as not having actually gone to her house at all, but as having only communicated with her by messenger.

-----

[ SECT. CLIV.—EMPEROR YŪ-RIYAKU (PART V.—STORY OF
THE WOMAN AKAWI-KO).]

Again once when the Heavenly Sovereign going out for amusement, reached the River Miwa,[1] there was a girl, whose aspect was very beautiful, washing clothes by the river-side. The Heavenly Sovereign asked the girl, [ saying ] : "Whose child art thou?" She replied, saying : "My name is Akawi-ko of the Hiketa Tribe."[2] Then he caused her to be told, saying : "Do not thou marry a husband. I will send for thee,"—and [ with these words ] he returned to the palace. So eighty years had already passed while she reverently awaited the Heavenly Sovereign's commands. Thereupon Akawi-ko thought : "As, while looking for the [ Imperial ] commands, I have already passed many years, and as my face and form are lean and withered, there is no longer any hope. Nevertheless, if I do not show [ the Heavenly Sovereign ] how truly I have waited, my disappointment will be unbearable;"—and [ so saying ] she caused mer chandise to be carried on tables holding an hundred,[3] and came forth and presented [these gifts as] tribute. Thereat the Heavenly Sovereign, who had quite forgotten what he had formerly commanded, asked Akawi-ko, saying: "What old woman art thou, and why art thou come hither?" Then Akawiko replied, saying: "Having in such and such a month of such and such a year received the Heavenly Sovereign's commands, I have been reverently awaiting the great command until this day, and eighty years have past by. Now my appearance is quite decrepit, and there is no longer any hope. Nevertheless I have come forth in order to show and declare my faithfulness." Thereupon the Heavenly Sovereign was greatly startled [and exclaimed]: "I had quite forgotten the former circumstance; and thou meanwhile, ever faithfully awaiting my commands, hast vainly let pass by the years of thy prime. This is very pitiful." In his heart he wished to marry her, but shrank from her extreme age, and could not make the marriage; but he conferred on her an august Song. That Song said:

"How awful is the sacred oak-tree, the oak-
    tree of the august dwelling!   Maiden of
    the oak-plain!"[4]

Again he sang, saying:                                        315

"The younger chestnut orchard plain of
    Hiketa:—o si dormivissem cum illâ in
    juventâ! Oh! how old she has become!"[5]

Then the tears that Akawi-ko wept quite drenched the red-dyed sleeve that she had on.[6] In reply to the great august Song, she sang, saying:

"Left over from the piling up of the jewel-
    wall piled up round the august dwelling,

—to whom shall the person of the Deity's temple go ? "[7]

316    Again she sang, saying :

"Oh! how enviable is she who is in her bloom like the flowering lotus,—the lotus of the inlet, of the inlet of Kusaka ! "[8]

Then the old woman was sent back plentifully endowed So these four Sngs are Quiet Songs.[9]

---

1. *Miwa-gawa*, It is the stream which flows past Hatsuse. For Miwa see Sect. LXV, Note 8.

2. *Hiketa-bo no Akawi-ko*. *Hiketa* is in Yamato. The etymology of the word is obscure. *Akawi-ko* signifies "red boar child;" but the appropriateness of the name to the woman in the story is not made to appear.

3. See Sect. XXXVII, Note 7.

4. Moribe says that, in this Song, the forgetful Monarch calls to mind the majestic and awful appearance of the sacred tree in the temple-grounds, and is moved by this religious thought to repent of his neglectful treatment as her who had so patiently waited for him through so many years. Motowori, on the contrary, sees in the words nothing more than a comparison of the old woman to some sacred tree of immemorial age, and the aversion felt by the monarch to an union with her.—The oak mentioned (the *Kashi*, *Quercus myrsinæfolia*) is an evergreen specie Both Motowori and Moribe consider that *mimoro* in the original Japanese of this Song should be taken, not as a proper name (see Sect. XXVIII, Notes 3 and 5), but simply as signifying "a sacred dwelling." As Miwa is mentioned in the earlier part of the story, it might seem more natural to regard *mimoro* as likewise being a Proper Name. But the word *mimoro* itself signifying "sacred spot," the difference between the two views does not amount to much, and it is best to follow a tive authority "Oak-plain" (*kashi-hara*) means "a place planted with oak-trees." The first sentence of the Song must be looked on as a sort of preface to the second.

5. The first words of this Song down to the colon and dash are a Preface to the Song proper, whose meaning stands in need of no explanation,—Moribe surmises that the word *kuri*, "chestnut," was formerly

a general name for all sorts of fruits, somewhat like our Euglish word "berry."

6. The drenching of the sleeve with tears is a common figure in Japanese poetry.

7. Or we might (following Moribe) render thus : "Left over from the guarding of the jewel-grove guard at the august dwelling," etc. The wording of his Song is far from clear. While Motowori sees in it a reference to the construction of a wall round the ground of a temple, the overplus of the materials for which sacred wall could not, it may be presumed, be applied to any profane purpose, Moribe disputes the propriety of such an interpretation of the word *kaki* which, according to him, denotes the grove planted in temple-grounds, temples never having been surrounded by walls such as Motowori assumes the existence of, nor even by "hedges" or "fences," which is the more usual acceptation of the term. He thinks, therefore, that the superficial signification of the actual words of the Song is that the priest, who has all his life been in the service of one particular shrine, cannot desert it for the adoration of some other deity. The underlying deeper significance of the little poem is in either case the same : Akawi-ko had, during her long waiting of eighty years, remained true to her first love, the Emperor. For every reason it had been impossible for her ever to give her affections to another, and she had now come up to the capital to demonstrate to him who had forgotten her the unchangeable nature of her feelings.

8. This pretty little poem is too clear to need any comment. Moribe supposes that some lotuses brought from Kusaka may have been among the presents made by Akawi-ko to the Emperor. In the original Japanese the reference to the lotuses comes first, as a sort of preface to the rest of the poem. The laws of English construction necessitate its being put last in the translation.

9. See Sect. CXXIV, Note 19.

[SECT. CLV.—EMPEROR YŪ-RIYAKU (PART VI.—HE MAKES A PROGRESS TO YESHINU).]

When the Heavenly Sovereign made a progress to the palace of Yeshinu,[1] there was on the bank of the Yeshinu river a girl of beautiful appearance. So having wedded this girl, he returned to the Palace. Afterwards, when he again made a progress to Yeshinu, he halted where he had met the girl, and in that place raised a great august throne,[2] seated himself on that august throne, played on his august lute, and made the maiden dance. Then he composed an august Song on account of the maiden's good dancing. That Song said:

> " Oh! that the maiden dancing to the lute-
> playing, of the august hand of the Deity
> seated on the throne might continue for
> ever! "[3]

---

1. See Sect. XLVI, Note 3.

2. See Sect. CXII, Note 2.

3. This Song presents no difficulties. In it the Emperor speaks of himself as a Deity, and is enthusiastically praised by the commentator Moribe for so doing.

---

317　　[SECT. CLVI.—EMPEROR YŪ-RIYAKU (PART VII.—THE HORSE-FLY AND THE DRAGON-FLY).]

When forthwith he made a progress to the Moor of Akidzu,[1] and augustly hunted, the Heavenly Sovereign sat on an august throne. Then a horse-fly bit his august arm, and forthwith a dragon-fly came and ate up[2] the horse-fly, and flew [away]. Thereupon he composed an august Song. That Song said:

> " Who is it tells in the great presence that
> game is lying on the peak of Womuro at
> Mi-yeshinu? Our Great Lord, who tran-
> quilly carries on the government, being

seated on the throne to await the game, a
horse-fly alights on and stings the fleshy
part of his arm fully clad in a sleeve of
white stuff, and a dragon-fly quickly eats
up that horse-fly. That it might properly
bear its name, the land of Yamato was
called the Island of the Dragon-Fly. [[3]]

So from that time that moor was called by the name [318]
of Akidzu-nu.[4]

---

1. *Akidzu-nu.* See Note 4 to this section.

2. Or, "bit."

3. The signification of the greater portion of this Song is clear
enough, and is sufficiently explained by the context. The word "who"
however admits of two interpretations, Motowori taking it to signify
'some one," whereas Moribe, keeping the literal meaning of "who?"
sees in it an angry exclamation of the monarch's at having been brought
out to the hunt under exaggerated promises of game. *Womuro* means
"little cave," but is here a proper name. *Mi-yeshinu* is a form of the
word Yoshino which is frequently met with in poetry, the syllable *mi*
being probably, as Mabuchi tells us in his "Commentary on the Collection of a Myriad Leaves," equivalent to *ma,* and therefore simply an
"Ornamental Prefix." The phrase "tranquilly carries on the government"
represents the Japanese *yasumishishi,* the Pillow-Word for *wa ga oho-
kimi,* "our Great Lord," which latter phrase descriptive of the Sovereign
is here put into the Sovereign's own mouth. "Of white stuff, *shiro-tahe
no,* is another Pillow-Word. The only real difficulty in this Song meets
us is the interpretation of its concluding sentence. The meaning apparently intended to be conveyed is that it was in order to prove itself
worthy of its name that the dragon-fly performed the loyal deed which
forms the subject of the tale. But it so, the author forgets that it was not
the dragon-fly that was called after Japan, but Japan that was called after
the dragon-fly (*Akidzushima,* "Dragon-fly-Island," from *akidzu,* "dragon-
fly"). What should be the point of the whole poem therefore fails of
application. The name "Island of the Dragon-Fly" has already appeared
in Sect. V (Note 26).

4. *I.e.,* Dragon-Fly Moor. See Motowori's remarks in his "Examination of the Synonyms for Japan," p. 26.

[SECT. CLVII.—EMPEROR YŪ-RIYAKU (PART VII.—ADVENTURE WITH A WILD BOAR).]

Again once the Heavenly Sovereign made a progress up to the summit of Mount Kadzuraki.[1] Then a large [wild] boar ran out. When the Heavenly Sovereign forthwith shot the boar with a whizzing barb,[2] the boar, furious, came towards him roaring.[3] So the Heavenly Sovereign, alarmed at the roaring, climbed up to the top of an alder. Then he sang, saying:

> " The branch of the alder-tree on the op-
> portune mound which I climbed in my
> flight on account of the terribleness of the
> roaring of the boar, of the wounded boar,
> which our great lord who tranquilly
> carries on the government had been
> pleased to shoot![4]

---

1. See Sect. LV, Note 1.

2. See Sect. XXIII, Note, 7.

3. This is the sense attributed by the commentators to the obscure word *utaki*, which seems to be only found written phonetically.

4. Our author cannot be right in attributing this Song to the Emperor, and we need not hesitate to accept the different version of the story given in the parallel passage of the "Chronicle," where the Monarch, as might be expected from all the other details that have been preserved concerning him, bravely faces the boar, while it is one of his attendants who runs away and climbs a tree to be out of danger, and afterwards composes these lines. This Song is a good instance of what Mr. Aston (in his "Grammar of the Japanese Written Language," 2nd Edit., p. 194) has said concerning some of the short poems of a later date: "These sentences are not statements of fact; they merely picture to the mind a state of things without making any assertion respecting it." Here we, as it were, simply see the frightened courtier sitting breathless and terrified amid the branches of the alder, and the whole verse has but the meaning of an exclamation. The term *ari-wo* rendered "opportune mound." is the only word in the text which raises any dif-

ficulties of interpretation. Moribe's exegesis has here been followed.
According to the older view it signifies "barren mound." For the words
our great lord who tranquilly carries on the government" see Sect
CLVI, Note 3.

———

[SECT. CLVIII.—EMPEROR YŪ-RIYAKU (PART IX.—REVELATION  319
OF THE GREAT DEITY OF KADZURAKI, LORD OF
ONE WORD).]

Again once, when the Heavenly Sovereign made a
progress up Mount Kadzuraki, the various officials[1] were
all clothed in green-stained garments with red cords that
had been granted to them. At that time there were
people ascending the mountain on the opposite mountain
acclivity quite similar to the order of the Heavenly
Monarch's retinue. Again the style of the habiliments
and likewise the people were similar and not distinguishable.[2] Then the Heavenly Sovereign gazed, and sent
to ask, saying: "There being no other King in Yamato
excepting myself, what person goeth thus?" The style
of the reply again was like unto the commands of a
Heavenly Sovereign. Hereupon the Heavenly Sovereign,
being very angry, fixed his arrow [in his bow], and the
various officials all fixed their arrows [in their bows].
Then those people also all fixed their arrows [in their
bows]. So the Heavenly Sovereign again sent to ask,
saying: "Then tell thy name. Then let each of us tell
his name, and [then] let fly his arrow." Thereupon
[the other] replied, saying: "As I was the first to be
asked, I will be the first to tell my name. I am the
Deity who dispels with a word the evil and with a word
the good,—the Great Deity of Kadzuraki, Lord of One

320 Word.[3]　The Heavenly Sovereign hereupon trembled, and said: "I reverence [thee], my Great Deity. I understood not that thy great person would be revealed;[4]—and having thus spoken, he, beginning by his great august sword and likewise bow and arrows, took off the garments which the hundred officials had on, and worshipfully presented them [to the Great Deity].[5] Then the Great Deity, Lord of One Word, clapping his hands,[6] accepted the offering. So when the Heavenly Sovereign made his progress back, the Great Deity came down the mountain,[7] and respectfully escorted him to the entrance[8] of the Hatsuse mountain. So it was at that time the Great Deity Lord of One Word was revealed.

---

1, Literally, "the hundred officials." This Chinese phrase has been met with before in the "Records," and recurs in this Section.

2. The original has the character 傾, out of which it is hard to make sense. Motowori's proposal to consider it put by error for 須, has therefore been adopted, though the translator feels by no means sure that it is a happy one. According to the strict Chinese sense of 領, it would not fit with this passage any better than 傾; but in Japanese we may be justified in understanding 不須 to mean "not distinguishable."

3. In the original: 吾者雖惡事而一言雖善一事而言言離之神葛城之一言主之大神者也. The import of the obscure expression "dispelling with a word the good" is not rendered much more intelligible by Motowori's attempt to explain it. For Kadzuraki see LV, Note. 1.

4. Literally, "that there would be a present (or manifest) great person."

5. *I.e.*, he kept nothing for himself, but from his own sword and bow and arrows down to the ceremonial garments in which his followers were clad, gave every thing to the god.

6. In token of joy, says Motowori.

7. The characters 滿山末, rendered by "came down the mountain," are evidently the result of a copyist's carelessness. The translation follows Motowori's proposal to emend the text to 降山來.

8. Literally "mouth."

[SECT. CLIX.—EMPEROR YŪ-KIYAKU (PART X.—THE MOUND
OF THE METAL SPADE).]

Again when the Heavenly Sovereign made a progress
to Kasuga to wed Princess Wodo,[1] daughter of the
Grandee Satsuki of Wani,[2] a maiden met him by the
way, and forthwith seeing the Imperial progress, ran and
hid on the side of a mound. So he composed an august
Song. That august Song said :

" Oh ! the mound where the maiden is
hiding ! Oh for five hundred metal spades !
then might [ we ] dig her out ! "[3]

So that mound was called by the name of the Mound 321
of the Metal Spade.[4]

1. *Wodo-hime* The signification of this name is obscure.
2. *Wani no Satsuki no omi.* For *Wani* see Sect. LXII, Note 11.
*Satsuki* is the old Japanese name of the fifth moon.
3. Moribe thus paraphrases this Song: "The Monarch had met a
girl carrying "a spade in her hand, and as she was beautiful, wished to
address her ; but she ran off and hid on the hill-side, leaving her spade
behind her. His words express a desire for five hundred spades like hers,
with which to break down the hill-side and dig her out.... It is in
joke that he talks of the maiden who was on the *other side* of the hill
as being *inside* it." That in ancient times all digging implements were
not made of metal will be seen by reference to Sect. CXXIV, Note 9.
4. *Kanasuki no woka..*

---

[SECT. CLX.—EMPEROR YŪ-RIYAKU (PART
XI.—THE LEAF IN THE CUP).]

Again when the Heavenly Sovereign made a copious
feast under a hundred-branching *tsuki*-tree[1] at Hatsuse,
a female attendant from Mihe[2] in the land of Ise lifted

up the great august cup, and presented it to him. Then
from the hundred-branching *tsuki*-tree there fell a leaf
and floated in the great august cup. The female attendant, not knowing that the fallen leaf was floating in
the cup, did not desist from presenting[8] the great august
liquor to the Heavenly Sovereign, who, perceiving the
leaf floating in the cup, knocked the female attendant
down, put his sword to her neck, and was about to cut
off her head, when the female attendant spoke to the
Heavenly Sovereign, saying: "Slay me not! There is
something that I must say to thee;" and forthwith she
sang, saying:

"The palace of Hishiro at Makimuku is a
palace where shines the morning sun, a
palace where glistens the evening sun, a
palace plentifully rooted as the root of the
bamboo, a palace with spreading roots like
the roots of the trees, a palace pestled with
oh! eight hundred [loads of] earth. As for
the branches of the hundred-fold flourishing
*tsuki*-tree growing by the house of new
licking at the august gate [made of]
*chamaecyparis* [wood], the uppermost
branch has the sky above it, the middle
branch has the east above it, the lowest
branch has the country above it. A leaf
from the tip of the uppermost branch falls
against the middle branch; a leaf from the
tip of the middle branch falls against the
lowest branch; a leaf from the tip of the
lowest branch, falling into the oil floating
in the fresh jewelled goblet which the maid

322

of Mihe is lifting up, all [goes] curdle-
curdle.  Ah! this is very awful, August
Child of the High-Shining Sun! The
tradition of the thing, too this! "[4]

So on her presenting this Song, her crime was 323
pardoned.  Then the Empress sang.  Her Song said :

"Present the luxuriant august liquor to the
august child of the high-shining sun, who
is broad like the leaves, who is brilliant
like the blossoms of the broad-foliaged five
hundred [-fold branching] true camellia-
tree that stands growing by the house
of new licking in this high metropolis of
Yamato, on this high-timbered mound of
the metropolis  The tradition of this thing,
too this! "[5]

Forthwith the Heavenly Sovereign sang, saying :                    324

"The people of the great palace, having put
on scarfs like the quail-birds having put
their tails together like wagtails' and con-
gregated together like the yard-sparrows,
may perhaps to-day be truly steeped in
liquor,—the people of the palace of the
high-shining sun.  The tradition of the
thing, too, this. "[6]

These three Songs are Songs of Heavenly Words.[7] 325
So at this copious feast this female attendant from Mihe
was praised and plentifully endowed.

---

1.  Said to be scarcely distinguishable from the *keyaki* (*Zelkowa keaki*)
2.  See Sect. LXXXIX, Note 7.
3.  Literally "still presented."

4. To understand the allusion at the beginning of this Song to the palace of Hishiro at Makimuku, which had been the residence of the Emperor Kei-kō (See Sect. LXXVI, Note 1), it must be known that in the account of the reign of that monarch as given in the "Chronicles" there is a story which, like that in the text, turns on carelessness in dealing with a goblet,—carelessness which Kei-kō graciously pardoned. Moreover the scene of the incident here related was in the immediate neighbourhood of the old palace of Hishiro. There was therefore a double reason for referring to that place; and the under-current of insinuation is, that as Kei-kō in the olden time forgave the courtiers who forgot his goblet, will not the present Sovereign forgive the maid of Mihe for letting a leaf fall into his? The poetess, after describing the splendour and solidity of the Imperial abode, passes on to a mention of the luxuriant and many-branching *tsuki*-tree growing near "the house of new licking," *i.e.*, the sacred hall where the Sovereign performed each year the ceremony of tasting the first-fruits of the harvest. The "gate" may either be taken in its literal acceptation, or else regarded as used by metonymy for the palace itself. The description of that which the middle and lowest branches "have above them" is somewhat obscure, and perhaps the words should not be too strictly pressed for a perfectly rational meaning, their chief use being as metrical parallelisms. The supposition of the commentators is however that the poetess, in speaking of this immense tree, meant to say that the middle branch (or branches) spread eastward, and the lowest branches westward. Next we are told of the fall of the fatal leaf into the oil, *i.e.*, into the liquor, contained in the Imperial goblet; and the poetess, before acknowledging the awfulness of her misdemeanour, skilfully brings in an allusion to the Japanese account of the creation, when the drops that fell from the spear used by the creator ond creatrix Izanagi and Izanami to make the brine "go curdle-curdle" did very good work indeed; for they were piled up and became the first-formed island for the Japanese archipelago (see Sect. III): for drops to fall down, or for leaves to fall into drops (of wine), must therefore surely be a good omen rather than a crime. Conformably with the hesitating nature of her allusion, the maiden leaves it quite uncertain what is conceived of as "going curdle-curdle" in the present nstance. In fact, neither must the thought be pressed too far, nor the entence searched too rigorously from a grammatical point of view. Such intentional vagueness is one of the specific characteristics of a great deal of the poetry of Japan. The words "the tradition of the thing,

oo, this!", which conclude the poem, are obscure in another and more usual sense; but, having been already treated of in Note 4 to Sect. XXIV, they need not detain us here. They do not affect the sense of the rest of the poem. Two points more remain to be noticed: one is that the word *Mihe* and *hi no mi kado* ("august gate of *chæmacyparis*") are respectively preceded by the Pillow-Words *ariginu no*, whose signification is disputed, and *makisaku*, which signifies "splitting true trees;" the other, that the original of the word "glistens" near the commencement of the poem only has that sense if, following Morihe, we identify *hi-gakeru* with *hi-kagayakeru*. As it stands, the word *kakeru* lends itself more naturally to the interpretation of "sets." But the logical difficulty of accepting the phrase "where the sun sets" in such a context, where on the contrary some phrase of good omen is alone appropriate, seems greater than the philological difficulty of deriving *hi-gakeru* by a process of contraction from *hi-kagayakeru*. The designation of the Emperor or Heir Apparent by the title of "august child of the high-shining sun" has been met with before, and needs no explanation when the solar ancestry claimed by the Japanese monarchs is called to mind.

5. The gist of this Song, which must be supposed to be addressed to the female attendant, is simply: "Present the goblet full of liquor to the Emperor."—In accordance with the rules of Japanese construction the Imperative "present," which is the chief Verb of the sentence, comes last, and is preceded by the comparison of the Monarch to the leaves and flowers of the camellia-tree, while the comparatively unimportant words describing the position of the tree come at the beginning. Thus in a literal English translation the climax is necessarily spoilt through the reversal of the order of the words. The "broad-leafed camellia" has already appeared in Sect. CXXIII, Note 11, the "house of new licking" has been explained in the note immediately preceding the present one, and the incomprehensible concluding exclamation has been discussed in Sect. XXIV, Note 4. The "high metropolis" of Yamato is of course the then capital. There is however some doubt whether the word *take-chi*, which is here thus rendered, should not rather be considered as a proper name. The expression *ko-dakaru*, rendered "high-timbered," is also doubtful. Motowori interprets it simply as "slightly high." Moribe seems right in explaining the word *tsukasa* to mean "a mound."

6. This Song is here out of place, and is supposed by Motowori to have been composed, not by the Emperor, but by some court-lady who was absent from the feast. The meaning simply is: "Ah yes," tis to-day that the court ladies are "drinking their fill of rice-liquo r〔.—and

would that I were with them)!"—The picture here presented of the manners of the court is not attractive; but the comparison of the ladies' appearance with that of various birds is quaint. The commentators tell us that the the appropriateness of the use of the word "scarfs" as applied to the quail lies in the peculiar plumage of that bird, which makes it look as if it had a scarf on. "Having put their tails together" means "standing with their trains in a row." The epithet "yard" applied to the sparrows paints the habits of that bird. The words "great palace" are in the original preceded by the Pillow-Word *momoshiki no,* whose signification is disputed. After lines

> *Kefu mo ka mo*
> *Saka-mi-dzuku-rashi.*

rendered "may perhaps to day be truly steeped in liquor," Moribe would like to consider the lines

> *Asu mo komo*
> *Saka-mi-dzuku-rashi,*

*i.e.,* "may perhaps to-morrow be truly steeped in liquor" to have been accidentally omitted. There is no doubt but that their insertion would add to the effect of the poem from the point of view of style.

7. 天語歌, read *ama-koto-uta.* This expression is altogether obscure, and the commentators differ in their interpretations of it. Mabuchi, following the characters, sees in them an allusion to the words "august child of the high-shining sun" which recurs in each of the three Songs thus bracketed together. Motowori thinks that *ama-koto* should be regarded as standing for *amari-goto* (餘語) "surplus words," in allusion to the meaningless *refrain* with which the Songs in question terminate. Other Songs, however, which end in the same manner, are not thus designated. Moribe's exegesis, though founded on Motowori's is preferable to it. Accepting *ama-koto* as a contraction of *amari-goto,* he would take he second half of the compound in the sense of "things," not "words" (事 not 語), and regard the whole as signifying that the Songs were composed or sung after the conclusion of the actual feast. Against this view must be set the fact that the Chinese characters lend it no support. The translator, has, as usual when in doubt, preferred to adhere to the sense given by the characters.

[SECT. CLXI.—EMPEROR YŪ-RIYAKU (PART XII.—SONGS BY
THE EMPEROR AND PRINCESS WODO).]

On the day of this copious feast the Heavenly Sovereign, when Princess Wodo of Kasuga[1] presented to him
the great august liquor, sang again, saying :

> "Oh! the grandee's daughter holding the
> excellent flagon! [If] thou hold the ex-
> cellent flagon, hold it firmly! Hold it quite
> firmly, more and more firmly, child holding
> the excellent flagon."[2]

This is a Cup Song.[3] Then Princess Wodo presented 326
a Song. That Song said :

> "Would that I were [thou,] the lower board
> of the arm-rest whereon our great lord
> who tranquilly carries on the government
> stands leaning at morn, stands leaning at
> eve! Oh! mine elder brother!"[4]

This is a Quiet Song.

---

1. *Kasuga no Wodo-hime* See Sect. CLIX. Note 1.

2. This Song is simply a reiterated and playful injunction to the
maiden to hold firmly the flagon containing the intoxicating liquor ; and
Motowori is, as Moribe remarks, putting more into the words than they
are really meant to convey, when he says that they imply *praise* on the
Monarch's part,—The English words " grandee's daughter " represent the
Japanese *omi no omina*, a somewhat remarkable expression, which is
interpreted by Motowori to signify " attendant maiden." The translator
prefers the view propounded in Moribe's comment on this Song, and has
therefore adopted it. The expression is in the original preceded by the
untranslatable Pillow-Word *minasossoku* (Moribe reads the last syllable
with the *nigori,—gu*). The word rendered " excellent flagon " is *ho-dari*,
the first element of the compound being explained by the commentators
in the sense of " excellent," i.e., " big," while the second is the same as
the modern word *taru*, " a cask." In ancient times, however, the signification of *tari* or *taru* was that of a vessel to pour liquor from, not

to store liquor in,—i.e., a flagon, not a cask. The words " quite firmly, more and more firmly " represent the Japanese *shita-gataku ya-gataku* according to Moribe's exegesis. Motowori's interpretation of them in the sense of " [take the] bottom firmly and the top firmly " is less acceptable

3. Thus does the editor of 1687, who is followed by Moribe, understand the original expression *uki-uta*. Motowori's interpretation, " Floating Song," seems less good.

4. So enamoured is the maiden of the Sovereign that she woulh fain be even the board of the arm-rest on which he leans.—The expression " lower board " is misleading, for it refers simply to the self-evident fact that the board forming the top of the little low table used as an arm-rest by one squatting on his mat is below the arm, as whose support it serves. The words "stands leaning" must probably be understood to signify " sits " or " squats leaning." The expression " our great lord who tranquilly carries on the government " is a frequently recurring periphrasis for the word "Emperor," and has been explained in Sect. LXXXVII, Note 4. The words " at morn " and " at eve " are literally in the original " at morning doors " and " at evening doors," the reference being to the fact that the coors of a house are respectively opened and closed in the early morning and at nightfall. The exclamation " Oh! mine elder brother " is addressed to the board of the arm-rest. *Conf.* the first Song in Sect LXXXIX, where Yamato-take apostrophizes a pine-tree in he same terms.

———

327 [SECT. CLXII.—EMPEROR YŪ-RIYAKU (PART XIII.—HIS AGE AND PLACE OF BURIAL).]

The Heavenly Sovereign's august years were one hundred and twenty-four. His august mausoleum is at Takawashi in Tajihi[1] in Kafuchi.

———

1. For Tajihi see Sect. CXXXII, Note 4. *Takawashi* signifies "high eagle."

[SECT. CLXIII.—EMPEROR SEI-NEI (PART I.—SEARCH FOR
A SUCCESSOR TO HIM).]

His Augustness Shiraka-no-oho-yamato-ne-ko dwelt at
the palace of Mikakuri at Ihare,[1] and ruled the Empire.
This Heavenly Sovereign had no Empress, and likewise
no august children. So the Shiraka-Clan[2] was established
as his august proxy. So after the Heavenly Sovereign's
decease, there was no King to rule the Empire. Thereupon, on enquiry [being made] for a King who should
rule the sun's succession, Oshinumi-no-iratsume,[3] another
name for whom was Princess Ihi-toyo, younger sister of
Prince Ichinobe-oshiha-wake,[4] [was found to be] residing
at the palace of Tsunusashi at Takaki in Oshinumi in
Kadzuraki.[5]

1. For Ihare see Sect. XLIII, Note 26. *Mika-kuri* signifies "jar-
chestnut."

2. *Shiraka-be*

3. In Sect. CXXXI (Note 7) this name appears as *Awomi-no-
iratsume*. Both *Awomi* and *Oshinumi* are supposed to be names of
places. The latter is the name of a district in Yamato. Its etymology
is obscure. For *Ihi-toyo* see Sect. CXXXI, Note 8.

4. See Sect. CXXXI (Note 5), where however the title of *wake*
("Lord") is omitted.

5. For *Kadzuraki* see Sect. LV, Note 1, and for Oshinumi see Note
3 to the present Sect. *Takaki* seems to signify "high castle," while
*Tsunusashi* is obscure. (See Motowori's remarks on these two names in
Vol. XLIII, p. 3 of his Commentary.)

[SECT. CLXIV.—EMPEROR SEI-NEI (PART II.—PRINCES OHOKE
AND WOKE ARE DISCOVERED.)]

Then Wodate, Chief of the Mountain Clan[1] when appointed governor of the land of Harima, arrived just at

328 [ the time of ] a rejoicing for the new cave of an inhabi-
tant called Shizhimu.² Hereupon, when the feasting and
the drinking were at their height, they all danced in
turn. So two young children³ [employed] to light the
fire sat beside the furnace.⁴ These young children were
made to dance. Then one of the young children said:
"Do thou the elder brother dance first." The elder
brother likewise said: "Do thou the younger brother
dance first." When they thus yielded to each other, the
people who were met together laughed at their manner
of yielding to each other.⁵ So at last the elder brother
danced, [ and when he had ] finished, the younger when
about to dance chanted, saying:

"On the bamboos on the mountain-slopes,
behind which are hidden as soon as they
appear my warrior-mate's sword, on whose
hilt red earth was daubed, •for whose cord
red cloth was cut, and his red flags that
were set up!:—Beggarly descendants of
King Ichinobe-no-oshiha, august child of
the Heavenly Sovereign Izaho-wake, who
ruled the Empire as it were cutting the
[bamboos'] roots and bending down their
extremities, and like playing on an eight-
stringed lute!"⁶

329 Then forthwith Chief Wodate, starting at the sound
[ of these words ], and rolling off his couch,⁷ drove away
the people of the cave; and having set the two⁸ princes
[ one ] on his left knee and [ the other ] on his right and
wept and lamented, he collected the people together, and
having built a temporary palace, and set [ the two princes ]

to dwell in that temporary palace, he sent a courier up
[ to the capital ]. Thereupon their aunt, Queen Ihi-toyo,
delighted to hear [ the news ], made them come up to the
palace.

1. *Yama-be no murazhiwodate.* *Yama-be* has already appeared.
*Wo-date* signifies " small shield."

2. For this name see Sect. CXLIX, Note 5. A similar festival at
the inauguration of a new cave is mentioned in Sect. LXXX.

3. Motowori's vain attempts to reconcile the dates with this statement of Princes Ohoke and Woke being " young children " at this time,
after an interval of two reigns since the death of their father, will be
found in Vol. XLIII, pp. 10-11, of his Commentary.

4. *I.e.*, as the commentators snppose, a place or vessel holding a
light with which to kindle other lights for the feast. The word can
scarcely here have its common signification of a " kitchen-range."

5. *I.e.*, at the fact of their being so courteous to each other.

6. This so-called " chant,"—it is not a Song, because not in metre,
and is accordingly not transcribed syllabically,—is at first sight so difficult as to seem to defy translation, and to make the student apply to
the whole of his interpretation Motowori's closing remark on his exegesis
of one of phrases contained in it,—" this is mere guess-work, and
the text demands further consideration." A little inspection shows, however, that the drift of the words is by no means so inscrutable as its
partly ideographic and partly phonetic transcription makes it appear.
The first part down to the colon and dash is a " Preface " to the second,
the " Pivot " joining the two parts in the original Japanese being the
word " bamboos." The laws of English construction unfortunately do not
admit of the force of the orginal, which entirely depends on the position
of the words, being rendered into our language. The appropriateness of
the Preface to the body of the chant rests on the consideration that the
*bright* articles mentioned in it, viz., the sword painted and decorated
with red streamers (or perhaps tied on with a red sash) and also the red
banners are easily *hidden* behind the thick leaves of a bamboo-grove, just
as the Imperial origin of the two young Princes was hidden beneath
the vile office which they filled in Shizhimu's household. The clause
" cutting the [bamboos'] roots and bending down their extremities " forms
the chief difficulty. Indeed the word " roots " is supplied by Motowori, and his interpretation of the phrase is merely tentative. We may,

however, until some better explanation is offered, see in it a reference to
the energetic manner in which the Empire was ruled by the young
princes' grandfather, the Emperor Izaho-wake (i-chiū), or else perhaps by
their father Ichinobe-no-Oshiha. This latter view is preferred by Motowori, though according to the history Ichinobe-no-oshiha never actually
ascended the throne. The position of the Verb "ruled" in the Japanese
text permits of either interpretation. The comparison of the government
of the Empire to playing on a lute is poetical and appropriate. It
shonld be noticed that in the Japanese text the construction of the
sentence forming the main body of the chant is the reverse of what it is
made to appear to be in the translation. The words "beggarly descendants," by which, as a climax, the singer reveals his own and his
brother's illustrious descent, therefore come last of all and produce on
Wodate the startling effect which we read of in the next sentence.

7. Or, "seat." In ancient times each person in a room sat on a
special mat, and it is that small mat which is here meant.

8. The Numeral is accompanied by the Auxiliary *hashira*, properly
used for gods and goddesses.

330            [SECT. CLXV.—EMPEROR SEI-NEI (PART.—THE
                        GRANDEE SHIBI).[1]]

So when the government of the Empire was about to
be assumed,[2] the Grandee Shibi,[3] ancestor of the Grandees
of Heguri[4] mixed in the Songs, and took the hand of
the beautiful person whom His Augustness Woke was
about to wed. This maiden was a daughter of one of
the Headmen of Uda,[5] and her name was Ofuwo.[6] Then
His Augustness Woke likewise mixed in the Song-Hedge.[7]
Thereupon the Grandee Shibi sang, saying:

(iv) "The further fin of the roof of the
        great palace is bent down at the
        corner.[8]

When he had thus sung, and requested the conclusion

of the Song, His Augustness Woke sang, saying :

(v) "It is on account of the great carpenter's <sup>331</sup> awkwardness that it is bent down at the corner. "[9]

Then the Grandee Shibi sang again, saying :

(viii)" The great lord, on account of the magnanimity of his heart, does not enter and stand in the eight-fold hedge of branches of the child of a grandee."[10]

Hereupon the Prince sang again, saying :

(i) "Looking on the breakers of the briny current, I see my spouse standing by the fin of the tunny that comes sporting. "

Then the Grandee Shibi, getting more and more angry sang, saying :

(ix) " [Though] the eight-fold hedge of branches of the Prince the Great Lord be made fast at eight places, be made fast all round, 'tis a hedge that shall be cut, 'tis a hedge that shall be burnt. "[11]

Then the Prince again sang, saying :

(ii) "Oh fisherman that spearest the tunny, the great fish ! He being [there], thou must be sad at heart, tunny-spearing fisherman ! "[12]

Having thus sung, the feast was concluded at dawn, 332 and they all retired. Next morning the two Deities,[13] His Augustness Ohoke and His Augustness Woke, took counsel, saying : "All the people of the Court go to Court in the morning, and assemble at Shibi's gate at noon. So[14] Shibi must surely now be sleeping, and,

333 moreover there will be nobody at the gate. So unless it be now, it were hard to plot against him,[115]—and forthwith they at once raised an army, and beleaguered the house of the Grandee Shibi, and slew him.

---

1. The student should compare the version of the story in this Sect. with that give in the "Chronicles of Japan," where it is placed some years later at the commencement of the reign of the Emperor Mu-retsu, and not only do many of the details disagree, but the arrangement and number of the Songs is different. It is impossible to make a consistent whole out of the story as here given; so, while noticing the linguistic peculiarities of each of the Songs in the order in which they appear in the present text, the translator has thought it advisable, following Moribe, to give in Note 12 a consistent scheme of interpretation for the whole. The small Roman numbers placed in brackets at the commencement of each Song indicate its place in the text as restored by Moribe.

2. By one or other of the two Princes Ohoke and Woke. "Each," we are afterwards told, "ceded the Empire to the other," and it therefore remained for some time uncertain which was to be the Sovereign.

3. *Shibi no omi.* In some of the Songs that follow there is a play on the identity of this name with that of the tunny-fish (*shibi*). But whether that be really the derivation it is difficult to ascertain.

4. *Heguri no omi.* Conf. Sect. LXI, Note 45.

5. *Uda no obito-ra.* Uda is the name of a place in Yamato.

6. *I.e.,* "big fish." But see the remark on this name in Note 12.

7. *Uta-gaki.* The derivation of this curious expression is disputed; but the meaning seems to be "strophic" or "choric song," or "a place where singing in which more than one takes part is going on."

8. In this Song the "further fin" (*woto tsu hata-de*, explained by the characters 彼鰭手 or 彼端手) is supposed to signify a pent-roof, or the eaves of the roof, or else an out-house connected by a slanting roof with the main building. The "great palace" is the palace of Prince Woke.

9. The "great carpenter" is the carpenter employed to build the roof above-mentioned.

10. The "eight-fold hedge of branches" is simply a "hedge," and the "child of a grandee" the Grandee Shibi himself,

11. The words "made fast" refer to the tying of the fence at certain places to give it strength. If we accepted Moribe's emendation of the final Verb *yakemu*, "burn," to *yaremu*, we should have to translate the last clause thus : " 'tis a fence that shall be broken."

12. "The great fish" (*ofuwo yo shi*) is the Pillow-Word for *shibi*, "tunny." The word "he" (which might also be rendered "*it*,"—the original being (*so*) must be taken to refer both to the fish itself and to the Grandee Shibi (*i.e.*, the grandee Tunny), who bore its name.—Following Moribe's acceptable restoration of the original story, which is founded on a comparison of the text of these "Records" with that of the "Chronicles of Japan," we find that in the first Song of the series the young Prince half jokingly remarks on the fact of the Grandee Shibi appearing in public with the damsel who was to have been his (the Prince's) bride. Shibi's name, which, as already stated, signifies "tunny," furnishes the occasion for the marine metaphors borrowed from the current and the breakers. Shibi's answer (Song II,—in the Records" wrongly ascribed to the prince), takes up the same strain, but in a more aunting tone : the prince is likened to a fisherman who would fain make a futile attempt to spear the great tunny, and his (the tunny's. i.e., the Grandee Shibi's) presence must indeed be pain and grief to him. In a third Song, which is given in the "Chronicles," but not in the "Records," the prince retorts that he relies on his good sword to win the girl for him in the end, and in Song IV the Grandee jeers at the dilapidated condition of his palace, and by implication at the sorry state of his fortunes,—a taunt to which the prince replies in Song V by saying that if the palace is dilapidated, and the Empire in disorder, the fault belongs to none other than to the Grandee himslf. Songs VI and VII, which are not found in the "Records," only serve to continue the growing war of words, which in Song VII (in the "Rocords" wrongly attributed to the Grandee) comes to a climax by the prince exclaiming that if he does not force his way into the Grandee's mansion to seize his lady-love, it is only on account of the magnanimity of his disposition. To this the Grandee replies in Song IX (in the "Records" erroneously attributed to the prince) by a sort of *tu quoque*, vowing that he will cut and burn his way into the prince's palace. This is not the end of the dispute in the pages of the "Chronicles," but it is all that need detain the reader of the "Records." It should, however, be mentioned that in the "Chronicles" the name of the girl is *Kage-hime* : *Ofuwo* "Big Fish," which is here given, would seem to be nothing more

than a nickname, which perhaps arose from the incidents of this metrical war of words.

13. The word used in the original is *hashira*, the Auxiliary Numeral for Deities. It recurs at the commencement of the next Section, where however it is not convenient to translate it.

14. The original here has the character 亦, " again " or " moreover." But this must be, as Motowori points out a copyist's error. Almost immediately below the same character recurs where it is equally out of place. The translator has followed Motowori in rendering it the first time by " so," and the second by " surely."

15. *I.e.*, There is no time like the present for plotting against him.

---

[SECT. CLXVI.—EMPEROR SEI-NEI (PART IV.—PRINCE OHOKE CEDES THE EMPIRE TO PRINCE WOKE).]

Then each of the two Princes ceded the Empire to the other, and His Augustness Ohoke [ finally ] ceded it to the younger brother His Augustness Woke, saying : " Had not Thine Augustness revealed our names when we dwelt in the house of Shizhimu in Harima, we should never have arrived at being the lords of the Empire. This is quite owing to Thine Augustness's deed. So, though I be the elder brother, do Thine Augustness rule the Empire first, "—and [ with these words ] he urgently ceded [ his claim ]. So, being unable to refuse, His Augustness Woke ruled the Empire first.

---

[SECT. CLXVII.—EMPEROR KEN.ZŌ (PART I.—THE OLD WOMAN OKI-ME).]

His Augustness Woke-no-ihasu-wake dwelt at the palace of Chika-tsu-Asuka,[1] and ruled the Empire for eight years. The Heavenly Sovereign wedded the Queen of Naniha,[2] daughter of the King of Ihaki.[3] He had no children. At the time when this Heavenly Sovereign was searching for the august bones of the King his father, King Ichinobe,[4] there came out from the land of Afumi [to the palace] a poor old woman, who said: "The place where the prince's august bones are buried is specially well known to me,[5] and moreover [his skeleton] can be known by his august teeth." (His august teeth were teeth uneven like a lily.) Then people were set[6] to dig the 334 ground and search for the august bones; and the bones having been forthwith obtained, an august mausoleum was made on the mountain east of the Moor of Kaya,[7] and they were interred, and the children of Kara-fukuro[8] were made to guard the august mausoleum. Afterwards the august bones were brought up [to the Capital]. So having returned up [to the Capital, the Heavenly Sovereign] sent for the old woman, praised her for having, without forgetting, kept the place in mind, and conferred upon her the name of the Old Woman Oki-me:[9] thus did he send for her into the palace, and deign to treat her with deep and wide kindness. So he built a house for the old woman to dwell in close to the palace, and always sent for her every day. So he hung a bell by the door of the great hall, and always rang it when he wished to call the old woman. So he composed an august Song. That Song said:

"Oh! the far-distant bell tinkles when she has past the moor with its low eulalias and the little valley. Oh! Oki-me must be coming!"[10]

Hereupon the old woman said: "I am very aged, 335

and would fain depart to my native land." So when the Heavenly Sovereign let her depart according to her request, he saw her off and sang, saying:

"Ah Okime! Okime from Afumi! from to-
		morrow [onwards] wilt [thou] be hidden
		behind the deep mountains, and alas! not
		seen!"[11]

---

1. See Sect. CXXXIII, Note 11.

2. *Naniha no miko.* For Naniha see Sect. XLIV, Note 26

3. *Ihaki no miko.*

4. Who had been treacherously slain by the Emperor Yū-riyaku (see Sect. CXLVIII).

5. *I.e.,* says Motowori, "it is known to me, and to none besides."

6. The character used is 起, which is more applicable to the *raising* of troops than to the *setting to work* of peasants. It seems however here to be used in the latter sense; or perhaps we should consider it to mean that people *were got together.*

7. See Sect. CXLVIII, Note 3. Possibly the "mountain east" should be a Proper Name,—Eastern Mountain,—but it is not taken as such by Motowori.

8. See Sect. CXLVIII, Note 1.

9. *I.e.,* "keeping an eye." *q.d.,* on the place of burial of the Emperor's father. Grammar would lead us to expect the order of the words forming the name to be reversed thus, *Me-oki;* but see Motowori's remarks in Vol. XLIII, p. 56.

10. This Song is not comprehensible except by reference to the text of the "Chronicles," whose author gives a somewhat varying version of the story. He tells us that, as a support to the infirm old lady, the Emperor had a string or rope stretched as a sort of hand-rest along the way she was obliged to pass in order to reach the Imperial apartments, and that at the end of the rope was a bell whose tinkling notified the Emperor of her approach. The conjectural exclamation which closes the little poem has therefore an obvious sense, which would be wanting if the bell were at the other end, as in the version here given; for the Emperor would not give expression to surprise at her approach, if he had himself just rung for her to come.—"Far-distant" is an imperfect attempt to represent the Pillow-Word *momo-dzutafu,* which here alludes to the stages

along which the old woman may be supposed to be travelling. The valley and the moor overgrown with short grass form an allusion to the way,—long and arduous for her,—which Oki-me had to traverse to reach the Imperial apartments, and they contain possibly a further allusion to her orginal journey to the capital.

11. The meaning of this Song is quite clear.—The second time the name *Oki-me* occurs, it might, instead of, being as here taken as an exclamation, be made the subject of the sentence, thus: "Oki-me from Afumi will by to-morrow, etc." The words "wilt [thou]," which represent *ka* of the original Japanese may be taken either as an exclamation properly so-called, or as a sort of rhetorical interrogation whose force is simply exclamatory. The meaning comes to the same in either case, and is literally rendered by the same English words; but according to the latter view, we should have to replace the point of exclamation by a point of interrogation.

----

[SECT. CLXVIII.—EMPEROR KEN-ZŌ (PART II.—HE
SLAYS THE BOAR-HERD).]

The Heavenly Sovereign searched for the old boar-herd who had seized his august provisions at the time when he first met with adversity and was fleeing;[1] and, having sought him out, sent for him up [ to the Capital ], beheaded him in the bed[2] of the River Asuka,[3] and cut the knee-tendons of all his kindred. Wherefore down to the present time his descendants, on the day when[4] they 285 come up to Yamato, always limp of their own accord. So the man's abode had been well seen and divined.[5] So the place was named Shimesu.[6]

----

1. See Sect. CXLIX.
2. Motowori would have us understand the text to mean "in the neighbourhood of the river." There is, however, no difficulty in accepting the author's statement literally, as any one who is acquainted with the broad, stony beds of Japanese rivers will readily admit.

3. *Asuki-gaka.* For Asuka see Sect. CXXXIII, Note 11.

4. *I.e.*, probably "whenever."

5. *I.e.*, discovered by augury" or else simply "found and pointed out,"—by whom does not appear.

6. The real etymology of this name is obscure, but the author's intention is to connect it with the "dividing" or "pointing out" mentioned in the preceding sentence, which is given phonetically as [*mi*] *shimeki.*

---

[SECT. CLXIX.—EMPEROR KEN-ZŌ (PART III.—THE EMPEROR YŪ-RIYAKU'S MAUSOLEUM IS DISFIGURED).]

The Heavenly Sovereign, deeply hating the Heavenly Sovereign Oho-hatsuse, who had slain the King his father, wished to be revenged on his spirit.[1] So when wishing to destroy the august mausoleum of the Heavenly Sovereign Oho-hatsuse, he [ was about to ] send people [ to execute this design ], his elder brother, His Augustness Ohoke, addressed[2] him, saying: "To demolish this august mausoleum thou shouldst not send other people. None but myself shall go, and I will demolish it according to the Heavenly Sovereign's august heart." Then the Heavenly Sovereign commanded: "Make thy progress, then, according to thy decree," Wherefore His Augustness Ohoke, having proceeded down himself, slightly excavated the side of the august mausoleum, and returned up [ to the capital ], and reported that he had dug up and demolished it. Then the Heavenly Sovereign, astonished at the quickness of his return up, asked how he had demolished it. He replied, saying: "I slightly excavated the earth at the side of the august mausoleum." The Heavenly Sovereign said: "Wishing to be revenged on the enemy of the King our father, I had counted on the complete demolition of the mausoleum, Why hast thou [ only ] slightly excavated it ? " He replied, saying : 337 " The reason why I did so was that the wish to be revenged on the spirit of the foe of the King our father is truly just. Nevertheless the Heavenly Sovereign Oho-hatsuse, though he were our father's foe, was still our uncle, and moreover was an Heavenly Sovereign who ruled the Empire. So if we now, simply from the con-sideration of his having been our father's enemy, were completely to demolish the mausoleum of an Heavenly Sovereign who ruled the Empire, after-generations would surely revile us. Meanwhile the wrongs of the King our father must not be unrevenged. So I slightly excavated the side of the mausoleum. This insult will quite suffice as a token to future ages. " On his thus addressing him, the Heavenly Sovereign said : " This also is very just, Be it as thou sayest. "

---

1. 靈, read *mi tama* or *tamashihi*. We might also translate it by the word "ghost."

2. The respectful character 奏 is used for this word, and again below we have the First Personal Pronoun represented by 僕, "servant."

3. This sentence ends in the original with the characters 以出參, which it is not necessary to render into English. They imply that the speaker will come back, and report on what he has done.

---

[SECT. CLXX.—EMPEROR KEN-ZŌ (PART IV.—HIS AGE AND PLACE OF BURIAL).]

So the Heavenly Sovereign died, and His Augustness Ohoke ruled the succession of Heaven's sun.[1] The Heavenly Sovereign's august years were thirty-eight years. His august mausoleum is on the mound of Iha-tsuki at Katawoka.[2]

1. See Sect. XXXII, Note 27.

2. For *Katawoka* see Sect. LX, Note 29. *Iha-tsuki* probably means "rockplatter," and seems to have been the name of a little plateau.

[SECT. CLXXI.—EMPEROR NIN-KEN.][1]

His Augustness Ohoke dwelt at the palace of Hirataka at Isono-kami, and ruled the Empire. The Heavenly Sovereign wedded Kasuga-no-oho-iratsume, the august daughter of the Heavenly Sovereign Oho-hatsuse-no-waka-take, and begot august children: Takaki-no-iratsume; next Takara-no-iratsume; next Kasubi-no-iratsume; next Tashiraka-no-iratsume; next His Grandeur Wo-hatsuse-no-waka-sazaki; next Prince Ma-waka. The child born to him by his next wife Naka-no-waku-go-no-iratsume, daughter of the Grandee Hitsmma of Wani, was: Kasuga-no-yamada-no-iratsume. The august children of this Heavenly Monarch numbered seven altogether. Of these His Augustness Wo-hatsuse-no-waka-sazaki [ was he who afterwards ] ruled the Empire.

[SECT. CLXXII.—EMPEROR MU-RETSU.]

His Grandeur Wo-hatsuse-no-waka-sazaki dwelt in the palace of Namiki at Hatsuse, and ruled the Empire for eight years. This Heavenly Monarch had no august children. So the Wo-hatsuse Tribe was established as

1. For the dicontinuance of explanatory foot-notes in this concluding portion of the translation see Translator's Introduction, Sect. II, near the top of page xv.

his august proxy.    His august mausoleum is on the mound of Ihatsuki at Karawoka.    On the death of this Heavenly Monarch there was no prince to inherit the Empire,    So His Augustness Ohodo, the fifth descendant of the Heavenly Monarch Homuda, was sent for down to the land of Afumi, and married to her Augustness Tashiraka, and presented with the Empire.

---

[SECT. CLXXIII.—EMPEROR KEI-TAI.]

His Augustness Ohodo dwelt in the Palace of Tamaho at Ihare, and ruled the Empire.    The (two) august children born to this Heavenly Monarch by Waka-hime, ancestress of the Dukes of Miwo, were: Oho-iratsuko, next Idzumo-no-iratsume.    The (two) august children born to him by his next wife, Meko-no-iratsume, sister of the Chieftain Ofushi, ancestor of the Chieftains of Wohari, were:    His Augustness Hiro-kuni-oshi-taka-kana-hi; next His Augustness Take-wo-hiro.kuni-oshi-tate.    The (one) august child born to him by his next wife (the Great Empress) Her Augustness Tashiraka, the august daughter of the Heavenly Monarch Ohoke, was: His Augustness Ame-kuni-oshi-haruki-hiro-niha.    The (one) august child born to him by his next wife Wo-kumi-no-iratsume, daughter of Prince Okinaga-no-mate, was: Sasage-no-iratsume. The three august children born to him by his next wife Kuro-hime, daughter of Prince Sakata-no-oho-mata, were: Kamu-saki-no-iratsume; next Mamuta-no-iratsume; next Uma-tsuta-no-iratsume.    The (three) august children born to him by his next wife Seki-hime, daughter of Womochi Grandee of Mamuta were: Mamuta-no-oho-iratsume; next Shira-saka-no-iku-hi-no-iratsume; next Wo-nu-no-iratsume, another name for whom is Naga-me-hime.    The (four) children born to him by his 339 next wife Yamato-hime, younger sister of Katabu Duke of Miwo, were: Oho-tratsume; next Prince Maroko; next Prince Mimi; next Aka-hime-no-iratsume. The (three) children born to him by his next wife Abe-no-haye-hime, were: Waka-ya-no-iratsume; next Tsuburà-no-iratsume; next Prince Adzu. The august children of this Heavenly Monarch numbered nineteen in all (seven Kings and twelve Queens). Of these His Augustness Ame-kuni-oshi-haruki-hiro-niha [was he who afterwards] ruled the Empire; next His Augustness Hiro-kuni-oshi-take-kana-hi ruled the Empire; the next, Queen Sasage, presided at the temple of the Deity of Ise. In this august reign Ihawi, Lord of Tsukushi, was disobedient to the Imperial Decrees, and was exceedingly disrespectful. So, the Great Chieftain Mononobe-no-arakawi and the Chieftain Ohotomo-no-kanamura were both sent to slay Ihawi.[1] The august years of this Heavenly Monarch were forty-three. His august mausoleum is at Awi in Mishima.

[SECT. CLXXIV.—EMPEROR KAN-AN.]

His Augustness Hiro-kuni-oshi-take-kana-hi dwelt in the Palace of Kanahashi at Magari, and ruled the Empire. This Heavenly Monarch had no august children. His august grave is at the village of Takaya in Furuchi in Kafuchi.

[SECT. CLXXV.—EMPEROR SEN-KUWA.]

His Augustness Take-wo-hiro-kuni-oshi-tate dwelt in the Palace of Ihorinu at Hinokuma, and ruled the Em-

---

1. Details of this struggle and its causes are given in the "Chronicles of Japan," and are discussed at length in Motowori's Commentary, Vol. XLIV, pp. 15-20. They are of no special interest.

pire. The august children born to this Heavenly Sovereign by his wife Her Augustness Tachi-bana-no-naka-tsu-hime, the august daughter of the Heavenly Sovereign Ohoke, were: Her Augustness Ishi-hime; next Her Augustness Wo-ishi-hime; next King Kura-no-waka-ye. The august children born to him by his next wife, Kafuchi-no-waku-go-hime, were: King Honoho; next King Weha. The august children of this Heavenly 340 Sovereign numbered altogether five (three Kings and two Queens). So King Honoho (was the ancestor of the Dukes Shihida.) Prince Weha (was the ancestor of the Dukes of Wina and of the Dukes of Tajihi.)

---

[SECT. CLXXVI.—EMPEROR KIM-MEI.]

The Heavenly Sovereign Ame-kuni-oshi-haruki-hiro-niha dwelt in the Great Palace of Shikishima, and ruled the Empire. The (three) august children born to this Heavenly Sovereign by his wife, Her Augustness Ishi-hime, the august daughter of the Heavenly Sovereign Hi-no-kuma, were: King Yata; next His Augustness Nu-na-kura-tama-shiki; next King Kasanuhi. The (one) august child born to him by his next wife Her Augustness Wo-ishi-hime, younger sister [ of the first one ], was: King Kami. The (three) august children born to him by his next wife Nukako-no-iratsume, daughter of the Grandee Hitsuma of Kasuga, were: Kasuga-no-yamada-no-iratsume; next King Maroko; next King Soga-no-kura. The (thirteen) children born to him by his next wife Kitashi-hime, daughter of the Prime Minister the Noble Inawe of Soga were: His Augustness Tachibana-no-toyo-hi; next his younger sister Queen Ihakumo; next King Atori; next

Her Augustness Toyo-mike-kashiki-ya-hime; next King Mata-maroko; next King Oho-yake; next King Imigako next King [of?] Yamashiro; next his younger sister Queen Oho-tomo; next King Sakurawi-no-yumi-hari; next King Manu; next King Tachibana-moto-no-waku-go; next King Tone. The five august children born to him by his next wife Wo-ye-hime, aunt of Her Augustness Kitashi-hime, were: King Umaki; next King Kadzuraki; next King Hashi-bito-no-ana-ho-be; next King Saki-kusa-be-no-ana-ho be, another name for whom was Sume-irodo; next His Augustness Hatsuse-be-no-waka-sazaki. Altogether the august children of this Heavenly Sovereign numbered twenty-five Kings and Queens. Of these His Augustness Nu-na-kura-futo-tama-shiki [was he who afterwards] ruled the Empire. Next His Augustness Tachibana-no-toyo-hi ruled the Empire. Next Her Augustness Toyo-mike-hashiki-ya-hime ruled the Empire. Next His Augustness Hatsusebe-no-waka-sazaki ruled the Empire. In all there were four Kings and Queens that ruled the Empire.

---

**341**  [SECT. CLXXVII.—EMPEROR BI-DATSU.]

His Augustness Nuna-kura-futo.tama-shiki dwelt in the Palace of Wosada, and ruled the Empire for fourteen years. The (eight) children born to this Heavenly Sovereign by his wife, his half-sister Her Augustness Toyo-mike-kashiki-ya-hime, were: King Shidzu-kahi, another name for whom was Kahi-dako; next King Takeda, another name for whom was King Wo-kahi; next King Woharita; next King Umori; next King Wohari; next

King Tame; next King Sakurawi-no-yumi-hari. The (two) august children born to him by his next wife Wo-kuma-ko-no-iratsume, daughter of the Headman Ohoka of Ise, were: Her Augustness Futo-hime; next Queen Takara, another name for whom was Queen Nukade-hime. The (three) august children born to him by his next wife Her Augustness Hiro-hime, daughter of King Okinaga-no-ma-de, were: King Osako-no-hiko-hito, another name for whom was King Maroko; next King Saka-nobori; next King Uji. The (four) august children born to him by his next wife Omina-ko-no-iratsume, daughter of Kasuga-no-naka-tsu-waku-go, were: King Naniha; next King Ku-hada; next King Kasuga; next King Oho-mata. Of the august children of this Heavenly Monarch,—seventeen Kings and Queens altogether,—King Hiko-hito begot by his wife his half-sister Queen Tamura, another name for whom was Her Augustness Nukade-hime, (three) august children, namely: the Heavenly Sovereign that ruled the Empire from the Palace of Wokamoto; next King Naka-tsu; next King Tara. The (two) august children born to him by his next wife, Queen Ohomata, younger sister of King Aya, were: King Chinu; next his younger sister Queen Kuhada. The (two) august children born to him by his next wife his half-sister Princess Yumi-hari, were: King Yamashiro; next Queen Kasanuhi,—altogether seven Kings and Queens, The august mausoleum [of the Heavenly Sovereign Nuna-kura-futo-tama-shiki] is at Shinaga in Kafuchi.

[SECT. CLXXVIII.—EMPEROR YŌMEI.]

His Augustness Tachibana-no-toyo-hi dwelt in the Palace of Ikenobe, and ruled the Empire for three years. The one august child born to this Heavenly Sovereign by his wife Oho-gitashi-hime, daughter of the Prime Minister the noble Iname, was: King Tame. The (four) 342 august children born to him by his next wife, his half-sister Princess Hashi-bito-no-anaho-be, were: His Augustness Uhe-no-miya-no-uma-ya-dono-toyo-to-mimi; next King Kume; next King We-kuri; next King Mamuta. The august children born to him by his next wife Ihi-me-no-ko, daughter of Tagima-no-kura-bito-hiro, were: King Tagima; next his younger sister Sugashiroko-no-iratsume. The august mausoleum of this Heavenly Sovereign, which had been by the borders of Lake Ihare, was afterwards removed to the middle sepulchre of Shinaga.

---

[SECT. CLXXIX.—EMPEROR SU-JUN.]

The Heavenly Sovereign Hatsuse-be-no-waka-sazaki dwelt at the Palace of Shibabaki at Kurahashi, and ruled the Empire for four years. His august mausoleum is on the mound of Kurahashi.

---

[SECT. CLXXX.—EMPRESS SUI-KO.]

Her Augustness Toyo-mike-kashiki-ya-hime dwelt at the Palace of Wohorida, and ruled the Empire for thirty seven years. Her august mausoleum, which had been on the mound of Ohonu, was afterwards removed to the great sepulchre at Shinaga.

# APPENDIX I.

JAPANESE TEXT OF THE SONGS PRESERVED IN THE
" KO-JI-KI, " OR " RECORDS OF ANCIENT MATTERS, "
TRANSLITERATED INTO ROMAN.[1]

## I. ( SECT. XIX, NOTE 6. )

Ya-kumo tatsu     Idzumo ya-he-gaki
Tsuma-gomi ni     Ya-he-gaki-tsukuru
     Sono ya-he-gaki wo

## II. ( SECT. XXIV, NOTE 4. )

| | |
|---|---|
| Ya-chi-hoko no | Kami no mikoto ha |
| Ya-shima-ḳuni | Tsuma magi-kanete |
| Toho-tohoshi | Koshi no kuni ni |
| Sakashi-me wo | Ari to kikoshite |
| Kuhashi-me wo | Ari to kikoshite |
| Sa-yobahi ni | Ari-tatashi |
| Yobahi, ni | Ari-kayohase |
| Tachi ga wo mo | Imada tokazute |

1. There are few various readings of the text of these poems'
Where any occur, the translator has been guided by the decisions of
Motowori and Moribe. Occasionally these two authorities differ as to the
division of the words into lines, and Moribe in particular does not hesitate
to propose such emendations as seem to him necessary. The translator
has in almost all cases adhered to the traditional text, but gives in foot-
notes such emendations as appear worthy of notice. Moribe's division of
the lines being in almost every case preferable to Motowori's, it has
however here been generally adopted.

| | |
|---|---|
| Osuhi wo mo | Imada tokaneba |
| Wotome no | Nasu ya ita-to wo |
| Osoburahi | Wa ga tatasereba |
| Hikodzurahi | Wa ga tatasereba |
| Awo-yama ni | Nuye ha naki |
| Sa-nu tsu tori | Kigishi ha toyomu |
| Niha tsu tori | Kake ha naku |
| Uretaku mo | Naku-naru tori ka |
| Kono tori mo | Uchi-yame-kosene |
| Ishitafu ya | Ama-hase-dzukahi |
| Koto no | Katari-goto mo |

Ko wo ba

### III. (SECT. XXIV, NOTE 5.)

| | |
|---|---|
| Ya-chi-hoko no | Kami no mikoto |
| Nuye-kusa no | Me ni shi areba |
| Wa ga kokoro | Ura-su no tori zo |
| Ima koso ha | Chi-dori ni arame |
| Nochi ha | Na-dori ni aramu wo |
| Inochi ha | Na shise-tamahi so |
| Ishi-tafu ya | Ama-hase-dzukahi |
| Koto no | Katori-gotomo |

Ko wo ba

### IV. (SECT. XXIV, NOTE 7.)

| | |
|---|---|
| Awo-yama ni | Hi ga kakuraba |
| Nuba-tama no | Yo ha ide-namu |
| Asa-hi no | Wemi-sakaye-kite |
| Taku-dzumu no | Shiroki tadamuki |
| Awa-yuki no | Wakayaru mune wo |
| So-dataki | Tataki-managari |
| Ma-tama-de | Tama-de sahi-maki |

Momo-naga ni        I ha nasamu wo
Aya ni              Na kohi-kikoshi
Ya-chi-hoko no      Kami no mikoto
Koto no             Katari-goto mo
              Ko wo ba

## V. (Sect. xxv, Note 2.)

Nuba-tama no          Kuroki mi keshi wo
Ma-tsubusa ni         Tori-yosohi                          345
Oki tsu tori          Muna miru toki
Ha-tatagi mo          Kore ha fusahazu
He tsu nami           So ni nugi-ute
So-ni-dori no         Awoki mi keshi wo
Ma-tsubusa ni         Tori-yosohi
Oki tsu tori          Muna miru toki
Ha-tatagi mo          Ko mo fusahazu
He tsu nami           So ni nugi-ute
Yama-gata ni          Magishi atane tsuki[2]
Some-ki ga shiru ni   Shime-koromo wo
Ma-tsubusa ni         Tori-yosohi
Oki tsu tori          Muna miru toki
Ha-tatagi mo          Ko shi 'yoroshi
Itokoya no            Imo no mikoto
Mura-tori no          Wa ga mure-i-naba
Hike-tori no          Wa ga hike-i-naba
Nakazhi to ha         Na ha ifu to mo
Yamato no             Hito-moto susuki
Unakabushi            Na ga nakasamaku
Asa-ame no            Sa-giri ni tatamu zo[3]

---

2. Motowori reads *Magishi    Atane tsuki as two lines.*
3. Motowori reads *Sagiri ni    Tatamu zo* as two lines.

Waka-kusa no        Tsuma no mikoto·
Koto no             Katari-goto mo
        Ko wo ba

## VI. (Sect. xxv, Note 3.)

Ya-chi-hoko no      Kami no mikoto ya
A ga oho-kuni       Nushi koso ha
Wo ni i-maseba      Uchi-miru
        Shima no saki-zaki
Kaki-miru           Iso no saki ochizu
Waka-kusa no        Tsuma motase-rame
A ha mo yo          Me ni shi areba
Na wokite           Wo ha nashi
Na wokite           Tsuma ha nashi
Aya-kaki no         Fuhayaga shita ni
Mushi-busuma        Nikoya ga shita ni
Taku-busuma         Sayagu ga shita ni
Awa-yuki no         Wakayaru mune wo
Taku-dzunu no       Shiroki tadamuki
So-dataki           Tataki-managari
Ma-tama-de          Tama-de sashi-maki
Momo-naga ni        I wo shi nase
Toyo mi ki          Tate-matsurase

## VII. (Sect. xxxi, Note 33.)

Ame naru ya         Oto-tanabata no
Unagaseru           Tama no mi sumaru
Mi sumaru ni        Ana-dama haya
        Mi tani futa watarasu[4]
Ajishiki            Taka-hiko-ne no
        Kami zo ya

---

4. Motowori reads *Mitani    Futa watarasu* as two lines.

### VIII. (SECT. XLII, NOTE 18.)

| | |
|---|---|
| Aka-dama ha | Wo sahe hikaredo |
| Shira-tama no | Kimi ga yosohi shi |

Tafutoku ari-keri

### IX. (SECT. XLII, NOTE 19.)

| | |
|---|---|
| Oki tsu tori | Kamo-doku shima ni |
| Waga wi-neshi | Imo ha wasurezhi |

Yo no koto-goto ni

### X. (SECT. XLVII, NOTES 16 AND 17.)

| | |
|---|---|
| Uda no taka-ki ni[5] | Shigi-wana haru[6] |
| Wa ga matsu ya | Shigi ha sayarazu |
| Isukuhashi | Kujira sayaru |
| Konami ga | Na kohasaba |
| Tachi-soba no | Mi no nakeku wo[7] |
| Kokishi hiwene | Uhanari ga |
| Na kohasaba | Ich-saka-ki mi no |
| Ohokeku wo | Kokida hiwene |
| Ye ye | Shi ya ko shi ya |
| [ Mo ha igonofu zo ] | Aa shi yo ko shi ya |

347

### XI. (SECT. XLVIII, NOTE 4.)

| | |
|---|---|
| Osaka no | Oho-muro-ya ni |
| Hito saha ni | Ki-iri-wori |
| Hito saha ni | Iri-wori to mo |
| Mitsu-mitsushi | Kume no ko ga |
| Kubu-tsutsu-i | Ishi-tsutsu-i mochi |

Uchite shi yamamu

---

5. Motowori reads *Uda no Taka-ki ni* as two lines.

6. Moribe emends *haru* to *hari*.

7. Motowori divides these lines thus: *Tachi-soba no mi no Nakeku wo.*

Mitsu-mitsushi  Kume no ko-ra ga
Kubu-tsutsu-i   Ishi-tsutsu-i mochi
   Ina utaba yorashi

## XII. (Sect. xlix, Note 2.)

Mitsu mitsushi  Kume no ko-ra ga
Aha-fu ni ha   Ka-mira hito-moto
So ne ga moto   So ne me tsunagite
   Uchite shi yamamu

## XIII. (Sect. xlix, Note 3.)

Mitsu-mifsushi  Kume no ko-ra ga
Kaki-moto ni   Uweshi hazhikami
Kuchi hibiku   Ware ha wasurezhi
   Uchite shi yamanu

## XIV. (Sect. xlix, Note 4.)

Kamu-kaze no  Ise no umi no
Ohishi     Hahi-motohorofu
Shitadami no   I-hahi-motohori
   Uchite shi yamamu

## XV. (Sect. xlix, Note 6.)

Tata namete  Inasa no yama no
Ko no ma yo mo I-yuki-mamorahi
Tatakaheba   Ware ba ya wenu.
Shima tsu tori  U-kahi ga tomo
   Ima suke ni kone

## XVI. (Sect. li, Note 17.)

Yamato no   Takasazhi-nu wo
Nana-yuku   Wotome-domo
   Tare wo shi makamu

### XVII. (Sect. li, Note 19.)

Katsu-gatsu mo      Iya-saki-dateru
Ye wo shi makamu

### XVIII. (Sect. li, Note 21.)

A me tsu tsu      Chi dori mashi to to [?]
Nado sakeru to-me

### XIX. (Sect. li, Note 22.)

Wotome ni      Taka ni ahamu to
Wa ga sakeru to-me

### XX. (Sect. li, Note 28.)

Ashi-hara no      Shigekoki wo-ya ni
Suga-tatami      Iyasaya shikite
Wa ga futari neshi

### XXI. (Sect. lii, Note 6.)

Sawi-gaha yo      Kumo tachi-watari
Unebi-yama      Ko no ha sayaginu
Knze fukanu to su

### XXII. (Sect. lii, Note 5.)

Unebi-yama      Hiru ha kumo to wi
Yufu sareba      Kaze fukamu to zo
Ko no ha sayageru

349

### XXIII. (Sect. lxvi, Note 7)

Ko ha ya      Mima-ki-iri-biko ha ya
Mima-ki-iri-biko ha ya   Ono ga wo wo
Nusumi shi semu to      Shiri tsu to yo
I-yuki-tagahi      Mahe tsu to yo
I-yuki-tagahi      Ukagahaku
Shirani to      Mima-ki-iri-biko ha ya

## XXIV. ( SECT. LXXXI, NOTE 4. )

Yatsumesasu          Idzumo-takeru ga
Hakeru tachi          Tsudzura saha maki
          Sa-mi nashi ni ahare

## XXV. ( SECT. LXXXIV, NOTE 8. )

Sanesashi          Sogamu no wo-nu ni
Moyuru hi no          Ho-naka ni tachite
          Tohishi kimi ha mo

## XXVI. ( SECT. LXXXVI, NOTES 3 AND 5. )

Nihibari          Tsukuha wo sugite
          Iku yo ka netsuru —
Ka-ga nabete          Yo ni ha kokono-yo
          Hi ni ha towo-ka wo

## XXVI.I ( SECT. LXXXVII, NOTE 3. )

Hisa-kata no          Ame no Kagu-yama
To-kama ni          Sa-wataru kuhi
Hiha-boso          Tawaya-gahina wo
Makamu to ha          Are ha suredo
Se-nemu to ha          Are ha omohedo
Na ga keseru          Osuhi no suso ni
          Tsuki tatanamu yo

## XXVIII. ( SECT. LXXXVII, NOTE 4. )

Taka-hikaru          Hi no mi ko
Yasumishishi          Wa ga oho-kimi
Aratama no          Toshi ga ki-fureba
Aratama no          Tsuki ha kihe-yuku
Ubena-ubena          Kimi machi-gata ni
Wa ga keseru          Osuhi no suso ni
          Tsuki tatanamu yo

### XXIX. (Sect. lxxxix, Note 6.)

| | |
|---|---|
| Wohari ni | Tada ni mukaheru |
| Wotsu no saki naru | Hito-tsu matsu a se wo |
| Hito-tsu matsu | Hito ni ariseba |
| Tachi hake-mashi wo | winu kise-mashi wo |

Hito-tsu matsu a se wo

### XXX. (Sect. lxxxix, Note 11.)

| | |
|---|---|
| Yamato ha | Kuni no mahoroba |
| Tatanatsuku | Awo-kaki yama-gomoreru |

Yamato shi uruhashi[8]

### XXXI. (Sect. lxxxix, Note 11.)

| | |
|---|---|
| Inochi no | Mata-kemu hito ha |
| Tatami-komo | Heguri no yama no |
| Kuma-kashi ga ha wo | Uzu ni sase |

Sono ko

### XXXII. (Sect. lxxxix, Note 11.)

| | |
|---|---|
| Hashikeyashi | Wagihe no kata yo |

Kumo-wi tachi-ku mo

### XXXIII. (Sect. lxxxix, Note 15.)     351

| | |
|---|---|
| Wotome no | Toko no be ni |
| Wa ga okishi | Tsurugi no tachi |

Sono tachi ha ya

### XXXIV. (Sect. xc, Note 3.)

| | |
|---|---|
| Nadzuki no | Ta no ina-gara ni |
| Ina-gara ni | Hahi-motorofu |

Tokoro-dzura[9]

. . . . .

---

8. Motowori reads *gomoreru* as a line by itself, and similarly *uruhashi* as a line by itself.

### XXXV. (Sect. xc, Note 5.)

| | |
|---|---|
| Asa-zhinu-hara | Koshi nadzumu |
| Sora ha yukazu | Ashi yo yuku na |

### XXXVI. (Sect. xc, Note 7.)

| | |
|---|---|
| Umi-ga yukeba | Koshi nadzumu |
| Oho-kahara no | Uwe-gusa |
| Umi-ga ha | Isayofu[10] |

### XXXVII. (Sect. xc, Note 8.)

Hama tsu chi-dori          Hama yo ha yukazu

Iso-dzutafu

### XXXVIII. (Sect. c, Note 18.)

| | |
|---|---|
| Isa agi | Furu-kuma ga |
| Itate ohazuha | Niho-dori no |
| Afumi no umi ni | Kadzuki sena wa |

### XXXIX. (Sect. cii, Note 2.)

| | |
|---|---|
| Kono mi ki ha | Wa ga mi ki narazu |
| Kushi no kami | Toko-yo ni i-masu |
| Iha tatasu | Sukuna mi kami no |
| Kamu-hogi | Hogi-kuruhoshi |
| Toyo-hogi | Hogi-motohoshi |
| Matsuri-koshi | Mi ki zo |

Asazu wose sa sa

---

9. Moribe restores the reading of the first line of this poem to *Nadzuki-ta no*, and both he and Motowori suggest conjectural concluding lines to supplement the evidently incomplete text. Moribe's are very elegant:

Shi ga tsura no     I-hahi motohori

Motohorite     Ne-naki tohedomo

Koto mo norasanu

10. Moribe reads *Umi-ga ha isahofu* as one line. It is difficult, on any method of division, to find rhythm in this Song.

## XL. Sect. cii, Note 3.)

| | |
|---|---|
| Kono mi ki wo | Kami-kemu hito ha |
| Sono tsudzumi | Usu ni tatete |
| Utahi-tsutsu | Kami-kere ka mo |
| Mahi-tsutsu | Kami-kere ka mo |
| Kono miki no | Mi ki no aya ni[11] |

Uta-danushi [ki] sa sa

## XLI. (Sect. cvi, Note 2.)

| | |
|---|---|
| Chiba no | Kadzu-nu wo mireba. |
| Momo-chi-daru | Ya-niha mo miyu |

Kuni no ho mo miyu

## XLII. (Sect. cvi, Note 8.)

| | |
|---|---|
| Kono kani ya | Idzuku no kani |
| Momo-dzutafu | Tsunuga no kani |
| Yoko-sarafu | Idzuku ni itaru |
| Ichiji-shima | Mi-shima ni to ki |
| Niho-dori no | Nadzuki iki-dzuki |
| Shina-dayufu | Sasa-nami-ji wo |
| Suku-suku to | Wa ga i-maseba ya |
| Kohata no michi ni | Ahashishi wotome |
| Ushiro-de ha | Wo-date ro ka mo |
| Ha-nami ha | Shihi (shi) nasu[12] |
| Ichihiwi no | Wanisa no ni wo |
| Hatsu-ni ha | Hada akarakemi |
| Shiha-ni ha | Ni-guroki yuwe |
| Mi-tsu-guri no | Sono naka tsu ni wo |

353

---

11. Motowori strangely makes *Mi ki no Aya ni* into two lines. The syllable *ki* in the last line of the Song is supplied by Moribe.

12. Motowori divides these lines thus: *Han ami ha shi Hishi nasu.* He also proposes here to divide the poem in two.

| Kabu-tsuku | Ma-hi ni ha atezu |
| Mayo-gaki | Ko ni kaki-tare[13] |

Ahashishi womina

| Ka mo ga to | Wa ga mishi ko-ra |
| Kaku mo ga to | A ga mishi ko ni |
| Utadakeni | Mukahi-woru ka mo |

Iso-hi-woru ka mo

### XLIII. (Sect. cvii, Note 9.)

| Iza ko-domo | Nu-biru tsumi ni |
| Hiru tsumi ni | Wa ga yuku michi no |
| Kaguhashi | Hana-tachibana wo |
| Ho tsu ye ha | Tori wi-garashi |
| Shi dzu ye ha | Hito tori-garashi |
| Mi-tsu-guri no | Naka tsu ye no |
| Hotsumori | Akara-wotome wo |
| Izasasaba | Yorashi na |

### XLIV. (Sect. cvii, Note 9.)

| Iza ko-domo | Nu-biru tsumt ni |
| Hiru tsumi ni | Wa ga yuku michi no |
| Kaguhashi | Hana-tachibana wo |
| Ho tsu ye ha | Tori wi-garashi |
| Shi dzu ye ha | Hito tori-garashi |
| Mi-tsu-guri no | Naka tsu ye no |
| Hotsumori | Akara-wotome wo |
| Izasasaba | Yorashi na |

### XLIV. (Sect. cvii, Note 10.)

| Midzn tamaru | Yasami no ike no |
| Wi-guhi uchi | [Hishi] ga-[ra no][14] |

---

13. Motowori divides these lines thus: *Mayo-gaki ko ni. Kaki tare.*

14. The defective text of this line is restored by the help of the parallel passage in the "Chronicles."

Sashi-keru shirani    Nunaha-kuri
Hahe-keku shirani    Wa ga kokoro shi
Iya woko ni shite    Ima zo kuyashiki

## XLV. (Sect. cvii, Note 11.)

Michi no shiri    Kohada-wotome wo
Kami no goto    Kikoyeshikadomo    354
Ahi-makuramaku

## XLVI. (Sect. cvii, Note 12.)

Michi no shiri    Kohada-wotome ha
Arasohazu    Ne-shiku wo shi zo mo.
Uruhashimi-omofu

## XLVII. (Sect. cviii, Note 2.)

Homuda no    Hi no mi ko
Oho-sazaki    Oho-sazaki
Hakaseru tachi    Moto-tsurugi
Suwe fuyu    Fuyu-ki no su
Kara ga shita-ki no    Saya-saya

## XLVIII. (Sect. cviii, Note 6.)

Kashinofu ni    Yokusu wo tsukuri
Yokusu ni    Kamishi oho-mi-ki
Umara ni    Kikoshi-mochi-wose
Maro ga chi

## XLIX. (Sect. cxi, Note 5.)

Susukori ga    Kamishi mi ki ni
Ware wehi ni keri
Koto nagu shi    We-gushi ni
Ware wehi ni keri[15]

---

15. Moribe proposes to emend the second half of this poem to
     *Koto nagushi we    Kokoro-gushi we*
     *Ware wehi ni keri.*

### L. (SECT. CXII, NOTE 10.)

Chihayaburu   Uji no watari no
Sawo-tori ni    Haya-kemu hito shi
  (Wa ga moko ni komu.)

### LI. (SECT. CXII, NOTE 15.)

Chihaya-bito   Uji no watari ni
Watari-ze ni tateru  Adzusa-yumi ma-yumi
I-kiramu to    Kokoro ha mohedo
I-toramu to    Kokoro ha mohedo
Moto-he ha    Kimi wo omohi-de
Suhe-he ha    Imo wo omohi-de
Iranakeku    Soko ni omohi-de
Kanashikeku   Koko ni omohi-de
355 I-kirazu zo kuru  Adzusa-yumi ma-yumi[16]

### LII. (SECT. CXXII, NOTE 4.)

Oki-he ni ha   Wo-bune tsuraraku
Kuro-zaki[17] no   Masazu-ko wagimo
  Kuni he kudarasu

### LIII. (SECT. CXXII, NOTE 8.)

Oshi-teru ya   Naniha no sakiyo
Ide-tachite    Wa ga kuni mireba

---

16.  Near the commencement of this Song Motowori divides the lines thus:

    *Watari-ze ni*  *Tateru*
    *Adzusa-yumi* *Mo-yumi*

and again at the end:

    *I-kirazu zo kuru* *Adzusa-yumi*
        *Ma-yumi.*

17.  See Sect. CXXII, Note, 4 for this doubtful word.

Aha-shima                Onogoro-shima
Ajimasa no               Shima mo miyu
          Saketsu-shima miyu

### LIV. (Sect. CXXII, Note 10.)

Yama-gata ni             Makoru awo-na mo
Kibi-hito to             Tomo ni shi tsumeba
          Tanushiku mo aru ka

### LV. (Sect. CXXII, Note 13)

Yamato-he ni             Nishi fukiagete
Kumo-banare              Soki-wori to mo
          Ware wasureme ya

### LVI. (Sect. CXXII, Note 14.)

Yamato-he ni             Yuku ha ta ga tsuma
Komoridzu no             Shita yo hahe-tsutsu
          Yuku ha ta ga tsuma

### LVII. (Sect. CXXIII, Note 11.)

Tsuginefu ya             Yamashiro-gaha wo
Kaha-nobori              Wa ga noboreba
Kaha no he ni            Ohi-dateru
Sashibu wo               Sashibu no ki
Shi ga shita ni          Ohi-dateru
          Ha-biro yutsu matsuba-ki[18]
Shi ga hana no           Teri-i-mashi
Shi ga ha no             Hirori-i-masuha
          Oho-kimi ro ka mo

356

18. Motowori divides this line in two, thus:
          *Habiro Yutsuma-tsubaki.*

## LVIII. (Sect. cxxiii, Note 14.)

| | |
|---|---|
| Tsuginefu ya | Yamashiro-gaha wo |
| Miya-nobori | Wa ga noboreba |
| Awoniyoshi | Nara wo sugi |
| Wo-date | Yamato wo sugi |

Wa ga migahoshi kuni ha

Kadzuraki Takamiya  Wagihe no atari[19]

## LIX. (Sect. cxxiv, Note 3.)

| | |
|---|---|
| Yamashiro ni | I-shike Toriyama |
| Ishike i-shike | A ga hashi-dzuma ni |

I-shiki-ahamu ka mo

## LX. (Sect. cxxiv, Note 5.)

| | |
|---|---|
| Mimoro no | Sono Takaki naru |
| Ohowiko ga hara | Ohowiko ga hara ni aru[20] |
| Kimo-mukafu | Kokoro wo dani ka |

Ahi-omohazu aramu

## LXI. (Sect. cxxiv, Note 6)

| | |
|---|---|
| Tsuginefu | Yamashiro-me no |
| Ko-kuha mochi | Uchishi oho-ne |
| Ne-zhiro no | Shiro-tadamuki |
| Makazukeba koso | Shirazu to mo ihame |

## LXXII. (Sect. cxxiv, Note 12.)

| | |
|---|---|
| Yamashiro no | Tsutsuki no mi-ya ni |
| Mono mawosu | A ga se no kimi ha |

Namita-gumashi mo

---

19. Instead of these concluding long lines Motowori divides thus:

    *Wa ga mikahoshi*    *Kuni ha*
    *Kadzuraki*    *Taka-miya*
        *Wagihe no atari.*

20. Motowori reads the words *Hara ni aru* as a separate line.

### LXIII. (SECT. CXXIV, NOTE 18.)

| Tsuginefu | Yamashiro-me no |
|---|---|
| Ko-kuha mochi | Uchishi oho-ne |
| Sawa-sawa ni | Na ga ihese koso |
| Uchi-watasu | Yagahaye-nasu |

Ki-iri-mawi-kure

### LXIII. (SECT. CXXIV, NOTE 18.)

| Tsuginefu | Yamashiro-me no |
|---|---|
| Ko-kuha mochi | Uchishi oho-ne |
| Sawa-sawa ni | Na ga ihese koso |
| Uchi-watasu | Yagahaye nasu |

Ki-iri-mawi-kure

### LXIV. (SECT. CXXV, NOTE 1.)

| Yata no | Hito-moto suge ha |
|---|---|
| Ko motazu | Tachi ka are-namu |
| Atara-suga-hara | Koto wo koso |
| Suge-hara to ihame | Atara-sugashi-me |

### LXV. (SECT. CXXV, NOTE 2.)

| Yata no | Hito-moto suge ha |
|---|---|
| Hitori wori to mo | Oho-kimi shi |
| Yoshi to kikosaba | Hitori wori to mo |

### LXVI. (SECT. CXXVI, NOTE 2.)

| Medori no | Wa ga oho-kimi no |
|---|---|
| Orosu hata | Taga dane ro ha mo |

358

### LXVII. (SECT. CXXVI NOTE 3.)

| Taka-yuku ya | Haya-busa-wake no |
|---|---|

Mi osuhi-gane

## LXVIII. (Sect. cxxvi, Note 5.)

Hibari ha                    Ame ni kakeru
Taka-yuku ya                 Haya-busa-wake
            Sazaki torasane

## LXIX. (Sect. cxxvi, Note 8.)

Hashi-tate no                Kura hashi-yama wo
Sagashimi to                 Iha kaki-kanete
            Wa ga te torasu mo

## LXX. (Sect. cxxvi, Note 8.)

Hashi-tate no                Kura-hashi-yama ha
Sagashikedo                  Imo to noboreba
            Sagashiku mo arazu

## LXXI. (Sect. cxxviii, Note 3.)

Tamakiharu                   Uchi no aso
Na koso ha                   Yo no naga-hito
Sora mitsu                   Yamato no kuni ni
Kari ko 'mu to               Kiku ya

## LXXII. (Sect. cxxviii, Note 4.)

Taka-hikaru                  Hi no mi ko
Ube shi koso                 Tohi-tamahe
Ma koso ni                   Tohi-tamahe
Are koso ha                  Yo no naga-hito
Sora-mitsu                   Yamato no kuni ni
Kari ko 'mu to               Imada kikazu

## LXXIII. (Sect. cxxviii, Note 6.)

Na ga mi ko ya               Tsuhi ni shiramu to
            Kari ha ko 'murashi

### LXXIV. (Sect. CXXIX, Note 8.)

| | |
|---|---|
| Karanu wo | Shiho hi yaki |
| Shi ga amari | Koto ni tsukuri |
| Kaki-hiku ya | Yura no to no |
| To-naka no | Ikuri ni |
| Fure-tatsu | Nadzu no ki no |

Saya-saya

593

### LXXV. (Sect. CXXXII, Note 5.)

| | |
|---|---|
| Tajihi-nu ni | Nemu to shiriseba |
| Tatsu-gomo mo | Mochite |
| Ko-mashi mono | Nemu to shiriseba |

### LXXVI. (Sect. CXXXII, Note 7.)

| | |
|---|---|
| Hanifu-zaka | Wa ga tachi-mireba |
| Kagirohi no | Moyuru ihe-mura |

Tsuma ga ihe no asari

### LXXVII. (Sect. CXXXIII, Note 10.)

| | |
|---|---|
| Oho-saka ni | Afu ya wotome wo |
| Michi toheba | Tada ni ha norazu |

Tajima-chi wo noru

### LXXVIII. (Sect. CXLI, Note 2.)

| | |
|---|---|
| Ashiki no | Yama-da wo tsukuri |
| Yama-dakami | Shita-bi wo washise |
| Shita-dohi ni | Wa ga tofu imo wo |
| Shita-naki ni | Wa ga naku tsuma wo |
| Kofu koso ha | Yasuku hada fure |

### LXXIX. (Sect. CXLI, Note 4.)

| | |
|---|---|
| Sasa-ba ni | Utsu ya arare no |
| Tashi-dashi ni | Wi-netemu nochi ha |

Hito hakayu to mo

Uruhashi to                Sa-ne shi sa-neteba
Kari-komo no               Midareba midare
         Sa-ne shi sa-neteba

360          LXXX. (SECT. CXLII, NOTE 7.)

Oho-mahe                   Wo-mahe sukune ga
Kana-to kage               Kaku yori-kone
         Ame tachi-yamemu

         LXXXI. (SECT. CXLII, NOTE 8.)

Miya-hito no               Ayuhi no ko-suzu
Ochi ni ki to              Miya-hito toyomu
         Sato-bito mo yume

         LXXXII. (SECT. CXLII, NOTE 12.)

Ama-damu                   Karu no wotome
Ita nakaba                 Hito shirinu-beshi
         Hasa no yama no hoto no
         Shita-naki ni naku[21]

         LXXXIII. (SECT. CXLII, NOTE 13.)

Ama-damu                   Karu-wotome
Shita-ta ni mo             Yori-nete tohore
         Karu-wotome-domo

         LXXXIV. (SECT. CXLIII, NOTE 2.)

Ama tobu                   Tori mo tsukahi zu
Tadzu ga ne no             Kikoyemu toki ha
         Wa ga na tohasane

---

21.  Moribe, following the reading in the "Chronicles," omits the
Postposition *no* after *Karu;* and Motowori reads *hato no* as a line by
itself.

## LXXXV. (Sect. cxliii, Note 4.)

| | |
|---|---|
| Oho-kimi wo | Shima ni haburaba |
| Funa-amari | I-gaheri-komu zo |
| Wa ga tatami yume | Koto wo koso |
| Tatami to ihame | Wa ga tsuma ha yume |

## LXXXVI. (Sect. cxliii, Note 6.)

| | |
|---|---|
| Natsu-kusa no | Ahine no hama no |
| Kaki-gahi ni | Ashi[22] fumasu na |

Akashite tohore

361

## LXXXVII. (Sect. cxliii, Note 7.)

| | |
|---|---|
| Kimi ga yuki | Ke-nagaku narinu |
| Yama-tadzu no | Mukahe wo yukamu |

Matsu ni ha matazhi

## LXXXVIII. (Sect. cxliii, Note 8.)

| | |
|---|---|
| Komoaiku no | Hatsuse no yama no |
| Oho-wo ni ha | Hata hari-date |
| Sa-wo-wo ni he | Hata hari-date |
| Oho-wo ni shi | Naga sadameru |

Omohi-dzuma ahare

| | |
|---|---|
| Tsuku-yumi no | Koyaru koyari mo |
| Adzusa-yumi | Tateri-tateri mo |

Nochi mótori-miru

Omohi-dzuma ahare

## LXXXIX. (Sect. cxliii, Note 9.)

| | |
|---|---|
| Komoriku no | Hatsuse no kaha no |

---

22. To the word *ashi* Moribe would prefix the Honorific *mi* which he finds in an old MS. The metre would gain by this emendation of the line.

23. This is Moribe's emendation of usual reading *ka*.

Kami tsu se ni          I-kuhi wo uchi
Shimo tsu se ni         Ma-kuhi wo uchi
I-kuhi ni ha            Kagami wo kake
Ma-kuhi ni ha           Ma-tama wo kake
Ma-tama nasu            A ga mofu imo
Kagami nasu             Aga mofu tsuma
        Ari to ihaba koso ni
Ihe ni mo yukame        Kuni wo mo shinubame[24]

## XC. (Sect. cliii, Note 4.)

Kusa-kabe no            Kochi no yoma to
Tatami-komo             Heguri no yama no
Kochi-gochi no          Yama no kahi ni
Tachi-zakayuru          Ha-biro kuma-kashi
Moto ni ha              I-kumi-dake ohi
Suwe-he ni ha           Tashimi-dake ohi
I-kumi-dake             I-kumi ha nezu
Tashimi-dake            Tashi ni ha wi-nezu
Nochi mo kumi-nemu Sono omohi-dzuma
            Ahare

## XCI. (Sect. cliv, Note 9.)

Mimoro no               Itsu-kashi ga moto
Kashi ga moto           Yuyushiki ka mo
        Kashi-hara-wotomo

## XCII. (Sect. cliv, Note 10.)

Hiketa no               Waka-kuru-su-bara
Wakaku-he ni            Wi-nete-mashi mono
        Oi ni keru ka mo

---

24. Motowori divides *Ari to ihaba koso ni* into two lines after the Particle *to*, and Moribe omits the Particle *ni* after *koso*.

### XCIII. (Sect. cliv, Note 12.)

Mimoro ni             Tsuku ya tama-kaki
Tsuki-amashi          Ta ni ka mo yoraumu
          Kami no miya-hito

### XCIV. (Sect. cliv, Note 13.)

Kusaka-ye no          Iri-ye no hachisu
Hana-bachisu          Mi no sakari-bito
          Tomoshiki ro ka mo

### XCV. (Srct. clv, Note 3.)

Agura wi no           Kami no mi te mochi
Hiku koto ni          Mahi suru womina            363
          Tokyo-yo ni mo ka mo

### XCVI. (Sect. clvi, Note 3.)

Mi-yeshinu no         Womuro ga take ni
Shishi fusu to        Tare zo oho-mahe ni mawosu[25]
Yasumishishi          Wa ga oho-kimi no
Shishi matsu to       Agura ni i-mashi
Shiro-tahe no         Sode ki-sonafu
Ta-komura ni          Amu kaki-tsuki
So no amu wo          Akidzu haya kuhi
Kaku no goto          Na ni ohamu to
Sora-mitsu            Yamato no kuni wo
          Akidzu-shima tofu

### XCVII. (Sect. clvii, Note 4.)

Yasumishishi          Wa ga oho-kimi no

---

25.  It seems less good to divide thus with Motowori:
          *Tare zo oho-mahe ni      Mawosu,*
or thus with Mabuchi:
          *Tare zo      Oho-maye ni mawosu.*

Asobashishi              Shishi no yami-shishi no
Utaki kashikomi          Wa ga nige-noborishi
Ari-wo no                Hari-no-ki no yeda[26]

## XCVIII. (Sect. clix, Note 3.)

Wotome no                I-kakuru woka wo
Kana-suki mo             I-hochi mo ga mo
          Suki-banuru mono

## XCIX. (Sect. clx, Note 4.)

Makimuke no              Hishiro no mi-ya ha
Asa-hi no                Hi-deru mi-ya
Yufu-hi no               Hi-gakeru mi-ya
Take no ne no            Nedaru-mi-ya
Ko no ne no              Ne-bafu mi-ya
Yahoniyoshi              I-kidzuki no mi-ya
Ma-ki-saku               Hi no mi kado
Nihi-nahe-ya ni          Ohi-dateru
Momo-daru                Tsuki ga ye ha
Ho tsu ye ha             Ame wo oheri
Naka tsu ye ha           Adzuma wo oheri
Shi dzu ye ha            Hina wo oheri
Ho tsu ye no             Ye no ura-ba ha
Naka tsu ye ni           Ochi-furabahe
Naka tsu ye no           Ye no ura-ba ha
Shimo tsu ye ni          Ochi-furabahe
Shi dzu ye no            Ye no ura-ba ha

---

26.  Motowori divides the lines of this Song thus:

| | |
|---|---|
| *Yasumishishi* | *Wa ga oho-kimi no* |
| *Asobashishi* | *Shishi no* |
| *Yami-shishi no* | *Utaki kashikomi* |
| *Wa ga nike* | *Noborishi* |
| *Ari-wo no* | *Hari no ki no yeda.* |

Ari-ginu no              Mihe no ko ga
Sasagaseru               Midzu-tama-uki ni
Ukishi abura             Ochi-nadzusahi
  Mina koworo-koworo ni[27]
Ko shi mo                Aya ni kashikoshi
Taka-hikaru              Hi no mi ko
Koto no                  Katari-goto mo
  Ko wo ba


C. (SECT. CLX, NOTE 5.)

Yamato no                Kono takechi ni
Ko-dakaru                Ichi no tsukasa                365
Nihi-nahe-ya ni          Ohi-dateru
  Habiro yo-tsu ma-tsubaki[28]
So ga ha no              Hirori-i-mashi
So no hana no            Teri-i-masu
Taka-hikaru              Hi no mi ko ni
To-yo mi ki              Tate-matsurase
Koto no                  Katari-goto mo
  Ko wo ba


CI. (SECT. CLX, NOTE 6.)

Momoshiki no             Oho-miya-hito ha
Udzura-tori              Hire tori-kakete
Mana-bashira             Wo yuki-ahe
Niha-suzume              Uzu-sumari-wite
Kefu mo ka mo            Saka mi-dzuku-rashi
Taka-hikaru              Hi no miya-hito
Koto no                  Katari-goto mo
  Ko wo ba

---

27. Motowori divides this line in two, thus :
  *Mina koworo*  *Koworo ni*
28. Motowori divides this line in two after the word *ha-biro*.

## CII. (Sect. clxi, Note 2.)

| | |
|---|---|
| Mina-sosoku | Omi no wotome |
| Ho-dari torasu mo | Ho-dari tori |
| Kataku torase | Shita-gataku |
| Ya-gataku torase | Ho dari torasu ko |

## CIII. (Sect. clxi, Note 4 )

| | |
|---|---|
| Yasumishishi | Wa ga oho-kimi no |
| Asa-to ni ha | I-yori-datashi |
| Yufu-to ni ha | I-yori-datasu |
| Waki-dzuki ga | Shita no |
| Ita ni mo ga | A se wo |

## CIV. (Sect clxv, Notes 8 and 12 )

| | |
|---|---|
| Oho-miya no | Woto tsu hata-de |
| | Sumi katabukeri |

## CV. (Sect. Notes 9 and 12 )

| | |
|---|---|
| Oho-takumi | Wojinami koso |
| | Sumi katabukere |

## CVI. (Sect. clxv, Notes 10 and 12.)

| | |
|---|---|
| Oho-kimi no | Kokoro wo yurami |
| Omi no ko no | Ya-he no shiba-kaki |
| | Iri-tatazu ari |

## CVII. (Sect. clxv, Note 12.)

| | |
|---|---|
| Sh ho-se no | Na-wori wo mireba |
| Asobi-kuru | Shibi ga hata-de ni |
| | Tsuma tateri-miyu |

## CVIII. (Sect. clxv, Notes 11 and 12.)

| | |
|---|---|
| Oho-kimi no | Mi ko no shiba-kaki |

Ya-fu-zhimari          Shimari-motohoshi
Kiremu shiba-kaki      Yakemu shiba-kaki[29]

### CIX. (Sect. clxv, Note 12.)

Ofuwo yo shi           Shibi tsuku ama yo
Shi ga areba           Ura-kohoshiki-kemu
            Shibi tsuku ama[30]

### CX. (Sect. clxvii, Note 10.)                   367

Asa-ji-hara            Wo-dani wo sugite
Momo-dzutafu           Nute yuraku mo
            Oki-me kurashi mo

### CXI. (Sect. clxvii, Note 11.)

Oki-me mo ya           Afumi no Oki-me
Asu yori ha            Mi-yama-gakurite
            Miyezu ka mo aramu

---

29. Moribe's proposal to emend *yakemu* to *yaremu* would be accept-able if it were supported by the authority of any texts.

30. Motowori's edition and most other texts have *shibi* as the final word. But Moribe's emendation to *ama* is necessary to ths sense, and has at least the authority of one MS. to support it,

APPENDIX II.

THE HITHERTO ACCEPTED CHRONOLOGY OF THE EARLY
JAPANESE SOVEREI NS MENTIONED IN THE "RECORDS
OF ANCIENT MATTERS" ("*KŌ-JI-KI*") AND IN THE "CHRO-
NICLES OF JAPAN" ("*NI-HONGI*").

[This "Accepted Chronology" is contained in the first three columns of
figures, whereof the first two, giving the corresponding dates according
to the European reckoning are transcribed from some Comparative
Chronological Tables by Mr. Ernest Satow, printed for private dis-
tribution in 1874. The ages of the monarchs in the third column
are from "The Digest of the Imperial Pedigree," a work published
by the Imperial Japanese Government is 1877, and therefore carrying
with it the weight of authority. It might perhaps be too much to
say that even its decisions are universally bowed to by the native
*literati ;* but the differences between various writers are all slight, and
excepting on points that affect only a very few years, the chronology
contained in the first three columns may justly be styled the "Accepted Chronology" both as far as natives and as far as foreigners
are concerned. It will be seen that it is founded in the main on
the statements contained in the "Chronicles of Japan," though sometimes differing therefrom as well as from the "Records." The fourth
column contains the ages of the monarchs according to the "Records" and the fifth their ages according to the "Chronicles." The
portion printed in italics, and including a little over a thousand years,
is that which has been shown in Section V of the Translator's Introduction to be undeserving of credence.

|        | Accession. | Death. | Age. | Age accord. to "Records." | Age accord. to "Chronicles." |
|--------|-----------|--------|------|--------------------------|------------------------------|
| *Jin-mu* | *660(B·C.)* | *585(B.C.)* | *127* | *137* | *127* |
| *Sui-sei* | *581* | *549* | *84* | *45* | *80* |
| *An-nei* | *548* | *511* | *57* | *49* | *57* |
| *I-toku* | *510* | *477* | *77* | *45* | *77* |
| *Kō-shō* | *475* | *393* | *114* | *93* | *113* |

| | Accession. | Death. | Age. | Age accord. to "Records." | | Age accord. to "Chronicles.' | |
|---|---|---|---|---|---|---|---|
| Kō-an | 392 | 291 | 137 | 123 | reigned | 102 | years |
| Kō-rei | 290 | 215 | 128 | 106 | " | 76 | " |
| Kō-gen | 214 | 158 | 116 | 57 | " | 57 | " |
| Kai-kuwa | 157 | 98 | 111 | 63 | " | 60 | " |
| Sū-jin | 97 | 30 | 119 | 168 | | 120 | |
| Sui-nin | 29 | 70(A.D) | 141 | 153 | | 140 | |
| Kei-kō | 71(A.D.) | 130 | 143 | 137 | | 106 | |
| Sei-mu | 131 | 190 | 108 | 95 | | 107 | |
| Chiū-ai | 192 | 200 | 52 | 52 | | 52 | |
| Jin-gō | 201 | 269 | 100 | 100 | | 100 | |
| Ō-jin | 270 | 310 | 111 | 130 | | 110 | |
| Nin-toku | 313 | 399 | 110 | 83 | reigned | 87 | years |
| Ri-chiū | 400 | 405 | 67 | 64 | | 70 | |
| Han-zei | 406 | 411 | 60 | 60 | reigned | 6 | years |
| In-giyō | 412 | 453 | 80 | 78 | " | 42 | " |
| An-kō | 454 | 456 | 56 | 66 | " | 3 | " |
| Yū-riyaku | 457 | 479 | age omitted | 124 | " | 5 | " |
| Sei-nei | 480 | 484 | 41 | not given | " | 23 | " |
| Ken-zō | 485 | 487 | age omitted | 38 | " | 3 | " |
| Nin-ken | 488 | 498 | 50 | not given | " | 11 | " |
| Mu-retsu | 499 | 506 | 18 | reigned 8 years | " | 8 | " |
| Kei-tai | 507 | 531 | 82 | 43 | | 82 | |
| An-kan | 534 | 535 | 70 | not given | | 70 | |
| Sen-kuwa | 536 | 539 | 73 | " | | 73 | |
| Kim-mei | 540 | 571 | 63 | " | reigned | 32 | years |
| Bi-datsu | 572 | 585 | 48 | reigned 14 years | " | 14 | " |
| Yō-mei | 586 | 587 | 69 | " 3 " | " | 2 | " |
| Su-jun | 588 | 592 | 73 | " 4 " | " | 5 | " |
| Sui-ko | 593 | 628 | 75 | " 37 | " | 75 | |

1. The reign of this Empress is in the "Records" not counted separately, but included in that of her son Ō-jin. For the mention of her age in the "Records" conf. Sect. CIII, Note 4.

# INDEX TO "KOJIKI."

—·—

### Kindly Prepared by the Rev. N. Walter, Osaka.

*N. B.*—The figures enclosed in parenthesis ( ) represent the pages in
the present edition. The figures without /parenthesis represent
the pages in the old editions previous to 1906.

## 2                    *Index to "Kojiki."*

*N. B.*—The figures enclosed in parenthesis ( ) represent the pages in the present edition. The figures without parenthesis represent the pages in the old editions previous to 1906.

Aketatsu [*Prince*], 169 (206), 193 (238). 194 (238).

Aki, 26 (33 n. 10), 131 (160 and 162 n. 16), 262 (327 n. 3).

*Akitsushima* [Island of the Dragon-Fly], 5 (2), 158 (195), 318 (397).

Alarming Female, Heavenly [*Ame-no-uzume-no-mikoto*], 57 (64), 58 (65), 108 (129), 110 (131), 113 (138), 114 (139).

Alder xxxiv. (xlvi), 257 (320 n. 19), 318 (398).

Altaic Language, i. (i), xiii (xviii). lxxii (xcvii).

*Ama* [*ame*], 47 (53 and 56 n. 12).

*Ama-nn-hi-boko*, 258 (321).

*Ama-no-uki-hashi* [Floating Bridge of Heaven], 19 (19), 93 (112), 111 (135).

*Ama-terasu-oho-mi-kami* [Heavenly Shining Great August Deity], 42 (46), 43 (50), 45 (52), 52 (61), 54 (63), 58 (65), 93 (112), 94 (114), 106 (128), 108 (129), 111 (135), 135 (165), etc.

*Amasu-hi-tsugi* [succession of Heaven's sun], 103 (123 and 126 n. 27).

*Ama-tsu-hi-daka hiko-nagisa-take-u-gaya-fuki-ahezu-no-mikoto*, 127 (157 n. 15).

*Ama-tsu-kume-no-mikoto* [Heaven's Round Eyes], see Oho-kume.

ambush. 254 (316). etc.

*Ame-kuni-oshi-haruki-hiro-niha*, 338 (423), 339 (424).

*Ame-nigishi-kuni-nigishi ama-tsu-hi-daka-hiko-no-ni-nigi-no-mikoto*, 106 (129 and 131 n. 5).

*Ame-no-fuki-wo-no-kami*, 26 (28 and 30 n. 5).

*Ame-no-hohi*, 49 (54), 50 (58), 94 (113).

*Ame-no-ko-ya-ne-no-mikoto*, 56 (67 n. 15), 57 (64), 108 (130), 110 (131)

*Ame-no-kumari-no-kami*, 27 (28 and 30 n. 13).

*Ame-no-mi-naka-nushi-no-kami*, 15 (15 n. 4).

*Ame-no-oshi-ho-mimi*, 48 (54 and 57 n. 18), 93 (112), 106 (129 n. 3).

*Ame-no-oshi-wo*, 25 (23 anp 27 n. 34).

*Ame-no-ta-jikara-wo-no-kami*, 57 (64 and 63 n. 27), 58 (65), 109 (130). 110 (130).

*Ame-no-toko-tachi-no-kami*, 16 (15 and 16 n. 10).

*Ame-no-uzume-no-mikoto*, see Alarming Female.

*Ame-no-wo-ha bari* [sword], 34 (37 and 38 n. 15).

*Ame-no-yasu-kawa* [River of Henven], lxix. (cxiii), 5 (3 and 3 n. 12), 47 (53 and 56 n. 12), 54 (63), 93 (112), 96 (115), 100 (121), etc.

N. B.—The figures enclosed in parenthesis ( ) represent the pages in the present edition. The figures without parenthesis represent the pages in the old editions previous to 1906.

*N. B.*—The figures enclosed in parenthesis ( ) represent the pages in the present edition. The figures without parenthesis ǀrepresent the pages in the old editions previous to 1906.

# Index to " Kojiki." 5

*N. B.*—The figures enclosed in parenthesis ( ) represent the pages in the present edition. The figures without parenthesis represent the pages in the old editions previous to 1906.

Beckoning Ancestor Lord [Heavenly] see *Ame-no-ko-ya-ne-no-mikoto.*

bees xxxiii, (xliv).

beginning of Japanese nation xliv, (lix).

bell [clapper] 25 (23 and 27 n. 31).

bell 109 (130 and 134, n. 25) *garter*, 312 (389), 334 (417).

Bi-datsu tennō 341 (426).

Bingo 157 (193 and 194 n. 13, 14).

birds [singing] 54 (63).

Biwa [lake] 237 (293). See sea of Afumi.

Bizen 161, (197 and 198 n. 21).

Blackberries 78 (92 and 94 n. 7).

Black, colour of mourning 80 (97, n. 2).

Black haired people 6, (2).

Blossoming-Brilliantly-like-the flowers of the Trees, [princess] 115-119 (140-143).

blue [green] clouds xxxvi (xlxiii).

blue, [green, sea] (xxxviii).

boar xxxii (xliii), 70 (83), 217 (269), 235 (292), 255 (317), 308 (385), 318 (398).

boat 20 (21), 101 (122), 236 (293), 255 (316), etc.

books first introduced to Japan. xliii, (lvii).

boots 262 (326).

boundary god 28 (29).

boundary marks of provinces. 6 (2), 152 (187 n. 5), 227 (282).

bow and arrows xxv (xxxiii), 46 (53), 71 (84), 74 (88)' 94 (114), 112 (125) 139 (170), 236 (293), 256 (317), 262 (326) see arrows.

bow-string 236 (293).

bracelets xxx (xli), 40 (45), 109 (134 n. 25).

branding xlii (lvi), 148 (180 and 182 n. 20).

Brave-Awful-Possessing-Male-Deity : *Take-mika-tsu chi-no-wo-no-kami,* 32 (36), 100 (121), 105 (124), 106 (129), 135 (165), 176 (216).

Brave-August-Name-Firm Deity 102 (122), 103 (123).

bravo [bandit] xxix (xxxix), 112 (135 and 137 n. 7), 141 (173), 206 (255).

bridge [floating] of Heaven. See *Ama-no-uki-bashi.*

broad brimmed xxx (xli).

bronze [age of] xxiv (xxxiii), xxxvi (xlviii).

Buddhism lx (lxxxi), 87 (105), 201 (248 n. 5).

N. B.—The figures enclosed in parenthesis ( ) reoresent the pages in
       the present edition. The figures without parenthesis represent
       the pages in the old editions previous to 1906.

*N. B.*—The figures enclosed in parenthesis ( ) represent the pages in the present edition. The figures without parenthesis represent the pages in the old editions previous to 1906.

colour, xxx (xli), xxxvi (xlviii), 187 (231), 278, 315.

comb xxxi (xli), xlvi (lxi), 35 (39), 36 (39), 61 (71 and 73 n. 9), 62 (72), 213 (263).

comb [superstition regarding] 35 (39), 62 (73).

computing time xlii (lvi).

concubine, mistress, wife equivalent xl (liii), 74 (90), 117 (143), 202 (249), 270 (337).

conduits [water] 296 (369), 305 (381 n. 8).

confiscations 190 (234).

conundrums 61 (71), 70 (83), 280 (349), 296 (369). see pillow-words, jeux-de-mots, songs, *passim.*

cook 105 (124), 163 (202 n. 16), see kitchen, furnace.

cooking pot xxx (xli).

copper xxxvi (xlviii), 55 (66 n. 9), 298 (371).

cormorant xxxii (xliv), 104 (124), 126 (155), 127 (155), 144 (177), 181 (222).

cormorant fishing xxxi (xliii), 137 (167), 144 (176).

cosmogony lv (lxxiv), 15 (15).

costume [see garments].

countries [great and small] 227 (282).

couriers 175 (215), 196 (239), 220 (271), 329 (411).

courtship of gods 19 (20), 68 (81), 69 (82), 75 (88), etc.

coverlets 81 (96).

cow xxxiv (xlvi) 259 (322).

crab xxxiv (xlvi), 246 (305).

crane xxxiv (xlvi) 300 (374).

creation 4 (1), 15 (15), 18 (17).

credibility of early Japanese records xliv (lix).

creepers xxxi (xli) 36 (39), 93 (112 n. 43), 209 (259).

crimes [unnatural] 32 (35), 230 (286).

crocodiles xxxiii (xliv), lxix (xciv), 69 (81), 124 (150), 127 (155), 167 (208. n. 11).

cross-beams 75 (88), 103 (123), 113 (136).

cross-swords 134 (164), 135 (165), 139 (170), 185 (227), 252 (313), 304 (379).

crow xxxii (xliv), xlviii (lxv), 6 (2), 136 (157), 138 (170), 175 (215).

Crumbling Prince [*Kuye Biko*] 86 (103).

cryptomeria [*sugi*] xxxiv (xlv), 61 (72), 192 (237).

crystal xxxi (xlii).

*N. B.*—The figures enclosed in parenthesis (  ) represent the pages in
       the present ledition The figures without parenthesis represent
       the pages in the old editions previous 10 1906.

*N. B.*—The figures enclosed in parenthesis ( ) represent the pages in the present edition. The figures without parenthesis represent the pages in the old editions previous to 1906.

forming his conscience 290 (361).

Forward [preiness] 72 (86), 79 (95).

fowl sxxxı (xliii), 54 (63).

fratricide 75 (85), 151 (185), 206 (254), 254 (316), 306 (383).

freak [imperial] 311 (389).

frog (toad) 86 (103).

*fude* xliii (lvii).

*fumi* xliii (lviii) 253 (314).

*fumi-bito* 252 (314 n. 3).

funerals xl (liv) 97 (116), 200 (245), 222 (275).

furnace : see kitchen.

Furnace [princess] *Kama no Kami* lxix (xciii) 90 (107).

*furu-koto-bumi* iv (vi).

*Futo-tama no mikoto* [Grand Jewel] 56 (64), 57 (64), 58 (65), 108 (130), 110 (131).

gable, 105 (124).

garlic, 213 (264), [chive], 248 (308).

garments of early Japanese xxx (xli), 40 (44), 53 (62), 79 (95), 296 (255), 253 (314 n. 11), 262 (326), 278 (345), 281 (350), 319 (399).

garter 298 (371)

gate 62 (72).

gate [august] 110 (130), 323.

Gemmio-tennō iv (vi), 20 (4 and 12 n. 33), 71 (85 n. 14).

gentile names [*Kabane*] xvi (xxi), xxxix (lii), lxii (lxxxv), 21 (24 n. 3), 50 (59 n. 5), 112 (137 n. 12), 137 (169 n. 8), 161 (199 n. 23), 197 (239), 203 (249), 227 (282), 253 (315), 268 (335), 295 (368), 310 (388), etc.

*gi, mi* [in pairs] 18 (17 and 18 n. 7).

giant 184 (226), 292 (364).

gin xxv (xxxiii) 140 (171).

ginger xxxiv (xlv), 143 (175) [*chive*].

girdle xxx (xlii), 40 (44).

girdle [inner] 191 (235 n. 12).

glass xxxi (xlii).

Go [country in China] 253 (314 n. 11).

goats xxxii (xliii).

gods see *Kami*, deity etc.

N. B.—The figures enclosed in parenthesis ( ) represent the pages in the present edition. The figures without 'parenthesis represent the pages in the old editions pervious to 1906.

Hand Strength Male Deity, see *Ama-no ta-jikara-wo-no-kami.*

*Hani-Yasu* [prince] see *Take-hani-yasu.*

*Hani-Yasu-bika-no-kami* 29 (32 n. 3.).

hanishibe 200 (24 n. 4).

*haniwa* 200 (247 n. 4).

Han-zei-tennō [Prince Mizuha-wake], 268 (334 n. 7), 292 (364).

hare xxxvii (xviii), xlvii (lxiii), 68 (81).

hare of Inaba xx (xxvii), 68 (81).

Harima 160 (169), 161 (197), 172 (207), 192 (237), 201 (248), 309 (387), 327 (409), 333 (416).

harvest god, 88 (107).

*hashira* 31 (34 n. 11), 130 (161 n. 12), 257 (321 n. 1).

Hatabi [prince] 243 (300), 268 (333).

hats xxx (xli). lix (lxxix), 40 (45), 161 (199 n. 23).

Hatsuse 164 (200), 302 (377 n. 8), 310 (388), 321 (401).

Hawk 192 (240 n. 8).

*Haya-aki-zu-hiko* [deity prince of swift autumn] 29 (28).

*hayabito* [court-jester] 118 (144), 125 (154).

*haya-bito* [man-at-arms] 289 (360), 290 (361).

*Haya-busa-wake* [King], 243 (300), 280 (349).

Hayashi channel 131 (160).

headdress 36 (39), 57 (64), 220 (271), 304 (379).

Heaven (lxxiv), 4 (1), 8 (2), 21 (22), 45 (52), 70 (83), 97 (116), 107 (129),

heavenly and earthly deities 4 (1), 6 (2), 16 (15), 18 (17, 19), 20 (22), 108 (130), 118 (144), 176 (216), 231 (287), *passim.*

heavenly bird boat, 28 (29), 100 (121),

Heavenly-Great-Ears, see *Ame-no-oshi-ho-mimi.*

Heavenly pillar 19 (20), 21 (22), 23 (23).

Heavenly Rock Boat 19 (20), 28 (29), 111 (136 n. 4).

heavenly-rock cave (54 65).

heavenly rock seat 111 (135).

heavenly seat 9 (3).

Heavenly Shining Great August Deity see *Ama-terasu-oho-mikami.*

heavenly sovereign, 5 (2), 7 (2), 9 (3), 117 (142), 1481 (80), 149 (181), 153 (189), 154 (189), 155 (190), 156 (193), 158 (193), 159 (194), 166 (201), 174 (213), 175 (215), 180 (221), 182 (224), 183 (225), 187 (230), 197 (239), 201 (248), 210 (271), 245 (305), etc.

*N. B.*—The figures enclosed in parenthesis ( ) represent the pages in the present edition. The figures without parenthesis ˌrepresent the pages in the old editions previous to 1906.

heavenly stairs [*Ama-no-hashi-date*] 19 (20).

Heavenly Young Prince: see *Ame-waka-hiko.*

Heaven's high plain: see *Takama-no-kara.*

Heaven's Sunheight-Prince-Wave-Limit-Brave-Cormorant-Thatch-Meeting-Incompletely [Augustness] 127 (155).

hedge 143 (175), 331, (413).

heir apparent [*Taishi*] 106 (128), 203 (249), 228 (283), 236 (293), 237 (295), 248 (308), 268 (333), etc.

hemp xxx (xli), lviii (lxxviii), 57 (68 n. 24).

herb-quelling-sword, [*Kusa-nagi-no-tachi*] lix (lxxx), 63 (73), 109 (130), 210 (260).

herd [boar, cow] 309 (389), 333 (416).

heron xxxii (xliv), 97 (116), 194 (238).

Hi [country] 23 (23), 152 (186).

Hi [river] 60 (71), 63 (72), 160 (196), 195 (238), 209 (258).

Hiba [mount] 31 (33).

Hibasu [empress] 200 (247).

Higashi-yama 88 (106).

High Integrating Deity [*Taka-gi-no-Kami*], 96 (115) 101 (121), 106 (128) 108 (129), 111 (135), 135 (165), 136 (167).

Hijiri no Komi 89 (108 n. 7).

*hiki* [ki] 30 (34 n. 11).

*hiko hime*, xv (xv,) xvi (xvi). 16 (16 n. 9), 25 (23 n. 33), 202 (249 and notes), 277 (344) *passim.*

*Hiko-ho-no-ni.nigi* 106 (131 n. 5), 107 (129), 111 (135).

hilt [sword] 32 (36), 304.

Hime [island] 25 (23), 283 (353).

Himuka [Hiuga] xlvi (lxii), 39 (44), 130 (159), 145 (179), 204 (250), 247 (308), (267 333), *passim.*

*Hino-haya-yagi-wo-no-kami,* see fire-god 29 (32 n. 26), 32 (36).

*hinoki* xxxiii (xliv) 61 (74 n. 12).

Hirata v (vi), ix (xii), lxii (lxxxiv), *passim.*

hiro [fathom] 19 etc (20).

historical criticism lxxii (xcvii).

historiographers, first appointed i (lxix), 10 (4).

Hitachi 51 (60 n. 16), 105 (128), 179 (222 n. 2,), 214 (266 n. 3)ﬁ.

Hiye [Mt.] 90 (107).

*N. B.*—The figures enclosed in parenthesis ( ) represent the pages in the present edition. The figures without parenthesis represent the pages in the old editions previous to 1906.

*N. B.*—The figures enclosed in parenthesis ( ) represent the pages in the present edition. The figures without parenthesis represent the pages in the old editions previous to 1906.

*N. B.*—The figures enclosed in parenthesis ( ) represent the pages in the present edition. The figures without parenthesis represen the pages in the old editions previous to 1906.

*N. B.*—The figures enclosed in parenthesis ( ) represent the pages in the present edition. The figures without parenthesis represent the pages in the old editions previous to 1906.

*N. B.*—The figures enclosed in parenthesis ( ) represent the pages in
the present edition. The figures without parenthesis represent
the pages in the old editions previous to 1906.

*N. B.*—The figures enclosed in parenthesis ( ) represent the pages in the present edition. The figures without parenthesis represent the pages in the old editions to 1906.

marriage with near relatives, xxxviii (li), xlviii (lxv), 129 (158). 226 (278), 268 (333), 296 (369), 304 (379).

*Masa-ka-a-katsu-kachi-hayabi-ame-no-oshi-ho-mimi-no-mikoto* see *Ame-no-oshi-ho-mimi.*

*Masaki* xxxiv (xlv).

mats, matting xvi (xxvi), 206 (255), 288 (358), 290 (301).

Matsu, see pine-tree.

Mausoleum [misasaki], 128 (156), 153 (188), 154 (189), 155 (190), 156 (192), 158 (193), 159 (195), 161 (197), 166 (201), 172 (207), 174 (213), 182 (225), 199 (246), 213 (263), 221 (274), 222 (275), 226 (281), 227 (282), 327 (408), 334 (417), 337 (421), 339 (424), 341 (427), 342 (428).

medicine, see physician xlii (lvii), 294 (567).

mediums 229 (284).

Medori [qneen], 242 (300), 280 (349), 281 (350).

medusa xxxiii (xliv), 15 (15).

melon 208 (257).

men with tails, 137 (167).

metals of early Japanese xxxvi (xlviii), 229 (285).

metal god, see *Kana-yama-biko-no-kami.*

metamorphosis, lii (lxxi), lvi (lxxv), 36 (39), 62 (72), 104 (124), 126 (155), 146 (179), 197 (239), 213 (264), 217 (269), 259 (322).

method of translating the Kojiki iii (iii), xii (xvi).

*mibube* 268 (334).

*miehinoku* 152 (185).

*Mifune no mahito* xix (xix n.).

*Miho* [cape], 85 (103).

Mikawa 171 (210 n. 61), 186 (227).

miko xv (xxi), xvii (xxiii), 203 (251), etc.

*miko* vi (xxii), xvii (xxiii).

*mikoto* xvi (xxii), 18 (19 n. i), 202 (251), etc.

millet xxx (xl), xxxilv (xlv), 60 (70), 143 (175).

*Mimaki-iri-biko-inime* 167 (205), 180 (220), see Sūjin tenno.

*mimi*, in names 48 (57 n. 18), 176 (217 n. 17).

Mimoro [Mt.] 88 (106), 176 (216), 277 (344).

mines 55 (63).

Minister (Prime) 227 (282), 229 (284), 248 (308), 289 (360).

Mino 98 (116), 171 (207), 193 (237), 204 (253), 216 (269 n. 6), 202 (300 :

N. B.—The figures enclosed in parenthesis ( ) represent the pages in the present edition. The figures without parenthesis represent the pages in the old editions previous to 1906.

*N. B.*—The figures enclosed in parenthesis ( ) represent the pages in
the present edition. The figures without parenthesis represent
the pages in the old editions previous to 1906.

*N. B.*—The figures enclosed in parenthesis ( ) represent the pages in the present edition. The figures without parenthesis represent the pages in the old editions previous to 1906.

N. B.—The figures enclosed in parenthesis ( ) represent the pages in the present edition. The figures without parenthesis represent the pages in the old editions previous to 1906.

N. B.—The figures enclosed in parenthesis ( ) represent the pages in
         the present edition.   The figures without parenthesis represent
         the pages in the old editions previous to 1906.

N.B.—The figures enclosed in parenthesis ( ) represent the pages in
the present edition. The figures without parenthesis represent
the pages in the old editions previous to 1906.

*N.B.*—The figures enclosed in parenthesis ( ) represent the pages in the present edition. The figures without parenthesis represent the pages in the old editions previous to 1906.

*N.B.*—The figures enclosed in parenthesis ( ) represent the pages in the present edition. The figures without parenthesis represent the pages in the old editions previous to 1906.

Shiki [Lord of], 154 (189), 156 (192).

*Shiki-tsu-hiko-tama-de-mi* [Augustness], An-nei tenno, 154 (189).

*shiko-me* [ugly old woman], 34 (41 n. 1) 36 (42 n. 13),

Shima 115 (139).

Shimosa 105 (127 n. 38).

Shinano 102 (123), 152 (186), 193 (237), 215 (267).

*Shina-tsu-biko-no-kami* 27 (31 n. 15).

shinto [origin obscure] xliv (lix), lv (lxxiv) etc.

shinto [false accounts of] lxi (lxxxii).

shinto priests viii (x), xxii (xxix) 176 (216) see priest and priestess.

shinto rituals ii (iii), xxvi (xxxv), lxv (lxxxviii).

shinto shrines xxvii (xxxvi), 42 (49 n. 22), 50 (58), 104 (124), 109 (130), 110 (131), 135 (165), 176 (216), 178 (219), 193 (238), 196 (239), 237 (295), 259 (322), 289 (359).

ships 10 (4), 197 (239) 212 (263), 231 (287), 237 (295), 293 (340), 285, (358) 294 (367).

Shiragi 1 (lxviii), 232 (289), 252 (313), 258 (321) 294 (367) see Korea.

*shirakata* 132 (160).

*shiratori-no-misasagi* 223 (275).

Shōgun 236 (292).

Shōko [King of Kudara] 252 (313).

Shōtoku Taishi 48 (57 n. 18), see prince Umayado.

shoulder blade of deer xxii (xxix), lix (lxxx), 21 (24 n. 2), 56 (64).

shrike (mōzu) 286 (356).

shrines : see shinto shrines.

shuttle xxv (xxxiv), 54 (63 n. 11).

sickle xxv (xxxiv), 215 (267).

Siebold liii (lxxii), lxix (xciv).

silk xxxii (xliii).

silk rugs xxvii (xxxvi), 122 (148), 212 (263).

silkworm xxxii (xliv), 60 (70), 151 (186 n. 4), 279 (345).

silver xxxvi (xlviii), 57 (68 n. 28), 226 (281 n. 36), 229 (285).

skins xxv (xxxiii), xxvii (xxxvi), xxx (xli), 122 (148), 212 (265).

skirts xxx (xli), 1 (lxvili), 40 (45), 179 (220), 206 (255), 233 (289).

slaves xli (lv), 133 (163 n. 34), 312 (389).

smiths 253 (314).

smith god [amatsu mara] 55 (63).

*N. B.*—The figures enclosed in parenthesis ( ) represent the pages in the present edition. The figures without parenthesis represent the pages in the old editions previous to 1906.

*Tomo no wo* 108 (133 n. 19), 295 (368).

*toneri* [retainers], 310.

top-knot xxxi (xli), 236 (293).

Torrent-Mist-Princess [*Takeri-bime-no-mikoto*], 48 (54), 82 (28).

tortoise xxxiii (xliv), 131 (160).

tortoise-shell [divination], xxii (xxtx).

Tosa 22 (22).

*Tōtōmi*, see *toho-tsu-afuui*.

*Totori* 185 (227).

towns xxv (xxxiv).

Toyo [province], 23 (23), 130 (159) 161 (197), 202 (249).

*Toyo-ashi-hara-no-Hehi-aki-no-noga-i-ho-aki-no-mitzu-ho-na-kuni*  xviii (xxv), 92 (112).

*Toyo-kumo-un-no-kami* 16 (17).

*Toyo-mike-kashiki-ya-hime* [empress Suiko], 342 (428).

*Toyora* 227 (283).

Tranquil River of Heaven, see *Ame-no-yasu-kawa*.

transliteration of Japanese words lxxiv (ci).

transmigration lx (lxxxi).

traps xxv (xxxiii), xxix (xl), 137 (167), see weir.

trays xxx (xl).

treachery xxxix (liii), 142 (173), 236 (295), 290 (361), see war tricks.

treasurer 291 (363).

treasury 10 (11), 291 (363).

treasures [Korean] xxxvi (xlviii), 261 (324).

tree god 27 (28).

tribe [*be*, clan], 151 (186), 152 (186), 164 (200), 170 (206), 171 (207), 172 (207), 185 (227), 200 (247), 205 (254), 243 (300), 251 (312), 268 (333), 291 (363) etc.

tribute 10 (4), 182 (224), 232 (289), 252 (313), 257 (320), 294 (367), 312 (389).

tribute on arrow-notches and finger-tips, 182 (224).

tribute on Japan from Korea, 232 (289), 252 (313), 294 (367).

tricks [war], 73 (87), 209 (259), 211 (261), 235 (292), 236 (293), 255 (317).

trousers xxx (xli), 40 (45), 255 (317), 262 (326).

trout [*aya*], xxxiv (xlv), 173 (213 n. 2), 234 (291).

*N. B.*—The figures enclosed in parenthesis ( ) represent the pages in the present edition. The figures without parenthesis represent the pages in the old editions previous to 1906.

*N. B.*—The figures enclosed in parenthesis ( ) represent the pages in the present edition. The figures without parenthesis represent the pages in the old editions previous to 1906.

*uneme* [palace waiting women] 145 (170 n. 7).

untrustworthiness of Japanese history xlv (lx), liv (lxxiii) see ère japonaise.

Usa 130 (159).

*uzu* [ornament] 57 (68 n. 28).

*Uzume no mikoto :* see *Ame-no-uzume-no-mikoto.*

vagueness [intentional] of Japanese poetry 323 (404).

valley god 28 (29).

value [historical] of Kojiki liv (lxxiv) etc.

van guard 103 (124), 108 (130), 112 (135), 113 (136).

vegetables xxx (xl).

vehicles xlii (lvi).

veils xxx (xli), 76 (91), 145 (178 n. 7), 281 (350).

vengeance, see Ohoke and the boar-herd 309-333 (386-414), 336 (420).

vine xxxiv (xlv).

violence [imperial] 206 (254), 309 (386), 321 (402).

void of heaven [sky] lv (lxxiv).

Wa-dō [*nengō*] 11 (5).

wager 262 (326).

wagtail xxxiv (xlvi), 324 (403).

waiting eighty years 314 (392).

*waka* [in names] 173 (213), see *wake.*

Waka-kusaka [queen] 268 (333), 304 (379), 310 (387), 311 (389), 312, (390).

Wakasa 237 (295).

Waka-tarashi-biko 202 (249).

*Waka-yamato-no-ko-hiko-oho-hibi* [Kaikuwa Tenno] 162 (199).

*Wake* [in names] xvi (xxi), xxxix (lii), 21 (24 n. 3), 50 (59 n. 5), 163 (200) 186 (223 n. 19), 201 (248), etc.

Waki [in names] see *wake.*

Wani [place] 80 (221), 269 (335).

*wani* [crocodiles] 269 (335 n. 7).

Wani-kishi or Hani [man] 252 (313).

warrior [female] 46 (53).

wasp 72 (86).

water caltrop xxxv (xlvi), 249 (309).

water-director [Mohitori] 141 (171), 273 (341).

water goddess [*mizu-ba-nome*] 29 (34 n. 4).

water gods, see Sumi.

N. B.—The figures enclosed in parenthesis ( ) represent the pages in
　　　the present edition. The figures without parenthesis represent
　　　the pages in the old editions previous to 1906.

water for Imperial household use 155 (191 n. 14), 285 (355).

waves stilled 212 (263).

war-tree xxxiv (xlv), 94 (117 n. 5).

weapons xxv (xxxiii), 46 (53).

weaving xxx (xli), xxxix (liii), 53 (62), 253 (314), 281 (350).

weaving maiden xxxiv (liii), xlvi (lxii), lxix (xciii), 54 (62), 99 (117).

wedding xxxix (liii).

wedge xxv (xxxiv), 71 (84).

weir 137 (167).

well [*wi*] lv (lxxv), 47 (53), 75 (83), 121 (147), 137 (167), 155 (191 n. 14) etc.

wept himself to death 199 (246).

wet nurses xxxix (lii), 70 (83), 128 (155).

whale 140 (171).

wheat 60 (70) etc.

why the emperors are short lived 116 (145).

wife [chief] 74 (88), 79 (95), 259 (322), 270 (337).

wife and younger sister xxxviii (li), see younger sister.

wife asserting her rights, see *Iwa-no-hime.*

wind-god 21 (24 n. 2), 27 (28).

window xxvi (xxxv), xxvii (xxxvi), xxxiii (xxxviii).

wistaria [*fuji*] xxvi (xxxvi), 262 (326).

witchcraft 180 (221).

woad xxx (xli)

*Wa-asatsuma-no-wake-go-no-sukune* 268 (333), 293 (365).

Wodo [princess] 320 (401), 325 (407).

Wohari [Owari] 153 (186), 157 (193), 163 (200), 173 (212), 185 (227), 192 (237), 211 (261), 215 (297).

Woharida 13 (5), 165 (200), 342 (428).

Wokada 131 (160).

Woke (King) 309 (386) see Ohoke.

woodcock 140 (171).

wooing 19 (20), 68 (81), 75 (91), 262 (326), 312 (390) passim.

worship [objects of], xlix (lxvi), lvii (lxxvii), see shinto shrines.

Wosana-goto lii (lxxi).

Wotsu [cape], 218 (270).

Wo-usu [prince], 201 (249), 205 (254), see *Yamato-Take-no-mikoto.*

*N.B.*—The figures enclosed in parenthesis ( ) represent the pages in
    the present edition. The figures without parenthesis represent
    the pages in the old editions previous to 1906.

DISCARDED
Richmond Public Library